BUSINESS ETHICS

Also by Janet Morrison and published by Palgrave Macmillan Higher Education

THE INTERNATIONAL BUSINESS ENVIRONMENT
INTERNATIONAL BUSINESS
THE GLOBAL BUSINESS ENVIRONMENT

BUSINESS

ETHICS

NEW CHALLENGES IN A GLOBALIZED WORLD

JANET MORRISON

macmillan
education

palgrave

First published 2015 by
PALGRAVE

Palgrave in the UK is an imprint of Macmillan Publishers Limited, registered in England, company number 785998, of 4 Crinan Street, London N1 9XW

Palgrave Macmillan in the US is a division of St Martin's Press LLC, 175 Fifth Avenue, New York, NY 10010.

Palgrave is a global imprint of the above companies and is represented throughout the world.

Palgrave® and Macmillan® are registered trademarks in the United States, the United Kingdom, Europe and other countries.

ISBN 978–1–137–30949–5

This book is printed on paper suitable for recycling and made from fully managed and sustained forest sources. Logging, pulping and manufacturing processes are expected to conform to the environmental regulations of the country of origin.

A catalogue record for this book is available from the British Library.

A catalog record for this book is available from the Library of Congress.

Typeset by Cambrian Typesetters, Camberley, Surrey, England, UK

Printed in China

CONTENTS

PART 1   THE BUSINESS ENVIRONMENT FROM AN ETHICAL PERSPECTIVE

PART 2   ETHICS AND BUSINESS

LIST OF ILLUSTRATIVE MATERIALS

FIGURES

TABLES

PHOTOS

AUTHOR'S ACKNOWLEDGMENTS

Although the writing of this book was down to me alone, I am grateful to a number of people who helped to make it a reality. Above all, I wish to thank my husband, Ian, for his support and encouragement. Thanks also to Rachel Dolan of St Peter's Library in the University of Sunderland, whose help in accessing research resources has been invaluable. I would like especially to thank my publisher, Ursula Gavin, and all the staff at Palgrave Macmillan Education whose skills went into the book's production. To the numerous anonymous reviewers who read the book's proposal and draft manuscript, I am grateful for the many helpful comments and suggestions you made. I have incorporated many of your suggestions, and I am confident the book has benefited as a result. Finally, I would like to thank fellow lecturers, researchers and students whose encouragement over the years gave me the confidence to embark on this book.

PUBLISHERS' ACKNOWLEDGEMENTS

The author and publishers are grateful for permission to reproduce the following copyright material:

Figure 4.7 Number of ratifications of human rights treaties from Pillay, N. (2012) 'Strengthening the UN human rights treaty body system: A report by the UN High Commissioner for human rights', United Nations Publications.

Figure 10.7 Access to Nutrition rankings, based on *Access to Nutrition Index 2013*, www.accesstonutrition.org.

Figure 11.4 Debarments and other sanctions issued by the World Bank for corruption and fraud, from Freshfields Bruckhaus Deringer LLP (2013) *World Bank Sanctions Investigations: Blacklist Revisited*, at www.freshfields.com.

ABOUT THE AUTHOR

Janet Morrison, now retired, was a senior lecturer in strategic and international management at Sunderland University Business School in the UK, where she enjoyed a long career in teaching, research, curriculum development and course administration. She taught international business modules at undergraduate and postgraduate levels. She also taught undergraduate modules in company law and a postgraduate module in international business law. She was programme leader for undergraduate international business degrees and the MBA in International Management.

Janet's academic background goes back to her first degree (in political science and history) at Mary Washington College of the University of Virginia in the US (now the University of Mary Washington), followed by a master's degree from the University of Toronto in Canada (in political theory). She later completed a law degree from the University of Newcastle-upon-Tyne in the UK.

Her published research includes articles in a range of areas, including corporate governance and corporate social responsibility. She is the author of the textbook, *The Global Business Environment*, the third edition of which was published by Palgrave Macmillan in 2011.

PREFACE

Business ethics as an academic subject and business priority has sharply risen in stature in the last decade. This is largely due to the growth in power and geographical spread of global companies, particularly in the wake of high-profile corporate failings. Shareholders, consumers, employees and governments now place companies in the moral spotlight, reminding business leaders that business behaviour is not above being subjected to standards of right and wrong that pertain to all in society. Much of this critical focus is framed in terms of corporate social responsibility (CSR), a multi-faceted approach to corporate behaviour which is itself closely associated with ethical principles. I devote considerable attention, therefore, to CSR and associated theories. But the growing complexities of the global economy demand both a broader and deeper view of business ethics than current management approaches which focus on reforming corporate behaviour.

This book places business ethics in a richer contextual setting than most texts in this subject area. While textbooks have focused on ethical issues facing western managers, the global business landscape has been shifting towards Asian and other emerging economies, which present new moral parameters and new business models. At the same time, in both developed and developing economies, ethical debate increasingly revolves around issues such as inequality, financial risk, outsourcing by global brands, climate change and human rights. While corporate profits soar and executives reap huge rewards, for ordinary workers in just about every country, low wages and job insecurity are continuing threats to improvements in well-being. Many millions of migrant workers around the world work in factories that make products for global brands, pick crops, mine the resources we depend on, and work on the construction sites that create gleaming new urban centres. Their precarious livelihoods and poor living conditions demand attention on human rights grounds, but who is responsible? A combination of government policies, political pressures and business interests perpetuate these arrangements, in which some players make financial gains, and those who come off the worst are the migrant workers. Their plight stems not so much from management failings as from the more fundamental problem of business models built on an underclass of low-cost labour.

These are some of the challenges that business ethics as a subject must now confront. This book therefore looks at a broad range of players and environments. Business decision-makers are nurtured in specific cultural, economic, legal and political environments, which impart values and standards of behaviour. Understanding these formative factors is essential to understanding the moral implications of how they behave. But behaviour and values are not set in stone. They can change over time, along with views of what constitutes the good actor and the good act. Dealing with ethical challenges involves going back to the foundations of ethics itself, one of the oldest branches of philosophy, on which business ethics builds. While concepts such as virtue and justice might seem abstract, the writers whose seminal works on basic concepts such as the moral individual in society, remain central to these endeavours. I take the view that explanations in relatively simple language will shed light on their relevance in current contexts.

Business ethics as presented here is neither a highly abstract academic subject nor, at the opposite extreme, a practical guide for western managers. Rather, it is a dynamic blend of theory and contemporary business situations. I have designed this book for use by students of business generally, at undergraduate and postgraduate levels. It will serve as an introductory text for those with little background in business studies, and, equally, it will be valuable for more advanced students seeking a wide-ranging grounding in business ethics. As an experienced author, I am well aware of the needs of students for whom English is a second language. This book is written in simple language, but in a style I would like to think is also inviting and engaging for readers. Key terms relevant to ethics and international business are defined clearly when they are introduced, and these definitions are recalled when the terms reappear in later chapters. Where explanations of business activities are needed, they are explained in plain language, with relevant and, I hope, interesting examples. Feedback from students and lecturers that I have been grateful to receive over the years suggests to me that readers want many things from a book. They are not seeking just a learning experience, but something more inspiring, that engages them directly, reveals some new insight, or shows a new way of looking at things around them. If I can do any of these things for readers, I will consider this book a success.

JANET MORRISON

LIST OF ABBREVIATIONS

AGM	Annual General Meeting
ATCA	Alien Tort Claims Act
BIT	bilateral investment treaty
BRIC	Brazil, Russia, India and China
CEO	Chief Executive Officer
CFO	Chief Financial Officer
CIS	Commonwealth of Independent States
CO_2	carbon dioxide
CSR	corporate social responsibility
ECHR	European Convention on Human Rights
EU	European Union
FCA	Financial Conduct Authority
FDI	foreign direct investment
FIPA	Foreign Investment Promotion and Protection Agreement
FSA	Financial Services Authority
GATT	General Agreement on Tariffs and Trade
GDP	gross domestic product
GMO	genetically-modified organism
GNI	gross national income
HMRC	HM Revenue and Customs
ICC	International Criminal Court
ICCPR	International Covenant on Civil and Political Rights
ICESCR	International Covenant on Economic, Social and Cultural Rights
ILO	International Labour Organization
IMF	International Monetary Fund
IP	intellectual property
IPO	initial public offering
IT	information technology
LSE	London Stock Exchange
MDGs	Millennium Development Goals
MNE	multinational enterprise
NAFTA	North American Free Trade Agreement

NGO	non-governmental organization
OECD	Organisation for Economic Co-operation and Development
PLC	public limited company
PPP	public–private partnership
PRA	Prudential Regulation Authority
PTA	preferential trade agreement
R&D	research and development
SEC	Securities and Exchange Commission
SME	small-to-medium-size enterprise
SOE	state-owned enterprise
SWF	sovereign wealth fund
TPP	Trans-Pacific Partnership
TRIPS	Trade-related Aspects of Intellectual Property
TTIP	Transatlantic Trade and Investment Partnership
UAE	United Arab Emirates
UDHR	Universal Declaration of Human Rights
UN	United Nations
UNCTAD	United Nations Conference on Trade and Development
US	United States of America
WTO	World Trade Organization

INTRODUCTION TO THE BOOK

OUTLINE

Why study business ethics?

Why does ethics matter for business?

What are the new challenges, and how is this book different?

Introducing key terms

Ethical themes throughout the book

The book's organization

How to use this book and the accompanying website

We begin this introduction by setting out the rationale for studying business ethics. We focus on the new challenges in today's world that reinforce the need for business and management students to gain a deeper and broader understanding of the ethical dimensions of business. There follows an explanatory section on some of the key terms which will be used in the book. Next, there is an introduction to the ethical themes which recur throughout the book. Finally, there is an explanation of how to use the book and the accompanying website.

WHY STUDY BUSINESS ETHICS?

The idea that business is simply about economic activities is widespread. It holds that making, growing or trading things in exchange for money is the essence of business. And it would seem to follow that focusing on how to do these things better is what business studies should be about. Business and management *are* about these activities, but they are about much more besides, as this book shows. Economic activities are necessary for societies to survive and prosper. They provide food, jobs, housing, transport and many other needs. In providing them, businesspeople make money for themselves, which enables their businesses to survive. If they had no possibility of making money, they would be discouraged from going into business in the first place or would not invest for the future. In a society where there is little or no prospect of a business reaping financial rewards for its owners, businesses will not thrive – and neither will the society. We might conclude that facilitating the pursuit of gain by business owners is thus key to a thriving economy. Their self-interested behaviour results in the economic benefits which a society enjoys. This is the thinking behind a belief in the free market. On the same reasoning, if their activities are curtailed or interfered with, then jobs will not be created and economic prosperity will be at risk. Whatever is good for business seems to be good for society. It is sometimes said that whatever is good for General Motors is good for the US. At first glance, this thinking looks plausible. A belief in these basic free-market principles has been a major influence globally. If the business enterprise is incentivized to come up with new products and services, then people in society benefit, through jobs, improved standards of living and a happier existence, at least in terms of material well-being. Ethics would not seem to come into the picture.

But think again. Happiness is not simply about money and material well-being, either for the businessperson or the ordinary person in society. People want a good income, but also other things which are harder to quantify, such as the prospect of a fulfilling life, meaningful relationships, a healthy natural environment and the confidence that their children will also enjoy healthy and happy lives. What if a firm launches a new product, such as a mobile phone, which involves production in unhealthy and unsafe factories, where workers receive little pay and are likely to incur long-term health problems as a result? The firm is likely to make big profits, which is good for the business. But our second assumption – that this is good for society – is not self-evident. The workers might benefit in that they have jobs rather than being unemployed, but their situation is far from most people's idea of happiness. What is good for the firm benefits *some* people (those rich enough to afford to buy its gadgets), but not others (those who make them). If workers are exploited to make things, grow crops, or extract resources from the earth, then most people would say that the firm's behaviour is wrong. It matters *what* the business is doing and *how* it is behaving in the process. The fact that the world needs the resources or products does not justify using exploitative means to produce them, or depleting the earth's supply of finite resources. The businessperson's desire to make money is not an unfailing compass pointing to the good of society. Indeed, it can be argued that the single-minded pursuit of money is probably not the best route to success even for the business. General Motors went bankrupt in the financial crisis of 2008, after all. Private goals and societal goals do not march automatically in harmony. Goals and means of achieving them involve a range of considerations which reflect values and views of right and wrong. Business decision-making has an inescapable ethical spectrum.

Whatever society we live in, and whatever role we play in that society – from lowly-paid labourer to powerful political leader – we regularly encounter situations in which we must decide on what is the right thing to do. These ethical dilemmas occur in every aspect of life: in the family, in schools, in the community, in government and in business. Ethics is about views of right and wrong, which affect the lives of everyone every day. Business decision-making does not take place in a value-free vacuum, but in social and cultural contexts. For a business, strategy and management increasingly encompass ethical concerns which can have profound impacts on its current and future prospects. For this reason, business ethics, which is the study of ethics applied to business, has become an important area for study and academic research. Business ethics focuses on the goals of the business, its organizational values and its behaviour. In today's world, this means taking into account both global and local factors, including cultural, legal and political forces which shape business structures and business behaviour.

The pervasive nature of business activities in today's world give business actors, whether individuals or organizations, critical roles in determining the kinds of lives we lead and the state of the planet which forms a legacy for future generations. Businesses play vital roles in employment, nourishment, housing, education, healthcare and many other aspects of life in most societies. And, increasingly, people affected by business decision-making are calling businesses to account according to ethical standards. It is not surprising that the subject of business ethics has grown to such an extent that there is now an extensive body of scholarship in both its theory and practice.

WHY DOES ETHICS MATTER FOR BUSINESS?

People easily see the relevance of ethics in an individual's personal life, as most societies recognize acts such as theft, assault or murder as wrongs. These are not just moral wrongs, but offences in national law: the person found guilty by a court could be liable to a jail sentence. Every society also recognizes many 'unwritten' rules such as a duty not to tell lies and to keep promises. Indeed, the feeling that we must conform to such rules is one of the main elements which help societies to function smoothly. It is easy to see how moral rules affect decisions we take as individuals, compelling us to tell the truth rather than to lie to our friends. But businesses seem to be different. While the people who run a business have an ethical dimension as human beings, it is sometimes said that this does not transmit to the business, which is separate. This view reflects the belief that the business exists to generate wealth for its owners. This is an economic function rather than a social or moral one. Decision-making by organizations is different from that of an individual. A firm's decisions are made within the framework of the organization and its goals. Its decisions further the firm's enterprise goals, rather than social ones. This outlook, which views social and moral perspectives as outside the sphere of business, has perhaps been accentuated by the expansion of international businesses, which have ties to many different societies. The global business stands astride numerous different societies, with their diverse cultural values. It seems to occupy a global domain, above these national environments. But does this mean that it is somehow 'above' ethical concerns?

This book starts from the fact that ethical questions are central to how the business sees its role in the world. They concern who we are and what we should be doing, both as individuals and members of an organization. The person who comes to work each day for an organization does not leave ethical concerns at the doorstep. The commonest business organization, the company, is recognized in law as a person, capable of acts with legal and moral implications. The company can be prosecuted for crimes which involve an element of intention, as in corporate manslaughter. And the individual working for the company cannot hide behind the company, but can be prosecuted in addition. National and international law thus recognize the capacity of the company, as well as its agents, for right and wrong behaviour.

Whatever its size, any business interacts with each society in which it operates, and is affected by the social, cultural and legal environment of each country. A business whose activities all take place in one country is a part of that society in a way analogous to an individual resident. In today's world such a business is becoming much rarer as, thanks to developments in technology and communications, even small firms can now do business outside their home country's borders. The horizons of a large company are much greater, bringing it into contact with a diverse range of national environments. The global company can take the view that it is somehow above the ethical frameworks of society. But, far from being an outsider in these different countries, it becomes enmeshed in the distinctive cultural environment of each. Moreover, as companies expand, they engage with a broader range of cultures. There is thus a compelling case for seeking and establishing ethical guideposts in the business sphere across national boundaries.

WHAT ARE THE NEW CHALLENGES, AND HOW IS THIS BOOK DIFFERENT?

Your day will probably have started with a breakfast product such as a packet cereal. The raw cereal ingredients will have been produced by farm workers, who are some of the most disadvantaged of all workers on the globe, only barely scraping a living, while the branded product yields profits for processors, distributors, wholesalers and retailers along the way. The clothes you put on were likely to have been made by garment workers in Bangladesh, working in dangerously unsafe factories. As likely as not, you reached for your smartphone – a gadget produced by migrant workers, probably in China, who work under conditions of duress, while global brand owners park profits in Caribbean micro-states. You could well have started the day with a coffee, another common product which generates large profits for a few dominant brand owners, commodity traders and processors, but little for growers. Each of these products raises issues which should be at the heart of any study of business ethics. But most business ethics textbooks make only passing mention of them. Instead, these texts focus on management issues which involve ethical decision-making, mainly in western organizations. They adopt the perspective of the business organization and focus on managing relations with employees, suppliers, governments and consumers. Authors typically point to aspects of the business environment, such as politics or 'the law', as external influences, overlooking the web of interactions between the business and its environment, in both local and global contexts. As this book dramatically shows, however, these interactions are key to shaping business ethics in today's world.

Business enterprises globally are far more varied in both structures and values than most western-oriented textbooks would have readers believe. Many of today's global companies have their roots in Asian and South American cultural environments, where state ownership and political goals are part of the business ethos. These are far removed from western ideas about the role of management and employee relations. So too are the strict discipline-oriented regimes used in large factory complexes of high-tech industries in China. Relying on migrant workers, they manufacture for global brands that demand high volumes of products within tight timeframes. These companies' methods raise ethical issues in relation to treatment of the workforce, and their expansion into other countries have brought these issues closer to home for western societies (see Chapter 9). But how do these ethical concerns impact on the global brands sought by consumers? Business ethics viewed from a western managerial perspective offers little understanding and analysis of such ethical challenges. Its focus on managerial issues is limited, sidestepping thorny questions such as a company's business model, ownership configuration and financial arrangements. Yet these issues are central to determining how managers behave in carrying out corporate goals.

This book delves into these core issues which shape a firm's ethics in practice. We examine the cultural, political and legal environments in which ethical issues arise (in Part 1), and apply ethical principles in a variety of business contexts as well as societal contexts (in Part 2). What are the new challenges which demand a broader approach to business ethics? Here are the challenges that will be discussed, with references to relevant chapters:

Migrant labour – Today's global economy depends on millions of migrant workers. Although the UN classifies migrants as people who move from one country to another (IOM, 2013), migrant workers can equally move from one region to another within a country. Examples of internal migration are factory workers in China, garment workers in Bangladesh, and miners in South Africa. Where migrant workers have entered a country from elsewhere, host countries are often dependent on their labour. Foreign workers drive buses in Singapore, work in Amazon warehouses in Germany, pick crops in the US, and work in the construction industry in rich Middle Eastern states. What all these migrant workers have in common is that, living far from their home regions, they are particularly vulnerable. Their living conditions, working conditions and pay are often problematic, and their human well-being suffers (IOM, 2013). Often hired by an employment agency, the migrant worker does not enjoy a straightforward employee relationship as depicted in management texts. It is often difficult to identify an employer, and thus difficult to hold anyone accountable for non-payment of wages or breaches of human rights (see Chapters 2, 7 and 9).

Privacy, data protection and surveillance – Information has become a valuable asset in today's world. Technological innovation has made it possible to gather, store and transmit volumes of data unfathomable in earlier generations. Governments and businesses have acquired technological capacity to acquire and use data, but there are growing concerns about the risks and responsibilities involved. The need for legal regulation is recognized by governments, but it fails to keep up with technological advances (see Chapter 4). And governments themselves are some of the most secretive accumulators of private data. Meanwhile, the accumulation of data, including that related to individual people, commercial interests and national security, proceeds unrelentingly. Personal data can be sold commercially, tapped into by government surveillance programmes and hacked into by criminals. Access to unprecedented amounts of information presents huge opportunities, but also raises ethical questions about the means of acquiring data, the ways it is used and the types of data collected.

Climate change – Climate change is a global issue with local impacts such as flooding, drought and food shortages that can be devastating, especially in poor developing countries. Yet most of the human activity which is blamed for rising temperatures and rising emissions, is taking place in the more industrialized advanced and emerging economies. Economic activities and consumer lifestyles which pay little heed to environmental impacts are increasingly recognized as unsustainable. Business strategists speak of sustainability, but in a context of business models which are known to be part of the problem. While some governments have imposed legal controls on emissions, many – including big emitters – are not inclined to do so, prioritizing economic goals over environmental ones (see Chapter 10).

Financial crises – In theory, when businesses compete with each other, markets function efficiently and economies benefit. However, in practice, market failure is not uncommon, and even supporters of free markets recognize the need for government regulation. When businesses engage in excessive risk and government regulation fails, financial crises can occur, bringing down whole national economies and causing catastrophic damage in society. The ripples can lead to global financial crisis, as happened in 2008. Recession, high unemployment and deprivation resulted in a number of countries. Governments were compelled to bail out banks and increase public spending to relieve economic hardship in societies. Belief in free markets was shaken, but so, too, was the ability of governments to regulate. Public hostility focused on the huge rewards enjoyed by bankers, even those whose banks had failed. The problems were deeper than could be fixed simply by changes in regulation. The assumption that everyone's self-interested pursuit of economic gains would ultimately benefit a society, needed urgently to be rethought (see Chapters 5 and 9).

Inequality – Inequality has been on the rise in the globalized world. The rich are getting richer almost everywhere, in both advanced and emerging economies. The wages of working people have not risen as rapidly, and many millions of middle-class people have seen stagnating or shrinking incomes. The assumption that economic gains derived from markets would 'trickle down' to all in society is now seen to be flawed. Growing inequality can have deep impacts on societies. People who work hard in low-grade jobs for a wage below their country's poverty line are discouraged, and even angry, when their bosses' pay is many hundred times that of their own. But the effects are not just on incomes. Concentration of wealth is usually accompanied by concentration of economic and political power, allowing wealthy élites to perpetuate systems which entrench inequalities. The feelings of impotence and injustice felt by those who feel they have been left behind can lead in extreme cases to social and political upheaval. It is no wonder that inequality is a worry for governments. It should also be a worry for businesses. Their strategies and policies determine how the responsibilities and rewards of the business are shared out (see Chapters 2, 9 and 11).

The challenges outlined above are all directly relevant for businesses, wherever they are located and whatever sectors they are operating in. Meeting these challenges calls for a rethinking of business models, goals and strategies in light of the theories and practices which make up business ethics as explored in this book.

INTRODUCING KEY TERMS

Key terms are shown in bold and defined throughout this book. Many of these are terms used in business ethics discourse, and many are related to international business activities. They are highlighted here to provide a useful reference point for discussion surrounding the issues, both for readers who have studied international business and for those who have no prior background in the subject. Here, we begin with a selection of the main terms and concepts.

The company is the favoured organizational structure used in international business. The company's spread of business activities across multiple locations makes it a **multinational enterprise (MNE)**, defined as a lead company, and/or known as a parent company, which owns or controls other businesses across national borders. The MNE can be quite complex organizationally, and might own subsidiaries in numerous countries. It might also license other companies to manufacture its branded products, giving it some control and responsibility over these manufacturing operations, even though they are not carried out by a company it owns. The companies with which it has licensing and other contractual agreements are known as 'affiliated' companies. A large MNE can consist of hundreds of companies and affiliates in numerous countries. MNEs are the drivers of international business, as is shown in Figure I.1. But other actors are also important in decision making, including governments and stakeholders (discussed below). The MNE designs a global strategy which

Figure I.1 *Actors, concepts and context in business ethics*

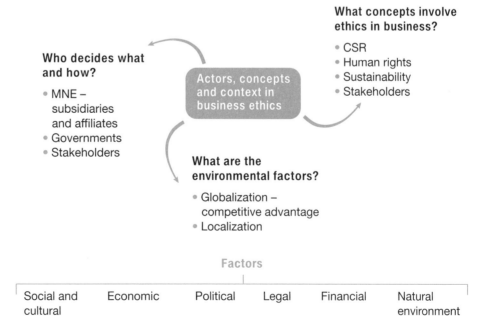

co-ordinates the activities of its many units and also the other organizations it does business. The MNE is typically linked with other companies, including suppliers of materials and components, in supply chains, which can span the globe. The factors which come into play in these differing locations are shown in the figure. How does the MNE design a strategy which takes account of local conditions but also meets ethical expectations of a wider audience at the global level? The conceptual tools which guide MNE ethical policies are set out in the top right of the figure. These are introduced below.

Business is used here in a broad sense, covering all types of economic activities, including agriculture, manufacturing, energy industries, trade and financial services. We will be examining MNE structures and decision-making in all these sectors. For now, we take an overview of their interactions in multiple national environments. Why would the MNE set up complicated arrangements and supply chains in different countries, rather than simply focus on the country most closely associated with its main business? The answer lies in the competitive advantages that particular countries enjoy in particular spheres of business activity, which make them attractive to MNEs. Every business involves numerous functions, such as finance, operations and marketing. The modern firm's executives now typically seek an advantageous location for each activity. Low taxes, low-cost labour and proximity to markets are some of the attractions which particular countries offer. Indeed, many countries pride themselves on just these advantages, in order to attract MNEs. MNEs' strategies of locating different functions in different locations are associated with globalization, a phenomenon which refers to the lowering of barriers to the movement of people, goods, services and information around the world. The MNE strategist sitting in the company's head office might point to this trend as evidence that its business is essentially global, not grounded in any one society. It is seeking economic advantages wherever they occur. It is a paradox, however, that the MNE strategist, faced with a welter of choices, chooses one location over another because of perceived *local* advantages. In other words, localization has become as much a reality as globalization. And with differing local environments come a plethora of interactions in which ethical issues arise. Moreover, with each strategic choice, corporate decision-makers encounter multiple dimensions of the business environment.

In looking at corporate decision-making, it is helpful to outline who the main players are, and where responsibility lies. These are matters of corporate governance (discussed in detail in Chapter 8). Corporate governance differs from country to country, but countries share basic principles. The shareholders are the legal owners of the company. The highest decision-making body is the board of directors, appointed by the shareholders. The company's senior managers and chief executive officer (CEO) are answerable to the board, whose members are expected to take decisions in the best interests of the company. This is usually interpreted as focusing on the shareholders' interests, although this perspective is now becoming broader. Although we speak of the company taking decisions, organizational decisions are not literally taken by the organization: they are taken by individual executives and managers, whose actions reflect moral values, whether in their personal lives or in business.

To take a simple example of corporate decision-making, suppose an executive of a company is considering whether to install a better safety system in the company's factory in an overseas location, which will reduce air pollution inside the premises and also reduce emissions. The new system is expensive to purchase, but some of the company's competitors have such systems. How should the company decide?

The CEO and chief financial officer are the key figures in taking this decision. A number of different environmental factors come into consideration, as shown in Figure I.1. At the economic level, the costs could be high, and the firm has a responsibility to shareholders to make profits. In terms of finance, it is possible that the firm could fund improvements through borrowing, but this too entails costs, and the financial officers would need to be convinced that the benefits would outweigh the costs. From the legal perspective, the country in which the factory is located will have safety legislation, which might or might not require the upgrading of systems. If the country's safety legislation is weak, the company's executives could well be complying with the law already, but they would know that an improved system would be justifiable on ethical grounds. Similarly, the country's environmental protection legislation might well be weak, but it could be argued that an ethical approach would involve improvements in pollution standards, even if not required by local law. In each of these dimensions of the business environment, ethical issues arise which influence businesses.

In this example, it is clear that many different people are potentially affected, including employees, the local community and customers. These considerations are often referred to as encompassing interests and groups of people known as **stakeholders**. In Figure I.1, stakeholders are depicted as influencing decision-making. This is a key concept in business ethics. Shareholders are often considered the most important stakeholder group, but any people directly or even indirectly affected by the company's activities are stakeholders. In this case, the factory's system affects not just the employees, but also other people who might be in the building, the surrounding area and the community at large. Impacts on people and communities raise issues of **human rights**, based on the fundamental respect for human dignity, which is a foundation concept in ethics. In the example, pollution can have long-term health implications, as well as environmental impacts, which can reach beyond immediate communities. Damaging impacts of operations on health is a human rights issue.

Stakeholder interests overlap with human rights issues, and are both covered in the notion of **corporate social responsibility (CSR)**. CSR sees the company has having multiple responsibilities in society, which will be discussed in detail in Chapter 7. The CSR perspective acknowledges that the company has economic responsibilities, but also legal and ethical responsibilities. The last of these, ethical responsibilities, would entail making decisions which potentially conflict with economic goals, at least in the short term. But, as we will see, corporate decision-makers might take a long view of environmental impacts, reasoning that sustainability should be one of the criteria in taking the decision. **Sustainability** is defined as taking into account the needs not just of today's inhabitants of the planet, but future generations as well. Environmental damage can be irreversible. If the national law does not require upgrading of safety systems, should the company go ahead with the upgrade on these other grounds, including ethical principles, stakeholder interests and sustainability?

The company could answer this question on the basis of the cultural values that exist in the country. In many countries, poor factory conditions and high levels of pollution are looked on as inevitable features of industrialization. They are usually associated with low-cost production, low wages and excessive overtime. In some countries, child labour is seen as acceptable, although legally prohibited. Most people today would criticize this attitude as being unethical. But on what grounds can we pass judgment on the norms of a particular culture? This is a challenge that ethical decision-making places in front of all of us, in business life as much as in private life. Indeed, for the businessperson, the issue is far more widely ramified than for the individual. I might be confronted with a decision whether to give back money to a shopkeeper who has handed over too much change for my purchase. That is an individual moral dilemma. I can simply keep the change, and although I know it is wrong, I am confident that no one will know and nothing will be done about it. For the business, however, the ripples of a moral dilemma may have social and environmental impacts not just locally but around the globe. For this reason, businesses are inevitably involved in social and moral issues in every location with which they are connected.

In fact, large MNEs nowadays often acknowledge a role in societies, stating that they take responsibilities towards communities seriously and wish to be good corporate citizens. But how much weight does this type of statement carry in practice? There is often a gap between their professed commitment to a particular community and the global picture of the company's behaviour in practice. CSR implies that the firm sees itself as a responsible player in society. However, the international business is likely to have links to many societies. And, as we noted above, it is more likely to see its strategy in terms of overarching global goals, in which the particular advantages of countries and communities are instrumental, that is, means to corporate ends.

The notion of the business as a focus of ethical concerns entails looking at the firm in its entirety, that is, in all its operations around the globe. Taking a view of the international business as a whole implies applying ethical standards which transcend national boundaries. A firm could well abide by local law in numerous locations but be considered to be acting unethically when its overall strategy and policies are taken into account. On what basis can we make such judgments, and, perhaps equally importantly, how can we advise firms to behave ethically in future? Answering these questions is at the heart of this book. As we have already seen, any business is confronted by a range of issues which arise in the environment at any given time and in any given place. These environmental factors impact on business behaviour, both directly and indirectly.

Crucial aspects of the environment which exhibit ethical dimensions are cultural, economic, political, legal, financial and the natural environment. Understanding how these environmental factors weigh on businesses plays a vital part in deciding how businesses should shape ethical responses. Part 1 of the book focuses on these environmental factors and their ethical dimensions, highlighting their relevance for international business. Ethical concepts and theories are introduced in cultural contexts, illustrating how they reflect cultural values and also frame ethical decision-making. In Part 2, we look at business responses in terms of strategy and behaviour. The rationale behind this approach is that understanding the context of a decision or action is key to making the right strategic choice in any set of circumstances. For the business, as for the individual, the right decision is not a decision taken in a vacuum or in a theoretical sense only, but the right decision in a context which presents itself. We might ask, what if the context is quite complex, with both local and global factors? At least part of the answer lies in understanding the interplay of local and global environmental factors, which is the focus of the chapters of Part 1. The book's ethical themes link the chapters in Parts 1 and 2.

ETHICAL THEMES THROUGHOUT THE BOOK

This book features six themes. Discussion of the issues arising throughout the book can be linked through these themes. They aid the reader in identifying and applying ethical concepts in business contexts. Some of these themes are so central that they have featured in ethical debate for many centuries. Others have arisen more recently, as economic, social and political changes have added to the complexity of the business environment.

Ethical themes can be visualized in broad groupings. The first two deal with normative issues underlying ethical principles. The second two deal with the social context of business activities. These focus on how economic activities evolve and how businesses and societies change. The last two focus on how governance is changing at various levels in the global economy. These three groupings are shown in Figure I.2.

There follows a brief introduction to each of the six ethical themes:

Interplay between the individual and society – This theme is at the heart of ethical theories over the centuries. Human dignity is the basis of the core foundation theories of business ethics. The ethical discourse surrounding individual values and the social context is central to identifying and applying ethical principles in the many different contexts in which businesses operate.

Moral rules and cultural divergence – Moral rules exist in any society, whatever the culture. Diverging values and norms of behaviour are crucial in the business environment. Business ethics is often about identifying, understanding and respecting the divergences, while being able to identify the right ethical approach which transcends cultural boundaries.

Economic development and changing societies – Most countries seek the benefits of economic development, and market reforms have played an important part in transforming many of those featured in this book. Industrialization, resource exploitation, changes in the

Figure I.2 *Overview of ethical themes*

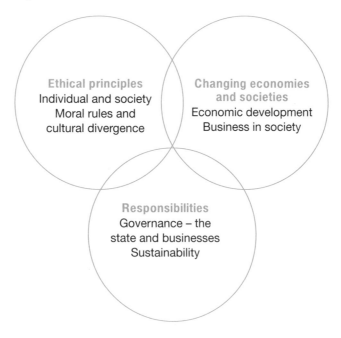

nature of work and changes in social interactions have resulted. While many benefits have flowed from these transformations, negative impacts and ethical challenges have also been aspects of development, raising ethical issues, including social justice and human rights.

Businesses as part of society – Businesses have been drivers of economic change, through industrialization and globalization. Businesses have multiple roles in society, extending beyond the economic activities which they consider their primary role. They often have strong political ties to government and influence public policy. Business activities involve social interactions with a variety of stakeholders, both internal to the organization and externally.

Governance and responsibilities – Governance is a broad theme, encompassing the way whole countries are governed and also the way businesses are run. In all governance processes, there are responsibilities within systems – both formal and informal – whereby the decision-makers are held answerable for their actions. Roles and responsibilities within a business take on wider perspectives when we look at the impacts of business in societies.

Sustainability guiding business and state actors – Steering a sustainable course is a responsibility of state actors, including governments, and, increasingly, business leadership

Table I.1 Ethical themes highlighted in the chapters

	Interplay between individual & society	Moral rules & cultural divergence	Economic development & changing societies	Businesses as part of society	Governance & responsibilities	Sustainability
1 Ethical theories and cultural contexts	●	●				
2 The global economy from an ethical perspective			●			●
3 The political sphere: societal and business goals	●				●	
4 Law and justice: diverse ethical perspectives for business		●			●	
5 Financial markets: what role for ethics?				●	●	
6 International trade and ethical considerations			●			●
7 Ethics and CSR in international business	●			●		
8 Corporate governance: how do ethical principles apply?				●	●	
9 Human rights and ethical business	●			●		
10 Sustainability and the ethical business				●		●
11 Conclusions: Business ethics and global challenges	●	●	●	●	●	●

is also seen as essential to the attainment of sustainability objectives. Sustainability in both long-term goals and day-to-day decision-making is central to the thinking of the ethical business in all its international activities.

The ethical themes are interrelated. Case studies and examples in the text show how these interrelationships arise. For example, sustainability is an issue in economic development, as is shown in the case study on Turkey which closes Chapter 10. Particular themes feature more prominently in some chapters than in others. Table I.1 shows the main chapters in which each theme is developed. The last chapter provides a synthesis of earlier discussions of each theme.

THE BOOK'S ORGANIZATION

The book is divided into two parts. Part 1 consists of Chapters 1 to 6, and Part 2 consists of Chapters 7 to 11. There follows a brief summary of the contents of each chapter.

PART 1 THE BUSINESS ENVIRONMENT FROM AN ETHICAL PERSPECTIVE

Chapter 1 Ethical theories and cultural contexts. This chapter introduces ethical concepts and their foundation theories. These will be featured throughout the book. The main theories are Kant's ethical theory, the utilitarians' theories, rights theorists such as John Rawls, Aristotle's virtue ethics and the theories of Confucius. The focus then shifts to cultural contexts, notably national cultures and religions. A final section brings together theoretical insights and cultural divergences in the context of international business.

Case studies

Evolving tobacco companies: Ethical questions in changing markets
Bangladesh factory collapse reveals plight of garment workers

Chapter 2 The global economy from an ethical perspective. The forces of globalization, including FDI, supply chains and outsourcing, are introduced, along with their ethical implications. Winners and losers from globalization are highlighted, and the implications for sustainable development are introduced. We discuss the ethical foundations of capitalism, and how capitalist systems have evolved in differing national cultures. There is a comparison with socialist principles, notably Marx's ethical philosophy, along with an explanation of socialist systems as implemented by states. Mixed economic models are discussed, with special reference to the emerging economies. A final section suggests ethical criteria for assessing economic systems.

Case studies

Apple: the exemplary capitalist company?
Tension between state and market in Brazil's oil industry

Chapter 3 The political sphere: societal and business goals. Basic concepts of politics are introduced, along with foundation theories of governance and the social contract. Democracy is discussed in both its ethical foundations and applications in actual political systems. These are compared to authoritarian alternatives, which have become influential in today's panoply of national political systems. The role of business in both democratic and authoritarian systems is highlighted. Accountability and legitimacy of governments are found to be essential for the achievement of economic and social goals, and in this respect, most governments, whether democratic or otherwise, have some way to go. Finally, international political relations are introduced, with specific reference to their impacts on international business.

Case studies

Qatar: a small state with global ambitions
Myanmar and the challenges of democracy

Chapter 4 Law and justice: Diverse ethical perspectives for business. Ethical concepts are placed in the framework of the rule of law, which is explained from a theoretical and practical point of view. Differing national legal systems are presented, with a focus on how they relate to business activities. Included are the main western traditions and also religious and customary legal systems. Legal aspects of business activities across borders are highlighted, including contracts, intellectual property and competition issues – all of which have ethical dimensions. International law is introduced, including human rights law and environmental law.

Case studies

Ethics and the death penalty
Data protection laws struggle to keep up with privacy concerns

Chapter 5 Financial markets: What role for ethics? Evolving ethical issues in finance are placed in historical perspective, indicating how the role of finance, and attitudes to it, have changed. Corporate status and personal responsibility are contrasted, in terms of accountability for wrongdoing. Players and processes in financial markets are analysed. Included are equities, bonds, sovereign borrowers and investors, and ethical investing. The regulation of financial markets, especially in relation to the financial crisis of 2008, is discussed, assessing what went wrong and how a rethinking of business ethics can contribute to reforms.

Case studies

China's shadow finance sector
The bank, the trader and the governor

Chapter 6 International trade and ethical considerations. World trade is presented in a historical context, highlighting ethical issues, especially the role of trading powers and imperialist expansion. National trade policies come under the spotlight, including protectionism and subsidies, assessing winners and losers in global trade. The continuing weak position of vulnerable developing countries is highlighted. The role of the World Trade Organization is assessed in the light of the Doha round. The recent developments in regional trade agreements bring numerous ethical issues into the frame, including protections of intellectual property, environmental protection and food safety. These reveal a wide range of ethical concerns which increasingly impact on MNEs.

Case studies

Indonesia gains from trade, but who is left behind?
Trading giants: the world at their feet

PART 2 ETHICS AND BUSINESS

Chapter 7 Ethics and CSR in international business. The chapter begins with an overview of the ethical challenges facing businesses. It then turns to a critical discussion of corporate purpose: what a company exists to do, and how answers to this question evolve over time. The shareholder primacy model of the company is introduced. An overview of business–society relations follows. There is a discussion of key concepts, theoretical foundations and business applications. Theories discussed include CSR, corporate social performance, corporate citizenship and stakeholder management. Social contract theory, discussed in Chapter 3, is revisited in the business context. Finally, the main ethical theories are considered in current business contexts, including the Kantian categorical imperative, utilitarian theory, rights-based theories and Aristotle's virtue ethics.

Case studies

H&M: Can the champion of cheap fashion also be ethical?
Serco and the privatization of public services

Chapter 8 Corporate governance: How do ethical principles apply? The ethical principles involved in corporate governance are presented at the outset of this chapter, including the different roles in public and private companies. The foundations of the shareholder primacy model of the company, including property theory and agency theory, are critically discussed. There follows a section on directors' duties to shareholders and other stakeholders, taking in differing national corporate governance frameworks. The evolution of thinking on executive rewards is discussed. A synthesis follows, highlighting interconnections between CSR, ethics and corporate governance.

Case studies

Volkswagen, a tale of engineering strength and governance weakness
Singapore and Temasek: A model for sovereign wealth?

Chapter 9 Human rights and ethical business. The chapter begins with the ethical foundations of human rights. Human rights in the global context, including international legal frameworks (introduced in Chapter 4) are then discussed. The main sections focus on company obligations in international human rights, and their relationship with CSR. There is an overview of legal processes by which companies can be treated as organizations liable for human rights abuses, and how these processes can influence corporate strategy. This is followed by detailed discussion of human rights in differing business contexts. The rights highlighted include the right not to be subjected to inhuman treatment, prohibitions on child labour, the right to organize in trade unions, and the right to a living wage.

Case studies

A better life for Walmart workers?
Human rights of miners in South Africa

Chapter 10 Sustainability and the ethical business. The multiple facets of sustainability are explored from an ethical perspective, covering economic and environmental aspects as well as issues of human well-being. Differing approaches to sustainable development are critically discussed. Environmental challenges, including climate change and meeting energy needs, are discussed, with particular reference to the vulnerabilities of poor countries. In a section on agriculture and food, producers' and consumers' perspectives are presented. Ethical initiatives such as fair trade are included. A final section looks as sustainability versus profits, turning towards an application of CSR and the role of social enterprises.

Case studies

Canada's oil sands: An energy source, but at what environmental price?
Assessing Turkey's sustainable development

Chapter 11 Conclusions: Business ethics and global challenges. The chapter begins with a review of the ethical themes and how they have featured in business examples. Each of the elements in the business ethics overview diagram (Figure I.1) is reviewed: actors, concepts and contexts. The chapter highlights the features of the changing environment which impact most strongly on business ethics. These are globalization and the spread of markets. The discussion throughout the chapters on the challenges highlighted in the Introduction are summarized, with a thought-provoking look at the prospects and possibilities for a more ethical future in international business.

Case study

Spain rejects Las Vegas-style casino project

CASE STUDY GRID

The opening and closing case studies all explore one or more of the global issues discussed in the chapter, highlighting the ethical challenges for businesses and their stakeholders. Each case study features one or more key locations and also a wide geographic spread of impacts, revealing the interconnectedness in today's globalized world.

Chapter and page number	Title	Geographic spread
1, p. 22	Evolving tobacco companies: ethical questions in changing markets	China, India, Indonesia, Brazil, Russia, Turkey, Nigeria, Uruguay, US, UK, Australia
1, p. 47	Bangladesh factory collapse reveals plight of garment workers	Bangladesh, UK, US, Spain, Pakistan, China, India and Turkey
2, p. 51	Apple: the exemplary capitalist company?	US, China, Taiwan, Caribbean, Hong Kong, Brazil, Mexico, Indonesia, Eastern Europe
2, p. 82	Tension between state and market in Brazil's oil industry	Brazil, China
3, p. 86	Qatar: a small state with global ambitions	Qatar, US, Iraq, Afghanistan, UK, Switzerland, Libya, Syria, Saudi Arabia, Kuwait
3, p. 116	Myanmar and the challenges of democracy	Myanmar, China
4, p. 119	Ethics and the death penalty	US, China, Denmark, Germany, Israel, UK
4, p. 147	Data protection laws struggle to keep up with privacy concerns	(Global) UK, Europe, USA

Chapter and page number	Title	Geographic spread
5, p. 151	China's shadow finance sector	China, US
5, p. 179	The bank, the trader and the governor	UK, Africa, Caribbean, US, Qatar, Middle East
6, p. 182	Indonesia gains from trade, but who is left behind?	Indonesia, Singapore, Malaysia, Cambodia and Vietnam, sub-Saharan Africa, India, China
6, p. 210	Trading giants: the world at their feet	(Global) Switzerland, China, Sudan, Iran, Singapore, US, Libya, South Africa
7, p. 216	H&M: can the champion of cheap fashion also be ethical?	Sweden, Spain, Europe, North Africa, Asia, Bangladesh
7, p. 246	Serco and the privatization of public services	UK, Australia
8, p. 250	Volkswagen, a tale of engineering strengths and governance weakness	(Global) Germany, US, Japan, Sweden
8, p. 274	Singapore and Temasek: a model for sovereign wealth?	Singapore, Switzerland, Asia, China, North America, Europe, UK, Australia, Hong Kong, Russia, Burma, Gambia, Bangladesh, Philippines, Sri Lanka, Indonesia
9, p. 279	A better life for Walmart workers?	US, China, Bangladesh, Brazil, India, Mexico
9, p. 308	Human rights of miners in South Africa	South Africa, US, UK
10, p. 312	Canada's oil sands: an energy source, but at what environmental price?	Canada, US, Asia
10, p. 342	Assessing Turkey's sustainable development	Turkey, Germany, Iraq, Iran, Saudi Arabia, Israel, US
11, p. 346	Spain rejects Las Vegas-style casino project	Spain, US, China, Singapore, Eastern Europe, Morocco

HOW TO USE THE BOOK AND ACCOMPANYING WEBSITE

Each chapter contains a number of features designed to aid the reader in understanding concepts and theories, applying them to business situations, and critically evaluating the issues raised. At the beginning of each chapter there is a chapter outline, a statement of the ethical themes covered in the chapter, and a set of learning objectives.

Within the text of each section of a chapter, there are highlighted terms, like those in this introduction. These are key concepts and other terms which form the basis of a discussion of the issues. An example of a concept would be human dignity. An example of term needed in discussion of international business is supply chain. Some organizations, such as the World Trade Organization (WTO) also feature among these highlighted terms. Readers are probably familiar with many of them already, and for these readers, the definitions will act as a reminder. For readers with no background in international business, the highlighted terms will provide the necessary foundation. All these highlighted terms are contained in the Glossary at the end of the book. There is also an Index at the end of the book.

References are listed at the end of each chapter. There are a few Notes at the end of chapters, which are explanatory in nature.

Throughout these chapters, there are features entitled 'Pause to consider ...', which present a question for readers to stop and think about. These pauses will help to bring together the points in the section, and also help readers to engage in critical thinking on the issues.

Callout boxes feature throughout the text, highlighting particular points. These are memorable points which are featured to make them stand out from the text. They will help in recalling the content of the section, and can be the focus of group discussion. Many are provocative.

At the end of each chapter, there are Review questions. Answering these questions is helpful in grasping the foundation knowledge contained in each chapter. The questions also raise issues from the chapter which involve critical reflection on its content. These questions can be used as an individual learning exercise or in group discussions, to complement the questions raised in the 'Pause to consider' boxes.

There is an opening case study and a closing case study for each chapter. The exception is the final chapter, which has only one case study. The case studies present issues which arise in the chapter where they are positioned, but they also raise broader issues. Some are related to each other, taking differing perspectives. Examples are the Rana Plaza case study in Chapter 1 and the H&M case study in Chapter 7. These can be looked at as a pair. There are other similar pairings. As with all case studies which involve current issues, there are continuing developments, and it is helpful to update each one as events unfold. The background provided in the case study feature will provide a good understanding of the issues which arise as new events unfold. There are discussion questions at the end of each case study.

An innovative feature, Spotlight on Ethical Business, presents structured interviews with people involved in business ethics globally, including management, monitoring and research. These interviews are available on the companion website for the book. They are introduced in boxes in relevant chapters. In each of these, readers will find background information on the interviewee and his/her role, background reading for the interview, and follow-up questions designed to spark critical thinking on the issues raised. Spotlight on Ethical Business offers valuable insight to the ways in which business ethics operates in the real world, through the eyes of people who are directly involved from a variety of perspectives. Here is a list of the interviews and where they are featured in the book:

> *Corruption and business*, interview with Peter van Veen, Director, Business Integrity Programme, Transparency International, UK; Chapter 1, p. 43.
> *The UN Global Compact and sustainability*, interview with Chris Harrop, Chair of United Nations Global Compact (UNGC) Network UK, and Director at Marshalls plc; Chapter 7, p. 236.
> *Garment workers in India*, interview with Jean Jenkins, Senior Lecturer in Employment Relations at Cardiff University, UK; Chapter 9, p. 298.
> *Sustainability and Fairtrade*, interview with Richard Anstead, Head of Product Management, Fairtrade Foundation, UK, Chapter 10, p. 335.

Also on the companion website is a range of other materials for lecturers and students. There are suggested lecture formats, suggested answers to case study questions, guidelines for discussing the 'Pause to consider' questions and guidelines for answering the Review Questions.

It is hoped that readers will find this book helpful and relevant not just for business ethics as an area of study, but in the many areas of business and management where issues of globalization and social impacts arise. It is also hoped that the book will be intellectually challenging and enjoyable.

REFERENCE

IOM (International Organization for Migration) (2013) *World Migration Report 2013* (Geneva: IOM).

PART ONE

THE BUSINESS ENVIRONMENT FROM AN ETHICAL PERSPECTIVE

The chapters in Part 1 set the scene for business ethics in context. **Chapter 1** explores the leading ethical theories that will feature in examples throughout the book. It also sets out cultural contexts in which ethical issues arise. Following on from cultural contexts, later chapters in this Part look in depth at other aspects of the business environment which impact on ethics in practice. In **Chapter 2**, globalization and economic integration are discussed, both in historical perspective and in the contemporary world. **Chapter 3** focuses on the political sphere as a source of ethical foundations and also an important area of activity in which businesses are increasingly involved. **Chapter 4** examines the legal environment as it affects business activities, including the role of companies in shaping laws. Law-making and enforcement are now more than ever seen to be key to changing business behaviour towards a more ethical approach. The next chapter, **Chapter 5**, takes up this challenge, in an exploration of global finance. This is perhaps the one function which has come most into prominence in recent years as in need of a renewed focus on business ethics. The last chapter in Part 1, **Chapter 6**, which focuses on trade and ethics, renews the discussion of cultural, economic and political factors which shape international business, with both positive and negative impacts. In each of these chapters, implications for business decision-making and societal goals are highlighted.

PART CONTENTS

CHAPTER 1

ETHICAL THEORIES AND CULTURAL CONTEXTS

ETHICAL THEMES IN THIS CHAPTER

- Interplay between the individual and society
- Moral rules and cultural divergence

THE AIMS OF THIS CHAPTER ARE TO

- Identify key ethical concepts
- Gain an understanding of the core ethical theories which underlie business ethics globally
- Appreciate the cultural contexts in which values and norms of behaviour evolve
- Begin to apply ethical concepts to business

EVOLVING TOBACCO COMPANIES: ETHICAL QUESTIONS IN CHANGING MARKETS

OPENING CASE STUDY

With the growth in smoking bans in restaurants and offices, people in many advanced economies might well get the impression that smoking is becoming less of a health problem globally. But this would be far from the truth. Some six million people die from smoking every year. Tobacco is the most widespread legal product easily available to consumers which is likely to kill up to half of its users. Moreover, some 600,000 people die each year from second-hand smoke. Many governments have recognized the public health issue and taken steps to curtail tobacco use, as is evident in the smoking restrictions in public places. But the extent of regulation varies a great deal from country to country. The smoker was once perceived, as in old Hollywood films, in a sophisticated setting. The truth about the typical smoker in today's world could not be more different. A typical smoker is more likely to be a poor inhabitant in rural India, probably with little or no education and unaware of the addictive nature of cigarettes. The less educated smoker is less able to quit the habit than the educated one (WHO, 2003).

Photo 1.1 *The health risks from smoking weigh with governments, but measures to curtail smoking are aggressively resisted by large tobacco companies.* (PhotoDisc/Getty Images)

Of the world's billion smokers, 80% live in developing and emerging economies. It is estimated that in China there are 350 million smokers, and smoking-related illnesses kill about a million people annually. Nearly three in five Chinese men are smokers. But, despite the health risks, regulation is relatively weak in China. This is because China National Tobacco, the world's largest tobacco company and one of the world's most profitable companies, enjoys a state monopoly, and the government takes in the equivalent of $95 billion in tax revenues from the sale of tobacco (Bloomberg, 2012).

Health risks and ethical issues weigh more heavily on many western governments and consumers. The large western tobacco companies, often referred to collectively as 'Big Tobacco', have been adapting to changing market conditions. The leading companies are Philip Morris, BAT (British American Tobacco) and Imperial. They resolutely defend their products as legal, offering consumers products for which there is steady demand, and resisting allegations that their business is unethical. As regulation has become stricter in some countries, the companies have shifted their marketing to countries with more lax regulation. They have faced accusations that they are behaving unethically by targeting poorer, more vulnerable, consumers. Their expansion into

emerging markets has been facilitated by trade agreements between countries which bring down trade barriers (WHO, 2012). This has given the tobacco companies access to larger potential markets. BAT had a turnover of £50 billion in 2011, generating profits of £4.9 billion, an increase of £600 million on the previous year (Thompson, 2012). Nearly two-thirds of BAT's revenues came from emerging markets, led by Indonesia, Brazil, Russia, Turkey and Nigeria. Is regulation becoming stricter in these markets? In 2012, Brazil introduced a ban on flavoured tobaccos, because of their greater attractiveness to young people. Uruguay now requires health warnings to cover 80% of a cigarette packet, and smoking there is banned in and around hospitals and schools. Such measures are vigorously fought by tobacco companies, who take their complaints to each country's courts, using their huge financial resources to contest the legality of regulation.

The companies have had some success. In the US, the Supreme Court has held that restrictions on advertising alcohol, a similar 'vice'-type of product, is in breach of the constitutional right of free speech enjoyed by the company. The court held that restrictions in respect of targeting children would still be lawful. This ruling on 'commercial speech' would seem to apply equally to tobacco companies (Quinn et al., 2011). Australia has introduced the most stringent regulation to date, in its Tobacco Plain Packaging Act 2011, which requires tobacco to be sold in plain packets without any manufacturer's logo, and containing graphic photos of smoking-related illnesses. The major tobacco companies are suing the Australian government, claiming they are being denied the right to brand their products. BAT's CEO, Nicandro Durante, from Brazil, says he accepts that some regulation is in order, but feels that the Australian example is going too far. Still, other countries are considering following the Australian example. He says, 'I think we are a very ethical industry and a very responsible industry ... . It's a risk product and I think regulation is good' (Thompson, 2012). A consideration for governments is their policy of taxing tobacco products heavily. This results in modest reductions in smoking, and, significantly, raises considerable tax revenues for government coffers.

Regulation and decline in smoking in western countries are factors leading tobacco companies to invest in alternative products, such as nicotine inhalers and electronic cigarettes, which so far are unregulated. Public health authorities have expressed concern about e-cigarettes, some of which come in flavours such as chocolate and strawberry, which could appeal to children (Quinn et al., 2011). Philip Morris sees these smokeless alternatives as becoming a significant market in the future. The company is planning on launching a Marlboro cigarette which only heats the tobacco, rather than burns it (Thompson and Wembridge, 2012). This will create less smoke and tar, and will be a healthier alternative for smokers. These initiatives, which reflect western consumers' health concerns, are at present only a small fraction of the overall market, and, if they gain ground, will probably attract regulation. They represent another strategy in the tobacco industry, which is constantly evolving. Asked whether he has any ethical misgivings about BAT selling tobacco, its CEO says, 'Never'.

Sources: Quinn, M., Mujtaba, B. and Cavico, F. (2011) 'Global tobacco sales dilemmas: the clash of freedom and markets with moraliy and ethics', *Journal of Business Studies Quarterly*, 2(2): 107–24; WHO (2012) *Confronting the Tobacco Epidemic in a New Era of Trade and Investment Liberalization* (Geneva: WHO); WHO (2003) *Tobacco and Health in the Developing World* (Brussels: WHO); Thompson, C. and Wembridge, M. (2012) 'Tobacco rush for smoke without fire', *Financial Times*, 13 August; Thompson, C. (2012) 'The running man of Big Tobacco', *Financial Times*, 1 October; Bloomberg (2012) 'China's tobacco monopoly bigger by profit than HSBC', 6 March, at www.bloomberg.com (18/09/14).

DISCUSSION QUESTIONS

- ▫ **What are the ethical issues raised in this case study?**

- ▫ **Do you agree with the stringent regulation introduced by Australia, or do you feel they have taken regulation too far? Give your reasons.**

- ▫ **Would you be happy working for a tobacco company, or would you refuse to work in the industry? Give your reasons.**

INTRODUCTION

This chapter introduces the main ethical concepts and places them in the theoretical frameworks with which they are associated. Looking at the prominent ethical theories over the years might seem to be a rather abstract exercise, unrelated to current ethical issues such as the ones just highlighted in the opening case study. However, the theories presented here are placed in the cultural contexts in which their authors lived, and it will be seen that, although the outward events in today's world seem very different, the underlying issues which gave rise to ethical theorizing are remarkably similar to issues faced by individuals, governments and businesses today.

Following a discussion of the relevant theories, we look more closely at cultural contexts, both historically and in the current environment. We highlight national cultures and religions as remaining highly influential in today's world, in which the growth of emerging markets is contributing to a more diverse cultural environment for international business. In an era of globalization, are national cultural differences becoming less significant? We find that national cultures and subcultures, with their divergent moral values, remain crucial in international business relations. For the MNE, clarifying and resolving ethical issues often involves evaluating a variety of cultural contexts. The last section therefore takes a practical approach to applying ethical concepts and theories in business contexts.

ETHICAL CONCEPTS IN CULTURAL CONTEXTS

Our ideas of right and wrong stem largely from the culture in which we have grown up. We learn from an early age that there are good and bad ways to behave, and that departing from these norms leads to social condemnation. These rules and norms of behaviour are referred to as a culture's morality. Cultures and moral standards differ from society to society. And this divergence can pertain to other types of grouping, including ethnic groups and religions. A cultural minority within a society, often known as a 'subculture', has its own moral standards. Immigrants often form subcultures in host societies, retaining the cultural norms of their home countries. But the longer they reside in their new country, the more likely they and their children are to adapt to the new culture. Urban dwellers and rural dwellers within the same country diverge in their cultural values. Culture change is a recognized phenomenon as societies shift from being mainly rural to urban. A radical change takes place as people move from family-based economic life to working as individuals for wages in factory conditions. A religion is another source of morality, and some religions are highly prescriptive in terms of moral codes. A religion's followers are likely to reside in numerous different countries, whose national social and cultural environments present a degree of conflict with religious values. It is usual for national governments to recognize the freedom of inhabitants to practise the religion of their choice, so long as its norms conform to national values. For example, a religion which recognizes polygamy will come into conflict with national law in most countries, as monogamy is more widely recognized in law. In any country, therefore, we are likely to find a range of approaches to morality, as well as changes in moral values which take place over time. The challenging task of ethics, by contrast, is to look beyond differing moral standards to basic concepts of good and bad which relate to all of us as human beings.

It could be argued that this task is impossible for two reasons. First, there is no such thing as absolute right and wrong. This is the position of the cultural relativist. Cultural relativism refrains from making judgments on moral values in different cultures. Second, it assumes we are able to be objective, to step outside our own cultural makeup, which is impossible. Dealing with the first of these objections, to study ethics does not assume there exist somewhere 'out there' absolute values which apply universally. It aims to understand the concepts of right and wrong, and how they work in practice, guiding the decisions and actions of people in everyday life. Turning to the second objection, to say that we all have moral values does not imply that we cannot conceive of any others. As we have noted,

Figure 1.1 *Ethical concepts in theory and practice*

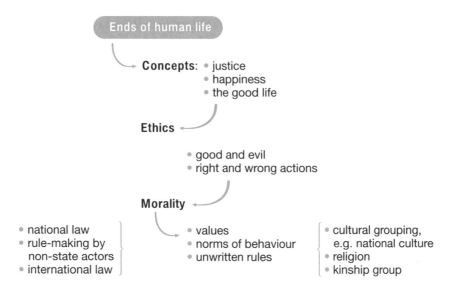

notions of right and wrong fluctuate among societies and over time. Shedding light on underlying concepts helps us to understand our own and other societies. It also helps in developing a critical perspective on ethical issues. The study of ethics goes back thousands of years, most notably to the ancient Greeks. Aristotle, whose ethical views will be discussed later in this chapter, felt uneasy that slavery existed in ancient Athens, as the practice was demeaning, treating human beings as property (Aristotle, 1962b: 34–5). This is an example of the philosopher looking beyond cultural norms to ethical principles. These concepts are depicted in Figure 1.1.

As Figure 1.1 shows, broad questions about the ends of human life inform ethical debate. Questions of morality, which bear on practical issues in our everyday lives, are matters of social, religious and other types of grouping within society. These are instilled in all of us from an early age, and are reinforced in social interactions throughout our lives. Moreover, many moral rules are incorporated into law. This can be through legislation within the state or through formal rules which are recognized by many groups and communities below state level. Rule-governed behaviour pervades all aspects of life in a modern society, from rules on shop opening hours to rules governing the duties of public officials. The moral element of rules is typically rooted in the society's cultural environment. For example, restrictions on shop opening hours on a Sunday stem largely from the Christian belief that one should not work on the Sabbath, or day of worship. In a second example, the public official who accepts a bribe is in breach of the duties of office. This would also be a crime in law, for which the perpetrator could be prosecuted. We would also probably say that this behaviour is unethical, as the act is dishonest. Dishonesty is generally considered an ethical wrong. However, in a number of countries, payments such as bribes tend to be seen as customary and acceptable practices in business, even though there is national legislation prohibiting the practice. This is a case where we would probably say that there is a divergence between ethical principles and the customary practice. Businesses often confront conflicts between

Rule-governed behaviour pervades all aspects of life in a modern society, from rules on shop opening hours to rules governing the duties of public officials.

cultural norms in a society and standards of ethical behaviour, especially in instances where an MNE's stakeholders in different countries take differing stances on what the company should do. Issues such as this are recurrent themes in the theories of the leading ethical thinkers whose insight and methods for tackling ethical questions are essential to business ethics.

We will look at a number of different ethical theories in this chapter, but one point of departure which they have in common is that they assume each of us is a rational human being, with feelings of pleasure and pain, a conscience, personal goals and a will to take the decisions which affect our lives. Rationality distinguishes humans from other living creatures. We are each of us capable of reflecting on our own lives, criticizing ourselves for bad decisions and deliberately changing our lives, irrespective of our cultural background. This does not lead to ethical absolutism, a view that there exists a universal human nature and a set of ethical rules which apply universally. The ways in which motivations, fears, rewards and deterrents affect behaviour differ between societies and also between individuals within a society, due to different psychological makeup. However, ethical theories over centuries have contributed to a greater understanding of ethical reasoning.

What are the arguments in favour of cultural relativism? Would you call yourself a cultural relativist? If not, what are the ethical absolutes which you feel should guide behaviour of both individuals and businesses?

ETHICAL THEORIES

In this section we discover the leading theories of ethics which have shaped ethical debate. The theories we highlight are Kant's ethical theory, utilitarianism, the rights-based ethical theory of Rawls, Aristotle's theory of virtue ethics and the teaching of Confucius. These theories span more than 2,500 years of history. Although most of these philosophers are western in their cultural backgrounds, Confucius is Asian. Of the theories discussed below, most represent a 'school' of thought, as there are several leading thinkers who have contributed to the general theoretical stance. This is particularly true of the utilitarians, who have influenced much moral philosophy from the eighteenth century to the present. In general, it is worth noting that each thinker writes in the context of the ideas and events that are current. Sometimes a theorist writes directly about the current situation, as Confucius and the English utilitarians did. Often, they are concerned that changes taking place in society are undermining moral standards. Some of these writers are highly prescriptive, pointing the way to a moral life. Kant and Aristotle are among them. We begin with Kant.

KANT'S ETHICAL THEORY

Immanuel Kant (1724–1804) wrote extensively on philosophical subjects, not just ethics, but also metaphysics and the theory of knowledge. His complicated sentences and use of many technical terms have meant his writings have posed challenges for translators and readers. But for the modern reader, perseverance is amply rewarded, as his views on ethical concepts have been among the most influential in ethical thinking. We begin with Kant's observation that people exist in the natural world, that is, the physical world of the senses, or sensible world, which they share with all other natural phenomena. The sensible world can be studied empirically. Understanding nature necessarily involves observing *what is*: we can observe what is, what has been, and, on the basis of that study, predict what will be.

However, it makes no sense to say that something in nature 'ought to be other than what in all these time-relations it actually is' (Kant, 1929: 473). *What is*, he asserts, can never imply *what ought to be*.

Kant recognizes that people naturally seek happiness, and have different ideas of what happiness is. No one can ever say definitively what he or she actually wishes, or whether it is attained. A person may wish to have riches, power and good health. But there are no definite principles of happiness, only our imagination based on our own empirical experiences in the sensible world. Everyone has feelings, wants and inclinations. The prosperity and private happiness which a person attains in the sensible world do not make a person good. Kant holds that values in this context have a 'market price' or value, in that a thing which has value can be replaced with another thing of equivalent value (Kant, 1948: 113). In the translation by T. Abbott, published in 1949, this concept is referred to as 'market value' (Kant, 1949: 51). These things of value have relative worth, which can be measured alongside other things considered desirable. But such value is relative; it does not represent intrinsic worth. Intrinsic worth Kant ascribes to human dignity.

Human beings are unique in nature in possessing rationality and will, that is, a sense of autonomy or freedom to act in accordance with principles that a person wills for himself or herself. Every person regards his or her own existence in a similar light, that is, as a being conscious of being an intelligence. Rationality relates to the intelligible world, and is contrasted with the sensible world. Every person is faced with a choice between actions based on inclinations and those based on moral duty. We can act on the basis of immediate inclinations, seeking happiness of the senses, or act on the basis of moral duty, which is obedience to law willed by a rational being (Kant, 1948: 72). The notion of duty is an important element in Kant's ethics. Indeed, Kant is a leading exponent of a philosophical approach known as deontology, which focuses on the intrinsic nature of right and wrong. For Kant, the morality of an act does not depend on the results, but on the sense of duty. He says that where a person finds happiness in helping others, this is valuable in spreading happiness, but has no moral worth. The reason is that the charitable person is acting from inclination rather than a sense of duty. Kant's uncompromising position can be contrasted with that of the utilitarians, whose view of morality was the opposite of Kant's and based on the results of actions (as discussed below).

For Kant, the morality of an act does not depend on the results, but on the sense of duty.

Kant holds that morality presupposes freedom and autonomy. He says, 'To the idea of freedom is inseparably attached the concept of autonomy, and to this in turn the universal principle of morality' (Kant, 1948: 135). This freedom is described by Kant as 'positive freedom', which he says is 'richer and more fruitful' than freedom in the negative sense (Kant, 1948: 127). Kant contrasts his notion of positive freedom as self-determination with negative freedom, which is 'independence of empirical conditions' (Kant, 1929: 476). He recognizes, however, that the two concepts are closely related, and his thinking contains elements of both. He recognizes that to act morally we must feel free, but when we act from a sense of duty, the moral law is perceived as binding, in which case freedom seems to be diminished. His answer is that the will's 'enactment of its own laws' preserves our autonomy. Negative freedom refers to the sensible world, while positive freedom relates to the intelligible world. The notion of two concepts of liberty which Kant raises has become a continuing theme in ethical discourse, and we will see it emerge again in the utilitarians. The difference between positive and negative liberty is sometimes described as freedom *to* act in a certain way versus freedom *from* impediments which stand in the way of one's actions (Berlin, 1958: 7). Kant's view of positive liberty as self-will is contrasted with the utilitarians' view of liberty as essentially freedom from impediments which will allow the individual to pursue his or her own goals.

Having established the principle of the freedom of the will, Kant goes on to describe the nature of ethical principles. Any rational being exists, he argues, as an end in himself, rather than merely as a means to an end. If an action is good only insofar as it is a means to something else, then it has no moral worth. Kant calls his principle of morality a categorical imperative, in that it is good in itself. The categorical imperative holds

> *The categorical imperative holds that each of us must treat each other always as ends in themselves, and never as means.*

that each of us must treat each other always as ends in themselves, and never as means (Kant, 1948: 105). Its essence is human dignity. In an alternative formulation of the principle, Kant says that we should act in such a way that our action could be universally followed: 'Act only on that maxim through which you can at the same time will that it should be a universal law' (Kant, 1948: 97). Put in terms of will, he calls this the 'idea of the will of every rational being as a will which makes universal law' (Kant, 1948: 109). This notion of universalizability has a rather different emphasis from the formulation that people should always treat each other as ends rather than means. Although we speak of the categorical imperative in the singular, we are in fact referring to two slightly different principles which are grouped under that heading. The two principles which make up the categorical imperative are perhaps the most important contribution of Kant's theory. These principles form the basis of what many later theorists would describe as a universalist approach to ethics, in contrast to the cultural relativism which was described earlier in this chapter. The universalist holds that ethical principles transcend cultural morals, offering a means by which differing cultures can be judged. For business ethics, the implication is that organizations can be judged by ethical principles which transcend the cultures of particular locations.

Kant speaks of a 'kingdom of ends' in which all members prescribe the law for themselves based on human dignity. For 'kingdom', the closest modern notion is probably 'state' or 'community'. He describes this grouping as a 'systematic union of rational beings under common objective laws' (Kant, 1948: 112). The mention of laws which bind all probably makes this closer to our concept of the state. In Kant's kingdom of ends, which he describes as an ideal only, each person is the maker of its universal laws and is also subject to these laws. He acknowledges that in practice, states are usually not governed in this way. Nonetheless, the concept remains a yardstick for judging actual governance of states. This idea of citizens' will being integral to the governance of the state has become an important concept in political philosophy, suggesting a moral role for the state. It is closely related to Rousseau's theory of the 'general will', which will be discussed in Chapter 3.

THE UTILITARIANS

Although it is common to group these theorists together under 'utilitarianism', this label is somewhat misleading, as it covers a number of different writers. They do share certain basic tenets, as we will see, but there are important differences between them. Kant's moral theory is often contrasted with that of the utilitarians (see Table 1.1). While very different in outlook and methodology, their theories are rooted in individualism, focusing on freedom and rationality, which define the individual human being. Their views on the individual are very

Table 1.1 *Comparing Kant and the early utilitarians*

Ethical issues	Kant	Utilitarians
View of the individual	Rational autonomy	Hedonistic; rational pursuit of self-interest
Nature of freedom	Positive: self-direction	Negative: freedom from impediments
Happiness	Obedience to moral duty	Seeking pleasure and avoiding pain
Ethical system	Universalist	Consequentialist
Basis of morality	Categorical imperative: treat people as ends rather than means	Greatest happiness of the greatest number
Nature of the state	Kingdom of ends	Minimal government intervention; democratic

different, but both schools of thought contributed to the foundations of liberalism, a blend of ideas about human dignity and natural rights which underpins much modern ethical thinking. Furthermore, they have been highly influential in shaping cultural, economic and political thinking, not just in western countries, but also in Asian countries. The early utilitarians wrote during an era of industrialization, changing economic landscapes and political upheavals across Europe. Although perhaps little remarked on today, these writers were influential in Japan during the Meiji period of modernization in the nineteenth century – an example of individualist thinking finding enthusiasts in a cultural environment which had been highly traditional and hierarchical.

The foundations of utilitarianism lie with a political philosopher who was not himself a utilitarian, but whose views permeate their thinking. Thomas Hobbes (1588–1679) took the view that all people seek happiness, by pursuing what gives them pleasure and avoiding what causes them pain. This became a central tenet of utilitarianism. Hobbes' view of the individual was one of egoistic hedonism. People pursue self-interested goals, and desire a maximum amount of freedom in which to do so. He postulates a state of nature, in which individuals are totally free to act, limited only by their means and strength. He recognizes that the state of nature would be far from secure, as the only rule would be 'might is right'.

Hobbes' state of nature would be far from secure, as the only rule would be 'might is right'.

He even describes the state of nature as a state of war of one person against another, in which no person could feel safe (Hobbes, 1960: 82). Not a very pleasant environment in which to live, and certainly not one in which a person could plan for the future. Having witnessed the horrors of the English civil war, Hobbes feared anarchy above all. He believed that the only solution would be a dictatorship based on absolute sovereignty of the ruler. He reasons that the state of nature is so unpleasant that people will submit to an absolute government. His proviso is that its aim is to maintain order, so that people can pursue their self-interest. If the sovereign fails to maintain order, the society could well slip back into the state of nature.

Hobbes offered a radically different view of morality from earlier moral philosophers. He parted company with those who see obedience to rules as leading to moral goodness or the development of a person's moral potential. He recognized the importance of freedom and rationality, but saw the rational person as chiefly a calculator, seeking self-interested goals which alone would bring happiness. The early utilitarians took this central tenet of Hobbesian thought as the starting point for their own thinking, but, as we will see, went on to take a different view of society and government.

The early utilitarians who set out the broad doctrine which we now consider the template for later theorists, were Jeremy Bentham (1748–1832) and James Mill (1773–1836). Of the two, Bentham is considered the more prominent figure, largely because of his zeal in support of democratic political reform. However, James Mill was perhaps the clearer theorist, whose written works offer a fuller and more coherent picture of the theory than we find in the writings of Bentham. In general, the two theorists make the following assumptions (Plamenatz, 1958: 72):

- That nothing is in itself desirable except pleasure and the relief of pain
- That one man's pleasure is in itself as desirable as any other man's
- That the right action is always the one which the prospective agent believes to be, under the circumstances, productive of the greatest happiness.

The first of these assumptions reflects the Hobbesian view of human nature, but the second two assumptions are what we would now see as characteristically utilitarian. They emphasize that one person's pleasure or pain is as relevant as any other person's. This implies a seemingly radical egalitarianism, quite revolutionary in a society which was highly unequal. A criticism of this view is that it assumes pleasure and pain can be measured, when in practice quantities of pleasure cannot be calculated in the way that commodities are measured. It is true that people do weigh up the possible consequences of alternative choices of action. Utilitarianism is often described as consequentialist for this reason. In contrast to the deontological approach of Kant, they hold that whether an action is good or not depends on the consequences. Consequentialism is depicted as the opposite of universalism in ethical theory, and is at the centre of much ethical debate. In business ethics, assessing the likely consequences of an action is often seen as a 'business case' for CSR. But critics argue that this is not truly an ethics-based approach, as self-interest, albeit long term, is still the guiding principle. In any case, the weakness of the utilitarian's attempts to measure happiness is a drawback of the theory. When a person is deciding on which course of action to take, he or she is not measuring up the alternatives in a quantitative way, as Bentham envisaged. The person chooses the course of action that he or she feels more strongly about. Bentham tended to 'confuse measurements of quantity with comparisons of effects' (Plamenatz, 1958: 74). In any case, people do not always behave rationally, and they are capable of behaving altruistically, acting out of charitable motives towards one another.

Utilitarians would agree with Hobbes that, in whatever terms people define their own happiness, they desire to maximize pleasure and minimize pain. This entails liberty in the negative sense. And conflicts are inevitable. James Mill observes that 'the objects of desire [are] not in sufficient abundance for all. The source of dispute is then exhaustless ...' (James Mill, 1955: 48). Government is necessary because without it, people would not be able to enjoy the fruits of their labour. Both Hobbes and the utilitarians feel that government represents an interference with a person's liberty. But, whereas Hobbes advocated an absolutist sovereign, the utilitarians envisage a government which is responsive to the people who inhabit its territory. Hence, the principle of government should be 'the greatest happiness of the greatest number' (James Mill, 1955: 47). This is often called the principle of utility. On this reasoning, if a government causes pain by restricting a person's liberty, it is justified if 'its coercive action creates less pain than it prevents' (James Mill, 1955: 83). The test of utility could be applied to any proposed law. This leaves open a wide range of possible interpretations. A minimalist interpretation is that government would be justified only in protecting the property rights of individuals. This view is advocated by economists who favour a *laissez faire* market economy. It was taken up by the classical economists, who assumed the pursuit of self-interest as the basis of their economic theories (see Chapter 2). But the classical economists arguably overlooked the wider implications of the theory. The utility principle could logically justify a more egalitarian approach (Robinson, 1962: 53). This interpretation could lead to an activist role of government in social welfare measures which benefit a large proportion of the population, as advocated by socialists. It is not difficult to see how early utilitarian theory underpinned both liberal and socialist economic perspectives.

By the nineteenth century, Britain had become an industrialized economy, characterized by new wealth accumulated by industrialists who were outside the existing establishment based on wealth in land. The latter had long dominated government. The growing middle class could identify with the views of the utilitarians in emphasizing the protection of property and seeking a greater responsiveness of government to the wishes of all in society. The 1832 Reform Act gave the franchise to the property-owning middle class. This was a watershed in democratic reform. But there remained a large working-class population, on whose labour the factories depended. Exploitative and degrading factory conditions prompted many political activists to press for more radical democratic reforms. James Mill was a more cautious democrat, believing that suffrage should be limited to those who were capable of rational action, a category which he interpreted as property-owning men over the age of forty. Despite his holding what we would now see as a highly restricted vision of who should have a democratic voice, he nonetheless fastened on democracy as the best possible government to realize his utilitarian principles.

James Mill's son, John Stuart Mill (1806–1873) was both a supporter of utilitarian theory and a critic of it. By the time he was writing, he was able to see that the democratic reforms advocated by his father were not as unqualifiedly beneficial to all as the elder Mill had believed them to be. What is more, J.S. Mill's moral philosophy had shifted away from the basic precepts of Bentham and James Mill. J.S. Mill had doubts about a number of the pillars of utilitarianism. He said that happiness is 'too complex and indefinite' to be pursued as if it were a single goal (J.S. Mill, 1962: 114). People in fact pursue a number of ends for their own sake, such as a desire for justice, for knowledge, for beauty or for love. In an essay on Bentham, he said that the idea that the morality of an act depends on its consequences does not go far enough, not taking sufficiently into account 'the consequences of the actions upon the agent's own frame of mind' (J.S. Mill, 1962: 115). For J.S. Mill, happiness is equivalent to development of the individual: 'it is only the cultivation of individuality which produces, or can produce, well-developed human beings' (J.S. Mill, 1955: 121). He said, 'It really is of importance not only what men do, but also what manner of men they are that do it' (J.S. Mill, 1955: 117).

J.S. Mill said, 'It really is of importance not only what men do, but also what manner of men they are that do it.'

These views represent a distinct departure from the utilitarianism of Bentham and James Mill. Although J.S. Mill was keen to defend the theories of his utilitarian predecessors, his own views on happiness and morality are more nuanced, placing greater emphasis on individual potential. Accordingly, he stressed the importance of freedom of the individual not just in respect of government interference, but also in respect to society's tendency towards conformity. He found in society a 'mass of influences hostile to individuality' (J.S. Mill, 1955: 131). 'The despotism of custom is everywhere the standing hindrance to human advancement', he said (J.S. Mill, 1955: 127). J.S. Mill's stress on human self-fulfilment sounds more akin to Kant's thinking, again suggesting that there is overlap between positive and negative definitions of freedom, as we found in the works of Kant.

The younger Mill was a supporter of democracy, but with more of a critical edge than his father. J.S. Mill was aware that there could exist a kind of 'good despotism', in which there was no great oppression, and the collective interests of the population are managed reasonably well (J.S. Mill, 1955: 204). Although citizens would enjoy an amount of freedom in the negative sense, they would know that they enjoyed it only as a concession from their ruler. Mill recognizes the fact that the negative concept of liberty does not necessarily imply democracy (see Berlin, 1958: 14). However, for J.S. Mill, individual expression and development would not be able to flourish in such a state. The despot dare not allow freedom of the press and discussion, as people would naturally clamour for a say in government, thus threatening the despot's rule. In giving way to calls for greater participation, the despot might well be transformed into a constitutional ruler. This turn of events was in fact just what was taking place in Britain.

The younger Mill favoured representative government, by which he meant the periodic election of representatives by 'the whole people, or some numerous portion of them', who have the 'ultimate controlling power' (J.S. Mill, 1955: 228). However, he warned of the dangers of democracy. Where there is rule by the majority, there is the risk that power will rest in the hands of a sectional interest or class. What would guarantee that they would govern in the interests of all? Mill was well aware that in most societies there is a minority of rich people and a great majority of poor people. Their interests are in opposition to each other. He observes that those in government might well justify their rule by saying that they are acting in the 'real' interests of the great mass of working-class people. But Mill had no time for such an argument, stating that only the individual can determine what his or her real interests are (J.S. Mill, 1955: 250). Kant would concur. Kant considered paternalism to be the 'greatest despotism imaginable' (in Berlin, 1999: 157).

Social justice is a theme in J.S. Mill's ethical theory. Mill considers 'social morality' to consist of 'a duty to others' (J.S. Mill, 1955: 140). This idea was quite radical in its day. It implies that justice is more than simply conformity with formal law. Justice also includes recognizing duties towards others to act in a way that reflects a basic sympathy. He says that, in addition to pursuit of 'self-regarding virtues', there is a need 'to promote the good of others' (J.S. Mill, 1955: 132–3). He says, 'the fact of living in society renders it indispensable that each should be bound to observe a certain line of conduct towards the rest' (J.S. Mill, 1955: 132). This is a notion which was taken up by later theorists such as John Rawls, discussed below. For the strict utilitarian, acting out of sympathy towards others is necessarily subordinate to self-interest. But J.S. Mill considers that the utilitarian view of what is expedient or inexpedient is separate from the rightness or wrongness of an action. Mill's views on justice seem far removed from those of Bentham. The distinction between justice defined as conformity with the law and the idea that justice is a higher ideal leads to the possibility of the 'unjust law' (Plamenatz, 1958: 142). This distinction is critical in arguments for social and political reforms. Law reflects the cultural norms of a society in a period in its history. Arguments about justice and human dignity spur reformers seeking changes in the law, such as women's right to vote. Social justice as a theme was further developed in the writings of the modern moral philosopher, John Rawls.

PAUSE TO CONSIDER...

What are the strengths of utilitarianism as an ethical theory? What are its weaknesses? To what extent is utilitarianism based on a view of human nature which you would agree with?

ETHICAL THEORY BASED ON RIGHTS AND JUSTICE: JOHN RAWLS

When we look at any society, observed John Rawls (1921–2002), we cannot help noticing pervasive inequalities, beginning at birth, which cannot be justified on grounds of 'merit or desert' (Rawls, 1971: 7). Every society consists of a basic set of institutions by which rights and duties are assigned, and advantages are allocated. Rawls is concerned about the social justice of these arrangements. How can a society in which justice as fairness be conceived? Such a society is a 'fair system of cooperation over time between generations' (Rawls, 1996: 18). He sees inter-generational justice as important in society (discussed further in Chapter 10). Social co-operation has three elements (Rawls, 1996: 16):

- It is guided by publicly recognized rules.
- It involves an idea of reciprocity. All do their part as the rules provide, and benefit in an 'appropriate way as assessed by a suitable benchmark of comparison'.
- It involves 'an idea of each participant's rational advantage, or good'.

Rawls uses the theoretical concept of the social contract to explain how societies are formed. In this, he follows a number of earlier philosophers, notably Locke and Rousseau, but going back as far as Plato. Hobbes had the beginnings of a social contract theory too. The social contract as envisaged by Locke or Rousseau (which will be discussed more fully in Chapter 3) rests on a notion of an agreement among free people to engage in social relations and to set up a government which is accountable to them. The social contract is often criticized as being a rather mechanical device, bearing little relation to reality. It is also sometimes seen as having little bearing on ethical theory. However, taken as a conceptual tool, it highlights the importance of liberty and justice, which are central to ethics (Barker, 1962: viii). Rawls is in no doubt that, 'without the ideas of society and the person, conceptions of the right and the good have no place' (Rawls, 1996: 110).

Rawls postulates an 'original position' in a way similar to that used by Hobbes in beginning with the state of nature. Of course, utilitarians used this hypothetical device as well. Rawls, however, takes issue with these philosophical predecessors in its conception. The original position is one of freedom and equality, in which people are rational but not pure self-interested egoists (Rawls, 1971: 13). Rawls assumes that there is a 'veil of ignorance' between people (Rawls, 1971: 136). No one knows anything about other people in the original position. People do not know the wealth or social status of others; nor do they know the values and aspirations of others. It is only in this way, he feels, that a principle of justice can emerge, in which each is treated equally and fairly as a person.

Each person has a wish to pursue his or her own conception of a good life, not just in the material sense, but embracing a view of 'what is valuable in human life' (Rawls, 1996: 19). This is a notion of self-fulfilment not unlike that of J.S. Mill or Kant. Each person also has a capacity for social co-operation. Rawls defines a sense of justice as 'a capacity to understand, to apply, and to act from the public conception of justice which characterizes the fair terms of social cooperation' (Rawls, 1996: 19). He rejects the utilitarians' principle of the greatest happiness, questioning whether anyone would willingly acquiesce in a detriment in order to bring about a greater amount of aggregate happiness in society. Two principles operate in his picture of the original position. The first is an equality of basic rights and duties. The second is that inequalities are 'only just if they result in compensating benefits for everyone, and in particular for the least advantaged members of society' (Rawls, 1971: 14–15).

Rawls believes that each person in society has basic rights founded on justice, or 'natural right, which even the welfare of everyone else cannot override' (Rawls, 1971: 28). Justice as fairness would not permit the loss of freedom suffered by some people to be compensated for by greater good enjoyed by others. Rawls points to what he feels is a basic mistaken belief of utilitarians – the extending to society as a whole the rational choices made by a single person. He takes issue with the view that utilitarianism is individualistic, finding that there is a contradiction in their thinking. Although individual self-interest is the basis of the happiness principle, and there is a strong emphasis on liberty, the principle of utility logically overrides individual values.

By contrast, Rawls argues that the moral worth of the person is rooted in having a rational plan of life which is consistent with principles of justice. Justice as fairness is thus elevated to pre-eminence as an ethical concept. Rawls feels that his notions of the just society can be used to judge the actual institutions in states. Like J.S. Mill, he finds weaknesses in democracy and constitutional government. Of course, Rawls was writing over a century after Mill, but finds that political inequalities can persist in a democratic system.

Rawls was writing during a turbulent period in the US, in which the civil rights movement sought equal rights for black citizens. Although slavery had been abolished by the constitutional amendments of the post-Civil War period (1865–68), discrimination remained a reality, particularly in individual southern states. Literacy tests and poll taxes were used effectively to restrict voter participation of black Americans. Both practices were banned in the 1960s, through a constitutional amendment to ban the poll tax and the Voting Rights Act 1965 to ban literacy tests. A result was to greatly increase the number of black registered voters. However, many states have introduced new forms of voter eligibility test, posing new obstacles in the way of voters. Rawls saw political inequality as eroding democratic institutions. Were he alive today, he would be concerned about the inequalities in US society which undermine the rights of all in society.

ARISTOTLE'S VIRTUE ETHICS

The ancient Greek philosopher, Aristotle (384–322BC), set out the ethical issues confronting all of us as human beings. He presents challenges for the modern reader largely because his works on ethics, which draw heavily on Plato and other Greek thinkers, are written in the context of the ancient Greek city state. Socially and culturally, this setting is very different from a modern society. On the other hand, Aristotle shares many of the concerns that modern readers can identify with, such as human goals, a moral life and how best to achieve happiness. Aristotle is considered a leading exponent of virtue ethics, in that the focus is on the qualities of virtue in the person, rather than on ethical actions (Nussbaum, 1999).

In *Nicomachean Ethics*, Aristotle's approach is to analyse important ethical concepts, including 'good', 'happiness' and 'virtue'. We begin with the term 'good'. He finds there are two meanings: things can be intrinsically good or they can be good in that they are conducive to the intrinsically good (Aristotle, 1962a: 12). Something is intrinsically good if it is pursued for its own sake, as an end. As human beings, we pursue many ends, such as wealth. Wealth is not a final end, but a means to an end. Happiness, Aristotle proposes, is a final end: it is above all else, and we do not choose it for the sake of anything else. This is rather vague, as people have varying views about what happiness consists of. He therefore looks at the distinctive characteristics that denote the human being, asking 'what is the proper function of man' (Aristotle, 1962a: 16). The flute player's function is performance on the flute, and therein lies his goodness in fulfilling his function. But this is not the final good. Aristotle considers that rationality, in conceiving and obeying rational rules, is the distinctive characteristic of humans. A person's proper function is a kind of life guided by the rational element. Happiness, for Aristotle, is attained through virtue: 'happiness ... requires completeness in virtue as well as a complete lifetime' (Aristotle, 1962a: 23). He envisages that a person needs to strive for all his or her life to attain happiness, and this involves a virtuous life.

The term 'virtue' for Aristotle denotes not just a person's intentions, but also excellence or skill in doing something. It covers many kinds of goodness, not just moral goodness (Huby, 1967: 21). So human achievement of any kind, as well as upright behaviour, are covered by virtue. Aristotle makes a distinction between intellectual and moral virtues. Intellectual virtues derive from the rational side of the person's soul. They include wisdom and understanding, and are gained with experience over time. Moral virtues derive from the irrational part.

Virtue for the human being lies in both being good and acting in a virtuous way.

They include generosity and self-control. They are connected to pleasure and pain which people experience throughout their lives. The person learns moral virtues through habit and education. Aristotle says that people have no moral virtues by nature: 'we do not by nature develop into good or bad men' (Aristotle, 1962a: 41). We have a capacity first, and we show activity later. Good habits contribute to virtue, but so too does reason. Every virtue has two characteristics, causing a thing to be good in itself and causing it to perform its function well. Virtue for the human being lies in both being good and acting in a virtuous way. Aristotle uses the principle of the 'median' or 'mean' to describe how people should act. Moral virtue is concerned with emotions and actions, in which a person should aim for a middle position between too much and too little. Acting excessively and acting deficiently are both extremes and constitute vices. We experience pleasure, pain, fear, confidence, desire, anger and a host of other feelings. The best course for behaving properly is to choose the right objects for the right reason and in the right manner: this is the characteristic of virtue.

Aristotle considers justice to be the highest of all virtues. This is because it focuses on the good of others. He says, 'the best man is not one who practices virtue toward himself, but who practices it toward others, for that is a hard thing to achieve' (Aristotle, 1962a: 114). He says that the lawbreaker is unjust, but so, too, is anyone who acts unfairly. Aristotle here alludes to a distinction we have mentioned earlier, which is between the law in the narrow sense of formal law, and the notion of a higher law meaning justice. Impliedly, one can be law-abiding, but act unfairly and thus be unjust. Of legal enactments, those that aim for the common good are said to be 'just'.

Aristotle considers that people by nature come together to form associations. The members of a family form a type of association, and families group together to form a village. The highest form of association, formed from a number of villages, is the polis, the basic political association characterizing the Greek city state. He thus considers the polis 'to exist by nature' (Aristotle, 1962b: 6).

The *polis* in ancient Greece was probably more like our notion of society, as the Greeks did not make the distinction we would make between state and society (Aristotle, 1962b: lv). The polis was based on face-to-face relations among citizens, in contrast to the large impersonal state with which we are familiar. Aristotle is clear that, although the individual and the family came first in order of time, the polis is prior and higher in nature. The state has a moral role: 'the end of the state is not mere life; it is, rather, a good quality of life' (Aristotle, 1962b: 118). He notes that the polis does not consist only of good people, but of a variety of different people. Each can be a good citizen, but it is possible to be a good citizen without having 'the excellence which is the quality of a good man' (Aristotle, 1962b: 102).

PAUSE TO CONSIDER...

Aristotle's virtue ethics represents a theory of social ethics which many feel should apply to businesses today. Assume a foreign company is setting up a factory in a developing country, where it must deal with the government and hire workers. The government is keen that the company should have good relations in the community. How could the company apply virtue ethics?

THE ETHICAL TEACHINGS OF CONFUCIUS

Confucius (551–479BC), the ancient Chinese philosopher, lived in an era when the vast area which now comprises China was composed of numerous independent states. It was a period of political turbulence, as the feudal system was collapsing, and with it, the cultural elements which had characterized civilization. Confucius is today thought of mainly as a teacher, but he also felt he had a political vocation, to bring about more enlightened government. In this latter vocation, he was unsuccessful, failing to gain political influence in the courts of the rulers of the day. However, his ethical teachings, on which his political views were based, have left an enduring legacy.

The ethics of Confucius focus on the exemplary virtue of the human being. In this respect, Confucian ethics are similar to Aristotle's virtue ethics. Every person should strive to attain a virtuous existence, exemplifying trust, humility, self-control, fairness and generosity. These qualities, he felt, could be acquired through education. He believed in a strong affinity between morality and education. Confucius was sceptical about the role of rules and laws in guiding virtuous behaviour. He believed that ritual was an important element in education, but by this he meant actions more like 'civilized usages' than the image which we might have of rites (Leys, 1997: xxv). Importantly, in keeping with his emphasis on virtue ethics, he believed that education was not simply a matter of accumulating knowledge: 'Education is not about having; it is about being' (Leys, 1997: xxix). The goal of education should be moral and intellectual qualities, and, Confucius thought, these are the qualities necessary for good leadership in society. Among his greatest legacies were his views that wealth and birth should not automatically bring power, and government positions should be based on meritocracy. He believed that education should be open to all, rich or poor, whether of high or lowly birth. The educated person deserved more respect than the person who is simply wealthy or powerful, but lacks education. The introduction of examinations for civil service positions, which were open to anyone, helped to erode the power of the hereditary aristocracy in China. Rule by an intellectual élite came to be established in China, acting as a kind of legitimating factor, which underpinned Chinese imperial rule for the next two thousand years.

Confucian ethics is also known for its espousal of the principle of filial piety. This notion of loyalty of the child to parents became a metaphor for rule by any superior over

For Confucius, the educated person deserves more respect than the person who is simply wealthy or powerful, but lacks education.

subordinates. It should be noted, however, that the elevation of this notion to a general principle of submission to one's superiors came long after Confucius' death. Confucius himself took a view of relations between parents and children more like one of dialogue, or give and take. He said, 'When you serve your parents, you may gently remonstrate with them. If you see that they do not take your advice, be all the more respectful and do not contradict them. Let not your efforts turn to bitterness' (Leys, 1997: 17). Understanding between generations, a notion which we have also seen in the thinking of John Rawls, is one of the many of Confucius' ideas which have a modern resonance.

In imperial China, Confucianism became officially recognized in ways similar to a state religion. However, official Confucianism, focusing on submission to state authorities, was not in keeping with the ideas which Confucius himself advocated, such as social justice and intellectual freedom. Inevitably, the country's communist leaders broke with the cultural heritage of Confucius, notably in the 'cultural revolution', a particularly dark era of 're-education' which led to widespread suffering and destruction of family ties (Leys, 1977). In Japan, Singapore and South Korea, Confucian thought has remained influential. Indeed, the ethical teachings of Confucius are now widely recognized as pivotal ethical principles in the humanist tradition. In China, too, Confucian precepts are now again recognized as part of the country's cultural heritage.

What advice could Confucius offer the current leaders of China which you feel would be relevant to the country's current situation?

CULTURAL CONTEXT

Ethical theorists can have dramatic impacts in the cultural, economic and political environments of countries where their views are influential. Philosophers pose ultimate questions about what constitutes the good life and how happiness can be achieved. Their answers diverge radically, as do the cultural contexts in which they wrote. Some of the contexts highlighted so far have been economic change, political turbulence and social upheaval. These remain recurring issues in today's world. They tend to crystallize in particular national contexts, which sometimes lead to a ripple effect, spreading to other countries. In Figure 1.1, we saw the main cultural contexts in which moral values are transmitted to people. The figure showed cultural groupings such as national cultures, religions and kinship groups.

NATIONAL CULTURES

We tend to think of a national culture as the culture of a nation state. This is true of states where there is a dominant culture and a fairly homogeneous society. Japan is an example, where the vast majority of people feel themselves to be Japanese. But a person's national culture need not be that of the country where the person lives or whose passport that person holds. A national culture can be defined as a sense of belonging to a distinctive group with its own cultural identity and history. Often, language is a key element for people's sense of national culture. In many countries, even where there is a dominant culture, there are residents who identify with minority cultures, often those of immigrants, but also cultures of indigenous peoples. People in minority groups tend to be among the poorest in society, and discrimination is a recurrent issue for government and businesses.

All societies are to some extent unequal, and, as we have seen among the ethical theorists, addressing inequalities involves ethical principles. In some countries, ethnic or religious differences are so great as to lead to conflict, threatening the very existence of the state. Such conflicts are difficult to resolve, as national loyalty in the form of patriotism can turn into extremes of nationalism, in which one group sees itself as superior to others. Intolerance of other cultures stems in part from a fear of the 'other' which takes a radical form. People tend to be sceptical of those with different lifestyles or appearance, which are the signs of differing cultural values and norms. A right to cultural identity is recognized as a human right. However, in practice, discrimination remains an issue in many countries.

It has been suggested that globalization is eroding national cultures, leading to a global society in which people are becoming citizens of the world, rather than identifying with particular nations. Is there evidence that this is occurring? We will look at the many phenomena associated with globalization in the next chapter, but it is relevant to look at this suggestion here, as the changing cultural context would bring about changing notions of ethics. Those pointing to an emerging global culture can point to globalized businesses, global brands and the growing middle classes around the world adopting similar lifestyles. On the other hand, cultural values run deeper than material consumer goods such as TVs and fridges. People eagerly embrace a higher standard of living, but moral values and national identity tend to be 'stickier' signifiers of culture. Certainly, in China, perhaps the chief example globalization, a priority of the central leadership has been to emphasize national pride as a unifying factor, especially in the context of the many minority ethnic and religious groups which continue to assert their own identities.

As an Asian country, China is considered a country which is traditionally more group-oriented than individualist. Western cultures in general give individual values a central ethical focus. The research of Geert Hofstede, which analysed data from over fifty countries, has contributed valuable insight into national cultures (Hofstede, 1994). Although now rather dated, the cultural dimensions which Hofstede used have become helpful tools in describing national cultures. Of Hofstede's cultural dimensions, two are particularly relevant in an ethical context. These are individualism/collectivism and power distance.

Individualism, which rests on individual responsibility, can be contrasted with a collectivist outlook, in which people see themselves and their goals as essentially part of a large group, which could be a whole nation or just an organization. The second dimension which can be highlighted is power distance, which relates to the inequality in a society (Hofstede, 1994: 24). By this, Hofstede refers to the sense that decisions which affect a person's life are perceived to be taken by himself or herself (in which case power distance is small), or are perceived to be taken at a higher level, for example, by the boss or the state. If power distance is large, the individual perceives he or she has little influence on the people who take the main decisions on policies which affect daily life. Hofstede found there to be a correlation between individualism and low power distance, and between collectivism and high power distance. These are shown in Figure 1.2. In grouping national cultures, the western cultures tend to fall in the first group, that is, the more individualist. Asian and Latin American cultures tend to be more collectivist and have larger power distance. These rather broad generalizations do not take account of changes over time, and also fail to take account of the different cultural heritage of each country. Countries in the same region can be highly diverse historically. This possibly accounts for the fact that the Asian countries which Hofstede surveyed show quite wide divergence although most fall into the top right quadrant of the diagram.

Figure 1.2   *Findings of Hofstede: cultural dimensions of selected national cultures*

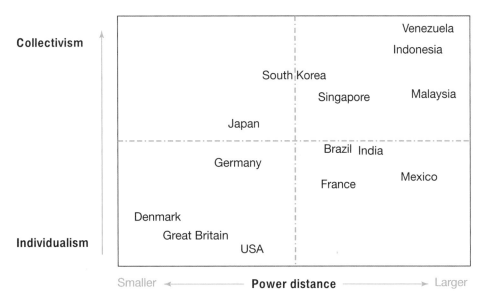

Source: Hofstede, G. (1994) *Cultures and Organizations: Software of the Mind* (London: HarperCollins), pp. 26, 53.

In societies that are individualist, the person as an individual is the centre of values. People are expected to look after their own needs, and those of their immediate family (Hofstede, 1994: 51). Ties between people tend to be loose, and a person's sense of identity is based on self-perception as an individual, rather than as a member of a group. Freedom in the negative sense is valued in the individualist society, and this can translate to advocacy of minimal government intervention, allowing maximum freedom for the individual to pursue his or her own goals. Often, freedom to pursue economic goals is referred to as economic freedom, which is the basis of capitalist markets (discussed in Chapter 2). At the same time, the inequalities which arise in market economies have led to concerns over social justice, highlighted particularly by John Rawls. A way of mitigating the effects of inequality in society has been to focus on equality of opportunity, in which equal access to education plays an important role.

The cultural underpinning of globalization has been in the values of capitalism, including economic freedom of individuals and companies operating in relatively free market environments. The success of market economies in achieving economic growth and prosperity has been emulated around the globe. Many countries in which the cultural heritage has not been one of individualist morality have adopted market principles. China and other Asian countries are examples. Looking at China, the cultural heritage in this vast country is highly diverse. Historically, the Confucian religious heritage can be cited as influential. China's communist revolution of 1949, seeking to make a cultural break with the past, enforced communist re-education, and emphasized the collectivization of the economy. In practice, however, the persisting cultural phenomenon of *guanxi*, which focuses on interpersonal ties, has remained a strong current in today's China. This is true even though the country's communist leadership has adopted market principles as a driver of the economy. Businesspeople from other countries wishing to do business in China soon become aware that personal ties and especially ties with members of the Communist Party are crucial to getting business done. Hence, the cultural heritage remains a strong force despite the overlay of both communist values and, more recently, market values. The Chinese leadership has allowed considerable market freedom to exist in the economy, within an environment where there remain high levels of state involvement.

South Korea is another country where Asian religious heritage, including Buddhism and Confucianism, have been influential. The country enjoyed a period of rapid industrialization and economic growth during the 1980s, during which its companies became global players in a number of industries, notably electronics. The impetus came not from individual entrepreneurs so much as from family-based businesses which grew into large conglomerates, known as *chaebol*. They included Samsung, LG and Hyundai. These industrial empires were favoured by governments, and, for many people, the influences of the company in everyday life became more significant than that of the state's institutions – such was the influence of the *chaebol*. They were not simply a source of employment, but a network of social institutions and values. The activities of their founding families were at the forefront of the news, and even when they were found to have been engaging in corruption, they retained prestige in the eyes of the public. South Korea's companies have proved themselves to be strong global competitors. They tend more to the collectivist than the individualist in Hofstede's dimensions (see Figure 1.2). The strength of these family empires, which have long historical roots, does not imply that they are backward-looking in terms of innovation. On the contrary, Samsung has shown that its innovative capacity – perhaps more closely identified with its great present-day global rival, Apple – is a daunting challenge for all competitors.

PAUSE TO CONSIDER...

Are national cultures inherently 'set' in your view, or can they change over time? Consider some examples, such as the US, industrializing Asian countries and post-communist countries.

RELIGION

Religion has played an important role in the national cultures of many countries. In Asian countries, religious beliefs and observances are seen as contributing to strengthening social ties. Japan is an example, where the national religion, Shinto, is a unifying force in society and closely identified with the sense of nationhood. Most of the world's religions are not so closely linked to a particular country, but form separate belief systems, whose adherents are found in a number of countries. An organized religion sees morality as stemming not from the individual, but from a higher force, either through a belief in a single God (such as Christianity, Judaism and Islam) or a panoply of gods (such as Hinduism). Religions tend to look to a sacred rule which is laid down to guide the faithful, often contained in a holy book, such as the Bible for Christians and the Qur'an for Muslims. Interpreting sacred scripture is itself an important task, as much of the detailed prescription for daily living and worship stems from scriptures.

Hinduism is rather different in this respect. Historically, there have been numerous teachers and groups of followers, forming sects within the overall grouping of Hinduism. There are also numerous written texts which guide followers of particular sects. Hinduism is itself culturally diverse. This diversity stems in large part from the ethnic diversity in India, where it originated. Diversity also characterizes the ethical elements of Hinduism. Hinduism is often criticized for its adherence to the caste system, the strict social stratification which remains a potent force in India, despite efforts to abolish it in law. In practice, however, the caste system is perhaps more linked with India's cultural heritage generally than with Hindu principles.

Morality for a religious believer consists of following the rules laid down by sacred scriptures and other sources of authority. Believers' approaches to religion vary; some are very strict in their observances and others more relaxed, observing some aspects of the religion, but not necessarily all. The strict adherents are sometimes called fundamentalists, and can be noted for their hostility to the more relaxed adherents. Among Muslims, the two main groups are Sunnis and Shias, both of whom have fundamentalist groups within their ranks. Among the Sunnis the Salafists have become a fast-growing group. These strict fundamentalist Muslims favour a return to the purist values of their forebears. In this group there are a number of strands, some of whom are highly politically motivated, promoting violent *jihad*, or holy war, while other Salafists emphasize peaceful struggle. In countries where Muslims predominate, as in the Middle East, there tend to be both Sunnis and Shias, and conflicts between them have been a cause of unrest. In Bahrain, for example, there is a Sunni minority which rules over a majority Shia population. Demonstrations against the government became a common occurrence during the period from about 2010, when uprisings against entrenched governments occurred in many Arab countries.

These uprisings, often referred to collectively as the 'Arab Spring', resulted from a combination of causes, including striving for religious freedom, political voice and economic opportunities. They have occurred in numerous Arab countries, including Egypt, Tunisia, Morocco, Algeria, Libya and Syria (see further discussion in Chapter 3). The presence of women in some of the demonstrations indicates dissatisfaction with the subservient role demanded of them in some of these societies. Restrictions on women's ability to move about freely and participate in economic and political life on equal footing with men can be seen as an ethical issue. It is arguable that although state and religious leaders invoke Islamic religious law, an ethical principle is at stake. Women in these societies argue they are entitled to the same basic rights as men, recalling the struggles of women for equality in western societies in the nineteenth century.

It is arguable that the Qur'an lends itself to many interpretations, upholding values of equality, tolerance and peace. However, these have tended to be overshadowed by the more radical pronouncements of Islamic clerics who wield considerable power over followers. Islam as a religion is all-encompassing in its application to everyday life of the believer. It is noteworthy that the Muslim Brothers, who have long been a strong force in Egypt, have seen

Photo 1.2 *Women have taken part in many of the protests in Arab countries, asserting rights to play more active roles in society.* (© iStock.com/jcarillet)

themselves not merely as a religious force, but in a social welfare role, and now in a political role. Islam encompasses a legal and political role, which brings followers into conflict with secular authorities in many states. In some countries, where Islam is the dominant religion, all state organizations conform to its rules, and the legal system is based on Islamic law, or Sharia law. For business transactions, it is important to observe the requirements of Sharia law, which forbid the making of loans for profits. Islamic finance has grown in importance in the global economy, along with the importance of Middle Eastern MNEs and government players in global finance (see Chapter 4). Finance is often highlighted as one of the most globalized of business functions, but the burgeoning of Islamic finance, including a whole parallel banking system based on Islamic law, shows the potency of cultural differences in the global economy.

Many religions, including both Islam and many Christian denominations, stress the importance of charity or philanthropy as a duty of the believer. This notion of giving to others is an ethical principle which seems to transcend religious divides. Many charities which work, for example, among the poor, provide for all the needy, regardless of religion. Although some charities see themselves as spreading a religious message along with their material aid, many do not. Businesses have long been upholders of the need to support charities. Are they acting out of genuine ethical principles or simply to promote a caring image of themselves? Aristotle would say that if they act merely out of enlightened self-interest, their actions have no moral worth. Their charitable giving would find more favour with the utilitarians, who would stress the consequences of maximizing happiness in society which stem from charitable giving.

Similarly, the principle known as the 'golden rule' is found in many of the world's religions. The golden rule dictates that we should 'treat others as you would have them treat you' (Duxbury, 2009: 1529). The golden rule can be found in numerous cultural contexts: it seems to cross national cultures and religious divides, suggesting that it has an ethical status above the level of simple homespun advice, which is how it is sometimes depicted. The golden rule is also similar to Kant's categorical imperative. However, Kant's categorical imperative stipulates obedience to a universal rule, whereas the golden rule states that the moral test is how we would like to be treated by others. Certainly, underlying the golden rule is a notion of human dignity in a social context (Duxbury, 2009). And it is arguable that this rule can form a moral prescription. We look at other examples in the next section.

Pause to consider... Religion is the main cultural identifier for many of the world's peoples, and some moral precepts such as the golden rule feature in many religions. Should this be an ethical principle applied in international business?

APPLYING ETHICAL CONCEPTS AND THEORIES TO INTERNATIONAL BUSINESS: A PRELIMINARY DISCUSSION

For the MNE, globalization has brought greater choice of location for various activities, including advantageous countries for manufacturing and fiscally advantageous countries for receipt of profits. In each location, the company encounters a different business environment, requiring understanding and adaptation. One of the more prominent issues arising in recent years has been the shift of manufacturing to low-cost countries. Many western MNEs have sought to engage with China – as a market or as a manufacturing location. They have encountered a range of ethical dilemmas along the way. Here are a few examples faced by a hypothetical MNE confronted with ethical dilemmas:

> ○ *An official expects a payment on the side to facilitate permissions needed to do business.*

This looks like bribery. Although it might be legally prohibited, officials in this country see this as customary. The MNE is compelled to pay if it wants to do business. The MNE could justify the payment by arguing that in the culture of the country it is seen as acceptable. This is an example of cultural relativism. The practice could be seen as ethically wrong, however, and an ethical firm might well decide not to do business in this country. How would the utilitarian approach tackle the issue? The company would need to consider the risk of reputational damage in its markets and among its shareholders.

SPOTLIGHT ON ETHICAL BUSINESS

Corruption and business *Peter van Veen*

Peter van Veen
*Director, Business
Integrity Programme,
Transparency
International, UK*

Originally trained as a development economist, Peter started his career at The Economist Intelligence Unit, monitoring political and economic risk and subsequently worked for the Chief Economist and Chief Political Scientist at Royal Dutch Shell. He then moved into management consulting and worked for Andersen Consulting (now Accenture) and SRI Consulting before running a services division for the Bertelsmann Group. After completing a postgraduate diploma in Corporate Governance and Business Ethics, Peter then shifted his focus to helping businesses and NGOs improve their governance and manage their strategic risk. Prior to joining Transparency International UK, Peter was responsible for monitoring and reporting external risk for SABMiller.

Visit **www.palgrave.com/companion/morrison-business-ethics** to watch Peter talking about facets of corruption and the work of Transparency International. He discusses the influence of national legislation and cultural contexts and reviews the most common challenges that face companies in reducing corrupt practices. He also explains why it is important for students of business and management to study business ethics.

You will find it helpful to look at other sections of the book which focus on these topics. They include sections on 'Diverse ethical perspectives in MNEs' legal relations' in Chapter 4, and on 'Interconnections: CSR, ethics and corporate governance' in Chapter 8.

When you have watched the video, think about the following questions:

1 In what ways does the level of corruption tolerated in a specific country environment impact on businesses operating there?

2 What roles and processes within a company are key to raising and maintaining ethical standards, even in high-risk environments?

3 Peter points out that companies often have high ethical principles in their policy statements, but fall short in practice. How can this slippage be prevented in practice?

Figure 1.3 *Corruption perception rankings*

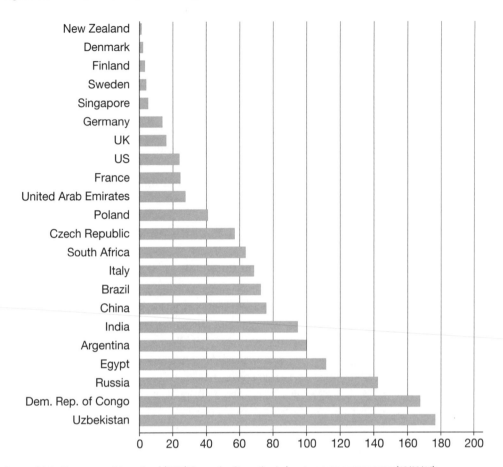

Source of data: Transparency International (2012) Corruption Perception Index, at www.transparency.org (18/09/14).

If a person wishes to do business in a country where corruption is prevalent, what is the best course of action: to go along with the practice, to insist on not paying bribes (in which case the firm may well not get very far in the country), or simply to stay away and concentrate on other locations? In today's world of international business, the unfortunate reality is that such forms of corruption are widespread, and are especially prevalent in emerging economies where the most business opportunities occur (see Figure 1.3).

Figure 1.3 shows the rankings compiled by Transparency International for their Corruption Perception Index, which calculates perceived levels of public sector corruption (Transparency International, 2012). They ranked 183 countries, the cleanest appearing at the top of the figure and the most corrupt appearing towards the bottom. These rankings will be referred to several times in this book. A ranking of 50 or lower indicates a high level of corruption in public life. The large emerging economies known as the BRICs – Brazil, Russia, India and China – are all in the lower half of the figure. Russia, in particular, is among the world's most corrupt countries, ranking 143 out of the 183 countries surveyed. Russia attracts considerable foreign investment, both financial investment (portfolio investment) and foreign direct investment (FDI) in which foreign companies acquire productive assets in a foreign country. Russia's wealth in gas and oil attracts large foreign investors such as BP and Shell. In Russia's gas and oil giant, Gazprom, ownership and control are dominated by the government, and senior management is linked to the country's political leadership. Foreign companies that operate alongside Russia's domestic energy companies are inevitably involved with the country's powerful business leaders, known as oligarchs, who in turn tend to be linked to the country's most powerful political leaders. Although we have highlighted Russia as an example, the links between business and political power are strong in many countries. It is notable that of the ethical theorists we have discussed, Confucius, Kant, the utilitarians, and John Rawls all criticized existing governments on ethical grounds and highlighted the need for political institutions to apply ethical standards, in terms of equality, fairness and justice.

○ *A company that manufactures the MNE's products at a low cost has a poor reputation for the ways it treats its workforce.*

The MNE is seeking to license a firm in the low-cost country to manufacture its products. The 'local' firm would be employing the workforce. The MNE might argue that as it is not the workers' employer, it has no control over working conditions. In many cases in China, the local employer is not a local Chinese company, but a foreign investor in China. In the case of Apple, the main manufacturer in China has been a Taiwanese company (see the opening case study of Chapter 2). A number of high-profile companies, such as Nike and Apple, have had to confront criticism from consumers. Local employment laws have gradually introduced greater worker protection in low-cost countries in respect of practices such as excessive overtime. Apart from the possible breach of local laws, the ethical issues concern treatment of the workforce. Kant's categorical imperative would be relevant, urging the firm to treat people as ends and not as means. These workers, although not employed by the brand owner, are part of the supply chain and are stakeholders. The categorical imperative is arguably relevant in this and other circumstances involving stakeholders. These stakeholders have a moral claim towards the brand owner, if not a legal one (see the closing case study). A concept that would also be relevant in these situations is Kant's formulation of the categorical imperative in terms of universalizability.

○ *The company manufacturing the MNE's products has a record of poor pollution control.*

Pollution is an issue everywhere, and firms are reluctant to invest in cleaner technology which involves high costs, especially in a country where legislation is weak and toleration of pollution is high. China became the world's largest emitter of greenhouse gases in 2007, largely as a result of its huge appetite for energy needed to power its factories producing goods for exports. The MNE in this example might well argue that as so much pollution is tolerated in the country already, this factory will make no difference. But of course, polluted air can travel across the globe, making this a global problem rather than a local one. In the Kantian tradition, the MNE might ask itself, 'what if everybody behaved as if it did not matter?' The answer could be catastrophic, as Kant would have pointed out in defining the universalizability aspect of the categorical imperative. Alternatively, J.S. Mill and John Rawls would both have urged that looking to the interests of others, and (in the case of Rawls) future generations, is an inherent aspect of living in society. The golden rule would also be relevant in this situation, echoing the concern for others that is the focus of ethical theories.

CONCLUSIONS

The ethical theories outlined in this chapter have all put forward ethical concepts which have a universal quality, transcending place and time. They have emphasized different perspectives. Kant, J.S. Mill and John Rawls, although all focusing on the individual human being, emphasized the social dimension of ethics. Aristotle's virtue ethics emphasized the moral life, but also stressed the need for social cohesion and justice. We tend to think of social groupings in cultural terms, usually national cultures that are dominant in particular countries, leading to economic and political institutions which reflect cultural values. But societies and national cultures change over time. Even in societies where individual freedoms are recognized in law, inequality can mean that the poorest inhabitants have little freedom in practice. Ethical concepts, such as human dignity and justice, underpin efforts to achieve changes in the law, and also changes in the way people behave towards each other.

Whatever kind of society we live in, we depend on social co-operation to make life liveable. This social dimension is the area of ethics. This is as true of organizations as it is of individuals. Businesses have tended to be among the exponents of cultural relativism, seeking advantages presented in particular locations where the cultural environment tolerates certain types of activity, such as harsh factory conditions. But, as we have seen, the cultural environment is a changing set of phenomena, and within cultures, changes occur, often because local voices within society raise ethical issues which lead to changes at government level. As we saw in the opening case study, when ethical standards rise, businesses can choose to move on to different locations where regulation remains lax. But increasingly, businesses are scrutinized in ethical terms, and held responsible for their actions, regardless of the particular location. Perhaps paradoxically, globalization, which has offered a host of diverse emerging markets, is also presenting a more universalized ethical perspective on business behaviour.

REFERENCES

Note on the references: For Aristotle, Hobbes, Kant, James Mill and John Stuart Mill, the dates of publication are the dates of the edition used. For the *Analects of Confucius*, the author cited is Simon Leys, the translator and editor, who sadly died in August 2014.

Aristotle (1962a) *Nicomachean Ethics*, translated and edited by M. Ostwald (New York: Bobbs-Merrill Co.)

Aristotle (1962b) *The Politics of Aristotle*, translated and edited by E. Barker (New York: Oxford University Press).

Barker, E. (1962) *Social Contract* (New York: Oxford University Press).

Berlin, I. (1958) *Two Concepts of Liberty* (Oxford: Oxford University Press).

Berlin, I. (1999) *The Roots of Romanticism* (London: Chatto & Windus).

Duxbury, N. (2009) 'Golden rule reasoning, moral judgment and law', *Notre Dame Law Review*, 84(4): 1529–605.

Hobbes, T. (1960) *Leviathan*, edited by M. Oakeshott (Oxford: Blackwell).

Hofstede, G. (1994) *Cultures and Organizations: Software of the Mind* (London: HarperCollins).

Huby, P. (1967) *Greek Ethics* (London: Macmillan).

Kant, I. (1949) *Fundamental Principles of the Metaphysic of Morals*, translated by T. Abbott, introduction by M. Fox (New York: Bobbs-Merrill Co.).

Kant, I. (1948) *The moral law: Groundwork of the metaphysic of morals*, translated by H.J. Paton (New York: Routledge).

Kant, I. (1929) *Critique of Pure Reason*, translated by N. Kemp-Smith (New York: Macmillan).

Leys, S. (1977) *Chinese Shadows* (Harmondsworth: Penguin Books).

Leys, S., translator and editor (1997) *Analects of Confucius* (New York: W.W. Norton & Co.).

Mill, James (1955) *Essay of Government*, edited by C. Shields (New York: Bobbs-Merrill Co.).

Mill, J.S. (1955) *Utilitarianism, Liberty and Representative Government* (London: J.M. Dent & Sons).

Mill, J.S. (1962) 'Bentham' in *Essays on Politics and Culture*, edited by G. Himmelfarb (New York: Doubleday & Co.).

Nussbaum, M. (1999) 'Virtue ethics: A misleading category?', *Journal of Business Ethics*, 3(3): 163–201.

Plamenatz, J. (1958) *The English Utilitarians*, 2nd edn (Oxford: Blackwell).

Rawls, J. (1971) *A Theory of Justice* (Oxford: Oxford University Press).

Rawls, J. (1996) *Political Liberalism* (New York: Columbia University Press).

Robinson, J. (1962) *Economic Philosophy* (Harmondsworth: Penguin Books).

Transparency International (2012) *Corruption Perceptions Index*, at www.transparency.org (18/09/14).

REVIEW QUESTIONS

1 What are the aspects of culture that influence morality?

2 What aspects of Kant's ethical theory are particularly relevant for business ethics, and why?

3 Explain the differences between the negative and the positive concepts of liberty.

4 The utilitarians are noted for embracing 'consequentialism' as a foundation of ethics. What are the pros and cons of consequentialism?

5 In what ways does John Stuart Mill depart from the utilitarianism of his predecessors? How are his views relevant to current issues in societies?

6 Explain Rawls' concept of justice as fairness. How is it relevant in business ethics?

7 Aristotle's virtue ethics is sometimes seen as focusing on personal ethics of the individual rather than on the social dimension? To what extent is this a fair analysis?

8 Two of the ethical theorists discussed in this chapter, Rawls and Confucius, discussed ethics between generations. Compare the two approaches.

9 Looking at dimensions of culture, to what extent is individualism linked to economic development?

10 Religion can be a source of ethics for guiding business behaviour, but it can equally be used to justify behaviour which could be considered unethical. Give an example of each.

CLOSING CASE STUDY

BANGLADESH FACTORY COLLAPSE REVEALS PLIGHT OF GARMENT WORKERS

Rana Plaza, a multi-storey building in Dhaka, Bangladesh, housed a bank on the ground floor and five garment factories on the floors above it. Most of the factories were producing clothes for well-known western brands. On 24 April 2013, bank staff saw cracks in the building, and were ordered to evacuate. The garment workers were forced to go back to the factories on the upper floors and resume work. Soon afterwards, the building collapsed, resulting in the deaths of over 1,100 people and injuries to 2,500. The scale of the disaster was slow to unfold, as the almost total disintegration of the building made it difficult to rescue people from the debris. The disaster was not an isolated incident. A fire five months earlier at Tazreen Fashions, a factory producing clothes for Walmart, resulted in the deaths of 117 people. In both cases, authorities reacted by saying that there had been violations of building regulations. Many buildings in Bangladesh do not comply with regulations, and fire safety regulations are often not adhered to. But inspectors tend not to look too closely, as the garment industry in Bangladesh, spread over 5,000 factories, accounts for 77% of the country's exports. The sector has grown rapidly in recent years, rising from $6 billion in export earnings in 2005 to nearly $19 billion in 2012.

Photo 1.3 *This shopper is looking for a new item for his wardrobe, but is he also thinking about where the clothes are made and in what factory conditions? (© iStock.com/Luminastock)*

Weak oversight of the construction and maintenance of buildings is not uncommon in developing countries, but carries heightened risks in Bangladesh, which is prone to natural disasters and flooding. Its garment industry, employing nearly four million workers, mostly women from poor rural areas, has been an economic success story, attracting numerous western brand owners because of its low wages. At $38 a month, the minimum wage of a garment worker is the world's lowest. The government has actively sought to attract brand owners to the country, and is accused of deliberately keeping minimum wages depressed. The last official rise was in 2010. In 2012, industrial protests spread throughout the country, closing factories for a week, but demonstrating workers were met with tear gas and rubber bullets. A labour organizer, who had complained he had been treated harshly by security forces, was murdered. No suspects have been pursued, and other labour organizers fear that his murder was meant to be a warning to other activists. In law, Bangladesh allows freedom of association and trade unions, but in practice, labour organizers face constraints.

The Rana Plaza factory was owned by a local politician closely linked to the country's ruling party. In fact, many political leaders are factory owners, including some 10% of the country's members of Parliament.

There is thus the potential for corruption between business and government interests. Bangladesh is among the world's most corrupt countries according to Transparency International's Corruption Perception Index, ranking 144 out of 183 countries (Transparency International, 2012). Any tightening of regulations, including building regulations, fire safety regulations and workers' rights, is seen as a cost which could deter the foreign businesses. One commentator says of the government, 'There is a very clear financial incentive for them to give the industry as much of a free pass as possible' (Kazmin et al. , 2013). The factory owners who ordered workers back into the building were very aware of the need not to miss a day of production, for fear of losing western customers. Should brand owners shoulder some of the blame?

They did not have direct legal obligations, but they had moral obligations, it could be said. NGOs have long complained of the plight of garment workers, noting especially the use of child labour, excessive overtime and unhealthy working conditions. They also highlight the fact that factories often send work out to subcontractors, who are not bound by the codes of conduct usually imposed by western brand owners. In some cases, the brand owner does not even know that a particular company is making its clothes. This was Walmart's defence in relation to the Tazreen factory fire. Brand owners have in place codes of conduct for suppliers which cover pay, conditions, health and safety matters. Fire risk and electricals tend to be covered, but not the structural soundness of buildings.

In the wake of the Rana Plaza collapse, over thirty western brands, including H&M, Marks & Spencer and Inditex, joined in a legally binding accord on fire and building safety in Bangladesh. Companies signing up to the accord offer to pay for independent inspection of buildings and rebuilding where necessary for safety. Some western brand owners have objected to the accord. US companies, Walmart and Gap, were reluctant to sign up to the legal and financial commitments it contains, but NGOs urge that a purely voluntary scheme, which is what these US companies would find acceptable, would not impose any accountability.

NGOs are also concerned about the huge number of injured workers in the Rana Plaza disaster. Medical costs, lost wages and compensation should be paid, but accident victims in developing countries are often left empty-handed. Some western retailers have agreed to pay 45% of compensation payments, in the hope that factory owners or the Bangladeshi government will pay the rest. Responses among brand owners have varied, however. Some, such as Primark of the UK, have said they will offer compensation to victims, but Mango of Spain has accepted no liability, despite its labels and invoices having been found in the Rana Plaza wreckage.

NGOs point out that the issues arising in Bangladesh are repeated in other countries which serve the global garment industry. Pakistan, China, India and Turkey all have poor records in terms of labour conditions and unsafe buildings. About 40% of clothing factories in China, India and Turkey have failed fire safety inspections (Butler, 2013). Walt Disney, the entertainment company, had used Bangladeshi factories to make clothing and merchandise, but has decided to leave the country. Only 1% of its production was taking place in Bangladesh, and none at the Rana Plaza. For Disney, the shift is less complicated than it would be for the brand owners which rely on hundreds

of factories in the country. These MNEs are faced with a dilemma of staying on in the country or facing huge costs of shifting to other countries, many of which have the same inherent problems of poor and unsafe conditions for workers.

Sources: Butler, S. (2013) 'Retailers urged to take Bangladesh safety deal further', *The Guardian*, 28 July; Kazmin, A., Jopson, B. and Lucas, L. (2013) 'Factory's collapse highlights failure to enforce basic rules', *Financial Times*, 26 April; Lucas, L. and Jopson, B. (2013) 'Rift opens up over textile worker safety in Bangladesh', *Financial Times*, 16 May; Kazmin, A. (2013) 'Bangladesh factory collapse a catalyst for workers' rights', *Financial Times*, 4 May; Palmeri, C. and Rupp, L. (2013) 'Disney Bangladesh exit pressure on clothesmakers who stay', *Bloomberg*, 3 May, at www.bloomberg.com; Transparency International (2012) *Corruption Perception Index*, at www.transparency.org (18/09/14).

DISCUSSION QUESTIONS

▫ **What factors in Bangladesh contribute to the poor conditions in the country's garment industry?**

▫ **To what extent is the fire and building safety accord deal among western MNEs likely to reduce the risk of further disasters like the Rana Plaza?**

▫ **What are the ethical dilemmas posed for western brand owners whose clothes are manufactured in Bangladesh?**

CHAPTER 2

THE GLOBAL ECONOMY FROM AN ETHICAL PERSPECTIVE

ETHICAL THEMES IN THIS CHAPTER
- Economic development and changing societies
- Sustainability guiding business and state actors

THE AIMS OF THIS CHAPTER ARE TO
- Identify processes of globalization and their implications
- Probe the underlying ethical assumptions of capitalism
- Compare divergent types of national economies, with focus on the role of markets
- Assess the social impacts of differing economic systems

APPLE: THE EXEMPLARY CAPITALIST COMPANY?

A pple is known globally for its iconic gadgets such as the iPhone and iPad. The brand's image rests on sleek design, high quality and continual innovation, making its products appealing to upmarket consumers the world over. Sales of iPhones alone amounted to 125 million in 2012, generating over $80 billion for the company (Apple 2012 Annual Report). That year saw Apple's overall sales increase 45% over 2011. Apple's success has arguably made it the company which all others would like to emulate. In short, the ultimate capitalist company. But the story behind Apple's success is more ambiguous, raising questions about whether it is really the capitalist model that should rule the world.

OPENING CASE STUDY

Photo 2.1 *The smartphone evokes a lifestyle image that contrasts sharply with the harsh realities of the huge factory complexes where high-tech gadgets are made.* (Thinkstock)

Based in Silicon Valley in California, Apple focuses on product research, innovation and development, in both hardware and software. It is here that its new iPhones, iPads and other products are conceived. It has also become a successful retailer, but it no longer makes any of the products which bear its logo. Founded in 1976, the company prided itself in its early years on making its products in California. Steve Jobs, its charismatic co-founder, boasted of the Mackintosh computer in 1983, that it was a 'machine that is made in America' (Chakrabortty, 2012). However, within two years, Jobs fell out with the company's directors and departed. Apple struggled to compete over the next decade, and Jobs returned in 1997. In one of the most successful turnarounds in business history, he refocused the company on innovation in products designed to excite the consumer. The iMac was still its prestige product. But the California factory which made iMacs until 2002 was gradually run down, and the building became a call centre, in an emblematic move which signalled the company's transformation to its current business model. From 2004, manufacturing was gradually shifted to China, where the company's products are now made by outsourcing companies under contract to Apple. A succession of successful products has transformed Apple into a corporate superpower. These include the iPod, iPhone and iPad, with new versions of each eagerly anticipated. First weekend sales of each iPhone are shown in Figure 1. Volumes on this scale are made possible by the hundreds of thousands of Chinese workers who make the company's products. The use of outsourced manufacturing now lies at the heart of Apple's business model. Apple's strategic shift was well timed to benefit from the Chinese government's promotion of export-oriented manufacturing to drive economic development. A chief beneficiary has been the Taiwanese contract manufacturer, Foxconn, which has become the major manufacturer of the iPhone and iPad.

Western MNEs typically outsource manufacturing as a way of reducing labour costs. But for Apple, the labour costs are relatively low in comparison to the overall cost of the product. It has been estimated that an iPhone 4 costs about $178 to produce, of which only about $6.50 is for Chinese labour. The phone sells for $630 in the US. Even if the phone were assembled by US workers at 10 times Chinese wages, the company would make sizeable profits. Tim Cook, Apple's CEO and former Chief Operations Officer, who took over shortly before Steve Jobs died in 2011, has pointed to two reasons for manufacturing in China rather than the US. They are the supply chain advantages and the fact that the Chinese factories can scale production up or down quicker than would be possible in the US (Duhigg and Bradsher, 2012). Foxconn's employees are almost all young migrant workers living in dormitories in factory

Figure 1 *Sales of iPhones in the first weekend after launch* (in millions of phones)

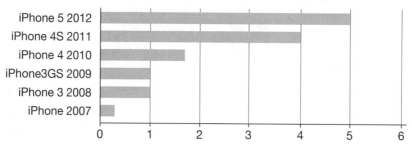

Source of data: Bradshaw, T. (2012) 'Apology takes brand into uncharted waters', *Financial Times*, 29 September 2012.

complexes. They can be available for work at short notice, and they can be shifted to other Foxconn factories in China. There are over a dozen, each employing up to 200,000 workers. The workforce at a factory can be increased rapidly to meet demand for particular products by shifting workers from other sites. Workers typically work 12 hours a day six days a week, allowing Apple to meet the huge consumer demand which follows a successful launch, such as that of the iPhone 5.

The outsourcing model has proved very profitable for Apple, as Figure 2 shows. Listed on the Nasdaq Exchange in New York, it had a market capitalization of $560.4 billion in 2012, making it the world's most valuable listed company, ahead of the oil giant, ExxonMobil, at $410 billion. Who are the beneficiaries of this wealth? The company's top executives are richly rewarded. CEO

Tim Cook received a remuneration package of $378 million in 2011. From its huge profits, Apple has accumulated impressive wealth: it sits on a cash mountain of $97 billion, $64 billion of which is located overseas. By channelling these overseas profits through low-tax jurisdictions in the Caribbean and elsewhere, its rate of corporation tax is under 2%, in contrast to the 35% rate it would pay in the US. But despite its successful launches and record profits, Apple's share price fell in 2012, suggesting that market analysts were doubtful that it could sustain its stellar performance. One reason for doubt is the gap left by the death of Steve Jobs, whose vision dominated the company. Other challenges are dealing with increasing competition in the mobile phone sector and responding to reports of poor labour standards in the manufacturing of its products.

Figure 2 *Apple's gross profit margins* (percentages)

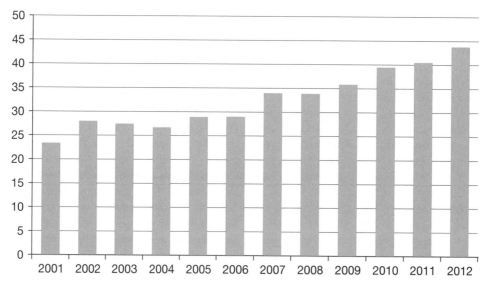

Sources of data: Apple Inc. (2012) *Annual Report 2012*; Froud et al. (2012).

Reports of poor working conditions and inhumane treatment of Foxconn employees have filtered out through global media. A series of suicides in 2010 was followed by improvements in working conditions, but incidents of rioting and strike action by workers in its plants have continued. Foxconn has responded with wage increases, but is constrained by the tight terms which Apple imposes on its suppliers. The iPhone 5 production was shifted to a factory in a central region, where wages are less than in the Shenzhen area near Hong Kong. But unrest followed, partly because workers were asked to move at short notice, and also because of the drop in wages. Worker shortages and skill shortages have become problems in the electronics industry in China, as prospective workers are tending to prefer other types of jobs, which offer better conditions and better career prospects. As China's manufacturing sector looks less sustainable, Foxconn is building factories in other countries, including Brazil, Mexico, Indonesia and countries of Eastern Europe. It is also planning to use more robots.

Although launched only in 2007, smartphones now account for about half of Apple's profits. But they face stiff competition from lower-priced rivals made by Samsung, whose products are more popular among the growing middle classes in emerging markets. Apple's continued success depends on strikingly innovative products, but this becomes more of a challenge over time as competitors have also become highly innovative. Apple's outsourcing model has rested on ruthless attention to cost reductions and profit maximization. Its sleek designs and functionality have sustained the brand and justified premium prices. But a brand image can lose its lustre if the company does not sustain the quality and integrity of its products in an increasingly competitive market. A quality problem with its maps application for the iPhone5 jolted Apple's management and damaged Apple's reputation. Although the company in 2012 outwardly seemed to be at the pinnacle of success, doubts about the ethics and sustainability of its business model remained. The US economy has lost factory jobs, while jobs created for migrant workers in China fall beneath ethical labour standards. Apple-branded products are imported into the US, widening the trade gap with China, whose consumers buy far fewer Apple products than their American counterparts. A former economic adviser to the US Government has said of Apple, 'If this is the pinnacle of capitalism, we should be worried' (Duhigg and Bradsher, 2012).

Sources: Apple Inc. (2012) *Annual Report 2012*, at http://investor.apple.com (26/09/14); Apple Inc. (2012) *Proxy Statement 2012*, at http://investor.apple.com (26/09/14); Duhigg, C. and Bradsher, K. (2012) 'How the US lost out on iPhone work', *New York Times*, 21 January; Chakrabortty, A. (2012) 'Apple: why doesn't it employ more US workers?', *The Guardian*, 23 April; Hille, K. (2012) 'Foxconn struggles with fresh labour disputes in China', *Financial Times*, 16 January; Froud, J., Soukhdev, J., Leaver, A. and Williams, K. (2012) *Apple Business Model: Financialization across the Pacific*, Centre for Research in Socio-Cultural Change, University of Manchester, Working Paper No. 111; Bradshaw, T. (2012) 'Apology takes brand into uncharted waters', *Financial Times*, 29 September 2012.

□ Why is Apple considered to be an exemplary capitalist company?

□ How sustainable is Apple's business model, in your view?

□ What ethical issues are raised by this case study?

INTRODUCTION

In this chapter, we focus on the economic activities which create wealth and jobs for countries, companies and individuals. Business activities, once mainly national in scope, have become globalized, bringing about possibilities for accumulating wealth on a huge scale. We look first at globalization, assessing it on grounds of ethical principles and sustainability. MNEs have benefited from new international strategies and an ability to shift activities to the most advantageous location. Countries, too, have benefited, attracting MNE investments which bring jobs to local citizens and income to national coffers. But globalization has raised questions of how benefits of economic activity globally are reaching societies, and how accountable the wealth creators are to the societies where their wealth arises.

National economies diverge in the ways they promote wealth creation and foster social well-being. We therefore look at differing economic models, their underlying ethical justifications and their relative ability to provide sustainable economic policies. Capitalism is the dominant model in today's world, but we find that it represents a number of different models with different ethical priorities. Furthermore, capitalism is constantly evolving, as governments are more conscious than ever of the limitations of markets in maintaining financial stability and dealing with global issues such as environmental degradation. The large emerging economies, with their state-centred economic models, have driven global economic growth, but ethical concerns are now rising up the agenda, engaging both governments and global companies.

THE CHANGING GLOBAL ECONOMY

Some of the ethical issues highlighted in the last chapter are linked to trends taking place in the global economy, such as the growth of manufacturing in low-cost economies. By shifting production to these economies, MNEs have been at the forefront of globalization. But globalization has come to take on widely ramified connotations in today's world, giving rise to both keen advocates and harsh critics. While advocates point to the economic benefits of new markets, critics point to loss of jobs in mature economies, and to the unsustainable nature of much of the new investment in developing and emerging economies. In this section, we aim to clarify the processes which fall under the broad heading of globalization, and to assess their ethical impacts.

GLOBALIZATION FROM CORPORATE AND COUNTRY PERSPECTIVES

Chief among the characteristics of globalization is the lowering of barriers between countries, making it easier to do business across national borders. These include cross-border finance, greater movement of technology among countries, greater exchange of information, lowering of trade barriers on goods, and improved transport. All of these improvements have been facilitated by advances in information technology (IT). MNE investments have been at the forefront of these developments, facilitated by governments through business-friendly policies. This trend has been one of the factors giving rise to talk of a 'borderless' world in which state sovereignty is withering as a force to be reckoned with. It is true that national borders deter businesses less than in previous eras, but it would be a mistake to underestimate the underlying authority of states to control businesses and individuals, should they wish to assert themselves. States remain key players in dealings with businesses and with other states. An example is in the movement of people across national borders.

Although flows of information, goods and finance have become globalized, control of the movement of people remains jealously guarded as an attribute of sovereign states. There has been movement of economic migrants, much of it organized, but globalization has not led to the mass movement of emigrants from poor countries to work in rich ones. In the main, developing countries have attracted inward MNE investment which is attracted to their abundant low-cost labour. Governments have sought benefits from co-operation with other players in the global economy. As a result, their economies are more integrated with those of other countries. But governments' perspectives remain focused on the *national* benefits which such integration brings.

The impetus for economic integration has come largely from the internationalization strategies of MNEs. Among these strategies are export, financial investment and foreign direct investment (FDI). FDI is the acquisition of productive assets in a foreign location with a view to gaining control of the operations. Policy decisions by governments affect the degree of openness in each location. A government can raise tariff barriers to discourage imports and protect local businesses (see discussion in Chapter 6). It can restrict capital flows. Governments can restrict FDI too. But FDI is attractive to most governments, offering employment, tax revenues and opportunities for economic development. When an investment looks to bring benefits to a country, governments are happy to welcome the investor, often with incentives. When it has doubts about the investor, it can say no, or negotiate different terms. Poor developing economies in need of capital investment are in a weak bargaining position in relation to a powerful MNE, but their location advantages, such as natural resources, can give them some degree of scope to negotiate terms which will benefit their country. It is notable that Mongolia, when targeted by China's state-owned coal company, tightened its regulatory framework and effectively closed the door to a Chinese company in 2012.

India has been in a strong position to make demands on prospective foreign entrants to its huge market. India's socialist-leaning governments have tended to be hostile to western MNEs. In India's rather turbulent social and political mix, there are anti-capitalist and anti-western feelings which have also resisted foreign investors. The country is now gradually opening to foreign investors. India, among others, has used the policy of requiring foreign investors to link up with a local company in a joint venture to enter the country, thus giving the local company considerable control over the operation. Starbucks entered India this way, opening its first shop in Mumbai in 2012, in a joint venture with Tata, the huge Indian conglomerate. In fact, by the time Starbucks launched in Mumbai, the requirement to use a joint venture had been dropped by the Indian government. Other western retailers are now targeting India, eyeing its fast-growing middle class, but India remains a challenging environment culturally, even though legal hurdles have been eased.

It is often observed that internationalization of business has been around for centuries, and that globalization is not a new phenomenon. However, the extent and depth of economic integration in our own era is qualitatively different from earlier eras. Trade between countries in earlier eras contributed to growing private wealth and also the wealth of rulers. The advent of industrial production contributed to a huge surge in trade. But FDI is the development that has led to greater economic integration.

A good example of FDI is the investment by Japanese car companies in the US. Japanese exports to the US met growing resistance in the form of import barriers in the 1970s. Their response was to set up production facilities in the US, on 'greenfield' sites, on which they built new factories to manufacture cars for the US market. The first of these was set up by Honda in the mid-1970s. This is the classic type of FDI project, which allows the MNE to own and control productive assets in a foreign market. The company becomes involved in the local economy, both in the building of the factory and the running of the operations. It has control over hiring staff and maintaining quality systems, but, it should be noted, it is subject to the relevant national laws in areas such as employment and safety. The company thus becomes involved in the local environment, creating a deeper presence than it would have as an exporter. As an alternative, the investing company can buy a whole existing company, or a stake in it, which gives the investor a similar control over the asset. This type of FDI is known as merger and acquisition activity. It is viewed as a quicker route towards establishing a presence in the host country. Which countries have been at the forefront of FDI, and what are the ethical implications of increasing FDI activity? We will take each of these questions in turn, looking first at where the investments go.

WHERE DOES FOREIGN INVESTMENT GO, AND WHY?

The world's outward flows of FDI, that is, the flows from a foreign country to a host country, are primarily from MNEs in the developed world. Relevant terms that are used to categorize countries are 'developed', 'developing', 'transition' and, more recently, 'emerging'. These categories are not precisely defined, and they can overlap. Lists can differ, but here, we use the UN's categories. The developed economies are the advanced, industrialized countries. These are the world's richest countries in terms of gross domestic product (GDP) per capita, defined as the total flow of goods and services produced by an economy, divided by the population of the country. The 34 members of the OECD (Organisation of Economic Co-operation and Development), sometimes known as the developed-countries' club, comprise these countries (Note 1). The leading economies in this group are the US, European Union (EU) countries and Japan. There are anomalies in these categories. China is the world's second largest economy and is highly industrialized and urbanized, but remains classified as a developing country.

The transition economies are economies making the transition from communism. They are countries of Eastern Europe and the CIS (Commonwealth of Independent States), which comprises Russia and states formerly part of the old Soviet Union. Developing economies refer to all the rest, in various stages of economic development. They make up the bulk of the world's countries. At the bottom end are the least-developed countries, which are mainly agricultural. Most developing countries seek development opportunities from industrialization or exploitation of natural resources, which is the route taken by many African and Latin American countries.

The countries that are making impressive strides in economic growth tend to be referred to as emerging economies. At the forefront of these have been the BRICs (Brazil, Russia, India and China). But others which would now fit that category are South Africa, Indonesia, Mexico, Nigeria and Turkey. These economies have all experienced dips in growth, however, and are wrestling with a number of issues, such as poverty and corruption, which affect the sustainability of their economic development (see case studies on South Africa, Indonesia and Turkey in this book).

The bulk of FDI flows have tended to be from developed countries towards other developed countries, but, as Figure 2.1 shows, investment in developed countries was affected by the financial crisis of 2008. Developing countries have grown in importance as both destinations of FDI and as investors. Figure 2.1 shows that FDI flows to developing countries were nearly half the total in 2011. MNEs from developing countries are still not as big outward investors as those from developed countries, but they are becoming global players.

Figure 2.1 FDI inflows to developed and developing countries (millions of dollars)

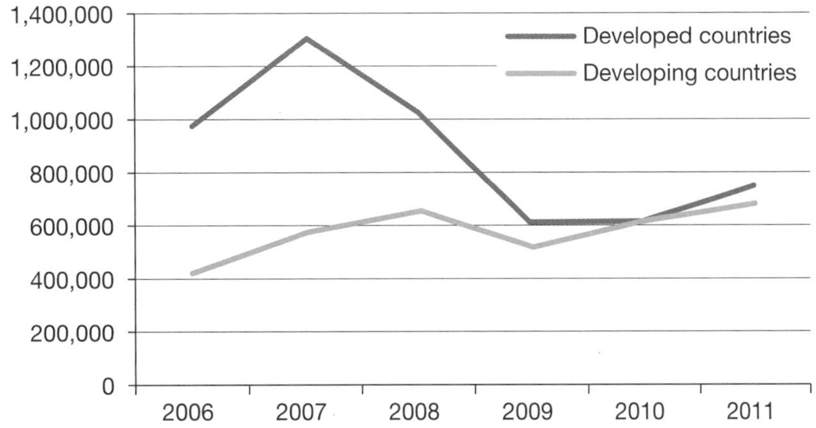

Source of data: UNCTAD (2012) *World Investment Report 2012* (Geneva: United Nations).

A feature of their strengthening role is the prominence of state-controlled companies in foreign investments, as will be discussed later in this chapter.

Takeovers such as the Indian and Chinese purchases of well-known UK companies are no longer unusual. Chinese companies are also making purchases in the US, reflecting the fact that these investors have abundant money to spend. These investments include both green-field projects and mergers/acquisitions, which have soared since 2010. However, such takeovers have strong political overtones in the US, where views towards China are ambivalent. China is a big investor in US sovereign debt, and the US is China's biggest export market. But US exports to China are dwarfed by Chinese exports to the US. Chinese FDI is a relatively recent phenomenon. China is viewed not simply as an economic predator in the way that Japan was viewed three decades ago, but with rather more hostility. In the eyes of American public opinion, the shift in manufacturing from the US to China caused the loss of US jobs. On the other hand, Chinese companies are now investing in the US, taking over enterprises and planning greenfield investments which create jobs.

Location advantages largely explain why FDI is targeted at one country rather than another (Dunning, 1993). Among them are proximity to natural resources, a large potential workforce, good transport infrastructure and relevant skills. For FDI in manufacturing, the countries with abundant low-cost labour enjoy advantages. China has been at the forefront of attracting manufacturing firms due to its low-cost labour provided by the country's millions of migrant workers. China's development model has rested on attracting FDI in manufacturing as an export platform. This model has been highly successful, its exports in sectors such as electronics, clothes and footwear now dominating global markets. This type of investment is greenfield investment as it involves the building of new factories and accommodation for workers. Most greenfield FDI targets developing countries, where costs tend to be lower. Lower levels of regulation and worker protection in developing countries are also factors which influence MNE decision-making, as these may aid in keeping costs down and giving management more latitude.

Advances in supply chains, by which a production is linked from one stage to another in an overall operation, have made it possible for a manufacturing process to involve inputs from a variety of sources. The supply chain resembles a network of linked firms rather than a hierarchical organization. The evolution of MNEs has led to more organizational flexibility than would be possible in the hierarchical organization. On the other hand, uncertainties arise with far-flung suppliers, including accidents, delays and quality problems. These have caused some companies to rethink supply chains with a view to reducing the risks.

Outsourcing of production, usually to a foreign location where costs are lower, is often criticized on ethical grounds. I have highlighted manufacturing in the opening case study, but other types of activity can also be outsourced. Textiles are typically manufactured in Asian locations for western markets, in conditions which are well beneath health and safety standards in developed countries (see closing case study of Chapter 1). Much of this production is outsourced by large retailers like Walmart. Sometimes companies shift business processes such as call centres and accounting services to outsourced locations. These need not involve FDI, but simply contracts for the supply of services of a foreign company.

Companies in the advanced economies which outsource to developing ones are often perceived as acting only out of economic motives, to reduce costs, and not considering the social consequences in the home country. Indeed, in some home countries, there can be backlash effects when people feel strongly that the firm has behaved irresponsibly. Looking at the longer term, the likelihood is that workers in the country which acquires the new outsourcing jobs will gradually obtain increases in pay and improved conditions. These improvements in conditions can start to alter the equation for the firm wishing to outsource. The firm can even find it more advantageous to take the process back in-house. Such choices are indicative of decision-making in a globalized world. Local advantages can come and go. The so-called foot-loose company can shift location as the competitive situation changes. For societies, these shifts can be highly disruptive. Companies which focus solely on reducing costs and maximizing profits might once have found favour with their shareholders, but shareholders and other stakeholders now ask whether this apparently short-term strategy is sustainable or ethical.

Location advantages serve to attract companies to developing and emerging economies, and governments tend to use extra incentives to attract MNEs. What are the ethical dilemmas posed for governments of developing countries that wish to attract FDI but also wish to pursue societal goals?

SUSTAINABILITY AND THE ETHICS OF GLOBALIZED PRODUCTION

Foreign direct investors have tended to be from advanced market economies. Traditionally, parent companies were registered in their home countries, where most of the shareholders were located. Shareholders and stakeholders, such as consumers, were culturally of the same mould, supportive of capitalist market values. When a manufacturing company saw opportunities to shift manufacturing to a cheaper location such as China, it looked like a 'win–win' situation. Shareholders would welcome the potential growth in output, benefits of scale economies and increases in profits. Consumers would welcome lower prices of imported goods. The calculation was an economic one. These impacts are shown in Figure 2.2. Many in advanced economies lamented the loss of jobs, but it was assumed that this was an inevitable feature of the increasingly globalized economy. It was thought, perhaps optimistically, that other jobs in the growing services sector would be available.

Figure 2.2 Winners and losers from globalization

What actually happened in many former manufacturing centres was a rise in unemployment due to the closure of factories, as well as the decline in other jobs which had depended on large numbers of factory employees. Britain lost two-thirds of its manufacturing jobs in the three decades following 1980 (Chakrabortty, 2011). The services sector – which includes administration, financial services, retailing, catering and tourism – has grown. The economy gradually became more focused on services, while manufactured goods were increasingly imported. In these circumstances, a country loses industrial expertise and skills. Small-to-medium-size enterprises (SMEs) which supply the large manufacturers also declined, along with their skills (Note 2). This trend contrasts with the continued existence of a strong manufacturing sector in Germany. Volkswagen has long sought to keep key components in-house, valuing the benefits of quality and reliability in supplies. This strategy has meant that manufacturing jobs in its home country of Germany have not been outsourced to the same extent as other MNEs. Similarly, the local SMEs which supply Germany's large manufacturers have been kept active. Germany has thus retained its industrial capacity to a greater extent that Britain.

Britain lost two-thirds of its manufacturing jobs in the three decades following 1980.

De-industrialization need not be detrimental to an economy if other good jobs are available. Many factory workers would say that they would gladly give up the repetitive work on assembly lines for a less strenuous job which is more interesting. But their skills might not be transferable to other jobs, and new jobs are often in locations some distance from the old manufacturing centres. There is also a broader concern that every country needs a variety of sustainable industries for jobs and growth. Governments fear the loss of whole industries, with the attendant reliance on imports, because their autonomy seems threatened when they are dependent on supplies from elsewhere. This has long been a worry in regard to food and energy (discussed in Chapter 10), but to a lesser extent, it applies to other goods. Governments of some countries use robust industrial policy as a tool to keep home industries alive and reduce imports. Should these national concerns weigh on the decision-making of the private-sector MNE?

The MNE shifting manufacturing abroad might lament the loss of jobs in the home country, but proceed nonetheless. MNEs have tended to believe that that their decision-making has to be based on economic realities, and that it is the task of governments to look after national interests. An ethical critic would argue, however, that a company should take into account social goods when making strategic decisions. The ethical company would be reluctant to close down an operation simply to reduce costs by using migrant labour in an overseas country.

Has FDI been a force for good for local economies, or simply a means of boosting the profits of the MNE? Figure 2.2 shows the winners and losers from globalization. While MNEs are among the winners, so are countries which attract FDI, and especially workers in sectors favoured by foreign investors. China has been a leading example, having experienced rapid economic growth and impressive poverty reduction. Life expectancy in China in 1960, during the hardline Maoist years, was 36 years. By 1999, life expectancy had risen to 70 years, close to that in the US (Rodrik, 2007: 238). However, China's coastal regions have fared better in terms of improved living standards, due to the concentration of manufacturing firms. As industries have migrated further inland in recent years, the benefits of China's economic growth have spread out from coastal areas. But China's leaders have not embraced globalization processes wholeheartedly. In terms of the features summarized in Figure 2.2, China has remained relatively closed: its financial markets have seen limited liberalization; it imposes many trade barriers on imported goods; and it operates controls on the internet. The Chinese example points to the gains specifically associated with abundant low-cost labour, which are benefits of localization.

The Chinese manufacturing model relies on huge factory complexes, but as we saw in the opening case study, conditions can be harsh for migrant workers. We have highlighted Apple, which uses the outsourcing model, but Samsung also stands accused of allowing breaches of employment law in the many factories in China which manufacture Samsung-branded products. Samsung's products are made by South Korean companies connected with Samsung which have operations in China. These are therefore more like in-house operations than Apple's outsourcing model, but despite Samsung's claims that they can better control conditions, numerous breaches of labour standards have been uncovered (Mundy, 2012). The ethical issues in all these operations, whether in-house or outsourced, concern how these workers are treated. Their lives are regimented, discipline is strict, and excessive overtime is not uncommon. Looking at workers merely as sources of cheap labour is abhorrent to notions of human dignity, treating people merely as means towards generating wealth for the companies in the supply chain.

Of course, manufacturing in a capitalist environment has always relied on people willing to exchange their labour in return for a salary. Waged labour is a core principle of capitalism, which might be held inherently unethical, especially by advocates of socialism (as will be discussed in the following sections). But if we accept that capitalist market values are justifiable, there is still much scope for arguing that enterprises should be responsible for managing their activities in an ethical way, treating workers with dignity, providing a healthy working environment and adhering to relevant national laws.

The capitalist assumption is that a person freely chooses to sell his or her labour in return for a wage, and that this employment contract creates duties on both sides. In fact, in most manufacturing, inequality of bargaining power is the norm: the factory owners determine the terms, and workers have little choice but to accept them, or be out of work. Chinese migrant workers are in a particularly vulnerable position. Although wages have risen in China, workers are now more inclined to strike to assert demands for better conditions. The Chinese government is well aware of the risks to social instability which can arise from poor working conditions and also from high levels of pollution which occur in areas where manufacturing is concentrated.

Ethical considerations regarding outsourced manufacturing have become a global issue. As Figure 2.3 shows, the brand owner's contract is with the manufacturer. The brand owner has no legal obligations to the manufacturing workers.

Only 38% of Apple's suppliers complied with the prohibition on excessive hours.

Furthermore, the contract manufacturer sometimes itself subcontracts to other companies, over whose employees it has no legal obligations. The brand owner might not even know that this further subcontracting is taking place. Nike, which outsources manufacture of its trainers, apparel and other products, has long sought to rebuff accusations of 'sweatshop conditions'. Apple has become embroiled in similar dilemmas. In its annual report, Apple highlights the risks involved in lack of direct control over its supply chain (Apple, 2012a). Following complaints about factory conditions, Apple has devised a code of conduct for suppliers, and it has carried out audits to root out poor safety standards, excessive hours and employment of underage workers. Its stated standards are high, but in practice, many suppliers do not reach them. For example, its code prohibits working hours in excess of 60 hours a week except in 'unusual or emergency circumstances', which allows for excessive hours when there are large orders to be filled (Apple, 2012b). Only 38% of suppliers complied with the prohibition on excessive hours, a percentage which includes those who exceeded the stated limits but came within the exception for 'unusual' circumstances. Overall, two-thirds of suppliers complied with its standards. Worryingly, it found six utilizing underage workers.

The waves of young Chinese workers heading for the factories from the countryside have slowed. The working-age population has shrunk from 82 million in the decade 2000–2010,

Figure 2.3 Outsourced manufacturing: where responsibilities lie

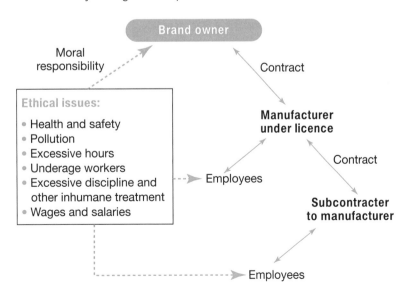

Sustainability implies the creation and maintaining of jobs which offer fulfilment and satisfaction to workers over a career.

to 23 million now, largely because of China's one-child policy. There are shortages of labour for the factories, and young people faced with a choice are tending to look for jobs in services. The government has turned its attention to sustainable development. This implies the need for continuing investment, but with an eye to the future viability of industries, both in terms of human values and environmental protection. Sustainability implies the creation and maintaining of jobs which offer fulfilment and satisfaction to workers over a career. Harsh factory conditions, which see high levels of turnover among workers, are the opposite of sustainable employment. It is entirely possible that China's factories will evolve to become better places to work. Wage rises are only part of the story. Workers also expect conditions to improve, along with attention to training and personal development. It is also true that automation is being introduced, replacing workers with machines and leading to greater efficiency. Pressures from the workforce, from consumers and from government are resulting in improvements in both sustainable business models and ethical practices, but in China the nature and pace of change are largely determined by the country's political leaders.

Improvements in working conditions that have occurred in western countries have often been the result of the activities of independent trade unions. From the nineteenth century, they have organized workers, aiming to achieve better terms and to bargain collectively on wages. The trade unions that are legally recognized in China are all linked to the Communist Party, and would not be considered independent. Although independent trade unions have a record of improving conditions in western countries, many have acquired reputations for disruptiveness. In the US, many companies, such as Walmart, have taken an anti-union stance (see Chapter 9). Where industrial relations become polarized between entrenched management and union positions, both sides risk losing sight of the overall goals which should unite them.

Decisions of MNEs based on short-term advantages have led to a 'race to the bottom', each location looking the best in terms of costs and environment until circumstances change. Industries run on this basis are not sustainable. Governments, employees, consumers and other stakeholders are beginning to value the more long-term perspective, which involves sustainable goals. This outlook could still be seen in terms of utilitarian principles, linked as it is to enlightened self-interest. Industries run on a more sustainable footing will not generate huge profit margins, but are better placed to maintain a steady level of profitability. For such firms, stakeholder considerations point to a more ethical business model as part of a sustainable approach. Advocates of capitalist markets point out that globalization of production is 'morally neutral', and workers in poorer countries have benefited from the jobs and wages that have resulted (Casson, 2003: 34). These supporters of capitalism express ethical concerns over the excesses of profit-seeking behaviour, which, they feel, run counter to capitalism's roots.

PAUSE TO CONSIDER...

A Chinese shoe company which has seen rising labour costs in China has shifted production to Ethiopia. This involves shipping out the expertise and materials, but the company saves on labour costs in Ethiopia. What are the ethical considerations involved?

CAPITALIST MARKET PRINCIPLES

The market reforms which are helping to drive economic growth in emerging economies such as China are derived from capitalism, although China itself could not be said to be a capitalist market economy. China's leaders have been astute in encouraging capitalist enterprises to realize economic gains, even though the country lacks the cultural and political institutional foundations which had nurtured capitalism in its early development. In fact, capitalism has long been evolving, and adapting to differing environments. Here we look at how capitalism has evolved, beginning with the ethical framework in which capitalism originated.

THE ETHICAL ROOTS OF CAPITALISM

Historically, many societies have been unified by cultural values derived from religion. All societies require that people behave according to socially accepted norms. Religion provides just such a set of norms. The religious moral framework is based on obedience to rules which rest on values of kindness to others, generosity and honesty. People may well be inclined to excessive behaviour and excessive focus on material goods, but religious precepts urge followers to obey a 'higher' voice which dictates that true values are spiritual, not material. The eighteenth-century Briton would read in the Bible, 'a rich man shall hardly enter into the kingdom of heaven' (King James Version, Matthew 19:23). Making money did not rest easily with being a righteous person. In The Fable of the Bees, a satirical poem of 1729 by Bernard Mandeville, the bees are first seen as avaricious, vain and prone to indulging in luxuries. But they then decided to convert to a virtuous life, avoiding over-indulgence and adopting frugal lifestyles. The result was a dramatic decline in prosperity. Britain at the time was not industrially developed. The notion of the luxurious lives of rich people creating jobs for the poor seemed a disturbing thought. Indeed, Mandeville's fable has been a debating point for later economists, including Adam Smith and John Maynard Keynes. Mandeville pointed out an uncomfortable truth: the double standard of people who claim to be Christian and accumulate wealth at the same time (Robinson, 1962: 21).

The notion of the luxurious lives of rich people creating jobs for the poor seemed a disturbing thought.

Capitalism rests on the idea of a market, which entails an exchange of something of value, such as labour, for something else, typically a 'price' in the form of wages. Anything of value has a price in the context of a particular market. For explanations of capitalist exchange, the writings of Adam Smith (1723–1790) are seen as the foundation stone. He found that landlords accumulate wealth from their lands, employing others to work for them, paying them for their labour and making a profit. Self-interest is enshrined as the key motivation of the capitalist:

> It is not from the benevolence of the butcher, the brewer or the baker, that we expect our dinner, but from their regard to their own interest. We address ourselves, not to their humanity, but to their self-love, and never talk to them of our own necessities, but of their advantages. Nobody but a beggar chooses to depend chiefly upon the benevolence of his fellow-citizens. (Robinson, 1962: 53, quoting Adam Smith)

In fact, Smith saw motivations as more complex than this, noting that people are influenced by established conventions and moral considerations (Sen, 2010: 187). Social norms of behaviour, he recognized, went beyond the notion of acting just out of self-interest. However, even these other motivations can be interpreted as rooted ultimately in self-interest. Smith's theory over time became simplified to this dominant motivation.

Weber wrote of the 'spirit of capitalism' as having originated in the Protestant ethic. He pointed to Calvinism, and specifically the English Puritans. Calvinism represented a new and revolutionary strand of Protestantism, rooted in individualism and the economic reality of market relations. In fact, it seems that Weber got these influences the wrong way round. Capitalism had already taken hold, including a growth in business enterprises, waged labour and individualist attitudes. Weber was looking at what was already a corruption of Calvinism, emphasizing an extreme individualism which Calvin himself and early followers would have found abhorrent (Tawney, 1922: 313). While early Calvinism espoused individualism, it also stressed rigorous discipline in economic affairs. Although Christians could find in Calvin an accommodation of capitalist accumulation, this was tempered by the need for self-control and social considerations. The ideal was 'a society which seeks wealth with the sober gravity of men who are conscious at once of disciplining their own characters by patient labour, and of devoting themselves to a service acceptable to God' (Tawney, 1922: 114).

Whereas the roots of capitalist thinking contained a notion of moral constraints, the religious roots gave way to a social scientific approach. This more comprehensively self-seeking view of human nature is reflected in laissez-faire capitalism (Fourcade and Healy, 2007).

PAUSE TO CONSIDER...

Why was Mandeville's fable of the bees so disturbing? Is there a place in today's capitalism for the religious dimension which would temper market motives?

LAISSEZ-FAIRE CAPITALISM

The economic individualism of the early Calvinists was moderated by moral restraint in the pursuit of economic self-interest (Tawney, 1922: 183). Rationality in earlier religious thinking was seen as part of a person's higher nature. For the early Protestants, human rationality implied that people could interpret religious truths for themselves, without reliance on the priests. But individualism came to take on a hedonistic Hobbesian view of human nature, which was adopted in economic thinking. This is the basis of laissez-faire capitalism. Smith held that markets were guided by an 'invisible hand', by which the self-interested behaviour of each would result in the overall good of society (Kay, 2003: 184). This has been interpreted as meaning that markets always balance supply and demand. Competitive markets, it was believed, would always be the most efficient way of organizing an economic system. This belief rested on an assumption about rationality which held that consumers and businesses have complete information on which to base decisions, and the ability to calculate accordingly. They are guided by rational expectations. Rationality came to refer simply to the rational economic agent, reflecting an extreme individualism. This developed into what economists refer to as rational choice theory. Rationality in the economics context thus lost its moral dimension.

Opting for a view of human nature which dwells on a person's lower nature fits readily with the study of competition for scarce resources, a preoccupation of the economist.

The economists' interpretation of rationality has been highly influential to the present day, reflected in the 'Chicago school', often referred to as the neoclassical school of economics. Rationality as used by an economist usually means 'self-regarding materialism' (Kay, 2003: 203). It can also mean simply consistency. As we discovered when looking at the utilitarians' thought, however, people do not always behave rationally. They are not always consistent, and they behave altruistically from time to time. Nonetheless, economists make the assumption of rationality, mainly, it is arguable, in order to impose a rigour in their discipline which gives it a scientific basis (Kay, 2003: 203). Opting for a view of human nature which dwells on a person's lower nature fits readily with the study of competition for scarce resources, a preoccupation of the economist. Economics came thus to be dominated by mathematics, squeezing out earlier moral considerations. Moral considerations, being qualitative and often worded in abstract terms, cannot be quantified, and did not have a place in a discipline seen as wholly logical, scientific and free from value judgments (Robinson, 1962: 57).

Cultures differ on perceptions of wealth accumulation. The societies which have embraced laissez-faire capitalism most enthusiastically have been in the Anglo-American cultural environment, where individualism is valued. As the US gained in economic prowess globally, its free-market capitalism became an example to the rest of the world. Its superiority over all other systems seemed to be sealed with the collapse of the Soviet Union in 1991. The US enjoyed not just economic success in the following decades, but also political and military influence globally. Its free-market values underpinned its global status.

FREE-MARKET CAPITALISM: THE AMERICAN MODEL

The American free-market model was built on the primacy of economic freedom, by which individuals are given maximum scope to pursue private enterprise (Friedman, 1962). The notion of the 'American dream' is reflected in the cultural underpinning of this model. This is the belief that in the US, any person, no matter how lowly, can rise to become materially successful (Corak, 2013). The elements are shown in Figure 2.4. Economic freedom refers to freedom in the negative sense, as an absence of impediments in the way of self-interested behaviour. The influential economist, Milton Friedman, is credited with articulating the importance of freedom as a value linked to capitalism (Palley, 2006). Other tenets flow from this view. Advocates believe that markets should have free rein and regulation should be kept to a minimum. Central to this model is the notion of 'small government'.

Figure 2.4 *The American model of free-market capitalism*

Individual person
- Individual self-interest
- Rationality in calculating self-interest
- Maximum economic freedom
- Personal morality based on religious beliefs

Society
- Social goods subordinated to individualism
- Mutual self-interest
- Charities provide social welfare

American model of free-market capitalism

Role of law
- Protection of private property
- Enforcement of contracts

Role of government
- Minimal
- Non-intervention in private enterprise
- No direct roles in business

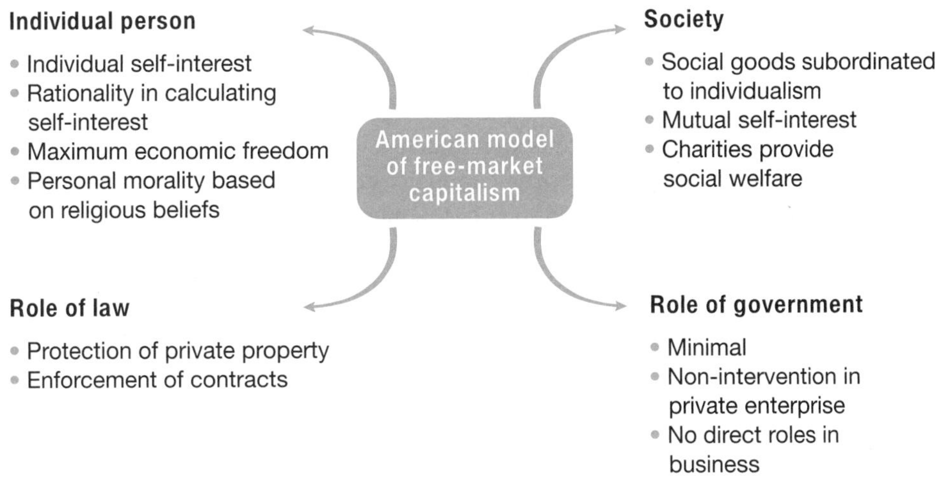

Governments, they feel, should not interfere with business, and should be limited to mechanisms for protecting private property and enforcing contracts. Governments, on this view, should not own assets, engage in business activities or provide goods and services. Taxes, therefore, should be low, in keeping with the minimalist state.

Proponents of the American business model believe that self-interested behaviour of individuals is paramount, and everything has a price (Sandel, 2012: 49). This applies not just to markets in goods and labour. Markets have crept into areas of health, education and environmental protection. Michael Sandel, lamenting the tendency of markets to commoditize everything, remarks that the market economy has turned into the 'market society' (Sandel, 2012).

Where do moral values fit into this model? Figure 2.4 refers to personal morality based on religious beliefs, and also to charities. Given the pervasiveness of markets in so many aspects of life in the US, it is perhaps surprising that most people are highly imbued with religious beliefs. This phenomenon has been the subject of research by sociologists, who find a paradox between the economic individualism of Americans and their collectivist tendency in religion and morals (Fischer, 2008). Approximately 79% of Americans identify with an established religious denomination (Pew Research Centre, 2012). This is a large proportion, but it has actually fallen from 92% in 1990. Even among the 20% of Americans who do not belong to a particular religion, over two-thirds say they believe in God, but they simply do not belong to an organized religion. The preponderance of active religious believers suggests the importance of moral standards in society, but it does not seem to extend to business behaviour or to the many aspects of life which have become commoditized.

Staunch supporters of free-market capitalism in the US have struggled to defend their philosophical position in recent years. Financial crisis, recession and increased government spending on welfare are indicators of market failures. Economists have tended to defend the market's ability to deliver growth, believing that there will be a 'trickle-down' effect, which will benefit all in society (Alvaredo et al., 2013). But inequality is widening (Corak, 2013). Between 2000 and 2007, incomes of the top 1% grew at 10.1% per year, while incomes of the other 99% grew at 1.3% (IMF, 2011). The figures for 2009–2012, which reflect the recession following the financial crisis, are more pronounced. The top 1% of incomes grew at 31.4%, while the bottom 99% grew at 0.4% (Saez, 2013). US median household income, adjusted for inflation, was 8% less in 2011 than in 2007, median earnings for full-time workers falling 2.5% in 2011 from a year earlier (US Census Bureau, 2012). Moreover, the number of people in full-time work has declined by 5 million since 2007. The lifestyle of the American middle class has long symbolized America's economic success story. But America's middle class has shrunk, become less affluent and less economically secure. Income mobility in the US has also declined, undermining another of the images of the US, that of the rags-to-riches life story. Research indicates that 43% of Americans in the bottom fifth of the population in terms of income are stuck there (Pew Charitable Trusts, 2012). While many in the bottom fifth will see rises in income, 65% of Americans in the bottom fifth will stay in the bottom two-fifths (US Census Bureau, 2012). By contrast, only 25% of Danes and 30% of British people in the bottom fifth will stay there.

America's middle class has shrunk, become less affluent and less economically secure.

In the US, the opportunities to realize one's potential depend on being able to pay for the better education, health, housing and amenities which have increasingly become subject to

Photo 2.2 Derelict homes are a reminder of the hardship caused by the collapse in the housing market in the US. This crumbling neighbourhood is in the state of West Virginia, one of the poorest states in the country. (© iStock.com/Lawrence Sawyer)

market forces (Corak, 2013). Inequalities in health and nutrition have deepened. The number of Americans who are so poor that they must rely on 'food stamps' provided by the federal government, has rocketed to 46 million (see Figure 2.5). This total has more than doubled since 1985, and the bill now amounts to $80 billion a year.

Free-market supporters advocate giving to others through charities and philanthropic activities. But charities struggle to deal with the demand for their services. Moreover, this is ad hoc giving, not institutional, and is often motivated by considerations such as favourable tax treatment of charitable donations. Milton Friedman, a supporter of charitable giving, stressed that these activities by individuals should be voluntary (Meyerson, 2006). He felt strongly that the government should not be involved in welfare state measures. And he rejected the idea that companies have social obligations, which he felt is against the business's paramount duty to create wealth for shareholders. Many American companies have supported CSR as a focus on philanthropic activities. In this respect, the social dimension is recognized as a voluntary additional activity, not as an element in the business model. This limited view of social responsibility echoes Friedman's idea of the primacy of markets.

Some of the critics of the free-market model are supporters of markets in general, but say that markets and pure profit-seeking strategies have gone too far. The labourer is earning wages in exchange for his work, which is morally acceptable, in contrast to the capitalist, whose role is exploitative. Criticisms of capitalism in principle have been voiced for a long time. We noted the concerns of J.S. Mill in the last chapter. As we have seen, Rawls, in particular, criticized the free-market model, urging redistribution and pointing to the need

Figure 2.5 *Numbers of Americans in receipt of 'food stamps' (millions)*

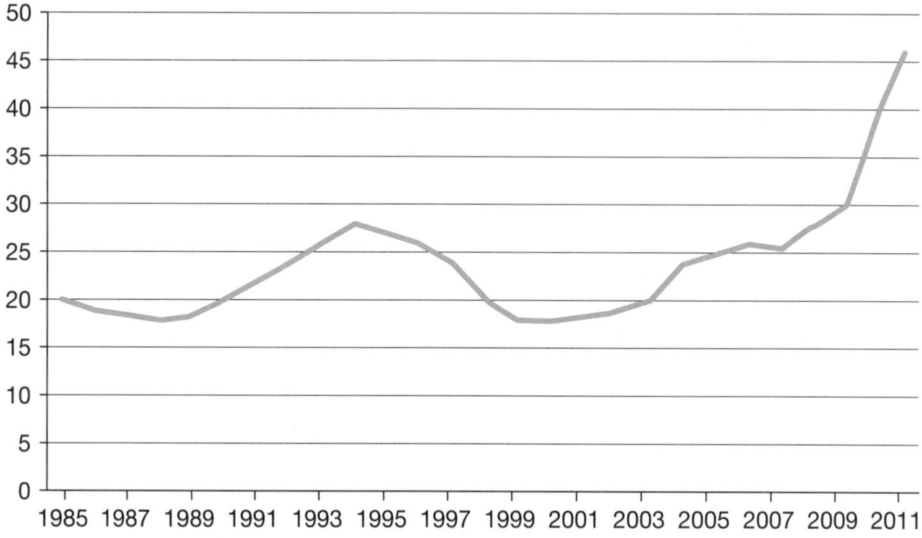

Source of data: US Department of Agriculture (2012) *Supplemental Nutrition Assistance Program Participation and Costs, 1969–2014,* at http://www.fns.usda.gov/pd/SNAPsummary (18/09/14).

for governments to redress the inequalities. But he would still support the market economy and its essential individualism.

What is the alternative? Following the 2008 financial crisis, belief in the stability of markets has been shaken. The moral issues raised by growing divisions between rich and poor need to be addressed, both within and between countries. If capitalism is losing its claim to legitimacy, does socialism offer a valid alternative?

The laissez-faire model of capitalism has been criticized by Sandel for turning US society into a market *society*, not merely a market *economy*. Yet there are high levels of government spending on welfare, which clash with the idea of a market society. How can this be explained?

SOCIALISM IN THEORY AND PRACTICE

Socialism rests on a belief that societal goals rather than private profit should be the basis of the economy. The socialist believes that capitalism has resulted in a concentration of wealth in the hands of the few, based on exploitation of the mass of working people. Although capitalism is premised on economic freedom, the mass of the population, dependent on waged labour, has little freedom and little voice. This is seen as ethically wrong, violating principles of human dignity. Socialism gathered support as a system which claimed to be superior to capitalism. But socialism has been more successful as a set of beliefs to rally those who are against capitalism than as an actual economic system in practice. Socialism was taken up by political movements, often with the aim of overthrowing existing governments. But, as we will see, the countries which have adopted socialism as a system have almost entirely failed to achieve a sustainable economy or social justice. In this section, we look first at the theory and then at how it evolved in practice.

MARX'S THEORY FROM AN ETHICAL PERSPECTIVE

The first and most influential socialist thinker was Karl Marx (1818–1883), whose works set out a vision of the ideal society of the future, in which all could enjoy freedom and self-determination. It would arise from the ruins of the capitalist system, which he believed would fall apart from continual crises and uprising by the working class, or proletariat. There was a utopian vision in Marx's philosophy which no doubt inspired early followers. Marx's more down-to-earth co-author, Friedrich Engels (1820–1895) was responsible for much of the popular interpretation of the theory.

Marx's vision of a perfect society owed much to the German philosophical tradition in which he was steeped. He did not specifically address individual ethics, but it underlies his theory of capital and labour, which is especially evident in his earlier works. His link between labour and the human essence is the ethical basis of his theory of a new era of social production (Kamenka, 1962). The worker's humanity, or 'species-being', exists in his labour, and in the process of exploitation by bourgeois owners, the worker gradually loses his essential humanity. Marx says the worker 'must sell himself and his human qualities' (Marx, 1963: 73). This is encapsulated in the notion of alienation, whereby the worker sees both the product of his work and the process of production as externalized, or standing outside himself like hostile forces (Marx, 1963: 123). The worker is thus debased by the capitalist system which treats him as a means. The distinction between treating people as ends and as means echoes Kant's categorical imperative. Also echoing Kant, Marx equates freedom with self-determination, in the tradition of the positive definition of liberty. Marx had contempt for the theories based on negative liberty and the rights of man. These, he felt, were linked with an egoistic view of human nature and a preoccupation with private property, as espoused by the classical economists.

Marx had a rather deterministic view of history and believed that capitalism was doomed to failure because of the 'contradictions' in the relations of production between capital and labour. The life of the worker, he felt, was so physically exhausting and mentally dehumanizing that the proletariat would inevitably revolt. A new classless society would result, which would transcend the notion of private property altogether. The well-known expression that the state would 'wither away' was in fact coined by Engels (Lichtheim, 1961: 373). Marx was firm in his belief in proletarian revolution and the revolutionary consciousness of the working class. Workers, he felt, had no desire simply to improve the existing system through reform. The notion of private property would disappear, and the result would be a pure form of communist society. As we will see, Marx was wrong in his assessment of class war. In reality, workers embraced the right to negotiate better conditions and welcomed job security. The Marxism adopted by activist political figures and new revolutionary groups bore little resemblance to the theories of Marx himself. The revolutions which did take place in the name of Marxism had little to do with proletarian revolt.

MARXISM IN PRACTICE

Marx's theory attracted followers, and socialist parties were formed across Europe, most of these developments taking place after his death. These parties, though revolutionary in their inception, became more reformist in practice. Socialist political parties have played important roles in the democratic politics of most European countries. The philosophies of these parties, however, have rested on an agenda which seeks reform of the existing system, not violent revolution. It is often observed that a weakness in Marx's theory is that he did not see that workers might be satisfied simply with improved conditions and pay. Through political pressure and also the activities of trade unions, better rewards and job security were achieved in Western European countries. In the final decades of the nineteenth century, trade unions had become part of the rising working-class consciousness. However, this was concentrated mainly in the large industrial complexes that had sprung up. Marx had referred to the proletariat in terms of class consciousness, which he felt would domi-nate workers' feelings of identity. In fact, the working class, or, perhaps more accurately, working classes, were diverse. They ranged from artisan workers who were highly skilled to less skilled workers in shipyards and construction. There were also religious differences, which remained strong, as well as differing national cultures among immigrant workers. The *Communist Manifesto*'s resounding call, 'Workers of the world, unite!', was more aspi-rational than realistic.

The chief example of an avowedly Marxist party with plans to lead a revolution was Lenin's Bolshevik Party in Russia. Lenin's Marxism owed little to Marx's theory, although the communist party platform which he inspired was called Marxism-Leninism. Russia was hardly ripe for proletarian revolution. The tsarist empire, with Russia at its heart, had seen little of the prosperity and industrial development which had taken place in Western Europe. The population was 80% peasantry. In the closing years of the nineteenth century, the tsarist government had belatedly adopted a policy of industrialization. Industrial centres did have concentrations of factory workers, but these were not the type of proletar-ian worker Marx had envisaged, pauperized by years of capitalist exploitation. In Russia, the peasantry, rather than industrial workers, came closer to the image of a downtrodden class, leading a miserable existence on the land and heavily taxed. Russia presented few opportu-nities to bring about change in a gradual, reformist way. The peasants had a history of upris-ings, and it was among these masses of poor people that there would be popular support for a revolutionary uprising. Lenin believed it would be best to 'seize the moment rather than wait for the development of capitalism' (Johnson, 1964: 14).

Lenin saw the peasantry as in the vanguard, establishing a democratic dictatorship of proletariat and peasantry. However, the dictatorship led by Lenin soon turned into a despotic regime supported by an ideology of Marxism-Leninism. The transformations of Marx's ideas are shown in Figure 2.6. Marx envisaged freedom being achieved by workers through the march of history. This notion became corrupted in the communist revolution which overthrew the tsarist monarchy in Russia. The transformation culminated in the new Soviet Russia, forming the USSR (Union of Soviet Socialist Republics). The rise of Joseph Stalin brought a further degeneration of Marxism-Leninism into a communist ideology based on a cult of personality. Stalinism aimed to achieve rapid industrialization in the USSR in the aftermath of the First World War. A state-planned economy was instituted, bringing in collectivization of production and collective farms in the name of the state, which, it was claimed, would achieve communism in one state. Stalinism, while still using the terminology of Marx, represented a corruption of Marx's ideals of freedom as self-determination.

Apart from the lack of legitimacy in ideological terms, the tyranny of the Soviet Union, based on the planned economy and all power concentrated in a centralized state, proved unworkable. Following the death of Stalin in 1953, reforms were introduced and Stalinism

Figure 2.6 *Marx's theory transformed into Marxism-Leninism*

Marx's theory		Marxism as practised by communist rule in the USSR
• Working-class consciousness as prerequisite for revolution	→	• Revolution in predominantly agrarian society
• Capitalist exploitation destined by history to collapse	→	• Communist party led revolution against tsarist imperial rule (few capitalists in Russia 1905–17)
• Liberty and self-determination defining human dignity	→	• State run be a small group of self-appointed communist party leaders
		• Lack of individual freedoms
• Communist society will be egalitarian and meet the human needs of all	→	• Unequal repressive regime, ruled by communist élite

as an ideology was officially refuted. But the Soviet state edifice remained in place, and in the years of the cold war, its ideology remained a driving force. But there were insurmountable problems with the centralized, heavily bureaucratic state, inefficient state-run industries and continuing poverty among the people. The many nationalities and diverse cultures which made up the USSR, each with its own aspirations, made it difficult to run a centralized system. Further reforms were instituted in the 1980s, introducing more flexibility in state-run enterprises, some element of private property and some democracy in the communist party. These proved insufficient to overcome the economic and political problems. It ultimately collapsed in 1991. Here are the main reasons for its ultimate failure:

- The system took insufficient account of the needs of people as individual human beings to realize their own goals. It became clear that private enterprise and private property were essential.
- The communist party, which had led the revolution, had ceased to have any vestige of legitimacy to govern, and remained unanswerable to the populace. Political infighting and corruption further damaged the party's ability to govern.
- State-run industries were inefficient, bureaucratic and weak in technological innovation.
- The diverse nationalities and cultures aspired to greater autonomy, which was insufficiently recognized in the centralized system.

The collapse of the Soviet Union was an indication of the inherent weaknesses of the planned economy, with its heavily bureaucratic controls and propensity to corruption. These destructive tendencies have been taken most seriously by the communist leadership in China, whose own revolution dates from 1949. Its revolution, too, sought to follow Marxism-Leninism, but its leaders have been keen to avoid the mistakes of their Soviet predecessors. Their embrace of market reforms while retaining communist controls, has been a distinguishing feature in their shift away from Marxist-Leninist orthodoxy towards a more market-oriented economy, bringing it within the broad category of mixed economy. The remaining nominally communist states in the world include North Korea, a repressive police state closed to the outside world, and America's close neighbour, Cuba, which has been subject to a US trade embargo for over half a century. In fact, communist Cuba, although a poor developing country in terms of income, outshines most developed countries in terms of health. Cuba is cautiously introducing market reforms, and the US government has taken small steps to resume relations with its communist neighbour.

PAUSE TO CONSIDER...

What ideas of Marx help to explain the problems of today's capitalist economies?

MIXED ECONOMIES

The mixed economy is one with elements of both open markets and state direction or ownership. It is hardly a 'model', as the balance can vary considerably. While we would consider most western economies to be closer to the market model, growing state involvement in economic activity has shifted these towards mixed economies. The liberal market economy reflects this trend, recognizing the need for government intervention to promote public goods. Meanwhile, the allure of markets has gripped most of the world's developing economies. Their leaders see the benefits of attracting foreign investors and encouraging private enterprises to create wealth and jobs. But, whatever the balance of state direction and market freedom, the role of government is crucial in ensuring that benefits to society are realized. Government policies are crucial not just for jobs, but for other social needs, such as health, education, living standards and opportunities for betterment among the population. Inherent in these concerns are ethical issues such as social justice and human dignity. Here, we look at the patterns emerging in mixed economies.

THE ROLE OF GOVERNMENT IN THE LIBERAL MARKET ECONOMY

All but the staunchest believers in free markets have had their faith shaken by the financial crisis of 2008 and the recession which followed. Among the causes were regulatory failures in globalized financial markets (to be discussed in Chapter 5). The US and UK, both home to large financial centres where light regulation has been a hallmark, were shattered by the collapse of large banks and the need for government bailouts. Regulation of financial markets is now recognized as an area in which governments and international organizations have a legitimate role to play. Another role which governments play in financial markets is to regulate competition, through laws on anti-competitive practices and monopolies (see Chapter 4). In these roles, the regulator acts like a referee, ensuring fair play in markets. Governments in market economies would prefer the tool of regulation over the direct intervention which occurred in 2008. However, direct action is not new to them: governments in most market economies have long played direct roles.

Government spending on defence and national security is recognized as essential by all sovereign states. But how far should governments go in social spending? This heading covers education, health, welfare benefits such as unemployment benefit and pensions. The answer depends in part on the picture of the 'good society' that each country holds. The liberal market economies all have democratic political systems. These will be analysed in the next chapter, but for now, it is important to note that the economic and political systems are interrelated. With universal suffrage came accountability of governments to an electorate which was in theory based on roughly one-person-one-vote. Political equality is not the same as social and economic equality. If a country values economic freedom to a high degree, it might well tolerate high levels of inequality (Fourcade and Healy, 2007). The US

Figure 2.7 *Share of top 1% in income distribution*

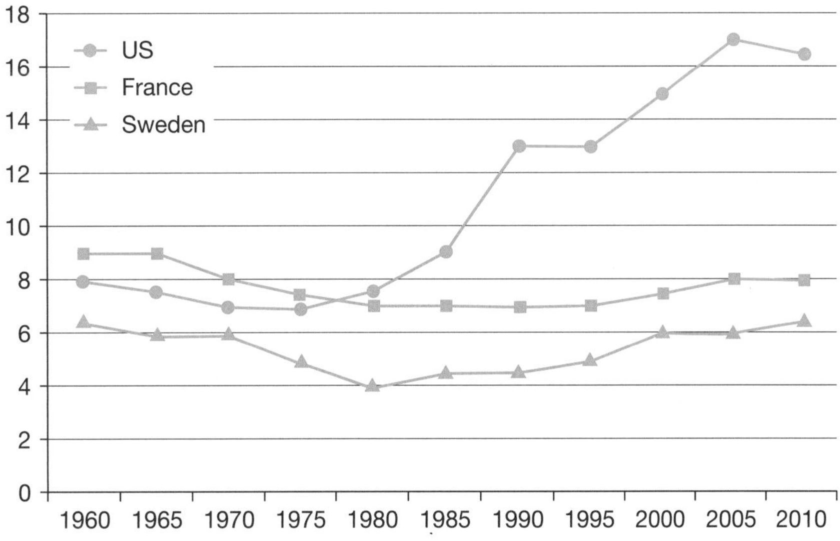

Source of data: IMF (2011) *Finance and Development*, 48(3), at www.imf.org (18/09/14).

and UK have long been in this category. Figure 2.7 shows the share of the top 1% in the national income of the US, France and Sweden. In the 1960s, their share was under 10% in all these countries, but the US saw a dramatic rise in inequality during the period of economic boom from 1985 onwards.

A country which prioritizes social equality is likely to spend more on social programmes. France is an example, discussed below in the section on the social market economy. Countries in the more liberal tradition have tended to have higher levels of inequality. In these countries, equality of opportunity is stressed, suggesting that each person should have opportunity for betterment, especially through education. This could well involve a lot of government spending on the school system. Much government spending in the more liberal tradition is seen as providing a social safety net, such as unemployment benefit. There are divergent views on spending for healthcare. Since 1948, the UK has had a national health service (NHS), brought in by the Labour government, which was socialist in economic thinking. The NHS has become immensely expensive, and recent governments have sought to outsource much of the provision to private contractors (see the closing case study of Chapter 7). But privatizing services is controversial in a country which has prided itself on a universal system. It also has ethical implications. As the market becomes ever more involved in healthcare, it looks like commoditizing health for profit, which can be seen as being unethical.

The US government has subscribed to the safety-net view of government spending in respect of healthcare, and has traditionally left it to employers to provide health insurance. This system has deteriorated with the reduction in the number of employers providing insurance. The decline in manufacturing jobs has been a big factor. Large manufacturers such as car-makers offered generous wage and benefit packages during the boom years of American manufacturing. But with the decline in manufacturing, the provision of health insurance became patchy. Meanwhile, healthcare costs have risen steadily. New legislation introduced during President Obama's first term of office features an insurance scheme which provides a safety net, but it still relies on employers' contributions. Opponents call this 'socialist' medicine, but this is rather misleading. It is not a universal health service run by the state, but an insurance system based on employer contributions, which is a less radical step in the American context. A universal health service is more likely to be found in the countries where the social market model of capitalism dominates.

THE SOCIAL MARKET ECONOMY

Within capitalist values there is an inherent tension. The capitalist wishes to maximize freedom, but the resulting concentration of economic power leaves those at the bottom of the ladder with little freedom. The historian R.H. Tawney has said, 'freedom for the pike is death for the minnows' (Tawney, 1964: 164). The social market economy sees a positive role for the state in fostering social goals within a market economy. The notion that democracy entails social justice is the basis of the systems which combine socialist ideals, such as equality and solidarity, with democratic government. These are sometimes called social democracies. They include Western European economies, Scandinavian countries and the post-communist transition economies of Central and Eastern Europe. They differ in many respects, but generally implement elements of socialism, including state ownership of companies in key sectors. These countries tend to have high public spending and high taxation, which funds health and welfare benefits. These are generally secular states in societies which have become multi-cultural. Governments in these countries stress the need for religious freedom and social inclusion. In general, these countries see government social policy and spending not in a negative light, but as a positive contribution to the good of society.

The United Nations rank countries in terms of 'human development' each year in its Human Development Index (HDI). These calculations take income into account, but attempt to make a broader assessment than that based on economic criteria alone. The index uses three main criteria: health, education and standard of living. The top ten countries are listed in Table 2.1. These calculations are based on an assumption of equality in the population of each country. In 2011, the rankings were recalculated, taking into account the inequality in each society. The recalculated rank of most of these ten countries remained the same, implying that they have relatively low inequality. The exceptions were Canada and the US. When inequality is factored in, Canada drops 7 places, and the US drops 19 places.

The health component of the Human Development Index is based on life expectancy, which has risen over the years in most countries, due to improvements in a number of areas, including nutrition, medicine and housing. For the OECD countries, which are the advanced economies, the average rise from 1983 to 2008 was 6 years, reaching an average age of 79.3 years (OECD, 2011). The lowest increase over that period among all OECD countries was in the US, where life expectancy rose only 3.3 years in the 25 years. There, the average lifespan is 77.9 years, about the same as the Czech Republic, but citizens of the Czech Republic have seen a rise in life expectancy of 6.6 years over

Table 2.1 *Human Development Rankings, 2011*

Rank	Country
1	Norway
2	Australia
3	Netherlands
4	US
5	New Zealand
6	Canada
7	Ireland
8	Liechtenstein
9	Germany
10	Sweden

Source: United Nations (2011) *Human Development Report 2011*, at www.undp.org (18/09/14).

that period – double that of the US. A number of factors are involved, including healthcare, lifestyle and nutrition. In the US, the annual health spending for each person is $8,362 (World Bank, 2011) which is far more than that of any other country. The annual health bill for a citizen of the Czech Republic is $1,480 (the World Bank's calculations include both public and private spending). The Czech Republic is a post-communist economy, independent since 1993. It is making the transition to democracy and a market-oriented economy. Its national health service is based on public insurance. The following principles underlie the system (Ministry of Health of the Czech Republic, 2012):

- Solidarity between healthy people and the sick
- Multi-source financing with major share of public health insurance
- Equal availability of healthcare for all insured persons
- The healthcare system strives to create the conditions where there are no differences in the availability of healthcare.

This statement, stressing solidarity and equality, is indicative of the ideals which countries aspire to in setting up a national health service. The same ideals extend to other areas of social spending. The social market economies tend to have large budgets for social spending, as shown in Figure 2.8. France and Denmark spend the largest proportion of GDP on social spending, but the UK and US also spend large sums, albeit more reluctantly. Australia is notable for its more modest outlays on public spending, amounting to 18.7% of GDP, while enjoying a ranking of second in the HDI.

Social spending reflects values of equality and human dignity in a society. The very rich are not as admired in the social market economies as they would be in the US. This does not mean that France or Denmark is essentially a socialist economy. These are market economies where equality of life chances is seen as important, and extremes of wealth and power are viewed as unethical. Generally, high taxation, notably 'social contributions', are designed to support the philosophy of solidarity.

State ownership of companies is an important aspect of the economies of many countries in this broad group. There are many different models of state ownership, and also divergent

Figure 2.8 *Government social spending as a percentage of GDP, 2012*

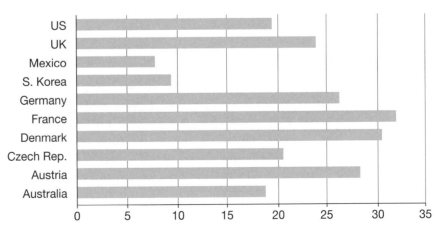

Source of data: OECD (2012) Government social spending 2012, at www.oecd-ilibrary.org (18/09/14).

models of corporate governance. We will look at the state's role in later chapters on politics and finance. Here, we look at how state-owned companies fit into the social market economy, and how they can support social values.

A government may own a company outright, and operate it as a government ministry. Most of the countries in this group do not adopt such a state-centric approach. Typically, the company is a registered company, but instead of private shareholders, the main shareholder is the state. A proportion of shares can be made available for purchase by private shareholders. In the case of EDF, 84.4% of the shares are in the hands of the state. Norway has many state-owned companies in key sectors, including petroleum, energy, transport and healthcare. These state-owned companies are operated on a commercial basis. They pay tax, are required to submit accounts and operate transparent systems of corporate governance which would be required of a company in the private sector. The policy in Norway, as in other countries, is to gradually privatize stakes in these companies, by inviting the public to buy shares. At the same time, state control emphasizes that these companies are established for social values.

Statoil is Norway's state-owned petroleum company. Its profits go into Norway's government pension funds. The Government Pension Fund – Global – amounts to some $444 billion, which is invested on behalf of the state. This is a sovereign wealth fund, which can be defined as any fund owned and managed by the state or an arm of the state. Norway's pension fund has become Europe's largest shareholder, holding about 1% of all European shares. Managed under the eye of the Ministry of Finance and a Council on Ethics, the fund aims to be an ethical investor. Its terms forbid investments in companies whose activities violate human rights, cause damage to the environment or are in other ways unethical. Consequently, it does not invest in the arms industry, and it has sold investments in tobacco companies which it had made before new, stricter ethical standards were brought in (2010). Norway's sovereign wealth fund is unusual in its accountability, transparency and ethical policies. Sovereign wealth funds generally have become a growing phenomenon in global finance. Often associated with non-democratic governments, they are usually more noted for their opaque ownership and governance. Norway is an example of state ownership focused on social goods and managed ethically.

PAUSE TO CONSIDER...

Compare the ethical foundations of the liberal market economy and the social market economy. What are the implications for business ethics in each of these broad types of economy?

STATE CAPITALISM

State capitalism refers to countries where the state is the main economic actor in the country, either through direct ownership or indirect control. Although these countries, in theory, view the state as representing the interests of the people as a whole, in practice, there is little accountability to the population. In ethical terms, this distinguishes these economies from those following the social market model, which are broadly democratic and prioritize social justice. The state-owned company and sovereign wealth fund are favoured structures whereby authoritarian and semi-authoritarian governments manage national wealth. In this section we look at two leading examples of state capitalism – China and Russia. In both cases, there have been policy moves towards market reforms and economic freedoms, revealing tensions between state control and market liberalization.

China's state-owned enterprises (SOEs) are now active globally, in both financial investments and FDI. They account for about 80% of China's outward FDI (OECD, 2009). Their investments in market economies are controversial. China's National Offshore Oil Corporation (CNOOC) failed in its attempt to purchase an American oil company, Unocal, in 2005, when a US government committee rejected the deal on national security grounds. It tried a different strategy in 2012, aiming to purchase a Canadian oil company, Nexen, which also has activities in the US. The rich North American oil fields are a major attraction for large oil companies. The Chinese company felt that Canada would be more amenable to its presence than the US had been. However, the takeover became a contentious issue in Canada. Apart from the doubts about the motives of Chinese state-owned companies, Canadians were concerned about foreign ownership of natural resources. Nonetheless, the takeover was approved.

Chinese SOEs have evolved from entities run as part of the government bureaucracy to companies which are more enterprise-oriented. This change reflects changes in government policy. In 1992, the government announced that it would be a 'socialist market economy'. Reforms of the state-owned sector were initiated. Numerous inefficient and unprofitable SOEs were to become more business-oriented and less linked to the bureaucracy. Many were transformed into companies and were listed on domestic stock exchanges. Some 80% of the top ten listed companies on the Shanghai Stock Exchange are in fact SOEs. As listed companies, a proportion of their shares are traded, but the bulk of the shares are non-tradable, held by the state. Individual shareholders have little scope for influencing how these companies are run. Despite market appearances, these companies are dominated by the Communist Party, whose leaders also control the central and local government agencies and other entities which dominate SOEs. SOEs' ownership remains opaque. Their corporate governance is weak, and they are prone to corruption.

Some 80% of the top ten listed companies on the Shanghai Stock Exchange are in fact SOEs.

Market reforms have allowed private businesses to spring up, gradually gaining greater importance in the Chinese economy. These firms have driven China's economic growth, although they have not enjoyed the favoured treatment, such as the advantageous loans lavished on the state sector. The large state-owned companies control assets worth an estimated $4.5 trillion, which is equivalent to 75% of the country's GDP (Rabinovitch, 2012).

Figure 2.9 *Revenues of China's stated-owned enterprises managed by the central government*

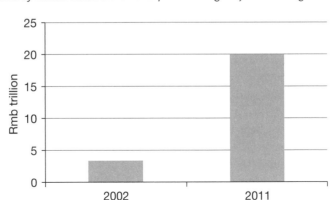

Source of data: Rabinovitch, S. (2012) 'March of the state presses private companies', *Financial Times*, 12 November.

Their revenues have also grown, as shown in Figure 2.9. Reformist voices have expressed concern that the state is now squeezing out the private-sector companies, which are crucial for the innovation and agility needed to build competitive advantage for the future. Further liberalization of the state sector would include allowing a greater proportion of shares to be traded. This would give the small shareholder a greater voice in the running of these companies, bringing in an element of accountability. However, such reforms would imply a loosening of the grip of the Communist Party in these corporations, and, for this reason, prospects for further liberalization are limited.

China has seen a huge reduction in poverty in the last three decades, lifting an estimated 600 million people out of poverty. However, poverty remains a problem, concentrated in rural areas and among ethnic minorities (World Bank report, 2010). In keeping with other Asian countries in the Confucian tradition, China has viewed social spending as an obligation for families rather than for the state, but this is changing. The state is now spending more on health and welfare, but China's citizens are becoming impatient with the patchy coverage and uneven quality. Spending per person on health in China is just $221 annually. Life expectancy is now 73 years, but China has a generally low ranking in the UN's human development index, at 101 out of 187 countries (United Nations, 2011). This low level of human well-being rather detracts from the pride the country takes in being the world's second largest economy.

The second leading example of state capitalism is Russia. Unlike China, Russia is a post-communist transition economy which introduced market reforms and democratic processes following the fall of the Soviet Union. However, Russia's progress, both economically and politically, has been uneven. A radical privatization of state assets in the 1990s led to the creation of a class of 'oligarchs', private individuals who benefited from the sell-off of state assets. Excessive expansion fuelled by debt led to a financial crisis in 1998. The government of Vladimir Putin, elected president in 2000, sought to stabilize the economy, but this involved bringing back greater state involvement. Although many companies appear to be independent, their ownership and management are linked to associates of the most powerful political leaders.

Russia's large companies are almost all in the natural resources sector, including oil, gas and metals. The gas giant, Gazprom, formerly the Soviet gas ministry, became a listed company on the London Stock Exchange in 1996. From its position as a gas monopoly, it has grown into a large conglomerate, reaching into other sectors like the media. The state has reasserted its grip on Gazprom, which is now effectively controlled by the government. Russia's resource-dependent economy is threatened by changing markets, as newer players enter energy markets. These include the US, which is now producing natural gas which can be transported as liquefied natural gas. The Russian government could launch another wave of privatizations, unleashing entrepreneurial potential in other sectors. Welcoming more FDI would also aid the economy. However, Russia has had a history of corruption and weak rule of law. Russia is ranked 176 in Transparency International's Corruption Perception Index (see Chapter 1). This implies a level of corruption worse than other emerging economies.

While Russia spends more than China on health for each inhabitant, at $525 per year, this figure, too, is low (World Bank, 2011). A Russian can expect to live just 69 years, a life expectancy which has remained virtually unchanged in the last 25 years. Russia ranks 66 in the UN's human development index, which is low for an industrialized economy. In terms of social provision and well-being, Russia is making little progress, despite its energy wealth. Russia, like China, has a growing middle class with aspirations for a better quality of life and more freedom. But the controls exerted through the state capitalist model probably inhibit rather than foster a better society for all inhabitants.

From the societal perspective, state capitalism can, in theory, bring benefits to the population if the wealth is channelled into improving living conditions and funding social welfare. In practice, partly due to corruption in these systems, societal gains are uneven.

PAUSE TO CONSIDER...

State capitalism has fostered economic growth, but its record in terms of societal goods and social ethics is less laudable. What are its weaknesses as a model?

IS THERE A BEST ECONOMIC MODEL?

We have considered a wide range of economic models, from extreme laissez-faire capitalism to the state-planned economy. We have looked at varying perspectives on freedom and differing levels of social spending, enabling people to live a healthy and fulfilled life. A wide range of industries and types of ownership have been considered. Every sovereign state faces issues of how best to organize economic activities. The example of the US seemed to show that markets topped any other system, leading many developing countries to open their markets more. The financial crisis and the rise of China, with its statist model, caused people to rethink what the best model is. A leading Brazilian economist has said of his own country, 'We want to consume like US consumers, we want to have the public services of the Europeans but we want to grow like an emerging market, so something has to give' (Leahy, 2012). Brazil's growth has slowed, and it has looked for ways to quicken industrialization and increase employment. Another Brazilian has said, 'It used to be that all of Latin America looked to Europe as its ideal model ... But now, China is becoming a more attractive or plausible model' (Leahy, 2012). Brazilians are aware that their country is competing against other BRIC countries. All veer towards the statist model, although India has now moved away from its socialist foundations. Unlike India, China is not democratic, and the foregoing discussion has shown that the more authoritarian states are less assiduous in safeguarding individual rights and social justice. On these grounds, therefore, one would probably not recommend China as a model. China's model has been effective in accelerating economic development, but states must move on from development models as growth begins to slow.

'We want to consume like US consumers, we want to have the public services of the Europeans but we want to grow like an emerging market, so something has to give.'

Any economic model, ideally, should be sustainable. This includes sustainability in terms of economic growth and jobs, environmental protection and provision of basic services. I have highlighted doubts about many of the models discussed here. High levels of public spending have placed large burdens on national treasuries in both the liberal market systems and the social market systems, but not always delivered the social goods they aspire to. The statist models have shown themselves to be weak in social provision and also weak in government accountability. There is probably no one best model for all countries. Rather, the best model is possibly dependent on the country's circumstances. Statist direction can clearly be effective, as in the case of China, but this model jeopardizes much that is of value to society and its individual inhabitants. They will tolerate these weaknesses for a time, but probably become less tolerant as time goes on. Social protests occur frequently in China, ranging from strikes of factory workers to demonstrations by middle-class groups against pollution. Such demonstrations of public sentiment have become easier to organize thanks to the phenomenal growth of social media in China. These grassroots activities are a warning that sustainability should be rising up the agenda for governments everywhere.

CONCLUSIONS

Globalization has been spearheaded by companies seeking advantages in diverse geographic locations to produce products, extract resources and make financial gains. The growing ease with which goods, money and information travels around the world has greatly facilitated their global aspirations. Their profits have grown with their markets, and corporate strategists have become adept at shifting activities to places where costs are low, while shifting profits to places such as offshore jurisdictions where taxes are minimal. In one of the paradoxes of globalization, profit-maximizing advantages have focused on local-ization, with trade-offs between locations. This aggressively capitalist strategy is admired when it succeeds, but is criticized when it fails, often because of excessive risk-taking in pursuit of greater rewards.

The world's economies represent divergent approaches to managing economic life. While capitalism on free-market lines has led many countries to introduce market reforms, the financial crisis reminded the world that markets carry risks. The exposure of the methods by which global companies have generated profits, such as the exploitation of armies of workers in Asian locations, has led to a debate on whether capitalist pursuit of self-inter-ested gain has gone too far. Moreover, the business models which rely on low-cost labour now look unsustainable in the long term, as well as being unethical in principle. Capitalists might say that their object is simply to make money within existing legal frameworks in each country, and that it is up to governments to change the law if they perceive social harms are being perpetrated. In the next chapter, we look at what governments and politi-cal systems are doing – or should be doing – towards ethical goals in relation to both soci-ety and businesses.

NOTES

1 The OECD is composed of the following members: Australia, Austria, Belgium, Canada, Chile, Czech Republic, Denmark, Estonia, Finland, France, Germany, Greece, Hungary, Iceland, Ireland, Israel, Italy, Japan, South Korea, Luxemburg, Mexico, the Netherlands, New Zealand, Norway, Poland, Portugal, Slovak Republic, Slovenia, Spain, Sweden, Switzerland, Turkey, UK and US.

2 SMEs are defined as follows: micro: 0–9 employees; small: 10–49 employees; medium: 50–249 employees. Large enterprises are those with 250 or more employees.

REFERENCES

Alvaredo, F., Atkinson, A., Piketty, T. and Saez, E. (2013) 'The top 1 percent in international and historical perspective', *Journal of Economic Perspectives*, 27(1): 3–20.

Apple Inc. (2012a) *Annual Report 2012*, at http://investor.apple.com (26/09/14).

Apple Inc. (2012b) *Apple Supplier Responsibility, 2012 Progress Report*, at http://investor.apple.com (26/09/14).

Casson, M. (2003) 'The Moral Basis of Global Capitalism: Beyond the Eclectic Theory', in Buckley, P. (ed.) *The Changing Global context of International Business* (Basingstoke: Palgrave Macmillan), pp. 5–38.

Chakrabortty, A. (2011) 'Why doesn't Britain make things anymore?' *The Guardian*, 16 November, at www.theguardian.com (18/09/14).

Corak, M. (2013) 'Income inequality, equality of opportunity and intergenerational mobility', *Journal of Economic Perspectives*, 27(1): 79–102.

Dunning, J. (1993) *Multinational Enterprises and the Global Economy* (Wokingham: Addison-Wesley).

Fischer, C. (2008) 'Paradoxes of American individualism', *Sociological Forum*, 23(2): 63–72.

Fourcade, M. and Healy, K. (2007) 'Moral views of market society', *Annual Review of Sociology*, 33: 285–311.

Friedman, M. (1962) *Capitalism and freedom* (Chicago: Chicago University Press).

IMF (2011) 'Inequality over the last century', *Finance and Development*, 48(3), at www.imf.org (18/09/14).

Johnson, C. (1964) *Revolution and the Social System* (Stanford: Stanford University).

Kamenka, E. (1962) *The Ethical Foundations of Marxism* (London: Routledge & Kegan Paul).

Kay, J. (2003) *The Truth about Markets* (London: Penguin Books).

Leahy, J. (2012) 'After the carnival', *Financial Times*, 10 July.

Lichtheim, G. (1961) *Marxism* (London: Routledge and Kegan Paul).

Marx, K. (1963) *Early Writings*, tr. and ed. T.B. Bottomore (New York: McGraw-Hill).

Meyerson, A. (2006) 'Milton Friedman on philanthropy', *Philanthropy*, November, at www.philanthropyroundtable.org (18/09/14).

Ministry of Health of the Czech Republic (2012) *General Principles of Health Care in the Czech Republic*, at www.mzcr.cz (no longer available).

Mundy, S. (2012) 'Samsung in China labour law breaches', *Financial Times*, 27 November.

OECD (2009) *State-owned Enterprises in China: Reviewing the Evidence*, at www.oecd.org (18/09/14).

OECD (2011) *Society at a Glance: Health Indicators*, at www.oecd.org (18/09/14).

Palley, T. (2006) 'Milton Friedman: the great laissez-faire partisan', *Economic and Political Weekly*, 41(49): 5041–3.

Pew Charitable Trusts (2012) 'Pursuing the American Dream: Economic mobility across generations', *Pew Economic Mobility Project*, 9 July, at www.pewstates.org (18/09/14).

Pew Research Centre (2012) '"None" on the rise', 9 October, *Pew Research Religion & Public Life Project*, at www.pewforum.org (18/09/14).

Rabinovitch, S. (2012) 'March of the state presses private companies', *Financial Times*, 12 November.

Robinson, J. (1962) *Economic Philosophy* (Harmondsworth: Penguin Books).

Rodrik, D. (2007) *One Economics, Many Recipes* (Princeton: Princeton University Press).

Saez, E. (2013) *Striking it Richer: the Evolution of Top Incomes in the US*, University of California at Berkeley, at http://eml.berkeley.edu/~suez/suez-UStopincorner2012.pdf (18/09/14).

Sandel, M. (2012) *What Money Can't Buy* (London: Allen Lane).

Sen, A. (2010) *The Idea of Justice* (London: Penguin Books).

Tawney, R.H. (1922) *Religion and the Rise of Capitalism* (Harmondsworth: Penguin).

Tawney, R.H. (1964) *Equality* (London: George Allen & Unwin).

UNCTAD (2012) *World Investment Report* (Geneva: UN).

United Nations (2011) *Human Development Report 2011*, at www.undp.org (18/09/14).

US Census Bureau (2012) *Income, Poverty and Health Insurance in the US*, 2011, at www.census.gov (18/09/14).

World Bank (2010) *China Poverty Reduction*, 19 March, at www.worldbank.org (18/09/14).

World Bank (2011) *Health Statistics*, at http://data.worldbank.org (26/09/14).

REVIEW QUESTIONS

1 What is meant by 'location advantage', and how is it linked to globalization?

2 What are the reasons behind FDI flows to developing countries? What do developing countries gain from inward FDI?

3 What are the main ethical criticisms of outsourced manufacturing?

4 What are the ethical assumptions underlying capitalism? To what extent is the idea of a rational economic agent derived from utilitarian thinking?

5 What are the ethical foundations of the American model of free-market capitalism?

6 How can free-market capitalism be criticized on ethical grounds?

7 What is the 'American dream'? Why has the dream turned sour for many Americans?

8 What is Marx's critique of capitalism? What is the ethical basis of his critique?

9 Why has Marxism in practice failed in the states which have attempted to adopt a state-planned economy?

10 To what extent does the liberal market economy adopt free-market capitalist principles, and to what extent are these tenets modified?

11 State capitalism would seem to be a contradiction in terms. Why?

12 In what ways is the UN's human development index a more revealing indicator of well-being than measures of income such as GDP per capita?

TENSION BETWEEN STATE AND MARKET IN BRAZIL'S OIL INDUSTRY

CLOSING CASE STUDY

Photo 2.3 *This oil rig within sight of Brazil's Sugar Loaf mountain symbolizes Brazil's hopes for oil production, and with it, hopes for future economic growth.* (© iStock.com/Brasil2)

Rich in natural resources, Brazil has become a leading global economy. Development policies of the socialist government led by former president, Luis Ignacio Lula da Silva, propelled Brazil to centre stage. His social welfare policies were instrumental in lifting over 30 million people out of poverty and swell a growing middle class. Nonetheless, Brazil remains one of the world's most unequal countries; the richest 10% receive 44.5% of overall income. Of a population of 190 million, 26% remain below the poverty line. A concern is that the average income of the white population is more than double that of the black and indigenous populations. Inequality is starkly highlighted by the sight of new luxury apartment buildings alongside the favelas, the urban slums where the very poor are concentrated.

Economic growth stalled under Lula's successor, Dilma Rousseff, and her response has been one of wielding greater government power to stimulate the economy. Rising demand for oil, reflecting a surge in car ownership, has been one of the major issues for Brazil's government and for energy companies. The country's largest oil company, Petrobras (Petroleo brasileiro), dates from 1953. It was a state-owned monopoly until 1997, when it was converted into a registered company in a wave of market reforms. It has grown to become Latin America's largest company. It still dominates Brazil's oil sector. Apart from oil production and refining, its activities include distribution 'midstream' processes. It has become internationalized, with acquisitions in some 27 countries, and it plans further expansion. Petrobras attracted headlines in 2010 when it issued shares worth $72.8 billion on the Brazilian stock exchange, which was the largest single share issue to date. Since then, however, its growth has slowed and its stock price has fallen, partly over the size of its debt burden. It has recently been attempting to sell off foreign assets, but buyers have not been plentiful, and it is feared that the sales will not realize as much money as hoped.

The Brazilian state directly owns 54% of Petrobras's shares. The Brazilian Development Bank owns 5% and the Brazilian sovereign wealth fund owns 5%, bringing the state's combined ownership to 64%. Compared to other global oil companies, it is perceived as inefficient and it has seen declining production. Brazil's government has long had a policy of placing a ceiling on domestic petrol and diesel prices, in order to control inflation, with the effect that prices are about 20% lower than global prices. Formerly self-sufficient, Brazil must now import oil to meet increased demand. This shift to importing has had a detrimental effect on Petrobras, which is importing at a loss, as it is compelled to sell the oil at less than it pays foreign suppliers. In June 2012, the government allowed a slight rise in petrol and diesel prices, the first since 2006.

Much publicity has surrounded the discovery of huge oil reserves off the Brazilian coast in 2007, which would help to enhance Brazil's role in global energy. The government sold the reserves to Petrobras at a price which seemed low to market observers (Leahy, 2012). Petrobras has been slow in exploiting the area, reflecting the difficulties of the extreme depths involved, which require specialist expertise. It had been envisaged that foreign oil companies would help to exploit these fields. However, the government introduced greater regulation in a new energy law in 2010, which has had the effect of holding back developments. The new rules state that Petrobras must have 30% ownership of the area, and must operate all drilling and production. Foreign companies' interests can be financial investments only, which will discourage them from coming forward. Brazil's limited refining capacity has been a concern. Petrobras has eyed the country's one privately owned refinery, the Manguinhos Refinery, reportedly making an offer for it in 2012, which did not go forward.

The Manguinhos Refinery, like other oil companies, has suffered from the cap on domestic fuel prices. Its plant became rundown and it struggled with losses, but following a takeover in 2008, it has been returning to viability. It has had plans to develop storage and pre-treatment, a midstream activity in which Petrobras has a near-monopoly. Manguinhos was successful in signing up Chinese company Sinopec for this development. Other companies, including BP, also expressed interest.

In October 2012, however, the fate of Manguinhos was dramatically altered. Without notifying its CEO in advance, the governor of the state of Rio de Janeiro announced the expropriation of its land and demolition of the refinery. Apart from the stunned CEO, there were protests from its shareholders, its 1,000 employees and from opposition politicians, who called for an enquiry. The governor said that the land would be flattened in order to build public housing for the poor, along with schools and other amenities. The governor was pursuing plans involving military police to drive out drug gangs in neighbouring favelas. Clearance of these areas has accelerated in the build-up to the 2014 football World Cup and 2016 Olympics. He claimed that because the refinery owed back tax to the government, there would be no compensation paid. The CEO has disputed the alleged tax bill and filed a lawsuit against the government in Rio. Lawyers have said that the governor possibly lacked the power of nationalization in any case, as the land was under the jurisdiction of the federal government, not that of the state of Rio. The CEO says that, in any case, the land is too contaminated to build houses on it. He has offered a strip of uncontaminated land on the site for public housing. It amounts to about 20% of the site.

The CEO has wondered why his company was targeted. He felt his operation was so small in comparison to Petrobras, which has a market value of $229 billion, that it could not possibly have been a threat. But some observers feel that the deal with Sinopec caused alarm bells to ring among the oil giant's government owners, and the result was that a viable company valued before the expropriation at just under $2 billion saw its value virtually wiped out in an instant.

Sources: Leahy, J. (2012) 'Brazilian stocks feel shockwaves of intervention', *Financial Times,* 12 October; Pearson, S. (2012) 'Refinery dispute puts focus on Brazil oil', *Financial Times,* 16 November; Pearson, S. (2012) 'From the favela to the top table', *Financial Times,* 8 October; Eisenhammer, S. (2012) 'Gasoline imports up as consumption grows', *The Rio Times,* 3 April, at www.riotimesonline.com; de Sainte Croix, S. (2012) 'Brazil strives for economic equality', *The Rio Times,* 7 February, at www.riotimesonline.com (18/09/14).

◻ How would you describe Brazil's economic model? What is the role of the government?

◻ What are the benefits and drawbacks of Petrobras as a state-controlled company?

◻ What ethical issues are raised in this case study, and what ethical principles are involved?

CHAPTER 3

THE POLITICAL SPHERE: SOCIETAL AND BUSINESS GOALS

OUTLINE OF THE CHAPTER

Introduction

Political theory: ethical foundations

Governance, political power and the business dimension
- Governance
- Power and authority

Theories of state–citizen relations
- Natural rights
- Social contract theories

Ethical foundations of democracy in state–society relations

Democracies in reality
- Democracies in Europe: National and EU perspectives
- Business lobbying in representative democracy
- American democracy and business dimension

The authoritarian alternative

Countries in transition: Assessing state–society relations in practice

International politics and business ethics

Conclusions

ETHICAL THEMES IN THIS CHAPTER
- Interplay between the individual and society
- Governance and responsibility

THE AIMS OF THIS CHAPTER ARE TO
- Evaluate the ethical foundations of politics
- Gain an overview of theories of state–citizen relations
- Contrast democratic and authoritarian systems of government in terms of business ethics
- Appreciate international political influences in international business activities

Photo 3.1 *Doha's impressive skyline symbolizes Qatar's growing wealth, but along with its rising global prominence has come greater international scrutiny of its government and companies.* (© iStock.com/ GeorgiaCourt)

QATAR: A SMALL STATE WITH GLOBAL AMBITIONS

Two decades ago, Qatar was hardly known outside the Middle East. This Arab state, smaller in area than Northern Ireland in the UK or Connecticut in the US, seemed destined to remain in the shadow of its larger neighbour, oil-rich Saudi Arabia. That all changed in 1995, when a palace coup saw the departure of its ruler, the emir, deposed by his son, Emir Hamad bin Khalifa al-Thani. The new emir promoted exploitation the country's oil and gas, and aspired to a role on the international stage commensurate with its energy wealth. In the years which followed, Qatar has enjoyed high economic growth, as shown in Figure 1. GDP per capita reached over $143,000 in 2011, making it the world's richest country by per capita income. Qatar became the one of the world's largest producers of liquefied natural gas (LNG). The money which flowed into its sovereign wealth enabled it to become active in global finance. The country was home to a large US base which became the central command headquarters for US military operations in Iraq and Afghanistan. Qatari satellite television company, Al Jazeera, has become a global broadcaster. Improbably for a state governed by an absolute monarch, Qatar has sponsored popular uprisings in other Arab countries. And perhaps even more improbably, Qatar was awarded the rights to host the football world cup of 2022. Having led Qatar to global prominence, the Emir stepped down in 2013, making way for his son, Sheik Tamim bin Hamad, to take over as ruler. The new Emir has taken over the reins of a much-changed country.

Wealth has been the key to development in Qatar. The conversion of its natural gas into LNG has allowed the country to exploit the world's growing thirst for gas, especially in the large emerging markets. The wealth of the state and that of the royal family are intermingled. Business and politics are inseparable. Qatar's sovereign wealth fund has invested heavily in financial institutions, becoming a large shareholder in Barclays Bank of the UK, and also a major shareholder in Switzerland's second largest bank, Credit Suisse. Following the financial crisis of 2008, these holdings have lost some of their attraction, especially in light of an investigation by UK regulators of possible irregularities in the Barclays acquisition. Qatar has more recently

Figure 1 Growth in Qatar's GDP (annual percentage change)

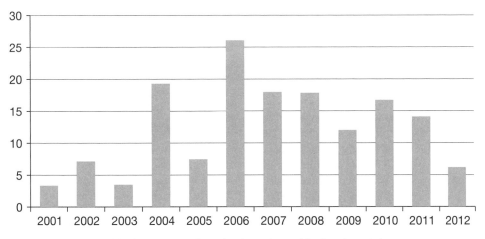

Source of data: World Bank, World Bank database: GDP annual growth, at http://.data.worldbank.org (26/09/14).

turned its attention to mining and commodities. It has been a key player in the takeover of Xstrata, a global mining company, by Glencore, the world's largest commodity trading company. As the country spreads its wings, its political and financial ambitions are attracting greater attention – and greater scrutiny.

Under the previous emir, modest political reforms were initiated. Municipal elections held since 1999 have allowed Qatari women to vote and to stand for office. A referendum approved a new constitution for Qatar. It provides for an Advisory Council, which would comprise 15 elected members and 10 appointed by the emir. Elections have not yet occurred. Only Qatari citizens would be eligible to vote. They are a minority in the country, numbering only 300,000 people. So far, these political reforms are only modest, leaving the absolute monarchy intact. Nonetheless, Qatar has backed popular uprisings in other Arab states in the region, including Libya and Syria. The thinking seems to have been that abusive dictatorships are unstable, unjust and threats to regional security. The invasion of Kuwait by Iraq in 1990 acted as a warning to other small states in the region. Syria's repressive regime has been supported by Iran, an important Shia Muslim state. Qatar, like Saudi Arabia, is a Sunni state. Regional religious tensions, as well as political unrest, have caused instability in the Middle East, and caused ripples of anxiety in countries across the region.

As a small, rich state, Qatar is perceived as stable. Qatari citizens, who make up only 15% of the population, have enjoyed growing prosperity. They have seemed content with the fact that they have only very limited political rights. Political dissent and political

parties are not allowed. The country's politics centres mainly on rivalries within the ruling family. The country is subject to Sharia law, which imposes restrictions in the social and cultural spheres. For example, drinking alcohol in public places is highly restricted. However, the influx of many western expatriates has brought more liberal cultural influences, which clash with local values. The country's rulers have been criticized for weak respect for human rights, especially in the case of the many migrant workers who work in the construction industry. The country's breakneck speed of development has led to strains in both its economy and society.

Qataris expect their country's increased wealth to be used for social goals, such as improved health and education. The country's health provision still lacks capacity in basic areas. The rulers have invested in prestige projects, while more mundane needs such as ordinary health clinics are spread thinly. In part, this is because the population has nearly tripled in the last ten years, and health provision has not caught up. Per capita spending on health was $1,489 in 2010, having fallen annually since 2008, despite rapid economic growth. Health spending is well short of the OECD average of nearly $3,000 per capita. For Qataris, healthcare, a key element of social spending, is one of the sensitive areas in which they wish to see marked progress. One Qatar journalist has expressed the view that 'Qataris want more hospitals than stadiums', referring to the huge programme to build football stadiums in the run-up to the world cup in 2022 (Peel and Khalaf, 2011).

The award of the 2022 football world cup to Qatar has brought into focus a number of issues which shine a critical light on the country. The country seemed an unlikely choice. Its mostly desert terrain suffers from searing heat of up to 50°C in June. Qatar has very high per capita carbon emissions, three times that of the US. Nine new stadiums are being built from scratch, along with associated infrastructure, including road and rail links. These challenges shine a spotlight on the ruling family, the government, and the society. There have been accusations of violations of the human rights of Nepalese construction workers on the large construction sites. With slowing economic growth, Qatar's global aspirations might now look optimistic. Energy markets are becoming less reliant on the Middle East, as other sources of gas and oil, including large reserves in

the US, are tapped. Moreover, the region's social and political turbulence remains a source of instability.

Sources: Kerr, S. (2012) 'End of boom saps Qatar confidence', *Financial Times*, 12 October; Peel, M. and Khalaf, R. (2011) 'Wealthy state with big presence', *Financial Times*, 17 December; Hall, C., Kerr, S. and Schafer, D. (2012) 'Qatar investors reel from bumpy ride on Barclays rollercoaster', *Financial Times*, 28 November; Hall, C. (2011) 'Medical care suffers from lack of capacity', *Financial Times*, 17 December; Stephens, M. (2013) *Qatar: Regional Backwater to Global Player*, BBC news, at http://www.bbc.co.uk/news/world-middle-east-20890765 (26/09/14); World Bank (2013) *Health Expenditure Per Capita*, at http://data.worldbank.org (26/09/14).

- In what ways do you consider Qatar a good example of how resource wealth should be used?

- What aspects of Qatar might be sources of social instability in the country?

- How is political reform contributing to better governance in Qatar?

INTRODUCTION

The political sphere concerns how societies are governed, including relations between political authorities, individuals and business organizations. Interactions between state and society raise key ethical issues, such as the freedom of individuals and their moral potential. Thus, political theory is a close relative of ethical theories. This chapter begins with the basic concepts of legitimacy, authority, notions of natural rights and the social contract as a model of governance. These ideas form an evaluative framework for assessing the differing governmental systems which exist in today's world.

This chapter seeks to uncover where the dynamics of the political sphere lie in differing types of society. We look critically at democracies and also at authoritarian systems, asking what societal goals are served in each, and also what negative aspects of each raise moral issues. Institutions are the backbone of government in the formal sense, but politics is much broader than the formal structures. In the broad processes of governance, there are many other players, including business organizations and networks. Their interactions shape the governance landscape. We look also at fragile states, where institutions and societal goals are in the formative stages. Nearly a fifth of the world's people and one-third of the world's poor live in these unstable social environments (OECD, 2012). Their hopes for a better life depend largely on improved governance. Their prospects have taken on a global dimension, as much of the world's energy and mineral wealth lies within these fragile countries. While ethical issues arise for businesses everywhere, they are perhaps most urgent in these countries.

Politics does not stop at national borders. In the last section, we look at the international dimension. Although economically powerful nations and companies are global players, politics, like global business, links countries in co-operative networks and international organizations. International politics, like international business, is seeing new players gaining influence, along with new outlooks on relations between the state, business activities and societal goals.

POLITICAL THEORY: ETHICAL FOUNDATIONS

A recurring theme in ethical theory is the importance of the social dimension in human life. The person living in isolation on a hypothetical desert island is not envisaged by philosophers as having the capacity for a moral life. Moral rules exist in a social context, guiding our behaviour towards other people. We have seen this perspective in the categorical imperative of Kant, based on treating people as ends rather than means. We have also seen it in the more prosaic principles of the utilitarians, who felt that the guiding principle should be the greatest happiness of the greatest number. Confucian principles, likewise, view social arrangements as critical to attaining moral virtue. As these philosophers appreciated, societies are based on relations among people. In writing about the value and capacities of the individual, they inevitably contributed to political theory. 'Ever since Plato first perceived that the inquiry into the nature of the good life of the individual was necessarily associated with a converging (and not parallel) inquiry into the nature of the good community, a close and continuing association has persisted between political philosophy and philosophy in general' (Wolin, 1960: 2).

Most people would probably agree with Aristotle's idea that people living in society desire a good life, not just a life which satisfies human needs in reasonable security from internal and external threats. Political theorists in all eras have been keen students of the laws, governments and customs of their day. They take a critical perspective and offer their reasoned theories about how political arrangements ought to be designed. They view existing institutions not as a social scientist, but from an ethical perspective, asking what 'ought to be' in relations among people in communities. The political theorist, like the ethical theorist, speaks of ideals not as ends which can be attained, but as benchmarks against which existing states can be measured.

Ethical theories in the deontological tradition take an absolute view of moral rules. In political theory, natural law is an example, defined as universal rules which are binding on all people as rational beings. Unlike the laws and customs of particular states, natural law considers that, whatever a person's position in society or citizenship status, people all have equal status as rational beings. Citizenship is the legal status which links an individual to a particular country, involving rights and duties. Natural law is above that of countries and is akin to the idea that each of us is a citizen of the world as well as of a particular state. Although going back to the Greeks and Romans, this notion of cosmopolitan citizenship has a strikingly modern feel. The era of globalization has highlighted issues like climate change which are global in nature, and call for co-operative solutions beyond states (Castells, 2008).

The civic dimension of natural law theory later gave way to other perspectives. From about the sixteenth century, individualism had an impact on political theory, as it had on ethical theories generally. Whereas the individual's value had been seen as deriving from civic status, the new interpretation of natural law saw human value rooted in the individual

The idea of a distinction between what is right and what the law says led to modern theories of natural rights and the social contract.

person. The person has two hats, in a sense, as a citizen of the state and as a human being, who, by virtue of an inherent rationality, can criticize the state and its laws. The idea of a distinction between what is right and what the law says led to modern theories of natural rights and the social contract, which are explained in this chapter. Ideas about the relations between people in a community are closely related to notions of moral well-being, which featured in Chapter 1. People routinely criticize their governments and laws, often, admittedly, because they simply feel the government is not serving their interests. But they also desire a better life, a life in which they can feel their dignity is recognized, and in which, simply, they can *be* somebody.

GOVERNANCE, POLITICAL POWER AND THE BUSINESS DIMENSION

Political power in any society is acquired and exercised in an environment inhabited by a number of different players, ranging from individual citizens to large organizations such as global companies. While we might think in simple terms of governments making laws or giving orders to be obeyed by all within the state's territory, in fact the relationship between ruler and ruled is much more complex. Formal and informal relations between governments, organizations and individuals create a dynamic political environment. As economic actors, producers and employers, businesses play important roles. The behaviour of governments and politicians directly affect the lives of those within the territory, in both physical well-being and moral aspirations. In this section, we look at political power and how to assess its legitimacy.

GOVERNANCE

People everywhere identify with multiple groupings. Families, business organizations, religious groups and associations such as trade unions, all have social norms and values, and all have systems, whether informal or formal, for allocating authority. They are examples of politics in that there are issues of what to do, who should lead, how leaders should be chosen, how much authority they should have, and how they should be held accountable to all in the group. In the company, these issues come generally under the heading of corporate governance (which is the subject of Chapter 8). Corporate governance involves frameworks determined by the company, bearing in mind that they must conform to the law of the place where it is registered.

Governance in the broad sense is about the processes by which communities and whole states are ruled. Government refers to the institutions by which rule is exercised, usually including lawmaking bodies and the executive to administer the law.

Although there is no world government, there are many inter-governmental organizations which play roles in governance at the global level, along with national governments and MNEs.

Sometimes 'government' means simply government in general, and in other contexts it means the individuals who make up the government of the day. The politics which characterize these institutions are of a 'public nature', relating to public life of all in a community, whether individuals, groups or organizations. These institutions can be elected bodies, civil service departments and government agencies. Politics also exists at international level, discussed later in this chapter. Although there is no world government, there are many inter-governmental organizations which play roles in governance at the global level, along with national governments and MNEs. Increasingly, MNEs are involved in all these levels of governance. We might say that their corporate goals are paramount, rather than societal goals. While this is true of many MNEs, others recognize the links between corporate and social values, including the role of politics. Many companies which are disinclined to recognize active social roles do recognize the importance of political interactions.

POWER AND AUTHORITY

We often hear the expression, 'politics is about power'. Even in authoritarian systems, where there is no open political debate, there is considerable political activity behind closed doors, as leaders and would-be leaders vie for ascendency (as shown in the opening case study). Power generally is about imposing one's will on others, often through physical superiority. *Political power* is about the exercise of power over others in the political context. Crucial to the exercise of power is whether it is acquired and exercised through some authority which is legitimate. The overlap between power, authority and legitimacy is shown in Figure 3.1. I discuss these relations in this section.

Politics typically involves conflict – between individuals, groups such as political parties and factions within parties. There is political competition for positions of authority within the state, whether they are elected posts or not. Political power can be gained in a variety of ways. In a democracy, political competition for elected office is open and public, whereas in the authoritarian system, the holders of political offices tend to be decided within closed circles of insiders.

What separates legitimate from illegitimate political power? A government which is perceived as having authority to govern is said to have *legitimacy*. If a government abuses its power, or if it has achieved power through force, it might claim to be legitimate, but will struggle to persuade public opinion. Legitimacy can be a matter of degree. A government may become authoritarian gradually, and its legitimacy gradually diminishes. Sometimes governments change suddenly, as in a coup d'état. This is the forceful takeover of executive

Figure 3.1 *The political sphere*

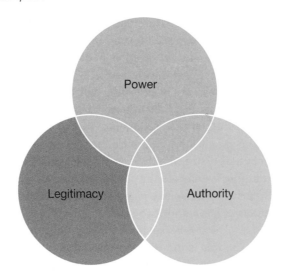

authority by an individual or small group of people who conspire to overthrow the leadership. The coup need not lead to much change of governmental style: one autocrat can replace another. Governments can also be overthrown by a military junta. The new military leaders might well state that their takeover is actually in the interests of society, as the previous government, whether elected or not, was corrupt. But the new government will have difficulty in establishing its own legitimacy.

Economic power can be linked to political power, either indirectly, by influence on governments, or more directly, when powerful business interests become involved in government activities. An MNE may have great influence in a country's economy, which brings it to the attention of policy-makers. For example, Samsung, a huge business empire in South Korea, accounts for 20% of the country's GDP (Yang, 2012). Samsung and other leading conglomerates have been favoured by government policies, due to their importance in the national economy and also their global market strength, which arguably enhances South Korea's global status. However, the conservative president, Park Geun-hye, elected in 2012, promised to rein in the power of the conglomerates and favour more 'economic democracy' (BBC, 2012).

In some countries, wealthy business people see their business empires as a platform to gaining political power. Examples are Silvio Berlusconi in Italy and Thaksin Shinawatra in Thailand, both of whom control business empires, and both of whom, also, have been prosecuted for corruption. Nonetheless, both are still active politically, although Thaksin exerts his political influence from a distance, as he lives in exile. The reverse process is also common: political leaders use their government positions to gain personal wealth and also enrich their families. When their businesses are preferred for government contracts, however, it is likely to be viewed as corrupt. Networks of personal relations between political and business leaders are often referred to as cronyism. Cronyism is usually associated with political systems which have weak regulation and lack of transparency. The political and business élite are the main beneficiaries from this type of system, while the needs of society are subordinated.

We expect government officials to focus on the public good rather than personal gain, but the link between political power and wealth is often strong, in both authoritarian systems and democratic ones. To what extent is this link corrupt or unethical? This is one of the issues underlying this chapter. Morally, political power should be exercised towards societal goals, but how to ensure that this occurs in practice is a conundrum for societies. It is one of the main issues addressed by political theorists through ideas about a social contract, discussed in the next section. In democratic politics, political parties seek support in the form of votes from the electorate, which gives them legal authority. Even so, that means only that they have been legitimately elected to office. How they use their office in practice raises further legal and ethical issues.

Authority is the rightful exercise of power. It can mean broadly a right to act in any of the groups or organizations we have mentioned above, such as authority of a company director or authority of a church leader. In the political sphere, authority carries legal weight in that the authority refers to the public domain. We would say that the government minister has authority to decide in a planning application, meaning that person is authorized by law. The minister has authority by virtue of the office, not in a personal capacity. However, if the minister takes a bribe, such as money or other personal benefit, for approving a planning application, this is in breach of the authority granted by law. Such breaches are not uncommon, however, and in some countries, can be seen as a 'perk' of office. They are a

Figure 3.2 *Authority to govern: how is it acquired, and lost?*

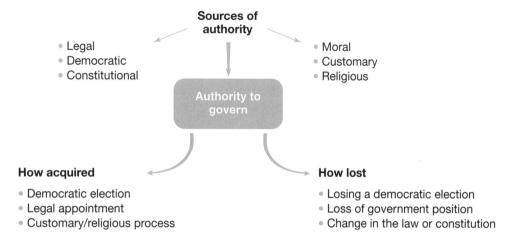

kind of corrupt practice, nonetheless, and the companies which pay them are also tainted. Nonetheless, companies might feel that the practice is simply an aspect of doing business in many countries.

Authority can derive from different sources, as shown in Figure 3.2. In a political system, an officer of the government has authority from a set of rules which specifically define rights and duties. These rules could be contained in a constitution, which contains the basic law of a country and is a source of legitimacy (Weatherford, 1992). Normally, the constitution is a written document. The UK is exceptional in that the constitution is unwritten, although many constitutional provisions are contained in legislation. Where a person has traditional authority, such as that derived from custom or religious belief, the rules are not enacted, but are recognized because people in that group or society believe in such authority (Raphael, 1970: 72). Authority can exist in the absence of power. A king may have authority to rule, but because of a rebellion, is unable to exercise it. On the other hand, constitutional monarchs are limited in the extent of their legal authority. Constitutional monarchs in today's world are mainly figureheads in countries which have representative democratic systems.

Autocratic rulers, such as military dictators or absolute monarchs, raise issues about their source of authority. They often claim to derive authority from the people, but they tend to preside over oppressive regimes, and, as they are not accountable to the people, their legitimacy can be questioned. The autocracy usually focuses on personalized leadership, backed up by authoritarian institutions. Authoritarian government, whether run by a single ruler or small group, is one that allows few civil and political liberties and is not responsible to the governed. At the opposite end of the governance spectrum is democracy, which recognizes civil liberties and accountability of governments to the people. In terms of legitimacy and authority, governments tend to fall on a continuum between the extreme authoritarian and the full democracy. Repressive measures are usually seen as a means to ensure security, and even democratic governments enact such laws to maintain national security. Governments of societies which are divided along ethnic or religious lines resort to repressive measures to promote security. But this can lead to greater disaffection. If these divisions are very deep, civil wars can result.

The World Bank estimates that one in four of the world's people live in areas affected by violent conflict and fragility.

Civil war and violent political change do not necessarily resolve all the issues which cause internal conflict. It is common for there to be continuing instability, especially if there are disaffected groups within the country who question the legitimacy of the new leadership. Conflicts can continue for years. The World Bank estimates that one in four of the world's people live in areas affected by violent conflict and fragility (World Bank, 2011). Every civil war which has occurred since 2003 has been a resumption of a previous civil war. The traditional picture of civil war is of violent conflict based on political and ideological differences between warring groups in society, typically a majority grouping and a minority separatist one. However, equally important in today's globalized world are terrorist activities, organized crime and trafficking of drugs, people and commodities which serve global markets. Groups such as radical Islamists in Africa use the proceeds of trafficking to fund their terrorist activities. These groups often link operations within a target country to networks of finance, arms, goods and people outside the country. There is thus potential for political destabilization of a number of countries.

Countries with weak state institutions are vulnerable to both internal divisions and the activities of militant groups who fund their activities through trafficking. Many of the countries of Africa are post-colonial states in which governments are perceived to lack legitimacy. It is not uncommon for revolutions to topple an autocrat, only to unleash a chaotic power vacuum in which different religious and ethnic groups seek power. This situation has been seen in the Arab uprisings of recent years. The autocrats had maintained stability, but at a cost of suppressing freedom. In what ways do political theorists shed light on how to solve the problem of ensuring stable government and a respect for individual rights? The social contract is one of their solutions. Although an old concept, 'the social contract between the state and society' is crucial in legitimate governance (OECD, 2012).

PAUSE TO CONSIDER...

Governments can derive legitimacy in different ways. And they can also lose legitimacy. Consider the situation where an elected government attempts to stamp out dissent, stifles the free press and becomes more authoritarian. How has it lost legitimacy?

THEORIES OF STATE–CITIZEN RELATIONS

In this section, we look at theoretical foundations of relations between the individual and rulers of states. Do people have inherent rights to have a say in how they are ruled? Should rulers be accountable to the people, and, if so, how? These are questions at the heart of politics.

NATURAL RIGHTS

If a person has authority to do something, it can be said that the person has a 'right' to do it. 'Right' is a broad concept, which can be used descriptively, but can also be used in normative theories. Legal rights or 'positive' rights are those which exist in law, such as the right to own property or to vote. Laws in this sense are promulgated by states in the form of legislation. According to this view, only rights recognized in law are valid. By contrast, natural rights are rights which all people are said to have by nature. Historically, the notion of natural rights is bound up with theories of natural law.

This notion of natural rights should be distinguished from the idea of human rights. The latter term has become widely used in recent years, and in more varied contexts than the political context in which natural rights theories emerged. Certainly, the notion of natural rights is an ancestor of human rights, but human rights refer to universal rights people hold by virtue of their inherent human dignity (discussed in Chapter 9). Human rights cover a wide spectrum, including civil, political, economic, social and cultural rights. They are now to be found enshrined in international law, as will be discussed in the next chapter. Early theorists of natural rights focused on their political implications (Macdonald, 1963: 47). They saw natural rights as a bulwark against arbitrary government, and almost all espoused some idea of a social contract between the people and government. They felt that if governments become tyrannical, natural rights entitle people to overthrow them. This idea can be a powerful tool, and has been used by pro-democracy activists over the years.

John Locke (1632–1704) was a leading proponent of natural rights. He highlighted the rights of life, liberty and property, which became central to theories of natural rights. Although remembered for his political and philosophical writings, Locke was active in political life and administration. He had lived through the turbulence of the Civil War in England, his family having sided with the parliamentarians against the royalists. Nonetheless, he favoured the restoration of the monarchy in 1660, as he had been alarmed by the brutality of the Commonwealth under Oliver Cromwell. Locke's leading work of political theory is the *Second Treatise on Civil Government*, first published in 1690. Locke begins with a description of the state of nature, in which people should adhere to the moral principles of natural law. He said, 'People being all equal and independent, no one ought to harm another in his life, health, liberty, or possessions' (Locke, 1956: 5). However, in practice, not everyone behaves morally, and in the state of nature, there is no ultimate superior to keep order and control immoral behaviour. Although Locke believes in the negative concept of liberty, he feels people will willingly give up some liberty to a government rightly constituted, in order to gain security which is lacking in the state of nature.

SOCIAL CONTRACT THEORIES

The social contract can refer to this coming together of inhabitants and also to the establishment of a government by consent, as shown in Figure 3.3. In this section, we look first at Locke's theory, and then at Rousseau's. Locke envisaged the coming together of people to form civil society as the main social contract. However, he goes on to discuss how to make governments responsible to society. The relationship between people and the government may be viewed as a second social contract, and one might criticize Locke for not focusing on this relationship as the main social contract (Marens, 2007). But Locke describes this relationship as a trust, in which the guiding principle is consent. The trust rests on people agreeing to the government having authority, which it must exercise on their behalf. Locke takes a strong stand against the absolute right of kings, which sanctions arbitrary rule and imperils people's lives and property without their consent. He feels that the legislature must be the supreme authority, and its authority should be grounded in consent of the people.

A difficulty with Locke's theory is that it tends to be presented as if it were a historical event, in which case the original parties to the contract bind later generations. But citizens

Figure 3.3 *Two social contracts, or one?*

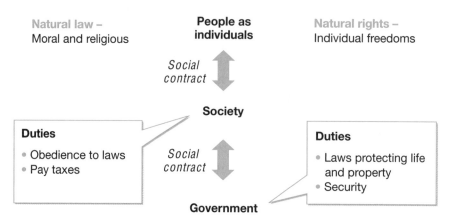

who come along later have not consented. Locke uses the device of 'tacit consent' to over-come this limitation, saying that anyone who lives in the state is impliedly agreeing to the original contract (Locke, 1956: 61). This is an unsatisfactory justification, as most people cannot simply leave the country where they reside. The artificial device of implied consent is a shortcoming, and perhaps highlights the hypothetical nature of the social contract. Lawyers might now call it an 'implied contract' (Barker, 1962: vii).

Notwithstanding its weaknesses, the theory has been influential in political discourse (Marens, 2007). Its influence in political life lies mainly in the prominence it gives to the principle of consent as a basis of political obligation. This implies that a society has a right to get rid of a ruler who betrays the trust between ruler and ruled. Although Locke was himself far from a revolutionary, his views lit up the eighteenth century's age of revolution, seized on by revolutionaries both sides of the Atlantic (Cranston, 1966: 77).

Also influential in later political developments was Jean-Jacques Rousseau (1712–1778), who was born in Geneva, but is more closely associated with France. More preoccupied with morality than Locke, Rousseau envisaged the attainment of a higher moral life in society. Locke defined liberty in negative terms and saw government inter-ference as a limitation on liberty. By contrast, Rousseau viewed the state as the embodi-ment of the true freedom of each person. What man acquires in the civil state, he says, is the 'moral liberty, which alone makes him truly master of himself' (Rousseau, 1913: 16). This is an eloquent statement of positive liberty, which sees liberty as moral self-direction (Putterman, 2006).

Like Locke and Hobbes, Rousseau's starting point is the state of nature, but his depiction differs from both predecessors. His state of nature is far from the state of war described by Hobbes or the state of nature described by Locke, which is governed by natural law, albeit with imperfections in practice. Rousseau sees the state of nature as pre-social. As people have few relations with each other, they do not come into conflict. This primitive existence based on subsistence becomes precarious as time goes on, and people come together to form a more enduring society. Rousseau appreciates that people would have to give up free-dom which they had in the state of nature, but seeks to find a way in which a person, 'while uniting himself with all, ... may still obey himself alone, and remain as free as before' (Rousseau, 1913: 12). His solution is the social contract. A summary of different views on the social contract appears in Table 3.1.

Table 3.1 *Comparative views of the social contract*

	Locke	Rousseau
The individual in the state of nature	Primacy of self-interest; moral principles should guide people, but conflicts arise	Self-interest, but a pre-moral, pre-social state; little conflict
Liberty	Negative: freedom from interference	Positive: freedom as self-realization
Social contract: how formed	Contract between people in the state of nature; followed by trust between people and government	Contract between people and government, creating the state
Morality and the social contract	Morality lies with the individual, not the state; state authority rests on consent	The state is a moral person embodied in the general will
Society and the social contract	Society of individuals pursuing self-interest, with minimal interference by the state	Society in which people attain a higher moral development through the general will

The social contract as envisaged by Rousseau allows a person to become part of a civil state, 'substituting justice for instinct in his conduct, and giving his actions the morality they had formerly lacked' (Rousseau, 1913: 15). In doing so, each person submits to be ruled by the general will, directed to the common good of society, rather than the particular goods of individuals, which is associated with the rule of tyrants. For Rousseau, the primary question of government is, 'Who is to govern us?' (Berlin, 1958: 45), whereas, for theorists like Locke in the liberal tradition, the main issue is, 'How far does government interfere with me?' (Berlin, 1958: 14). Berlin presents these as opposing concepts, favouring negative liberty himself. In truth, both these questions matter to people: the first concerns legitimacy of governments and the second, the pursuit of individual goals.

In his theory of the general will, Rousseau emphasizes sovereignty of the people, which is central to democracy. The state, Rousseau says, is a 'moral person whose life is in the union of its members' (Rousseau, 1913: 24). In contrast, Locke's theory of natural rights was more individualistic. Locke himself was a believer in representative government and majority rule, but did not advocate universal suffrage, believing that the right to vote should be confined to property owners. His views were followed by the English utilitarians. Rousseau's approach tends towards the collective. He saw Geneva, the city-state where he was born, as the ideal of democratic governance (Cranston, 1983). Geneva was relatively small (about 40,000 inhabitants), and homogeneous. Although Rousseau envisaged the general will as embodied in the state, the idea of a collective will can apply to a group of people with a sense of identity and shared aspirations. They could be a class or a people sharing a national identity. Movements for self-determination of peoples, such as those aimed at overthrowing colonial rule, have embraced Rousseau's idea of popular sovereignty. People seeking self-determination might be willing to tolerate a loss of some freedom in the negative sense in order to be part of a larger moral entity which allows them to realize themselves as human beings.

The implications of this theory have attracted criticism as justifying tyrannical rule in the name of freedom (Williams, 2005). Most notably, Berlin makes the link between positive liberty and abuses of dictatorship (Berlin, 1958: 22). However, abuses of *both* positive and negative concepts of liberty are not difficult to find. China enshrines free speech in its constitution, yet party censors have blocked 'freedom of speech' as a search term on the internet (Gapper, 2013). The US displays both extremes. The Obama presidency has used treason legislation (the 1917 Espionage Act) to clamp down on journalists in more cases than all previous presidents combined. At the other extreme, free speech has been legally defined to allow an individual, company or group to make unlimited, secret donations for political causes, arguably undermining the democratic values that the constitution was intended to uphold (discussed later in this chapter).

PAUSE TO CONSIDER...

In what ways is social contract theory relevant in today's world? Give some examples.

ETHICAL FOUNDATIONS OF DEMOCRACY IN STATE–SOCIETY RELATIONS

Most people think of democracy as a good thing, although they will often have very different interpretations of what it means. Whatever the interpretation, democracy is perceived as having an ethical underpinning which values people as moral beings, and asserts the right of people to self-government. Those broad values are derived from a diversity of moral theories. In the tradition of Rousseau, there is a view of democracy as set of social and ethical principles bound up in the state. In the more liberal tradition, democracy is seen as a set of structures and processes which make up a political system. The former view is more about ends, and the latter view is more about means, focusing as it does on political institutions. Both ends and means come into any discussion of democracy, as they are interrelated.

Democracy in a broad sense of 'participatory governance' has a long and diverse history (Sen, 2010: 323). We tend to think of democracy as originating with the Greek city-state, but in fact it was more widespread. 'Government by discussion' has taken place since ancient times in Persia, India and other parts of Asia. The village meeting is a kind of direct democracy, as people participate directly in governance. These early examples of participatory governance are the ancestors of the democratic institutions in today's world.

Direct democracy is possible only in a small unit like a Greek city-state. But balloting for an elected council or assembly was also an aspect of ancient democracies. In larger states, balloting formed the basis of representative democracy. Representative democracy allows people to vote for office holders to represent them in assemblies which have law-making authority. Government is therefore said to be based on consent, and participation takes the form of voting. This implies free choice, free participation in the electoral process, and responsibility of government to the governed. These are the elements which are central to liberal democracy. But no government, even an elected one, can please all the electorate, given the diversity of interests in society. For this reason, majority rule has long been considered central to democratic government.

In large democratic states, elections of political office holders take place periodically. Voters elect representatives to a legislative body. In a parliamentary system, the executive is the prime minister, who is from the main party. In a presidential system, the president is elected separately. We could say that each voter has a small amount of political power in the act of voting, but, after that, has no means of directly influencing policy until the next election. Elected politicians are acutely aware of the supporters who voted for them. But for democracy to thrive, they should serve all the people, not just the sectional interests that formed the bulk of their electoral support.

It might be assumed that the majority of an electorate represents the widest spectrum of different interests. But the majority could represent a dominant interest group which, once it obtains authority, feels it has a mandate to pursue its policies, regardless of the impact on

Legislators should maintain a focus on the common good, above sectional interests, but they are strongly influenced by the nature of their power base.

minorities. This is clearly unsatisfactory and can lead to divisiveness. In many countries, ethnic divisions and class interests are challenges for democratic institutions. Legislators should maintain a focus on the common good, above sectional interests, but they are strongly influenced by the nature of their power base. The authors of the US Constitution were alert to this problem, and instituted a system of checks and balances between the different branches of government. Thus, legislation must be passed by both houses of the legislature and signed by the executive. But getting legislation over these political hurdles can sometimes cause paralysis, or what is termed 'gridlock' in American politics (discussed in the next section).

Pluralism is central to democracy. Democracy flourishes in an environment where all interests have a voice which the government must listen to. This is arguably the strongest moral justification for democracy (Benn and Peters, 1964: 414). People in any society identify with a number of groupings. They include religious groups, political parties, trade unions, people at work and other associations based on interests. This panoply of associations is referred to as civil society. Free association in groups of our own choice is central to a functioning democracy. Closely associated with freedom of association is religious freedom, freedom of speech and freedom of the press. These freedoms encourage political debate, including criticism of the government. Of course, political discussion depends on people agreeing on fundamental principles such as tolerance of views that are different from our own. Democracies are sometimes said to be mature when parties of opposing views can discuss rationally, and accept that, when the one party wins an election, it will consider the interests of all in governing.

Democracy can be seen as a set of institutions that include free and fair elections, a legislature which functions in a law-making role, and checks and balances which safeguard the institutions' legitimacy. These institutions are shown in Figure 3.4. Also shown in the figure are the individual freedoms essential to democracy. The freedoms are commonly set out in

Figure 3.4 *Elements of democracy*

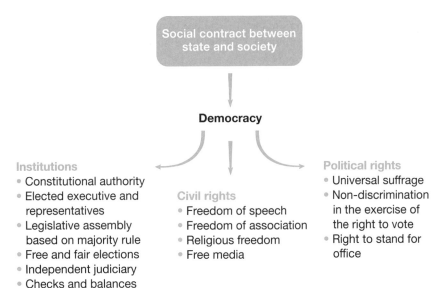

a bill of rights, such as the first ten amendments to the US Constitution. Is it possible to separate the basic freedoms from democracy? Democracy cannot thrive without these freedoms, but it is possible for these freedoms, notably civil rights, to exist to some degree in a non-democratic state (Gray, 2012). This is the realm of negative freedom, it will be recalled. These freedoms are those to pursue one's own personal goals without undue interference by governments. The autocratic leader might well allow some personal freedoms to flourish, to contribute to people's sense of personal well-being. Citizens of the autocrat's state have freedoms within strictly-defined bounds, but not democracy.

Popular sovereignty as interpreted through representative institutions gives citizens a voice, but this does not necessarily mean that they feel empowered. Citizens are aware that voting for political leaders provides only a brief opportunity to express consent. The institutions of liberal democracy would certainly not impress Rousseau. He felt that the moral authority of the state rests in the common good expressed in the general will, which rises above the particular wills of individuals. Falling within the tradition of the positive liberty, the state embodying the general will would be morally superior to the liberal democratic state. Oppressed peoples the world over have looked on this ideal of self-determination as being democratic and ethically justified. This idea is shared by Locke, who defended the right of people to overthrow tyrannical rule. But Locke's ideal state was not a moral entity as envisaged by Rousseau. For the liberal Locke, ethical capacity rests with the individual person. In his view, society is an aggregate of individuals, each with a moral value, while the state is seen as instrumental (Cranston, 1953: 71). To find the common good, he thought, one must look to the will of individual people.

What are the ethical principles of democracy? The capacity for individuals to have a voice in government is an ethical foundation of democracy, in keeping with the principle of treating people as ends rather than means. The one-party state which allows no dissent might claim to be democratic, but is not in reality, as people have no real voice. Democratic theory is also indebted to Rousseau for the idea that the common good of a people also has moral worth, rising above the clamour of voices seeking to be heard. In today's world, this is perhaps a useful reminder. Citizens now have numerous ways of making their voices heard as individuals. The internet and social media provide a forum for anyone to make their views known, even in societies where there is media censorship. And it seems clear that democratic movements are using these means to organize in countries with limited civil society. Governments are also using the media, both to listen to grassroots views and to communicate directly with citizens. In practice, democracies vary a great deal, in both their institutions and their ideas of a good society.

PAUSE TO CONSIDER...

Many different ethical principles are used as criteria in deciding how democratic a society is. Among them are free speech and the right of association in civil society. But these rights are curtailed in most societies to some degree. To what extent does this make them less democratic?

DEMOCRACIES IN REALITY

The principle of sovereignty of the people usually translates into representative institutions in which there are elected members of a legislative assembly and, in many cases, an elected president. The democracies of Europe and North America are among the most long-standing examples. These countries, in the main, are capitalist market economies, and have traditions of recognition of natural rights. Most of these democracies emerged from revolutionary turmoil, involving the overthrow of kings and colonial rule. Mature democracies, however, did not spring up overnight, but evolved over long periods. There was considerable upheaval along the way, including a civil war (in America), periods of royalist resurgence (in France), and the period of Nazi rule in Germany. The growth of democracy coincided with the growing importance of markets in national economies. In this section we look at democracies in practice, including the role of business.

DEMOCRACIES IN EUROPE: NATIONAL AND EU PERSPECTIVES

Democratic politics assumes a political system in which all citizens are equal in their political voice. Each citizen has a unique set of interests and moral values, and each is presumed to be free to join with others to put forward views and choose candidates for elections. In reality, political equality can be undermined in countries where there is a high level of economic and social inequality (Rawls, 1971: 16). When ranking the quality of democracy in different countries, one of the leading ranking organizations uses political indicators as well as indicators used for the UN's human development index, which include health and education. On these rankings, the Scandinavian countries take three of the top five rankings, while the UK is thirteenth and the US is fifteenth (Democracy Ranking, 2012).

The democracy of the social market economies, with their strong welfare programmes and emphasis on equality, is known as **social democracy**. In these economies, large public-sector companies are seen as serving the common good. They are big employers and big investors, and are thus crucial to the national economy. They are active in key industries such as utilities, telecommunications and infrastructure. They tend to have close links with governments, and their executives are likely to be of the same educational background as members of the government. In France, for example, it can seem that policy is determined by the nexus of big business and government. Government is dominated by one of the two main parties, the Socialist Party on the left and an alliance of conservative parties on the right. The 'establishment', or network, of political leaders and business leaders may seem remote from ordinary citizens. However, there are factors which provide counterweights to this establishment perspective. A sizeable proportion of voters support smaller parties, including extreme nationalists, revolutionary socialists and green parties. Another factor is the propensity of French people to engage in street demonstrations to make their views known. These demonstrations are seen as part of the political process, rather than simply ephemeral 'letting off steam', and they sometimes influence governments to change their policy.

Institutions of the European Union can also seem remote, despite the fact that the European Parliament is now directly elected by EU citizens. The European Parliament was heralded as a supra-European institution, focusing on the common good of all its citizens. However, it often seems mired in rather narrower national and sectional interests. One could say that this is to be expected in any democracy. As we noted in the last section, pluralism is characteristic of societies in which democracy flourishes. But a sense of the common good is also necessary, to unite all interests in wider goals. On this criterion, the European vision is proceeding more slowly than was envisaged. The EU has a tradition of weighting political power towards the Council and the Commission. This tilts the power in favour of the executive institutions. The Council is composed of ministers from the governments of member states, of which there are now 28. The Commission, which is composed of unelected officials, has both important legislative and executive authority. Most legislation originates with the Commission, and it manages the spending on programmes within the EU and abroad. The Commission has been criticized for weak accountability. In 1999, an independent committee of enquiry reported that financial mismanagement and fraud were widespread, implicating most of the commissioners. The Parliament had the authority to dismiss them, but in the event, all twenty commissioners resigned (Walker, 1999). This crisis was a low point in public confidence in the Commission and signalled a shift in power towards the Parliament.

The perceived intrusiveness of unelected 'eurocrats' is one of the causes of the allegation that the EU has suffered from a 'democratic deficit'. The European Parliament now has greater authority in checks and balances on the other bodies. Has this helped ordinary Europeans to feel they have an effective voice in the EU?

Research indicates that a majority of European citizens feel that the European Parliament 'best represents the European Union' (European Parliament, 2012). And more than two-thirds feel it has an important role to play in the functioning of the EU, but that percentage has gone down from 77% to 71%. Asked about their feelings of identity, 44% felt they have only a national identity, not an EU one. This figure went up 5% over the period 2011 to 2012. Those who feel both EU and national identity amount to 43%, a percentage which went down 3% over the period. It is perhaps heartening that, when asked what are the main values represented by the EU, the one which came top was values of democracy and freedom. However, as Figure 3.5 shows, a minority of EU citizens feel that their voice counts in the EU.

Citizens were also asked whether their voice counts in their own country. A selection of these results appears in Figure 3.6. It seems that citizens of the countries which are closer to social market economies are more likely to feel that their voices count. The percentages for the Scandinavian countries are particularly high. These countries have relatively low inequality and high levels of social spending by governments. At the opposite end of the figure lies Italy, where people seem to have little belief that the government listens to their views. This also implies a lack of confidence in the government to look after interests of ordinary people. Successive governments of rightist populist politician and multi-millionaire, Silvio Berlusconi, whose colourful lifestyle and lingering taint of corruption attract a great deal of media attention, have not helped to raise the moral esteem in which politicians are held in Italy.

Although the UK has relatively high social spending, its economy is more of a free-market model than the four countries in Figure 3.6 where citizens feel they have a greater voice. One might

Figure 3.5 *Perceptions of the European Union*

Respondents were asked whether they agree or disagree with the following statement: 'My voice counts in the EU'.

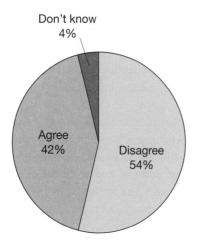

Don't know
4%

Agree
42%

Disagree
54%

Source: European Parliament (2012) *European Parliament Eurobarometer*, 20 August (Brussels: European Parliament).

Figure 3.6 *Perceptions of citizens of EU countries on their say in their own countries*

Respondents were asked whether they agree or disagree with the following statement: 'My voice counts in my country'. Percentages given are for those who agree with the statement.

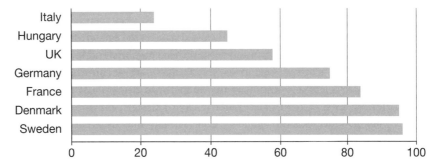

Source: European Parliament (2012) *European Parliament Eurobarometer,* 20 August (Brussels: European Parliament).

expect that the emphasis on economic freedom that characterizes the UK would foster greater pluralism in civil society, reflected in a sense that the majority represents a wide range of views. But the survey suggests that people do not necessarily feel the common good is being served. Both the UK and US, discussed below, are dominated by two main parties, representing the broad right and left of the political divide. The policies of the US Democratic Party and the British Labour Party are on the left, that is, associated with social priorities. The US Republicans and the British Conservative Party are on the right, favouring greater economic freedom, lower taxes and lower social spending. Note, however, that, although economic freedom is historically a liberal value, in US political discourse, confusingly, 'liberal' has taken on the opposite meaning, that is, a preference for more social welfare.

BUSINESS LOBBYING IN REPRESENTATIVE DEMOCRACY

The functioning of representative democracy depends to a great extent on law-makers and other decision-makers being well informed about the activities, needs and objectives of those to whom they are ultimately responsible. Groups, businesses and other interests provide detailed information to law-makers, which aids the legislative process. They also seek to make their particular cases for favourable treatment. This recalls the issue raised earlier in this chapter about the tension between corporate and societal goals. For law-makers and government officials, there is a constant balancing act between gathering relevant information needed for legislation, which is legitimate, and being swayed to support a particular group over others, which is contrary to the public interest. Lobbying refers to the ways businesses and other interest groups seek to influence politicians. A company might have its own in-house lobby specialist, or it might hire a specialist firm to lobby on its behalf. Access to law-makers is recognized in law in most countries, often enjoying constitutional protection as free speech. But countries have different approaches to lobbying, in terms of its alleged benefits and the need to regulate the activities of lobbyists (Holman and Luneburg, 2012).

For law-makers and government officials, there is a constant balancing act between gathering relevant information, which is legitimate, and being swayed to support a particular group over others, which is contrary to the public interest.

In the US, lobbying is a huge business, said to account for estimated $9 billion annually (Attkisson, 2012). Lobbying has been subject to growing regulation in recent years, mostly with the aim of making it more transparent. Transparency is seen as an essential element in preventing corruption. Lobbyists must register and make quarterly financial reports. But there are many people working as lobbyists who identify themselves in other ways, for example, as lawyers, and thereby avoid having to register (Luce, 2012). Regulation in the US is thus more relaxed in practice than the regulatory framework would suggest.

Many European countries have taken an accommodating approach to lobbying. Registration is voluntary in many, such as the UK, and usually results in few lobbyists registering. In some countries, particularly in Eastern Europe, the aim has been to encourage business interests through easy access to law-makers, indicating that in these post-communist systems, the role of business in economic development is seen as a positive force, rather than one which needs curtailing. This might seem to an outsider to open the way for corruption, and, indeed, corruption can be a problem. In the EU, the pattern of voluntary registration and weak transparency has been the norm, but the EU is now moving towards a stronger model of regulation. As more power has shifted to the European Parliament, lobbyists, not surprisingly, have focused their activities on Members of the European Parliament (MEPs), raising awareness of a need for a regulatory regime in which transparency is more to the fore.

While it might be assumed that lobbyists are against regulation, research by Holman and Luneburg has found that in both the US and EU, a majority of lobbyists surveyed welcomed a lobbyists' registry. This is largely because lobbyists see transparency as a way to persuade the public that their activities have a legitimate role in governance, and are not seen as behind-the-scenes activities which arouse suspicion of corruption.

Figure 3.7 *Perceptions of US citizens on their voice in government*

Respondents were asked whether they agree or disagree with the following statement: 'People like me don't have any say about what the government does'.

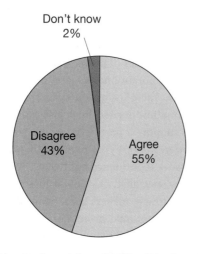

Source of data: Pew Research Centre (2012) *Pew Values Survey 2012*, at www.pewresearch.org (18/09/14).

AMERICAN DEMOCRACY AND THE BUSINESS DIMENSION

Americans seem to lean towards pessimism when asked whether their voices are being heard in government, as shown in Figure 3.7. Are they simply disenchanted with politicians or disenchanted with the whole system?

The increasing importance of money in US politics has coincided with rising inequality. While median incomes of Americans have fallen, politicians' wealth has increased. The median net wealth of the 94 newly elected members of Congress in 2012 was $1,066,515 (Center for Responsive Politics, 2013). This is almost exactly $1 million more than the wealth of the average American household. Nearly a half of all legislators in Congress are worth over $1 million; many are multi-millionaires. On measurements of wealth alone, they are hardly representative of ordinary people.

A reason why legislators are getting richer is that getting elected to office now requires large sums of money. About $6 billion was estimated to have been spent on the general election of 2012, setting a record (Tett, 2012). Both main parties now rely heavily on contributions of wealthy donors. The share of the top 0.01% in total income stands at about 5%, but their share in political contributions has risen to over 40% (Bonica et al., 2013). This rise in reliance on wealthy donors applies to both the Democratic and Republican parties. A Supreme Court decision in 2010, known as the 'Citizens United' judgment, held that unlimited spending for political purposes is an aspect of free speech, and thus protected by the Constitution. The court ruling meant that individuals, companies, trade unions and other groups can give without limit to political causes, so long as they are not co-ordinated with a political party. Two types of group have benefited. The super-Pacs (political action committees) take in huge sums of money from wealthy donors, whose donations must be disclosed. The other type of group is the not-for-profit organization, which is legally a charity set up for welfare purposes. These are tax-exempt and can raise unlimited money without disclosing the donors. Sheldon Adelson, the casino tycoon, and his wife, Miriam, contributed over $100 million to Republican spending in 2012. This flow of funds has helped Republicans to retain a majority in the House of Representatives, the lower house of the US Congress. However, a large majority of Americans, amounting to 80% of those questioned in a leading survey, are unhappy with allowing unlimited donations from rich individuals, along with the lack of transparency (Tett, 2012).

It has been argued that the new organizations are now eclipsing the political parties (McGregor, 2012). Over time, the two main political parties became broadly based, with wide geographical spread and many different interests under each party umbrella. Within each party, there would be debate and disagreement on goals. Now, the new groups are more highly focused on particular issues which their contributors feel strongly about, often with ideological zeal. Much donor spending is on strident negative advertising, targeting candidates who oppose their views. Political communication traditionally relied on cheap, low-technology devices such as posters and bumper stickers. Nowadays, the American voter is bombarded with negative advertising on television and personalized internet advertising, both of which, like lobbying, indicate the influence of business on politics.

Much donor spending in political campaigns is on strident negative advertising, targeting candidates who oppose their views.

For many businesses, buying influence in Washington and spending large sums on political campaigns have become accepted as ways to further business objectives. A company could well claim to take CSR seriously while engaging in lobbying. Almost every large American company engages in lobbying to some extent. Activities designed to inform legislators are helpful. But these practices, which are technically legal and beneficial in principle, raise ethical questions. Bribery is considered corrupt, but lobbying practices are, in reality, not far removed from paying for favours: lobbying often leads to changes in the law and funding decisions which favour the lobbyist's interest. Apart from the problem of skirting bribery allegations, lobbying, large donations and super-Pac activities could be seen as subverting democratic values. Individuals, not companies, cast votes, but, as we have seen, much of the information the voter receives is filtered through these less-than-transparent partisan groups funded by business interests.

The World Bank carries out an assessment of governance worldwide, based on an aggregate of international surveys featuring five key indicators. These are voice and accountability,

Figure 3.8 *Governance indicators in selected countries*

Countries are rated from 1 to 100, 100 being the top score.

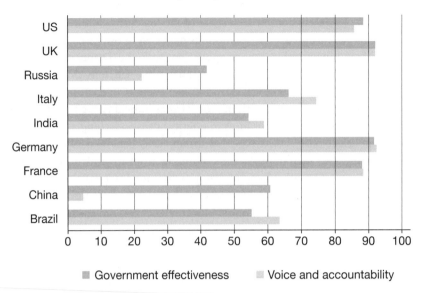

■ Government effectiveness   ▨ Voice and accountability

Source of data: World Bank (2012) *Worldwide Governance Indicators*, at www.worldbank.org (18/09/14).

political stability, rule of law, corruption and effectiveness of government. Since 1996, the US has fallen from the top tier of countries in all these categories. Figure 3.8 shows two of the criteria. The BRICs are all much lower on governance criteria generally, but it is notable that India and Brazil, both democracies, are relatively higher in terms of accountability than China and Russia. Of the BRICs, China has the highest ranking in government effectiveness, but a very low score in voice and accountability. How stable is this situation in the long term?

Lobbying by businesses and business donations for political purposes are important aspects of American political life. Assess their impacts on democracy.

THE AUTHORITARIAN ALTERNATIVE

Two of the BRICs, India and Brazil, are democracies. China is non-democratic. Russia has a democracy in form, but its 'managed democracy' has become authoritarian. Of these emerging economies, China has enjoyed the most successful economic growth over the last three decades. Observers could well conclude that this confers a legitimacy to its authoritarian model. The party's ideology remains officially Marxism-Leninism, but the introduction of market reforms by Deng Xiaoping in the 1980s marked the beginning of China's rapid ascent up the economic ladder. In the last decade, average incomes have tripled in China, bringing a better quality of life and better prospects for future generations. Basic medical insurance now extends to 432 million people, whereas in 2000, it covered only 38 million. But this is still well under half the population of 1.3 billion.

China's top-down political model has allowed its leaders to control how resources are directed and control state-owned industries. It also allows the government to invest on a lavish scale in infrastructure, which the democratic system in India, for example, cannot match. These improvements have undoubtedly contributed to China's economic development. Its policy of welcoming FDI in chosen sectors has lifted employment and exports (as discussed in Chapter 2). Challenges for this state capitalist model are sustaining growth in the long term and introducing more accountability and transparency.

Rising living standards help authoritarian leaders to maintain stability. Chinese people enjoy considerably more freedom than they did even a decade ago. The rise of social networking has played a key role in a new freedom of expression, despite the widespread censorship imposed by the government. China's microbloggers have shown considerable ingeniousness in sidestepping the controls. And social networks have also allowed people to voice complaints. Although China has a very low score for voice and accountability in the World Bank's governance indicators (see Figure 3.8), its citizens voice complaints about many issues, including corruption, inequality

The Chinese government spends more on its domestic security budget than it does on military spending against external threats.

and pollution. Does this mean that they want democracy? In fact, there are elections at local level in China. Although controlled by the party, they indicate some experience with democratic processes. A majority of Chinese respondents in a major survey carried out in 2012 said they liked American ideas of democracy (see Figure 3.9). This does not mean that Chinese people would support a democratic revolution to overthrow the current system. But there is a good deal of unrest at local level, and there has been factory unrest. The Chinese government spends more on its domestic security budget than it does on military spending against external threats (Anderlini, 2012). And censorship, for example, blocking search terms such as free speech, noted earlier, can seem ridiculous. Unrest does not necessarily translate into political agitation, but many would now consider that political reform is a necessary adjunct to continuing economic progress.

China and Russia are both large countries in which ethnic and religious divisions threaten the unity of the state, and also threaten the sense of legitimacy of the central government. In both countries, regions with separate identities have asserted separatist aspirations, and have been met with violent repression. People who live in provinces such as Tibet consider their claims for self-determination to be based on cultural identity and history. They consider rule by the Chinese outsiders to be illegitimate. A federal approach can be a solution in some cases, allowing regions some autonomy, but under a central government which has ultimate control. However, this is an aspect of democratization, delegating powers to the regions, and is usually incorporated in a constitution. The closing case study on Myanmar highlights the difficulties in combining democratization and aspirations for federalism.

Autocratic rule is arguably more stable in small, homogeneous countries. The 'benign despot' who is seen as a paternal figure can be perceived as having legitimacy. Qatar, featured in the opening case study, is an example. States like Qatar benefit

Figure 3.9 Do Chinese people like American ideas about democracy?

Percentages of respondents

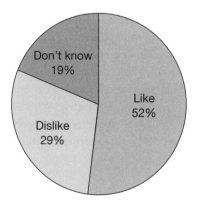

Source of data: Pew Research Centre (2012) *Global Attitudes Survey 2012*, at www.pewresearch.org (18/09/14).

from resource riches. Their companies and sovereign wealth funds are influential players in international business. In these countries, there is little distinction between a state-owned company and one owned by the ruler or the ruler's family, as the ruling families control state finances. Is there a kind of social contract between ruler and people in these countries? Citizens of these states often benefit from high levels of services, including health, education and infrastructure. Their generally high standard of living is a kind of compensation for the fact that they have few civil and political rights. On the other hand, there are large numbers of non-citizens working in industries such as construction. These workers, usually from Asian countries, often outnumber citizens. They do not enjoy the same benefits as citizens, and there have been concerns about possible breaches of human rights, as the opening case study showed.

The turbulence in Arab countries which has seen the overthrow of governments in Egypt, Tunisia and Libya, has led to political instability. In these countries, there were a number of different political and religious groups seeking to overthrow existing autocratic regimes. When the regimes fell, the result was a rather chaotic political scene. Leaders of the 'Arab spring' uprisings had differing goals. Many wanted democracy, but some favoured fundamentalist Islamic rule. Creating a new government recognized as legitimate by all groups is a challenge. Autocratic regimes which had ruled these countries had been relatively stable. They had overseen economic development, and many of these countries had reached middle-income levels, that is, per capita income of over $4,085 (see Note 1). Widespread uprisings seemed unlikely, but unemployment, especially among the young, helped to trigger the uprisings.

The participants in the uprisings used the internet and social media (OECD, 2012), which have grown rapidly in the Middle East. The World Bank suggests that 'respect and status' are important factors in the minds of the people who joined rebel movements in the Arab spring (World Bank, 2011). This seems to confirm that the idea of wanting to *be* somebody transcends cultural differences. Rising levels of education are influential, as education imparts an ability to think independently. These countries' hopes for economic development are now overshadowed by political uncertainty. Businesses are wary of the political uncertainties and weak legal framework, but they see early entry into these economies as a source of competitive advantage. New political leaders welcome investors, as economic development is needed in order to create jobs and wealth. Large oil companies have long been active in the region, and have become accustomed to operating in unstable environments. In some of these states, such as Egypt, democratic elections have been held, but this is only the beginning of a transition to democratic institutions. In other Middle Eastern countries, such as Jordan and Kuwait, there are monarchies which have introduced elected legislatures in moves towards democratic reform. But supporters of more radical reform are impatient with these tentative steps. In countries where discontent is simmering beneath the surface, the examples of the Arab spring uprisings have contributed to feelings of empowerment on the part of the discontented – and fear on the part of existing governments.

Desire for respect and status are important factors in the minds of the people who joined rebel movements in the Arab spring.

PAUSE TO CONSIDER...

What are the factors contributing to instability in authoritarian countries? How do these factors impact on businesses?

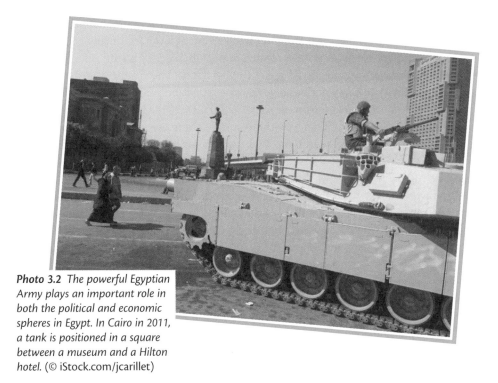

Photo 3.2 *The powerful Egyptian Army plays an important role in both the political and economic spheres in Egypt. In Cairo in 2011, a tank is positioned in a square between a museum and a Hilton hotel.* (© iStock.com/jcarillet)

COUNTRIES IN TRANSITION: ASSESSING STATE–SOCIETY RELATIONS

Transition within a state or society can take many different forms. Societies are always changing, often in ways which are hardly perceptible over a short period. Transition refers to deliberate changes instigated by governments to shift the whole country from one type of system to another. Transition can refer to economic transition, notably the transition from communist planned economies to market economies. The new states created by the breakup of the Soviet Union are the largest category of transition economies. Here, we are looking mainly at political transition. This often takes the form of democratization, building democratic institutions in countries with an authoritarian past, for example, as a result of colonialism. Political transition can be a part of a wider process of rebuilding in states where there have been conflicts and social and economic upheaval. These states, known as fragile states, are looking at transforming themselves in multiple dimensions.

It is often felt that market reforms and democratization go together. The post-communist states of Central and Eastern Europe, including Poland, the Czech Republic, Slovakia and Hungary, instituted democratic reforms along with economic transition. However, it is easier and quicker to set up formal institutions than it is to develop the attitudes and values which underlie the formal system. Now EU member states, these countries have been more turbulent politically than the mature two-party systems. In some, such as Hungary, divisive political parties such as extreme nationalists have posed a risk to fragile democratic institutions. Russia has formal democracy which masks an increasingly authoritarian government, in which state control of the economy is also a component. Russia and other former Soviet republics have witnessed strains among different ethnic and religious groups, as well as movements for greater democracy. State–society relations are strained in this situation, as many groups feel that the central government lacks legitimacy.

There are many states in which poor state–society relations have led to instability. These countries are considered to be fragile states. The fragile state is one which has a 'weak capacity to carry out basic governance functions and lacks the ability to develop mutually constructive relations with society' (OECD, 2012: 15). Governments of these states elicit little sense of legitimacy within society. There are estimated to be 47 fragile states in the world, mostly in Africa, South Asia and the Middle East. The economies of a sixth of them depend on energy or minerals. Oil, gas and mineral wealth can transform a country's economy, but in a fragile state, a risk is that the wealth is captured by the leaders and their cronies, and society sees little of the benefit. These states often have high levels of economic growth, but such growth has been termed 'discordant development' (Joseph, 2013). Where there is discordant development, rapid economic growth is combined with deepening inequality and group distress, which can lead to uncertainty and violent conflict. Nigeria is an example, where there are multiple ethnic, linguistic and religious groups making up society. Despite the resource riches, the country remains poor. Although many fragile states are middle-income economies, a widening poverty gap is a common feature, contributing to instability (OECD, 2012).

Where there is discordant development, rapid economic growth is combined with deepening inequality and group distress.

Fragile states have received considerable international development aid (IDA) from rich countries. Donor countries have consistently stressed the need for democratic institutions in these states, but in these historically diverse societies, democratic politics and electoral competition can sometimes lead to violent conflict. Elections in Kenya in 2007 and Nigeria in 2011 were followed by serious communal violence and loss of life. Would autocracy be better? Some experts raise this possibility, but reject it on the grounds that it does not work in an ethnically diverse society (Collier, 2008: 49). The autocrat usually depends on the support of a particular ethnic group, undermining legitimacy in the eyes of other groups. One might also say that this is a problem with democracy, as majority rule can jeopardize the interests of minorities. In a democracy, if one group controls the government, checks and balances can function to control the misuse of power. In this way, the democratic government can maintain a sense of legitimacy in society.

The world's fragile states are no longer viewed as simply cases of failed state institutions which require institutional solutions. It is now recognized that the problems go deeply into the issues of authority and legitimacy. Rebuilding states requires addressing the quality of state–society relations (OECD, 2012). Under the guidance of the OECD, a New Deal for fragile states was launched in 2011, which sets out peacebuilding and statebuilding goals. This appears in Figure 3.10. As the figure shows, political solutions are only part of the picture. Most of the goals focus on society, including security, justice, employment and services. There is a need for legitimate political solutions which will help to maintain peace and resolve conflicts. The underlying issues which these goals address are the causes of fragility, which lie in simmering conflicts between groups over power and resources. Solutions must involve all groups recognizing the benefits of statebuilding.

An added factor in resource-rich fragile states is the role played by foreign investors. MNEs are active in almost all these countries. Mining companies are active in resource-rich African countries, such as the Democratic Republic of Congo (DRC). Here, central political authority is threatened by incursions from groups coming across its borders from

Figure 3.10 *New Deal for fragile states*

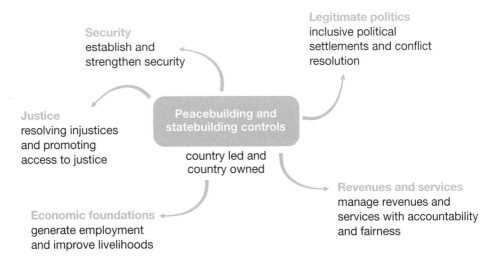

Source: OECD Development Assistance Committee (2011) *New Deal for Peace*, at www.newdeal4peace.org (18/09/14).

neighbouring countries, and the UN has established peacekeeping operations. Regional conflict has a long history in central Africa. The quest for energy and minerals, like those needed for high-technology products, leads these companies into politically unstable countries. They are sometimes criticized on ethical grounds in these circumstances, as their activities can contribute to the tensions in society, especially if inhabitants feel they are not benefiting from the wealth being produced. Adding to the instability, political leaders often seek personal enrichment from resource wealth, rather than ensuring the benefits are channelled towards social goals. For investors, a CSR approach will raise awareness of the social dimension, but broader solutions to social tensions require the development of legitimate governance (see case study on South Africa in Chapter 9).

What should be the ethical principles guiding governance in fragile states? Why are they proving difficult to realize in practice, and what can be done by foreign direct investors and host governments?

INTERNATIONAL POLITICS AND BUSINESS ETHICS

In theory, the world's states have equal legal status, as each has sovereign authority over its territory. But in terms of power, they are highly unequal. The small, weak state has little autonomy in practice. The bigger state, although enjoying greater relative power, faces numerous economic and political constraints in relations with other states, as leaders recognize that give-and-take helps to further national interests. Although there is no world government, this does not mean that there is a vacuum in global governance. There is considerable international law (discussed in the next chapter), supported by international institutions to which states have committed themselves. There are also ethical principles lying behind the law. Leaders of states do not normally speak as if they feel unbound by any rules. They refer to both legal and moral rights and wrongs in their dealings with other states. A chief influence has been the United Nations (UN), to which most of the world's

Figure 3.11 *The countries with the highest military expenditure (billions of dollars)*

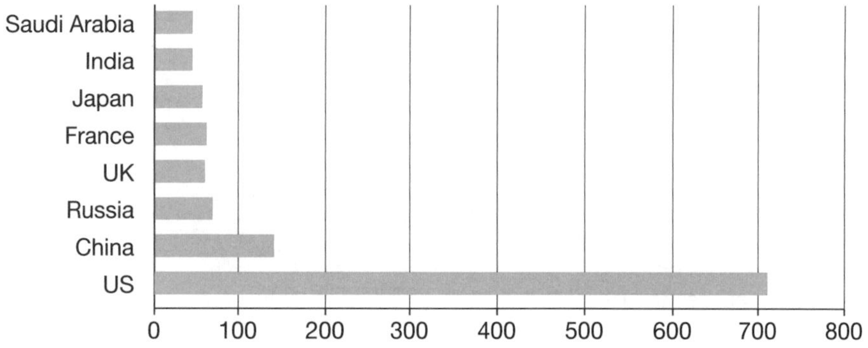

Source of data: Stockholm International Peace Research Institute (2011) at www.sipri.org (18/09/14).

countries belong. In the aftermath of the Second World War, the UN set itself optimistic goals of bringing states together to ensure global peace and security. The UN recognizes state sovereignty as its foundation, and strives to instil in member states respect for each other and for international law. Unilateralism in state behaviour, for example, when one country invades another, is a fact of life, but the UN has endeavoured to bring such interventions within the ambit of its own institutions, for example, in authorizing humanitarian intervention. It has not always been successful. One of the more disappointing aspects of international relations has been the fact that the US supported the UN at its inception in 1948, but has tended since then to reduce its sense of obligation to UN mechanisms and international law (Johnson, 2004: 73).

The military sphere is both a major influence in international politics and a huge global business. Sales of weapons and military services have risen 60% since 2002, bringing in sales of over \$411 billion to the 100 largest producers of arms and military services (SIPRI, 2012). Globally, 8 out of the top 10 arms companies are based in the US. As Figure 3.11 shows, the US is by far the largest military power. It has some 725 military bases in over 130 countries (Ferguson, 2004: 16). China's military prowess is expanding rapidly, leading to tension with neighbouring countries. Japan's national security is based partly on its own defence establishment, but mainly on its treaty alliance with the US, which is committed to defend it in case of attack. The US has maintained a substantial presence in Japan, with 90 facilities and 50,000 military personnel. This presence has aroused criticism among many Japanese people (Fackler, 2012).

Since the Second World War, the US has been the dominant political, economic and military player in the world. A word commonly used to describe US superpower status is hegemony, which implies a dominant power in international relations (Ferguson, 2004: 8). As is often pointed out, however, American goals have tended to be those of a 'liberal empire', wishing to spread its own vision of liberty and democracy, which its leaders believe will bring security and stability in various parts of the world, ultimately serving US national interests. In practice, American military interventions have contributed little to nation building in countries such as Iraq and Afghanistan (Bueno de Mesquita and Downs, 2006). These countries face mammoth tasks of rebuilding in an environment of economic and political instability as well as ethnic conflict. Both Iraq and Afghanistan are fragile states.

American companies are generally in the private sector, owned by individuals and institutions other than the government, unlike the large state-owned enterprises of China, for example. American companies are not instruments of US foreign policy. They would be expected to take their own strategy decisions independently of government and based on their own corporate goals. Indeed, leading American industrialists, the Koch brothers, have traded with Iran, using intermediary companies to get round a US trade embargo imposed in response to Iran's nuclear programme (Adams, 2011).

Today's world is witnessing a shift in international political influence towards the large emerging countries, based on their increased economic power. This is sometimes referred to as a shift to a 'multipolar' world (US National Intelligence Council, 2012). Nonetheless, American businesses remain powerhouses in many sectors. Think of Google, Microsoft, Coca-Cola and Walmart. However, for all these companies, global markets are increasingly important. The rise of the emerging markets, including the BRICs, is providing some indication of the new political powers on the block. In all the BRIC countries, the state plays an active role in business, and this role is perceived as morally justified, for the benefit of the country as a whole. The executive chairman of Google, Eric Schmidt, has criticized China for sponsoring cybercrime on a large scale, threatening international business relations (White, 2013). He observes that the Chinese state is much more interventionist than the US government would be, and seemingly uninhibited by moral qualms. He says that China's companies are seen directly as contributing to national goals. In the case of Huawei, the Chinese telecoms company, he says, 'When Huawei gains market share, the influence and reach of China grow as well' (White, 2013). On the other hand, it has emerged that the US National Security Agency has carried out surveillance of Huawei by means of 'backdoors' into their networks (Pengelly, 2014).

'When Huawei gains market share, the influence and reach of China grow as well.'

Other emerging and developing countries have also seen the state as important in economic development. For business ethics, therefore, the norms are evolving. Free-market values often clash with social values, including the importance of personal relations and a sense of community. The relational dimension is more likely to be articulated by the newer companies from emerging economies, which are defining today's competitive landscape. Also important are values of national interest and national competitive advantage, which have strong political dimensions. These values diverge from the traditional notions of corporate self-interest and shareholder value associated with western companies. This does not mean that emerging MNEs are more attuned to CSR than western counterparts. They can be as ruthlessly capitalist in their behaviour as any western MNE. What it does mean, however, is that governance within emerging MNEs is based more on relational ties intertwined with the country's overall governance, which include national and political goals.

CONCLUSIONS

This chapter has highlighted the importance of legitimacy in governance and politics. As we have seen, it is not an all-or-nothing concept. A formal democratic government may be strongly criticized by parts of the citizenry, and an autocratic one based on traditional authority might enjoy public support. It matters whether citizens feel their voices are being heard and interests being taken into account. This state–society interaction is the basis of the ethical dimension in politics. The social contract as a concept captures the reciprocal obligations which lie at the heart of this relationship. Although an old concept, it resonates in today's political environment, especially in the context of pro-democracy movements around the world.

Democratic stirrings, featuring calls for elected governments, constitutions and individual freedoms, would seem to suggest that quintessential American values are taking root around the world. But democracy in these new contexts stem from peoples' desires for self-determination, free from the influences of existing world powers. The desire of the individual person to *be* somebody captures this idea. The political influence of the US in today's world is actually waning. The balance of political power internationally is gradually shifting away from the post-war system dominated by the US to one in which the new emerging economies are stamping their own identities on political relations, both in their domestic systems and in international relations. They are redefining the global political landscape, most notably in asserting the importance of the state in global business. Whether they will also be rewriting the social contract with their peoples to reflect changing societal goals is a question whose answer will gradually emerge over time.

NOTE

1 The World Bank classifies countries according to income levels, based on gross national income (GNI) per capita. Low income is $1,035 or less; low-to-middle income is $1,036–$4,085; middle income is $4,086–$12,615; and high income is $12,616 or more (World Bank (2012) 'How we classify countries', at www.worldbank.org: 18/09/14)).

REFERENCES

Adams, G. (2011) 'Billionaire Koch brothers in the dock over trades with Iran', *The Independent*, 4 October, at www.independent.co.uk (18/09/14).

Anderlini, J. (2012) 'New leaders face tough challenges', *Financial Times*, 12 December.

Attkisson, S. (2012) 'Behind the closed doors of Washington lobbyists', *CBS news*, 7 October, at www.cbsnews.com (18/09/14).

Barker, E. (1962) *Social Contract* (New York: Oxford University Press).

BBC (2012) *South Korea's Presidential Candidates*, BBC news, 18 December, at http://www.bbc.co.uk/news/world-asia-20491418 (26/09/14).

Benn, S. and Peters, R. (1964) *The Principles of Political Thought* (New York: Collier).

Berlin, I. (1958) *Two Concepts of Liberty* (Oxford: Oxford University Press).

Bonica, A., McCarty, N., Poole, K. and Rosenthal, H. (2013) 'Why hasn't democracy slowed rising inequality?', *Journal of Economic Perspectives*, 27(1): 103–24.

Bueno de Mesquita, B. and Downs, G. (2006) 'Intervention and democracy', *International Organization*, 60(3): 627–49.

Castells, M. (2008) 'The new public sphere: Global civil society, communication networks and global governance', *Annals of the American Academy of Political and Social Science*, March, 616: 78–93.

Center for Responsive Politics (2013) *Millionaire Freshman make Congress even Wealthier*, 16 January, at http://www.opensecrets.org/news/2013/Q1/new-congress-new-and-more-wealth (26/09/14).

Collier, P. (2008) *The Bottom Billion* (Oxford: Oxford University Press).

Cranston, M. (1953) *Freedom: A new analysis* (London: Longman).

Cranston, M. (1966) 'John Locke and government by consent', in Thomson, D. (ed.) *Political Ideas* (Harmondsworth: Penguin), pp. 67–80.

Cranston, M. (1983) 'Rousseau and the ideology of liberation', *The Wilson Quarterly*, 7(1): 146–57.

Democracy Ranking (2012) *The Democracy Ranking of the Quality of Democracy*, at http://www.democracyranking.org (26/09/14).

European Parliament (2012) European Parliament Eurobarometer, 20 August (Brussels: European Parliament).

Fackler, M. (2012) 'Curfew is imposed on U.S. military in Japan amid rape inquiries', *New York Times*, 19 October, at www.nytimes.com (18/09/14).

Ferguson, N. (2004) *Colossus: The rise and fall of the American empire* (London: Penguin).

Gapper, J. (2013) 'Censorship is making China look ridiculous', *Financial Times*, 10 January.

Gray, J. (2012) *A Point of View: The Trouble with Freedom*, at http://www.bbc.co.uk/news/magazine-19372177 (26/09/14).

Holman, C. and Luneburg, W. (2012) 'Lobbying and transparency: a comparative analysis of regulatory reform', *Interest Groups and Advocacy*, 1(1): 75–104.

Johnson, C. (2004) *The Sorrows of Empire* (London: Verso).

Joseph, R. (2013) 'Discordant development and insecurity in Africa', *Foresight Africa*, Brookings Institute, January, pp 14–16.

Locke, J. (1956) *The Second Treatise of Government*, ed. J.W. Gough (Oxford: Blackwell).

Luce, E. (2012) *Time to start thinking* (London: Little, Brown).

Macdonald, M. (1963) 'Natural Rights', in Laslett, P. (ed.) *Philosophy, Politics and Society* (Oxford: Blackwell), pp. 35–55.

Marens, R. (2007) 'Returning to Rawls: social contracting, social justice and transcending the limitations of Locke', *Journal of Business Ethics*, 75(1): 63–76.

McGregor, R. (2012) 'Fully funded', *Financial Times*, 2 July.

OECD (2012) *Fragile States 2013: Resource Flows and Trends in a Shifting World*, at http://www.oecd.org (18/09/14).

Pengelly, M. (2014) 'NSA targeted Chinese telecoms giant Huawei – report', *The Guardian*, 23 March, at www.theguardian.com (18/09/14).

Putterman, T. (2006) 'Berlin's two concepts of liberty: a reassessment and revision', *Polity*, 38(3): 416–46.

Raphael, D.D. (1970) *Problems of Political Philosophy* (London: Macmillan).

Rawls, J. (1971) *A Theory of Justice* (Oxford: Oxford University Press).

Rousseau, J.-J. (1913) *The Social Contract*, tr. G.D.H. Cole (London: J.M. Dent).

Sen, A. (2010) *The Idea of Justice* (London: Penguin).

SIPRI (Stockholm International Peace Research Institute) (2012) *The SIPRI Top 100 Arms-producing and Military Services Companies, Excluding China, 2011*, at http://www.sipri.org (18/09/14).

Tett, G. (2012) 'Absence of transparency sparks unease with $6bn poll', *Financial Times*, 6 November.

US National Intelligence Council (2012) *Global Trends 2030: Alternative Worlds, NIC 2012-001*, at http://www.dni.gov (18/09/14).

Walker, M. (1999) 'EU chiefs resign en masse', *The Guardian*, 16 March, at www.theguardian.com (18/09/14).

Weatherford, M.S. (1992) 'Measuring political legitimacy', *American Political Science Review*, 86(1): 149–66.

White, G. (2013) 'China, the world's most sophisticated hacker, says Eric Schmidt', *The Telegraph*, 2 February, at www.telegraph.co.uk (18/09/14).

Williams, D.L. (2005) 'Modern theorist of tyranny? Lessons from Rousseau's system of checks and balances', *Polity*, 37(4): 443–65.

Wolin, S. (1960) *Politics and vision* (Boston: Little, Brown).

World Bank (2011) *World Development Report 2011*, at www.worldbank.org (18/09/14).

Yang, J. (2012) 'Samsung's family feud', *Bloomberg Businessweek*, 7 June, at www.businessweek.com (18/09/14).

REVIEW QUESTIONS

1 In what ways does the idea of natural law support a belief in individualism?

2 What are the criteria you would use to determine whether a government is legitimate or not? Give some examples of current governments.

3 What is the ethical basis of the social contract as a political theory?

4 Locke and Rousseau espoused differing views on the social contract. How have their differences led to lingering divisions in moral thinking?

5 On what principles is liberal democracy based? Is it suitable for any country, or just ones with individualist traditions?

6 How is social democracy different from liberal democracy? In what type of system are citizens most likely to feel that their voice counts?

7 Think of your own country. Do you feel your voice matters in determining how it is run?

8 What was the effect of the Citizens United judgment on US democratic politics?

9 Looking at the governance indicators in Figure 3.9, government effectiveness seems to be stronger where voice and accountability are weaker. What does this indicate for the business environment?

10 To what extent is China's authoritarian political system stable, and why?

11 What were the factors which saw the eruption of Arab spring uprisings? In what ways are these factors still important?

12 What are the challenges faced by formerly authoritarian states wishing to introduce democratic systems?

13 Explain what is meant by a 'fragile state', and assess the challenges for businesses in these environments.

14 What are the implications of a 'multipolar' world for the global business environment?

MYANMAR AND THE CHALLENGES OF DEMOCRACY

When people think of Myanmar nowadays, the first image that comes to mind is that of Aung San Suu Kyi, famous for her pro-democracy stance during the country's long dark period of military rule. She was detained under house arrest for fifteen years, from 1989 to 2010, the year in which the ruling generals decided to embark on a transformation of the country to a democracy. Suu Kyi's National League for Democracy (NLD) had been banned, but was allowed to register as a party in 2011, and she won a by-election in 2012, becoming an opposition member of parliament in the fledgling democratic state. As the daughter of the country's independence leader, General Aung San, who was assassinated in 1947, just before the country became independent, she has long aspired to see its democratic transformation. She still calls the country Burma, its old name, although the military junta changed its name to Myanmar in 1989. That transformation now seems to be genuinely taking place, but the country faces formidable challenges along the way.

Photo 3.3 These young Buddhist monks look nervous. In Myanmar's new democracy, there are tensions between the Buddhist majority and numerous other ethnic and religious groups.

Burma of the 1980s was a turbulent country, stirred up by democracy protests against the ruling military dictator, involving diverse groups in society from Buddhist monks to farmers. Suu Kyi organized pro-democracy rallies, calling for free elections and gradual democratic reforms. The protests were forcefully put down by the army, which seized power in 1989, installing a military junta to rule the country. They held elections in 1990, which were won by Suu Kyi's NLD, but the party was not allowed to take its seats, and their leader was placed under house arrest.

Having ruled for nearly two decades, the generals gave up power to an elected president in 2011. The military's running of the country and its economy had long been condemned internationally. The society was very poor, and the government paid little attention to social needs and basic services. Even during the devastation of Cyclone Nargis in 2008, they refused to co-operate with international relief workers. The generals' management of the economy became noted for corruption, often through government-controlled businesses. Myanmar suffered from deforestation through uncontrolled logging, and became known for trafficking of commodities, animals and people. The generals were condemned for human rights abuses, including the imprisonment of political prisoners. The country was subject to international sanctions, but nonetheless the generals were able to carry on business activities, mainly because of growing ties with China. When observers now wonder why the generals have seemingly passed on power to an elected government, it is thought that the growing influence of China is a factor which persuaded them that a democratic government would be the strongest option for the country.

However, the challenges are monumental. In addition to the extreme poverty and lack of infrastructure, perhaps the greatest issue for Myanmar is the multiplicity of ethnic and religious groups. The population is split into 135 ethnic groups, many of which speak languages unintelligible to the others. Although the main groupings are Burman people (68%) and Buddhism (89%), other groupings, which have their own geographic areas, are highly restive and armed. The government has used force to suppress protests, but such methods seem to set back hopes for democracy. Twenty armed groups have signed peace deals with the government, but these deals have not resolved all the issues. The Kachin state in the north has sought a federal solution to achieve some autonomy, but the government has resisted, and the constitution of 2008 would need to be amended. Unrest has also occurred at a copper mine jointly owned by a Chinese company and the Burmese military, where villagers claim their land was forcibly taken from

them. Police tactics including the use of military munitions in dealing with these protesters have been criticized (Fisher, 2013).

It is sometimes said that the generals have not actually withdrawn from political power, but are lurking in the shadows. After all, the new president, Thein Sein, was a military man himself. Moreover, 25% of the seats in the parliament are given over to the military. He says, 'this is an armed forces [that] the country has had to rely on for a very long time for security ... so it was important at this time that they were not left behind entirely' (Thein Sein, 2012). The generals, however, were the source of corruption which was devastating for the economy and society. Myanmar's per capita GDP is just $750, and 26% of the population live in poverty. The new era of democracy is expected to bring economic development, which will allow free competition. This will be a major challenge. Outside investors are eager to invest in the country, but they face numerous challenges, including poor infrastructure, lack of modern banking, a legal system which is only just getting established, and a general lack of skills in the population. Above all, however, there is a need for the new government to peaceably resolve the ethnic tensions.

Sources: Fisher, J. (2013) *Burma Police used White Phosphorous on Mine Protesters*, BBC, 14 February, at www.bbc.co.uk (18/09/14); Robinson, G. (2013) 'Myanmar admits to air strikes on Kachin rebels', *Financial Times*, 4 January; Buncombe, A. (2012) 'Lives still in limbo for Burma's forgotten cyclone victims', *The Independent*, 3 December, at www.independent.co.uk; Pilling, D. and Robinson, G. (2012) 'A nation rises', *Financial Times*, 5 December; Thein Sein (2012) 'Interview: Myanmar leader promises fresh wave of reforms', 12 July, *Financial Times*.

DISCUSSION QUESTIONS

▫ **To what extent is the new government in Myanmar legitimate?**

▫ **Assess the relative strengths of the main centres of political power now emerging in Myanmar.**

▫ **What challenges for democracy lie ahead in Myanmar?**

CHAPTER 4

LAW AND JUSTICE: DIVERSE ETHICAL PERSPECTIVES FOR BUSINESS

ETHICAL THEMES IN THIS CHAPTER
- Moral rules and cultural divergence
- Governance and responsibility

THE AIMS OF THIS CHAPTER ARE TO
- Identify the elements of the rule of law
- Grasp divergences in legal systems, along with the implications for business
- Assess impacts of international law in business
- Raise awareness of MNEs' divergent perspectives on ethics and law

OPENING CASE STUDY

Photo 4.1 *The governor of the state of Maryland is pictured here in February 2013, along with campaigners against the death penalty. Shortly afterwards, the state's legislature passed the law repealing the death penalty in Maryland. (Jiva Manske/ Amnesty International)*

ETHICS AND THE DEATH PENALTY

The death penalty is legal in many countries, but is criticized on ethical grounds. Deliberately putting a person to death for committing a crime, however heinous, is arguably like committing another terrible offence in violation of human dignity (Camus, 1965). While the death penalty has a long history in many countries, global public opinion is now shifting against it. Of the UN's 193 member states, 100 have abolished it, and another 40 have ceased carrying out death sentences. In 2011, executions took place in 21 countries under national laws permitting capital punishment (Amnesty International, 2013). In China, it is estimated that thousands are executed every year. States with Islamic foundations also endorse the death penalty. Historically, many western countries have had the death penalty, but most have now abolished it. The US is the exception, but debates on the ethics and efficacy of execution as a punishment have long taken place. Proponents point to the deterrent effect of the death penalty, and to the importance of retribution for crimes such as violent murder. Opponents point to evidence that it is ineffective as a deterrent: the states using the death penalty most are also the ones with the most murders. They also stress that courts sometimes wrongly convict, but they cannot put right a miscarriage of justice once a person is dead.

The eighth amendment to the US Constitution prohibits 'cruel and unusual punishment'. The Supreme Court has interpreted its role rather narrowly, delivering judgments on surrounding issues rather than the ethical question of whether the death penalty should be declared unconstitutional per se. It has forbidden its use against children and the 'mentally retarded' (Death Penalty Information Centre, 2013). The court has recognized that interpretation of the law could change with 'evolving standards of decency' (Goldberg and Dershowitz, 1970). But it has preferred to look at shifts in public opinion rather than to address the ethical issue in normative terms. The death penalty is largely subject to the legal jurisdiction of the 50 individual states, in which public opinion varies considerably. They are obliged to adhere to the federal constitution, and to abide by the decisions of the US Supreme Court. The wide scope for variation has left a patchwork of different regimes. A murder might incur the death penalty in one state, but not in the adjoining state.

The federal government and the majority of US states recognize the death penalty, but there has been a trend towards abolishing it. Connecticut abolished it in 2012, and Maryland followed in 2013, becoming the eighteenth state to do so. The electorate in California, which has 724 prisoners waiting on 'death row' to be executed, voted in a referendum in 2012 to keep the death penalty. A thin majority of 53% supported retaining it, suggesting a moral divide in society on the issue.

Most of the US states which apply the death penalty rely on lethal injections to carry out executions. This has been considered preferable to electrocution, where the level of pain could be considered cruel and thus unconstitutional. However, difficulties in obtaining the necessary drugs from pharmaceutical companies have affected their ability to continue executions. A number of drug companies now refuse to supply drugs which they know will be used in executions. When US company, Hospira, stopped producing one of the drugs used for lethal injections, prisons turned to the Danish company, Lundbeck. Lundbeck took a strong ethical position, banning the use of its medicines in executions. Similarly, Fresenius Kabi, a German maker of propofol (a drug implicated in the accidental death of Michael Jackson), decided in 2012 to change its distribution network so that prisons in the US would not be able to buy the drug for lethal injections. These companies have taken the view that their medicines are designed to save lives and help people, not kill them. Teva, the Israeli pharmaceutical company, has imposed a similar ban on supplying US prisons. European governments have taken a lead internationally in incorporating a ban on the death penalty in the European Convention on Human Rights. The European Commission has banned the export of 'torture goods', including drugs that are known to be destined for carrying out executions.

American prisons have found their sources of lethal drugs increasingly restricted. They can resort to importing from third-party countries to get round manufacturers' bans on exports, and they can buy from unofficial sources. However, state laws require them to certify the legitimacy of their sources, and the drugs must be approved by the US Food and Drug Administration (FDA). Non-FDA-approved drugs obtained from doubtful producers risk being contaminated. In 2011, a consignment of drugs destined for prisons was seized in Georgia by drug enforcement officials. The consignment had been obtained from a UK company called Dream Pharma, which operated in London behind a storefront of a driving instructor. Georgia is now proceeding with legislation which will declare the sources of lethal-injection drugs to be 'state secrets'. This bill is described as protecting the privacy of people involved in executions, but critics fear that it will be used to conceal information from the public in cases where the drugs used were not of the right quality. Georgia has also been criticized for its legislation on the execution of mentally handicapped prisoners. Although the US Supreme Court ruled in 2002 that such prisoners should not be put to death, Georgia applies a very strict test, requiring that condemned persons must prove learning difficulties beyond reasonable doubt. Medical experts have asserted that this is almost impossible to do.

A moratorium on executions across the US occurred in the 1970s, following the Supreme Court's questioning of racism in the trials of accused people. However, racist bias remains an issue. Research in North Carolina has found that the odds of receiving a death sentence rose 3.5 times among defendants, whether white or non-white, who murdered white victims, as opposed to non-white victims (Unah and Boger, 2001). In 2009, North Carolina passed the Racial Justice Act, aimed at eliminating racial bias in the judicial process. Following a political shift to the Republican Party in the legislature and the governor's office, however, this act was repealed in 2013. Most of the 161 inmates on death row in the state had filed complaints under the former law. They could now be a step closer to execution. However, the state's three-drug lethal injection method faces legal challenges in the courts, and prison authorities have run into difficulties in obtaining the drugs in any case. Meanwhile, opinion polls in North Carolina show unease with the death penalty: over half of those questioned would prefer prisoners to serve life sentences instead (Clark, 2013).

There are thus multiple legal and ethical issues surrounding the death penalty, including the trial process, the sentencing and the legalities of the prisoner's execution. These issues have been the subjects of debate across the US and also globally. At international level, there is now a growing body of human rights law, by which national governments are increasingly being scrutinized. Pharmaceutical companies have shown that taking a stand on ethics can lead to rethinking by governments, legal authorities and the public generally.

Sources: Camus, A. (1965) Réflexions sur la guillotine, in *Essais* (Paris: Gallimard); Rankin, B. and Abbey, M. (2013) 'Bill would cloak lethal injection in secrecy', *Atlanta Journal Constitution*, 21 March, at www.ajc.com; Goldberg, A. and Dershowitz, A. (1970) 'Declaring the death penalty unconstitutional', *Harvard Law Review*, 83(2): 1773–819; Unah, I. and Boger, C. (2001) 'Race and the death penalty in North Carolina, 1993–1997', *North Carolina Death Penalty Study*, the University of North Carolina (Chapel Hill), at www.unc.edu; Topping, A. (2012) 'Californian death penalty fight goes on despite vote', *The Guardian*, 8 November, at www.guardian.co.uk; Woodford, M. (2012) 'Corporate ethics are a matter of life and death', *Financial Times*, 22 October; Clark, M. (2013) 'Some states speed up death penalty', *Stateline News*, Pew Charitable Trusts, 18 June, at www.pewstates.org; Death Penalty Information Centre (2013) *Facts about the Death Penalty*, at www.deathpenaltyinfo.org; Amnesty International (2013) *The Death Penalty in 2011*, at www.amnesty.org (18/09/14).

DISCUSSION QUESTIONS

- On what grounds can the death penalty be defended in the countries where it is legal and regularly used?

- Why is the death penalty criticized in the US? Should it be prohibited across the US? Give your reasons.

- Explain the ethical reasoning of the companies which have stopped exporting drugs used in lethal injections.

INTRODUCTION

International business depends on legal relations – between firms, with governments and within communities. The law which governs them is usually determined by national legal systems, each with its own cultural and political background. The law in any country is applied and interpreted in a set of institutions. Behind every written law or institution there lies an ethical foundation, whether obvious or not, which shapes views of right and wrong, reveals a picture of the individual and reflects a view of individual–society relations. These are ethical issues which are embedded in the law as it applies to individuals and companies. The company which engages in legal relations is thus inevitably involved in the moral dimensions of a society. On an international scale, a firm's legal relations across national borders raise not only complicated legal issues but a host of cross-cutting moral issues.

This chapter shows how national legal systems diverge, and how these divergences reflect cultural differences. It looks at business law and ethics in practice, analysing how norms and practices are changing as businesses become more involved in cross-border activities. It is often said that globalization spells a diminishing role for the state and its institutions. We find, on the contrary, that states play an important role in businesses' global strategies. On an ethical level, international law plays an important role, transcending the particular legal and cultural environments of states. For international businesses, this growing role of international law and ethics, especially in crucial areas such as human rights and environmental protection, is taking a lead.

ETHICAL FOUNDATIONS OF LAW

Cultural values and norms of behaviour are influential in shaping a society's legal environment. A culture's moral rules about what is right and wrong may stem from religion, as we saw in the concept of natural law in the last chapter. Many, like the 'golden rule', discussed in Chapter 1, are traditional in many societies as well as many religions. If a person breaks one of these rules by, for example, failing to keep a promise, this attracts opprobrium from others in society. In most cases, the person suffers criticism from family members or other associates, as a way of conveying that this type of behaviour is immoral. Where the immoral behaviour is more serious, it becomes a matter of law. Declaring any act to be subject to law raises it to a level of public authority. Law thus consists of rules defined and administered by public authorities, usually the state.

The state's laws are known as positive law, enacted by state law-making authorities. 'Legal positivism' as a school of thought is associated with the utilitarians, especially Bentham. It holds that positive law enacted by a sovereign authority is the only real law. This 'law of the land' is backed up by the coercive force of the state's enforcement institutions and courts. When people say that an activity is 'against the law', this is usually the type of law they have in mind. Obedience is based on coercion, not on any moral reasons for obedience. Legal positivists concede that many of the state's laws are influenced by morality (Hart, 1961: 181). And, if the government is democratic, one could say that consent is the ultimate basis of authority, which gives the law legitimacy. The utilitarians thought that positive law should be based on the utility principle as its ethical foundation, aiming always to achieve the greatest happiness of the greatest number. This could be termed 'utility-based ethics' (Sen, 2010: 362). This view, as pointed out in the first chapter, is associated with 'consequentialism': whether the law is good or bad is based on the consequences, rather than on any ethical principle in itself.

However, the underlying ethics of law has been interpreted in much broader ways. As with ethical theories generally, law has come to have numerous normative implications, and the state's laws are not uncommonly criticized for violation of some higher ethical standards. Natural law is one of these normative perspectives, often linked to religious beliefs. But natural law need not be specifically derived from religion. It can have an ethical basis in the idea of human dignity (Hart, 1961: 190). Natural law in this sense is linked to notions of justice and human rights (discussed in Chapter 9).

Justice as a concept focuses on the value of each individual human being, implying that all are morally equal. Rawls' theory of justice invokes two principles. These are, first, a system of basic rights and duties, and, second, equality of opportunity (Rawls, 1971). Personal liberty is enshrined in the first principle, reflecting his liberal view of rights (Sen, 2010: 59). Rawls' idea of justice is based on fairness to all in society, who share an essential human dignity. He criticized the inequality inherent in the utilitarian principle of the greatest happiness of the greatest number, which would sacrifice some people's happiness for others'. Rawls' view of social justice was rooted in liberal democratic society. His principles of justice as fairness can be used to assess the state's laws and workings of its legal system. Rawls considered his principles of justice to be categorical imperatives in the Kantian tradition, as each person is 'a free and equal rational being' (Rawls, 1971: 253).

Justice is closely associated with the idea of due process, by which people are entitled to a fair, unbiased consideration of any case in which they are involved in relation to state authorities. This is most obviously relevant in accusations of crime, but is also relevant in administrative processes between an individual, group or company and the state. Due process should ensure that, despite the power of the state and the relative weakness of the other party, the legal procedure should have a balanced and fair approach. This principle is central to the rule of law.

The **rule of law** holds that equality before the law should be the basis of the country's legal system. Thus, no one is above the law, and even rulers cannot sidestep the law. A **constitution**, setting out rights and duties of both rulers and ruled, is a pillar of the rule of law. The rule of law has its basis in the inherent value of human dignity. The rule of law can be seen from two perspectives. First, it represents a set of values, or ends, which have a clear normative dimension. These values are shown in Figure 4.1. Second, the rule of law can be seen as a set of institutions which are formal mechanisms (Carothers, 1998). There is over-lap between the values approach and the institutional approach. For example, the law should be clear and predictable, and not retrospective. These are formal requirements. Equality before the law is a value, resting on an ethical principle, but it requires certain formal institutions to be effective. If most people are too poor to go to the courts to assert their rights, then the system does not uphold equality before the law.

Although we tend to think that institutions are the means and values are the ends, insti-tutions are often seen as ends in themselves (Belton, 2005). For example, independence of the judiciary is a hallmark of the rule of law, as shown in Figure 4.1. Judges should be selected independently of government or other interests, and on the basis simply of legal qualifications, rather than political views. This technical approach is formal only: it cannot guarantee unbiased judges. A country can technically have an independent judiciary, but informal pressures on judges can lead to bias. This might well be the case in countries where the institutions are in the formative stage. This issue has come to prominence as a growing number of countries are becoming integrated into the global economy and reforming their legal systems to improve the rule of law.

Businesspeople look on the institutions of the rule of law in each country as crucial to their business activities. Contractual relations are at the heart of business transactions, and

Figure 4.1 *Principles of the rule of law*

businesses stress the need for a stable and reliable legal environment, in which they can, if the need arises, pursue claims in the country's courts. Many countries are making the transition to market economies and democratic political systems. The rule of law as a criterion is increasingly used in assessing the legal environment in a country. It is used by the World Bank to assess governance. It is also used by aid agencies which target poor developing countries. And it has been used by the EU in assessing the legal systems of applicant countries, such as the post-communist transition economies of Central and Eastern Europe. Agencies have tended to take the formalist approach to the rule of law, looking at institutions. Moreover, different agencies use different institutional criteria (Skaaning, 2010). The US Agency for International Development (USAID) considers the existence of a market economy to be an aspect of the rule of law (Upham, 2002). This reflects its assumption that only market economies are able to ensure the rule of law. This approach has attracted criticism, however, as market-friendly institutions need not necessarily be best suited to a country's development needs (Stiglitz, 2002).

In pluralistic societies, home to more than one culture, the rule of law should, in theory, reinforce justice and fairness for all, rather than uphold particular cultural paradigms. Each person, even one from a minority culture, should feel that he or she has equal access to the justice system. The rule of law can take different institutional forms. Law as an institutional system interacts with the cultural and political environment. Legal systems around the world, while implementing similar basic principles, produce very different legal outcomes in practice. In this section, we look at how different systems work in business contexts.

Figure 4.2 Sources of national legal systems

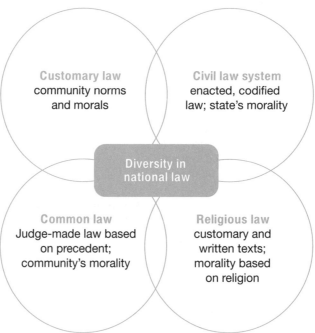

ETHICAL UNDERPINNINGS OF LEGAL SYSTEMS

A legal system is essentially a set of institutions, but its dynamism stems in part from the cultural and political environment of the country. For this reason, countries whose legal systems look similar might be very different in practice. A country's government is the major driver behind its legal system. Political sovereignty of states (introduced in the last chapter) is related to legal sovereignty. Sovereignty is the attribute of states which enables them to make the law, design institutions to administer the law and enforce the laws, backed up by coercive force.

There are several broad types of legal system discussed in this section. The two main types are common law systems and civil law systems. Other types of legal system, such as customary and religious systems, operate in many countries, sometimes alongside a dominant state system. The national legal system in any country is likely to have assimilated elements from a variety of different types of law over the years, as shown in Figure 4.2. The ethical environment has been an influence on the evolution of law and legal institutions in every country. As the figure shows, the community, the state, customary groupings and religion are all sources of ethics which influence how law evolves.

THE COMMON LAW LEGAL TRADITION

The common law tradition originated in England and spread to other parts of the world through British colonial expansion. Common law countries include the US, India, Australia, New Zealand, Ghana and Nigeria. Common law is judge-made law, that is, decisions handed down by judges in dealing with the cases that come before them. Common law courts deal with disputes between citizens, including corporate entities. Dispute resolution is at the heart of the common law (Joireman, 2001). But over time, general principles evolve. A system of precedent operates to ensure consistency. Judges examine precedents relevant to each case, and the decision of a higher court is binding on lower courts.

The common law court is adversarial. The court is presented with two sides, whose lawyers put forward the strongest case they can muster. The plaintiff is the party who initiates the case against the defendant. The judge, or panel of judges, must decide on the basis of the evidence which precedents are applicable and why. The judges are not primarily seeking the truth in a disinterested way. They are looking at the plausibility of the arguments on both sides. This method might seem messy and inefficient, especially as it is based on a context of cultural understandings (Merryman, 1985).

The common law system is rooted in the morality of the community (Cotterrell, 2000). The common law thus develops as values change. The community in some cases might be an abstraction, but the moral principle remains intact. Take the landmark case of *Donoghue v Stevenson* (Coleman, 2009; [1932] AC 562). May Donoghue suffered illness from drinking a soft drink containing a decomposed snail, and sued the manufacturer of the drink. The court held that the manufacturer had a duty of care towards the consumer as a 'neighbour'. Lord Atkin asked, 'Who is my neighbour?' The answer was anyone whom I could reasonably foresee is likely to be affected by my actions. With this, the modern law of negligence was born. The ripples have extended across the globe, from the Gulf of Mexico, where the Deep Horizon oil rig disaster took place in 2010, to India, where a gas explosion

'Who is my neighbour?' The answer was anyone whom I could reasonably foresee is likely to be affected by my actions.

in Bhopal in 1986 cost hundreds of lives. The oil company, BP, has been sued in the US courts for billions of dollars in damages following the Deep Horizon disaster, while the chemical company, Union Carbide, was sued in the US as well as India. The US legal action failed, but the legal possibilities it unleashed taught global companies a lesson in legal liabilities of international business (see Chapter 9).

Membership of the EU, which has extensive law-making authority, has impacted on the legal systems of all member states, whose number reached 28 with the admission of Croatia in 2013. EU law is supranational, in that it represents authority above the sovereign state. Its authority derives from each state ratifying the EU treaties and enacting legislation which recognizes EU law. Some EU law, in the form of regulations, is directly applicable in member states, and other legal instruments known as directives, oblige the member state to incorporate them in domestic law. EU law poses challenges for the different member states, each of which has its own cultural background and legal traditions. The European Court of Justice, the highest court in the EU, is the final interpreter of EU law. New law emanating from the EU can be a source of tension within member states, especially when new laws are perceived as being imposed from above, and lacking a sense of legitimacy which national law is afforded. However, EU law has taken a lead in many areas, such as consumer protection and employment protection. As we will see in the closing case study, a new regulation on data protection is an example of how the law of all member states is directly affected by the EU.

CIVIL LAW SYSTEMS

The development of the law of negligence is a classic example of adaptation of the common law to changing circumstances. Civil law systems, by contrast, are based on legal codes handed down by the sovereign. The tradition of codified law goes back to the Romans, but the ancestors of most modern codes date from the French Napoleonic codes. Rather than the community-based moral context of common law, civil law is in the tradition of legal positivism, separating law and morals. A civil law system focuses on the state and its relationship with its citizens. In practice, this takes a more administrative and bureaucratic approach to applying the law. It is said to be fairer and more efficient than the common law (Merryman, 1985). But its efficiency depends on the existence of a smooth-functioning bureaucracy.

An inquisitorial approach is adopted by courts in civil systems. The judge, who represents the state, is a key figure, investigating the evidence and questioning witnesses. The task of the judge is to apply the relevant law. In this way, like cases are treated alike. Most European countries have adopted civil law systems. As these systems depend on enacted law, they are favoured by countries setting up new legal systems from scratch, whatever the cultural background in the society. There are separate codes for different areas of the law, such as a criminal code and commercial code. The administrative machinery is important because of the crucial role of the bureaucracy in the civil law system. Where this is lacking, the efficiency of the system is much diminished. Former colonial powers, including the French, German, Portuguese, Dutch and Italians, left legacies of civil law systems in their colonies. In Africa, there has tended to be a mixture of systems, reflecting the multi-cultural nature of society. Traditional courts that applied customary law existed alongside courts introduced by colonial powers (Gluckman, 1963).

A general trend across legal systems has been towards more enacted law. It offers a promise of certainty and consistency, and it is an effective way to introduce changes quickly.

Figure 4.3 *Safety and the rule of law in selected African states*

Scores out of 100

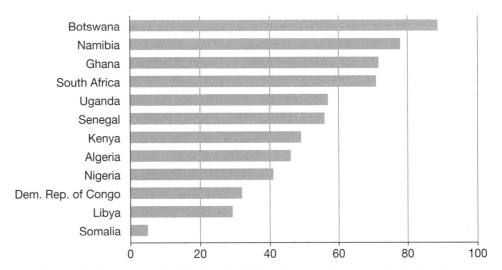

Source of data: Mo Ibrahim Foundation (2012) *Ibrahim Index of African Governance 2012*, at www.moibrahimfoundation.org (18/09/14).

Codified law is easy to access, and is clearly set out. These are important elements of the rule of law. In the US, initiatives towards harmonizing the common law of the 50 separate states have led to the Universal Commercial Code. These have nudged common law closer to the countries with civil codes. At the same time, countries with codified law have witnessed a degree of flexibility in how the law is applied, adapting it to changing circumstances. Civil law is inherently less contextual than common law. This can be seen as an advantage in a multi-cultural state, as the state's legal system can be applied uniformly.

An annual assessment of governance in African states is carried out by the Mo Ibrahim Foundation. Figure 4.3 shows a selection of scores for safety and the rule of law. Among the higher scores are countries in Southern Africa in which common law systems were established. However, note that Senegal, a civil law country, ranks higher than Kenya and Nigeria, both countries with common law legacies. Deep-seated ethnic divisions have been a factor in these latter two countries, hampering the development of stable institutions. Recent elections in Kenya have seen the election of a president who was indicted by the International Criminal Court for crimes against humanity after the last election in 2007, when violent ethnic clashes erupted. Kenya and Nigeria are both countries which are experiencing impressive economic growth. The Ibrahim research, which examines four categories of indicators, has found a growing imbalance between scores for its first two categories (economic opportunity and human development) and its second two categories (safety & rule of law and participation & human rights). Scores in the first two categories are rising, while those in the second two are declining. This trend, observable over the last six years, has featured in almost half of the 52 African countries surveyed. This suggests that prioritizing economic growth and human development (including welfare, education and health) have yielded positive results, but at the expense of building legal institutions to safeguard fairness in systems of justice, judicial independence, civil liberties and human rights.

The African countries which have achieved higher scores for the rule of law do not have unified legal systems in either of the two traditions discussed here, but, rather, mixed legal systems. These are often dual legal systems, reflecting indigenous customary law and structures, as well as legal systems inherited from colonial times. Legal history in Botswana and Namibia also includes Roman–Dutch law, which was superseded by English common law. The dual system of customary and common law, which also operates in Ghana, uses customary law in social and community matters among indigenous peoples, while the common law system applies to commercial and administrative matters. The two systems can function alongside each other, through 'mutual adaptation' (Griffiths, 1983). The ability of common law to assimilate customary law and ethical traditions is indicative of the community context in which common law has traditionally operated.

PAUSE TO CONSIDER...

What are the benefits of a civil law system from the business ethics point of view?

CUSTOMARY AND RELIGIOUS LEGAL SYSTEMS

Common law and civil law systems are both western in inception, and their spread has been mainly through colonization. This has been particularly evident in Africa, which had existing customary legal forms. Indigenous legal systems, whether in Africa, Asia or the Americas, can be loosely grouped together as customary systems, although they represent a huge variety of forms and cultural backgrounds. Another broad category is religious legal systems, of which Islamic law is an example. Customary and religious law are not self-contained categories. For example, much customary law contains religious elements. In Senegal, customary law has traditionally incorporated Islamic influences, and the imposition of a civil law system by French rulers recognized customary and religious influences.

Customary law draws on cultural values and norms in the community for maintaining continuity and cohesion. In any society, conflicts arise. Settling them peacefully in ways

The notion of due process, which western legal systems stress, is also present in customary law, helping to establish the system's legitimacy in the eyes of the relevant community.

recognized by all in the community, and achieving reconciliation between the parties, are important for social cohesion. Mechanisms for peaceful conflict resolution reinforce the moral values of the community. Customary courts often rely on respected elders in a community to dispense justice, and this is typically a transparent and public process. The notion of due process, which western legal systems stress, is also present in customary law, helping to establish the system's legitimacy in the eyes of the relevant community. Also important in local legal systems is its participatory nature, involving the parties actively in the process. Much resolution of disputes in this context is achieved by arbitration, which seeks to bring the parties together to reach a peaceful agreement through the offices of a third party. As communities evolve, especially through economic development, customary law recedes in importance. In African countries, both in the civil law and common law traditions, customary law has been assimilated gradually into the main legal system.

Customary law can overlap with religious law. Formal religions have legal systems which are rather more developed than those in customary settings. Among them are Christianity, Islam, Judaism and Hinduism. Formal religious law is derived from sacred documents and interpreted by jurists steeped in the relevant religious tradition. Religious law exists in states alongside other religions and state legal systems which are essentially secular. An exception is Islam, which is a national religion in some states. However, its influence extends beyond these Islamic states, as it is also an important source of law in many secular states which have large Muslim populations. In these latter states, Islamic law is recognized within the national legal system.

Islamic law, the Sharia, is written law. The sacred text of the Qu'ran guides followers in moral living generally, covering both legal and non-legal matters (Reinhart, 1983). The Qu'ran as a source of law is analogous to codified law, but much of it is not set out explicitly as law, and legal interpretation by jurists is necessary to discern the law. Islamic jurisprudence is highly developed, and the use of precedent is one of its features. While its methods have affinity with common law and civil law systems, Islamic law differs from both in its universal approach. Sharia represents the whole spectrum of life and ethical values, both temporal and spiritual (Mohammed, 1988). All countries with large Muslim populations recognize Islamic law, but most of these countries are secular states with national legal systems in one of the main western traditions. The national legal systems in Jordan and the United Arab Emirates (UAE) are based on civil codes, but both have incorporated Sharia elements. By contrast, Dubai and Qatar are common law countries with Sharia elements. In these states, the Sharia law relates to personal law, including family matters.

As noted above, in some states, Sharia law has been adopted as the main legal system, creating a theocracy. Iran is an example, having created an Islamic Republic in its revolution of 1979. Saudi Arabia is another example. In the predominantly Muslim northern states of Nigeria, Sharia law has been instituted, creating Islamic states within Nigeria's federal system. This Islamization has raised constitutional issues in Nigeria (Iwobi, 2004). These states were conceived as part of a federal system in the country's constitution of 1999, which was adopted following fifteen years of military rule. However, they now seem to be taking a more autonomous legal position in the adoption of the Sharia. Relations between Christian and Muslim communities in Nigeria have been fraught with tension. The decision to adopt the Sharia as a legal system reflects a fundamentalist view of Islam, which is associated with a reaction against perceived westernization. Questions over human rights arise in states where Sharia is the only recognized law. In these contexts, discriminatory treatment of women and minorities is a major concern. Another human rights concern is the imposition of Islamic criminal penalties such as amputations, which international law designates as cruel and inhumane.

In states which recognize Sharia law as existing alongside national legal systems, a more open and international approach is evident. This internationalism, when applied to legal obligations, adapts to the globalization of international business, recognizing transnational law and contracts (Bälz, 2008). More generally, Islamic law has shown itself to be adaptable to changing political, economic and social conditions. Some Arab countries, such as Qatar and Dubai, have become highly globalized, especially in global finance. Their rise has coincided with a rise in Islamic finance, which refers to the specific rules applying to commercial transactions.

The world of international business has seen the ease with which Islamic notions of obligation and Islamic finance have adapted to changing business practices.

The legitimacy of trade and commercial activities has long been recognized in Islamic law. Usury is prohibited on ethical grounds. Usury can refer simply to the levying of interest, but it also includes profiteering and fraudulent trading generally. As a consequence, transactions which might involve interest in a western context, such as a loan, must be framed in a way which does not involve interest. Interest-free banking has grown since the 1970s, meeting the need for Sharia-compliant financial products. Islamic finance has grown up in centres where there is a relatively liberal regulatory environment, such as London and Dubai, rather than in Islamic states. The Sharia element can be seen as an ethical addition in a transaction (Bälz, 2008). In this way, a religious requirement is transformed into an essentially ethical one, and can be incorporated in legal instruments in any appropriate financial centre. The world of international business has seen the ease with which Islamic notions of obligation and Islamic finance have adapted to changing business practices.

In this section, we have seen that the major legal traditions of common law and civil law have shown themselves to be adaptable in pluralist societies around the globe. While the two main traditions have differing sources and legal outlooks, both subscribe to the rule of law, recognizing the importance of due process and institutional integrity. They have also shown themselves to be adaptable in countries where religious and cultural traditions play important roles in legal institutions. Increasingly in international business, the rule of law is seen as a set of criteria which determine the capacity of a country to support business relations, whether among domestic businesses or internationally.

BUSINESS LAW ACROSS BORDERS AND ITS ETHICAL IMPLICATIONS

Businesses seek a stable environment in which their contractual transactions and other activities can be carried out with some confidence that property will be protected, laws will be upheld, and agreements will be enforced. When things go wrong, they seek impartial and efficient judicial proceedings to resolve the issues satisfactorily. The institutions which provide these assurances form the basis of the rule of law (Carothers, 1998). In this section we look at some of the ethical dimensions in the key areas of law which are of concern to international business.

TRANSNATIONAL CONTRACTUAL RELATIONS

Contractual relations fall within the broad area of private law. Private law covers family law, the law of inheritance, property law and the law of obligations, including contracts and torts. For a business, property law, the law of contract and the law of torts are paramount. Of these, contract law is the area that covers most business transactions. Torts cover a range of other obligations in society, such as a duty of reasonable care, discussed in the last section. Contract law differs from one national system to another. Although many basic principles are similar, specific rules can vary between civil law and common law countries. Moreover, countries within the same legal tradition also differ from one other. These differences arise partly from differing cultural and political environments. For example, the importance of personal relations over written contracts is a feature of much Asian business practice, encapsulated in the notion of *guanxi* in China. China has developed a system of codified law, but its cultural environment is inevitably important in the practical aspects of business relations.

To facilitate business across borders, businesses need some degree of certainty over what the law is in relation to each transaction. But this can be more of an aspiration than a reality. Firms can face high transaction costs and legal uncertainty in international contracts (Rödl, 2008). A business would ideally like the body of contract law to be the same everywhere and to remain settled, but even then, it would be applied differently in different locations.

Figure 4.4 *Business choices in transnational contract law*

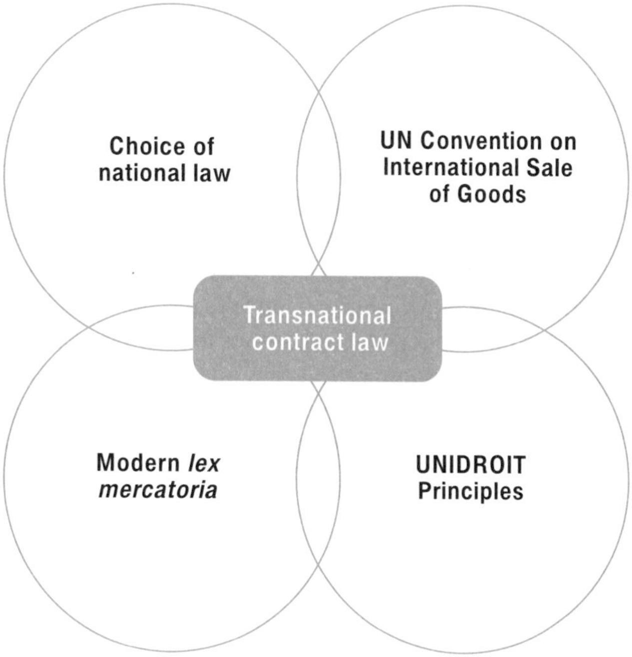

Figure 4.4 shows the main elements of transnational contract law. Progress has been made in harmonizing contract law among differing legal systems. Under the auspices of the UN, there is the Convention on Contracts for the International Sale of Goods (CISG) of 1980. This treaty applies in the 79 countries that have ratified it. They include the US, China, Russia, Germany, and, most recently, Brazil. The UK, India and South Africa, all common law countries, remain outside the CISG. The CISG covers the essential aspects of contracts for the sale of goods, including contract formation, performance of the terms and remedies in cases of breach of contract. The CISG represents a step forward in harmonization of contract law between common law countries and civil law countries. In cases of disputes between parties, it falls to national courts to interpret the convention (Lookofsky, 2011). Parties to international contracts are can choose the law that they wish to apply to their contract, through choice-of-law clauses, and they can also choose the jurisdiction they wish to have disputes decided in. Businesses thus have freedom to determine the law which pertains to the contract. They can also provide for arbitration in the case of disputes, whereby a third party is brought in to resolve the issues.

Freedom of contract has long been a recognized principle in both civil and common law systems. Historically, trade has relied heavily on custom and practice in contracting across borders. In the medieval period, these customary rules became known as *lex mercatoria*. This idea of law created and administered by the traders themselves has long appealed to businesses and has enjoyed a revival in recent years, as it seems to offer a viable means of transcending national legal systems. Research suggests that *lex mercatoria* in the medieval period was not entirely self-regulatory, but rested on a combination of customary and official institutions (Michaels, 2007). Still, the possibility of non-state law does seem to offer possibilities for international business. In fact, the idea of people agreeing privately what terms they wish to apply to their contracts is established in international commercial transactions. This principle lies behind the use of the UN's UNIDROIT Principles of International Commercial Contracts, which can be seen as the new *lex mercatoria*. They pertain to all types of contract, and can be used and adapted by parties as they wish. Last revised in 2004, the UNIDROIT Principles have considerable appeal to businesspeople on economic grounds. They are an efficient means of representing the wishes of the parties, and disputes can be settled through arbitration, which is a cheaper and less formal process than court proceedings. Transaction costs are thereby reduced. The appeal of this approach seems to accord with globalization.

Law-making by parties to a contract has an ethical appeal in that, in theory, people are free to design their own contracts and resolve their disputes in a participatory environment. But it could be questioned how law thus formed derives its legitimacy. Does individual freedom alone confer legitimacy? Parties might conceivably contract in terms that invite criticism on grounds of violating human rights, for example. Legitimacy of the law is associated with legitimacy of the government, as the last chapter showed. Statutory legal frameworks are constraints in many types of contract, such as building, finance and other services. In these areas, state regulation conveys a sense of legitimacy in the eyes of the public. It is therefore not realistic to contend that parties are free to contract outside the system of state laws. States recognize the use of customary practices and self-determined arrangements, but their legitimacy derives from the state, rather than from the parties themselves (Michaels, 2007).

Freedom of the individual is an ethical foundation of capitalist systems. More specifically, capitalism came to emphasize economic freedom and minimal state interference. But despite the growth in global markets, states remain important players. Some states offer legal and financial advantages over others. A company might register subsidiaries in a country not because it does business there but because taxes are low. Businesses, rather than lamenting the existence of a diversity of national laws, have come to thrive on the plethora of differing national legal systems. However, when they opt for countries with lax regulation, they invite criticism on ethical grounds.

INTELLECTUAL PROPERTY LAW

Products protected by intellectual property law have grown in importance with global competition. Indeed, in today's world, these rights are often part of the global scanning just highlighted. Intellectual property (IP) covers a wide range of property rights, but all have in common the fact that they are intangible assets, that is, products of human mind rather than physical property. They are embodied in physical products, however, and the intellectual property is often the key component of a product which gives it its value. A complex product embodies a number of different types of intellectual property. Think of the smartphone or other high-tech gadget sold under a global brand such as Apple or Samsung. A trademark, consisting of a logo or name which identifies the brand, can be registered under national law in each market. However, counterfeit products are huge business, and difficult to curtail. Goods bearing false logos, which constitute trademark infringement, are sold in many markets. As Figure 4.5 shows, in the last decade, the number of cases in which counterfeit goods were seized in the EU has risen 1,000%. A total of 114 million articles were seized in 2011, with an estimated retail value of 1.2 billion euros. China was the origin of

Figure 4.5 *Customs interception of counterfeit goods in the EU*

Number of cases

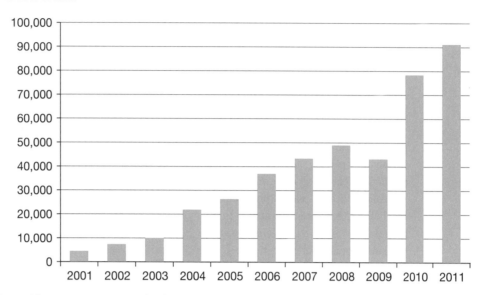

Source of data: European Commission (2012) *Report on EU Customs Enforcement of Intellectual Property Rights 2011*, at www.ec.europa.eu/taxation_customs (18/09/14).

73% of these goods. The largest category was medicines, accounting for 24% of the articles seized. The growth in the market for counterfeit goods can be explained largely by the growth in e-commerce.

Luxury goods and electronic gadgets are also favoured products of counterfeiters. The smartphone embodies considerable technology, much of it at the forefront of innovation, and the owner is keen to protect this IP from competitors. Software can be patent or copyright, two further types of IP. It has generally been considered copyright. Certainly, application programmes are copyright. Books, films and music are also copyright, protecting authors and composers from unauthorized publication. Copyright comes into existence automatically on creation of the original work, although it can be difficult to prove. A patent must be applied for, and this process can be long and expensive. The patent protects inventions, aiming to ensure that the inventor or the owner of the patent can enjoy a monopoly on the exploitation of the invention for a reasonable time. When that time is up and the patent lapses, others are free to use the patent, but, by then, the product will probably have been superseded by more innovative products. Much software, especially programmes integral to the functionality of a high-tech gadget, is considered patentable. The functioning of a smartphone depends on numerous patents, which cover the hardware and functionality. Often, patentholders license other manufacturers to produce their products, but there is a risk that products will be copied by unlicensed manufacturers.

It is sometimes said that patents provide too much protection for owners, stifling innovation, and that research and development (R&D) would be better promoted without them. This is rather a double-edged argument. Proponents of patents say that the right to exploit the invention and reap the rewards is an incentive to inventors. Critics argue that the monopoly created by the patent gives the owner too great a grip on the technology. There is an ethical issue in the idea that the inventor should be entitled to the rewards. This seems to be in keeping with the value placed by capitalism on property rights. But capitalism also values individual freedom. Much software is 'open-sourced', made available freely. And applications, or 'apps', for smartphones and tablets are usually developed not by the brand owner, but by independent developers. Legally, each has a copyright in each application, but these rights are transferred to the brand owner. The growth of user-developed software has presented challenges for companies like Apple, as the products are sold partly on the attractions of the applications available, which are, in a sense, outsourced and not within the control of the company.

An ethical debate has focused on medicines and vaccines. A company might hold the patent for the only vaccine for a particular disease. This monopoly gives it total control over supply and pricing. Is there an ethical case for restricting patent rights in cases where the public good is at stake? Developing countries, in particular, urge that they are disadvantaged in dealing with the global pharmaceutical giants. High prices render many medicines out of reach for the poorer countries. In many countries, medicines produced by unauthorized manufacturers are a problem, especially as these can be unsafe. In exceptional cases, a country can compel a patent owner to grant a compulsory licence to another firm to produce the medicine for that country's population. India issued its first compulsory licence in 2013. It was issued to a domestic company, Natco, to produce a cancer drug which is patented by Bayer AG of Germany. The aim was to make the drug cheaper and more widely available to those who need it (Chatterjee, 2013). Bayer's price was the equivalent of US$5,098 for a month's dose, while Natco's price was US$160. Bayer would still have to be paid a royalty under the compulsory licence. This decision has been welcomed by medical practitioners, but for the pharmaceutical industry, it is a warning that other states could follow India's example.

Research in biotechnology, promising breakthroughs in testing and treatment, also raises ethical issues. Scientists have made significant advances in their knowledge of human genetics. As a result, some have formed companies which have succeeded in obtaining gene patents, most notably in the US. Gene patents give them effective control of the use of this knowledge, possibly curtailing future research. US patentholders in some fields have gained financially from their monopoly over the genetic testing of patients for the gene sequence protected by the patent. Some 40% of the human genome has been patented, and this includes gene sequences relevant to a number of diseases such as cancer, Alzheimer's disease and epilepsy (BBC, 2013). These patents have been the subject of lawsuits in the US. Critics of gene patents argue that an isolated gene sequence which is unmodified should not have been granted patent protection in the first place, as it is a discovery rather than an invention. The gene patent has not been widely recognized outside the US. In 2013, the US Supreme Court ruled gene patents invalid, in a landmark judgment which will have implications for future research and testing of patients (Bravin and Kendall, 2013). This decision was welcomed by professionals and patients, who had been concerned about corporate monopolies – and high prices – prevailing in the testing for many diseases. It will also have implications for patents of plants and animals.

In 2013, the US courts ruled gene patents invalid, in a landmark judgment which has implications for future research and testing of patients.

The route by which most developing countries acquire medicines is through the production of generic versions. These are medicines whose patents have expired. Generic manufacturers are thus free to produce them. Natco is a generic manufacturer, and India is home to many such companies, which are generally perceived as threats to the large, research-focused

Figure 4.6 *Growth in volume of patents in key technology fields*

The year 2000 = 100

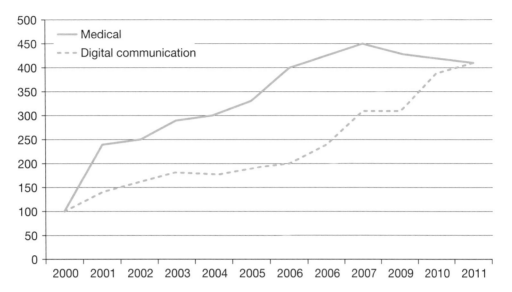

Source of data: WIPO (World Intellectual Property Organization) 2012, *Promoting Access to Medical Technologies and Innovation*, at www.wipo.org (18/09/14).

companies. The latter companies argue that they invest huge sums in R&D, and should be entitled to the rewards from exclusive rights to use the patent for its duration. Generic companies aim to make drugs widely available. They do not have large R&D budgets and are not likely to come up with a breakthrough discovery. For this reason, some system of patent protection is needed in the public interest, to provide incentives to research-intensive companies. But the companies with big R&D budgets are increasingly facing price resistance in national markets, and discovery of new drugs becomes harder. As Figure 4.6 shows, the volume of medical patent activity globally has decreased, while R&D in digital communication, by way of comparison, has risen. Pharmaceutical companies are therefore being forced to rethink their business models. Many are trimming primary research budgets, locating R&D in cheaper countries and also producing generic products themselves. Controversially, GlaxoSmithKline (GSK) has entered 'pay-to-delay' agreements with generics manufacturers, to prolong patent protection that is close to expiry. Bayer, noted in the example above from India, still produces aspirin, a drug it discovered in 1897, and probably the most commonly used medicine in existence.

Legal frameworks for protecting IP should protect researchers and also benefit consumers. But there is a tension between these goals. Excessive zeal in protecting IP can stifle research rather than encourage it, and excessive R&D costs are difficult to recoup in markets. For large companies in sectors such as pharmaceuticals, the costs of litigation can be a huge component of the company's overall costs. Companies which rely heavily on IP assets are finding increasingly that their defence of proprietorial rights is threatened by challenges on grounds of wider access to public goods.

PAUSE TO CONSIDER...

Assess the benefits and drawbacks of generic medicines from an ethical point of view.

COMPETITION LAW

The last subsection highlighted a reality of markets: the monopolist is in a strong position to control supply of a product and its price. It need not worry about rising costs as it can just raise prices; it need not worry about brand image, as there are no competitors; and it has few worries that more innovative rivals will eat into its market, as its monopoly is an effective barrier to newcomers. This might be good news for the monopolist, but it is not for consumers, who might well end up paying high prices for mediocre products or services. Many countries have legislated in the broad area known as competition law (called 'antitrust' law in the US), curtailing monopolists and restrictive business practices. Competition law can encourage businesses to remain competitive and innovative, benefiting the national economy in the long term. In countries where monopolies, either state-owned or private sector, are allowed to flourish, international competitiveness suffers and consumers pay higher prices than in more competitive national environments. Mexico is a good example of this phenomenon, where monopolists have long held a grip in key sectors such as telecommunications and energy.

The two elements of competition law are anti-monopoly laws and control of the use of restrictive practices, such as price fixing. The two areas are related, as restrictive practices are tools favoured by monopolists. Anti-monopoly laws cover reviews of proposed mergers between companies which might lead to abuse of a dominant market position. Although competition law differs from country to country, these elements are generally present. Judicial interpretation differs considerably from country to country, and over time. We now look at some concrete examples.

In some industries, a pattern of mergers and acquisitions has led to consolidation globally, in which a few large companies have become dominant. This has occurred in mining, commodity trading (the subject of a case study in Chapter 6) and energy. A company could well have a nearly 20% share of a global market, but a share closer to 50% in its major national markets. The brewing industry is an example. In 2000, only one company, Anheuser Busch (AB), had a global market share of over 5%, but by 2011, the four leading brewing companies (AB InBev, SAB Miller, Heineken and Carlsberg) each had shares of over 5%. The upshot is that the four companies control nearly half the global beer market. The largest, AB InBev, formed when InBev of Belgium acquired AB in 2008, now controls 19.5% of the global market and 47% of the US market.

From its 200 brands, AB InBev had revenues of $40 billion in 2012. This market power alone had not alarmed US regulators. However, the company's proposal in 2013 to acquire another large brewer, Modelo of Mexico, prompted a lawsuit from the US Department of Justice. It is not simply the size of the company's market presence that matters, but its real or potential abuse of a dominant market position. Modelo had a 6% US market share; adding it to AB InBev's 47% was felt to be detrimental to consumers, stifling competition and leading to higher prices. AB InBev redesigned its takeover bid, promising to divest itself of some key brands, which seemed to satisfy the US authorities (Wembridge, 2013). The US beer market remains highly concentrated, nonetheless. AB InBev and MillerCoors, the other large player, together control 80% of the market. Small brewers have protested, especially in light of the large companies' grip on distribution as well as production.

AB InBev and MillerCoors, the other large player, together control 80% of the US beer market.

The EU's competition authorities, guided by the competition commissioner, take a rather more robust line than US counterparts. Google has been criticized for the way it presents its search results, tending to feature its own services more prominently than those of other companies. Google was cleared by US authorities, but encountered accusations of anti-competitive practices from the EU commissioner. Google's share of the EU search engine market is over 90%. Its grip is lower in the US, but still 67%. After extended negotiations, the EU commissioner has obtained an agreement with Google to alter the way it presents results. This should avoid costly legal proceedings like those which entangled Microsoft for a decade. The commissioner also has in his sights investigations of banks colluding to rig interest rates and an investigation of anti-competitive practices by Russian energy giant, Gazprom.

Meanwhile, China has also become more robust in applying new anti-monopoly laws, which date only from 2008. In 2009, its competition authorities halted a proposed takeover of Huiyuan, a Chinese juice company, by Coca-Cola. More recently, its regulator has launched an investigation into possible abuse of a dominant position by two state-owned telecommunications companies, China Telecom and China Unicom, for blocking possible competitors who wish to offer broadband services (Hille, 2011). Consumer complaints have played a part in persuading authorities that they are being disadvantaged by dominant companies. Chinese authorities might have been expected to uphold state-owned companies; recognizing the importance of competition in delivering better services is a big step. It also shows that consumer complaints can make themselves felt in China.

Criticism of the huge power of global companies is an aspect of the criticism of capitalism generally. Global companies can often seem to be so powerful economically that they dwarf the national regulators set up to police competition. An absence of regulation at the global level allows the dominant companies to pursue aggressive growth strategies in multiple markets.

Critics of liberal markets take the view that economic activities should serve society, rather than the particular interests of large capitalists. As we noted in Chapter 2, capitalist incentives are based on the pursuit of self-interested enterprise in an environment of economic freedom. The growth of super-size global companies is an inevitable consequence, it could be argued. Global companies would say that this trend is beneficial, as they deliver products desired by people the world over, efficiently and at low cost, due to their economies of scale. However, they are still criticized on ethical grounds. And this criticism comes from market supporters as well as opponents. Many businesspeople support a 'level playing field' in markets, allowing competition to thrive. Consumers desire choice and variety in the marketplace. There is potential for unethical exploitation in concentrated markets, whereby the global company is able to determine products, supply and prices charged to consumers. This view of the company is one in which a shareholder perspective dominates, in contrast to a more ethical approach in which other stakeholders are taken into account. Whether international law offers a more ethical approach is a possibility to which we now turn.

There is potential for unethical exploitation in concentrated markets, whereby the global company is able to determine products, supply and prices charged to consumers.

PAUSE TO CONSIDER...

What are the shortcomings in the legal regulation of monopolies, takeovers and restrictive practices?

INTERNATIONAL LAW: IMPACTS ON GOVERNMENTS AND BUSINESSES

To the positivist, law is an order of the sovereign authority in the state. This provenance ensures its legitimacy, and it is enforced by the coercive power of the state. When individuals or companies are reminded of the obligation to obey the law of the land, this is the law referred to. We have seen, however, that law as a concept is broader than an order backed by coercion. The notion of natural law evokes a moral law which transcends the orders of governments. Natural rights are linked moral precepts which uphold the inherent value of the individual. Some theorists of natural rights, such as Rawls, stress the importance of social justice as a necessary adjunct to individualism. Rawls thought in terms of societies, nations and peoples, rather than in the international sphere (Rawls, 1999). But other theorists, notably Sen, have seen the international dimension of justice (Sen, 2010). Sen recognizes the divergence of societies, but feels that an international perspective involves recognizing a notion of global justice. The positivist would have little time for such an idea. There is no global sovereign giving orders and no global police to back them up. The positivist would therefore be sceptical of the idea of international law, saying that it is not really law at all. Yet there is a growing body of international law, and states repeatedly recognize obligations thereby created. In this section, we examine how this comes about and what these obligations involve.

HOW DOES IT WORK?

For companies, national law is paramount, but international law provides more ethically focused standards to which they, like governments, are increasingly expected to adhere.

International law is more diverse than its national counterparts. It is also more complex in the types of obligation created. While much international law either reflects existing national law or becomes converted into national legislation, much consists of norms and governance structures, which are influential in guiding state behaviour, but do not have the legal force of national law. A crucial difference between international and national law is that, in general, the parties directly bound by international law are states, rather than individuals or companies. For companies, national law is paramount, but international law provides more ethically focused standards to which they, like governments, are increasingly expected to adhere.

Formal international law consists mainly of treaties and conventions, to which states alone are parties. There are also many co-operative groupings among nations which govern particular areas of law. These groupings devise both treaty law and other agreements on issues such as international standards, which also involve non-governmental organizations (NGOs). International labour standards are contained in conventions initiated by the International Labour Organization (ILO). International initiatives often take the lead in encouraging countries to change their laws, for example, in raising labour and environmental standards. Many countries legislate accordingly. Hence, standards agreed at international level on ethical grounds can be said to be 'positivized' by being adopted into national law.

The UN is one of the lead players in bringing together sovereign states to co-operate in tackling international issues. The treaty is an agreement between sovereign states which obliges state parties to implement its provisions in their territories. The treaty as an instrument is in fact much older than the UN, and has long been used by countries for purposes such as ending hostilities after a war. The unique aspect of the UN's role that makes it relevant for business ethics is that it brings together a multiplicity of states to deal with global issues such as human rights and climate change. These treaties are multi-lateral instruments, often termed conventions. A multilateral treaty can take years to come into force. A treaty is negotiated and signed by an initial group of country represen-tatives. Countries then ratify it, often through a vote in the legislature, although some countries recognize treaties automatically. When the treaty is ratified, it becomes national law. Each treaty specifies the number of ratifications needed before it is said to be part of international law. The treaty remains 'open' for further states to ratify it. Some countries ratify treaties many years after they have become international law, possibly in recogni-tion of a growing international consensus on the subject.

Critics of international law stress the weak powers of enforcement at international level (Nickel, 2002). However, there are numerous bodies which oversee the implementation of treaties, and there is an international court system, which includes the International Court of Justice and the International Criminal Court. Their authority is accepted by most coun-tries, and their judgments carry the weight of international law. Hence, the combination of structures and legal instruments at international level are contributing to a growing body of supranational obligations.

From the ethical perspective, international law plays a crucial role, in that it looks to ethical principles beyond the particular laws of states. In this section, we look at two areas in which this ethical dimension is evident, which are human rights and environmental protection.

HUMAN RIGHTS LAW

The ethical foundation of human rights lies in the inherent value of the human being. This concept has underpinned a number of ethical theories (discussed in Chapter 1). These theo-ries take different views of the person in society, a consequence of which has been differing ideas about human rights. In this chapter, we introduce the main international conventions on human rights. In Chapter 9, we will look more closely at human rights in relation to busi-ness. The main categories of human rights are contained in the conventions. They include traditional natural rights and the newer concept of economic and social rights. Among the traditional rights are the rights of free speech, religious freedom, the right of association and the right to property. Also in this category is the right to life, which includes rights not to be tortured, treated inhumanely or enslaved. The rights in this category all attach to 'personhood' as their ethical foundation. They are recognized in international human rights treaties. They are also enshrined in the written constitutions of many states as a 'bill of rights'. The first ten amendments to the US Constitution constitute a bill of rights. In the UK, the Human Rights Act of 1998 was passed to incorporate the European Convention on Human Rights (ECHR). These fundamental rights derive legal force from their presence in either the constitutions or the domestic law of states.

Right to life and the right to due process refer to all people as human beings, but when incorporated into national law, tend to be referred to as rights of citizens. A consequence has been that in some contexts, citizens' rights are valued more highly than rights of non-citizens. Immigrants, especially those who enter a country illegally, typically suffer discrimination. In some countries, their rights are curtailed by law, but in many they suffer discrimination in situations where the law formally protects them.

The UN Charter in 1945 affirms in its Preamble 'faith in fundamental human rights, in the dignity and worth of the human person ...' These are not defined in the Charter, but were set out in greater detail in the Universal Declaration of Human Rights (UDHR) in 1948, discussed in detail in Chapter 9. The declaration became the basis of two conventions which followed, albeit much later, taking effect in 1976. Ratifying states are obliged to implement these conventions in their national law. We now summarize these two major treaties. The International Covenant for Civil and Political Rights (ICCPR) features the following provisions:

- A people's right to self-determination
- The right to life, including freedom from cruel, inhuman, degrading or harsh punishment
- Freedom from slavery or forced labour
- Freedoms of movement and association
- Freedom of speech and peaceful assembly
- Freedom of conscience and religion
- Right to privacy
- Equality before the law – the right to be presumed innocent; protection against discrimination on any ground such as race, colour, sex or political opinions
- Rights of citizens to vote in elections with universal and equal suffrage

As of 2012, 167 states had ratified the ICCPR. China was not among them. Although the ICCPR includes the right to life, it expressly allows the death penalty for the most serious crimes. An optional protocol banning the death penalty was voted by the UN General Assembly in 1989, and this has been ratified by 74 countries. The US ratified the original treaty, but not the optional protocol. The right to privacy has a significant proviso in that it upholds 'lawful interference', discussed in the closing case study. Other rights of particular concern to international business include the right not be subject to inhuman treatment or forced labour.

The second convention, the International Covenant for Economic, Social and Cultural Rights (ICESCR), contains the following rights:

- A people's right to self-determination
- The individual's right to work
- The right to a decent living
- The right to safe and healthy working conditions
- The right to join a trade union
- The right to adequate food, clothing and housing
- The right to education
- The right to healthcare
- The right to take part in cultural life

The ICESCR had been ratified by 160 states by 2012. China is among the ratifiers, but not the US, where there has been resistance to the concept of economic and social rights. These rights have a different emphasis from the traditional civil and political rights, and are more focused on the quality of life in society, touching on both political and business actors.

Figure 4.7 *Number of ratifications of human rights treaties*

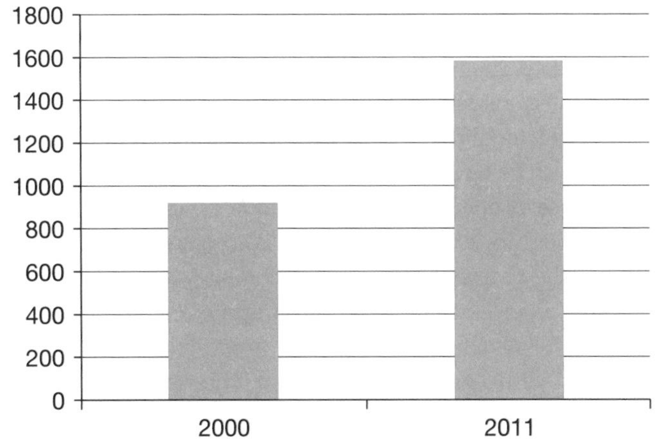

Note: 2000 – 6 treaties
2011–9 treaties and 3 optional protocols

Source of data: Pillay, N. (2012) *Strengthening the UN Human Rights Treaty Body System: A Report by the UN High Commissioner for Human Rights*, at www2.ohchr.org (18/09/14).

Economic and social rights are relevant in business activities, employment and the welfare of workers and their families. They relate closely to businesses' sense of social responsibility (discussed in Chapter 9).

Human rights treaties are overseen by UN treaty bodies and a UN High Commissioner for Human Rights. Despite the abundance of law, these offices have little power to compel states to comply. However, the existence of the law acts as a persuasive force in relation to both governments and businesses. Ratifications of the main treaties have risen significantly, as shown in Figure 4.7. Ratifying countries are obliged to submit regular reports to the treaty bodies on their compliance. As in other areas of international law, the role of NGOs is important in the governance process, involving governments, UN bodies and companies. Amnesty International and Human Rights Watch are highly respected NGOs that play important roles in the governance system. Their reporting of human rights abuses has been one of the factors that leads to changes in state and business behaviour.

Enforcement of human rights has been enhanced by the establishment of the International Criminal Court (ICC), which prosecutes individuals for war crimes, crimes against humanity and genocide. This court, based in The Hague, has supranational jurisdiction which complements that of national judicial processes. This 'complementarity' is one of its distinctive characteristics (Sands, 2013). Its jurisdiction extends to the 122 states which have ratified the treaty, the Rome Statute of 1998.

The US has not ratified the Rome Statute, although President Obama has supported the efforts of the ICC in capturing war criminals and bringing them to justice. On the other hand, the US record in human rights gives cause for concern. Since the terror attacks in New York in 2001, the US has engaged in policies against suspected terrorists which are strongly criticized as human rights violations, including torture and indefinite detention without trial. Conclusions reached by a bipartisan taskforce, the Constitution Project, criticize the continued existence of Guantánamo Bay detention facilities and the use of unmanned aerial vehicles (UAVs), known as drones, to kill suspected terrorists

(Constitution Project, 2013). Secret drone attacks authorized by the president have killed between two and three thousand people, mainly in Pakistan.

The use of drones in warfare has been subjected to legal and ethical criticism (Kreps and Kaag, 2012). A high court judgment in Pakistan has held that the drone strikes in its territory are international war crimes (Stafford Smith, 2013). Following the US precedent, other countries, including China, are acquiring drone technology for military purposes. The technology is also being applied in civilian activities: miniaturized drones are produced commercially for use by companies and individuals. While they can have legitimate uses, the private use of drones, for example, in surveillance, has potential for misuse, as pointed out by Eric Schmidt, the chairman of Google, a company itself embroiled in privacy issues (Ball, 2013). Mass surveillance of telephone and internet communications by the US National Security Agency (NSA) has been questioned on legal grounds. Assurance that these activities were carried out with legal authority have not quelled public criticism, and there have been calls for greater oversight of surveillance activities. The NSA's senior lawyer has said that the collection of data was carried out with co-operation of the large tech companies, such as Google and Yahoo, but this has been denied by the companies (Ackerman, 2014).

ENVIRONMENTAL PROTECTION LAW

Environmental protection is both a global and a local issue. Governments legislate in this area for a number of reasons, among which are national security, health and economic prosperity. Energy has become a key factor in global economic growth. China's spectacular growth has been fuelled by increased use of non-renewable fossil-based fuel, notably coal, which is a major emitter of CO_2, the main greenhouse gas. Industrialization has created jobs and fostered prosperity, but the detrimental effects of industrialization have become evident. These include pollution of air, water and soil; degradation of the ecosystems and contamination of the marine environment. Their impacts are compounded by the damaging effects of climate change. Global warming affects the entire planet, and logic dictates that global solutions are needed. But international co-operation to reduce damaging CO_2 emissions has been painfully slow.

The most important international law on climate change has been the Kyoto Protocol, a treaty which was agreed in 1997. At the heart of the Kyoto Protocol is the commitment to reduce greenhouse gas emissions. The treaty committed designated rich countries, mainly in North America and Europe, to reducing emissions to 5% below 1990 levels by 2012. Developing and emerging countries were excluded from this commitment. The treaty received widespread support from governments. The 55 parties needed to ratify it had done so by 2005. It has now been ratified by 192 countries. The US has not ratified, however, and Canada, which had, has withdrawn its ratification.

A second phase of the Kyoto Protocol aims to address emissions targets afresh, encompassing the emerging economies. Negotiations are continuing under the auspices of the UN's Framework Convention on Climate Change, which dates from the Earth Summit in 1992. That summit stressed the principle of sustainability, urging countries to ensure that the well-being of future generations should not be jeopardized by short-term goals. Despite high-profile UN meetings in Copenhagen, Durban and Doha, there has been little progress on the second phase of Kyoto. This is partly due to the unwieldiness of the

Despite high-profile UN meetings in Copenhagen, Durban and Doha, there has been little progress on the second phase of Kyoto.

gatherings. The Copenhagen talks in 2009 had 10,591 delegates from 194 countries. The largest countries tend to have the largest delegations. The smaller countries, which are often the most vulnerable to the ravages of climate change, have smaller delegations, creating an imbalance in numbers and influence. The UN's approach to these meetings is to reach agreement by consensus, not by voting. However, the large size of the gatherings makes achieving a consensus difficult. The Durban meeting in 2011 agreed that by 2015 there should be a binding agreement to succeed Kyoto. The Durban Platform, as the agreement was called, was a breakthrough in that both developed and developing countries supported it. However, Canada, Japan, New Zealand and Russia expressed unwillingness to go along with it.

The 2012 Doha meeting of delegates from 195 countries was again criticized for unwieldiness, and little progress was made towards a consensus on emissions reductions. However, an agreement was reached for aid to be channelled to poor countries for 'loss and damage' due to climate change (Harvey, 2012). For a country such as Bangladesh, which is estimated to have as many as 10 million people displaced due to natural disasters, this was a welcome breakthrough. The UN's head of climate change concluded that, in light of the limited progress of Doha, country-based initiatives are the most effective way forward to deal with the issues (Clark, 2013). Climate change legislation has been passed in a number of countries. An example is the UK's Climate Change Act 2008, which imposes carbon reduction targets. But the national route can be criticized as too weak in view of the urgent challenges of climate change.

In international efforts to deal with climate change, the ethical case has been overshadowed by national interests. From an ethical perspective, the case for emissions reductions is based on sustainability, set out in the Earth Summit in 1992. Governments recognize the need for sustainable development. China's political leaders are now more concerned than ever with the threats posed by pollution. But this concern stems less from ethical principles than from the realities of social unrest sparked by deteriorating urban conditions, especially where pollutants threaten health. China's leaders' reluctance to submit to international targets for reducing emissions reflects their focus on economic growth, but that growth is now jeopardized by environmental problems. At the same time, China's growing middle classes are becoming more concerned with qualitative issues such as pollution, which affect health and well-being. They have seen rising incomes and changing lifestyles – with more material goods, home ownership, car ownership and opportunities to travel. But the question of how sustainable these lifestyles are is now being asked in China, just as it has caused concern to people in the older industrialized countries of Europe and North America. Business responses to sustainability issues will be the focus of Chapter 10.

DIVERSE ETHICAL PERSPECTIVES IN MNES' LEGAL RELATIONS

MNEs are involved in legal relations in virtually every aspect of their business activities, from purchasing resources and services to delivering finished products to customers. National law is the dominant influence on the formation of contracts, and on the liabilities which the company incurs in a location. Companies which operate in a number of countries encounter a variety of legal systems, and also diverse cultural environments which influence how legal processes are carried out on a day-to-day basis. The company is obliged to abide by the law of the location, but this is not as straightforward as it seems. In many places, formal law and informal practices diverge. Breaches are often tolerated in practice, and businesses might find it expedient simply to go along with local practices. In some situations these practices are unethical as well as illegal, involving the payment of bribes or falsifying records. Companies which outsource manufacturing, especially in low-cost locations, are often caught up in accusations of tolerating either illegal or unethical practices of subcontractors. The MNE chooses locations for their economic advantages and takes risks, knowing that it does not control the employment of the workers who make its products. In a narrow sense, it can distance itself legally from unethical practices such as child labour because it is not the direct employer. But it cannot escape accusations of unethical conduct.

The MNE has become skilful at choosing differing countries for particular activities, taking into account the advantages (and disadvantages) of the legal system in each. Many global companies lobby governments actively to achieve changes in laws to suit their interests, including relaxation of anti-pollution laws. Where laws on environmental protection are weak, the country might well attract foreign investors who see the benefits of less regulation – whether by law or because inspection is haphazard. Is this MNE strategy itself unethical? We would probably say that it is, because the socially responsible company would take into account the impacts of its activities in local communities, whether required to do so by law or not. This approach to MNE strategy can operate in a variety of areas, from the legal registration of the company to the residence of the company for tax purposes. Although associated with globalization, this strategy is more accurately described as localization, as it rests on weighing up national differences.

The supremacy of national legal systems facilitates MNE strategy based on location advantages. The MNE can arrange its finances so that its profits arise in offshore locations such as Caribbean islands where little or no tax is payable, even though it has no activities there. If countries were to harmonize tax laws, the allure of the so-called 'tax haven' would disappear (discussed in the next chapter). Such harmonization on a global scale is highly improbable, but on a more limited scale, it is more likely. Bilateral agreements on tax between countries are common, and the EU is considering harmonization of tax laws. Many MNEs will always seek financial and other advantages among differing national environments. The company's shareholders might applaud, but such strategies are increasingly perceived by stakeholders as unethical.

Technological innovation often raises new legal and ethical issues. We have seen this in relation to medicines. Other examples are the internet and telecommunications, which are subject to differing national systems of regulation. These, too, involve ethical issues, including censorship, privacy rules and anti-competitive practices of dominant companies. Although, on ethical principles, Google has objected in the past to complying with censorship in China, it has now agreed to comply (Halliday, 2013). As we have seen, some global companies consider themselves 'above' national law when regulators are perceived as impediments to their activities, but they are eager to seize on differing national laws when there are financial advantages to be enjoyed. The phenomenon of playing off national systems against each other has long been practised. Once seen as an example of the strengths of the MNE, it is now coming to be seen in a more negative light, as a manipulative approach in which stakeholders are sacrificed for the benefit of corporate insiders.

PAUSE TO CONSIDER...

Do you consider the global company to be 'above' the law? Does it matter whether the law in question is national or international?

CONCLUSIONS

Ethical foundations of law determine its content and the ways in which it is applied. They also influence the perceptions of legitimacy and the sense of moral obligation to obey felt by governments, companies and individuals. Law is mainly a phenomenon of states and societies, and this chapter has emphasized that national law is the basis of most of an MNE's international transactions. However, the chapter has also highlighted the differing historical, cultural and political environments that determine the content of the law and how it is applied. These, as we have seen, can be highly diverse. There are some common ethical themes, but moral issues tend to be viewed differently in different cultures, with inevitable impacts on the legal system. Justice in one location is sometimes far removed from what would be seen as justice in another. It is perhaps no wonder that in a globalized world, international agencies and MNEs alike seek to measure national legal systems against criteria under the broad heading of the rule of law. Of course, these, too, are subject to fluctuation. But they indicate a genuine tendency to identify universal principles to which all national legal systems should adhere.

The rule of law as a set of principles is essentially ethical, stressing human dignity and equality before the law. The rule of law is not an all-or-nothing phenomenon, and it is true to say that it is more of an ideal than a set of criteria which are measurable. States must continually respond to internal and external threats as they perceive them. But most state governments now appreciate that legal reforms to establish and maintain the rule of law benefit society and also benefit business activities. The country with an efficient, fair and transparent legal system is likely to be seen as an attractive place to do business by foreign investors.

Countries are keenly aware of national competitive advantage, but this does not imply a go-it-alone attitude. They are increasingly engaged in international governance structures, often to enhance their own domestic credentials. This co-operative activity indicates a willingness to tackle global issues through international agreement, with the result that national laws become modified to conform to international standards. A state sometimes subscribes to internationally agreed principles, but makes exceptions in practice if it senses national interest might be at stake. A shift in this behaviour can come about through states perceiving a growing international consensus. It can also come about through governments taking an enlightened view of long-term national interest. Similarly, international firms are now accepting the validity of looking beyond national law to internationally recognized ethical principles.

REFERENCES

Ackerman, S. (2014) 'US tech giants knew of NSA data collection, agency's top lawyer insists', *The Guardian*, 19 March, at www.theguardian.com/world/2014/mar/19/us-tech-giants-knew-nsa-data-collection-rajesh-de (26/09/14).

Ball, J. (2013) 'Drones should be banned from private use, says Google's Eric Schmidt', *The Guardian*, 13 April, at www.theguardian.com/technology/2013/apr/21/drones-google-eric-schmidt (26/09/14).

Bälz, K. (2008) 'Sharia risk? How Islamic finance has transformed Islamic contract law', *Harvard Law School Occasional Publication 9*, Islamic Legal Studies Programme, at www.law.harvard.edu/programs/ilsp/publications/balz.pdf (26/09/14).

BBC (2013) *Human genome: US Supreme Court hears patent case*, 15 April, at www.bbc.co.uk/news/world-us-canada-22157410 (26/09/14).

Belton, R. (2005) *Competing Definitions of the Rule of Law, Carnegie Paper No. 55*, Carnegie Endowment for International Peace, at www.carnegieendowment.org/2005/01/21/competing-definitions-of-rule-of-law-implications-for-practitioners/1uv5 (26/09/14).

Bravin, J. and Kendall, B. (2013) 'Justices strike down gene patents', *Wall Street Journal*, 13 June, at www.wsj.com (18/09/14).

Carothers, T. (1998) 'The rule of law revival', *Foreign Affairs*, 77(2): 95–106.

Chatterjee, P. (2013) 'India's first compulsory licence upheld, but legal fights likely to continue', *Intellectual Property Watch*, 4 March, at www.ip-watch.org (18/09/14).

Clark, P. (2013) 'Progress at glacial pace in UN talks on emissions', *Financial Times*, 23 January.

Coleman, C. (2009) 'The legal case of the snail found in ginger beer', *BBC*, 20 November, at www.bbc.co.uk.

Constitution Project (2013) *Report on Detainee Treatment*, at http://detaineetaskforce.org (18/09/14).

Cotterrell, R. (2000) 'Common law approaches to the relationship between law and morality', *Ethical Theory and Moral Practice*, 3(1): 9–26.

Gluckman, M. (1963) *Custom and Conflict in Africa* (Oxford: Basil Blackwell).

Griffiths, A. (1983) 'Legal duality: Conflict or concord in Botswana?', *Journal of African Law*, 27(2): 150–61.

Halliday, J. (2013) 'Google's dropped anti-censorship warning marks quiet defeat in China', *The Guardian*, 7 January, at www.guardian.co.uk

Hart, H.L.A. (1961) *The Concept of Law* (Oxford: Clarendon Press).

Harvey, F. (2012) 'Doha climate change deal clears way for damage aid to poor nations', *The Observer*, 8 December, at www.guardian.co.uk

Hille, K. (2011) 'China expected to increase antitrust probes', *Financial Times*, 14 November.

Iwobi, A. (2004) 'Tiptoeing through a constitutional minefield: the great Sharia controversy in Nigeria', *Journal of African Law*, 48(2): 111–64.

Joireman, S. (2001) 'Inherited legal systems and effective rule of law: Africa and the colonial legacy', *The Journal of Modern African Studies*, 39(4): 571–96.

Kreps, S. and Kaag, J. (2012) 'The use of unmanned aerial vehicles in contemporary conflict: A legal and ethical analysis', *Polity*, 44(2): 260–85.

Lookofsky, J. (2011) 'Not running wild in the CISG', *Journal of Law and Commerce*, 29(2): 141–69.

Merryman, J.H. (1985) *The Civil Law Tradition*, 2nd edn (Stanford: Stanford University Press).

Michaels, R. (2007) 'The true Lex Mercatoria: Law beyond the state', *Indiana Journal of Global Legal Studies*, 14(2): 447–68.

Mohammed, N. (1988) 'Principles of Islamic contract law', *Journal of Law and Religion*, 6(1): 115–30.

Nickel, J. (2002) 'Is today's international human rights system a global governance regime?', *The Journal of Ethics*, 6(4): 253–71.

Rawls, J. (1971) *A Theory of Justice* (Oxford: Oxford University Press).

Rawls, J. (1999) *The Law of Peoples* (Cambridge, MA: Harvard University Press).

Reinhart, K. (1983) 'Islamic law as Islamic ethics', *Journal of Religious Ethics*, 11(2): 186–203.

Rödl, F. (2008) 'Private law beyond the democratic order?', *The American Journal of Comparative Law*, 56(3): 743–67.

Sands, P. (2013) 'Introduction' to Lauterpacht, H., *An international bill of rights of man* (Oxford: Oxford University Press).

Sen, A. (2010) *The Idea of Justice* (London: Penguin).

Skaaning, S.-E. (2010) 'Measuring the rule of law', *Political Research Quarterly*, 63(2): 449–60.

Stafford Smith, C. (2013) 'Will Pakistan finally stand up against illegal US drone attacks?', *The Guardian*, 12 May, at www.guardian.co.uk (18/09/14).

Stiglitz, J. (2002) *Globalization and its Discontents* (London: Allen Lane).

Upham, F. (2002) *Mythmaking and the Rule of Law Orthodoxy, Carnegie Paper No. 30*, Carnegie Endowment for International Peace, at www.carnegieendowment.org/2002/09/10/mythmaking-in-rule-of-law-orthodoxy/47s4 (26/09/14).

Wembridge, M. (2013) 'AB InBev rejigs Modelo offer in effort to win DoJ support', *Financial Times*, 15 February.

REVIEW QUESTIONS

1 In what ways is equality before the law an ethical principle? How does it impact on international business?

2 Common law legal systems are prevalent in many advanced economies that are home to large MNEs. In what ways does this suggest that such systems are attractive from a business perspective?

3 What are the risks to the rule of law in African states highlighted in the chapter, and how do

these affect the business ethics of foreign investors?

4 Mixed legal systems are found in many emerging economies. What challenges do they pose for international business?

5 What are the ethical issues facing the large pharmaceutical companies which have traditionally focused on R&D?

6 In industries where there are a few large players, practices such as price-fixing and carving up markets are possible, and difficult for regulators to detect. What is unethical about these practices?

7 Why is the positivist dismissive of international law? On what grounds could supporters of international law take issue with the positivist approach?

8 What are the differences in the types of human rights covered by the two UN conventions outlined in this chapter?

9 What are the weaknesses of the UN's approach of trying to achieve a consensus on emissions reductions in climate change talks?

10 Why are MNE strategies of looking for the most advantageous legal environments attracting criticism on ethical grounds?

CLOSING CASE STUDY

Photo 4.2 *Who is using your personal data, and for what purposes?* (Getty)

DATA PROTECTION LAWS STRUGGLE TO KEEP UP WITH PRIVACY CONCERNS

Users of the internet are well aware of advertisements targeted at them personally, which regularly appear on web pages. Companies such as Facebook, Twitter and Google, count on advertising to bring in profits. Tracking technology has become highly refined, allowing companies to gather and send users' information to numerous locations. A website can turn names and email addresses into code which is sent to third parties, who also receive encoded personal data from email lists of advertisers. The two datasets can be matched, and the website shows the targeted advertisement, even though no actual email addresses have been sent. Social media networks, in particular, facilitate tracking. Advertisers gain large amounts of information collected online regarding the user's browsing habits, online purchases and other information which users are often unaware is being systematically collected. This information is gathered, collected and sold to other firms, which gain valuable insights about the user's private life. A user must agree to the terms and conditions set out by the company. Typically, these are lengthy statements, in which crucial terms do not stand out. A company such as Facebook or Google, has a single set of terms which all users must agree to, whatever their location in the world. However, the terms are still subject to national law, as is the use of data by these companies.

The right to privacy is recognized as a human right, but it is not absolute. The UN Convention on Civil and Political Rights speaks of the right to privacy against 'arbitrary or unlawful interference'. This broad principle can refer to data obtained by private-sector companies or public authorities. Governments justify interception of personal data on grounds of national security or suspected criminal activity. Still, state access to personal data can cause controversy, and a balance must be struck between security and individual privacy. A proposed UK Communications Data Bill in 2012 aroused much criticism as a 'snoopers' charter'. Under the scheme, internet service providers and telecoms companies would log customers' emails, text messages and browsing habits. Access would be limited to the police, security officials, and tax authorities, but other bodies, including local councils and other public-sector bodies also wished to have access. In response to criticisms, the government redrafted the bill, but it was rejected in 2013 by the coalition partners, the Liberal Democrats, who are traditionally strong advocates of civil liberties (Watts, 2013).

Regulation of the handling of personal data by private-sector companies has been revised as technology has progressed, but the law tends to lag behind technological developments (Burn-Murdoch, 2013). For example, cloud computing services and cloud-stored data would now possibly warrant separate legislation. The UK Data Protection Act 1998 sets out data protection principles. In principle, data must be collected for specific purposes and used only for those purposes. These purposes should be conveyed clearly to the person whose data is collected (the data 'subject'). However, companies have become adroit at interpreting this principle broadly, to include other purposes they deem to be legitimate, giving themselves maximum scope to collect and sell personal data in ways that would probably come as an unwelcome surprise to many people (Burn-Murdoch, 2013). A European Directive of 1995 (which the UK's 1998 Act implements) applied to both public and private bodies, and

allowed collection of data for specified, explicit and legitimate purposes, but this is now perceived as in need of tightening up to redress the balance more towards the individual.

The directive has been implemented in different ways in different member states, creating a patchwork of laws. A new EU regulation has been proposed, which would supplant these national laws, creating a single data protection law for the EU. The proposal from the Justice Commissioner would tighten up controls on companies considerably. It would require consent to be explicit in each case of data transfer. It would also contain a 'right to be forgotten', allowing individual users to compel social media companies to erase their personal data. There would be flexibility: if the company has passed on the data to third parties, it can only request that the data be removed. Under the original proposal, a breach could result in a fine of up to 2% of global turnover. Such a punitive fine has been one of the most controversial aspects of the proposal. Large US technology companies, including Google, Facebook, Amazon and Yahoo, have lobbied European Members of Parliament (MEPs) for changes to the regulation to allow them more flexibility.

The US Government has also exerted pressure on EU authorities of the proposed regulation. However, many MEPs have reacted adversely to the intense lobbying, especially in light of their own concerns about US legislation. New anti-terrorist measures were enacted in the Patriot Act of 2002, which gives US law enforcement agencies power to access personal data held outside the US by any company based in the US. Microsoft and Google, which have operations in Europe, have admitted that they would have to divulge data about Europeans held by their cloud-computing services in Europe, even though this would be in violation of EU law. UK defence company, BAE Systems, decided against contracting for Microsoft's cloud-based service because of this risk. The new regulation would make clear that non-European companies will be covered by European data protection law when they hold data on European individuals and companies, and this protection extends to data sent to destinations outside Europe.

Several governments, including the UK and Germany, have expressed concern over the workability of the proposed regulation, including the administrative burden it would place on the technology companies. The UK has even spoken of opting out on certain measures, such as the right to be forgotten. The use of strong legislative powers reflects EU concerns over privacy of data and also concern over the huge power enjoyed by the large technology companies. In 2013, revelations obtained through leaks showed largescale electronic surveillance by the US National Security Agency, penetrating telephone and internet communications in countries considered friendly as well as those considered enemies. These revelations sounded alarm bells around the world, implicating US companies in these activities. Following these revelations, US companies are now likely to face even greater scrutiny over their adherence to privacy terms.

Sources: Batchelor, C. (2012) 'Privacy: US and EU clash on confidentiality', *Financial Times*, 22 May; Fontenalla-Khan, J. (2013) 'Brussels fights against US data privacy push', *Financial Times*, 10 February; Burn-Murdoch, J. (2013) 'Data protection law is in danger of lagging behind technological change', *The Guardian*, 12 April; Bowcott, O. (2013) 'Britain seeks opt-out of new European social media privacy laws', *The Guardian*, 4 April; Watts, R. (2013) 'Home office faces legal challenge unless it reveals details of snoopers' charter', *The Telegraph*, 20 April, at www.telegraph.com/uk (18/09/14).

DISCUSSION QUESTIONS

- **What is the ethical reasoning behind data protection law?**

- **In what ways can the large technology companies be criticized for their practices? Is there are risk of 'backlash' from users?**

- **How confident are you that your own personal details are not being misused by technology companies, including social media?**

CHAPTER 5

FINANCIAL MARKETS: WHAT ROLE FOR ETHICS?

ETHICAL THEMES IN THIS CHAPTER

- Businesses as part of society
- Governance and responsibility

THE AIMS OF THIS CHAPTER ARE TO

- Identify the ethical issues in global finance
- Become familiar with the processes taking place in global finance which have ethical implications
- Appreciate the role of regulation in ensuring fairness and transparency in financial markets
- Consider measures for reforming finance globally from social and ethical viewpoints

CHINA'S SHADOW FINANCE SECTOR

Although China has introduced dramatic market reforms in its economy, the government has a reputation for keeping a tight grip on major financial institutions through ownership and regulation. Its leading banks are all state-owned. They have grown rapidly in their domestic market and are now expanding globally through acquisitions. However, strict banking regulation has led to the rise of a more informal sector known as 'shadow finance', which, although offering alternatives to the official banks, is becoming enmeshed in mainstream banking. The extent to which this might cause financial instability is a cause for concern in China – and internationally.

OPENING CASE STUDY

Photo 5.1 *At risk of collapse? The financing of China's booming construction industry depends on a variety of investment mechanisms whose soundness raises concerns.* (© iStock.com/bo1982)

Growing demand for financial services from both individuals and businesses across China is a reflection of deepening domestic markets and increasing wealth among the new middle class. However, ironically, it poses a dilemma for the government, which wants to maintain control and stability but at the same time encourage growth. China has experienced a housing boom, fuelled largely by ambitious property developers. In measures designed to cool the market, the government has made it more difficult for developers to obtain loans to finance their projects. But new developments continue to appear, as the industry taps into loans from the unofficial banking sector, through channels which operate as shadow banks. Also having difficulty obtaining loans are China's millions of small businesses, who are vital to economic growth. They, too, have turned to shadow banking. The unofficial sector has grown rapidly, and is estimated to be worth between 13.6 trn and 24.4 trn yuan, which would amount to 50% of GDP (Rabinovitch, 3 December 2012).

Should the growth of shadow banking be a cause of worry? There is no precise definition of shadow banking. It covers numerous types of firm, including finance companies and pawnbrokers, which are legal businesses, but not legally banks, therefore escaping banking regulations. Chief among these businesses are companies referred to as 'trusts', which operate like investment funds. They take in investors' money for

specific projects, offering returns that are higher than they would get from a bank. Trusts lend the money to high-risk customers such as property developers. The risk of default is a concern, especially in the context of a volatile housing market. If the borrower defaults, investors are at risk. This risk has been compared to that which caused the crash in the US housing market in 2008, following a housing boom which was encouraged by the easy availability of loans (Bloomberg News, 2013).

In moves similar to financial institutions elsewhere in the world, shadow banking has also expanded the range products it offers. Ordinary Chinese people, disappointed with low returns on bank deposits, are increasingly tempted by 'wealth management products' (WMPs). WMPs offer guaranteed returns higher than ordinary deposits, but they are opaque. They can be spread among equities, bonds, money markets or inter-bank markets. They can also be invested in shadow banking activities such as non-bank loans. The risks are difficult to assess, for both the customers and those offering the products. These products are offered by mainstream banks as alternatives to deposits, but customers are often unaware that their money is finding its way into the shadow sector. Banks offer their own WMPs and also act as intermediaries, offering WMPs of third parties such as trust companies. Many of these WMPs do not specify the nature of the investment. One that did specify the investment was the Bank of Hebei, which sold WMPs to finance a trust loan to the parent company of RiseSun Real Estate, a property developer. In Langfang, a city within commuting distance from Beijing, RiseSun is building a 10,000-apartment complex, and five other similar ones in the area. For development on such a huge scale, the firm would not have obtained loans from banks directly, but banks are now involved in its financing – through the back door.

The Bank of Hebei WMP was one year duration, but WMPs are typically shorter term, lasting one to three months. Banks have tended to place the incoming money in a funding pool, which takes in inflows from selling new products and pays out on mature products. This practice, likened to a Ponzi scheme, is highly risky, and has been banned by a new regulation in 2013 (Yong and Sweeney, 2013). A worry is that in the case of default, the bank would be unable to pay out. Customers are likely to assume that, as WMPs are sold by the bank, the bank's guarantee applies as if the money were in an ordinary deposit. They trust the bank with their investment, but the status of the investment could be unclear. Some WMPs have failed, and customers have suffered losses. The WMPs which the banks sell on behalf of the trust companies fall outside the regulatory system. The banks tend to channel WMPS into off-balance sheet vehicles, making their status opaque.

The Chinese government has allowed the growth in WMPs to take place, as they fulfil roles in the economy which the official sector cannot meet. China's state media have warned investors that WMPs are not guaranteed by the government. However, regulators are now concerned about the risks. Should banks themselves be liable on the losses from shadow banks whose products they handle? A difficulty is that official banking and shadow banking are entwined in practice, and risk spreads to the mainstream banks. Ordinary Chinese people have flocked to invest their savings in products which they assume are low-risk.

The growing popularity of banking and investment services among ordinary citizens in the advanced capitalist economies has led to a debate on the balance between encouraging investment and safeguarding individual investors. Financial institutions are obliged to give customers accurate information regarding the nature of the investment and level of risk. Even so, these countries have seen numerous financial scandals, including misselling of financial products, in which ordinary citizens have suffered losses. Shadow banking has risen in importance in these countries too, largely in response to the greater regulation imposed on banks following the financial crisis of 2008. Regulators in these markets are keenly aware that citizens can turn on elected leaders when there is a banking scandal, voicing a common view that governments are ultimately responsible for the country's financial stability. China's leaders could well start to feel the weight of blame from ordinary citizens for a shadow banking system whose rapid growth now calls for greater transparency and regulation.

Sources: Davies, P. (2013) 'Appetite grows for overseas acquisitions', *Financial Times*, 25 March; Yong, X. and Sweeney, P. (2013) 'China issues new rules targeting wealth management fund pools', *Reuters*, 10 May, at www.reuters.com; Rabinovitch, S. (2012) 'Uncertain foundations', *Financial Times*, 3 December; Rabinovitch, S. (2012) 'China hit by wealth product scandals', *Financial Times*, 28 December; Bloomberg (2013) *Soros Sees China Shadow-Banking Risks Similar to Subprime*, 8 April, at www.bloomberg.com; Alloway, T. (2011) 'Traditional lenders shiver as shadow banking grows', *Financial Times*, 29 December; PwC (2012) *Report on Foreign Banks in China*, July, at www.pwccn.com (18/09/14).

DISCUSSION QUESTIONS

- What is shadow banking, and why has it grown in China?

- When the bank sells a WMP to an investor, is there a moral obligation to warn of the risks, or just the duty to abide by legal regulations?

- How does China differ from other countries in which there is a shadow banking sector?

INTRODUCTION

International business depends on finance to raise funds and carry out transactions, but finance as a function has grown far beyond these roles. It has become a global sphere in its own right, and one which is so powerful that, if things go wrong, the stability of companies, countries, and indeed the whole global economy, can be threatened. On the good side, global finance has opened up opportunities for businesses and societies to prosper. The growing pervasiveness of market values and culture change has invigorated economies and helped to deliver social goods. Emerging economies are examples of the benefits of greater financial integration globally, but also the risks. Finding a balance between market values and social ethics is key to retaining the benefits of financial globalization while controlling the destabilizing risks.

This chapter will present relevant aspects of global finance in relatively simple terms, focusing on the players and processes which highlight the ethical dilemmas posed by financial markets. It begins with an overview of how ethical perceptions of finance have changed. It goes on to discuss the principles of company incorporation and personal responsibility, which lie at the heart of business ethics. Much of this discussion draws on legal distinctions, reminding us that law and ethics are often entwined. We then look at financial markets, their players and the people who benefit, as well as those who lose out. The later sections focus on ethical principles and regulation in the financial sphere. The image of finance as an activity closer to gambling than any other in the panoply of business activities presents challenges for regulators. But the ethical dimension is now more relevant than ever, as companies, governments and ordinary citizens are urging an ethical reconfiguration of international finance.

THE EVOLVING ETHICAL PERSPECTIVES OF FINANCE

Businesses, governments and individuals: every organization and individual must engage in finance at some level. Even religious organizations dedicated wholly to other-worldly goals need to sustain themselves financially. Finance as a function involves money transactions – buying, selling, lending, investing and many other related activities. In a for-profit enterprise, these transactions managed as a whole aim to grow wealth, allowing the gains to be used as owners desire. The ethical foundations of finance are associated with those of capitalism, based on the idea of individuals and organizations pursuing their own self-interest. From the religious and moral perspective, however, not all finance is the same. Historically, loans of money involving the payment of interest, or usury, has been considered immoral by Christian churches (and also in Islam, discussed in the previous chapter). Churches have gained in wealth through property ownership and trading activities, which deal with real assets, producing products of value to society. In contrast to productive activities, purely financial activities are viewed as more dubious morally, as they appear to focus on money for money's sake. The aura of money has a distinctly unethical tinge: wealth and ethics are uncomfortable partners.

Banking has existed since the middle ages. Bankers and their services have been essential in the running of governments, industries on every scale, and services that everyone needs. Financial services can be a means to an end, the end being something more than simply making more money. Prices reflect values and serve to allocate resources, fulfilling a socially

Whereas making money for some other purpose can be justified ethically, making money as a goal in itself – suggesting greed for its own sake – cannot.

legitimate role (Raines and Leathers, 1994). Bankers and financial intermediaries are important business players, doing the deals which finance productive economic activities. Finance plays a crucial role in the growth of businesses, and is part of the capitalist ethos. But finance also plays a role in delivering societal goods. As economies develop, bankers provide services for ordinary consumers, such as mortgages for house purchase. Financial investments also fund the pensions on which people depend in retirement. Hence, finance is multifaceted, serving business goals and also social ends. A development which we will highlight in this chapter is the transformation of finance into an end in itself. The ethical implications have been dramatic. Whereas making money for some other purpose can be justified ethically, making money as a goal in itself – suggesting greed for its own sake – cannot.

In recent decades, finance has become globalized, greatly expanding its activities, geographic scope and investment products. Financial globalization has been facilitated by advances in information technology and communications, leading to greater interconnectedness between financial markets. The established market economies in Europe and North America have led the way in financial developments, signalling a spread of market values globally, as shown in Figure 5.1. The figure highlights the roles of companies and regulators. Corporate players have played lead roles in global capital markets, often through speculative activities. They have been encouraged by national authorities whose liberalization agendas extol the benefits of markets. Liberalizing a domestic economy does not necessarily lead to the opening of the economy to foreign participation and ownership. Some economies, such as the rapidly developing economies of Asia in the 1990s, opened their financial markets too hastily, exposing their economies to new risks from globalizing financial flows. The Asian 'tiger' economies had seen the opportunities of foreign investment, but the Asian crisis of 1997–8 alerted the world to the risks of globally mobile capital.

Figure 5.1 *Finance and the spread of market values*

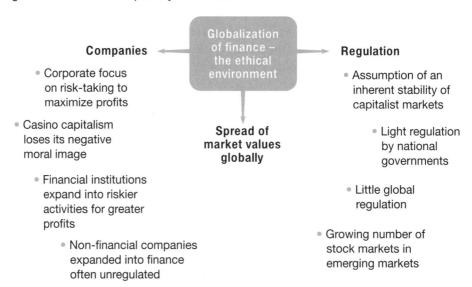

In the Asian economies, liberal reforms overlaid institutions in environments which are traditionally more group-oriented than individualist, creating moral tensions. These were aggravated by the market-oriented reforms dictated by the IMF, and known as the 'Washington consensus'. Financial liberalization, one of the main tenets of IMF policy, proved disastrously destabilizing in a number of Asian and Latin American economies in the 1980s and 1990s (Arestis, 2004). More recently, emerging economies have implemented domestic reforms guided by strong state policies, partly from a perspective of cultural values based on the state as an ethical force. Markets are viewed with some suspicion as being motivated only by self-interested companies. These countries are also suspicious of flawed IMF liberalization policies of the past. State capitalism, as we saw in Chapter 2, embraces capitalist markets within a context of national priorities. In China, whole sectors, such as energy, banking and telecommunications, are predominantly state-owned, although increasingly globalized in reach. **Privatization** has been crucial to liberalization in post-communist economies, transforming state-owned enterprises into listed companies which offer shares to private investors. Privatization signals a cultural shift to market-driven strategies, although in many of these new companies the state still has a significant owner-ship stake.

The growing financial sector in many western countries, most notably the US and UK, has been facilitated by light-touch regulation, as shown in Figure 5.1. Financial institutions in these countries have been at the forefront of global finance. They reflect the ethics of the utilitarian view of markets – that social welfare is achieved by limited regulatory interfer-ence, allowing the maximization of benefits. But the utilitarian's view of benefits is rooted firmly in the wealth maximization of the individual, rather than any higher sense of social ethics. The evolution of business forms such as companies, MNEs and other entities has enabled individuals to utilize channels for maximizing financial gain for themselves, while minimizing liabilities and risks which their businesses incur. Advantages stem from the corporate form, as we discuss in the next section. Also advantageous for businesses has been the new geographical scope which is opened up by globalization.

Businesses with international aspirations have benefited from the new financial opportu-nities. A business might struggle to get a loan from the banks in its home country to fund expansion, but it can now look to multiple foreign investors and also loans from overseas sources. A company can now register in a country other than its home country. It can list on a stock exchange in yet another country, possibly near its main markets. And it might attract shareholders from a number of countries. These possibilities are not confined to businesses from advanced economies. Companies from emerging economies are among those seeking to grow by tapping global capital markets.

SMEs are able to internationalize more rapidly because of developments in global finance. While these financial advantages are applauded by SMEs, there are also drawbacks. It is arguable that in earlier eras, the SME which was firmly rooted in the home country operated in an identifiable cultural context which provided the foundations for its corpo-rate culture. For such a company, customers were close at hand, and its managers often had personal ties with them. Customer ties had an immediate moral dimension. The company which seeks to globalize from the outset is operating outside this societal context. Its values are dominated by market considerations, and its customers are envisaged in greater abstrac-tion: they are seen as markets rather than as individual consumers. With globalization, market considerations tended to crowd out moral contexts.

Finance has shifted from being instrumental in nature – a means to achieving some other goal – to being an end in itself.

Financial institutions have expanded the range of investments on offer. Innovative investments include derivatives, which are products that depend on the value of another asset which itself can be difficult to measure. For example, debt can be packaged as securities and traded, but the underlying security for the debt could well deteriorate, as in the case of mortgage-backed securities in the US housing boom of 2006–7.

Derivatives offer greater potential for gain, but also carry greater risk than traditional investments such as simply purchasing shares in a company. Much of this development has occurred under the radar of regulation. Stock exchanges are regulated by national authorities, but much trade in derivative products has been largely unregulated. Finance has shifted from being instrumental in nature – a means to achieving some other goal – to being an end in itself (Soppe, 2004). Many companies whose core businesses are in other sectors have become involved in financial activities, often unregulated. General Electric of the US is an example: an industrial company whose financial subsidiary became its most profitable division. Finance has moved more to centre stage, now seen as more lucrative than activities such as primary production and manufacturing. Its potential for wealth maximization has gone hand in hand with more speculative – and risky – strategies. The analogy with gambling is often made, as in the term, casino capitalism (Raines and Leathers, 1994).

The early 1900s saw the introduction of innovative financial products similar to today's derivatives, but there was considerable hostility in the US to such products on moral grounds because of their similarity to gambling. This was a period in which morality infused ideas of social welfare: gambling was socially harmful, and this outweighed the gains which might be enjoyed from alternative investments (Raines and Leathers, 1994). Regulation was considered desirable to promote public goods. The Sherman Antitrust Act of 1890 was passed in an era of huge business empires. It was intended to curtail monopolists and anti-competitive practices, thus benefiting consumers and promoting fairer markets. But courts have tended to take a lenient view of business interests in interpreting the legislation. Legal distinctions were established between gambling and other financial activities deemed to be legitimate. As markets became ever more influential and profitable, the voices of moral critics grew fainter. Gambling – now a large industry further boosted from online gaming – is ringfenced by legal frameworks, and is no longer subject to the moral condemnation it had a century ago. Even states operate national lotteries to fund public goods. The benefits of markets triumphed over moral criticisms. The analogy between gambling and risky financial investments no longer seems shocking. In 1985, even the US regulator, the Securities and Exchange Commission, was speaking of self-regulation as the goal, with a code of ethics for unregulated markets (Raines and Leathers, 1994). At about the same time, however, an analysis of the dangers of global finance, *Casino Capitalism*, was published by Susan Strange (Strange, 1986). The risks she highlighted did not lead to a retreat. Global finance continued to grow, reaching wider markets and growing in size. Its surge was halted only by the crisis of 2008.

The crisis shone a spotlight on practices in the financial sector which had become globalized and highly interconnected, in an environment of limited and patchwork regulation. Along with the feeling that global finance had spun out of control was the feeling that this somehow symbolized a crisis of capitalism itself, where the culture of greed and profits-at-all-costs had come to dominate. Governments played a significant role in shoring up the banks and imposing regulatory reforms, including the bolstering of banks' capital bases.

Debate centred on the extent to which banking and finance should be reined in to serve societal goals. Can the culture and values of finance be reshaped to bring ethical principles back in? An implication of any restructuring could see institutions retreating from global aspirations and becoming more national in focus (Wolf, 2012). It would also imply greater oversight of markets and companies, which governments have been reluctant to do in a world which worships national competitive advantages.

PAUSE TO CONSIDER...

Who are the winners and losers from the globalization of financial markets? To what extent is it fair to say that an ethical vacuum lies at the heart of global finance, and that this has been responsible for much of the excessive risk which has led to global financial instability?

COMPANY STATUS VERSUS PERSONAL RESPONSIBILITY

A recurring theme in the ethics of finance is where risk and responsibility lie. Every business must manage risk, from the micro-firm to the large MNE. The company as a legal form allows risk to be dispersed and also spreads personal responsibility for the running of the business. This has greatly facilitated business expansion, but it has also attracted critics, who see personal accountability as an ethical principle which is being eroded.

The company is a highly versatile organizational form, with flexibility to grow from a small enterprise to a complex multinational based on the same essential structures. The company or corporation as an entity is an artificial person with a separate legal existence from the people who form it. It is conceptually different from an association of people who come together to do business. An implication of this distinction is the notion of the interest of the company as a whole, as distinct from the aggregate of the interests of individual owners. Owners tend to see a company as furthering their personal interests, but the logic of separate legal identity implies that these are not the same as that of the company (discussed further in Chapter 8). The company takes on a life of its own: it endures beyond the lives of owners, who come and go.

The company can be free-standing or linked to a group of companies, each treated legally as a separate entity. The multinational comprises numerous separate companies in different locations: a parent company with oversight of the group, and many subsidiaries. The parent company is typically a shareholder in its subsidiaries. A company can invest in other companies as a financial investment or as a means of exerting control through an ownership stake (discussed in Chapter 2). A company which is part of a supply chain is likely to invest in linked companies, forming a network of ownership ties. In today's globalized environment, a company might have numerous such investments, and affiliate companies will also have numerous ties. The company is likely to have disparate owners with divergent interests, and its executives themselves have their own interests. The notion of the company as owing responsibilities to *stakeholders*, rather than just *shareholders*, fits in with the legal and philosophical view of the company as a separate person: the shareholders are not privileged in the way that the merely economic view of the company would assume.

The origins of the modern company go back to the era of growing trade in Europe in the seventeenth century (Ferguson, 2009). The joint-stock company allowed people to come together as investors, to embark on business activities greater than any of the individuals could achieve separately. Each investor would become a shareholder in the enterprise. The most illustrious early example was the Dutch East India Company, established by state charter in 1602. Its organization displayed an astonishing array of innovations which were catalysts in later capitalist development, and which are crucial to the modern MNE. These include the idea of permanent capital in the company, the separation of ownership and management, limited liability of shareholders and tradable shares. The Dutch East India Company was able to mount largescale trading activities, often linked to colonization, which, although risky, offered the prospect of payouts to the investors from the profits, now known as dividends (Gelderblom et al., 2012). This company was closely intertwined with the Dutch state, and its expansionist activities were based on warfare as much as trade. A forerunner of today's ethical investor, one shareholder, a Mennonite, withdrew from the company in 1605 because it was profiting from warfare (Ferguson, 2009: 132) (Note 1).

An advantage offered to investors was limited liability. This meant that if the project failed, the shareholder would lose the money invested, but would not be liable for the company's debts. The concept of limited liability is an advantage that the company enjoys over unincorporated businesses. It is also an advantage over traditional partnerships, which involve people entering business together for common gain, although there is now a form of limited partnership open to businesses, which has grown in popularity.

In the two centuries which followed the early trading companies, companies proliferated as capitalist economies developed. But limited liability was slow to be generally adopted in national legislation. Unlimited liability was linked to the principle of personal responsibility for the business, implying a moral view that the person who forms a company should be responsible if it fails. Owners of unincorporated businesses and partnerships faced the liabilities of the business, and it was thought morally wrong that a businessperson whose company failed could retain personal wealth while creditors got nothing. This viewpoint was especially strong in banking. In a banking collapse, depositors stood to lose all, and it seemed morally repugnant that the personal wealth of owners would be untouched, especially as they are ultimately responsible for the running of the company. Only by the end of the nineteenth century had most countries adopted limited liability. Until the early twentieth century, banks had unlimited liability, but converted to limited liability following numerous bank failures in the closing decades of the nineteenth century.

There are still firms that retain unlimited liability, among them Swiss private banks. But this situation is changing following the closure of a Swiss private bank, Wegelin, in January 2013. Wegelin had been investigated by the US Justice Department in relation to the bank's possible liability in helping US citizens to avoid tax. Following Wegelin's closure, two of Switzerland's remaining private banks announced they were converting to limited companies (Marriage, 2013). The managing partner of one said that the traditional private banks 'contribute to the stability of the financial system. If we take too much risk, we lose our shirt' (Schäfer and Shotter, 2013). Where business owners face personal responsibility, they tend to take fewer risks and are less inclined to aggressive expansion (Freedman, 2000). Because of their conservatism, Swiss private banks withstood the financial crisis better than the more ambitious global banks exposed to volatile markets.

'If we take too much risk, we lose our shirt.'

The link between personal responsibility and the principle of unlimited liability highlights a principle which is sometimes overlooked. In a small company, the owners and shareholders are likely to be the same people. Here it is arguably justified that the owners, who are both the directors and shareholders, should take on the risk of failure. Through limited liability, that risk shifts to the creditors, creating 'moral hazard' (Freedman, 2000).

Moral hazard operates to give owners a sense of freedom from responsibility, as others will have to bear the losses. In a large company with many shareholders, by contrast, directors and managers run the company, and shareholders are not directly involved. They perform a monitoring function, but their oversight is necessarily limited. When the company fails, the managers, not the shareholders, are mainly to blame. For this reason, limited liability seems more justifiable in principle.

There are risks that directors will act irresponsibly, hiding behind the corporate identity. Businesspeople can set up companies in offshore locations for purposes such as funnelling profits away from tax authorities. The 'special purpose entity', which provides secrecy and anonymity for a variety of purposes, can be kept off a company's accounts, as noted in the opening case study. The device featured strongly in the case of Enron, the energy-trading company which collapsed in 2001. A body of law on exceptions to the principle of limited liability has developed, enabling courts to look behind the 'veil of incorporation' to the individuals involved, holding them personally liable. They will be liable in cases of criminal wrongdoing such theft, false accounting and fraudulent trading. The CEO of Enron was sentenced to 24 years in prison. More common than outright crime is the grey area of management decisions on matters such as acquisitions or high-risk investments which, with hindsight, were misguided. Many bank executives, especially in the US and UK, have been criticized for excessive risk-taking and a culture of greed in the years leading up to the financial crisis. Over-expansion financed by debt was ill judged, but this does not mean that it was criminal, and boards acquiesced in these strategies. Nonetheless, investors and shareholders who suffered losses can and do launch lawsuits, as directors and executives were arguably in breach of their duties to the company (discussed in Chapter 8). Bankers lost sight of prudential principles which in earlier times would have made them more cautious. They certainly lost sight of the fact that they were meant to serve clients and other stakeholders, as highlighted in the closing case study. Regulatory failures loom large in these banking disasters. Large banks were globalized, and were perceived as too big to fail. It is no wonder that personal accountability has arisen as an issue following the financial crisis.

Large banks were globalized, and were perceived as too big to fail.

The corporate form benefits every conceivable size of company, from the micro-firm of only one person to the global company with thousands of shareholders. The young business is likely to register as a private company, gaining the benefits of limited liability, but without onerous disclosure requirements (see Figure 5.2). Family businesses are often private companies, retaining ownership and control within the family. The shares of private companies cannot be traded, and, for this reason, they are less in the limelight. Large businesses can choose to incorporate as private companies. Well-known private companies include Ikea of Sweden, the furniture and furnishings company. Some owners who want to retain tight control of their companies deliberately choose to remain private. However, choosing to become a public company is financially tempting. The valuation of the company can be greatly enhanced if the shares trade successfully and the stock price rises. Founders decide when and where to list through an initial public offering (IPO), taking into account the national law and the rules of the particular stock exchange.

The companies behind most familiar global brands are public companies. The public limited company (PLC) must register in a particular country, and fulfil the legal requirements of the national law, such as disclosure and financial reporting. The public company should not be confused with a 'public sector' company. Most PLCs are in the private sector.

Figure 5.2 *Legal control and disclosure in differing forms of business*

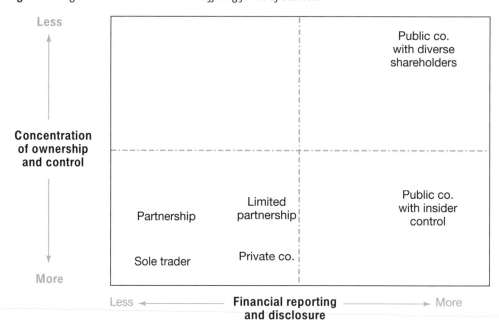

The PLC is 'public' because, in principle, its shares are tradable by ordinary investors. The company's shares, known as its equity, are bought and sold on stock exchanges. PLCs differ widely in their ownership, as shown in Figure 5.2. Public companies are usually envisaged as owned by a diversity of shareholders, but this is often not the case. Swiss pharmaceutical giant, Roche, is family dominated. Internet companies, including Google, Facebook and Twitter, have ownership structures whereby the founders retain control by ownership of shares with weighted voting rights, while shares offered publicly have very limited or no voting rights.

Another way of retaining control is to offer few shares to the public. The public company might need to offer only 25% or less of its shares as a 'free float' to outsiders. This allows founders to retain control, but raises corporate governance issues, as dominant owners are able to use the PLC form to further individual interests rather than those of the company as a whole. Both London and New York stock exchanges have allowed companies to list which are dominated by oligarchs, allowing them to sidestep listing rules and regulatory hurdles. One of these, an oligarch-dominated mining company, Eurasian Natural Resources Company (ENRC), was listed on the London Stock Exchange (LSE) in 2007, although offering only 19% of the shares as free-floating. ENRC became embroiled in allegations of fraud, leading to criticism of the exchange and of the UK's regulatory framework (Armitage, 2013).

PAUSE TO CONSIDER...

The joint-stock company with limited liability is a boon for businesspeople, but it can also facilitate wrongdoing such as setting up sham companies. These are legally and ethically wrong, but are difficult to uncover. To what extent do the benefits of limited liability outweigh the disadvantages?

FINANCIAL MARKETS: WHO DO THEY SERVE?

The nature of finance dictates that the interactions are essentially those of markets, matching buyers and sellers of all kinds, and offering all manner of securities. These include shares, bonds, foreign exchange, commodities and derivative products. Participants in financial markets are diverse in their status and interests. These are the main ones:

- Individuals – Individual investors invest in shares, bonds and other products mainly for financial returns. People often invest via mutual funds, which spread the risk among a range of companies.
- Financial services companies – Banks, insurance companies and other companies in this sector offer services to companies and also to individuals. The 'universal' bank has tended to be divided into an investment bank, which handles the more risky (and also more profitable) corporate business, and a retail bank, which serves consumers. Most banks are public companies. Banks issue bonds which attract a range of investors, and bank loans are an important source of capital for non-financial companies.
- Other private-sector companies – PLCs offer a proportion of their shares on stock exchanges. Companies do not trade in their own shares directly, but executives and directors often own shares and options. The option is a futures contract, allowing the recipient to purchase shares at a future date. Companies commonly raise money by issuing corporate bonds. And companies are also engaged in contracts for hedging foreign-exchange risk, to protect themselves from currency fluctuations in cross-border transactions.
- State-owned companies – These companies have become important players in global markets, supported by their sovereign owners. There are now 54 Chinese state-owned companies in Forbes 500 list of the world's biggest companies. These companies are often listed on stock exchanges, and the trend is for them to behave more like market entities than limbs of the state. Often, however, their corporate governance and ownership structures are opaque.
- Investment funds – Investment funds such as pension funds are managed funds which invest on behalf of their members. The funds can be companies in their own right. Fund managers have differing investment policies which vary with the purposes of the fund. Sovereign wealth funds, managed on behalf of state owners, also fall into this category.
- Governments – Governments borrow money in financial markets by issuing bonds, which can be attractive to long-term investors. Governments are also a source of finance, lending money to companies and to other countries. Lending by Brazil and China to numerous countries, notably in Africa, has helped to build ties with African countries.

Financial activities thus involve organizations whose main purposes vary greatly. For-profit companies in the private sector seek gains for their owners. With state-owned companies, the picture is more ambiguous: ownership is often opaque, and national goals come into play. Pension funds seek to invest for financial gains, as they must continuously pay out pensions against a backdrop of ageing populations in most countries. Governments both borrow and invest. They increasingly rely on borrowing to fund public spending. These public and private players have driven a growth in finance globally. All the players highlighted here must weigh the risks in finance: how do the benefits desired by the organization or individual justify the risks involved in any financial move? We next focus on two main types of investment: shares and bonds.

EQUITIES AND CORPORATE BONDS

When a company lists on a stock exchange, it invites outsiders to take a stake in its ownership. Many investors choose a stock because they believe in the company's products, goals, culture and values. These investors are likely to welcome a voice in the Annual General Meeting (AGM), as well as the dividends. Investors seeking only a financial return often invest via mutual funds. Share prices tend to reflect perceptions about the financial prospects of particular companies and sectors. We look at US stock markets as an example, as they are the world's largest. When share prices are rising, investors will tend to invest in them. But sometimes there is a bandwagon effect, and the flow of money into a sector leads to a bubble. Then there is a correction, bringing values back down to earth. The correction can be sudden. This happened following the bursting of the 'dot-com' bubble in 2000, following sharp rises in internet and IT stocks. This crash is shown in the Figure 5.3, which highlights movements of share prices on the S&P 500 Index. This index covers 75% of US equities, and is therefore a good indication of the total market.

As the figure also shows, there was a recovery in share prices from 2004, leading to further highs in 2007. But there followed a crash in 2008, marked by the spectacular failure of Lehman Brothers bank in the US. A burst in the housing market bubble led to a crash in the values of derivatives known as mortgage-backed securities, threatening all the companies which traded in these risky products. AIG, an insurance company, was a casualty. The housing market crash brought it to the verge of bankruptcy. AIG was perhaps the most extreme example of betting the whole company. It stunned the financial world by the depth

Figure 5.3 *The S&P 500 Index, 1980 to 2012*

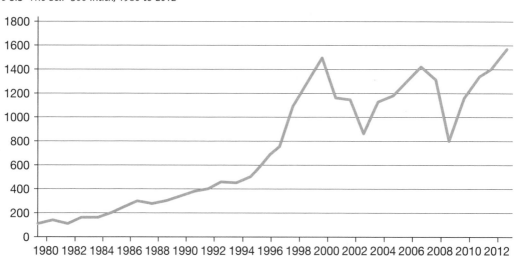

Source of data: S&P Dow Jones Indices, at eu.spindices.com (18/09/14).

AIG stunned the financial world by the depth of its exposure to derivatives trades, which amounted to $2.4 trillion – more than double its balance sheet.

of its exposure to derivatives trades, which amounted to $2.4 trillion – more than double its balance sheet.

The AIG collapse was symbolic of the gambling ethos which gripped the financial sector, concentrated in Wall Street, the centre of New York's financial district. The repercussions of a failure of this size, which would affect businesses as well as ordinary people holding its insurance policies and retirement accounts, made it 'too big to fail'. It was where 'Wall Street met Main Street' (Sender, 2012). The US government pumped a total of $182 billion in rescue funds into AIG. The government also became the company's main shareholder. The fact that AIG's disgraced directors collected large bonuses brought the image of Wall Street into further disgrace. Public opinion turned against the values encapsulated by Wall Street, prompting 'Occupy Wall Street' protests, which brought together numerous groups, including anti-capitalists and anti-globalization protesters. Central to their message was the rise in inequality. Although not a coherent movement, such protests sprang up in numerous countries, including those in which austerity measures were causing hardship to ordinary people.

The US Federal Reserve, the central bank, brought in a team of experts to unwind all the transactions and stabilize AIG. The company is now back in business, and the government's stake is reduced to 16%. But the employees now number 57,000, less than half the number in 2008. The company's shares were trading at $28 each in 2013, in contrast to a share price of close to $1,200 before their crash in 2008.

Emerging markets have enjoyed higher growth rates than the advanced economies and did not suffer to the same extent in the financial crisis. But they were affected nonetheless, as their exports to the big western markets slowed. Equity markets in emerging economies slumped following the crisis, and IPOs virtually dried up. Companies in these countries have turned to bonds to obtain finance, taking on considerable debt, as shown in Figure 5.4.

Photo 5.2 In 2011, Occupy Wall Street protesters set up makeshift tents in Zuccotti Park in New York's financial district. New York authorities forced them to leave after nine weeks, by which time they had become the global focal point for the stand against inequality. (© iStock.com/wdstock)

Figure 5.4 *Emerging-market corporate issuance by non-financial companies*

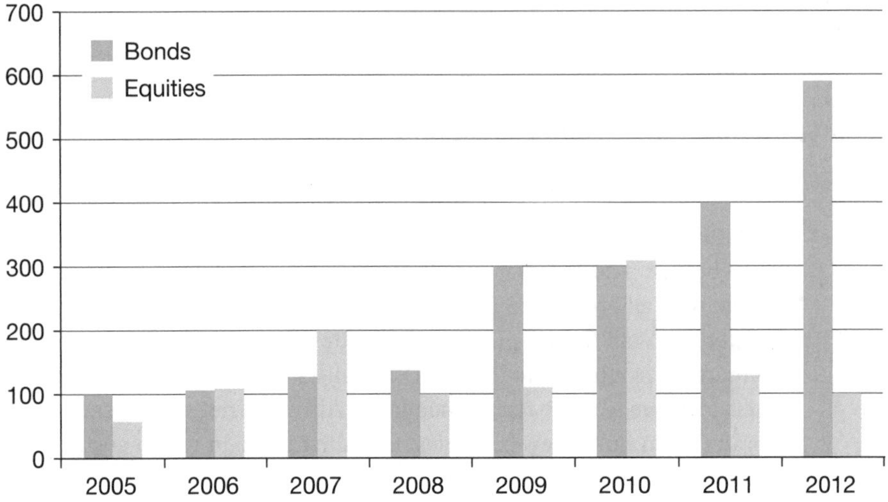

Source of data: IMF (2013) Global Financial Stability Report, April, at www.imf.org (18/09/14).

As an alternative to bank loans, companies can raise money through issuing corporate bonds, fixed-term debt instruments which pay investors a fixed rate of return. They are considered low-risk investments, but much depends on the strength of the company itself, usually measured as debt-to-equity ratio. Although emerging-market shares are mainly owned by domestic investors, these companies are looking beyond their own borders for debt finance. Corporate bonds in local currencies have become popular, and so, too, have corporate bonds denominated in US dollars. Low interest rates in North America and Europe, which governments have relied on to boost growth, have attracted emerging-market companies. They can issue dollar-denominated bonds and sell them to foreign investors. In the last five years, total foreign currency borrowing by companies in emerging markets has risen 50% (IMF, 2013).

For companies, corporate bonds at relatively low rates offer better opportunities for finance than bank loans (which require security) and equities markets (which are volatile). But when profits are weak, companies can face problems paying them back. For investors, bonds are considered lower-risk investments than shares, as bonds have guaranteed returns. Companies have no obligation to pay dividends to shareholders, but they do have to make interest payments to bondholders. The investor in shares is a member of the company and has an interest in the company as a whole. The bondholder is merely a creditor, with only a financial interest.

In 2013, Petrobras of Brazil, the state-controlled oil company, issued the largest ever dollar-denominated corporate bonds, totalling $11 billion. These bonds, likened to Brazil's sovereign debt, proved popular with investors around the world. There are risks, however, including those attached to the massive offshore oil exploration projects which the money is being used for (see closing case study in Chapter 2). Petrobras is the most heavily indebted of the publicly traded oil companies, and will be issuing more bonds in the future. Are its finances sound? There is foreign exchange risk, in that Brazil's currency could fall against the dollar. Political instability could also affect its strategy. Investors have been satisfied that Brazil's economic and political stability make this a good investment, especially compared with equities. Large pension funds face a dilemma in this respect, needing to go for low-risk investments, but also aware that their funds are depleted by poor returns from equities. From 2001 to 2012, US public pension schemes of the defined-benefit type suffered a shortfall of 28%. These funds should gravitate to low-risk bonds, but have tended to favour equities. Funds in this position might be tempted to go for riskier investments, in a 'gamble for resurrection' policy (IMF, 2013: 30).

PAUSE TO CONSIDER...

What factors lead a company to refrain from inviting investors to buy more shares and instead issue corporate bonds to raise money? What ethical concerns are involved in this choice?

SOVEREIGN BORROWERS AND INVESTORS

Governments issue bonds to fund public spending. The ease with which countries can borrow has led to an accumulation of debt, which is often criticized as imprudent. The national debt of countries, known as sovereign debt, has reached high levels. There has been an increase of $15.4 trillion in government debt since 2007 (McKinsey Global Institute, 2013). It is higher in the advanced countries than in the emerging markets. It can amount to more than 100% of a country's GDP, as shown in Figure 5.5. The rise in govern-ment debt has become a political as well as economic issue in the three countries shown in Figure 5.5. In all of them, debt spiralled and growth slowed. Greece, a eurozone country, reached a point where it was unable to make interest payments, and required a bailout arranged by the IMF and European Central Bank. The Chinese government has been a major purchaser of US sovereign debt, drawing on its vast foreign exchange reserves esti-mated to be $3.2 trillion. When levels of debt are very high, servicing it becomes an issue, especially in a context of slow economic growth and weak state revenues. States are usually

Figure 5.5 *Government debt as a percentage of GDP in the US, UK and Greece*

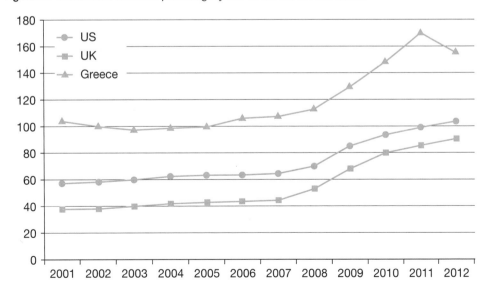

Sources of data: Eurostat, *General Government Debt*, at epp.eurostat.ec.europa.eu; *US Government Spending, US Federal Debt*, at www.usgovernmentspending.com (18/09/14).

advised by economists to introduce austerity measures such as cutting spending and raising taxes (Wolf, 2013). But opinion is divided: austerity measures inflict further pain on society, and do not necessarily bring growth in jobs, which is a critical element in economic growth.

For a country like Greece, which was on the brink of default, the prospect of sovereign bankruptcy would have had even more severe social consequences than the austerity measures which were already severe. The risks of social upheaval were high, especially in a context of high unemployment. Countries can and do default on debt. A number of Latin American countries have suffered financial crisis and defaulted on international bonds. Argentina is a notable example of sovereign default, having defaulted on $100 billions-worth of bonds in 2001. As of 2013, the position of the creditors was still in doubt, 'hold-out' creditors battling in the US courts for a better deal than that offered by the Argentine government. Argentina has placed itself in a difficult position with foreign investors when it needs to return to financial markets for further borrowing. Just as companies can be viewed as acting irresponsibly in their financial affairs, governments are sometimes accused of mismanaging their country's finances. The creditors suffer in these circumstances, but then they undertook the risks of these investments. Moreover, holdout investors tend to be hedge funds which target these situations in the hope of eventually obtaining a favourable payout. These tactics are criticized by the IMF (Harding and Wigglesworth, 2013). The most unfortunate losers are the people in the society who lose their jobs, homes or pensions when a national economy collapses, as these are the victims of the government's irresponsible financial management. It has been unfortunate that political leaders have often gained plaudits for prestigious projects funded by debt, leaving the bills to be paid by their successors in office.

Not every country is able to tap international financial markets: those that are fragile and unstable must rely heavily on foreign aid. But some countries which have been recipients of aid have become more stable and can now tap bond markets. In 2013, Rwanda, a country devastated by genocide in 1994, had recovered sufficient stability in its economic and political systems to launch a bond issue of $400 million. But there remain underlying issues of governance and rule of law in the country, which must be taken into account by potential investors. Rwanda has seen impressive economic growth, of 8% per annum, and, like other Sub-Saharan African countries, is attracting global investors.

For countries rich in resources and without legacy debt problems, investments offer many opportunities. Sovereign investors are active in global markets, usually seeking financial returns rather than more active roles. Sovereign wealth funds (SWFs) are investment vehicles controlled by the state which invest in financial markets. They invest in a range of assets, including equities, bonds and real estate. Sovereign investors are often from countries rich in energy assets. Middle Eastern countries rich in oil and gas are active investors. Qatar investment funds are among the active investors (see case study in Chapter 3). Asian countries with large foreign exchange reserves form another group of sovereign investors. Singapore's SWF, Temasek, is an active investor (see closing case study of Chapter 8). While these investors are seeking mainly good financial returns, they can take active roles on company boards if they hold a significant stake. SWFs can be obscure in their ownership and governance structures, as well as their investment policies. An exception in terms of transparency and ethical policies is the Norwegian state oil fund, the world's largest SWF, discussed in Chapter 2. The fund remains mainly a financial investor. However, its role is now evolving into one of greater engagement with the management of the companies in which it has significant stakes, and it is scrutinizing the ethics in target companies (Milne, 2013).

ETHICAL INVESTING

By buying shares or investing in bonds, the investor supports the aims of the company. Many investors look only to potential gains in share price and dividends, while others see the investment as an ethical choice. Ethical considerations now influence a large segment of investors. The potential investor can focus on the type of business, the way the company is managed, its view of stakeholders, and many other factors.

Ethical investing, often called 'socially responsible' investing, is an approach to investment which weighs ethical concerns about the company more heavily than monetary returns. Companies can be screened negatively and positively. Negative screening automatically excludes certain sectors. Among these are the 'sinful' industries, mainly tobacco, alcohol, gambling, and pornography. There are other industries which investors might exclude, such as weapons and nuclear power. Positive screening includes companies 'only if' they adhere to certain criteria, such as not using child labour (Michelson et al., 2004). Many shareholders support 'green' investments, avoiding oil and gas companies. Other companies which investors avoid are those involved in sweatshop manufacturing. The ethical investor could be concerned about all these issues, or only, say, green issues. Under the UK's Pensions Act 2000, trustees of occupational pension schemes must declare the extent of the social, environmental and ethical considerations that go into their decision-making on investments. This type of legislation encourages contributors to the fund to take an interest in where their money is going, and press funds for information justifying particular investments.

Many mutual funds now offer investments designed for ethical investors. The mutual fund is a bundle of investments which is managed by fund managers. The mutual fund is less risky than a single-company investment, because it spreads the risks. The investor who wishes more direct involvement can make a deliberate choice of a particular company. Ethical funds are marketed to the public as investment products with ethical credentials in particular sectors. These funds do not necessarily offer better financial returns than ordinary funds without an ethical slant. Industries such as tobacco and alcohol usually deliver among the highest returns for investors. But the ethical investor is more concerned about the substance of the investment than the return. When investing via a mutual fund, the investor is indirectly investing in the target company, and is not a shareholder with rights in the company itself. Mutual funds designed for ethical investors are often active shareholders, selecting companies to invest in according to the concerns of their investors. However, a UK survey of the 20 largest ethical fund providers in the UK has found that many investors are unhappy with the level of information they receive and the responsiveness of the funds to their ethical concerns.

The ethical investor is more concerned about the substance of the investment than the return.

Figure 5.6 shows the results of screening by the funds surveyed. While 63% screened out alcohol companies, only 11% operated a screen for child labour, even though this was an issue of particular concern. It is easier to simply rule out certain industries like tobacco than to assess whether a company co-operates with an oppressive regime. But the weak attention

Figure 5.6 *Screening by UK ethical funds*

Percentages

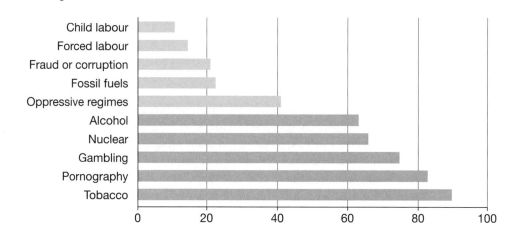

Note: the top five issues in the chart were of the greatest concern to investors.

Source of data: FairPensions (2012) *Ethically Engaged: A Survey of UK Ethical Funds,* at www.shareaction.org (26/09/14).

to these concerns indicates that many ethical funds could do more to reflect ethical views of investors, and, thus, more effectively influence corporate behaviour of the companies in which they are shareholders. This survey concerned shares, but it should also be noted that many investors also invest in bonds, including government bonds. Bonds of emerging economies are growing in popularity, but as we noted above, carry risks relating to country factors. The Rwandan government's bond issued in 2013 was intended to raise money to build a hydro power station and a convention centre in the capital (Wigglesworth, 2013). The country's government has been tainted with accusations of authoritarian rule and a poor human rights record. Also relevant is the fact that Rwanda remains a very poor country with low levels of societal well-being. The country ranks 167 out of 186 countries in the UN's human development index. Rwanda has made progress in human development, but a Rwandan child can expect only 3.3 years of schooling. Questions about government's public spending priorities would be added to the other ethical issues arising in relation to this, and other, Sub-Saharan African countries.

PAUSE TO CONSIDER...

Assume you are thinking about investing ethically. Would you invest in shares or bonds? What criteria would you use, and why?

REGULATING STOCK MARKETS

For any registered company, the investment by shareholders is the financial foundation of the business. The public company's shares can be traded both on official stock exchanges and in unofficial markets, or 'dark' markets. The world's stock markets are fragmented, each managing its own exchange, and each regulated by national regulators. It is only in the last decade that exchanges themselves have become listed companies, leading to a greater sense of competition among them to attract listings and investors. The New York Stock Exchange and the Nasdaq exchange, also in New York, which concentrates more on technology stocks, are by far the world's largest exchanges in terms of the value of shares traded (World

Federation of Exchanges, 2012). The two together handle over half the share trading of the top ten biggest stock exchanges.

Whereas markets were formerly driven by individual trades between human beings, the big markets now use automated platforms, in which ultra-fast computer systems can deal with huge volumes of trades. Trading on exchanges has thus become depersonalized and dependent on technology. Volumes have increased greatly with high-frequency trading. Technology glitches have affected these highly complex operations. Even a minor glitch can affect thousands of trades, affecting the companies involved and also denting the public's confidence in the exchange. A technical glitch halted trading on the day of the high-profile Facebook IPO in 2012 on the Nasdaq exchange. As a result, many trades were lost. The regulator, the Securities and Exchange Commission (SEC), fined Nasdaq $10 million, the largest fine it has imposed on an exchange.

An increasing proportion of trading in equities is now taking place outside exchanges, using the services of 'dark pools' offering private trading. Private trading venues now account for nearly 40% of trade in US equities, as shown in Figure 5.7. These platforms, often run by large banks, tend to be cheaper than official exchanges, and, not surprisingly, are seen as a threat by the regulated exchanges. Regulators in the US, Europe and Australia are concerned that private trading venues could undermine the transparency of markets, damaging public confidence and deterring private investors from investing in equities.

Regulation aims to ensure transparency and fairness in the dealings an exchange handles. It aims to maintain the confidence of investors and public generally. An exchange is itself part of the regulatory framework, enforcing its own rules on those who use the exchange's services. Critics might argue that there is a conflict of interest in the new global competition among exchanges: they are no longer non-profit public services, but for-profit players in the markets which they oversee. Confidence in an exchange depends on principles of honesty and transparency. It also depends on provision of accurate information and efficient processing of transactions. The SEC had encouraged technological developments and off-market trades, to bring about greater competition and to 'democratize' investing

Figure 5.7 *The rise of off-exchange trading in the US*

Percentage of all US equities trading volume

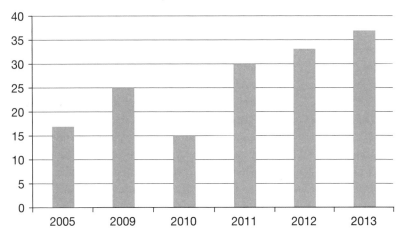

Source of data: Massoudi, A. and Mackenzie, M. (2013) 'Investors turn to the dark side for trading', *Financial Times*, 26 April.

(Mackenzie et al., 2012). However, the technological revolution and the growth in off-market trading have dented confidence in the regulator, in a period when Main Street investors are wary of the perils of Wall Street and its big players.

One of the major risks of stock exchanges is their use by unscrupulous traders for fraudulent purposes such as 'laundering' the proceeds of crimes, known as money laundering. Market abuse can take the form of **insider dealing** (or trading), which is the use of inside information to influence trading, thus achieving a financial advantage over players who lack the relevant information. Asymmetry of information is an almost inevitable aspect of markets: some people have inside information, such as advance knowledge of a takeover bid, which they can exploit, for example, by timing a sale of shares before the news becomes public. Insider dealing is a criminal offence in most countries. A company can be prosecuted, and so can an individual: the veil of incorporation offers no protection. However, it is difficult to prove, and difficult to stamp out, all the while undermining confidence in the market. An exchange might turn a blind eye to the practice, but when the practice becomes widespread, it poses a risk to the integrity of a market. National regulators and prosecutors have become more dedicated to rooting out market abuses in recent years. From 2009 to 2012, the UK regulator, the Financial Services Authority (FSA), had nine successful prosecutions for insider dealing, and another 16 are ongoing (Note 2). Hong Kong, through its Market Misconduct Tribunal, has become stricter in monitoring for possible market abuse and prosecuting those caught, in its efforts to dispel an impression that it takes a soft line on such practices. The US has pursued a number of high-profile cases of insider dealing.

Hedge funds, which are investment funds whose managers are noted for their aggressive investment strategies, are some of the main targets of efforts to stamp out insider dealing. In 2011, Raj Rajaratnam, who managed Galleon, a hedge fund, was prosecuted in the US for insider dealing and securities fraud in the trading of shares in numerous companies, including the bank, Goldman Sachs, Google and Intel. Whereas sentences of two years had been the norm in earlier cases, Rajaratnam received a prison sentence of 11 years. The judge said that the crimes pointed to a 'virus in our business culture that needs to be eradicated' (Hilzenrath, 2011). Further convictions followed, as prosecutors pursued links with Galleon. The Galleon prosecution was intended to give a strong signal to traders, but 2013 saw another insider dealing case by another hedge fund. That company, SAC Capital, agreed to a fine of $1.2 billion in a negotiated settlement for pleading guilty to pervasive fraudulent behaviour: 'SAC not only tolerated cheating, it encouraged it', said an investigator (Scannell et al., 2013). However, the company's founder and leading trader was spared prosecution (Stewart, 2013). After six years of investigation and the large fine imposed on his company, some action against him was expected. It is urged by some that the best way to ensure that justice is done is to go through with a court hearing (Gapper, 2013). After all, it is the people behind the company who commit wrongdoing. Why should they escape? The negotiated deal with prosecutors tends to look as if it is simply a matter of a money calculation, whereas following a trial and a guilty verdict, the conviction carries more moral weight. This trend of agreeing outcomes in criminal trials reflects the sense of markets pervading other spheres of society, highlighted by the political philosopher, Michael Sandel, and noted in Chapter 2. With oversight of national markets, regulators are trusted with safeguarding fairness and transparency of the market mechanisms. They prefer

It is the people behind the company who commit wrongdoing. Why should they escape?

light-touch regulation, but many companies seize opportunities for making gains which are presented where there is an absence of strict regulation.

A survey of 500 professional people in the financial services sector in the UK and US shows that a culture of integrity is still lacking, and misconduct is still widespread (Labaton Sucharow, 2012). Nearly 25% said they would have to engage in unethical or illegal conduct to be successful, and 26% said they had first-hand knowledge of wrongdoing in their organizations. When asked whether they would commit the crime of insider trading to gain $10 million if they could get away with it, 16% said they would. Only 55% said they definitely would not. Clearly, the perception that regulation is weak contributes to the scant respect for legal and ethical rules. Regulators in both countries operate whistleblower schemes, whereby people with knowledge of wrongdoing are encouraged to report to the authorities. However, many of the respondents in this survey were unaware of the schemes. Only 26% of financial service professionals in the US thought the SEC was effective, and only 29% in the UK thought the FSA was effective.

When asked whether they would commit the crime of insider trading to gain $10 million if they could get away with it, 16% said they would.

Prior to the financial crisis of 2008, the then regulator, the FSA, adopted a lax approach to the high-risk activities of UK banks. The result was a near failure of three banks, the Northern Rock, the Royal Bank of Scotland (RBS) and HBOS, which was taken over by Lloyds Bank. Barclays Bank was able to raise capital independently to ward off government intervention (discussed in the closing case study). The Bank of England has now set up a new regulatory framework under its direct control (see Note 2). Britain had prided itself on the reputation of London as a financial centre, but these banking disasters dented that reputation. The reputation of the London Stock Exchange (LSE) has also been affected by cases in which it allowed companies to list which fell beneath its standards for corporate governance and transparency.

PAUSE TO CONSIDER...

The culture of the financial services sector seems still to be focused on weighing up risk versus gains. What elements of cultural change would help restore public confidence?

SEEKING COMPETITIVE ADVANTAGE THROUGH FINANCE: COMPANIES AND COUNTRIES

The example of the LSE above is indicative of the attitudes which countries adopt to attract large companies. We have seen national competitive advantage in attracting manufacturing activities to low-cost countries. Finance, too, offers opportunities to gain competitive advantage in particular locations. These are countries which have designed laws and policies which are particularly business-friendly. The competition among countries to offer low corporation tax rates has led to global reductions in corporation tax, as shown in Figure 5.8. Many of the most attractive locations are in small countries, grouped together loosely as tax havens. These include offshore countries such as British overseas territories, notably in the Caribbean and the Channel Islands. There are also small European countries, such as Luxembourg, Ireland and Cyprus. The EU has sought to impose greater transparency on these jurisdictions. Switzerland and Singapore are noted for their banking secrecy, although pressure from foreign governments has now led to more exchange of information with Swiss banks.

Figure 5.8 *Comparison of tax rates for corporation tax and individual tax*

Percentages

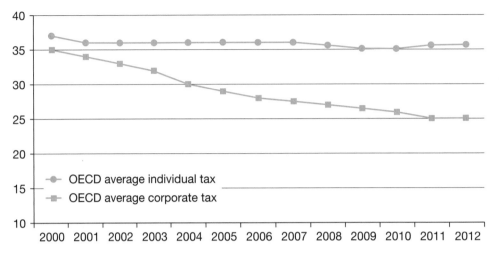

Note: Individual tax rate is the combination of personal income tax and social charges for a single person on average earnings with no children

Source of data: OECD, *OECD Statistics*, at www.oecd.org (18/09/14).

The Netherlands has also built up a position of competitive advantage, attracting hundreds of multinationals. Many of these are 'letterbox companies', which have little or no activity in the country. There are 23,000 letterbox companies in Holland, managed through trust firms, which take advantage of the favourable tax treatment, especially on the royalties paid on intellectual property. This policy has been criticized by Holland's politicians, who point out the comparison between the tax rate of 39.5% paid by Dutch citizens and rates of 1–2% paid by large multinationals which funnel money through Holland. While the government is now under pressure to change its policy, it is reluctant to do so, as any change might deter foreign companies which bring real investment and jobs. Companies are now required to have some business presence in the country.

Multinational companies can arrange their finances to benefit from the tax differences between countries. American companies, in particular, have strong incentives in this respect. The full rate of American corporation tax is 35%. Complex legislation offers many allowances and deductions which allow firms to escape the force of the full rate, but for the large global company, it is still worthwhile devising tax schemes to avoid it. Crucially, foreign profits of US multinationals are not taxed until the money is 'repatriated'. There are thus incentives for these global companies to hoard money abroad. US companies hold in total an estimated $1.7 trillion offshore. Apple has accumulated $102.3 billion offshore. A US Senate investigation found that it used a number of non-tax resident subsidiaries in Ireland, to receive the bulk of its international profits (Politi, 2013a). But when it wished to pay a dividend to shareholders, it did not repatriate any profits. Instead, it borrowed the money in a massive bond issue of $17 billion, to avoid a tax bill. It had to make interest payments to the bondholders, but these are tax deductible. Tim Cook, Apple's CEO, when appearing before the Senate committee investigating the company's tax affairs,

Apple's CEO says, 'We not only comply with the laws but we comply with the spirit of the laws.'

was nonetheless unapologetic. He said, 'We don't depend on tax gimmicks', and also responded to questions about the company's legal obligations, saying, 'We not only comply with the laws but we comply with the spirit of the laws' (Politi, 2013b). But most people would say that the company is circumventing the spirit of the laws through its massive tax avoidance, estimated to 'save' the company $44 billion over four years.

Aided by tax advisers, corporate financial officers have become skilled at setting up links in low-tax jurisdictions to funnel profits made in high-tax jurisdictions. Large companies such as Google, Starbucks and Apple are vociferous in stating that such tactics are legal, as they are simply taking advantage of differences in international taxation afforded by governments. This line underplays the fact that these companies lobby governments intensively to secure advantageous policies (Stiglitz, 2013). Google paid UK tax totalling £10 million over five years to 2011, during which it enjoyed UK revenues of £11.9 billion. Its chairman is adamant that this is legal, and is 'just capitalism', citing the company's responsibility to shareholders (Dico, 2013). He has also claimed that the policy is not unethical (Warman and Waterfield, 2013). Many would disagree. The company devised complex schemes to avoid tax by recording transactions in Ireland when in fact both parties were in Britain. But it did not stop at that. An Irish subsidiary collects revenues from the UK, France and other countries. It then pays royalties to another Irish subsidiary legally resident in Bermuda. The money is then channelled to Bermuda through a subsidiary in the Netherlands which has no employees.

Tax avoidance is arranging financial affairs to reduce tax liabilities. This is considered legal, while schemes which have no purpose other than reducing tax liabilities are usually considered tax evasion, and are not legal. Hence, it is arguable that such schemes are indeed tax evasion. But the UK government has taken a lenient line on tax liabilities of large multinationals in the UK. These large companies have often been able to negotiate their tax bills with the UK tax authority, HM Revenue and Customs (HMRC). The result has been opaque deals to pay agreed sums to HMRC. Such deals have been criticized by the Public Accounts Committee of Parliament, as they raise suspicions that the companies are being let off lightly (Syal, 2013). In 2012, Starbucks took the unusual step of volunteering to pay HMRC £10 million in tax, mainly as a result of reputational damage suffered because of its tax avoidance strategy. Starbucks, unlike the technology companies, has a very visible presence, with 735 coffee shops across the UK. Although the company's executives have often spoken of the success of its UK outlets, Starbucks UK has recorded losses for 10 of the 14 years it has existed in the country. It has paid £8.6 million tax on sales of £3 billion since 1998, mainly for disallowed deductions. The inconsistency between its executives' pronouncements and the company's balance sheet owes much to practices of transfer pricing.

Transfer pricing occurs when the MNE organizes transactions among its units across borders to suit its tax objectives. A company in a tax haven can buy an asset at a low price from another company in the group. It then sells the asset at a high price to one in a high-tax country, such as the UK. The UK company then sells it at the same high price to a UK retailer, making no profits. Starbucks has successfully used this policy. The coffee beans used in UK outlets are bought from a Starbucks subsidiary in Switzerland at premium prices. Payments for roasting are made to a subsidiary in the Netherlands, as are royalties payments made by Starbucks UK for use of the brand. Starbucks UK is also heavily indebted, paying off loans made by subsidiaries within the group. When all these payments are taken into account, it is not difficult to see why Starbucks UK appears to be unprofitable. UK competitors have criticized its practices. It is competing across the UK against domestic coffee chains which pay far more tax, and have become vocal in alleging unfair competition.

Artificial devices to avoid and manipulate tax liabilities are widely used and defended by the companies which use them as being wholly legal. But these practices are widely perceived to be unethical. Companies like Google, Amazon and Apple which do business in a country benefit hugely from taxpayer-funded benefits, such as infrastructure, an educated workforce, high-speed internet and reliable administration. These benefits enhance their profitability, while ordinary taxpayers, including local businesses, pay for them (Picciotto and Shaxson, 2012). The tax multinationals would pay in the absence of tax avoidance schemes would amount to huge sums, which could help to fund public services such as education. US companies celebrated a victory when they were declared to be analogous to ordinary people in the *Citizens United* judgment (see Chapter 3). But they are keen *not* to be treated like ordinary citizens for tax liabilities (Stiglitz, 2013). Mr Schmidt of Google blames governments for the tax system that allows his company to escape tax. However, his company devotes itself to manipulating the system, and would logically continue to do so, whatever tax reforms might be put in place. Moves are now under way to work towards accord among countries through the OECD and EU to harmonize rules and clamp down on tax havens. A possible solution is the unitary tax, which taxes a company on the genuine activities it conducts in each country (Picciotto and Shaxson, 2012). This type of solution would tax a company according to its physical assets, workforce and sales in a country, as a proportion of global profits. Such a system would better reflect the activities of a company in each location, and would benefit developing countries. These countries are often disadvantaged by MNE tax avoidance and other technically legal but ethically doubtful policies. And these societies are the main losers, as funds that should find their way to public coffers are funnelled to corporate treasuries.

A unitary tax would tax a company according to its physical assets, workforce and sales in a country, as a proportion of global profits.

Which of the following would be most effective in changing MNE tax avoidance behaviour, and why?

a. Federal legislation in the US lowering the rate of corporation tax to 25%;

b. EU legislation to impose a tax regime across the member states, which taxes the MNE on the business activities in each state;

c. A criminal prosecution against a large MNE for tax evasion.

d. A 'boycott Starbucks' campaign at grassroots level.

REFORMING GLOBAL FINANCE: IS REGULATION PROMOTING MORE ETHICAL BEHAVIOUR?

Countries have pursued national competitive advantage in numerous ways, as this chapter has shown. They have used lenient regulatory systems to attract global banks and investors such as hedge funds. Some have lowered corporate tax rates to lure MNEs. Some have attracted banking activities by upholding banking secrecy to shield individuals and companies from investigation by other governments into possible tax evasion and fraud. There is a growing consensus against countries which defend banking secrecy, as they are perceived to be complicit in the crimes of banks' clients. There is pressure within the EU to harmonize corporation tax rates, which would adversely affect Ireland's current competitive advantage. The EU has announced plans to impose greater transparency and disclosure rules on MNEs' tax positions in member states. This would require them to disclose profits and taxes in each member state where they have activities. This new law would shine a spotlight on tax anomalies, which, when they are publicly disclosed, could lead to pressure for the tightening of regulation. Companies and governments that, in alliance, have perpetuated elaborate systems of tax avoidance, are unlikely to be converted overnight to an ethical perspective. But public opinion and political activism have highlighted the issues.

The financial crisis of 2008 showed up a financial sector which had grown rapidly through globalized activities, such as derivatives markets, but whose capital foundations were weak. When they came under pressure, they crumbled. Regulators in many countries, through their lenient approach to banks and other companies heavily involved in finance, are partly to blame: their trust in corporate managers, directors and market mechanisms proved misguided. Following bailouts and restructuring, banks have become smaller institutions, with stronger capital bases. But changing the banking culture and norms of behaviour is more of a challenge. A pessimistic view would be that financial professionals have adapted their practices to the changed environment, but this need not imply that their attitudes and values have changed. A major concern for finance globally has been to restore stability. The IMF sees overall principles of more transparent financial reporting and disclosure as key to restoring confidence in the financial sector. However, it recognizes that political commitment is key to bringing about reforms (IMF, 2013). Many countries have expressed willingness to co-operate, but their actions have tended to reflect national interests more than a wish for stronger international regulation. Calls for greater regulation have come from the G20 countries, a grouping of developed, emerging and developing countries which comes together regularly to focus on global issues (Note 3).

All agree in principle that capital requirements of banks need to be raised and that greater co-operation is needed in the funding of failures. And it is clear that the regulation of derivatives trading needs to be strengthened. These reforms could be considered moves towards sustainable banking, restoring to banking a business model based on more ethically sustainable principles of serving society. Other issues are more contentious. These include legislating structural changes. The 'universal' bank with both retail banking and trading subsidiaries has been a model in the US and UK, but is now seen as risky, because the trading limb can jeopardize deposits in the retail limb. The two types of activity have different cultures, reflecting the distinction described at the outset of this chapter between serving clients, which is seen as ethically grounded, and financial trading, which is the 'casino' limb of the business. The implicit guarantee is that these huge universal banks are too big to fail, and that they will be bailed out by taxpayer money. But why bail out reckless casino trading? It has been said, 'it is a funny casino where gamblers can play with other people's money' (*The Guardian*, 2013). These issues are highlighted in the closing case study. Requiring the two activities to be broken up into separate banks is a drastic solution, but ringfencing the retail activities is a possible solution that would protect retail operations while avoiding breaking up large banks.

'It is a funny casino where gamblers can play with other people's money.'

Financial regulators from 27 countries met in Basel, Switzerland in 2010, aiming to achieve agreed measures to strengthen global finance and prevent a recurrence of the crisis two years earlier. Their agreement, known as Basel III, specified high levels of bank capital, overseen by a group of regulators in Switzerland. However, since then, fragmentation has taken place, and countries have devised different schemes. Moreover, the US reforms under the Dodd–Frank Act include rules that are extra-territorial: they affect overseas subsidiaries of US banks and US subsidiaries of overseas banks. For its part, the EU has proposed new rules on hedge funds which the US feels will disadvantage its funds. New EU regulators, the European Banking Authority and a European Securities and Markets Authority, are not welcomed by all member states, who wish to feel free to set their own regulatory standards. The many new sets of rules being hammered out by national regulators are making for a complex mix. A fund manager, for example, would need to comply with different sets of rules in each country, leading to a bureaucratic quagmire. While the goal was uniform standards at the global level, this still seems a long way off. Moreover, the public perception of the finance sector remains negative, focusing on excessive rewards and little sense of responsibility towards clients and other stakeholders. The EU has legislated to introduce caps on bankers' bonuses – a measure objected to by the UK. It is indicative of the cultural challenges that banks are devising other ways of paying the sums which would have been given as bonuses.

As we have seen in this chapter, the chance to make huge personal gains encourages dishonesty. These opportunities are now thinner on the ground within the more risk-averse banking models. And it should not be overlooked that responsibility and monitoring are aspects of any business that encourage more transparent and moral behaviour. The notion of personal responsibility that the unlimited banking model had in earlier eras had the virtue of making bankers ultimately responsible for their risks. In the limited company, bank executives are responsible to their boards, and directors have a monitoring function. Board monitoring of executives was woefully inadequate in the years leading up to the financial crisis. In Ireland, board members of failed banks, including non-executive directors, were warned that they could face investigation for wrongdoing and possible legal proceedings (Masters, 2012). Corporate governance is itself a regulatory issue, and board members should be better informed and more pro-active in monitoring executives (this will be discussed in Chapter 8). Monitoring within the organization and regulation from outside depends on people who are willing and able to exert robust, independent judgment on executives and others in the organization. A culture of self-interested behaviour thrives in an environment where there are few checks and little accountability. Cosy relationships between financial players, global corporate executives, regulators and tax authorities foster an environment of arrangements based on perceived self-interest rather than greater public goods.

CONCLUSIONS

Global financial markets have opened up new opportunities for wealth creation and rewarded handsomely those who have driven innovations in finance. Faith in markets to continue to develop in an orderly and stable manner, while expanding to encompass more countries and environments, proved over-optimistic. Numerous national financial crises of the 1980s and 1990s, followed by a global financial crisis in 2008, stunned governments and societies. A new critique of finance and its leading actors was a result. Finance may seem remote to most ordinary people: they see the realities of household expenditures and taxes, but do not see the movements of global capital markets. But these markets increasingly affect ordinary people, in their jobs, welfare services and pensions. Suspicion and fear of global finance has led to accusations against both large companies and governments. A groundswell of hostile public opinion has ensued. Much of the criticism has focused on unethical behaviour.

Governments face multiple challenges in putting in place regulatory frameworks to prevent another financial crisis. But a more difficult challenge is the deep-seated profits-at-all-costs culture which this chapter has highlighted. Even as banks were cleaning up the toxic derivatives and bad loans, more innovative financial products were being devised to facilitate new potential profits, and off-exchange trading has boomed. As this chapter has shown, regulation has been a response of governments, but all would agree that cultural changes also play a crucial role in creating a more sustainable business model in the financial sector. One lesson that governments and international bodies have taken on board is that finance is not simply about business and governments: it is about societies.

NOTES

1 The Mennonites, a Protestant group, are noted for their pacifist views.
2 In 2013, the FSA was disbanded and replaced by the Prudential Regulation Authority (PRA), which oversees financial stability, and the Financial Conduct Authority (FCA), which oversees financial behaviour. The PRA is under direct control of the central bank, the Bank of England.
3 The G20 members are South Africa, the US, Canada, Mexico, Brazil, Argentina, China, Japan, South Korea, India, Indonesia, Russia, Turkey, Germany, France, the UK, Italy, Saudi Arabia, Australia and the EU. Note that the EU is treated as a member separate from its own member states for this purpose.

REFERENCES

Arestis, P. (2004) 'Washington consensus and financial liberalization', *Journal of Post Keynesian Economics*, 27(2): 257–71.

Armitage, J. (2013) 'City standards watchdog is roasted by MPs over ENRC', *The Independent*, 26 November, at www.independent.co.uk (18/09/14).

Dico, J. (2013) 'Google tax policy is "just capitalism"', *The Independent*, 26 May, at www.independent.co.uk (18/09/14).

Ferguson, N. (2009) *The Ascent of Money* (London: Penguin).

Freedman, J. (2000) 'Limited liability: Large company theory and small firms', *Modern Law Review*, 63(3): 317–54.

Gapper, J. (2013) 'Wall Street justice should be delivered in open court', *Financial Times*, 23 May.

Gelderblom, D., De Jons, A. and Jonker, J. (2012) *The Formative Years of the Modern Corporation: The Dutch East India Company Voc, 1602–1623*, Erasmus Research Institute of Management, www.erim.eur.nl (18/09/14).

Guardian (2013) *Barclays: No Way to Run a Banking System*, 31 July, at www.theguardian.com.

Harding, R. and Wigglesworth, R. (2013) 'IMF reviews role of state in debt crisis', *Financial Times*, 23 May.

Hilzenrath, D. (2011) 'Raj Rajaratnam, hedge fund billionaire, gets 11-year sentence for insider trading', *The Washington Post*, at www.washingtonpost.com (18/09/14).

IMF (2013) *Global Financial Stability Report*, April, at www.imf.org (18/09/14).

Labaton Sucharow (2012) *Wall Street, Fleet Street and Main Street: Corporate Integrity (US and UK Financial Services Industry Survey)*, at www.secwhistlebloweradvocate.com (18/09/14).

Mackenzie, M., Massoudi, A. and Foley, S. (2012) 'Rage against the machine', *Financial Times*, 17 October.

Marriage, M. (2013) 'Swiss banks alter structure after Wegelin', *Financial Times*, 10 February.

Masters, B. (2012) 'Clampdown on cheats aimed at restoring faith', *Financial Times*, 14 June.

McKinsey Global Institute (2013) *Financial globalization: Retreat or Reset? (Financial Globalization Report)*, March, at www.mckinsey.com (18/09/14).

Michelson, G., Wails, N. and van der Laan, S. (2004) 'Ethical investment and outcomes', *Journal of Business Ethics*, 52(1): 1–2.

Milne, R. (2013) 'Norwegian state oil fund focuses on greater corporate engagement', *Financial Times*, 26 April.

Picciotto, S. and Shaxson, N. (2012) 'Tighten the rules so that corporate tax is fair for all companies', *Financial Times*, 20 November.

Politi, J. (2013a) 'US senators accuse Apple of elaborate tax-avoidance moves, *Financial Times*, 21 May.

Politi, J. (2013b) 'Apple: We pay all the taxes we owe, every dollar', *Financial Times*, 22 May.

Raines, P. and Leathers, C. (1994) 'Financial derivative instruments and social ethics', *Journal of Business Ethics*, 13(3): 197–204.

Scannell, K., McCrum, D. and Braithwaite, T. (2013) 'Prosecutors bring criminal charges against SAC Capital', *Financial Times*, 26 July.

Schäfer, D. and Shotter, J. (2013) 'An end to 200 years of Swiss banking life', *Financial Times*, 2 May.

Sender, H. (2012) 'An improbable profit', *Financial Times*, 23 October.

Soppe, A. (2004) 'Sustainable corporate finance', *Journal of Business Ethics*, 53(1/2): 213–24.

Stewart, J. (2013) 'SAC: a textbook case of corporate prosecution', *New York Times*, 5 November, at www.nyt.com (18/09/14).

Stiglitz, J. (2013) 'Globalisation isn't just about profits. It's about taxes too', *The Guardian*, 27 May.

Strange, S. (1986) *Casino Capitalism* (Oxford: Blackwell).

Syal, R. (2013) 'Revealed: "Sweetheart" tax deals each worth over £1 bn', *The Guardian*, 29 April, at www.theguardian.com (18/09/14).

Warman, M. and Waterfield, B. (2013) 'Google chief Eric Schmidt: "the tax regime is not up to us"', *The Telegraph*, 22 May, at www.telegraph.co.uk (18/09/14).

Wigglesworth, R. (2013) 'Rwanda's bond issue reflects progress after 1994 genocide', *Financial Times*, 25 April.

Wolf, M. (2012) 'Seven ways to fix the system's flaws', *Financial Times*, 22 January.

Wolf, M. (2013) 'Austerity loses an article of faith', *Financial Times*, 24 April.

World Federation of Exchanges (2012) *WFE Market Highlights*, at www.world-exchanges.org (18/09/14).

REVIEW QUESTIONS

1 Why is finance looked on as morally dubious?

2 What is financial globalization, and what are the main forces behind its growth?

3 What is the 'veil of incorporation' in company law, and what are the ethical implications?

4 Explain the differences between the public company and the public-sector company.

5 Why did AIG collapse and what were the lessons?

6 What are the ethical factors associated with sovereign debt?

7 What can companies and fund managers do to attract more interest in ethical investing and respond better to their ethical preferences?

8 How effective are stock markets at regulating their activities, and why has regulation become a key issue for investors?

9 Large companies that engage in tax avoidance by using tax havens state that they are abiding by the law and doing nothing wrong. Do you agree or disagree with this stance, and why?

10 What is transfer pricing, and is it unethical?

11 Why is the culture of professionals in financial services apparently resistant to changes which would be more in keeping with ethical and socially responsible values?

12 What is sustainable banking, and is it achievable? Explain.

THE BANK, THE TRADER AND THE GOVERNOR

CLOSING CASE STUDY

Barclays Bank of the UK traces its origins back over 300 years, to its founding by Quakers. The cultural imprint of its Quaker legacy remained in the company long into the twentieth century. As a minority religious group with pacifist beliefs, Quakers in the seventeenth century could not enter occupations such as the law and the army. They gravitated towards banking and established a reputation for integrity and trust, reinforced by their religious beliefs. A family-dominated bank, Barclays grew through acquisitions in the nineteenth century, acquiring banks in Africa, the Middle East and the Caribbean, reflecting British colonial presence. In the twentieth century, Barclays was still family controlled, upholding the traditional values of its founders, but in the 1980s it underwent radical changes which have led it progressively away from its founders' culture.

Deregulation of equities trading on the London Stock Exchange (LSE) brought new opportunities for investment banking in the 1980s. Barclays ventured into an equities business. It hoped to integrate its existing conventional banking with its new investment banking in a universal bank similar to the large American banks. This combination proved to be uneasy, as the differing cultures were not easily integrated. The investment bankers were essentially dealmakers, highly ambitious and unafraid of risks. But the investment limb struggled, and by the 1990s, the CEO concluded that it lacked the scale to compete in both operations. The investment banking side was strengthened with the creation of Barclays Capital in 1997. By that time trading in securities and derivatives were becoming highly lucrative, and traders were rising in the banking hierarchy, not just at Barclays, but in banking generally. The rather staid image of banking culture was shifting more towards the culture of the traders, whose high-octane lifestyles and bonus-driven attitudes were transforming banking. It was from the trading side that Bob Diamond, Barclay's rising star, emerged. Bob Diamond had come to Barclays from CS First Boston in New York, having resigned following his bonus award in 1995, which, although several million dollars, he considered unreasonably small. This reaction was later seen as indicative of how he would change things at Barclays.

Mr Diamond built up the investment division, Barclays Capital. A crowning achievement was the acquisition of the US business of the failed bank, Lehman Brothers, in 2008. But the plaudits he received for steering Barclays towards greater recognition on Wall Street were soon overshadowed by the financial crisis which impacted on all the British banks. Barclays alone did not reach for a bailout, but its salvation came in the form of funding from Qatar, in a deal which was

Photo 5.3 The UK's central bank, the Bank of England, came under pressure in the financial crisis of 2008, when regulatory systems seemed to fail. (© iStock.com/ dynasoar)

controversial at the time and has since been the subject of an investigation by the Serious Fraud Office. Mr Diamond, who was appointed CEO in 2011, also courted controversy for his extravagant pay awards, notably his pay of £17 million for 2011, to which was added the provision that Barclays pay his tax bill. At the time, an emerging scandal was encompassing a number of banks, accused of fixing of an important benchmark lending rate, the London interbank offered rate (Libor). Barclays was fined $290 million for its part in the Libor fixing by the FSA. The bank suffered reputational damage as a result, which was compounded by other revelations, including the extent of its tax avoidance business, which, while technically legal, was perceived to be unethical. Its tax unit contributed a large portion of the profits of the investment banking business, but whistleblower revelations regarding the huge sums channelled through offshore networks led to the accusation from former Chancellor of the Exchequer (minister of finance), Lord Lawson, of a tax avoidance business on an 'industrial scale' (Lawrence, 2013). The company was also compelled to set aside £3.4 billion to cover liabilities for the misselling of payment protection insurance products to customers.

In July 2012, the Governor of the Bank of England spoke to the Chairman of Barclays Bank, Marcus Agius, and conveyed to him that Bob Diamond would have to depart as CEO. Both Diamond and Agius resigned. The Governor was belatedly asserting regulatory authority which, he acknowledges, had been lacking. He has said that, 'with the benefit of hindsight, ... banks had grown too quickly and borrowed too much, and ... so-called 'light-touch' regulation hadn't prevented any of this' (Giles, 2012). Of the banking culture, he said, 'From excessive compensation to deceitful manipulation of the most important interest rates, we can see we need a change of culture in the industry' (Giles, 2012). Media reaction highlighted that, although other banks were also involved in the rate-fixing scandal, Barclays was unjustly singled out, and its executives made scapegoats (Armitage, 2012). Why was that? Possibly, the larger-than-life character of Bob Diamond, with his confidence that the Libor troubles would simply blow over, suggested an arrogance that made public opinion turn

on him personally. Like the former CEO of RBS, Sir Fred Goodwin, Diamond seemed to sum up 'the unacceptable face of banking' (Sorkin, 2013).

Has Barclays' culture changed? The new CEO, Antony Jenkins, came from the retail banking business. He has launched a Project Transform and promised to make ethical behaviour a priority. He admitted the bank had made mistakes and announced that any new activities would be screened for reputational impact as well as profitability. The tax unit would be closed due to 'negative media and political attention', he said (Jenkins and Schäfer, 2012). Appearing before a Parliamentary committee in 2013, he said he was 'shredding' the legacy of Bob Diamond (Lawrence, 2013).

Bob Diamond was interviewed in New York in 2013, having had time to reflect on what had gone wrong at Barclays. He expressed the view that the Governor of the Bank of England had no authority to sack him: only the board had that authority. He feels the image of himself portrayed in the media is unfair, saying, 'I never did anything for money. I never set money as a goal' (Sorkin, 2013). A photo in the article shows him travelling in an ordinary subway train, but the interviewer notes that his is not the life of an ordinary commuter: Diamond's New York home is a $37-million penthouse overlooking Central Park.

Sources: Sorkin, A. (2013) 'Robert Diamond's next life', *New York Times*, 2 May, at www.nyt.com; Armitage, J. (2012) 'Barclays hits back after "hounding out" of Bob Diamond', *The Independent*, 4 July, at www.independent.co.uk; Plender, J. (2012) 'How the traders trumped the Quakers', *Financial Times*, 7 July; Giles, C. (2012) 'The bank that roared', *Financial Times*, 14 July; Jenkins, P. and Schäfer, D. (2012) 'Barclays to cut back tax unit in ethics push', *Financial Times*, 11 September; Lawrence, F. (2013) 'Barclays secret tax avoidance factory that made £1bn a year profit disbanded', *The Guardian*, 11 February, at www.theguardian.com (18/09/14).

□ Which aspects of Barclay's pre-crisis strategy and management would you consider the most unethical and why?

□ To what extent was lax regulation a cause of Barclay's descent into scandals?

□ Do you consider the post-Diamond reforms at Barclays are turning it into a more ethical bank, or simply focusing more on repairing its reputation?

CHAPTER 6

INTERNATIONAL TRADE AND ETHICAL CONSIDERATIONS

ETHICAL THEMES IN THIS CHAPTER

- Economic development and changing societies
- Sustainability guiding business and state actors

THE AIMS OF THIS CHAPTER ARE TO

- Identify the ethical dimensions of world trade
- Appreciate the power relations which impact on trade
- Assess critically national trade policies from an ethical viewpoint
- Compare multilateral and regional trade agreements in their impacts on societies

INDONESIA GAINS FROM TRADE, BUT WHO IS LEFT BEHIND?

The Asian financial crisis of 1997–8 was devastating for the Indonesian economy and society. In 1998, the country's GDP contracted by 13.8%, and half the population suffered from poverty. That year saw the overthrow of Suharto, Indonesia's long-reigning dictator, giving way to a fragile democratic system – one in which patronage and business dynasties, which characterized the Suharto period, were still pervasive. Since then, Indonesia has been admired as a success story of economic recovery, thanks largely to its export success. Economic growth reached pre-crisis levels by 2003, and it has grown at relatively consistent rates of 6% since then, dipping to 4% in 2009, and reaching up to 7% since then. Natural resources are key to its comparative advantage. Coal, oil, numerous minerals, and agricultural products such as palm oil and timber have seen rising demand in global markets. The companies behind this success are Indonesia's powerful family-owned conglomerates, aided by close ties to the government. The government of President Yudhoyono, which reaches the end of its second term in 2014, had promised to reduce the corrupt links between politicians and big business which had become endemic. And it had also promised to improve economic and social conditions for the vast majority of Indonesians. But there have been disappointments in both respects. The wealth and economic strength of the business tycoons has continued to dominate, while poverty and deprivation remain huge challenges.

Photo 6.1 *Toxic foam from river pollution is one of the many environmental problems in Indonesia, impacting most heavily on the poorest in society.* (© iStock.com/Herianus)

Environmental concerns are also concerns for the government. Logging and palm oil production have both caused deforestation, which is heavily criticized by environmentalists. Palm oil is extensively used by global food companies such as Nestlé. Nestlé and other companies have announced policies of using only palm oil from sustainable sources, but, in practice, this is difficult to verify. Sinar Mas, a large Indonesian conglomerate with major activities in palm plantations and pulp and paper, is one of the companies frequently cited as responsible for deforestation. The Indonesian government declared a moratorium on deforestation, but the rules are sometimes waived by local politicians, who give permissions to companies in return for unofficial payments, which tend to find their way into campaign coffers as elections approach. This seems to have happened in 2013, when 'slash-and-burn' practices led to the destruction of forests as a way of clearing the land cheaply for palm plantations. But the price was a dangerous pollution haze which spread over neighbouring Singapore. The haze strained relations with Singapore. Sinar Mas was cited as one of the companies involved, but there were many others, among them companies registered in Singapore and Malaysia.

The years of strong economic growth have led to changes in Indonesian society, but the benefits are not evenly shared. The country is an archipelago of over 17,000 islands. The western islands have been the traditional economic centre, and this is where the capital, Jakarta, is located, but recent economic growth has occurred in eastern cities where ports are thriving. Indonesia is the world's fourth most populous country, with a population of 250 million. Home to the world's largest Muslim population, the country has been lauded as 'proof that democracy and prosperity can live alongside Islam' (Bland, 2012). However, as economic recovery has progressed, inequality has widened. In 2002, the top 10% of the population accounted for 25.6% of the country's income, while in 2012, their share had risen to 30.6% (World Bank Development Indicators). Rising numbers of people are entering the middle class, clustering in the growing urban areas in the east of the country, where hypermarkets and shopping malls are springing up. But the prosperity has not trickled down. Poverty has been reduced, but remains high, especially in rural areas, which have not seen the benefits of economic growth. The percentage of people living below the official national poverty line was 12.5% in 2012, down from 18% in 2006. However, this still represents 30 million people, 70% of whom live in rural areas. Moreover, this figure understates the extent of poverty due to the low level at which the national poverty line is set – less than $1 a day (*The Economist*, 2011). It is estimated that about 100 million Indonesians get by on $2 a day or less, which is triple the number of people officially in poverty (*The Economist*, 2011). The government subsidizes fuel and food for the poor, and, when fuel subsidies were reduced, it introduced a large cash transfer programme to compensate. But cash handouts do not provide a long-term solution.

Given Indonesia's large and growing population, job creation is a particular concern. The country has a manufacturing sector, but this sector, which was 29% of GDP in 2009, has contracted since then, mainly due to the rise of competing locations in Asia, such as Cambodia and Vietnam. Poor educational provision is a factor in holding back job creation. The country has need of educational development which will provide skilled workers and build technological advancement. But whereas most countries with Indonesia's impressive growth would be expected to be spending more on education, Indonesia has actually spent less on education over the last three years. Its spending on primary education fell from 13.4% of GDP per capita in 2009 to 8.7% in 2011, a level comparable with the poorer countries of Sub-Saharan Africa (World Bank Development Indicators). Although formal employment is rising, most employment in Indonesia is still in the informal sector. This means that work is highly precarious and unregulated, involving no employment status or job security.

Despite its relatively high growth, Indonesia remains in a lowly ranking of 121 out of 186 countries in the UN's human development index. Less than half the rural poor population have access to clean water, and in rural areas only about half of children complete junior high school. Child labour is a concern, with 1.5 million children engaged in full-time work (Bland, 2013). Emblematic of the plight of Indonesia's poor are the 1,500 families who scrape a living as waste pickers at Bantar Gebang, one of Jakarta's vast landfill sites, looking for material that can be sold for recycling. Here, even pupils in primary school work part-time at the dump, and only 40% stay in school past age 11. This is a world away from the luxury hotels, shopping centres and private hospitals being built in fast-growing urban areas in the eastern part of the country.

Indonesia's boom has been built on commodity exports and rising domestic consumption, but its oil production is dwindling, and demand in its export markets, such as India and China, is slowing. These threats bring into question its growth model, which assumed a continuing commodities boom. Any faltering in growth would also risk political turmoil. Indonesia's poorest inhabitants, the hundred million living on $2 a day or less, had aspirations that the post-1998 recovery would bring them a better life, better jobs and better prospects for the future. They are still waiting.

Sources: World Bank (2013) *Indonesia Economic Quarterly: Adjusting for Pressures*, at www.worldbank.org; *World Bank Development Indicators*, at www.worldbank.org; *The Economist* (2011) 'To make a million people unpoor', 3 August, at www.economist.com; ILO (2013) *ILO Trade and Employment Report on Indonesia*, at www.ilo.org (18/09/14); Bland, B. (2012) 'Archipelago apprehension', *Financial Times*, 30 August; Bland, B. (2013) 'Life is rubbish for Indonesian poor left behind in boom times', *Financial Times*, 20 March.

□ **What ethical issues arise for the Indonesian government?**

□ **What ethical issues arise for the large companies which dominate the Indonesian economy?**

□ **Companies which trade with those in Indonesia could be accused of being complicit in unethical practices. What advice would you give them?**

INTRODUCTION

Trade is a cornerstone of international business. Whatever product a firm makes or whatever service it provides, it must find buyers and deal with trading intermediaries to turn sales into lucrative markets. Globalization has seen companies looking further afield for buyers and also looking to source raw materials from more advantageous locations, seeking primarily to reduce costs and improve efficiency. Trading activities play a crucial role in this decision-making. But trade is much more than the mechanics of exchange transactions: it involves societies, consumers and governments, each with sets of interests and values. It also involves a range of ethical considerations that transcend particular situations. This chapter sets out the different interests and ethical perspectives of these distinct players.

The chapter begins with an overview of the ethical dimensions of trade, and their historical antecedents. We look at the historical context, including imperialism, past and present. We then look at globalization, in which trade and FDI have been twin drivers. While many countries and many groups within countries have benefited, the impacts are uneven. As trade has grown, corporate gains have not been matched by gains in welfare within societies. Ethical issues for countries and companies centre especially on groups which have little scope to exert pressure on governments and MNEs. The last major section is on the changes taking place in international trade and WTO oversight. As multilateral trade agreements to liberalize trade have encountered strong headwinds from national governments, moves towards bilateral and other more limited trade agreements are taking place. While these moves might be taken to signify a new liberalization which could potentially benefit societies, there remain concerns over the impacts of trade deals on human rights, IP rights, labour standards and environmental protection.

WORLD TRADE AND ETHICAL DIMENSIONS

Trade is one of the oldest business activities, going back to ancient times. Over history, it has been one of the most assured routes to increased wealth. From the empires of the ancient Romans and Greeks to the empires of the nineteenth century, trade has enriched imperial countries' rulers and also the merchants who did the deals. The last chapter noted the rise of the Dutch East India Company, pointing out the link between trade and national expansion. Although some imperialistic countries have simply invaded and plundered other territories, most see trade as advantageous, offering payment of some kind for the resources they appropriate. Trade is about the exchange of goods or services across borders, usually for some price, although not necessarily money. Exports are destined for other markets, while imports are products entering a country from abroad. In a barter transaction, goods are exchanged for other goods. While trade can take place between regions within a single country, we adopt the view of trade as essentially international, that is, between countries. The subject matter of trade can be just about anything. Agricultural products, minerals, energy and manufactured goods come to mind. In today's world, services have become an important element of trade, as this chapter will highlight. There is a darker side too. There is a long history of trade in human beings, for slavery or forced labour. Slavery was abolished in the middle of the nineteenth century in most countries, but informal variants of slavery persisted. There is also a thriving global trade in arms, illegal drugs and counterfeit goods, which also fund crime, insurrections and terrorist activities. It is sometimes thought

Figure 6.1 Who, what and why of trade from ethical perspectives

that trade is simply about economic transactions on a large scale: the trader is a businessperson, and commodities can be interchangeable, even as between people and goods. While some traders will always persist in this view, the ethical issues revolving around trade have become more and more evident in public opinion and consumer sentiment globally.

Trade is older than capitalism, but capitalism has grown through trade. Industrialization and the growth of capitalist enterprises from the eighteenth century onwards were greatly enhanced by the potential for trade. Some of the largest businesses over the following century rested on export and import businesses, often raw materials from abroad destined for industrial processing in Europe. While companies could grow powerful gradually in their own countries, they could grow dramatically through exports of goods, and imports of raw materials. Governments intervene in these activities routinely. They protect domestic industries through imposing tariff barriers on imported goods and by subsidizing local producers. **Protectionism** is thus perceived as creating distortions in markets. Nonetheless, protectionism is common, and is one of the aspects of trade which the World Trade Organization (WTO) was set up to limit through co-operation among member states. As we will see, companies rely on trade in global production networks and global markets. But trade is not merely about economic exchange. It has a moral dimension, in the products, the producers themselves, the traders and the interests they represent, as shown in Figure 6.1.

Trade makes a link not just between the people directly involved but between societies. The societies of both parties, the seller of goods and the purchaser, are affected by trade. Trade is not morally neutral between these societies. There are benefits to be gained, not just in money terms but in qualitative impacts on societies, many of which are linked to development. The benefits are not usually equally shared: one side gains more than the other, although the effects might take a long time to become apparent. Ideally, when a country's businesses export successfully, the wealth generated contributes to the country's GDP, fostering economic growth and swelling government coffers. This allows the government to invest in social goods such as education and health. But this ideal situation is often far from reality. Countries can enjoy economic growth without their societies seeing tangible benefits, either because their governments take most of the profits, or the revenues go to foreign businesses that control the assets. Trade thus raises a wide range of ethical questions, in addition to the issues of subject matter just mentioned. How are exported products produced? If through poor labour conditions or environmentally damaging practices, they are unethical. If the workers who produce crops for export are paid very little, and large profits are channelled to rich owners overseas, this, too, is unethical. This highlights a recurring characteristic of trade: that of asymmetry, a stronger power and a weaker one.

THE HISTORICAL CONTEXT: IMPERIALISM

Trade has grown in harmony with the growth of empires. Imperialism is 'the domination and exploitation of weaker states by stronger ones' (Johnson, 2004: 28). This domination can be military, political or economic. These three aspects of domination can reinforce each other. Mercantilism is the approach taken by a stronger power which focuses on national economic benefits through trade. The imperialist can exert controls over economic and political life, and also over existing cultures. Empires are sometimes praised as being benign, bringing the benefits of the culture and institutions of the imperial power to populations. This assumes a superiority of the cultural values of the imperial power, which are imposed on the weaker country. The Roman empire is an example of this view. So too is America in the post-war era, in that the US has been the dominant economic, political and military power, or hegemon (see discussion in Chapter 3). Cultural imperialism takes an ethnocentric view of the world: the stronger power feels justified in subduing others on grounds of moral superiority which denies the validity other peoples' cultures and values. The large MNE, especially the global business with large market shares in different sectors across many countries, can be analogous to the imperialistic country. The 'business empire' is often united by a strong corporate culture, usually that of its home country, which pervades the organization, whatever the country location. Many business empires have grown in periods of national economic ascendancy, often benefiting from close relations with governments.

The large MNE, especially the global business with large market shares in different sectors across many countries, can be analogous to the imperialistic country.

Imperialism tends to be used interchangeably with colonialism (Landes, 1998: 423). The imperial power might not take over the whole running of a country, but controls it sufficiently to exert its will over the territory. Imperialism is usually linked to military dominance. Wars are fought for control of trade routes, key ports and territories rich in resources. Colonialism implies a degree of occupation of foreign territory and also control of formal institutions of governance. But occupation and control are not the same. The British ruled India with a relatively small British colonial service, amounting at its peak to 168,000 people, or just 0.05% of the population, but this was a colony nonetheless (Maddison, 2001: 119).

Colonialism tends to have a more negative connotation than imperialism. For this reason, the supporter of benign imperialism would probably refrain from calling it colonialism. Figure 6.2 depicts colonialism as essentially exploitative, and this would also pertain to imperialism. In terms of exports, the weaker party is the exporting country, whose goods are sold cheaply and shipped to the colonial power. Colonialists benefit from cheap imports, but the benefits are likely to be unevenly distributed: the businesspeople involved in the

Figure 6.2 Winners and losers in colonial trade

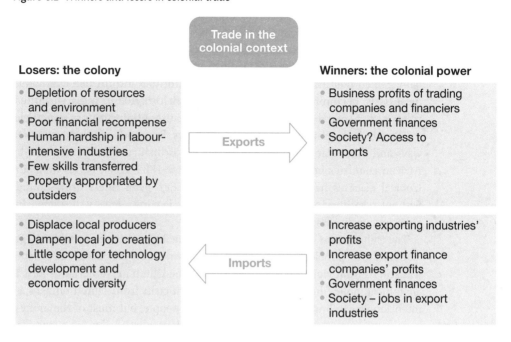

relevant industries benefit the most. Businesses also benefit by exporting their goods to subservient countries which are captive markets. The ethical perspective of the imperialist is that of the home country. Trade with other countries is designed to serve national interests of the home country, whether through imports of resources or exports of goods. The pursuit of national interest, however, can equate to enriching the businesspeople and financiers who are involved, as well as the governments which collect taxes. For societies, the picture is different. As the figure shows, a colony's social welfare and economic development almost inevitably suffer. The gains for society in the home country of the colonial power are more ambiguous. Imports from the colony benefit its citizens. Wealth from the colony could be used to do much more, improving social conditions, but it is likely to find its way into the coffers of large businesses and the political élite. Historically, empires have been highly unequal societies, both in their home countries and in their colonies.

Exploitation and drain of resources characterize trade between strong aggressive powers and weak territories. Dating from 642, Islamic rule of North Africa was bolstered by the strength of religious and cultural identity. Its economic power derived largely from trade in gold extracted in African territories, but the slave trade was also highly developed. In over eight centuries of Arab rule in North Africa, 4.3 million slaves were transported from Sub-Saharan Africa to destinations north of the Sahara, and another 2.2 million were shipped from East Africa to Arabia (Maddison, 2001: 222). European traders sought to make inroads into the Muslim trade routes, partly because of the financial gains from the gold trade and also for religious motives, as they felt a sense of mission to push back Islamic influences. From about 1500, trade between European countries and Africa grew, mainly in coastal cities. The Portuguese became early leaders in these trading activities, and also engaged in missionary activities to convert local people to Christianity. The Dutch, British and French followed the Portuguese into Africa. These later traders were active in the slave trade, relying on a network of African slave traders. Some 4.5 million slaves were shipped from Africa to the Americas from 1500 to 1870 (Maddison, 2001).

The period of European countries' outward expansion only reached peaks of imperial consolidation in the late nineteenth century. In the British penetration of India, trade came first, organized by the East India Company, which was formed in 1600. The company gradually gained political power, which was transformed into British colonial rule on a piecemeal basis, becoming consolidated in 1857. British rule in India was often through local rulers rather than direct, but controlled by British administrators nonetheless. India benefited from development in many material ways. But much of the development, such as railways and other transport, served mainly the British rulers. Colonization by Europeans of African countries became significant only after 1880, when better medicines to deal with tropical diseases had been developed. New European rulers drew boundaries in Africa without regard to local cultures and ethnicity, leaving a legacy of states which lack natural cohesion, as discussed in Chapters 3 and 4.

The subjugation of indigenous peoples evokes criticism on ethical grounds. Forced labour of local people, though a slight improvement on the dismal life prospects of the slave, was still flagrant violation of human rights. The Dutch in Netherlands East Indies launched an 'ethical' policy in 1900, in response to criticism from Dutch citizens in Holland. The intention was to improve the welfare of local people, but most of the money seems to have gone on better salaries for bureaucrats and better irrigation for sugar plantations which were owned by westerners. The poor labour conditions on sugar plantations, along with poor social services and education, were typical of the time.

Most ethical theorists would criticize colonialism in the forms just described as unethical, mainly because whole peoples are subjugated to foreign powers. But not all would agree, many people holding that a form of benign imperialism can benefit a society (see Ferguson, 2003, 2004). An ethical critique of empire could begin with the basic principles of liberty discussed in Chapters 1 and 3, which involve freedom of self-determination. The natural rights theorists acknowledged a right to overthrow despots. Applying Kant's categorical imperative, colonialism amounts to treating other people as means and not ends. Colonialism would also be condemned by the social justice theorists like Rawls and Sen.

Can imperialism be defended? Imperial powers in the past have justified their colonialism in paternalistic terms, alleging that they had a cultural superiority or even destiny which justified their activities. Many even adopted a religious dimension, believing that they were fulfilling God's mission through enlightening peoples who were considered morally backward. The Chinese empire which reached its height in the eighteenth century was built on a 'civilizing mission' based on religion, and it suppressed religions it perceived as threatening, such as Christianity, Islam and Tibetan Buddhism (Waley-Cohen, 1998). John Stuart Mill's views in favour of the British empire have aroused criticism, largely because they seem to conflict with his liberal stance on the value of individualism and self-development.

J.S. Mill did not support imperialism as an end in itself, but as a means of guiding Indians towards a more civilized and tolerant existence.

A career employee of the East India Company, Mill supported a 'tolerant imperialism', which could be distinguished from forced assimilation (Tunick, 2006). He felt that Indian cultures should not be suppressed, but that India had not yet reached a level of civilization where it would be capable of self-government. He did not support imperialism as an end in itself, but as a means of guiding Indians towards a more civilized and tolerant existence. His stance would still probably be criticized on ethical grounds: even benevolent imperialism is still imperialism. Mill took a strong stand against colonialism in Jamaica, and criticized treatment of slaves (Kohn and O'Neill, 2006). And he opposed mercantilism. Historians now look back on the British colonial legacy in India as having left some enduring benefits such as the legal system and respect for the rule of law (Maddison, 2001: 131). But for Indian society, there were few benefits in terms of improved standards of living.

India became a sovereign state in 1948, and Indonesia, in 1949. African colonies became independent states slightly later. But, although former colonies are now sovereign states, imperialism as a phenomenon is not dead. American economic and military dominance has persisted throughout the post-war period, bolstered by the supremacy of the US dollar in world markets. US imperialism, although different from that of the European empires, is real and has shaped much of world trade, along with its influence in global politics. Like earlier imperialisms, the American self-image as the world's only superpower has been justified at home by its stated commitment to liberty and democracy. The US government has portrayed itself as upholding liberal values in the world, promoting open markets and democracies in place of authoritarian regimes. But liberal imperialism is still imperialism, and its interventions in many countries, nominally sovereign, have left them worse off as societies (see Chapter 3). The massive scale of surveillance activities carried out by its National Security Agency and affiliated organizations has undermined its claims to uphold liberal values. Major beneficiaries of US military interventions around the globe have been large American companies with links to the military and national security sectors. For an imperial power, the US position in world trade has become incongruous. It has huge levels of national debt, and a huge trade deficit (meaning that it imports more than it exports). The British empire, by contrast, had a huge trade surplus. Power in world trade is now shifting away from America towards emerging economies, but America's resurgence in oil and gas production indicates that it remains a powerful actor, as do the global companies that are based in the US.

PAUSE TO CONSIDER...

'Benign imperialism' is sometimes supported on grounds that it offers solutions to instability and poor local governance in fragile states. How would this position be criticized on ethical grounds?

TRADE AND GLOBALIZATION

Two world wars saw the disintegration of the empires of the last two centuries. Since the Second World War, many new developing countries have become active in trade. World trade has grown and has become more open. Globalization has brought expansion of trading ties by both countries and companies. However, the proliferation of new independent states has not led to the sharing of benefits which many might have expected. An underlying assumption in trade in a world of sovereign states is that trade benefits all countries. Every country is assumed to be better off trading than not trading. This assumption goes back to the views of the classical economists, notably Ricardo, whose theory of comparative advantage showed that a country should export products in which it has advantages, and import other products it needs which it cannot produce as efficiently as other countries (Kitson and Michie, 1995). In theory, a country can gain wealth from exports, and use this money to pay for needed imports. This view represents a rather idealized picture, however, presupposing that countries compete equally and that markets always function perfectly. In fact, there are disparities in bargaining power, markets are sometimes distorted, and sovereign states often engage in protectionist policies. For example, a country might have to sell its commodity exports cheaply when relevant markets are falling. It could then find it must pay dearly for imports. It is also the case that economies of scale come into play in manufacturing, leading to cumulative advantages in international trade, whereas weaker trading nations suffer from a cumulative deterioration in their trading position (Kitson and Michie, 1995). Gleaning benefits from trade, on the one hand, or suffering detriments from trade, on the other, raises ethical issues. We look first at the impacts of globalization and then at the ethical implications.

TRENDS IN TRADING RELATIONS: WHO IS BENEFITING AND WHO IS NOT?

In the early post-war period, developed economies dominated world trade. The US was a pioneer in the production of mass-market consumer goods. Its manufacturing companies grew in the context of rising domestic demand. American consumers were eager to acquire the latest household appliances. Demand from affluent consumers abroad also boosted US companies. But America's lead in consumer goods such as washing machines, refrigerators and televisions, amounted to more than simply selling products consumers desired: America was selling its lifestyle (Domosh, 2004). This period saw the export not just of consumer goods but of the American way of life. The heyday of American consumerism was the 1950s and 60s, epitomized by the large industrial centres such as Detroit, the centre of the motor industry. But their place in the sun gradually dimmed as challengers appeared on the horizon – mainly from Asia. From the 1970s, Japan was gaining in economic power through industrial development, the first of the Asian high-growth economies. State guidance, which was based not on state ownership but on reciprocity between government and industry, played a crucial role in its success (Johnson, 1982). While the US attempted to keep Japanese imports at bay, Japanese car manufacturers established greenfield sites in the US to produce cars for the US market (discussed in Chapter 2). Their success contributed to reduced market shares for the powerful US carmakers. Two of these companies, General Motors and Chrysler, faced humiliating bailouts by government in 2008. In the 1980s, South Korean companies followed the lead of Japan, focusing on manufacturing FDI in the US and Europe. Japan, an original G8 member, has long been recognized as a developed country (Note 1). South Korea has also achieved the status of a developed country and is a member of the OECD (see note, Chapter 2). Both are also democracies. By contrast, China, although now the world's second largest economy, is still considered a developing country.

China's rise to become an industrial superpower followed a different pattern from its Asian neighbours. From the time of its market reforms in the 1990s, China welcomed inward FDI, attracting companies in sectors involving low-cost, labour-intensive manufacturing. Its exports, which have flooded into western markets, have included products which involve low skills such as textiles, but also electronics such as TVs and smartphones. China grew to become the world's manufacturing superpower, toppling the dominance of the advanced economies known as the 'triad' countries, comprising North America, Europe and Japan. Developed countries' aggregate share of world trade was 55% in 2010, down from

America did more than sell products: America was selling its lifestyle.

69% in 1995 and 60% in 2008 (UNCTAD, 2012a). China has been the world's leading merchandise exporter since 2009, with a 10% share of global exports. Its strength in export-oriented manufacturing has been responsible for a long period of high economic growth, averaging 10% annually for two decades.

China's growth has now slowed, and the country faces many of the issues which preoccupy the developed countries, such as expectations of continuing improvement in quality of life. China's economic success has created a growing middle class, whose changing lifestyles largely reflect an updated version of the powerful American image of earlier decades: household appliances and gadgetry, fast food, new family cars and leisure pursuits such as travel. These consumers are some of the winners in the China success story. Poverty has been reduced, but the migrant workers on whom the country depends have not enjoyed the dream lifestyles of richer city dwellers. Conditions in China's vast manufacturing complexes (discussed in Chapter 2) have been criticized, much blame falling on the global brands whose products are assembled in China. Negative aspects of China's global rise have been rising inequality and rising levels of pollution. China's growth has been fuelled by exploitation of its own resources, especially coal, but also by huge energy imports, notably oil. Chinese demand for energy and raw materials has helped to enrich resource-rich exporting countries, many of which are also developing countries. As Figure 6.3 shows, exports from emerging economies, although falling in 2009, have rebounded, while those from developed countries have not strengthened to the same extent. World trade as a whole grew only 2% in 2012, affected by weaker economic growth and also by protectionist measures of governments. China's manufacturers have come under pressure to improve wages, working conditions and employee representation in factories. Taking into account that they also face higher prices for imported raw materials and energy, China's exports have become more expensive. This comes at a time when consumers in its large western markets are lamenting stagnant wages and are not as free-spending as they were in the boom years before the financial crisis.

Figure 6.3 *Growth in volume of exports from developed and emerging economies*

100 = Base in 2000

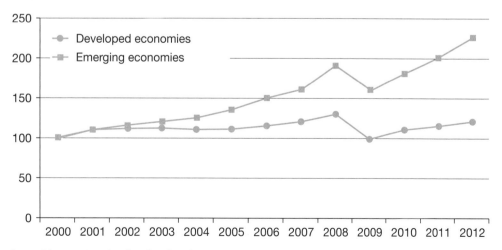

Source of data: UNCTAD (2012) *Trade and Development Report,* at www.unctad.org (18/09/14).

China's lead in low-cost manufacturing has gradually dwindled, and globalized companies have looked for location advantages elsewhere. Much of the manufacturing of textiles and footwear has shifted to poorer Asian countries, which are cheaper. They include Cambodia, Vietnam and Indonesia (featured in the opening case study). Wages in Cambodia are about $110 to $130 per month, compared with $400 in China. These countries have seen the benefits of employment, but it has been concentrated in low-skill industries, often in poor and unsafe working conditions. Workers striking for higher wages in Cambodia have been met with aggressive police tactics. There have been accusations of forced evictions to make way for factories (Jacob, 2013). Cambodian garment factories are smaller than Chinese counterparts, but they still contribute significantly to the economy and employ 500,000 people. Cambodia's textile exports in 2012 were $4.3 billion, while China's were $270 billion. Governments in Vietnam and Cambodia have actively encouraged companies in the garment industry, resulting in a rush of FDI. Factory owners, often foreign investors, are among the main winners. In Cambodia, these are frequently companies from Hong Kong, Taiwan or Japan. These companies, like those in China, face demands not just for higher wages, but for more union representation. Meanwhile, pursuing global strategies, brand owners and foreign investors are continually looking for cheaper and more advantageous locations elsewhere. The Rana Plaza collapse in Bangladesh, in which over 1,000 people lost their lives, was an indication of the 'race to the bottom' in sectors based on cheap labour (see case study, Chapter 1).

The factory collapse in Bangladesh, in which over 1,000 people lost their lives, was an indication of the 'race to the bottom' in sectors based on cheap labour.

In more complex products such as cars, who are the winners and losers? Globalization in the current era, in contrast to that of the empires of earlier eras, has seen FDI become more closely linked to trade, as supply chains are divided into stages of production, each taking place in different countries. Countries have become more interconnected, and much economic power has shifted to the MNEs who co-ordinate global production in dispersed locations. Almost all countries export 'intermediate' goods as well as finished products. And in general, about one-third of each country's imports are destined for exported products (OECD, 2013). The percentage tends to be higher in smaller countries. A developing country may well have little scope in practice to exert influence over the industry or to gain in technological innovation, as it is simply producing components as part of global supply chains. Much power has shifted to the MNE, which sees each country merely as part of the chain. The UN's Trade and Development Conference (UNCTAD) sees this phenomenon as a kind of 'offshoring' of production, with detrimental consequences for the countries in the chain (UNCTAD, 2012a). The MNE is looking at short-term profitability and could well relocate an operation to a different country if circumstances change. Countries involved in trade might see few benefits: the profits are exported by the MNEs and the society sees few long-term gains. Although it might gain employment, these jobs do not represent the development of a depth in technology skills and innovation.

Increasingly, the motor manufacturers are seeking to produce vehicles in low-cost locations. Mexico serves the US market, while Moroccan and Romanian car factories serve the European market. As Chinese imports have become more expensive for US consumers, Mexico has seized opportunities to increase exports to US markets. Mexico had a share of over 14% of US imports in 2012, whereas China's share, still huge at 26%, had fallen from 29% in 2009 (Thomson, 2012).

Whereas it is usually pictured as the poor southern neighbour of the US, Mexico has become a threat to China's export dominance. China's rising wage bills, along with the cost and time involved in shipping goods to western markets, have boosted the attractions of Mexico. Other factors have been China's heavy-handed bureaucracy and complaints of leakage of intellectual property. Mexico has been gradually improving its educational system, developing engineering skills needed for making complex products like cars and airplanes. It has also benefited from its many free trade agreements with other countries, which allow it to import parts and other inputs with little or no import duty. Mexico has embraced openness in trade, concluding 44 free trade agreements with other countries – twice as many as China and four times as many as its Latin American rival, Brazil. An unlikely celebration occurred in 2012, when a new Chrysler car factory in Mexico began exporting Fiat 500 cars to China. Few Mexicans would have thought this possible, and Chrysler could also celebrate. The US car company went bankrupt in 2008 and was rescued by Fiat of Italy, which has a long experience of exporting in highly competitive global markets.

An unlikely celebration occurred in 2012, when a new Chrysler car factory in Mexico began exporting Fiat 500 cars to China.

In trade between developing countries, resource-rich countries have enjoyed advantages, but resource riches do not automatically benefit societies. A number of African countries are major exporters of energy and commodities, meeting high demand from emerging economies such as China and Brazil. In the last decade, trade between China and Africa multiplied 20 times, reaching $200 billion in 2012. This trade is dominated by Chinese imports of raw materials and fuel from Africa, while African countries import mainly manufactured goods from China.

Manufactured goods from China include clothing, food, electronics, furniture, building materials and plastic goods. Many of these products could easily be made in Africa by African workers, but they stand little chance of competing against the tide of cheap Chinese imports. As a result, manufacturing in Africa has shrunk. Although the rise in Chinese demand for oil has led to impressive economic growth in some African countries, this is not the kind of growth which is sustainable or creates jobs. Nigeria, the continent's most populous country, with a population of 160 million, is an example. Crude oil is Nigeria's biggest export, but ordinary people see little benefit in their lives. Chinese investment in roads and infrastructure has been welcome, but both the machinery and the workers are brought in from China. China's trade policies are now causing concern among African political leaders. Their governments have encouraged Chinese initiatives in the past, often as a political policy to counteract the influence of former colonial powers who tended to look on FDI and trade as linked to the development of western liberal values. Now the risk is from a 'new form of imperialism', Nigeria's central bank governor has warned. He says, 'China takes from us primary goods and sells us manufactured ones. This was also the essence of colonialism' (Sanusi, 2013). China, he says, 'is no longer a fellow under-developed economy – it is the world's second-biggest, capable of the same forms of exploitation as the west' (Sanusi, 2013). The woes in Nigeria, including ethnic unrest, stem from multiple causes, including poor governance and corruption. Deals between exploitative oil companies and corrupt politicians have cost the country dearly over the years. Other African oil-producing countries are attempting to learn the lessons of how to manage resource wealth in transparent processes which channel funds to social goods.

'China takes from us primary goods and sells us manufactured ones. This was also the essence of colonialism.'

Nigeria is rich in oil, which is extracted by large oil companies, foreign owned. Its crude oil is largely exported. Nigeria remains a very poor country, and its people resent the fact that they see little benefit from the oil riches. Nigeria has little oil refining capacity and has to import oil, which is costly. It also imports tomato paste, which it could produce at home, but is compelled to import from China. What ethical principles are raised in this example?

ETHICAL ISSUES CHALLENGING COMPANIES AND COUNTRIES

Trade is conducted largely by for-profit companies, seeking wealth creation for their share-holders. These corporate players are mostly registered companies in the private sector, but there are also state-controlled listed companies active in trade and FDI. Many publicly-listed MNEs have a wide shareholder base, but there are some which, although listed, are dominated by a few insiders. There are also a number of private companies, which disclose little about their ownership and activities. The business activities involved in trade are diverse. Trading companies act as intermediaries, but are also involved in primary produc-tion. They are highly influential, although their names are not necessarily well known to consumers as they do not promote themselves as brands. Extraction industries such as oil, gas and mining are dominated by a few large companies globally. Even so, there has been considerable consolidation among these large players. The takeover of Xstrata by a trading company, Glencore, in 2012, is an example, and perhaps an indication of the ascendancy of the trading companies (discussed in the closing case study). As we have seen in the last section, global manufacturers are also involved in trade, which has grown with the exten-sions of global supply chains. Agriculture and food have become industrialized and global-ized in tandem. Much agriculture globally is dominated by the large trading companies such as Cargill, a private family company. Nestlé is the biggest food company, whose brands, unlike the names of the trading companies, are well known to consumers, as are those of Procter & Gamble (P&G), the second-largest food company.

Food companies are keenly aware of ethical issues. Food processing is similar to manu-facturing in that there can be an extended food chain. MNEs in the industry aim to produce food products for global markets that are safe, priced competitively and appealing to consumers in different countries. They are aware of popula-tion growth and the need to increase production. At the same time, consumers expect high standards and also ethical practices in food production. They are concerned about sourcing and the welfare of farm-ers and workers in the processing industry. Food companies are mainly processors, but are now taking an active role in food production, the first link in the supply chain. Nestlé now buys produce directly from 680,000 farmers, like cocoa growers in the Côte d'Ivoire (Lucas, 2012). These deals are not simply sales of primary products. The company provides technical expertise and finance where needed. Working with farmers, its experts can help to increase yields, and the company can also be confident that the farmer's business is sound, assuring stability of supplies. This link with producers makes business sense for the company, but it also has an ethical dimension. The company is in a position to ensure that there is no child labour employed and that social welfare is provided. This can mean building schools and other facilities. While some would consider these activities in keeping with a CSR approach, it could also be said that the companies are taking over provi-sion of services which should be the job of government, although the level of social welfare

Nestlé now buys produce directly from 680,000 farmers, like cocoa growers in the Côte d'Ivoire.

in African countries is often low. The companies are sometimes criticized for creating a dependency relationship with the farmer, who may be paid little by the company. The company is ultimately concerned more to generate profits for its owners than to better the lives of farmers. Fairtrade initiatives, discussed in Chapter 10, are aimed at providing a better deal for producers and maintaining a sustainable approach to trade.

Energy, resources, agriculture and food are all areas which are central to governments' concerns, as they directly impact on societies. As we have seen, governments of resource-rich countries do deals with outside investors. Governments look to social goods, while the corporate players are looking to corporate interests. There is potential conflict between these goals. One might think that governments would always have the upper hand, but the power of global companies has given them consider-able leverage over governments. A leading authority, Paul Collier, has said, 'Harnessing resource wealth requires a chain of decisions to go right, of which the most fundamental is to capture revenues for society' (Collier, 2013). He points out that, whereas profits are seen as a legitimate return on capital, the mining industry also extracts rents, taking the resources of poor countries (Collier, 2013). Rent-seeking activities of mining companies which exploit their business advantages in poor countries are frequently condemned as unethical, although the companies themselves tend to fall back on the defence that they are acting within the strict letter of the law. In Peru, the government hopes that the development of copper mining will lead to exports which could one day rival those of Chile. But Chile has experienced social unrest in mining areas, and Peru is also having to confront angry residents in copper-mining areas, who are unhappy about being shifted off their land. The mine owner, the state-owned Chinese company, Chinalco, is building new housing for displaced residents, but they still feel they are being victimized for the sake of the mining industry (Schipani, 2013). This situation is common in mining areas around the world, presenting dilemmas for governments (see closing case study on South Africa in Chapter 9). Governments in some large emerging economies, including China, India and Brazil, have taken strong stands against large foreign corporations. India is one.

> *'Harnessing resource wealth requires a chain of decisions to go right, of which the most fundamental is to capture revenues for society.'*

India has been keen to impose regulations which protect small domestic retailers against a possible onslaught from global retailers who wish to enter the country. It has only reluc-tantly allowed large western retailers to enter, and required them to do so with a local part-ner. India's protectionism can be seen as an ethical response to globalized capital, reflecting its socialist political heritage. By contrast, Walmart had little difficulty in purchasing a supermarket group based in South Africa for $2.4 billion. Massmart has 377 stores in 12 African countries. Eyeing Africa's booming urban population, the supermarket chain can look to growth potential. Africans could well take to a re-branding of the stores with the Walmart logo, as the American brand is perceived as having a better lifestyle image than the South African brand the stores have had. For Walmart, this acquisition could be more successful than some of its other foreign ventures, which have run into difficulties on ethi-cal and legal grounds. It faces bribery accusations in Mexico, Brazil, China and India. In its home market of the US, it has been embroiled in numerous allegations of breaches of employment law and discrimination (see Chapter 9). For Africans, the American company does not bring the same connotations of colonialism that European companies bring. Nonetheless, from an ethical perspective, Walmart, the world's largest retailer, could be cast in an imperial light without much stretch of the imagination. Furthermore, Walmart is one of the largest purchasers of low-cost manufactured goods from China and other Asian countries. African leaders who are unhappy about the floods of Chinese goods in shops and markets could find these products are even more in evidence as Walmart expands across the continent.

National governments are highly influential players in global trade. They tend not to trade directly, but they act through state-owned companies and companies with close ties to government (discussed in the next section). Although the big trading powers would not admit to being empire builders in the historical sense, they view trade as strategically important and a matter of national security. In strategic goods in which they are not self-sufficient, they are keen to secure reliable supplies. For energy and food, this has become a priority. Some relatively rich countries which must import food acquire land in other countries to grow food which is exported back to their populations. African countries are some of those targeted by 'landgrab' activities (see Chapter 10). They are invariably poorer countries, characterized by weak institutional protection of land rights and prone to succumb to the opaque land deals proposed by richer countries, many from the Middle East and Asia (Oxfam, 2012). Some of these investments risk jeopardizing the food supplies of poor African populations. The World Bank, which is the international authority most able to regulate these activities, has received numerous complaints from targeted countries.

Commodities markets are notoriously volatile. Three factors can be highlighted, all with ethical implications:

o Corn farmers in the US receive subsidies for growing crops for ethanol production, a biofuel. The boom in corn production for ethanol in 2007–8, 2011 and 2012 resulted in a reduction of crops produced for food, sending global prices higher. The effects were devastating for poor food-importing countries (UNCTAD, 2012a).

o Commodities are the subject of purely financial investment, through commodity derivatives trading. Investors in commodities futures markets are akin to speculators, betting on price movements. Their effects are to cause volatility and rises in prices (UNCTAD, 2012b).

o In addition to commodities derivatives trading, banks have engaged more directly in commodities markets, trading physical commodities and also assets such as mines and warehouses. Wall Street banks were thus in a position of advising on investments in trading and production in which they were active players.

Legislation in the US was intended to curtail the conflicts of interest which arise when investment banks hold significant stakes in the assets traded, but Wall Street banks have been able to navigate the legal constraints to develop trading businesses. Some have used private warehouses to hold 'dark inventory' of metals, which creates an impression of scarcity, raising prices (Gapper, 2013). Commodity price movements result in winners and losers between countries and within countries. Commodity-importing developing countries can face sharp rises in prices for food and fuel. In the poorest countries, food can account for up to 80% of a household's spending. The rise in global food prices of 2007–8 was made worse by activities of financial players. Exporters gain from price rises, but the winners in these cases could well be a small number of private owners of natural resources. The effect in the exporting country can thus be to increase inequality, widening the divide between the élites who control resources and ordinary members of society who see few benefits. In commodity-producing developing countries, the ownership of resources is typically in the hands of private owners, and trade is dominated by large MNEs and trading companies. Gains tend to be captured by these owners and their financial investors, with few benefits for workers in the producing economy, or for governments in those countries.

PAUSE TO CONSIDER...

When a society suffers from poverty, poor health and limited educational opportunities despite increasing wealth in an economy, who is most to blame: the government or corporate investors? Who should be responsible for re-focusing on societal goals?

NATIONAL TRADE POLICIES AND ETHICAL CONCERNS

No country is self-sufficient. All governments now recognize that trade relations are important to the economy and the society. A country's trade balance, representing the balance between its exports and imports, is an indicator of the competitiveness of the economy. If a country has a trade surplus, that is, a surplus of exports over imports, then its industries are viewed as competitive globally. If it has a trade deficit, importing more than it exports, its economy is viewed as less competitive, and dependence on imports can imply precariousness of supplies.

Governments play both direct and indirect roles in trade. Acting directly, state-controlled companies both export and invest in foreign production. These companies are integral to the state capitalism model which prevails in a number of emerging economies, among

The flood of Chinese products in world markets owes much to the country's policy of pumping state funds into export industries.

which China is the most active exporter. Exports of goods and services are over 30% of China's GDP and the country has a large trade surplus. Its state-centred development model uses subsidies extensively to support both domestic companies and foreign investors who manufacture products intended for export. The flood of Chinese products in world markets owes much to the country's policy of pumping state funds into export industries. Government largesse includes direct subsidies, tax incentives, government-sponsored research, subsidized loans, cheap land for greenfield investment and fuel subsidies. China's exporting companies thus enjoy considerable advantages in global markets. Government funding not only gives them resource advantages which allow them to undercut foreign competitors, it allows them to build up scale of production rapidly, which is often key to conquering global markets. For small firms, both within China and abroad, there is scarcely a level playing field in market sectors where the competition is dominated by large state-financed companies. Subsidies to exporters are therefore trade distorting. They are also accused of promoting over-production, over-use of resources such as water, and environmental damage. Moreover, China's manufacturing industries are dependent on migrant workers, whose poor living conditions and harsh employment regime are criticized on human rights grounds. How do more liberal market economies compare?

Most countries, even those based on free-market principles, prioritize national interests in trade relations. In these countries, the state's role is usually seen as indirect, but it is widely ramified and involves many of the measures associated with state capitalism, such as subsidies (Beattie, 2012b). Private-sector companies can be aided by state subsidies and also by protectionist national trade policies, which deter foreign imports and also foreign investors in some cases. The distinction between direct and indirect state activity has become more blurred in recent years. In the US, where large companies are mainly in the private sector, one might expect less state involvement. But, in fact, the federal government aids companies which are important exporters. Many private-sector companies are heavily involved in government activities, and others are in strategic industries which receive preferential treatment. In the US, there are many private-sector companies which carry out large amounts of work for government, such as the aerospace industry, weapons industry and military services companies. In these sectors, there are close relations between companies and government departments. Large companies in all sectors are influential in lobbying members of Congress for their particular interests (discussed in Chapter 3). Where these companies are major exporters, they are directly involved in determining trade policy.

The US farm lobby is influential in maintaining high levels of subsidies, which mainly go to large agribusiness companies. Subsidies are concentrated on the major commodity crops, including wheat, corn, soya beans, rice and cotton. They include direct payments, advantageous loans, government-funded research, subsidized farm insurance and market access promotion. Money for market access is provided to companies to help them promote their products in foreign markets. They have been very successful, as shown in Figure 6.4. Farming subsidies amounting to $20 billion or more each year have helped to facilitate dramatic growth in US agricultural production, 23% of which is destined for export.

As Figure 6.4 shows, US agricultural exports almost tripled in just over a decade, rising from about $50 billion in 2000 to over $140 billion in 2012. Compare this stunning growth to the lacklustre export growth from developed countries generally, shown in Figure 6.3, earlier in this chapter. One might ask what societal purpose the billions of dollars in subsidies serve, especially in the context of America's huge national debt burden. The subsidies to commodity crops benefit the food processing industry, and also benefit the meat and dairy industries, as subsidized crops go into animal feed. American agricultural exports

Figure 6.4 *Value of US agricultural exports*

Billions of dollars

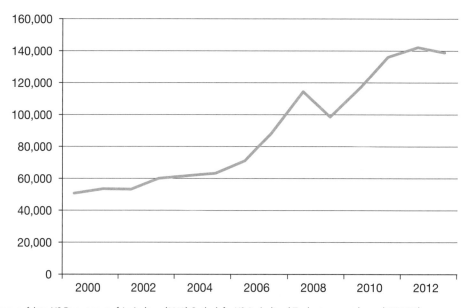

Source of data: US Department of Agriculture (2013) *Outlook for US Agricultural Trade*, at www.usda.gov (18/09/14).

have boomed largely because of growing demand in emerging economies. While China has a large agricultural sector, it must import large amounts of food. In particular, it cannot meet the growing demand for meat, which America produces in abundance. China's meat consumption is rising, while America's is not, suggesting that America's meat producers should focus on exports. But China has now gone a step further, with the acquisition by Shuanghui International, China's largest pork producer, of Smithfield, the US's largest pork producer. This takeover is the largest acquisition of a US company by a Chinese one. It faced regulatory hurdles, as US law and political sentiment are both stacked against foreign takeover in strategic industries. However, pork does not raise the security concerns that telecommunications, for example, would raise. An outcome for the enlarged company is an explosion in pork exports from the US to China. The combined company would create a global giant in pig farming: these companies each slaughter more than 15 million pigs annually. It would also confirm the dominance of factory-farming methods which Smithfield has relied on and which are now used by Shuanghui in its Chinese operations.

Both Shuanghui and Smithfield have been embroiled in legal and ethical controversies for safety issues and animal welfare. In China, the rush to increase production, combined with weak regulation, has resulted in health scandals and accusations of contaminated meat. Media reports of thousands of pigs found floating dead in rivers caused uproar in 2012, undermining the Chinese public's confidence in food safety. Earlier, Shuanghui was accused of using dangerous additives in pig production. Smithfield has been criticized for its animal welfare practices, including extreme confinement of animals, which were exposed in an undercover video (Humane Society of the United States, 2010). Like other meat producers in the US, Smithfield has used the drug, ractopamine, a drug originally developed to treat asthma in humans, which promotes lean muscle in pigs. Ractopamine has been declared safe by the US Food and Drug Administration, but there remain doubts about the long-term impacts on consumers. Countries including China, Russia and the EU have barred pork imports containing it, and US producers, including Smithfield, have begun to produce ractopamine-free pork to retain export markets. Perhaps ironically, this policy change could have nudged Shuanghui towards making its takeover bid. The use of drug additives in meat production in the US has reflected a growing involvement of large pharmaceutical companies, whose drugs designed for humans are increasingly used in animal production, creating a lucrative income stream, but raising concerns from consumers, both in the US and in other countries. The US government faces a dilemma in this respect. It wishes to support global pharmaceutical companies such as Eli Lilly, which now derives significant profits from drugs for animal feed. However, the meat industry is facing growing concern over its use of drugs in meat production, both at home and in export markets.

The use of drug additives in meat production in the US has reflected a growing involvement of large pharmaceutical companies, whose drugs designed for humans are increasingly used in animal production.

Figure 6.5 sets out the priorities which national governments must juggle in trade policies. As the figure shows, internal issues represent domestic interests, but governments are also concerned about mutually beneficial relations with other countries, both in the region and globally. This is especially true where vital imports are concerned. At the same time, ethical issues stride both internal and external priorities. Ideally, governments seek to design trade policies to suit all these national goals, although the influential industries in

Figure 6.5 *National priorities in trade*

each national economy are likely to have the greatest sway. Outright protectionist measures, such as tariffs in the form of duties on imported goods and export subsidies, have given way to non-tariff barriers, as we have just seen. Health and safety requirements on imported products, including sanitary requirements for food, now abound. These are barriers to trade which are qualitative rather than a matter of levying an import duty. For a government, a drawback of protectionist measures is that of retaliation by the other country, which is likely to be damaging for other domestic industries. Protectionist measures reached a zenith in the 1930s, when countries, crippled by the depression, sought to strengthen domestic industries through the imposition of tariffs. Dramatic falls in world trade resulted, leading to high unemployment and continued depression.

Following the Second World War, trade liberalization, which would see a gradual opening of borders, was envisaged as promoting peace and prosperity. It was thought that countries which trade with each other are less likely to start wars against each other (McDonald, 2004). But, although trade became more open, as will be discussed in the next section, governments were no less concerned to prioritize national interests. Issues such as jobs, nurturing domestic companies and nurturing vital industries remained priorities. Many of the subsidies of the 1930s, such as US farm subsidies, remained in place, but became increasingly anomalous. Whereas in the 1930s, the large US farming population consisted of small farmers with incomes of roughly half of the national average, today, the farm subsidies go mainly to large owners and companies, and farm incomes are 28% *above* the national average. In sharp contrast, hired workers on US farms are described by the US Department of Agriculture as 'one of the most economically disadvantaged groups in the

US' (USDA, 2013). About 50% of hired crop workers are non-citizens who are not legally entitled to work in the US. Mainly Mexican, they are poorly paid, earning about 50% the wages of an industrial worker. There is no legal minimum age for children working on family farms in the US with parents' consent, and children can work on *any* farm from age 12 with parents' consent. Children work on large industrial farms, where they make up an estimated 9% of hired farmworkers. This work is dangerous and carries serious health risks, involving heavy machinery and extensive pesticide spraying. Furthermore, child farmworkers work long hours, which in other industries would be considered only suitable for adults. Human rights groups have highlighted the plight of hundreds of thousands of children at risk from doing heavy farm work in the US. They have called for child labour on farms to be subject to the same age limits, hour restrictions and restrictions on hazardous work as US labour laws generally (Coursen-Neff, 2011). For most jobs, children under 16 cannot be employed, and those under 18 cannot be employed in hazardous jobs. The US was a signatory of the UN Convention on the Rights of the Child, but has not ratified the treaty.

Hired workers on US farms are described by the US Department of Agriculture as 'one of the most economically disadvantaged groups in the US'.

Duties on imports were reduced on many manufactured goods through a succession of agreements under the General Agreement on Tariffs and Trade (GATT), but non-tariff barriers proliferated. Non-tariff barriers can be viewed from different perspectives. As we have seen, the US views its industrialized farming as safe, but its practices are questioned on health and safety grounds in many countries. Apart from ractopamine-fed pork, other controversial issues are the use of genetically-modified organisms (GMOs) and hormone-treated beef. The US takes the view that foreign markets prohibiting these products are acting in an unwarranted way (US Trade Representative, 2013). The issues, however, are not merely scientific, but also ethical. Countries which take a firm stance against GMOs tend to support traditional farming, sustainable agriculture and animal welfare. They are also sensitive to consumer concerns and the livelihoods of agricultural smallholders. EU countries have been among the main markets which have resisted US agricultural exports on these grounds. The supporters of GM crops urge that their methods, which are based mainly on large-scale, industrialized agriculture, are necessary to feed the world's growing population. But these methods involve a dominant role played by large MNEs in agribusiness, and, most importantly, their patent monopolies which affect the whole food production chain. Monsanto, a major agribusiness company, depends on the acceptance of GM crops internationally. IP protection is one of their major assets in maintaining a grip on GM agricultural production, but, as we found in Chapter 4, IP monopolies benefit large companies in the developed world, while adversely affecting people in poor developing countries (see further discussion in Chapter 10). And it is in these countries in particular that the precariousness of food supply is critical. Thus, trade liberalization is often viewed as benefiting exporters in rich countries and disadvantaging poor countries which rely on imports. This has been one of the biggest challenges facing the WTO.

PAUSE TO CONSIDER...

Food safety concerns have been used by many countries as a means of preventing imports of food. Which safety concerns do you feel are ethically valid, and which are simply means of blocking imports to protect domestic farming?

CHALLENGES FOR THE WTO IN ITS OVERSIGHT OF WORLD TRADE

The origins of the WTO go back to the aftermath of the Second World War, when three bodies, known as the Bretton Woods institutions, were agreed. The IMF and the World Bank were created to provide oversight of financial stability and development. But the third institution, known then as the International Trade Organization (ITO), which was to oversee trade and related issues, did not win the approval of key countries, notably the US, and was shelved. Instead, GATT (the General Agreement on Tariffs and Trade) became the chief means of reducing trade barriers. The GATT was not an organization itself, but a treaty mechanism, by which countries came together to negotiate multilateral trade agreements, known as 'rounds' of trade negotiations. The GATT was succeeded in 1995 by the WTO (World Trade Organization), a new organization which took over the oversight of multilateral agreements. It has also expanded its trade role and has a permanent organization and director general. Besides sponsoring multilateral treaties, the WTO oversees a dispute settlement procedure in trade matters between countries. Both areas of activity have become more challenging in recent years, as its membership has grown and national interests have tended to diverge. The WTO has struggled to keep up with the changing landscape of trade, and its unwieldy procedures have slowed progress in reaching agreements and solving disputes. An effect has been that countries are seeking trade agreements on a smaller range of issues and among fewer countries. Some countries might welcome a shift from multilateral agreements to more limited agreements among fewer countries, but a weakening of multilateral institutions would result in greater influence by the richer countries, to the detriment of the poorer ones.

MULTILATERAL AGREEMENTS

Most governments acknowledge in theory that open markets benefit both exporting and importing countries. But governments are selective in their support for trade liberalization. Most seek open markets for their own exporters, but are more protectionist when those industries are at risk from competition. The WTO has promoted trade liberalization as a goal through multilateral agreements, that is, treaties to which there are many ratifying parties. They are based on the principle of 'the most favoured nation'. This involves equal access to all parties: favourable terms for one implies the same terms for all. This can be contrasted with the preferential treatment enshrined in bilateral and plurilateral agreements, which freeze out non-parties. However, multilateralism has foundered, as it has proved difficult to persuade sovereign member states to lower trade barriers in many sectors which are key to national economies. Moreover, as noted in the last section, trade is no longer a simple issue of open markets, but surrounded by normative concerns which make achieving consensus difficult.

Trade liberalization rests on the proposition that all countries will gain. Barriers to trade have been dismantled through multilateral agreements. But most of the successful reductions have come in manufactured products. Agricultural products have been far more affected by continuing barriers. This has become an increasingly important issue because of the growth in membership. The WTO has grown from the 23 countries which were parties to the original GATT in 1947 to 159 WTO member countries. Most of these member states are developing and emerging countries, whose interests tend to diverge from those of the rich countries.

The Doha Round of trade negotiations, commenced in Doha, Qatar, in 2001, was intended to be a development round to focus on the needs of developing countries in world markets. But this agenda was overwhelmed by the interests of the most powerful trading nations. The aim to produce a wide-spectrum multilateral agreement was ambitious, covering agriculture, manufacturing and services. Developing countries were particularly concerned about access for their agricultural produce in developed countries' markets, and developed countries sought free access for their goods and services to developing countries. There was also a divergence between the interests of the large emerging economies and smaller developing economies. The appointment of Brazilian diplomat, Roberto Azevêdo, as the WTO's new director-general, signified the growing influence of emerging economies. His appointment was seen as a move towards giving the organization a greater sense of legitimacy, as he is seen as enjoying the confidence of the many developing countries (Subramanian, 2013). Contrary to expectations, the Doha round was concluded with an agreement in December 2013. This was a more modest agreement than many had hoped, concentrated on smoothing procedures for businesses. It contained some provisions designed to help developing countries (Donnan, 2013).

The 1990s saw the concluding of a regional free trade deal for North America, the NAFTA (North America Free Trade Agreement), between the US, Canada and Mexico. While it did not include labour conditions and environmental protection in the core text, they were in side agreements. NAFTA also broke new ground in including protection of IP rights as part of a free trade agreement. These include not just protections for patents and trademarks, but also protection for industrial designs and copyright material. These areas of intangible property rights can be very lucrative for companies which have ownership of significant rights, but they raise fears among governments in developing countries that IP-protected imports will swamp domestic markets.

The NAFTA precedent was soon followed in the WTO with an agreement on Trade-related Aspects of Intellectual Property (TRIPS), mainly due to pressure from the rich countries who own the bulk of IP rights. The TRIPS agreement of 1995 was intended to enforce high standards of protection of intellectual property throughout the world, but developing countries felt strongly that these protections placed them at a disadvantage. In particular, they were concerned about their ability to fight serious diseases, as they lack the resources to pay prices demanded by the large pharmaceutical companies. They demanded the right to use the compulsory licence in the interests of public health (explained in Chapter 4). The TRIPS agreement bowed to this pressure, and allowed a transition period during which developing countries would be exempt from the agreement. This deadline was extended, and the agreement has been subject to further high-level negotiations on interpretation (Sykes, 2002). In 2013, the plight of the poorest countries was again the subject of WTO negotiations. Haiti, ravaged by disease following a devastating earthquake in 2010, led the battle to obtain a further extension. Haiti's case to obtain life-saving drugs

Haiti's case to obtain life-saving drugs was aided by the UN Commission on Human Rights, which had argued that access to medicine is a human right.

was aided by the UN Commission on Human Rights, which had argued that access to medicine is a human right (Sykes, 2002). Despite tough resistance from the developed countries, the least-developed countries won an extension of their exemption from the whole of TRIPS for another eight years. Concerns about the TRIPS agreement are indicative of the divergent interests and ethical issues now overshadowing world trade and future trade agreements.

DISPUTE SETTLEMENT PROCESSES

The WTO established a rather cumbersome dispute resolution process, whereby a member country can submit complaint that it is the victim of unfair trade practices by another country. The main complaints are allegations that a country is '**dumping**' goods on another country for prices less than the cost of production. The country which is suffering from the dumping of goods seeks to impose 'antidumping' duties by way of retaliation. Related to complaints of dumping is the allegation that a country is subsidizing a particular export industry excessively, in order to make it more competitive, with the effect that the country's exports distort trade. The country whose industries are prejudiced by these exports seeks to apply 'countervailing duties' (CVDs) to goods from the offending country, which need not be related to the products complained of. Applications to the WTO to apply CVDs have doubled since 2004. Many new subsidy-related cases have been started in recent years at the WTO. A reason for the surge in such cases is partly the increasing activity of emerging economies in global trade, aided by their state capitalist economic models in which state subsidies play a major role. However, as we have seen, most countries subsidize domestic industries to some extent, and WTO rules allow this if the subsidies are to keep industries alive and protect livelihoods. The EU holds that its agricultural subsidies fall into this category, as most European farmers operate on smallholdings. If EU countries individually subsidize bigger industries as national champions, they can fall foul of EU law as state subsidies are anti-competitive, and they also breach WTO rules. The government funding which went into the aerospace industry to develop the Airbus has been a cause of complaint by the US at the WTO. But the EU counterclaimed that the US government subsidized Boeing in building its Dreamliner aircraft. Following an expensive decade-long legal battle, the WTO concluded that both countries had engaged in excessive subsidies, a conclusion which was predictable from the start of proceedings, and which probably indicated that the legal action was ill-judged. That case was complicated by the fact that both companies were at the centre of extended supply chains which involved numerous suppliers: Boeing uses European parts, and Airbus uses American parts. On a lesser scale, this situation has become typical of many trade disputes. The country which complains is almost always risking harm to its own industries. Undeterred, the US president launched a WTO complaint against Chinese car parts manufacturers, but at the same time praised the successful government bailout of the US car manufacturers (Beattie, 2012b).

The US president launched a WTO complaint against Chinese car parts manufacturers, but at the same time praised the successful government bailout of the US car manufacturers.

BILATERAL AND OTHER TRADE AGREEMENTS AMONG COUNTRIES

The weakening mandate of the WTO has prompted national governments to bypass multilateral solutions in favour of more limited trade agreements, increasing the spectre of protectionism. An effect of the stalemate in the Doha trade round was a proliferation of bilateral trade agreements, which are quicker and less complex to negotiate. The **bilateral trade agreement** is a treaty between two countries, but one of the two can be the EU, which now has 28 member states. There has also been a rise in agreements among groups of countries. Some of these are regional trade agreements, which exist in all of the world's major regions. They bring together countries which share roughly the same geographical region, and focus mainly on reducing trade barriers among themselves. The EU is the biggest and most deeply integrated of these, extending beyond trade to legal and political structures. The EU is now endowed with legal personality to enter trade agreements as a sovereign power in its own right. NAFTA's coverage of issues such as IP rights has set a precedent for future trade deals led by the US. NAFTA also introduced the Foreign Investment Promotion and Protection Agreement (FIPA), by which foreign investors from one of the member countries can have recourse to an arbitration tribunal in disputes in another member country.

The US has taken the initiative in drafting free trade agreements with a number of individual countries. These 'preferential trade agreements' (PTAs) are mainly with countries in Asia, Central and South America. The US has in place 20 of these agreements, all with countries whose economies are a fraction the size of the US. While they reduce tariff barriers and other barriers on specific products traded between the two countries, they also contain stringent protections for IP which are designed mainly to benefit US corporations. In terms of trade liberalization globally, these preferential trade agreements are problematic. They pertain only to the parties involved, creating disparities between insiders and outsiders. Bilateral agreements are also criticized on the grounds that they are usually one-sided. The stronger party invariably gains more than the weaker one. Indeed, the weaker country can find itself disadvantaged by the terms. In US bilateral agreements, the other country is typically bound to accept terms which benefit US farm commodity exporters and owners of IP rights.

A further type of agreement among countries, which could be called a 'plurilateral' or 'mega-regional' agreement, has emerged in the years of the stalled Doha negotiations. These are trade agreements among a number of countries which need not be in the same region. Two such agreements have been promoted by the US: a Trans-Pacific Partnership (TPP) and a US–EU free trade agreement, known as the Transatlantic Trade and Investment Partnership (TTIP). The TPP has been under discussion since 2010, initially including the US and 11 Pacific Rim countries (see Note 2). The TPP would overlap with the Asean trade pact (the Association of South East Asian Nations) and the Apec (the Asia-Pacific Economic Co-operation Group), as well as US PTAs with some of these countries. Although termed a 'partnership', this agreement would be dominated by the US. The economies of the other 11 countries in total have a GDP of only 37.2% of US GDP. In 2013, Japan joined the discussions, introducing a much larger economy to the discussions, but even including Japan, the combined GDP of the other countries is only 75% of US GDP. Some of these other countries have developed doubts about their continued participation. In 2012, Chile cited concerns about increased protection for IP. Chile's trade representative said that the IP clauses give more extensive legal rights for IP proprietors than either the TRIPS agreement or the bilateral agreement which the country already has with the US (Flynn, 2012). These extensive rights represent the interests of powerful pharmaceutical, software and entertainment industries in the US. The extra protections would increase burdens for Chile, but bring no benefits, he said (Flynn, 2012).

The entertainment sector, which is now being driven by the digital revolution, eyes large potential gains for the US from the export of films and other media content, as Figure 6.6 shows. The balance of trade in services greatly favours American exporters, and is perceived

Figure 6.6 *US–TPP countries services trade*

Billions of dollars, 2011

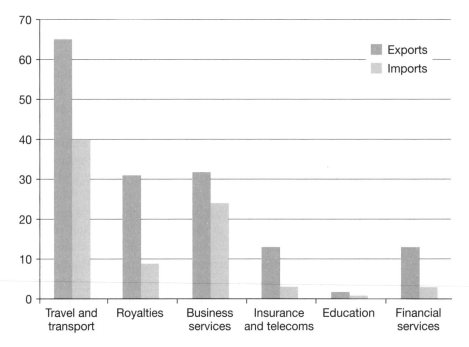

Source of data: Williams, B. (2013) 'Trans-Pacific Partnership Countries: Comparative Trade and Economic Analysis', Congressional Research Service, at www.loc.gov/crsinfo/ (26/09/14).

as one of key benefits for the US in the TPP. Royalties are huge earners for the entertainment companies such as Disney and Universal. Royalties from exports earned by these companies in TPP countries are triple the amount of imports. Chile has recently passed legislation giving protection for internet service providers and users against actions for copyright infringement, which would potentially clash with the TPP proposals.

A notable absentee from the TPP discussions is China, suggesting that the US is keen to obtain favourable terms with other countries in the Pacific as a counterweight to China's power in world trade. TPP discussions have been shrouded in secrecy. However, leaked documents raised fears of environmentalists, health experts concerned about access to medicines, and labour leaders concerned that there seemed to be no mention of core labour standards in the proposed agreement. Members of the US Congress have criticized the secretive process as undemocratic, expressing concern that large US corporations were insiders to the discussions, but they were not.

It has been thought that the US intends the TPP to be a template for future free trade agreements, such as one with the EU (Beattie, 2012a). The US intended for this agreement to cover all areas of trade, including manufactured goods, agriculture and services. But this broad scope might prove to be optimistic, as both the EU negotiators and many of the EU's 28 member states have particular issues on which they are not prepared to give way. In agriculture, the EU has stood by its objection to GMOs and hormone-treated beef. The EU also objects to the US laws on internet privacy (discussed in the closing case study in Chapter 4). Disclosures that American technology companies such as Google, Microsoft and Apple have co-operated with the US government in surveillance programmes have contributed to suspicions about excessive intrusion into privacy. The EU has objected to the US 'buy American' law, which discriminates against EU companies. Furthermore, the agreement contains an 'investor–state dispute settlement mechanism', following the FIPA model. France's trade minister has been concerned that this provision will allow American companies to challenge national environmental and social laws (O'Connor and Chaffin, 2013).

France has taken a strong stand against the inclusion of cultural industries, such as film and music, in the US–EU trade talks. The French position is that audio-visual should be excluded from the talks. France has a system of subsidies, tax incentives and quotas for local content in film, television and music, which aim to prevent these industries from being swamped by English-language content. The 'cultural exception' is of particular concern to France, but EU negotiators fear that the ringfencing of any one sector will make it more difficult to secure an overall agreement. The US has expressed the view that all issues must be on the table in order for negotiations to proceed. Recalling the TPP precedent, IP rights are seen as critical, as digitalization and the internet are transforming the creative industries. The US trade surplus in royalties and licence fees, which was over $80 billion in 2012, is far more than its trade surplus in agricultural products, which was $25 billion.

The US trade surplus in royalties and licence fees, which was over $80 billion in 2012, is far more than its trade surplus in agricultural products, which was $25 billion.

Opposition to the inclusion of IP rights kept the subject out of the Doha round, but by then, a separate TRIPS agreement had been concluded. The TRIPS agreement remains under fire in many respects, and the two new plurilateral trade agreements sought by the US are re-igniting the debate. But in talks aiming to achieve a TTIP, the US faces a different bargaining situation from the TPP. The EU is the world's largest trading bloc; its combined GDP is approximately equal to that of the US. And there are strong policy positions established within the EU which clash with US strategic objectives in trade talks. Unlike the TPP, a US–EU free trade agreement is more akin to an agreement among equally powerful states. In this chapter, we have seen numerous examples of inequality of bargaining power among trading nations, and the stronger one usually has the power to get its way. However, in organizations such as the WTO, the democratic setup gives the smaller nation a voice, which can be used as a blocking voice. Similarly, in the EU, the 28 member states could have the final say.

Although the two initiatives championed by the US to achieve trade deals with Pacific countries and the EU are ostensibly aimed at liberalizing trade, agriculture is a particularly difficult sector in which to achieve agreement, with ethical concerns to the forefront. What are the ethical concerns, and why do they loom so large?

CONCLUSIONS

Much of the history of trade reveals an ethical ambiguity. Types of trade once thought defensible are now considered unethical, and ethical thinking continues to evolve. There are now far more ethical concerns about health and safety issues which form the basis of non-tariff barriers. On the other hand, ethical issues such as child labour struggle to alter the business models of large exporters, even in countries such as the US, which would claim to honour human rights. Both governments and companies are responsible for the effects that trading relations have on home societies and societies of trading partners. Impacts include issues of access to medicines, affordable food imports, precariousness of local producers competing against imports, and the sustainability of local culture against global media companies protected in trade agreements. We have also seen that governments in many countries are active in trade, directly or indirectly. They can behave in ways that benefit societies, but are often inclined to favour some groups and companies rather than others.

Governments set economic goals and trade policies, and are also concerned about societal impacts. While all might, in theory, welcome a regulatory system overseen by the WTO, competing national interests and globalized MNEs make it difficult to achieve agreement. MNEs must act in a trading environment with cross-cutting trade regimes and ethical considerations. While a government might conclude a deal with an MNE which both sides regard as advantageous, such as the award of mining rights, this does not make the deal an ethical one. It could well entail displacement of people's homes and environmental damage, while government officials are likely to reap financial rewards. International opinion expects ethical behaviour of companies despite their dealings with political leaders who place personal gains above societal goods. For the MNE, identifying ethical guideposts, therefore, is increasingly challenging.

NOTES

1 The G8 is an informal grouping of the main economic powers in the world at the time of its foundation in 1975. These countries were the US, UK, Germany, France, Italy and Japan. Canada joined a year later, and Russia joined in 1998. The G8 holds annual summit meetings to discuss current issues of global importance.
2 Countries involved in the Trans-Pacific Partnership (TPP) are Australia, Brunei, Canada, Chile, Japan, Malaysia, Mexico, New Zealand, Peru, Singapore, US and Vietnam.

REFERENCES

Beattie, A. (2012a) 'A new world of royalties', *Financial Times*, 24 September.

Beattie, A. (2012b) 'Tricks of the trade law', *Financial Times*, 29 October.

Collier, P. (2013) 'How we can help African nations to extract fair value', *Financial Times*, 13 May.

Coursen-Neff, Z. (2011) *Child Farmworkers in the US: A 'Worst Form of Child Labor'*, Human Rights Watch, at www.hrw.org (18/09/14).

Domosh, M. (2004) 'Selling civilization: Toward a cultural analysis of America's economic empire in the late nineteenth and early twentieth centuries', *Transactions of the Institute of British Geographers*, 29(4): 453–67.

Donnan, S. (2013) 'WTO comes back to life with signing of trade deal', *Financial Times*, 9 December.

Ferguson, N. (2003) *Empire: How Britain made the modern world* (London: Penguin).

Ferguson, N. (2004) *Colossus: The Rise and Fall of the American Empire* (London: Penguin).

Flynn, S. (2012) *Chile Threatens to Pull Out of TPP because of US Demands*, at www.infojustice. org (18/09/14).

Gapper, J. (2013) 'Banks should keep out of mines and warehouses', *Financial Times*, 25 July.

Humane Society of the United States (2010) *Undercover at Smithfield Foods*, at www.humanesociety.org (18/09/14).

Jacob, R. (2013) 'Cambodia reaps benefit of China's rising wages', *Financial Times*, 8 January.

Johnson, C. (1982) *MITI and the Japanese Miracle* (Stanford: Stanford University Press).

Johnson, C. (2004) *The Sorrow of Empire* (London: Verso).

Kitson, M., and Michie, J. (1995) 'Conflict, cooperation and change: the political economy of trade and trade policy', *Review of International Political Economy*, 2(4): 632–57.

Kohn, M. and O'Neill, D. (2006) 'A tale of two Indias: Burke and Mill on empire and slavery in the West Indies and America', *Political Theory*, 34(2): 192–228.

Landes, D. (1998) *The Wealth and Poverty of Nations* (London: Little, Brown).

Lucas, L. (2012) 'A shift from subsistence', *Financial Times*, 18 August.

Maddison, A. (2001) *The World Economy: A Millennial Perspective* (Paris: OECD).

McDonald, P. (2004) 'Peace through trade of free trade?', *The Journal of Conflict Resolution*, 48(8): 547–72.

O'Connor, S. and Chaffin, J. (2013) 'Paris raises legal fears over US trade talks', *Financial Times*, 11 September.

OECD (2013) OECD-WTO Trade in Value Added (TiVA) database, at www.oecd.org (18/09/14).

Oxfam (2012) *Our Land, Our Lives: Time Out on the Global Land Rush*, at www.oxfam.org (18/09/14).

Subramanian, A. (2013) 'Why too much legitimacy can harm global trade', *Financial Times*, 14 January.

Sanusi, L. (2013) 'Africa must get real about its romance with China', *Financial Times*, 12 March.

Schipani, A. (2013) 'Andean concessions', *Financial Times*, 6 February.

Sykes, A. (2002) *TRIPS, Pharmaceuticals, Developing Countries and the Doha 'Solution'*, Olin Law and Economics Working Paper No. 140, at www.law.uchicago.edu (18/09/14).

Thomson, A. (2012) 'China's unlikely challenger', *Financial Times*, 20 September.

Tunick, M. (2006) 'Tolerant imperialism: John Stuart Mill's defense of British rule in India', *The Review of Politics*, 68(4): 586–611.

UNCTAD (2012a) *Trade and Development Report 2012*, at www.unctad.org (18/09/14).

UNCTAD (2012b) *Development and Globalization: Facts and Figures*, at www.unctad.org (18/09/14).

USDA (2013) *Farm Labor: Background, Economic Research Service*, at www.ers.usda.gov (18/09/14).

US Trade Representative (2013) 2013 *Report on Sanitary and Phytosanitary Measures*, at www.ustr.gov (18/09/14).

Waley-Cohen, Joanna (1998) 'Religion, war and empire-building in eighteenth century China', *The International History Review*, 20(2): 336–52.

Williams, B. (2013) 'Trans-Pacific Partnership Countries: Comparative Trade and Economic Analysis', Congressional Research Service, at www.loc.gov/crsinfo (26/09/14).

REVIEW QUESTIONS

1 In what ways does trade support imperialism of states?

2 Which groups within a country tend to benefit from trade, and which tend to lose out? Look at both exports and imports.

3 China has been at the forefront of globalization and trade. What have been the positive and negative effects in the country?

4 In what ways are other countries now threatening China's dominance in low-cost manufacturing for export? What are the ethical considerations involved in these shifts?

5 When large trading companies expand into production and other related activities, what are the ethical issues?

6 Why has India pursued policies which deter large foreign investors?

7 Protectionist measures of national governments are designed to benefit domestic interests, but to what extent do they chiefly benefit large companies rather than all members of society?

8 A goal of the Doha multilateral trade agreement was to benefit the trading activities of developing nations. Although all parties would agree with this goal in principle, it was difficult to reach agreement in practice. Why?

9 Bilateral trade agreements have proliferated, but do they foster 'free' trade, given the inequality in bargaining power between the parties? Give your reasons.

10 Intellectual property rights were a focus of both the NAFTA and the TRIPS agreements. What ethical issues are raised by the treatment

of IP rights in each? In what ways do they promote healthcare for people unable to afford the prices charged by large pharmaceutical companies?

11 Smaller countries in the proposed Trans-Pacific Partnership have objected to US proposals for IP in the pharmaceuticals, software and entertainment sectors. What are their objections, and on what ethical principles do they rest?

12 What is a Foreign Investment Promotion and Protection Agreement (FIPA), and what issues does it raise for corporate responsibility?

TRADING GIANTS: THE WORLD AT THEIR FEET

CLOSING CASE STUDY

Traders form a vital link between producers and consumers of a variety of essential commodities in the global economy. The main industries in which they operate are agriculture, energy (including oil and gas) and mining. Despite their pivotal role in the global economy, the large trading companies are little known by the general public, and their names are hardly recognized. Most people would recognize Nestlé or Starbucks, but few would recognize Ecom Agroindustrial, the world's largest coffee milling company and second largest coffee trader, which counts the two global brands, among many others, among its customers. Ecom Agroindustrial is a family-owned trading company based in Switzerland, a hub for trading companies. Among its attractions are its low taxes and light-touch regulatory environment. Some of the world's leading trading companies are based here, including Vitol (oil), Glencore (mining) and Cargill (agricultural commodities). These companies, like the majority of the world's 20 largest trading companies, disclose little public information, generally because they are private or unlisted companies, traditionally controlled by families and employees.

Photo 6.2 These huge grain silos are symbols of the growing presence and power of global trading companies. (© iStock.com/ ollirg)

Trading as a business is centuries old, and the trading companies, or 'houses', would probably not expect – or welcome – the public attention that they are now receiving. What has brought their activities into the limelight, and also attracted unwanted critical attention, has been the extraordinary rise in profits that they have generated in little more than a decade. Vitol, the oil trader, which is a private partnership, made $296 million in profits in 2000, but in 2009, its profits reached $2.28 billion (Blas, 2013). Sales of the top ten traders totalled $1.2 trillion in 2012 (Blas, 2013). Cargill, a family-owned private company which is mainly an agricultural commodity trader, achieved record sales of $3.95 billion in 2008, while Glencore, a trading and mining giant, publicly listed but 70% owned by employees, recorded sales of $5.2 billion in 2007. The net profits of the top ten trading companies from 2003 to 2013 totalled $243.6 billion, outshining the giant Wall Street banks, which themselves made bumper profits during the global financial boom.

The profits bonanza for the owners and associates of the top trading companies can be attributed largely to increased demand from China in all these sectors – energy, commodities and metals. The trading companies themselves are no longer pure traders. Their ambitions have taken them deep into buying productive assets such as plantations, mines, smelters and shipping operations. Extending their grip over assets and supply chains has proved financially beneficial. But many of the activities and policies of these companies have raised controversies over ethical issues. They run extensive intelligence networks, gathering information on movements of commodities. They are often criticized for their dealings with countries with poor human rights records, such as Sudan and Iran. They are also criticized for complicity in environmentally damaging activities. Trafigura, the world's second largest metals trader (after Glencore), and third largest oil trader (after Glencore and Vitol), was alleged to be involved in the dumping of oil waste products in the Côte d'Ivoire in 2009. The company reached an undisclosed settlement with complainants, which left questions unanswered. The employee-owned company has issued bonds, the latest in 2013, and its tapping into capital markets raises the prospect of greater public scrutiny. Trafigura has also shifted its incorporation from Geneva to Singapore, reflecting the changing perceptions of the big trading houses. It announced in 2013 that it will be issuing semi-annual results for the first time since its founding in 1993, by a former associate of Glencore's founder.

Switzerland made headlines in 2013 when it had a referendum on capping the wages of corporate executives. The measure was rejected but the fact that the vote was held suggests a shifting of public perceptions against large companies. The commodities trading companies, once welcomed in Switzerland, now feel a coolness in the air. Switzerland is raising tax rates and asking for greater transparency and attention to human rights. Other trading companies are likely to follow Trafigura in shifting to Singapore. Singapore has actively promoted itself as a trading base and offered lower taxes as an incentive. These considerations are rising up the agenda in the context of slowing growth in China, which has dented profits. The aggressive takeover by Glencore of mining giant Xstrata for $80 billion raised eyebrows among the world's competition regulators, taking up to a year to clear regulatory hurdles. The huge deal shone a light on Glencore's past. Its founder, Marc Rich, who died in 2013, just as the takeover was nearing completion, was a successful trader, but often on the edge of legal and ethical rules. He became a fugitive from US justice, having been indicted in 1983 on 65 criminal counts, including tax fraud and trading with Iran when it was holding 52 American hostages. Rich fled to Switzerland, and carried on his successful trading business there, seemingly unfazed by criticisms of trading with Libya and the apartheid regime in South Africa, in violation of an international embargo. Rich maintained that his trading was legal under Swiss law. On his last day in office, President Bill Clinton issued a pardon to Rich, which was alleged to be connected to donations to the Democratic Party, although Clinton denied any connection. Rich never returned to the US, probably fearing for his safety following the media coverage of the pardon, which highlighted his past. Many companies traditionally look back with pride to the values of their founder. Glencore, by contrast, would prefer to keep this chapter of its corporate history in the shadows.

The large commodities traders have long been in the shadows in global business, but their growth in profitability and power has now led to calls for greater transparency and regulation.

Sources: Martin, D. (2013) 'Marc Rich, financier and famous fugitive, dies at 78', *New York Times*, 26 June; Blas, J. (2013) 'Tougher times for the trading titans', *Financial Times*, 15 April; Terazono, E. and Blas, J. (2013) 'Swiss question role of commodities traders in economy', *Financial Times*, 27 March.

- In what ways can the large commodities trading companies be compared with global banks?

- What are the concerns about transparency and corporate governance that arise particularly in the case of the commodities traders?

- What are the ethical issues that arise in commodities trading?

PART TWO

ETHICS AND BUSINESS

The chapters in Part 2 focus on how businesses globally should address ethical challenges in practice. **Chapter 7**, CSR and ethics, examines theories of the business in society, including CSR, corporate citizenship, stakeholder management and social contract theories. We then apply these theoretical perspectives in today's world of international business, asking in particular how ethics and law work together in shaping business behaviour in societies. Ethical theories introduced in Chapter 1 are applied in a variety of business contexts. **Chapter 8**, on corporate governance, delves more deeply into how business purpose is determined, including differences among types of company and differing countries. We look critically at the shareholder primacy model of the company, asking whether reforms along stakeholder principles would lead to more socially responsible corporate behaviour. The following chapter, **Chapter 9**, focuses on human rights, a key element in business ethics, and a major challenge for businesses in many contexts, including low-cost manufacturing and the extraction industries. This chapter builds on international human rights law, introduced in Chapter 4, looking at how businesses are increasingly viewed as liable for breaches of human rights in operations in which they exert control. In particular, we examine the right not to be subjected to inhuman treatment, the prohibition on the use of child labour, the right to join an independent trade union, and the right to a living wage. **Chapter 10**, on sustainability, follows from the previous chapter in stressing that sustainability relates to both the natural environment and the provision of means for future generations to achieve levels of human well-being that the current generation enjoys. Environmental challenges, including climate change and energy needs, are examined in a context of sustainable development. This chapter looks also at initiatives such as social enterprise and Fairtrade as ways in which sustainability and CSR goals can combine. The final chapter, **Chapter 11**, reviews the ethical themes of the book and draws conclusions on the ethical challenges set out in the Introduction. We highlight inequality, both within and among societies, as a challenge to all decision-makers, both in business and the corridors of government, suggesting that social goals and economic goals can, and should, go hand in hand.

PART CONTENTS

CHAPTER 7

ETHICS AND CSR IN INTERNATIONAL BUSINESS

OUTLINE OF THE CHAPTER

Introduction

Managing global business activities: what are the ethical challenges?

- Ethical capacity and the company
- Ethical choices from the start
- Ethical challenges as the business grows

How has thinking on corporate purpose changed?

Business–society relations: concepts and theories

- Corporate social responsibility (CSR)
- Corporate social performance
- Corporate citizenship
- Stakeholder management theory

Social contract theories

Political CSR: does democratic theory offer new insights?

Applying ethical theories in international business

- Ethics and law: mutually reinforcing
- Ethical theories in the business context

Conclusions

ETHICAL THEMES IN THIS CHAPTER

- Moral rules and cultural divergence
- Businesses as part of society

THE AIMS OF THIS CHAPTER ARE TO

- Identify ethical challenges in global business
- Appreciate the role of business in society
- Relate CSR principles to international business in differing societies
- Apply ethical theories in international business

H&M: CAN THE CHAMPION OF CHEAP FASHION ALSO BE ETHICAL?

Hennes & Mauritz, better known by its brand, H&M, is a fashion retailer founded in Sweden which has grown to become a global leader in the 'fast fashion' sector. The rise of Spain's Inditex (owner of Zara) in this sector has now seen H&M drop to second place globally. Fast fashion has been driven by the mastery of global supply chains by these large companies. The time required to produce a garment, from the design phase through to delivery to outlets, has been reduced to only a few weeks in some cases. Sourcing raw materials in volume and production in low-cost environments are key to these companies' success. Inditex sources much production in Europe and North Africa. H&M has relied largely on Asian suppliers, which are more distant from European markets, but claims to be as fast as Inditex (Milne, 2013b). However, H&M prides itself on much more than fast fashion. It has sought to establish itself as a champion of sustainability in a sector which would seem to contradict the very values associated with sustainability.

Photo 7.1 H&M stores are a familiar feature of shopping centres, but the ethical challenges of 'fast fashion' remain unresolved. (© iStock.com/JenGrantham)

These values include ethical sourcing, concerns for health and safety, concerns for environmental protection and human rights. The textile industry has notoriously relied on cheap labour in poor countries such as Bangladesh, where legal regulation of working conditions is weak. In Bangladesh, unsafe conditions were dramatically brought to the public's attention by the collapse of the Rana Plaza which took the lives of nearly 1,200 people in 2013. As the largest customer of the Bangladesh garment factories, H&M attracted much media attention. Its garments were not produced in the Rana Plaza building, as its code of conduct prohibits doing business with manufacturers in residential buildings. Nonetheless, H&M has been quick to sign up to the accord on fire and safety which has been one of the initiatives launched in the wake of the disaster. It is also rethinking its supply chain strategy in light of its sustainability goals.

H&M has produced CSR reports since 2002, all of which highlight the difficulties of dealing with manufacturers in low-wage countries where it is difficult to monitor conditions. From 2009, the report has been titled the 'sustainability report', possibly suggesting a more environmental focus. The 2012 sustainability report lists seven commitments (H&M, 2013a). Serving customers and working with partner firms in manufacturing are the first two. The third is 'be ethical'. The next three are environmental: climate change policies, recycling, and using natural resources responsibly. The last one is to 'strengthen communities'.

H&M has been at the forefront in its sustainability policies. It is the world's biggest user of organic cotton in manufacturing, and aims to increase its use of organic cotton, as well as to promote more sustainable practices in conventional cotton production. But its huge and increasing demand for cotton seems in contradiction with sustainability goals. A cotton garment could conceivably last for many years. But underlying the company's strategy is the fact that customers view fashion items as having a short lifespan. One of H&M's responses is a garment collecting scheme, introduced in 2012, which encourages customers to return old clothes to the stores for recycling. In European stores, customers bringing old clothes are given a voucher for 15% discount off new purchases. The scheme thus relies on incentives which encourage further purchases. The old clothes are recycled, but, as sceptics point out, textile recycling is very limited (Balch, 2013).

Under its ethical policies it highlights transparency, integrity, honesty and human rights. In fact, under its second commitment, on relations with manufacturers, it highlights many ethical issues, such as overtime and wages. It has stressed human rights in earlier reports, highlighting these same issues. In the 2012 report, these processes are subjected to a rating system, from 'started', to 'more to do', to 'on track'. Higher wages, reduction in overtime and health improvements are all rated in the middle category, 'more to do'. These issues have been in the company's Code of Conduct for suppliers for many years, and it is something of an admission that little progress seems to have been made. In the 2012 report, it concedes, overtime 'remains a core issue' (H&M, 2013a: 43). The nature of fast fashion requires rapid responses and filling orders quickly. Ethical principles are difficult to implement in practice, given the existence of hundreds of different suppliers. For 2012, H&M took the further step of making public the list of suppliers in the report. H&M also takes a stand against corruption, noting that corrupt 'facilitation payments' for shipments are common in the sector. A prohibition on such payments was included in its Code of Conduct in 2012.

The head of sustainability at H&M stresses that 'we can make a difference to hundreds of thousands of people working in our supply chain' (H&M, 2013b). She goes on to say that there are structural issues associated with the supply chain which would require an industry response. Many western brand owners, both luxury and mass-market, use the same manufacturing companies. She says, 'the truth is that the price of a garment does not tell us much about how it is produced' (H&M, 2013b). H&M's CEO confirms this observation, saying that they see medium to luxury brands in the same factories, but these charge 10, 20, or even 100 times more than H&M (Milne, 2013a). H&M itself has a number of brands, including new brands such as COS (Collection of Style) aimed at the more upmarket customer.

In common with other Swedish companies, H&M is a family-dominated business. Its current CEO, Karl-Johan Persson, is the third generation of his family, his grandfather having founded the firm in 1947. H&M's IPO was in 1974, on the Swedish stock exchange, where it is the country's largest listed company. There are two classes of shares, the A shares carrying ten times the voting strength of the B shares. The Persson family own 38% of the shares, but control nearly 70% of the vote. Although the company's business is fast fashion, which has a short-term perspective, its CEO takes a long-term perspective on the family business.

Figure 1 H&M's expansion

Number of stores

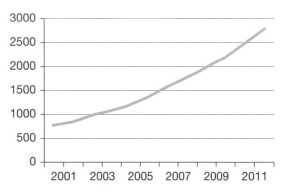

Source of data: H&M (2013) Annual Report 2012, p. 40 at www.about.hm.com (18/09/14).

The company has expanded aggressively in the past decade, increasing the number of stores by 10–15% each year (see figure), even following the financial crisis of 2008. The number of stores increased by 304 in 2012, and ten countries have been added in the past two years. There are now 2,800 stores in 48 countries. The first H&M store to open in the southern hemisphere was in Chile in 2013, and the CEO foresees expansion in Latin America. He is also thinking about production in Latin America or possibly Africa. Although this rethink is not necessarily linked with the disaster in Bangladesh, he is aware of the challenges. The company has invested in improving worker conditions in Bangladesh and has supported rises in wages. But it cannot guarantee labour conditions which conform to its stated policies. Its head of sustainability says of 'guaranteeing' labour conditions, 'Of course we cannot when we are such a huge company operating in very challenging conditions' (H&M, 2013b). She goes on, 'Remember that H&M does not own any factories itself. We are to some extent dependent on the suppliers – it is impossible to be in full control' (H&M, 2013b). These admissions acknowledge the bigger issue, which is the business model itself, which has been called 'the elephant in the fitting room – a business model predicated on producing millions of units and of a fashion cycle that favours 30–50 trend-driven fashion seasons a year' (Siegle, 2012). H&M's branded production amounts to over 500 million garments a year, and it produces none of them itself. The CEO invites consumers to ask themselves the following when shopping: 'Is this a decent company that acts in a responsible way?' (Milne, 2013a).

Sources: H&M (2013a) *Conscious Actions Sustainability Report 2012,* at www.about.hm.com; H&M (2013b) *Interview with Helena Helmersson, Head of Sustainability,* at www.about.hm.com; Milne, R. (2013a) 'A defender of fast fashion', *Financial Times,* 20 May; Milne, R. (2013b) 'H&M rethinks sourcing policy', *Financial Times,* 20 May; Siegle, L. (2012) 'Is H&M the new home of ethical fashion?', *The Observer,* 7 April; Balch, O. (2013) 'H&M: can fast fashion and sustainability ever really mix?', *The Guardian,* 3 May, at www.theguardian.com (18/09/14).

DISCUSSION QUESTIONS

□ What ethical issues stand out in the case study?

□ The 'elephant in the fitting room' is the business model of fast fashion. To what extent has H&M overcome the ethical challenges in fast fashion?

□ Look at the question posed by the CEO at the end of the case study. Would you buy clothes from H&M? Why?

INTRODUCTION

In this chapter, ethical concepts and theories are applied in a variety of international business settings. Modern discourse on business ethics focuses particularly on the relationship between business and society. Large MNEs typically operate in numerous societies. They do more than merely 'exist', however: they are active forces in economic life and often active forces in governance and the shaping of legislation. While these are potentially forces for the public good, companies can also have negative impacts in societies, perpetuating poor working conditions and environmental degradation. What is more, they often take legal steps to avoid regulatory hurdles and minimize liabilities such as tax. Globalization has been the driver of much of this global scanning. Corporate profits have benefited, but critics among consumer, environmental and employee groups have raised ethical criticisms.

These criticisms have led to widespread rethinking of ethics in business. Numerous recent theorists have addressed these issues of business–society relations, bringing in the role of governments and regulation. In this chapter, we look at recent theories of corporate social responsibility (CSR), corporate citizenship and stakeholder management, with a view to applying them in the current world of globalized supply chains. We also take into account the rise of emerging economies with state-guided industries and a proliferation of state-controlled companies. Ethics might seem to be overshadowed in the rapid developments of the global economy. However, we find the contrary is true. Ordinary people are more and more concerned with basic issues like integrity of corporate leaders, decent work practices, humane working conditions and ethical sourcing.

MANAGING GLOBAL BUSINESS ACTIVITIES: WHAT ARE THE ETHICAL CHALLENGES?

Ethics is about consciously making distinctions between right and wrong and following them through in practice. Ethical behaviour rests on applying values that have a universality which transcends the numerous cultural environments in which an international business might be involved. This is a broad view of the sphere of ethics, encompassing businesses as well as individuals. When managers are asked about their ethics, it is not uncommon to point to the staff's code of ethical conduct, and how effectively wrongdoers within the firm are held to account for activities such as harassing other staff or falsifying expenses. Although matters such as staff honesty and transparent advertising are important in the overall picture, they are only part of that picture.

ETHICAL CAPACITY AND THE COMPANY

While it is generally accepted that a natural person has moral capacity, moral capacity of a company is often contested (Wartick and Cochran, 1985). The company is sometimes said to be merely an association which is 'amoral', capable of neither right nor wrong. It is made up of real people, however. A natural person has a conscience and will, but, it is argued, a company, which is a separate artificial entity, does not. This view that companies are some-how above standards of right and wrong has gained ground in conjunction with the view of the company as solely an economic entity which acts in pursuit of the self-interest of its owners. Advocates of this view say the company exists for economic purposes only, and cannot legitimately be judged on ethical or social criteria. They do accept, however, that companies are subject to law, and can be faced with penalties for legal wrongdoing. There are large bodies of corporate law in most countries, which recognize the company as a distinct legal entity, for example, for tax and regulatory purposes. But there is also a growing amount of evidence that the company is not an ethical and social 'black box' separate from those who run it.

The company in law is an artificial person, or 'juridical' person, which has a separate existence from the people who set it up, its directors and shareholders (see Chapter 5). The company has perpetual existence, which carries on despite changes in owners and managers. The company has no independent will: it acts only in the ways which real people dictate. Because of limited liability, they are not generally liable for its debts, but if fraud is committed in the company's name, they can become personally liable. Company directors are often accused of wrongs committed by the company, and face the consequences, even though, in some cases, they personally have not been involved. As we have seen in Chapter 5, where there is a serious wrong such as insider dealing, the company incurs a fine, and the guilty directors can go to jail. But recall the discrepancy in the case where the company admitted crimes of insider dealing, while its leading trader claimed innocence.

When moral wrongs are committed by the company, consumers are quick to blame the executives. And in practice, many directors accept responsibility. This is largely because of potential damage to corporate reputation, of course, which can impact on profits if consumers feel so strongly that they stop buying from them. Economic goals themselves are thus not as unambiguous as they might seem to those who rely on assumptions of rational self-interest driving the company.

ETHICAL CHOICES FROM THE START

Ethical challenges affect all aspects of the business: how it makes products, how it organizes people and how it respects the environment. An entrepreneur with a business idea

Figure 7.1 *Ethical choices start with the birth of the business*

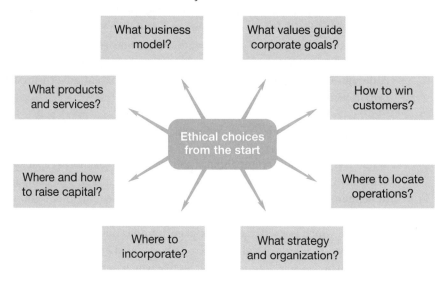

faces numerous choices in getting the enterprise up and running. These choices are laden with ethical implications. Indeed, ethical challenges arise even before the business is founded. Entrepreneurs must address a range of questions in which some of the alternatives are superior on ethical grounds than others. These ethical choices are shown in Figure 7.1.

Perhaps the most influential of the questions posed in Figure 7.1 is the nature of the business model, as answers to other questions flow from it. Many new businesses originate in the highly competitive high-tech sector, relying on innovative ideas to launch either products or services. The company in this sector is likely to envisage a core set of key employees as the creative heart of the organization, and rely on outsourced manufacturing for products such as high-tech devices. But a business model based on outsourced manufacturing in advantageous locations such as Asia raises ethical questions over working conditions and human rights. A closely related question which must be addressed is core values. What matters most to the founders? Great, innovative products which delight customers in all markets? Most technology entrepreneurs would probably identify with this goal, and most people would consider it worthy. After all, the products are good because they are bringing real benefits to users, improving people's daily lives. But this goal, ostensibly laudable in principle, is more problematic when applied in the real global competitive environment. Smartphones and other high-tech devices are almost all manufactured in low-cost, outsourced manufacturing environments. Brand owners who do not manufacture their own products are good examples of globalization in practice. Producing great products is a means of generating wealth for the insiders in the company. Making money for owners is at the heart of the capitalist business. This in itself does not make it unethical, but how far is too far for entrepreneurs to go in seeking to maximize profits?

Making money for owners is at the heart of the capitalist business.

Global choices of location come into play for every aspect of the business. Where to register the company is one, as laws on disclosure, financial reporting, taxation and governance come into the equation. It used to be assumed that corporate founders would register their business as a company in the country where they founded it, or in the individual state in the US. But this has ceased to be the case. Countries now present themselves as advantageous locations for companies, offering minimal regulation, light taxes and legal protection of owners' controlling rights. The British government states that it is 'committed to creating the most competitive tax regime in the G20' (Schmidt, 2013). The G20 is a loose grouping of advanced and emerging countries, which meets to air issues of common concern, but has no legal authority over governments (see Note 1). In the US, the state of Delaware has become the favoured jurisdiction for registering companies. Similarly, when the founders think of listing the company, they can choose a stock exchange which is similarly advantageous. As was discussed in Chapter 5, the company need not be active in either the country of registration or the country of listing. But, as Figure 7.1 suggests, these decisions in fact present ethical challenges. In ethical terms, it seems wrong for a company to carry on business activities in a country, but register itself offshore and shift profits offshore in order to reduce tax burdens. Companies can register subsidiaries in tax havens for this purpose, and also use charitable foundations for ownership purposes due to their advantageous tax positions. The charity, of course, is founded on a worthy cause, but, as we have seen in Chapter 3, charitable forms can be used as an umbrella to cover a range of other activities which serve self-interested purposes of individuals.

PAUSE TO CONSIDER...

If you were launching a company, would you do either of the following, and why?

a. Register the company in a Caribbean tax haven
b. Outsource manufacturing to a low-cost Asian country

ETHICAL CHALLENGES AS THE BUSINESS GROWS

A start-up is likely to focus on a few core products or services at the outset, and keep decision-making concentrated on the founders and their associates. It is likely to be looking at targeting multiple markets as the firm grows. As Figure 7.2 shows, in a global environment, opportunities are greater than ever.

Global corporate strategy constantly reviews location advantages and disadvantages as they change over time. We have seen in the first part of this book how low-cost manufacturing environments find their comparative advantages difficult to sustain. There are inevitable pressures on factory owners to improve conditions and wages of workers, which send up costs. And government incentives which might have helped in the early stages of setting up operations eventually run out. Other locations with lower wages are sought. New suppliers also come on the scene. It is not long before a company starts to think about how it can extend success in one product range to other products or services which are complementary, especially if it is building a strong brand. It might also diversify into other businesses as opportunities arise.

Organizationally, the MNE enjoys the flexibility to set up subsidiaries and invest in affiliate companies, which help to spread both opportunities and also dilute risks. But new businesses present new risks, and also raise ethical challenges. Much financial thought goes into a company's decision to establish subsidiaries or branch offices in a new location. A subsidiary is a separately registered company, subject to national law where it is registered, whereas in many countries a branch office is not subject to the same regulation. It also follows that the subsidiary established in an offshore location offers advantages for receiving profits and

A nondescript building in Wilmington, Delaware is the registered address of 278,000 companies.

Figure 7.2 *Encountering ethical challenges as the business grows*

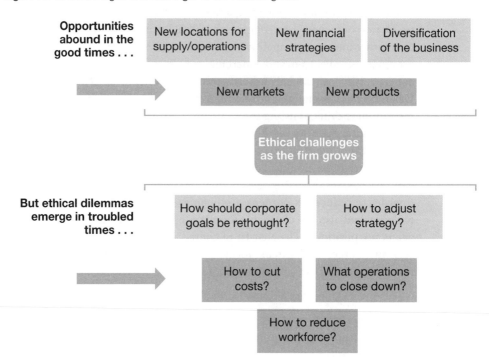

royalties, as we have seen in Chapter 5. A nondescript building in Wilmington, Delaware is the registered address of 278,000 companies. Such subsidiaries exist on paper, but might have little real existence and hardly any employees. The function they serve is nonetheless valuable, potentially 'saving' millions in tax. Shifting from one manufacturing centre to another to cut costs invites accusations that the firm pays little heed to ethical standards. While workers in an outsourced factory are not employed by the brand owner, consumers are nowadays likely to see the brand owner as at least partly responsible for their conditions, as we discuss later in this chapter.

Just as expansion presents challenges, so does the necessity to deal with downturns and shocks to the business, as shown in Figure 7.2. Companies which run into difficulties financially or find their products have been overtaken by rivals in the marketplace face challenges in turning around performance. But as cost-cutting is involved, decisions must be made about where to trim costs, including employees and even whole units. No firm likes to lay off staff, and employment laws offer some protection to workers in most countries. The ethical firm will respond to a crisis with transparency and even-handedness, helping workers to find employment in other sections of the organization. Indeed, this is a legal requirement in some countries. Such a firm views employees as stakeholders and is also likely to have a sense of social responsibility. But many firms profess to take social responsibility seriously and nonetheless proceed with downsizing on purely economic considerations. This gives the impression that managers consider CSR desirable 'if we can afford it'. Viewed as a cost, CSR gives way to 'bottom line' considerations which appear in accounts.

Many of the troubles that arise are difficult to foresee and plan for. These include natural disasters and government action. But some spectacular corporate failures have resulted from managerial negligence, over-risky financial strategies or misconduct within the company. Banks and other financial services companies highlighted in Chapter 5 are examples. There are others, including energy trader, Enron, which collapsed in 2001. As became well known in the aftermath of the Enron scandal, the company had a CSR policy and code of ethical conduct which looked impeccable on paper (Beecher-Monas, 2003). But in practice, these turned out to be worthless. A superficially ethical approach which has little bearing in reality can undermine general public confidence in corporate communications. When corporate scandals erupt, consumers are now accustomed to firms putting out statements that they take law and ethics very seriously, and that what happened is an aberration. These firms assure the public that they simply need to tighten their systems so that there is no repetition. But consumers are justifiably sceptical. Nike assured consumers along these lines in the 1990s, when they were accused of tolerating sweatshop labour practices, but there were further scandals. BP, which had a record of safety lapses, similarly assured the world that there would be no repeats after a serious refinery fire in 2005, but the Macondo oil spill in the Gulf of Mexico followed in 2010. Is the capitalist enterprise essentially one of profit maximization, in which ethical considerations are an add-on?

HOW HAS THINKING ON CORPORATE PURPOSE CHANGED?

We found in Chapter 5 that companies such as Google are forthright and unapologetic in stating that they are doing nothing wrong in shifting profits to low-tax jurisdictions. Indeed, they assert that they are taking legal obligations seriously, reminding critics that they owe an obligation to shareholders to maximize profits. Google is a public company, having listed in 2004. It exemplifies the shareholder primacy model, reflecting the view that the capitalist company exists for maximizing returns to shareholders as owners. This is also called the economic model of the company because of its primary aim to make money. The shareholder focus itself involves multiple interests, some in conflict with each other, as we will discuss in the next chapter on corporate governance. Hence, the 'economic model' is perhaps a more accurate way of identifying this type of company, serving to contrast its profit-maximizing purpose with CSR perspectives. The rise of the economic model to a position of supremacy is a fairly recent development, dating from the 1970s. Before then, the mix of capitalist enterprise and social purposes was a subject of lively debate which has been rather overshadowed in today's finance-driven business environment. Here, we revive the arguments about corporate purpose afresh, with a view to seeing how recent theory on CSR and stakeholders fits into a continuing debate.

Many decades ago, it was common for companies, when asked what purposes they serve, to reply with a list of goals which revealed corporate values (Stout, 2012). Although producing great products would be included, also included were providing employment, improving people's lives, and contributing to the community. In the post-war period of rapid growth in the US, the founder of the retailer, Sears, listed four parties in the business in order of importance: customers, employees, community and stockholders (Clarkson, 1995). He said that if the needs of the first three are looked after, then profits will flow to stockholders. The 1920s and 30s in the US was an era of vibrant academic debate on the nature of the company in society. Up to then, companies had been mainly private companies, owned and controlled like personal property. By the 1920s, American companies had grown large and had become public corporations with numerous small shareholders who played no role in running the company. These corporate giants controlled large amounts of wealth, which led to a view that the existence of many small shareholders turned these companies into social institutions with responsibilities to the public (Bratton, 2001). With the stock market crash of 1929 and the ensuing Great Depression, government intervention on grounds of public welfare became accepted, and corporations were seen as part of this effort (Bratton, 2001).

A famous debate took place in the 1930s, between a leading corporate law specialist, Adolph Berle, who championed shareholder primacy, and Merrick Dodd, a corporate law professor who held that the corporation is 'an economic institution which has a social service as well as profit-making function' (Stout, 2012: 17). Social legislation in the form of the New Deal dates from this period. It included social security, housing regulation, recognition of trade unions, and labour standards. Regulatory frameworks such as the Securities and Exchange Commission date from this period. So too do government subsidies of agriculture, designed to support farming livelihoods (see Chapter 6). Although these programmes were considered 'liberal' in the American context and were opposed by supporters of the Republican Party, many endured and continue to exist to this day. However, in mainstream corporate thinking, the trend was in the opposite direction.

From the 1970s, largely under the influence of the Chicago School of neoclassical economics, led by Milton Friedman, the ideas of shareholder primacy and profit maximization became the predominant view of the purpose of the company. Friedman believed that making money is the company's only legitimate goal, subject to basic legal and ethical constraints imposed by society. When the company spends money on social purposes, it is, in effect, acting illegitimately, as it takes away wealth which is due to shareholders (Wartick and Cochran, 1985). This economic paradigm gained a grip on thinking in academic scholarship as well as in business practice. Its academic influence extended from economics to law and management. The manager, according to this orthodoxy, should follow market indicators, referring back to utilitarian assumptions and also libertarian views of economic freedom (Ostas, 2001). Faith in markets was central to this model, and share price became a convenient measure of corporate value, allowing comparative performance to be assessed between companies and over time. The theory chimes with classical economic theory, going back to the foundations of capitalism. As we have seen in Chapter 2, the pursuit of rational self-interest has a theoretical simplicity and objectivity. The neoclassical economists of the Chicago School went further, however, in defence of profit-maximizing behaviour. Not only was profit maximization legitimate, they asserted that it was imposed by law (Stout, 2012). In response, lawyers in both the US and UK stress that this view of the company's obligation is wrong in law. In both the US and UK, legal duties are owed to the company itself, not to individual shareholders or to shareholders as a whole (Kay, 2013). But the view of legal obligations to shareholders has been accepted uncritically in both academic and business circles nonetheless. So assured were adherents of the shareholder-oriented model that theirs was the only valid model of the public corporation, that it was seen as universally applicable (Stout, 2012).

However, other interpretations of corporate purpose, though overshadowed, had not disappeared. Evidence abounded of corporations' activities in social and political life in the US, suggesting that companies at an empirical level engage in active roles in society. Even in the 1970s, there was considerable legislative activity in the US in areas of equal opportunities, health and safety, environmental protection and consumer product safety. In all these

Friedman believed that making money is the company's only legitimate goal.

areas, companies are involved in applying the law, thus becoming part of the structure of social life. One could say that these activities are consistent with the economic model, which accepts that companies have legal obligations. But they are also active in lobbying (see Chapter 3), suggesting a more active role in shaping public policy. Their activities are mainly directed at reducing regulatory burdens, but, whatever their motives, they are playing social roles. Any company which has employees and physical operations exists in a social and ethical context, whatever the country. The development of a coherent body of theory on social purpose and ethical business practices has grown up over the last several decades, recognizing this fuller picture of the business in society.

The neoclassical approach to corporate purpose has been undermined by a succession of market failures, the largest of which was the financial crash of 2008, which call into question its assumptions about markets operating efficiently (see Chapters 2 and 5). It has been challenged from outside its heartlands by the evolution of different approaches to the corporation in countries where market reforms are taking place in the absence of foundations in individualist cultures or capitalist economic development. One of the older of these is Japan, which has a long history of recognizing social responsibility as an essential aspect of corporate culture. More recently, there are post-communist countries, such as Russia, the states of the former Soviet Union, and states in Central and Eastern Europe. In China, market reforms are taking place in the context of continuing domination of the Communist Party. Capitalist enterprises abound in all these countries, and many are listed on stock exchanges. However, despite legal forms which look similar, these companies have differing views on the role of the company in society. State-owned enterprises, also listed on stock exchanges, are explicitly associated with social and political goals, as well as economic activities, with a focus on guided economic development (see Chapters 2 and 3). The idea of the company as an independent economic entity grew up in liberal market economies, giving rise to a perceived dichotomy between the company on the one hand, and government intervention on the other. This rather polarized way of thinking was characteristic of neoclassical economic theory. It is much less relevant in economies where the state is perceived as guiding development and is seen as a good thing in that role. But even in liberal economies, it has become evident that 'business and society are interwoven, rather than distinct entities' (Wood, 1991: 695).

PAUSE TO CONSIDER...

Although the Berle–Dodd debate on shareholder primacy vs social purpose took place in the 1930s, the topic is highly relevant today. What points would be made on each side in a modern re-run of their famous debate?

BUSINESS–SOCIETY RELATIONS: CONCEPTS AND THEORIES

Interactions between business and society have been the focus of theories in a number of academic areas which attempt to move beyond the economic model. As noted already, lawyers have been active. Some have looked at the concepts in legal and economic contexts (Ostas, 2001). Management theories have explored CSR as a concept and also how it can be applied in practice, through corporate social performance (CSP) (Wood, 1991). Economists have contributed to questioning the economic orthodoxy in terms of stakeholder interests (Preston and Sapienza, 1990). In this section, we look at three of these theories.

CORPORATE SOCIAL RESPONSIBILITY (CSR)

Corporate social responsibility (CSR) as a concept rests on the idea that the company has a broader range of responsibilities in society than merely economic obligations. These responsibilities 'rest on an ethical understanding of the organization's responsibility for the impact of its business activities' (Maon et al., 2009). The range of responsibilities has been set out by Carroll in a model of CSR which comprises economic, legal, ethical and philanthropic responsibilities. Carroll's pyramid model, shown in Figure 7.3, suggests an order of priority among the four components of CSR. His model has served to lay the conceptual groundwork of CSR, and has become a basis on which later theories have been built.

Carroll begins with economic responsibilities, including generating profits, maintaining a strong competitive position and maintaining a high level of efficiency. Without economic success, the company will falter, but Carroll notes the transformation of 'profit motive' into 'profit maximization'. Set against this dominant paradigm was a growing body of literature which highlighted the importance of the company in the social environment. His analysis of legal and ethical responsibilities is more nuanced than appears in the figure itself, which suggests entirely separate categories. Both 'embody ethical norms', he points out, and represent expectations of those in society (Carroll, 1991: 41). Legal responsibilities, including a broad duty to obey the law, rest on expectations of obedience. The phenomenon of firms obeying the letter of the law, but managing to get round the legislators' intent has always been a challenge for law-makers, and is highlighted in a more recent article co-authored by Carroll, which points out the opportunistic attitude of some companies (Schwartz and Carroll, 2003). Recently, tax avoidance has attracted much negative

Figure 7.3 Carroll's pyramid of CSR

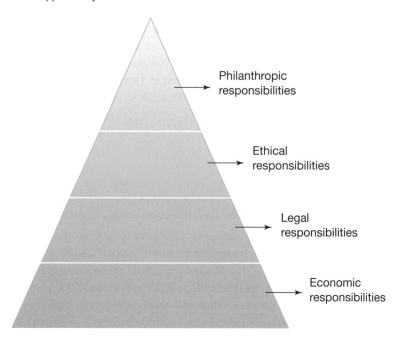

Source: adapted from Carroll, A.B. (1991) 'The Pyramid of Corporate Social Responsibility: Toward the Moral Management of Organizational Stakeholders', *Business Horizons*, 34: 39–48, at p. 42.

media attention. Carroll stresses that it is important for a company to be a law-abiding corporate citizen. In Carroll's CSR typology, corporate citizenship relates to three of the sets of responsibilities: legal, ethical and philanthropic. Carroll has also contributed a theory of corporate citizenship, which rests on the same four sets of responsibilities as his CSR pyramid, suggesting that he sees these concepts as interchangeable (Carroll, 1998). Corporate citizenship, however, implies that the company is a member of society in a way analogous to a human being, which is rather more precise than simply a social role, as will be discussed below.

Carroll sees *ethical responsibilities* in a number of different perspectives. Environmental concerns, civil rights and consumer protection are highlighted as areas where ethical concerns are voiced, and followed up by legal enactment. There is thus a dynamic interaction between law and ethical principles. Businesses are expected to meet 'newly emerging values and norms' (Carroll, 1991: 41). He also distinguishes between moral values of groups in society and the ethical principles of moral philosophy. Recall the opening case study of Chapter 4, on the death penalty in the US. The death penalty is legal in numerous individual states, but some companies are refusing on ethical grounds to supply the drugs used in killing people. The US Supreme Court has taken a view that the law reflects changing ethical norms in society, rather than transcendent ethical principles. Carroll says that businesspeople are constantly being pushed to higher ethical standards than required by law.

Similarly, companies are fulfilling expectations of society when they give to charities and take part in charitable activities. *Philanthropic responsibilities*, the final element of the pyramid, represent discretionary spending by the company on items like cultural goods, which improve the quality of life in communities. These activities, too, are said to be those of the good corporate citizen. Carroll says that contributions to charities are not an ethical obligation. Companies often contribute money, facilities and time to charities, but if they do not, they are not regarded as unethical organizations. He notes a growing trend among companies to equate corporate citizenship with charitable giving. This narrow interpretation, he says, is not a socially responsible approach. The three other elements of CSR are more important than philanthropy, which is merely the 'icing on the cake' (Carroll, 1991: 42). In Carroll's later re-working of his CSR theory, he omits philanthropy as a separate level, highlighting the three main 'domains' of CSR (Schwartz and Carroll, 2003). His later view is that philanthropy is probably now an aspect of ethical responsibilities, as it is expected by society, rather than merely discretionary. Nonetheless, it is helpful to retain philanthropy as a separate category, as it differs in essence from other aspects of ethical responsibilities, for the reasons given by Carroll in his original pyramid model. Society might expect companies to give to charities, but responses to expectations are not the same thing as acting out of ethical duties.

The three other elements of CSR (economic, legal and ethical) are more important than philanthropy, which is merely the 'icing on the cake'.

Carroll applies the pyramid model in terms of *stakeholders*, arguing that stakeholders are the 'social' in CSR. Stakeholders are often seen in terms of economic claims on the company, but Carroll broadens their relevance to include legally and ethically legitimate claims, which in some cases can seem to give rise to conflicts. A difficulty which other theorists have addressed is how to apply CSR concepts in practice, in the many situations highlighted at the start of this chapter as ethical challenges. This is especially true of the MNE which operates in different societies.

Transnational CSR becomes complicated in that societies in which an MNE operates are likely to have differing expectations of CSR and differing ethical concerns (Artaud-Day, 2005). Conflicts between them can arise. Cultural and social differences, as well as differing legal requirements, impact on the ways in which societies view CSR. In some developing countries, it is often thought that economic concerns come first, and CSR can wait until the company is established financially. The MNE is tempted to think that CSR policies should be addressed only to western markets, where consumers are perceived to be more sensitive to the issues. However, as MNEs are now seeing stronger growth in emerging markets than in more established ones, it is arguable that a rethinking of transnational CSR is needed. Theories of political CSR, discussed later, are part of this rethinking.

PAUSE TO CONSIDER...

Many companies consider CSR to be focused on philanthropic activities. How would Carroll argue against this position?

CORPORATE SOCIAL PERFORMANCE

While the CSR conceptual framework highlights corporate responsibilities, some theorists have developed these principles into applied theories of corporate social performance (CSP). The CSP approach involves social responses in practice, bringing in all the ways in which a firm goes about meeting challenges for business in society (Wartick and Cochran, 1985). Critics of CSR have tended to argue that the principles are vague, and there is little indication of how to apply them in practice. But CSP theory is best seen as complementing the CSR framework, not replacing it (Wood, 1991: 703). Exploring the ways in which corporate involvement in society takes place is the main focus of CSP theorists. Social responsiveness is one of the processes which CSP seeks to address. Whereas corporate responsibility suggests normative principles, social responsiveness suggests acting in a context of social norms which present themselves in particular situations. Social responsiveness is thus linked closely to stakeholder management (discussed below). It takes place in a social context in which moral issues arise, but its focus is on social responses rather than ethical actions. A firm could conceivably be socially responsive but acting unethically. It has been argued that this is a limitation in CSP theory (Scherer and Palazzo, 2007). Critical analysts of CSP argue that the theory is more instrumental than normative, focusing as it does on outcomes in a context of economic goals, rather than on normative principles associated with CSR (Scherer and Palazzo, 2007).

Social responsiveness serves to highlight a process of engagement with social issues. Wartick and Cochran give an example of a firm which prioritizes the safety of its products but is suffering from quality problems, resulting in its products having to be recalled. Each time its product is found unsafe, it responds by recalling it. After ten recalls, one could still say the firm has been socially responsive, but not socially responsible (Wartick and Cochran, 1985: 763). It responded to immediate concerns, but failed to address the wider issues of CSR strategy. The two concepts are both necessary. Responsibility plays a macro role, and responsiveness a micro role. CSP adds an 'action' dimension to complement the normative content of CSR. Wood provides a comprehensive definition of CSP. Corporate social performance, she says, can be defined as 'a business organization's configuration of principles of social responsibility, processes of social responsiveness, and policies, programs, and observable outcomes as they relate the firm's societal relationships' (Wood, 1991: 693).

In her definition, CSR principles remain the first element. Wood sees three facets to social responsiveness: environmental assessment, stakeholder management and issues management. Managing the three elements involves having processes in place, for which methods of analysis and assessment have been developed. Scanning techniques are used for environmental assessment, while there are frameworks for assessing stakeholder salience (Mitchell et al., 1997). Issues management, which would seem to have more of a policy orientation, has also been the subject of monitoring and assessment techniques. These have focused on external and internal relations of the company. External issues include political strategies and public affairs. As companies become more involved in political discourse and interactions with governments, these become more important and also more susceptible to scrutiny by stakeholders. Internal processes include the design and use of corporate codes of ethics. Whether formal codes of conduct contribute to better CSP is one of the issues addressed. These methods of assessment give indications of outward processes associated with CSP, so that empirical assessments of social responsiveness can be made. One of the outcomes has been an increase in the inclusion of these elements in company reporting. Companies increasingly include in annual reports their social and environmental performance measures, in addition to financial disclosures. The three elements make up triple bottom line reporting. Indeed, in some countries, social and environmental reporting are now legally required.

CORPORATE CITIZENSHIP

Corporate citizenship rests on the analogy that the company is a member of society in a way analogous to the individual citizen. As we have seen, good corporate citizenship features in Carroll's CSR model. Many companies have latched onto the concept as related to philanthropy only, and hold themselves out as good corporate citizens in communities. They draw attention to charitable activities such as improving local environmental amenities. This shallow approach to corporate citizenship seems to have become popular among businesses, but academic scholarship has attempted to define corporate citizenship as a deeper theoretical approach (Matten and Crane, 2005). Given Carroll's linking it with CSR, how helpful is corporate citizenship in its own right?

The international business is involved in different ways in numerous societies. It seems to be stretching common sense to say that a company is a corporate citizen in all of them. Citizenship in relation to human beings is an administrative category, linking a person with a particular sovereign state, which is the person's nationality. Only rarely is a person a citizen of multiple countries. In most societies, the distinction between citizen and non-citizen is a sensitive one. Non-citizen residents, such as immigrants, are likely to have fewer civic rights and welfare entitlements. They are also likely to suffer from discrimination. As is often pointed out by advocacy groups, immigrants have human rights recognized in international law even though they do not have citizenship rights in the countries where they reside. The citizen has political rights recognized most fully in democracies. The citizen can vote in elections and stand for office, but normally the non-citizen resident in a country cannot. It is usually said that the citizen of a country must pay taxes and obey the law of that country, but paying taxes and obeying the law applies to any residents of a country, citizens or not. How do these points apply to the company? The company's nationality is the country where it is registered. The MNE operates in many societies, and plays an economic and social role in them, sometimes a highly important role, but this does not make it a citizen in ways similar to a human being. It must abide by the law in any society where it has operations. So must any organization in society, from a church to a sports club.

It has been suggested that the company's citizenship lies in the social services it performs in society, which have been on the rise in many countries (Matten and Crane, 2005). Both for-profit companies and non-profit organizations carry out many public services. Companies also often commit themselves to welfare services in conjunction with their employees or customers in a country. This can be seen in a context of CSR, recognizing social as well as economic responsibilities. For example, Novartis, the Swiss pharmaceutical company, runs a health education programme in one of China's poorest regions, the far-western rural Xinjiang province, where the ethnic Uighur population, with its distinctive culture and Islamic religion, is concentrated. Novartis is using CSR 'to build a brand in a region that has gone from zero to almost universal health insurance coverage in recent years' (Waldmeir, 2013). However, poverty, poor health and weak educational attainment are challenges recognized by the local government. The programme, the Health Express project, which is run as a public–private partnership (PPP) between the government and Novartis, aims to educate school children in the basics of hygiene, such as washing hands. It is hoped that they will persuade their parents to take up these basic hygiene habits, which will lead to general improvement in health. Novartis see this programme as a CSR project. It is run on a zero-profit basis, and ultimately the company hopes to gain a positive awareness of the brand among the population. This is a long-term goal for Novartis in China's growing healthcare market.

Novartis is using CSR 'to build a brand in a region that has gone from zero to almost universal health insurance coverage in recent years.'

The Novartis Health Express project can be differentiated from the PPP and outsourcing of public services that is taking place in many countries. Novartis offers its health visitor services as an adjunct to its business, whereas for the companies which specialize in providing social services, this is their main business. Some governments have sought as a matter of policy to privatize or 'outsource' public services. Companies typically take over services in health, education and prisons, formerly carried out by government agencies. The companies which operate in these sectors do so for profit. Their business models are based on contracting with governments to offer services, stepping into quasi-governance roles rather than citizenship roles. Real citizens are on the receiving end, and when there is a breakdown in services, people tend to blame the government as much as the company in charge of the services on the ground. These companies have been criticized for lack of transparency and weak accountability in relations with government bodies (see the closing case study).

An issue which arises in connection with corporate citizenship is how it operates in different societies, including authoritarian regimes. Some authors have seen corporate citizenship as similar to the participation of individual citizens in a democracy (Moon et al., 2005). This limits the application of corporate citizenship to countries with democratic political systems. All countries have citizens, not just democratic ones. How does a company go about being a good corporate citizen in China, for example? In the context of China's one-party rule, the good Chinese citizen would comply totally with what the party leadership dictates. Companies such as Yahoo, which co-operate with Chinese government censorship of political dissent on the internet, are accused by people outside China of flouting ethical principles. But any company which does business in China faces legal obligations. It might disagree with them on ethical grounds. Internet companies have long seen themselves as empowering individuals in the freedom of a borderless cyber environment. They face particular ethical challenges when governments impose internet controls or use surveillance mechanisms to gather private data on individuals. Although reluctant, they must comply with government requirements.

An important element in democratic politics is civil society, which covers the many organizations which people voluntarily join and through which democratic participation and political debate can thrive (see Chapter 3). A principle of democracy is political equality – every person's voice should be heard. The richness of civil society organizations is an indication of pluralism in political life. Countries where rulers suppress political dissent set back democratic participation, but what about ostensibly democratic countries where corporate money plays a major role in politics? Corporate actors with their deep pockets can shape political debate and dominate election campaign advertising in some countries such as the US. They also cultivate links with civil society organizations. An organization called the European Privacy Association, which was set up in Brussels, looks on the surface like a grassroots group wishing to participate in the EU's privacy policy debate. However, it emerged in 2013 that the group is financed mainly by US technology companies. This tactic, known as 'astroturfing', is familiar in Washington's lobbying circles, but new in Brussels. One Member of the European Parliament says, 'They have brought Washington-style campaigning infused with a lot of Silicon Valley money' (Fontenella-Khan, 2013). After its financing was revealed, the organization registered itself in EU's voluntary register of lobbyists.

'They have brought Washington-style campaigning infused with a lot of Silicon Valley money.'

The idea of the company as analogous to the individual citizen received legal endorsement from the US Supreme Court in 2010, when it was held that the corporation enjoys the constitutional right of free speech in the same way that a natural person does. The *Citizens United* judgment, mentioned in Chapter 3, paved the way for unlimited secret donations to political causes. This judgment seemed to run counter to legal precedent, which had held that too much corporate money would risk undermining individual citizens' faith in the electoral system.

The majority decision in *Citizens United* was strongly criticized in a dissenting opinion by Mr Justice Stevens (Supreme Court of the US, 2010). He reiterates that the company is not like a human being in terms of citizenship. It cannot vote in elections or hold office. The company may be foreign controlled, and is treated in law in almost every respect as being a separate artificial entity, not a human being. He stresses the economic role of companies in society, but expresses concern about their growing political role in the US. His concerns are echoed by surveys of US voters. A Demos poll, shown in Figure 7.4, shows that over 80% of registered voters felt corporations have too much political power, leading to corruption and the jeopardizing of political equality (Kennedy, 2012).

PAUSE TO CONSIDER...

Think about a civil society organization which you have had contact with. It could be a sports club, a religious group, a trade union, or a single-issue group such as a society against animal cruelty. What role, if any, has business played in the group?

Figure 7.4 *Corporations' influence on democratic processes in the US*

Respondents were asked, 'Do corporations and corporate CEOs have too much political power and influence?'

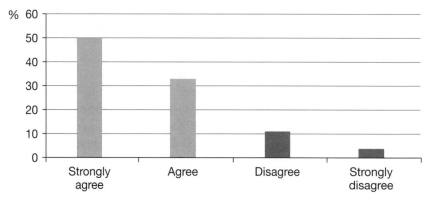

Source of data: Demos Analytics Poll, 2012, at www.demos.org (18/09/14).

STAKEHOLDER MANAGEMENT THEORY

Responsibilities of companies to stakeholders feature strongly in management theories as well as CSR theories. Freeman is one of the early theorists of stakeholder management whose work has become highly influential. He defines the stakeholder as 'any group or individual who can affect or is affected by the achievement of the organization's objectives' (Freeman, 1984: 46). Stakeholders, he says, are 'those groups which make a difference' (Freeman, 1984: 42). Freeman justifies this broad definition by saying that the stakeholder is an 'umbrella' concept in both business strategy and corporate social responsiveness. The strategist must deal with the people who affect the firm's business directly, but to be effective in the long term, the business must look to those groups it affects or can potentially affect. This distinction gives us a clue to the different uses of the concept, in both descriptive contexts and normative contexts.

Stakeholders are those groups which make a difference.

Freeman makes a distinction between primary and secondary stakeholders which has been followed by other theorists. Primary stakeholders are those who are directly involved in the business, and whose interests are essential to its success (see Figure 7.5). They include shareholders, employees, suppliers and customers. These groups have different roles. Among them, shareholders stand out as being distinctive. In a company, they are legally the owners, but, with the separation of ownership and management, they play little role in running the business (see Chapter 8). Employees are central, but their status can be ambiguous, especially in supply chains and networked organizations, where employees can move from one organization to another. Many companies have relatively small workforces employed full-time, but many more marginal workers, who are part-time workers, agency workers or workers on fixed-term projects.

Theorists highlight criteria which apply to these diverse stakeholders, which help to identify them and assess their impacts. Two of these criteria are legitimacy and power. The stakeholders listed all have legitimate interests, and they are in positions to exert pressure.

Figure 7.5 *Stakeholder management*

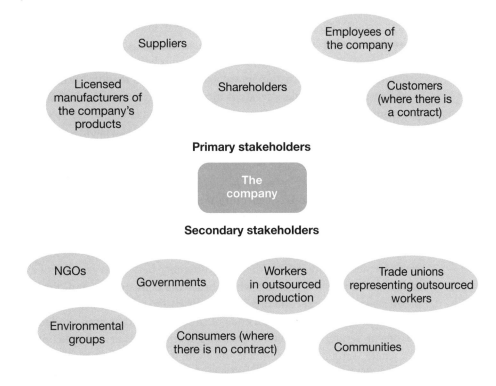

For example, if customers are dissatisfied with a firm's products and stop buying them, this directly affects corporate performance. A third criterion is urgency (Mitchell et al., 1997) which refers to time sensitivity. A claim that is urgent can take precedence over other legitimate claims. Identifying, evaluating and managing their interests in relation to the firm's goals are central to stakeholder management. Stakeholder theory thus fulfils a descriptive function, in that it describes how managers deal with these groups. Clarkson describes the corporation itself as a system of primary stakeholder groups (Clarkson, 1995: 107).

Secondary stakeholders fall within the broad umbrella of stakeholders described by Freeman, but their interests are not so vital to the survival of the company. As he noted, the company's activities affect these stakeholders over the long term, but the interactions are not as direct. The media and special interest groups would fall into this category, according to Clarkson. So too would NGOs. Although Clarkson considers public stakeholders such as governments and communities to be primary stakeholders, for most companies in market economies, they would be secondary stakeholders. For an internet service provider, for example, the extent of public investment in high-speed internet infrastructure is important,

Taking these stakeholder interests into account involves an ethical perspective rather than merely descriptive criteria of urgency and power.

but this does not make the government a primary stakeholder. On the other hand, for a company which specializes in outsourced public services, such as Serco, the government is a primary stakeholder, as it contracts with governments as part of its business (see the closing case study). Secondary stakeholders tend to represent community interests, which give rise to issues of social responsibility. Environmental concerns should be taken into account by the company, as these are legitimate stakeholder issues, but there could well be few powerful stakeholders speaking for environmental concerns. They might include community groups and NGOs, but these are not primary stakeholders. Taking these stakeholder interests into account involves an ethical perspective rather than merely descriptive criteria of urgency and power. Stakeholder management in respect of these stakeholders thus becomes more normative than descriptive.

Conflicts can arise. Customers value cheap clothes manufactured in low-cost locations. Brand owners and retailers seek out manufacturing centres such as Bangladesh, where the government has sought to attract these companies (see opening case study). On a stakeholder analysis of a retailer such as Primark, primary stakeholders are customers who buy their clothes and licensed manufacturers who make the clothes. Both are contractually tied to the company. Workers in the factories are not contractually linked to the brand owner, and would thus seem to be secondary stakeholders, as are the trade unions which press for safer working conditions. Even more remote are subcontractors who acquire work from licensed manufacturers, a practice which makes it even more difficult for brand owners to keep track of factory conditions (see Figure 2.3). Some brand owners consider the manufacturers of their products to be mere suppliers, and have codes of conduct for suppliers which cover factory conditions. But there is a difference between a supplier of a component and a supplier of a finished product which bears the company's brand. Both are suppliers in a broad sense, but the second one is more closely linked to the brand. Gap refers to its manufacturers as 'vendors', and has a code of conduct for outsourced production which is called a 'Code of Vendor Conduct' (at www.gap.com). The code is about conditions in the factories where Gap's brands are made, including the issue of child labour. There is a conflict between the interests of primary stakeholders, which are to keep costs down, and the stakeholder interests of those who work in the factories.

Normative stakeholder theory views stakeholders as having moral claims. It has been argued that each stakeholder group can be thought of in terms of Kant's categorical imperative, that is, having a right to be treated as an end and not as a means to an end (Donaldson and Preston, 1995). This normative approach reflects a focus on the philosophical foundations of ethical theories and also the rights-based social contract theorists (discussed in Chapters 1 and 3). We now turn to these business ethics theorists, beginning with social contract theories.

For each of the following stakeholders, assess whether it is a primary or secondary stakeholder, and to what extent it exerts moral claims on the company:

o A patient in a hospital run by Hospitals-4-you, a for-profit company.
o Wildlife in a river next to a carpet factory in China owned by Sun Carpets, a Taiwanese-owned company which manufactures carpets under licence for Carpets-R-Us, a London-listed company. The factory uses chemicals which occasionally escape into the river.

SOCIAL CONTRACT THEORIES

Carroll refers to ethical environments in communities, as well as theories of moral philosophy, as sources of ethical principles. The tension between cultural relativism and universal ethical theories has been discussed in Chapter 1. The tensions become particularly apparent in international business. The cultural relativist would argue that practices such as militaristic disciplinary regimes in factories are acceptable because this is the way factories

'The Foxconn structure is very autocratic and can be, I think to some people, somewhat demeaning.'

in the country routinely operate. In other countries, these practices are seen as contrary to values of human dignity. Hon Hai, the Taiwanese owner of Foxconn, which operates factories in China, has found that its militaristic regime does not go down well with workers elsewhere, including the US, Eastern Europe, and Latin America. A senior Foxconn manager in the US has said, 'they really wanted to employ/deploy the management strategy that they had in China and that just didn't work very well here ... The Foxconn structure is very autocratic and can be, I think to some people, somewhat demeaning' (Mishkin and Pearson, 2013). Foxconn has recognized the need to understand and adapt to differing cultures. This is a management response rather than a principled stance on adopting higher ethical standards. In China, where the vast bulk of Foxconn's outsourced manufacturing takes place, CSR has been seen as a western import, applying employment and labour standards demanded by western brand owners (Wang and Juslin, 2009). It is only in the last decade that Chinese companies have come to embrace social responsibilities more positively, often prompted by governmental pressures to improve working conditions. In some cases, these moves have stemmed from worker unrest and strikes, suggesting that local employment conditions are influential.

Responding to worker dissatisfaction is a management challenge arising from the importance of employees as stakeholders. A strike or riot indicates a breakdown in relations between management and workers. Workers' expectations change over time. While migrant workers put up with poor conditions and humiliating treatment in the early years of the manufacturing boom, new recruits nowadays do not share the same attitudes. Cultural changes taking place in China indicate a growing desire for a better quality of life, including one's working life. Companies can respond in a short-term way, doing the minimum required by changing laws. But they could take a longer-term view, asking themselves deeper questions about their role in society. Foxconn now operates in several different cultural environments, and seems to be responding in each of them in ways that simply deal with the immediate local issues.

The social and moral norms of communities are recognized in social contract theory, which is based on a contractual view of the company in society. The idea of the social contract is a familiar one in political theory. We found in Chapter 3 that social contract theorists such as Locke and Rousseau took up the idea of a whole community consenting to government, in an 'original contract'. Donaldson and Dunfee, theorists of business ethics, hold that there are two levels of social contract which operate in the business environment. At a local level, people consent to microsocial contracts reflecting local moral norms, which equates to 'moral free space' (Donaldson and Dunfee, 1994: 260). Informed consent is a crucial element, giving the microsocial contract its authenticity, and it is important that there is a right of exit. They do note the difficulty, however, where jobs are scarce and people take jobs which involve poor working conditions. These workers stay on because they need the money, so that any right of exit is more theoretical than real. The extent of their consent could be questioned in these circumstances. Above this level there is consent to a macrosocial contract, which represents all rational contractors. The macrosocial contract is seen as an implicit contract similar to that envisaged by earlier theorists.

While the microsocial contract rests on cultural relativism, the second contract rests on a transcendent view of ethical principles, which the authors call hypernorms. Hypernorms, they state, 'are principles so fundamental to human existence that they serve as a guide in

SPOTLIGHT ON ETHICAL BUSINESS

The UN Global Compact and sustainability   *Chris Harrop*

Chris Harrop
*Chair of United Nations
Global Compact (UNGC)
Network UK, and Director
at Marshalls plc*

Chris Harrop is Group Marketing Director and the Director of Sustainability at Marshalls plc, a leading supplier of hard landscaping products. In his roles at Marshalls, he has been instrumental in promoting sustainability in the company's strategy and operations. Chris is also chairman of the UN Global Compact UK Network, and a non-executive director at the Ethical Trading Initiative. He holds a BA Hons Business Studies, an MBA, and several professional qualifications. He is a chartered director of the Institute of Directors and a chartered marketer of the Chartered Institute of Marketing.

Visit **www.palgrave.com/companion/morrison-business-ethics** to watch Chris talking about the UN Global Compact in general and the activities of the Global Compact's UK network in particular. Chris discusses the key areas of the Global Compact: human rights, labour rights, the environment and anti-corruption. He emphasizes the links between the four areas, and the challenges raised by extended global supply chains. Although the challenges are daunting, notably in contexts of resource constraints, he stresses the potential benefits to businesses – and societies – of a focus on sustainability.

Before watching this video, take time to look again at related sections in the chapter and elsewhere in the book. Look at the section on 'Comparing CSR and legal frameworks' in Chapter 9, where there is a discussion of the UN Guiding Principles for Businesses, which Chris mentions. The four key areas of the Global Compact are featured in Figure 7.6. In Chapter 10, there is a detailed discussion of sustainability. Look particularly at the first three sections. The Millennium Development Goals (MDGs) are featured in Figure 10.2.

When you have watched the video, think about the following questions:

1 For a company which relies on sourcing through a global supply chain, how can participating in the Global Compact help it to raise ethical standards?

2 Recession has posed challenges for companies. Some might say that they should just focus on the bottom line and leave CSR until later. How can a re-focus on sustainability and responsibility help a company in formulating a post-recession strategy?

3 Chris distinguishes between a 'do-no-harm' approach and a 'do-good' approach. From an ethical perspective, how is the do-good approach preferable?

evaluating lower level moral norms' (Donaldson and Dunfee, 1994: 265). Hypernorms help to bridge the gap in the so-called 'naturalistic fallacy', which is deriving 'what ought to be' from 'what is'. The two authors wish to base obligations on consent in ways similar to the earlier contract theorists, but they wish also to develop a normative approach to business ethics. Hypernorms represent a convergence of principles from religious, cultural and philosophical sources. They share a view of human dignity and rights which transcend specific beliefs and values. For the business, these act as a guide. Microsocial contracts

Figure 7.6 The UN Global Compact

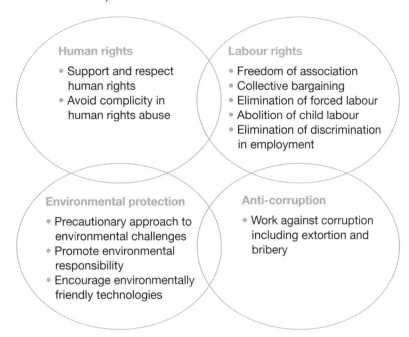

Human rights

- Support and respect human rights
- Avoid complicity in human rights abuse

Labour rights

- Freedom of association
- Collective bargaining
- Elimination of forced labour
- Abolition of child labour
- Elimination of discrimination in employment

Environmental protection

- Precautionary approach to environmental challenges
- Promote environmental responsibility
- Encourage environmentally friendly technologies

Anti-corruption

- Work against corruption including extortion and bribery

Source: United Nations (2013) 'The Ten Principles', the *UN Global Compact*, at www.unglobalcompact.org (18/09/14).

should be compatible with hypernorms. A difficulty is the practical one of how to apply these broad principles in practice. Some companies seek to adopt a universal code of conduct. This is the approach of the UN Global Compact. It reflects the idea that there are universally agreed principles in areas of human rights, labour rights, environmental protection and anti-corruption, shown in Figure 7.6.

The principles listed in these four broad areas are derived from international law and conventions. For labour standards, they are contained in the ILO's Declaration of Fundamental Principles (1998). Environmental principles are in the Rio Declaration (1992). Anti-corruption principles are in the UN Convention against Corruption (2003), and the human rights principles are in the UN Declaration of Human Rights (UNDHR). The UNDHR is discussed in Chapter 9. The company which signs up to the Global Compact accepts the application of these principles in all its operations, whatever the location. The standards, however, are not legally enforceable. Legal commitments in each area are the responsibilities of governments. Law in many places falls short of these standards. For the company, therefore, this commitment is to higher ethical standards.

Integrated social contracts theory, as Donaldson and Dunfee's theory is known, offers a normative approach to business ethics which focuses on global ethics, while recognizing the role played by local community norms in business relations. The idea of contracting based on rights and expectations has thus moved from the political sphere envisaged by earlier theorists to wider social groupings. It has also moved from geographically-defined entities such as communities and states to relational ties which are unbounded by geography. Companies recognize fundamental rights and duties among stakeholders in locations scattered across the globe.

POLITICAL CSR: DOES DEMOCRATIC THEORY OFFER NEW INSIGHTS?

Critics of integrated social contract theory argue that there are no universally recognized hypernorms, only standards which differ between cultures and countries. Similarly, echoing the positivist position, they argue that law-making and enforcement are essentially national, as there is no global legislature. Hence, both moral and legal authority seem to be lacking at global level. Is it still possible to derive a normative basis for CSR which takes a transnational approach and avoids a presumption of universal norms? Some theorists feel that the answer lies in the views of deliberative democracy held by Jürgen Habermas. Scherer and Palazzo put forward a theory of CSR that envisages the company as a political actor in a globalized society (Scherer and Palazzo, 2007). They point out that globalization is eroding the roles of traditional national governments, while companies are taking on wider roles in society formerly carried out by governments. These roles were highlighted in the section above on corporate citizenship. In this context, companies are becoming part of a wider participative process, also involving civil society and governments.

This deliberative concept of CSR sounds similar to stakeholder dialogue, but its advocates point out that it goes beyond stakeholder considerations, based as they are mainly on interests of particular groups. The key to this new concept of CSR lies in the theory of Habermas, for whom the deliberative democratic process itself constitutes ethical discourse and confers legitimacy. Democratic procedure is not merely an expression of political will, but a wider deliberative process (Habermas, 2001: 110). Habermas criticizes traditional views of liberal democracy, which tend to focus on institutions such as elections and take a limited view of citizens' roles. His view of deliberative democracy derives its legitimacy from the involvement of all groups, so that the corporation becomes a player in this new democratic interaction. A sceptic might ask, however, what assurance is there that the corporation will not continue to behave as a mainly economic actor in exerting its influence through these processes?

Habermas's thinking has evolved over a long period, and in early works he was rather more pessimistic about democracy than he has been in his later works. In early works, he observed the power of dominant industrial élites that put particular interests above those of the public good (Staats, 2004). His later work sees corporations as embedded in the democratic process, but it could be argued that companies still see themselves as economic actors, and wield corporate power which outweighs civil society voices (Staats, 2004). As we have noted, companies have become adept at utilizing organizations ostensibly grounded in civil society to exert influence over agenda setting in public debate on issues which affect them. As Habermas has himself observed, national cultures and states remain strongly linked to democracy (Habermas, 1999). However, most of the world's people live in countries where economic and political élites are dominant, even where there are democratic constitutions. And there is little trust in politicians to focus on the public good rather than self-interest (see Chapter 3). A contribution of political CSR is that it stresses the importance of normative legitimacy in business behaviour, but this process-based normative framework looks rather idealistic. Scherer and Palazzo, it could be argued, underestimate the evolving consensus on global standards and international law that this book has highlighted (see also Chapters 4 and 9). These standards reflect ethical principles which transcend cultural differences, with legal support in international law. They perhaps represent a sounder way forward for changing business behaviour in practice.

APPLYING ETHICAL THEORIES IN INTERNATIONAL BUSINESS

Hypernorms reflect ethical principles which transcend cultural differences. This way of looking at the foundations of ethics has a long history, dating back to the leading philosophers introduced early in this book. This approach highlights a challenge of applying ethical principles in practice: they seem vague and non-specific, and it is difficult to apply them in practice. On the other hand, if principles, such as those contained in laws, are highly specific, then actors are inclined to take a rule-governed approach to them, applying particular laws but not necessarily staying true to the principles. A tension between rule-governed behaviour and principle-governed behaviour can result. In this section, we look first at how law and ethics reinforce each other. We then apply the main ethical theories to the challenges facing international business.

ETHICS AND LAW: MUTUALLY REINFORCING

The prospect of a personal gain of $10 million, we saw in Chapter 5, is likely to tempt financial services professionals to commit an act of insider dealing, which they know to be a crime. Insider dealing is widespread, difficult to prove, and there is a low likelihood of being caught. Setting these factors against the possible gain, it looks to many like a risk worth taking. The person who thinks and acts this way has little sense of morality and integrity, and is deterred from wrongful acts mainly by the thought of the policeman round the corner. Many businesses have similar attitudes. They see the obligation to abide by the law in principle, but skate on the edge of legality and sometimes go to great lengths in setting up schemes to circumvent the law. They claim to abide by the letter of the law, but they do not adhere to the spirit of the law. Cadbury, the confectionery company taken over by Kraft Foods in 2010, was such a company. It had a long tradition of ethical and philanthropic values, but, it later emerged, had been artificially setting up aggressive tax avoidance structures for years before the takeover (Ford et al., 2013). Cadbury, along with many other companies, took the view that profit maximization was the only measure of corporate performance, and any means was acceptable as long as it did not involve breaches of formal law. The law is viewed as a hurdle to be overcome or circumvented, and, as long as the company seems to be successful in avoiding legal and regulatory infringements, it can assert that it has done nothing wrong. We found in Chapter 5 that such practices have become common among MNEs.

The more socially-nuanced version of this view holds that ethics in business consists of abiding by standards imposed by society, often in the form of governments and regulators. But this, too, comes down to a legalistic approach which skirts round the ethical issues. Business is seen as a kind of game, and the business plays by the rules of the game – an outlook made famous by Friedman (Boatright, 2000). This attitude overlooks the fact that the rules are not imposed from outside, but derive from interactions which take place in society, among businesses, governments and multiple stakeholders. Businesses play active roles in shaping the laws and, importantly, shaping the values which inform the laws. In the area of data protection and privacy, for example, technology companies are aggressive in making their preferences for future legislation known to law-makers in the US and the EU. The large technology companies, including Google, Microsoft, Facebook, Yahoo, Apple and eBay, spent an estimated seven million euros in 2012 in lobbying EU law-makers, and this is

'You would expect any tech company to actively participate in the discussion over the rules that will shape the future of our industry ...'

thought to be an underestimate (Fontenella-Khan, 2013). The privacy officer of one of these companies says, 'You would expect any tech company to actively participate in the discussion over the rules that will shape the future of our industry' (Fontenella-Khan, 2013). Their activities are much more developed in Washington, where they were estimated to have spent over $35 million in lobbying the US federal government. These are companies which, as in the Cadbury example above, adopt elaborate tax avoidance schemes. They thus hold ambivalent views of the law. They acknowledge their input when they press their own corporate interests to legislators, but when those interests involve legal contortions to avoid tax, they portray the legislators as too interventionist. Legal interference is thus justified if it benefits the company, but not if it imposes obligations which add to costs. This approach is not based on ethical considerations or ideas of social responsibility, but in business terms it has proved highly profitable. These technology giants are now powerful global corporations. But globalization, coupled with the internet, has also enhanced the power of individuals and societal groups (Boatright, 2000). These individuals and groups, including consumers, employees and ordinary citizens, increasingly draw attention to ethical issues in globalized business and demand greater transparency in governance – which includes corporate players as well as governmental ones.

In reality, MNEs are continually engaged in social and legal interactions in multiple locations and at international level. As we have seen in Carroll's theory, a CSR approach views legal and ethical responsibilities as a continuum, the law often reinforcing ethical values. Companies are confronted with ethical and social issues which are often intertwined, as we found when looking at ethical challenges in the early sections of this chapter. Moreover, ethical decision-making and behaviour involves both the attitudes of the decision-makers and the decisions which flow from them. To return to the financial services professional who is tempted to pass on insider information for a gain of $10 million, a decision not to go ahead with it does not necessarily reflect a morally right choice, but just a decision that it is not worth the risk.

ETHICAL THEORIES IN THE BUSINESS CONTEXT

Four major theoretical strands stand out in business ethics: the utilitarian school of thought, the deontological theorists such as Kant, rights-based theories and Aristotle's virtue ethics. These theories were introduced in Chapter 1. They are shown in Figure 7.7. Here, we revisit these theories in order to apply them in business and society. Applying these theories to international business today might seem far-fetched, as these theorists were concerned mainly about the individual in society and the role of governments. We noted in Chapter 1 that theorists were not purely 'ivory tower' philosophers. Most were sensitive to social issues of their time, and were influenced by events happening around them, often criticizing governments. With the exception of Rawls, they could not have imagined the growing power of business over people's lives, not to mention the extent of globalized businesses. But this is the reality which current ethical theorists must address. Issues of the individual in society are still relevant, even though the circumstances are very different from those envisaged by earlier theorists. Similarly, the concepts remain valid, and can help us to understand the ethical challenges of changing circumstances. We look at each type of theory in turn.

Figure 7.7 The right act and the good person

	The Right Act	The Good Person
Consequentialist (utilitarians)	Material benefits outweigh costs	Seeks to maximize self-interested benefits
Categorical imperative (Kant)	Fulfils moral duty to treat others as ends and not means	Fulfils a higher moral purpose
Rights-based (Locke, Rawls)	Recognizes natural/human rights	Upholds moral responsibility for social justice
Virtue ethics (Aristotle)	Knowingly chosen for its pure virtue	Develops virtuous character

Figure 7.7 shows the main ethical theories arising in business ethics. The utilitarians' theories are the most closely linked to business activities, as they are associated with the emergence of the capitalist enterprise. The self-interested individual is the focus, usually linked to the egoism of Hobbes' state of nature (see Chapter 1). But whereas Hobbes envisaged an authoritarian state as the solution, utilitarians looked to the opposite solution, urging the maximum of individual freedom and minimum of government interference. They saw the market as resolving conflicts, along the lines of Smith's 'invisible hand'. The utilitarians' consequentialist ethics flows from their assumptions about human nature. Actions are considered good to the extent that they maximize pleasure and minimize pain. People are assumed always to make rational calculations and choices which result in maximizing happiness for themselves. However, people act for various reasons, not just rational calculations, and they are also capable of altruistic behaviour. One person's happiness might come at the expense of another person's pain. For critics, even those such as J.S. Mill, who was part of this tradition, the ethical shortcomings of the theory were apparent in the absence of any sense of moral duty and the failure to recognize in human nature an ethical capacity towards others in society.

The second theory in Figure 7.7 provides an ethical framework in the way the utilitarians could not. Kant sees moral development of the individual as the highest form of existence. This development equates to a sense of freedom in recognizing a higher law. This transcendent quality of morality places Kant's theory in the deontological school of thought. From an ethical perspective, it benefits from its universality. The categorical imperative, to treat all human beings as ends rather than as means, recognizes an innate human dignity and applies to people everywhere. Kant recognizes that all people desire happiness, but that this in itself does not make them good. Only obedience to a higher moral duty leads to a good life, in contrast to a life of material well-being only. This moral development culminates in the kingdom of ends which Kant envisages in the state.

The categorical imperative is generally accepted as an ethical principle which is relevant to business ethics. Its relevance can be seen in situations where global companies are engaged in activities such as extraction and outsourced manufacturing in countries with weak rule of law and poor governance. Abiding by the law in these locations might mean little, serving to give an appearance of right behaviour to business activities which are ethically wrong. In these cases, employees and inhabitants in target countries are seen as instrumental. Workers matter only as production operatives, not real people. Pressures from consumers, journalists and NGOs bring poor conditions into the public domain, highlighting the failures to abide by principles of human dignity. As we noted at the outset of this section, applying broadly-worded ethical principles in specific situations is not something managers and decision-makers are trained to do. They would prefer to have a set of specific rules or laws to apply, in which case they can rely on a 'compliance' officer to do the job. Ethical issues are nonetheless real, even in the absence of a specific rule. The call for transparency which is now being heard from users and consumers of corporate goods and services is an indication that people in general have an idea of the difference between right and wrong in specific circumstances, even when companies seem not to.

We turn next to theories which offer a principled view of ethics, but somewhat outside the deontological approach. These are rights-based theories which adopt a view of human dignity as their starting point. This is similar to Kant's categorical imperative, but it takes a different view of social ethics. Kant's views of the moral state are seen by many as conflicting with the value of individual freedom. The utilitarians stressed negative freedom to too great an extent, but Kant's views of positive freedom tend to underestimate the need for individual freedom of action. Rights-based theories lay stress on rights of individuals in societies and social justice. They often begin with the idea of a social contract which represents an agreement among people to recognize the natural rights of each other and the need for social co-operation. The just society is one in which people respect the inherent worth and goals of other people. Rawls' idea of justice as fairness implies equality of opportunity. In a grossly unequal society, the poor and least advantaged people have little freedom and little scope for self-fulfilment. Rawls values individualism and the idea of freedom in the negative sense, as implying space to achieve our own goals, but tempers these values with a concern for others. He invokes what he calls his Aristotelian principle, saying that each person enjoys the realization of moral capacity over time. Despite this nod towards Aristotle, Rawls' theory focuses on rights and duties towards others in society, rather than on the development of the moral capacity of the individual person.

> *In a grossly unequal society, the poor and least advantaged people have little freedom and little scope for self-fulfilment.*

From a Rawlsian perspective, inequality in societies globally is an ethical concern, in both developed and emerging economies. Despite poverty reduction, inequality has grown in China (OECD, 2012). In the US, the very rich have become richer while the bulk of the population has seen falling living standards. Protests by Walmart workers and fast-food employees over their 'starvation wages' swept through a number of cities in 2013, giving some indication of the impacts of what Rawls would see as social injustice (see Chapter 9). While the political dimension was Rawls' focus, the politics of inequality encompasses the growing power of corporate interests, which have gained enormous influence in political decision-making. Today's Rawlsian would agree with Mr Justice Stevens that the influx of corporate money 'undermines the integrity of elected institutions' (Supreme Court of the US, 2010). The risks to political equality in the US have also increased with the judgment by the US Supreme Court to abolish crucial elements of the Voting Rights Act 1965, which was intended to eliminate racial discrimination in voting arrangements (Supreme Court of the US, 2013).

> *Today's Rawlsian would agree with Mr Justice Stevens that the influx of corporate money 'undermines the integrity of elected institutions.'*

As we found in Chapter 3, politics is about power relations, whether within a country or internationally. Business, too, involves power relations, now played out on a global stage and routinely involving political interactions in both local and international spheres. The capitalist enterprise has triumphed: communist political systems embrace capitalism, and state-owned companies worship profit maximization. But in emerging economies, like advanced ones, consumers and residents have seized the idea of having rights against companies as well as governments. They feel they have *rights* to safe food, safe consumer products, a clean environment and high standards of healthcare. They criticize greedy politicians, financiers and industrial tycoons whose power and money help to channel scarce resources into private coffers rather than public goods. They call for socially responsible businesses which pay taxes and offer decent employment, but they also call for integrity and honesty in the people who run them. These might seem old-fashioned values, but they are perhaps due for a renewal in corporate executive suites. Recall Barclays Bank, featured in the closing case study of Chapter 5, whose new CEO said the company needed a change of culture, shredding the legacy of the recent past (Lawrence, 2013).

Aristotle recognized the importance of personal character and integrity in his **virtue ethics** (see Chapter 1). Virtue for Aristotle is an internalized value. Acts matter, but the motive is crucial. The person must choose a way of acting knowingly because it is virtuous, not for any personal gain (Whetstone, 2001). And the virtuous act is part of a bigger picture of character development over a person's whole life (Nussbaum, 1999). Theorists of business ethics who focus on virtue ethics tend to highlight the personal and individual approach. The emphasis on the actor's character rather than the rule can be applied in management of people (Bertland, 2009). The virtuous manager promotes the capabilities of employees, allowing them to develop as human beings, rather than focusing on rights and duties. The same approach could be applied to other stakeholders, viewing interactions as encouraging moral development, rather than simply dealing with material interests, as stakeholder relations are often depicted. Virtue ethics as focused on the individual, however, was only one aspect of Aristotle's theory. He saw virtue in a social and political context, which is essential to the moral fulfilment of the individual. Aristotle's conception of the Greek city state, as noted in Chapter 1, was more akin to our notion of 'society'. He would not have had in mind the business corporation which modern business ethics focuses on. Indeed, Aristotle criticized business activities which pursue materialistic goals and rest on greed (Boatright, 1995). The modern corporation, based on capitalist values, is not conducive to the good life in the way that the civic values of Aristotle would have been.

Modern theorists of virtue ethics tend to highlight Aristotle's personal ethics at the micro level while disregarding his political views. This overlooks an integral element of this theory, but it need not undermine the relevance of virtue ethics as part of an overall approach to business ethics. Virtue ethics' focus on character of the person, while not providing guidance for specific actions nor relating to organizations of the type we are familiar with, nonetheless provides an essential insight into ethics: the 'doing' matters outwardly, but so does the 'being' of the person.

Recall the example of the financial professional tempted by $10 million for passing on insider information. Insider dealing is a criminal offence as well as a moral wrong. How would the following philosophers view the person who refrains for fear of being caught as opposed to the person who refrains because of a sense of moral duty?

a. Kant

b. Aristotle

CONCLUSIONS

One of the commitments listed by H&M in the opening case study of this chapter was to 'be ethical'. As we have seen, however, laudable principles are difficult to translate into practice, and situations which present themselves are usually more complex than first meets the eye. Challenges abound at every turn in international business, and many of these stem from the social dimension of business activities. The socially desirable decision can often conflict with economic goals. H&M chose to sign up to the safety accord in Bangladesh because it was the right thing to do, but the company is also aware that future accidents could damage its reputation. Businesses must now weigh up not just economic responsibilities, but also social and ethical impacts. There is emerging a changing perception of the company, from one which is focused on economic goals, to one in which economic goals are intertwined with social and ethical goals, as envisaged by CSR theorists. Indeed, it is becoming clearer that the company intent on pursuing competitive advantage is best advised to take a CSR approach to strategy as the most sustainable economically over the long term.

The social dimension of business tends to be analysed in terms of stakeholders, a broad category which includes just about any interest or claim that a company could face. These interests cover economic impacts as well as social and environmental claims. They have a moral aspect too, in that right behaviour is behaviour which reflects social values. In international business, the commitment to be ethical is not capable of being achieved in absolute terms. Ethical behaviour, as we have seen, is not just about actions, but intentions and attitudes. Managing stakeholder interests involves weighing up differing claims, some of which conflict with each other. Ethical theories show us that interests are not simply material interests of some groups over others. Moral choices matter in the social context of every business. A just and fair society is as much in the interests of business enterprises as it is in the interests of ordinary people.

NOTE

1 G20 members are Australia, Argentina, Brazil, Canada, China, European Union, France, Germany, Japan, India, Indonesia, Italy, Mexico, Russia, Saudi Arabia, South Africa, South Korea, Turkey, United Kingdom, and the United States.

REFERENCES

Artaud-Day, M. (2005) 'Transnational corporate social responsibility: A tri-dimensional approach to international CSR research', *Business Ethics Quarterly*, 15(1): 1–22.

Beecher-Monas, E. (2003) 'Corporate governance in the wake of Enron: an examination of the Audit Committee solution to corporate fraud', *Administrative Law Review*, 55(2): 357–94.

Bertland, A. (2009) 'Virtue ethics in business and the capabilities approach', *Journal of Business Ethics*, 84(1): 25–32.

Boatright, J. (1995) 'Aristotle meets Wall Street: the case for virtue ethics in business', *Business Ethics Quarterly*, 5(2): 353–9.

Boatright, J. (2000) 'Globalization and the ethics of business', *Business Ethics Quarterly*, 10(1): 1–6.

Bratton, W. (2001) 'Berle and Means reconsidered at the century's turn', *Journal of Corporation Law*, 26: 737–70.

Carroll, A.B. (1991) 'The pyramid of corporate social responsibility: toward the moral management of organizational stakeholders', *Business Horizons*, 34: 39–48.

Carroll, A.B. (1998) 'The four faces of corporate citizenship', *Business & Society Review*, 100(1): 1–7.

Clarkson, M. (1995) 'A stakeholder framework for analysing and evaluating corporate social performance', *Academy of Management Review*, 20(1): 92–117, at 106.

Donaldson, T. and Dunfee, T. (1994) 'Toward a unified conception of business ethics theory: integrative social contracts theory', *Academy of Management Review*, 19(2): 252–84.

Donaldson, T. and Preston, L. (1995) 'The stakeholder theory of the corporation: concepts, evidence, and implications', *Academy of Management Review*, 20(1): 65–92.

Fontenella-Khan, J. (2013) 'Astroturfing takes root', *Financial Times*, 27 June.

Ford, J., Gainsbury, S. and Houlder, V. (2013) 'The great tax fudge', *Financial Times*, 21 June.

Freeman, R.E. (1984) *Strategic Management: A Stakeholder Approach* (Boston, MA: Pitman).

Habermas, J. (1999) 'The European nation-dtate and the pressures of globalization', tr. G.M. Goshgarian, *New Left Review*, Vol. 235: 46–59.

Habermas, J. (2001) *The Postnational Constellation* (Cambridge: Polity Press).

Kay, J. (2013) 'Directors have a duty beyond just enriching shareholders', *Financial Times*, 5 June.

Kennedy, L. (2012) 'Citizens *actually* united', *Demos brief*, October, at www.demos.org (18/09/14).

Lawrence, F. (2013) 'Barclays secret tax avoidance factory that made £1bn a year profit disbanded', *The Guardian*, 11 February, at www.theguardian.com (18/09/14).

Maon, F., Lingreen, A. and Swaen, V. (2009) 'Designing and implementing corporate social responsibility: an integrative framework grounded in theory and practice', *Journal of Business Ethics*, 87(1): 71–89.

Matten, D. and Crane, A. (2005) 'Corporate citizenship: toward an extended theoretical conceptualization', *Academy of Management Review*, 30(1): 166–79.

Mishkin, S. and Pearson, S. (2013) 'Foxconn challenged as global reach grows', *Financial Times*, 3 January.

Mitchell, R.K., Agle, B.R. and Wood, D. (1997) 'Toward a theory of stakeholder identification and salience: defining the principle of who and what really counts', *Academy of Management Review*, 11(4): 853–86.

Moon, J., Crane, A. and Matten, D. (2005) 'Can corporations be citizens? Corporate citizenship as a metaphor for business participation in society', *Business Ethics Quarterly*, 15(3): 429–53.

Nussbaum, M. (1999) 'Virtue ethics: a misleading category?', *Journal of Ethics*, 3(3): 163–201.

OECD (2012) China in Focus: Lessons and Challenges, at www.oecd.org (18/09/14).

Ostas, D. (2001) 'Deconstructing corporate social responsibility: insights from legal and economic theory', *American Business Law Journal*, 38(2): 261–300.

Preston, L. and Sapienza, H. (1990) 'Stakeholder management and corporate performance', *Journal of Behavioral Economics*, 19(4): 362–75.

Scherer, A.G. and Palazzo, G. (2007) 'Toward a political conception of corporate responsibility – business and society seen from a Habermasian perspective', *Academy of Management Review*, 32(4): 1096–120.

Schmidt, E. (2013) 'Why we need to simplify our corporate tax system', *Financial Times*, 17 June.

Schwartz, M.S. and Carroll, A.B. (2003) 'Corporate social responsibility: a three-domain approach', *Business Ethics Quarterly*, 13(4): 503–30.

Staats, J.L. (2004) 'Habermas and democratic theory: the threat to democracy of unchecked corporate power', *Political Research Quarterly*, 57(4): 585–94.

Stout, L. (2012) *The Shareholder Value Myth* (San Francisco: Berrett-Koehler).

Supreme Court of the US (2010) Citizens United v. Federal Electoral Commission, Number 08-205.

Supreme Court of the US (2013) Shelby County, Alabama v. Holder, Number 12-96.

United Nations (2013), 'The Ten Principles', *The United Nations Global Compact*, at www.unglobalcompact.org (18/09/14).

Waldmeir, P. (2013) 'Novartis builds for future by educating China's rural poor', *Financial Times*, 18 June.

Wang, L. and Juslin, H. (2009) 'The impact of Chinese culture on corporate social responsibility: the harmony approach', *Journal of Business Ethics*, 88(3): 433–51.

Wartick, S. and Cochran, P. (1985) 'The evolution of the corporate social performance model', *Academy of Management Review*, 10(4): 758–69.

Whetsone, J.T. (2001) 'How virtue fits with business ethics', *Journal of Business Ethics*, 33(2): 101–14.

Wood, D. (1991) 'Corporate social performance revisited', *Academy of Management Review*, 16(4): 691–718.

REVIEW QUESTIONS

1 What is the 'economic model' of the company? In what ways has this model become dented in recent years?

2 Explain Carroll's pyramid model of CSR. How are legal and ethical responsibilities interrelated?

3 What are the strengths and weaknesses of corporate social performance (CSP) as a complementary theory to CSR?

4 To what extent is the concept of corporate citizenship helpful in analysing the position of a company in society?

5 What are the differences between primary and secondary stakeholders? Which are more important in stakeholder management: economic interests or moral claims?

6 In what ways does the theory of integrated social contracts take in both cultural differences and international ethical standards?

7 What are the four areas covered by the UN Global Compact? Why is it considered a benchmark even though it is not legally binding?

8 How does the normative approach of political CSR aim to improve on both normative CSR theories and stakeholder theories of management? What criticisms can be made of political CSR?

9 In applying ethical theories to business, which matters most: the right act of the good actor? Explain.

10 Which of these ethical theorists are most relevant to business ethics: the utilitarians, Kant, Rawls or Aristotle?

SERCO AND THE PRIVATIZATION OF PUBLIC SERVICES

CLOSING CASE STUDY

Serco is a large international company, listed on the London Stock Exchange and employing 120,000 people in 30 countries. In the UK, it employs 53,000 people and is active in a wide range of services used by millions of people. Yet many people would probably not be familiar with the name or know much about it. This is largely because its services are not offered under its own brand, but as public services which it operates on behalf of government agencies. Although the company logo appears on signs at establishments which it runs, members of the public are not necessarily aware that a service such as a healthcare is being provided by a for-profit outsourcing company. However, the outsourcing of public services has grown around the world and has become big business. Serco's UK contracts are worth an estimated £750 million. Serco and G4S, its main rival, are among the few companies big enough to take on large government contracts.

Photo 7.2 The running of prisons like this by private-sector companies for profit has given rise to criticisms. (© iStock.com/ compassandcamera)

Serco is the largest provider of services in the UK. It is active in delivering public services in numerous sectors, including security, healthcare, prisons, education, trains, immigration removal centres, the national nuclear laboratory, and the management of the UK's ballistic missile early warning system. It even runs hire bicycles, known as 'Boris bikes' in London. Its activities in other countries include an immigration detention centre run on behalf of the Australian government. As outsourcing has grown, so have Serco's profits, which were up 27% in 2012. Its revenues were up 41% in 2012 (Serco, 2012).

Serco's growth and diversity of services could well cause some alarm. How can it possibly have expertise in all these specialized areas? And how can it take on so many new contracts so quickly? Serco benefits from the fact that governments which are hard pressed to control public spending are keen to outsource services in order to save money. Typically, there are only one or two bidders and little competition. These contracts create 'quasi-monopoly private providers' (Harris, 2013), and the duration of the contracts can be several years. The contracts specify levels of performance of the services, but companies are invariably stretched to provide a high level of service and also generate profits. The bulk of employees of Serco UK are former civil servants, and the company is legally bound to offer them the same employment terms as their former public employers. But it is common for the new private-sector employer to reduce the number of staff, as happened when Serco took over community health services in Suffolk from the National Health Service (NHS). The company aimed to reduce bureaucracy, utilize technology to a greater extent and deliver services more efficiently. New staff were hired to implement changed systems, but they were hired on less good pay and conditions than those transferred from the public sector (Harris, 2013). It might be asked why the new approach involving greater technology could not have been introduced under the NHS. Private providers face pressures to cut costs while also generating profits. Although Serco asserts its commitment to first-class public services, many failings and criticisms have come to light, suggesting difficulties in balancing tight budgets against standards people expect in public services.

Thameside Prison, a new prison run by Serco, is rated one of the three worst in Britain, and a cause of 'serious concern' by the Ministry of Justice (Travis, 2013). The Prisons Inspectorate found that a large number of prisoners were locked up for longer hours than should have been the case. However, the Ministry of Justice was content that Serco was working hard to deliver the contract.

The company has also had contracts for the electronic tagging of offenders who are subject to curfew orders. Both Serco and G4S have been accused of serious overcharging under their contracts for electronic tagging. The companies were alleged to be charging for tagging a number of offenders who had died, had been placed back in custody, or had left the country (Morris, 2013). This overcharging, which could amount to many millions of pounds, has possibly been taking place over several years, in which case staff at the Ministry of Justice might have been able to question the overcharging. A fraud investigation into the two companies was announced by the Minister of Justice in 2013, leading to falls in the share prices of both companies. Serco had bid for more tagging contracts, and but withdrew from the bidding process on the announcement that it was being investigated.

A concern which arises often in relation to privatized public services is that of accountability of the companies for poor performance. The contracts with the government are subject to 'commercial confidentiality', which means that their terms are shrouded in secrecy. Although a government agency is subject to a request for information from public under the Freedom of Information legislation, this does not apply to the private-sector companies which carry out government services.

Parliament's Public Accounts Committee has taken an interest in the performance of public services by outsourcing companies. In one of its reports, it found failings in out-of-hours medical services in Cornwall. Serco had a five-year contract worth £32 million with the primary care trust. The report by the Public Accounts Committee found it had lied about its performance and altered data on 252 occasions (Public Accounts Committee, 2013). By falsifying data, it was effectively overstating its performance. Serco blamed two members of its staff for the wrongdoings, and said they had left the company, but the terms of their departure were subject to a confidentiality agreement and could not be revealed. The two staff were not paid bonuses, but the contract manager was paid a performance-related bonus. Serco itself had received performance-related bonuses in 2012, but offered to repay them.

Serco also runs detention centres for immigrants. It runs two removal centres in the UK (Colnbrook and

Yarl's Wood) and the Christmas Island detention centre, run on behalf of the Australian government. Its treatment of people in these centres has been criticized on human rights grounds. The conditions in which people are confined have been compared to prison conditions, although the people being detained are not criminals. A report on Yarl's Wood by the UK Children's Commissioner in 2009 showed poor treatment of children, especially those with healthcare needs (Dugan, 2009). The Commissioner called for the end of detention of children, and the coalition government has agreed in principle with this goal, but as of 2013, children were still being detained in facilities which hold those awaiting deportation (Gower, 2013).

Serco describes its business model as incorporating its four governing principles (Serco, 2012). The first is to be entrepreneurial; the second is to enable 'our people' to excel. The third is to deliver on its promises, stating, 'we only promise what we can deliver' (Serco, 2012: 13). The fourth is to build trust and respect, stating that the company never compromises on safety and always operates in an ethical manner. The company does not have a policy described as CSR, nor does it see its role in terms of corporate citizenship. Serco does have web content on 'corporate responsibility', which includes sections on 'our people', health and safety, the environment and the community (at www.serco.com). The section on the community is entirely about philanthropic activities. It states a commitment to invest 1% of pre-tax profits to give back to society, and describes other charitable activities.

The announcement of the investigation into possible fraud in electronic tagging was potentially highly damaging for the company. The CEO resigned late in 2013, in the hope that the company's reputation could be restored. Having received compensation of £2.5 million, including bonuses, in 2012, he left with a combined package worth over £6.5 million: a payout of £2.6 million, a pension pot of £2 million and share options worth £2 million at the time of his departure.

Sources: Lawrence, F. (2013) 'Private contractor fiddled data when reporting to the NHS, says watchdog', *The Guardian*, 7 March; Harris, J. (2013) 'Serco: the company that is running Britain', *The Guardian*, 29 July; Public Accounts Committee (2013) *The Provision of Out-of-Hours GP Service in Cornwall*, Parliament, at www.publications.parliament.uk; Dugan, E. (2009) 'Inside Yarl's Wood: Britain's shame over child detainees', *The Independent*, 26 April; Travis, A. (2013) 'Two private prisons among worst three jails, inspectors find', *The Guardian*, 25 July; Gower, M. (2013) *Ending Child Immigration Detention: Commons Library Standard Note*, 2 January, at www.parliament.uk; Morris, N. (2013) 'G4S and Serco face £50 million fraud inquiry', *The Independent*, 12 July; Serco (2012) *Annual Report 2012*, at www.serco.com; Treanor, J. and Syal, R. (2013) 'Serco CEO quits before investigation into electronic tagging charges', *The Guardian*, 25 October, at www.theguardian.com (18/09/14).

DISCUSSION QUESTIONS

□ Some of the failings and poor performance in public services highlighted in this case study suggest failings by both the outsourcing company and the government oversight. Highlight examples.

□ What are the pros and cons of outsourcing public services to private-sector companies?

□ How would you assess Serco in terms of corporate social performance in the societies where it has become crucial in delivering public services?

CHAPTER 8

CORPORATE GOVERNANCE: HOW DO ETHICAL PRINCIPLES APPLY?

ETHICAL THEMES IN THIS CHAPTER
- Businesses as members of society
- Governance and responsibility

THE AIMS OF THIS CHAPTER ARE TO
- Establish the links between corporate governance and ethical conduct
- Understand the roles of directors and shareholders in companies
- Assess critically the shareholder-versus-stakeholder approaches to corporate purpose
- Relate CSR and ethical theories to corporate governance

VOLKSWAGEN, A TALE OF ENGINEERING STRENGTHS AND GOVERNANCE WEAKNESS

Volkswagen (VW), one of Germany's most famous companies, has become a global force in the motor industry, among the world's top three car manufacturers, its rivals being General Motors (GM) of the US and Toyota of Japan. Each of these three global carmakers produces close to 10 million vehicles annually, and each is looking to increase market share in the large emerging markets, where car ownership is growing among the burgeoning middle classes. All three are listed companies. All

Photo 8.1 *The iconic VW Beetle, dating back to the 1930s, is still a familiar image to people world-wide.* (© iStock.com/mrohana)

are long established: GM dates from 1908, while Toyota and Volkswagen both date from 1937. In their long histories, all have had their good times and bad times. Toyota is famed for its lean manufacturing system, but has had numerous quality problems and a string of recalls. GM suffered in a general decline in competitiveness of the US motor industry, which culminated in its near collapse in 2008. The company is now regaining global competitive strength. Volkswagen has not experienced reverses on this scale, but suffered competitive setbacks in the 1970s and 80s with lacklustre sales outside its home market. It has restructured and turned to global markets since then, with robust sales in a range of segments, from small cars in the Skoda brand to luxury vehicles in the Audi and Porsche ranges. It also has controlling stakes in two large truck companies, MAN of Germany and Scania of Sweden. At first glance, Volkswagen might seem to have an edge over its rivals as a stock, but in fact, among the three, Volkswagen stands out as the least favoured share in attracting investors. When the would-be investor looks at VW's ownership and corporate governance, doubts soon emerge about how the company is run, despite its manufacturing prowess.

Volkswagen's history from the 1930s has been dominated by two families – the Porsche family and the Piëch family. Ferdinand Porsche designed the iconic Beetle as a 'people's car' in the 1930s, and also founded the Porsche sports-car company. His grandson, Ferdinand Piëch, led Volkswagen's revival in the 1990s, building on its engineering strengths. At 75, he is no longer CEO, but is chairman of Volkswagen. He is also a major shareholder in Porsche SE. The histories of VW and Porsche are thus entwined. Porsche is the smaller of the two companies, but in 2008, under Wolfgang Porsche, a cousin of Mr Piëch, Porsche attempted a takeover of VW by secretly purchasing options on over 70% of VW's shares. The attempt failed, leading Porsche into financial disaster and legal actions over its takeover plans. As a result, two Porsche executives were dismissed and faced criminal prosecutions. A Qatari

sovereign wealth fund acquired a stake in Porsche SE and most of the share options in VW held by Porsche, which in turn gave it a 17% share in Volkswagen. Volkswagen gained ascendency and bought out Porsche's car-making subsidiary, Porsche AG. As a result, Volkswagen now runs the entire stable of brands, whose sales amounted to 9 million vehicles in 2012. In 2013, the Qatari fund sold its stake in Porsche SE, but retained its stake in Volkswagen. It is the company's third largest shareholder. Volkswagen's controlling shareholders are the Porsche and Piëch families.

Porsche SE, the holding company in which the two families control 90% of the voting rights, owns 50.7% of VW's voting shares. A 20% stake in Volkswagen is controlled by the state of Lower Saxony, as a result of an agreement with the state when the company was listed in 1961. Known as the 'VW law', this blocking vote is designed to deter takeovers. The EU considers the law to be against the free movement of capital in the EU. It was reworked in 2008, but the 20% blocking vote remains in place. The outside investor considering buying shares in Volkswagen would find that outside investors account for only 9.9% of the voting rights in the company. One analyst has said, 'Outside investors are always going to be in the passenger seat' (Tait and Kirk, 2012).

How does this ownership structure impact on the way Volkswagen is governed? As in other large German companies, Volkswagen has two boards, the higher being its supervisory board and the lower, the management board. By German law, half the seats on the supervisory board must be held by employee representatives. Volkswagen has a supervisory board of 20. There are 10 employee representatives elected by the workforce, 3 of whom are from the trade union, IG Metall. The 10 shareholder members include Ferdinand Piëch, the chairman, and 4 other members of the Porsche and Piëch families, including Piëch's wife. There are 2 members from Lower Saxony and 2 from the Qatar sovereign wealth fund. Finally, there is one independent member, the CEO of a Swedish bank, SEB.

The families are dominant in the supervisory board. Ferdinand Piëch remains chairman although he was found to have been in breach of his duty of care as a supervisory board member by a Stuttgart court in 2012, over the ill-judged failed takeover of VW. His wife was elected to the board in 2012, replacing the CEO of Tui, the German travel company. Commentators have criticized the predominance of the two families, pointing out that there is only one outside voice on the board, that of the Swedish CEO. In terms of stakeholder representation, the employees represented are those employed in Germany, despite the fact that 46 of VW's 102 car plants are outside Germany. However, the company's policy, supported by IG Metall, its major trade union, is that workers in other VW factories around the world should have union representation and vote for members of works councils along the pattern which exists in Germany. The company faced criticism in 2012 over the remuneration of its CEO, Martin Winterkorn, whose pay is linked to financial performance. His pay would have been over 20 million euros in 2012, but the company cut back his bonuses, bringing his pay and bonuses down to 14.5 million. Even so, such high pay was frowned on by public opinion in Germany.

Sources: Tait, N. and Kirk, S. (2012) 'Volkswagen', *Financial Times*, 6 September; Bryant, C. (2013) 'Volkswagen throttles back on bonuses', *Financial Times*, 23 February; Bryant, C. (2012) 'VW's governance irks investors', *Financial Times*, 18 April; Matussek, K. (2013) 'Porsche faces crucial court day in suit over VW trades', *Businessweek*, 16 April, at www.businessweek.com; *The Economist* (2012) 'VW conquers the world', 7 July, at www.economist.com; *Volkswagen Group Annual Report 2012*, at www.volkswagenag.com (18/09/14).

□ What have been the effects of the failed hostile takeover of Volkswagen? Look at both the restructuring and the ethical and legal issues.

□ In what ways can the makeup of Volkswagen's supervisory board be criticized?

□ Would you consider buying shares in Volkswagen, and why?

INTRODUCTION

Decision-making and accountability are central issues for any company, whether large or small. How are decisions taken, and to whom are decision-makers liable? The answers depend largely on answering a prior question: what is the purpose of the company? As we saw in the last chapter, there are differing types of company and differing perspectives on how they should be run. There, we highlighted two distinct schools of thought. The one that has become dominant is the shareholder primacy model, which holds that the company is essentially economic in purpose and run for the benefit of shareholders. The other is that the company exists in society and thus has social and ethical responsibilities. The CSR view of the company takes in stakeholder interests and also has a strong ethical perspective, in that significant stakeholders exemplify moral claims. How do these contrasting views of corporate purpose influence decision-making and accountability in the company? That is the focus of the broad area of corporate governance.

We begin by defining corporate governance, highlighting the social and ethical contexts. We then examine critically the foundations of the shareholder primacy school of thought, and its implications for corporate governance. We then move on to discuss the nature of directors' duties and the practicalities of corporate governance in differing national environments. In particular, we examine alternative stakeholder models of corporate governance. We then look at how CSR and ethical theories are linked to corporate governance.

CORPORATE GOVERNANCE IN AN ETHICAL CONTEXT

Corporate governance refers to the highest decision-making processes and organizational structures in the company. Governance is a concept derived from political analysis. As we found in Chapter 3, it focuses on where legitimacy and authority lie, and how legitimate power is exercised. Here is a summary of the major points. Governments exert sovereign authority. They can use coercive power, demand taxes to be paid and apply criminal law to serious wrongdoers. Governance in the political context concerns the whole of a political unit, such as a country or sub-national region. Political authorities oversee public welfare and, in cases of democratic authority, there is accountability to the electorate. Political theorists stress that governments derive their authority from the consent of those governed. This consent is often depicted as a social contract. Indeed, in non-democratic systems, too, there can be an implied social contract. Citizens might be content with life under the autocrat who governs fairly and promotes public goods.

Governance within the company is rather different, as the company is not a sovereign authority. The company comes within the jurisdiction of the state, and must abide by the state's laws. Its governance structures are authorized by the company's internal constitutional documents, and its processes are overseen by the company itself. Still, the company's governance is a matter of broader concern in society. In most countries there is legislation on corporate governance, and there are also many less formal regulatory frameworks with which companies must comply. It is now common for corporate governance regulation to take in a range of stakeholder interests. The social dimension of companies, which CSR theories link to management, is now being addressed in the wider sphere of corporate governance. The linking of CSR and stakeholder concerns to corporate governance now shapes much debate on future regulation.

Ethical concerns have risen up the corporate governance agenda as the issues are increasingly perceived in the wider context of society. It is now felt that directors and managers should be accountable not just to shareholders, but to other stakeholders, and should act in ways which can be justified on ethical grounds. Spiralling executive pay and poor decision-making are criticized not just by shareholders, but by a broad range of people in society. Rising executive pay is also perceived as unfair in the context of rising inequality in society and stagnant wages in the general working population. The way companies are run is now as much a concern as their economic performance. If they are run in ways which benefit the few insiders at the expense of broader stakeholders, they are criticized on ethical grounds, even if they generate large profits. Corporate governance is no longer seen as simply a matter for the company itself. It is now part of a wider context in which ethical issues are central.

ROLES IN PUBLIC AND PRIVATE COMPANIES

There can be thousands of registered companies in a country. They vary not just in size, but in the ways they are governed and held accountable for their actions. Private companies can be distinguished from public companies (see Chapter 4). In the private company, there are typically only a few owners and they are likely to take a hands-on role in the company. For these companies, the requirements for disclosure of information and financial reporting are less comprehensive than those for public companies. Corporate governance in the private company is less concerned with structures and more concerned with informal agreements among the people at the heart of the company. Personal relations matter more than corporate structures. The owners, directors and managers tend to be the same people in multiple roles. This is shown in Figure 8.1, where their roles are depicted as continuously interacting.

The public company, by contrast, is marked by a separation between the investors, directors and managers. The directors are the highest decision-makers in the company, and are entrusted with safeguarding the best interests of the company as a whole. The directors are accountable to shareholders for how the company is run, but the running of the company is in the hands of managers. The CEO and other senior executives are usually directors. They thus interact with other board members on a regular basis, and, ideally, are kept informed about what the company is doing. Shareholders, by contrast, have little contact with the board, meeting annually in the annual general meeting (AGM), which is a formal event rather than an ongoing engagement with shareholders. In their landmark work, Berle and Means highlighted the shift in the nature of the company from the classical economic model of the entrepreneur and owner to the large company in which there was

Figure 8.1 Corporate governance roles in the private and public company

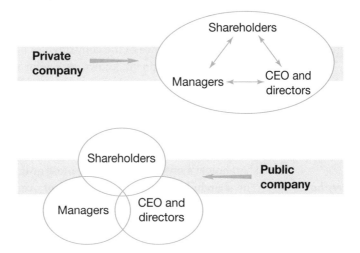

a separation between ownership and control. The numerous individual shareholders were owners, but they took no role in the business, which was run by managers (Berle and Means, 1932). These divergent roles are shown in Figure 8.1. Governance becomes more challenging in the public company, as people in each of these roles have particular interests which can collide. It is easy to lose sight of the purpose of the company as a whole. This is one of the issues addressed by theorists of corporate governance. The prevailing theory rests on the shareholder primacy model, which we examine in the next section. We will find that, despite its influence, it has been shown to be flawed in key assumptions. It is also increasingly challenged on social and ethical grounds.

FOUNDATIONS OF THE SHAREHOLDER PRIMACY MODEL

A starting point of corporate strategy and decision-making is the fact that shareholders own the company. This is the bedrock of the shareholder primacy model of the company introduced in Chapter 7. The model holds that the company's purpose is to maximize shareholder wealth. A number of theories have been used to support this model, including property theory and agency theory. They are based on analogies which look as if they are legally established, but they owe more to economic thinking than legal principles. It is helpful, therefore, to take a fresh look at what today's shareholders own and what their roles are in reality. It is also essential to ask who exactly is the shareholder at the heart of the shareholder-centred model.

PROPERTY THEORY AND THE SHAREHOLDER

Property theory, based on the idea that a company is a kind of property, has been highly influential, and has largely shaped the principles of corporate governance recognized in law and practice around the world. It holds that the shareholders are owners, and the company should be ultimately run for their benefit, in the way that the owner of a property such as a hotel derives benefit from running it. If a person 'owns' a thing, that person has rights over it, and can resist the wishes and interests of others over it. But ownership itself is a contentious issue. Owners typically do not have absolute rights over the object owned, but must act within legal and moral constraints. The hotel owner must address a range of issues, from health and safety to how the premises are used. While shareholders-as-owners remain a relevant starting point, it is helpful to look at what their ownership entails, and how their interests are translated into governance of the company.

The registered company was originally known as a joint stock company, and for this reason shares are often referred to as stocks, notably in the US. The shareholder owns a portion of the company's shares, along with the rights which accompany that specific holding. There is thus a contract between the shareholder and the company. Employees, suppliers and other stakeholders also have contracts with the company. Property theory suggests that the shareholder's contract is one of ownership, unlike these other stakeholders, but the

Many shareholders have either no voting rights or highly diluted voting rights in their companies.

shareholder's ownership is unlike most ordinary meanings of ownership. The shareholder does not exert control over the company as an asset in the way that the owner of property might expect. The shareholder's share certificate represents a limited set of rights in respect of the company. Most shareholders hold 'ordinary' shares, which give the holder a right to vote in the AGM. But in many companies, such as Google and other technology companies, they have either no voting rights or only diluted voting rights in a dual class structure. H&M, discussed in the opening case study of the last chapter, is an example. Where they have voting rights, they vote on the appointment of directors, but almost always their choice is limited to candidates chosen by the management. They have a right to a dividend, which represents a portion of the profits, but their entitlement is contingent on the company's board of directors declaring a dividend, which they have no obligation to do. Many do not. Apple, a highly profitable company, existed for 17 years before declaring a dividend. Shareholders in a public company can sell their shares (known as the right of 'exit'), and, in the case of successful companies, realize a profit on the sale. But, despite being called 'owners', they cannot sell the company itself or any of its assets. Because of limited liability, they are not liable for the company's debts; nor are they liable for wrongs committed by the company. By investing their money in the company, they have taken a risk and have contractual rights against the company. They are able to sue it and also directors for breach of duties to the company. Some theorists also hold that they are 'residual claimants' on the company's profits, but this claim is rather misleading. To appreciate why, it is useful to look at the role of debtholders in the company.

The debtholder can be anyone who has lent money to the company. Debtholders, or creditors, are important stakeholders, and like shareholders, have contracts with the company, often secured on the company's assets. Indeed, the debtholder can be in a better position than the shareholder, as the company is obliged to pay the bondholders their interest due, while it is not bound to pay a dividend. To say that the shareholder is the 'residual claimant' on the corporation's profits means that when all obligations such as paying interest to bondholders have been made, whatever is left is due to shareholders (Fama and Jensen, 1983). However, the category of residual claimant comes from bankruptcy law, rather than from the running of an ongoing business. In the existing business, it is likely that profits will be used for re-investing in the business. They may also be used to pay bonuses to executives. Shareholders are among the many groups which have claims to profits. The board could decide not to pay them dividends, thinking, for example, that it is better to pay off debt. Or it could make donations to charities it favours. The shareholder-centred model holds that directors should be focused primarily on maximizing shareholder wealth. But, in practice, shareholders have little power over them. The theory that has addressed this issue is agency theory.

AGENCY THEORY

The application of agency theory to corporate governance is attributed mainly to Jensen and Meckling, whose article in 1976 became one of the most frequently cited sources in corporate governance literature (Jensen and Meckling, 1976). Their 'theory of the firm' is set out in economic terms, but it relies on well-known legal concepts in what has become known as the principal–agent model of the company. Their theory is both descriptive and normative. We look first at the law of agency, from which it derives. As shown in Figure 8.2, the principal grants authority to an agent to act on the principal's behalf. The principal must exist and have legal capacity prior to the agent entering the scene, and is independent of the agent. There is a contract between principal and agent setting out terms such as duties and payment. When the agent has carried out what the contract requires, the agent drops out

Figure 8.2 How agency works in law

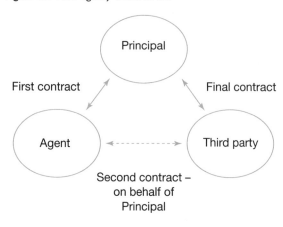

First contract

Final contract

Second contract –
on behalf of
Principal

of the picture legally, and the final contract is between the principal and the third party. This describes a one-off deal, such as using an agent to buy a property. If the agency agreement is a continuing relationship, the agent carries on making contracts under the continuing legal authority.

In law, the principal is bound by the contract made by the agent, although if the agent acts outside his/her authority, the principal can sue the agent. Agents abound in international business. Financial agents make investments on behalf of investors. Senior employees make contracts on behalf of the companies they work for. The company thus becomes a party to contracts with numerous third parties, as in Figure 8.2. But how does the principal–agent model apply to shareholders? Jensen and Meckling start from the proposition that the shareholders as owners of the company are the principal, and they hire managers as agents to run the company. The two have different interests. Owners seek maximization of shareholder value. Directors and managers are concerned above all to preserve their own positions. This flows from the separation of ownership and control highlighted by Berle and Means. The managers who run the business are inclined to shirk and behave opportunistically, creating costs for the principal, known as 'agency costs'. The key to reducing agency costs is said to be to incentivize directors and managers, so that their interests are more aligned with those of shareholders. The rise in equity-based remuneration for executives has been a result.

Agency theory makes assumptions about shareholders owning the company which we found to be flawed. They do not actually own the company in any but a highly restricted sense. Neither are they the residual claimants on the company's profits, except in limited situations involving bankruptcy. Agency theory views shareholders as the principal in a way similar to the triangular relationship depicted in Figure 8.2. Similarly, managers are seen as the agents. It is possible that this model would fit a private company with one dominant owner and no debt. However, within the large corporation, both shareholders and managers cover a range of individuals and interests. Neither group can be depicted as a unified entity in the way which would fit this simple model. We look first at shareholders.

Shareholders are not legally a principal in the way that a company or a natural person is. Both companies and natural people have legal capacity to make contracts. The company as a legal entity routinely enters into contracts – otherwise it could not carry on business. Usually, these contracts are negotiated by employees as agents. Shareholders do not constitute a legal entity: they are members of the company, which is itself a separate entity. They are a diverse group of investors. The image of the shareholder depicted by the shareholder primacy model is a single-minded investor focused on wealth maximization as reflected in returns and measured by share price. The picture is one of 'rational economic man', with a short-term perspective. In fact, shareholders are highly disparate in their values and interests. Some look for long-term stability and others look for short-term returns. Many investors do not own stocks directly, but invest in managed funds. While it used to be the case that a company's shareholders were mainly its own nationals, investors are nowadays likely to be geographically dispersed, and reflect priorities and values of their own national environments. Many shareholders are themselves corporations, for whom portfolio investment is an element of corporate strategy. We will highlight further the changing profile of shareholders when we look at UK equities later in this chapter.

We now turn to managers. How do the diverse interests of shareholders impact on managers in terms of agency theory? Recall that in law, the principal is entitled to control the agent's activities. This assumes a principal with the legal capacity to control the agent and a clear set of contractual objectives. We have seen that shareholders do not fit these assumptions. A confusion which arises in the agency model is that it does not distinguish between the roles of directors and managers. Looking back at Figure 8.1, note that these roles are separate in the public company. The directors are the custodians of the best interests of the company itself, which is not legally the same as serving the shareholders' particular interests. Figure 8.3 shows a single-tier board. Directors include both full-time executives and part-time non-executive directors, who take no part in the day-to-day running of the company. Still, like all directors, they have responsibilities of oversight of the company's best interests. They also sit on important committees, including the remuneration committee and audit committee. Senior executives tend to be both directors and employees of the company, while most managers are employees only. Executives owe duties to the company, and are answerable to the board. In practice, boards of directors tend to acquiesce in executives' decisions.

Agency theory holds that managers are inclined to be self-serving, to the detriment of shareholders' interests. The solution to the problem of agency costs is to better align the interests of managers with those of shareholders. More specifically, the use of equity-based remuneration (or 'compensation' in the US) such as stock options would incentivize managers. An article by Jensen and Murphy in 1990, making the case for the use of stock options, seemed to mark a gathering pace in the shift towards equity-based incentives

Figure 8.3 *The single-tier board of directors*

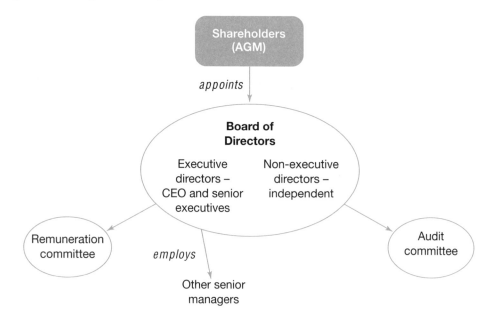

(Jensen and Murphy, 1990). It makes the assumption that all parties rationally pursue financial self-interest. According to the theory, if incentives are aligned, agency costs are reduced and shareholder value is maximized. The market is thus seen as a means of monitoring managers and improving performance.

But has the adoption of agency theory led to shareholder value maximization? The expectations were that corporate performance would improve in companies which adopt these governance rules. In the space of less than two decades, equity-based remuneration in the US S&P 500 companies went from nothing to 66% (Stout, 2012: 20). Shareholders would expect to see higher share prices and greater returns. But empirical research has been inconclusive on the links between agency theory and improved corporate performance, finding that corporate performance rests on a complex range of factors, a significant one being just plain luck (Yermack, 2006).

A rethinking of corporate governance has followed. Many commentators have said that the principles of shareholder value remain valid, and that the problem lies with the excessive risk-taking by executives (Hill, 2012a). They recommend reforming executive incentive schemes. However, the issues are deeper than this, lying in the weakness of the theory itself.

As has been shown, agency theory does not capture the legal and economic relationships in the large corporation with multiple shareholders. 'The shareholder' as envisaged in the theory is an abstraction, envisaged as covering a coherent set of identifiable interests, but that coherence is absent in fact. The assumption that shareholders as principals own and control the company is also a misrepresentation of their ownership status. Shareholders in US companies have seen a stark weakening in their voice within their companies. Their returns have diminished while equity-based executive rewards have risen. Between 2006 and 2011, not one management-nominated candidate for a US board has failed to be elected (Milne, 2013). Paradoxically, the fixation with shareholder value maximization has resulted in a deterioration in shareholder welfare. A response has been a rise in shareholder activism, often through advisory groups which bring together investors to gain a greater voice than they would have individually.

PAUSE TO CONSIDER...

Would you be attracted to buying shares in a company such as Google, which asserts the importance of shareholder wealth, but offers non-voting shares to the public? Why?

HAS SHAREHOLDER PRIMACY UNDERMINED BUSINESS ETHICS?

Maximizing shareholder wealth as the purpose of the company rests a view of human nature much like the Benthamite utilitarians discussed in Chapter 1, acting entirely out of perceived material self-interest, without a shred of ethical or 'pro-social' motivation. But scientific research, as well as common observation of people in everyday situations, shows that the vast majority of people act in ways that are pro-social, that is, reflect social values and norms of behaviour (Stout, 2012: 96). The phenomenon is well known among shareholders. Many invest in ethical funds, and many criticize the ethical misdeeds of executives. One might say that this is because they see a loss to shareholder value associated with reputational damage. But this confirms the fact that values matter in the eyes of society. The owner-entrepreneur of a private company feels these moral pressures directly, and feels accountable for any misdeeds: there is nowhere to hide. But in corporate structures of large companies, the moral messages can get lost. It has been argued that legal compliance in a society generally cannot be explained without social and moral sanctions which act as restraints on would-be lawbreakers (Elhauge, 2005). People feel moral pressures in everyday life among family, friends and associates. They refrain from breaking the law not merely for fear of being caught, but because they will be frowned on by the people who matter most in their lives. Similarly, shareholders have social and moral values as well as desires to receive a return on their investments. But in the large public company, they face impediments in impressing their values on managers, in what is called a 'collective action problem' (Elhauge, 2005: 759). Individually, they are in a weak position to press moral considerations on managers. They inevitably lack detailed information on the company's activities, and each shareholder is inclined to think he/she is only one of many. How can one voice make an impact? Shareholders thus appear uninterested in anything except share price, as this is the most visible indicator they have of the company. Managers thus feel justified in their focus on maximizing profits. The result, however, is that corporate governance risks being reduced to the 'lowest possible moral denominator' (Elhauge, 2005: 800).

Corporate governance risks being reduced to the 'lowest possible moral denominator'.

Another factor which distances investors from corporate decision-making is the rise of investment funds, which invest in a portfolio of shares. Individual investors are direct shareholders only in the fund, not in the individual companies in which it invests. They have no ownership rights in those companies, and thus do not feel 'engaged' in the individual companies. The main shareholders in many large listed companies are funds such as pension funds, rather than individual investors. Fund managers take the decisions about which shares to buy and sell. Because they are large investors, they have considerable potential influence on boards, but tend to go along with management decisions, thus further entrenching the profit maximization ethos.

A survey of people in the top quarter of wage earners in different countries gives an indication of what informed members of the public think about Milton Friedman's famous statement 'The social responsibility of business is to increase profits' (*The Economist*, 2011). As Figure 8.4 shows, the country showing the greatest enthusiasm for Friedman's views was the United Arab Emirates, where 84% of respondents agreed with Friedman. But while the rich Gulf state embraces Friedman's capitalist values, it is also noted for suppression of political dissent and accusations of human rights violations. Perhaps surprisingly, the US, the home of Friedman's strongest advocates, is ambivalent in its views of him. Only 56% of the top quarter of wage earners agreed. Britain, where free-market principles are also established, is even less enthralled with him; only 43% of Britons agreed. Significantly, people in the two strong emerging economies, China and Brazil, largely disagreed with Friedman, while Indians showed a much more pro-capitalist way of thinking.

The financial crisis of 2008 was a blow to shareholder primacy thinking. Especially in the finance sector, companies came in for sharp criticism on ethical grounds. This was most marked in institutions such as banks which had a traditional image of prudence and caring for customers. The crisis had many causes (as explained in Chapter 5). Weak governance, excessive risk-taking by managers and acquiescent boards came in for criticism, as well as weak regulation. The growth in executive compensation based on stock options and other equity-based incentives is singled out for criticism, research suggesting that stock options encourage unethical behaviour by rewarding greed (Harris, 2009). Some of the loudest outcries against unethical corporate behaviour have come from outside corporate structures, in the form of popular demonstrations such as the 'Occupy' protests which

Figure 8.4 What does the informed public think is the responsibility of business: a selection of countries?

'The social responsibility of business is to increase its profits.'
Percentage for each country consists of those who 'strongly agree' and 'somewhat agree' with this statement.

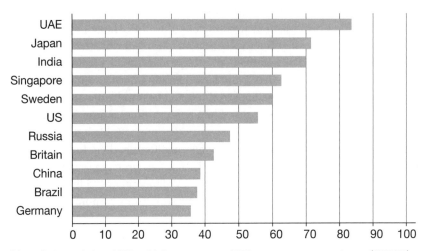

Source of data: The Economist (2011) 'Milton Friedman goes on tour', 27 January, at www.economist.com (18/09/14).

started in Wall Street in New York and have occurred in numerous other cities. Protesters, of course, are a minority, but they can send out signals of general unease in public opinion, from which the occupants of executive suites of large companies might otherwise feel insulated.

Since then, regulatory reform has been debated, but also important, if more elusive, is the change in culture that is needed to bring social and ethical considerations into decision-making. As noted above, legislation and regulation have inherent limitations. In the mentality fostered by shareholder primacy thinking, managers have become adept at altering their behaviour to get round legal constraints in their pursuit of profits. And many would treat future regulatory reforms with similar disdain. Bringing back ethical standards requires a change of culture, but this is easier said than done. Changing structures, regulatory reforms and changing the leadership of companies can play a role (Hill, 2012b). Also important is educating boards to do their jobs of oversight of managers. It might also be added that the entrenched position of shareholder primacy thinking in MBA syllabuses needs to be questioned (Murray, 2013).

> *Bringing back ethical standards requires a change of culture, but this is easier said than done.*

The shareholder primacy model owes its dominance to an engrained belief among both businesspeople and academics that managers have a legal duty to increase shareholder wealth. The manager who focuses single-mindedly on short-term share price tends to say that he/she is simply fulfilling fiduciary duties in law. Although wrong in law in both the US and UK, this view is highly persistent. In the next section, we find that directors have considerable discretion in the exercise of their duties.

There is extensive law and policy in national corporate law systems. These systems take a broader view of corporate purpose than that of the agency model. Governments have had to bail out large companies (many of them banks) and to deal with public unease at corporate excesses and the inequalities in their societies. National regulators in many countries are taking a more active interest in corporate governance reforms. We look next at the main approaches to corporate governance in national environments.

PAUSE TO CONSIDER...

Think of the region and country in which you live. What proportion of the higher income earners in that region and the country as a whole would be likely to agree with Friedman's statement in Figure 8.4, and why?

DIRECTORS' DUTIES TO SHAREHOLDERS AND OTHER STAKEHOLDERS

Directors' duties are the subject of legislation and other types of regulation in national legal systems. The body of corporate law in this area is most developed in the US and UK, both of which fall in the broad tradition of liberal market economies, in which the shareholder primacy model has become widely accepted. We look first at these models, which have become influential globally. Corporate governance structures based on a single board of directors is a hallmark of these systems. By contrast, two-tier boards of directors have predominated in many countries in Europe, encompassing broader stakeholder interests. These latter countries fall more into the tradition of social market economies. The contrast in economic environments is some indication of the ways in which directors and managers view their roles in their companies and their companies' roles in society.

US PERSPECTIVES ON DIRECTORS' DUTIES

It is common to find that directors of US companies assert they have a legal duty to maximize profits. There is considerable law, including state law, federal law and an abundance of case law on the subject. However, legal authorities point to the fact that corporate managers have never had an enforceable legal duty to maximize profits. They have always had discretion to take decisions which might sacrifice profits in the public interest. The American Law Institute (ALI) sets out the position as follows:

American Law Institute Principles of Corporate Governance (cited in Elhauge, 2005: 763)

Para 2.01(b)(2)–(3)

Even if corporate profit and shareholder gain are not thereby enhanced, the corporation, in the conduct of its business:

(1) Is obliged, to the same extent as a natural person, to act within the boundaries set by law;
(2) May take into account ethical considerations that are reasonably regarded as appropriate to the responsible conduct of business; and
(3) May devote a reasonable amount of resources to public welfare, humanitarian, educational, and philanthropic purposes.

This statement of the law is not itself legally binding, but reflects a welter of case law on the subject. Most significantly, the Delaware courts, which are highly influential in corporate law due to the large number of companies registered in their jurisdiction, has held that shareholder interests are 'not a controlling factor' (Elhauge, 2005: 765). The ALI provisions apply even if an economic loss results. Directors are thus obliged to pursue the best interests of their companies, but these do not simply equate with shareholders' interests. Moreover, shareholders' interests are not merely financial.

In the US, directors are legally subject to the 'business judgment rule'. This means that they are entitled to use their own best judgment in deciding what is best for the company, always bearing in mind that they must not simply take benefits for themselves personally. If they act in good faith, their actions are not likely to be struck down in the courts, even if the effect is to harm shareholders. They might, for example, decide that employees should be paid more, even though it means less money for dividends. Directors and executives owe a fiduciary duty to the company as a whole, not just to the shareholders.

> *If directors act in good faith, their actions are not likely to be struck down in the courts, even if the effect is to harm shareholders.*

Shareholders can – and do – sue the company and its directors for serious mismanagement. If they sue simply for bigger dividends they would probably fail, as there has been no breach of fiduciary duty on the part of directors.

Those who assert a legal duty to maximize profits are articulating the position of Milton Friedman, noted in the last section. In effect, they deny that social and moral considerations have a place in their decision-making. This is, in effect, a licence to commit worse behaviour than they would be subject to under a regime of being accountable to shareholders. Moreover, law differs from country to country. Take as an example the fact that slavery was legal in Sudan until 1924. Engaging in slavery in Sudan in 1920 would have maximized profits. However, no US court would have held that a company was therefore obliged to engage in slavery (Elhauge, 2005: 803). Shareholders, as we have seen, do take social and moral issues seriously, but are ineffective in influencing corporate boards and managers. Some supporters of the view that a company has a legal duty only to maximize profits urge that a duty to take account of social and moral considerations could be written into the law. But this overlooks the point raised earlier, concerning the limitations of law as a means of controlling behaviour. Legal regulation is important but insufficient as a means of controlling behaviour. Behavioural norms are enforced as much by a sense of social and moral obligation as by legal regulation. The mentality that law is the only means of regulating behaviour leads to behaviour oblivious of social or moral sanctions.

Most managers, in practice, believe they should weigh shareholders' profit maximization against other interests, and act accordingly. Stakeholder considerations are a routine aspect of business, but stakeholders have no formal role in corporate governance structures in the US. Some thirty US states have enacted 'constituency statutes', however, which explicitly state that directors can take into account other stakeholders besides shareholders, including employees, customers and suppliers. Delaware has not passed such a statute, but state case law exists which has the same effect. These laws came into existence following a series of takeovers in the 1980s, when there was some alarm about a growing market for corporate control among public companies. In fact, directors in the US have devised a number of mechanisms which give them the power to thwart takeovers. The use of different classes of shares is one. In many companies, notably technology companies, there are classes of shares, typically with one class having much more voting power than the other class. The dominant shareholders control the company through owning most of the shares with multiple votes. The prospect of a market for corporate control, which might serve as a monitor of poor management, is thereby diminished.

The dual share structure has been criticized for its dilution of shareholder rights. In the UK, the dual structure is very rare, and there is a more active takeover market. A clash of perspectives was evident in 2013, with the IPO of Manchester United, Britain's most successful football club. The company which owns the club is dominated by the Glazer family of the US. Having piled a huge debt burden onto the company, they raised money through an IPO in 2012. The IPO proved controversial. The Glazers registered the company in the Cayman Islands, registering it as an 'emerging growth' company and also a 'controlled company', in order to benefit from reduced disclosure requirements. The listing was on the New York Stock Exchange, where 10% of the shares were offered to the public, but these were shares with limited voting rights and little expectation of a dividend, especially in view of the millions which had to be paid each year in servicing the debt. The company has a dual-class share structure, whereby the Glazers control the shares with greater voting rights. Football has had limited following in the US, and it might have seemed logical to list the club in Britain, but it was not feasible because of the dual-class structure. Football, or 'soccer' in the US, is growing in popularity worldwide, but is considered to be a risky investment, dependent as it is on the performance of the team. There seemed to be little attraction for the ordinary investor, except the prospect of selling the shares later at a profit. The shares were destined for institutions and other super-rich investors drawn by football's glamorous image, rather than for ordinary football fans.

PAUSE TO CONSIDER...

Would you buy Manchester United shares? What ethical criticisms can be directed at the Glazers?

THE UK AND THE ENLIGHTENED SHAREHOLDER

Corporate governance in Britain is a good deal more amenable to shareholder rights than that in the US. In the main, dual-class structures do not exist. This does not mean, however, that one-share-one-vote vests much more power in the shareholder than his/her American counterpart. The UK has seen a marked change in the makeup of share ownership over the years. In the 1960s, the individual shareholder was common, and shares were held on average for eight years. Two-thirds of shareholders were individual households in 1957, and one-third institutions. By 2003, the proportions were reversed, and institutions, largely pension funds, owned 85% of shares, while households owned only 15% (Collison, 2011: 14). The holding period has fallen dramatically since then, to just seven-and-a-half months in 2007 (Kay, 2012). The rise of short-term perspectives is due partly to the growth of hedge funds, which have very short-term investment horizons. Similarly, the rise in high-frequency trading has led to a huge increase in the volume of trading on stock exchanges, while the value of transactions has shrunk. Two-thirds of UK equities are now owned by hedge funds and high-frequency traders. Bear in mind that, as was highlighted in Chapter 5, there are technological challenges associated with high-frequency trading, and exchanges can be forced to close down due to glitches from time to time. One technological glitch closed the Nasdaq for over three hours in August, 2013. Risks such as these discourage the individual shareholder, who is more-than-ever likely to invest in managed funds rather than specific companies. Another factor that has changed the profile of share ownership is globalization. In 1963, only

Two-thirds of UK equities are now owned by hedge funds and high-frequency traders.

7% of UK equities were held by non-UK owners. By 2010, 41.2% were held by non-UK owners. Many legal owners, moreover, are offshore entities set up in part to conceal the identities of the actual people behind them. How does this changing picture of the UK shareholder affect directors?

UK directors, like their American counterparts, owe fiduciary duties to the company, not individual shareholders. However, the perception that they have a duty to maximize profits has gained ground. In the UK Companies Act 2006, duties of directors are set out as follows:

Section 172(1) Duty to promote the success of the company

A director of a company must act in a way he considers, in good faith, would be most likely to promote the success of the company for the benefit of its members as a whole, and in doing so, have regard (amongst other matters) to:

a. the likely consequences of any decision in the long term,
b. the interests of the company's employees,
c. the need to foster the company's business relationships with suppliers, customers and others,
d. the impact of the company's operations on the community and the environment,
e. the desirability of the company maintaining a reputation for high standards of business conduct, and
f. the need to act fairly as between members of the company.

This statement of the legal position represents a compromise between those who wished the law to say that directors have a duty to maximize profits, and those who wished to see a duty extended to stakeholders as well as shareholders (Kay, 2013). The list of matters that the directors must take into account makes it clear that they cannot hide behind the law when engaging in policies such as tax avoidance by saying that this is the way they *must* behave. They engage in tax avoidance because they *choose* to, not because they must. Professor Kay, who carried out a review of UK equities in 2012, says the law could be described as 'enlightened shareholder value' (Kay, 2013). The enlightened shareholder is presumed to view long-term self-interest as encompassing the interests of other stakeholders and also the reputation of the company, which implies upholding high ethical standards. The wording, however, suggests that reputation is what matters, and high standards are a means to that end.

Although the law seems to make it clear that directors have a duty towards the company, this is not how it is interpreted. Research has shown that it is generally interpreted as a duty to maximize shareholder value, and that among corporate executives the law is thought to mean that the duty is maximizing share price in the short term (Collison, 2011). Professor Kay interviewed the chairman of Cadbury at the time of its takeover by Kraft, and found that Cadbury board members felt they could not legally reject a high bid for the business, even if they disagreed with it, feeling that in the long term, it would have been better for Cadbury to remain independent (Kay, 2012). He comments that it was once thought that institutions with large stakes in companies such as Cadbury would take a long-term view of the company's interest. However, in the case of Cadbury, a large proportion of the shares at the time of the bid were being held by hedge funds and other short-term investors seeking a quick profit. For this reason, Britain has been perceived as an attractive market for hostile takeovers. This implies a deterioration in attentiveness to long-term corporate goals. The fact that the law is perceived as fostering short-term gain possibly represents a shortcoming in the way it is written. The law review group which drafted the 2006 version of directors' duties received submissions from across the spectrum of

Cadbury board members felt they could not legally reject a high bid for the business, even if they disagreed with it.

views on the purpose of companies. They included many who felt that stakeholder interests should be part of directors' duties, in a more 'pluralist' approach – one that is familiar in many European countries but would represent a departure from the shareholder primacy model associated with Britain. The formula chosen was intended as a recognition of pluralism, but as interpreted in practice, has not had this effect.

Professor Collison suggests that further reform towards stakeholder values would be in order (Collison, 2011). His research highlighted the fact that in the market economies of the US and UK, where shareholder primacy has reigned, quality of life issues associated with high levels of income inequality were more in evidence than in countries with a more pluralist view of the purpose of the company. He asked interviewees whether they thought that this evidence was relevant to reform of corporate governance in Britain. Most of them said yes, and felt it should be taken into account in reforming the law on directors' duties. Stakeholder recognition is now taking place within British companies on a piecemeal basis. An example is transport company, First Group, which has appointed a train driver to sit on the board and on the remuneration committee.

Guidelines for UK corporate governance are contained in the UK Corporate Governance Code, which is descended from the corporate governance code first issued by the Cadbury Committee in 1992 (FRC, 2012). The approach taken is to recommend best practice and leave companies the flexibility about implementing its guidelines. They must 'comply or explain' in respect of key principles. The code stresses the need for boards to be well informed, composed of a mixture of knowledgeable and independent members, and recognize their collective responsibility for board decisions. The code also stresses the importance of committees, including the remuneration and audit committee, and urges the maximum transparency and dialogue with shareholders. Important principles include the need for a balance between executive and non-executive directors, and the separation of the offices of chairman and CEO. On remuneration, it stresses that CEO remuneration, where linked to performance, should be geared to the long-term best interests of the company. The UK Code has been used in a number of countries as a template for best practice in corporate governance. It makes no mention of stakeholders other than shareholders. It stresses the importance of engagement with shareholders, but in practice, this is difficult to achieve.

The Kay review highlighted areas of possible reform. The ownership of UK equities has now shifted towards shareholders interested only in short-term share prices. These owners have little sense of long-term monitoring of corporate directors. Professor Kay has recommended that long-term investors such as pension funds might be given greater weight in voting strength. In the context of a takeover bid, he recommends that only shareholders who have held their shares for a specified length of time should be able to vote, although the UK Takeover Panel rejected this idea in 2010. The idea that some shareholders' votes should count more than others is considered wrong by many. Such structures have propped up family owners of companies in the past, and these structures have now become very rare in Britain. For many, weighted voting would be considered a retrograde step.

A more modest recommendation made by Kay was that a shareholder forum could be set up in large companies, in which major shareholders could engage in dialogue with company directors. This type of gathering is possible in any case, but he feels that encouraging these groups would help to further the goals of promoting the best interests of the company. In fact, an Investor Forum was set up in 2013, consisting of representatives of 15 large investors, including asset managers, pension funds and charities.

STAKEHOLDER APPROACHES TO CORPORATE GOVERNANCE

Countries in which social market economies are the norm are more likely to adopt corporate governance principles and structures which cover a broader range of stakeholders than those in the US and UK traditions. Many European countries have adopted a two-tier board of directors. The lower board is the management board, and the higher board, or supervisory board, takes the big strategic decisions of the company. Stakeholder groups are represented on the supervisory board. Germany is a leading example of this model. In Germany, 50% of members of the supervisory board must be representatives of employees and trade unions, and 50% represent shareholders. German corporate governance rests on a view of the company as a community, in which employees are central. This model is known as 'co-determination', suggesting that employees have equal say in decision-making with the company's shareholders. Although this model gives stakeholders a direct role in governance, it has faced criticism. Trade unions can themselves build power bases within companies, which do not necessarily serve the best interests of the company in the long term. As in the other jurisdictions we have looked at, directors have legal duties to the company as a whole, but the heavy weighting of the board towards employee representatives can cloud the focus on long-term perspectives. Only German trade unions are members of the supervisory boards. Workers in a company's other locations globally have no direct voice. However, the German carworkers' union, IG Metall, is now becoming active in the US states where German companies have plants. A globalized car company can play off one country against another, whereas trade unions tend to be country-based. IG Metall is now pressing for better working conditions and voice for workers, including those in the US.

Shareholders on some German supervisory boards have become more vocal in their questioning of the board's decision-making. In a non-binding vote, 40% of the shareholders in Deutsche Bank rejected the CEO's remuneration package in 2010. In 2013, shareholders staged another rebellion, this time against the reappointment of a well-known industrialist to the board. Again, the rebellion failed, and he was duly elected, but the signs of disquiet were palpable. Those against his appointment argued that he was a member of five other boards, and would not have the time to do the job properly. Among the dissenting shareholders were a large British pension fund and a large Dutch pension fund. The rebellion signalled that shareholders consider it unacceptable that outside directors sit on many different boards, creating a club-like atmosphere in the boardroom, which discourages scrutiny of directors. This is in fact a common practice in many countries, and has contributed to boards' failures in monitoring executives.

While it might be expected that the EU would seek harmonization of corporate governance across its 28 member states, this has not been the case. The European Commission has taken the position that in corporate governance, one size does not fit all, and that varying law, culture and traditions must be taken into account. As was highlighted in Chapter 2, economic systems vary across Europe. Social market economies prioritize social welfare over market values. But the EU Commission has been concerned that in many European countries, entrenched owners, often families, control large companies. These dominant owners far outweigh the voices of other shareholders, and their power can lead to a kind of crony capitalism and corruption. These structures act as a barrier against takeovers, and certainly provide continuity against the short-termism which prevails in the UK. However, the opening case study on Volkswagen highlighted the weaknesses of corporate governance in this type of ownership structure. On the other hand, H&M, the Swedish company featured in the opening case study of Chapter 7, showed the strengths of a long-term perspective where the family owners prioritize CSR.

Sweden is among the world's highest-ranking countries in quality of life, and it prides itself on its social values. The Swedish model of corporate governance can be seen as supporting the social values of the country, but is also criticized for the role it bestows on dominant shareholders. Two large holding companies dominate the corporate landscape in Sweden. Between them, they control hundreds of companies, amounting to more than half the companies on Stockholm's stock exchange. The two holding companies, both dominated by insiders, are active shareholders, electing board members and taking part in the big decisions of companies. In some cases, their shares are 100 times the voting weight of ordinary shareholders. This situation promotes stability in decision-making, and aids companies in focusing on long-term goals. But its vesting of corporate power in so few individuals means that there is a very cosy relationship between the company and its dominant shareholders, and smaller shareholders are overlooked. Moreover, it is difficult to see how the holding companies, which control hundreds of companies in many different sectors, can effectively engage with all of them. In response to this criticism, the large shareholders say their accumulated expertise is invaluable to the running of each company. The system works on trust between shareholders and directors. The CEO of one of the two large holding companies says that, 'You have to share your power' (Milne, 2013). Observers of the Swedish model of corporate governance tend to think that, while it suits Swedish society, in which there is a consensus on social values, it would probably not suit larger countries with more diversified societies.

'You have to share your power.'

Do Asian examples of corporate governance shed light on balancing shareholder and other stakeholder voices, while maintaining a focus on the long-term goals of the company? Japan has long had a view of the company which falls more into the stakeholder mould. Its companies see themselves as a kind of family, and employees have a sense of belonging which they lack in countries where employment relations are driven by contracts and rulebooks. Personal relationships are important in Japanese companies, as in Asian companies generally. Personal ties of loyalty, however, can cloud a person's view of what is right behaviour in a given situation. Japan has seen scandals arising from cover-ups of wrongdoing out of loyalty to senior staff. South Korea's companies, too, although more in the tradition of family domination, have suffered from scandals which might have been averted if people were willing to speak out against superiors. In both Japan and South Korea, formal corporate governance structures tend to be just that – formal only. The real decision-making takes place among dominant insiders. In these circumstances it is usual to conclude that corporate governance is weak, in that there are few effective means for monitoring and accountability. Similarly, in China, governance is closely linked with those in political power, often in ways that are opaque. They might have governance structures which look similar to other companies, but decisions are influenced by political masters. Recall the divergence between Japan and China which appears in Figure 8.4 on the importance of profit maximization. Japanese people surveyed, perhaps surprisingly, were more profit-oriented than those in China, who were more pro-social.

An issue which has galvanized public opinion as well as shareholder concern in many countries, whatever corporate governance processes are in place, has been executive pay.

PAUSE TO CONSIDER...

What are the benefits and drawbacks of the Swedish model of corporate governance? How could it be criticized on ethical grounds?

EXECUTIVE REWARDS UNDER THE SPOTLIGHT

The ascendency of managers in the modern company led to an assumption that complacent managers had become entrenched, presiding over weak shareholder returns but protected by a complacent board. The solution recommended by agency theory was to better align the interests of managers and shareholders, by rewarding managers through long-term incentive plans, share options and performance-related bonuses. Mixes of market-based remuneration for executives thus became the norm. In a sense, the solution was successful, in that executive pay soared, but this was not necessarily good news for shareholders. It has been argued that the high wages have attracted the wrong sort of CEO, that is, people who are essentially risk-takers. The incentives acted as an 'enticement to cheat, to commit fraud or otherwise cook the books' (Harris, 2009: 152). Managers became adept at manipulating the system, for example, to trigger bonus payments.

Shareholder returns have been worse at companies where executive remuneration is heavily tilted towards market incentives than at companies where managers have lower incentives (Hill, 2012a). The financial sector, in particular, has come under the spotlight. Executives in banks and other financial institutions have made the most striking gains in rewards, largely on the strength of the globalization of financial markets. As Figure 8.5 shows, however, shareholder returns in UK banks have been poor in comparison to executive rewards.

Figure 8.5 *Pay and dividends in UK banks*

Billions of pounds

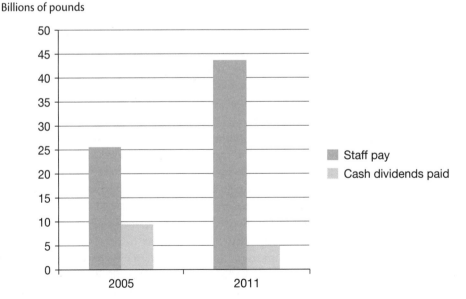

Source of data: McCrum, D. and Burgess, K. (2012) 'Shareholders lose patience on executive pay', *Financial Times*, 21 April.

'Aspiration to make big bucks is part of the American dream.'

Research has also shown a link between high levels of stock options and financial misconduct (Harris, 2009). A firm that pays over 92% of CEO compensation in stock options was shown to have a 40% chance of having to make an accounting restatement in the following ten years (Harris, 2009). Monitoring by boards has not been effective. They have tended to acquiesce in the proposed remuneration of executives. Huge rises in CEO pay have been particularly in evidence in the US, where high CEO pay has not been criticized to the same extent as in European countries. One US fund manager explains, 'Aspiration to make big bucks is part of the American dream' (Oakley, 2013). However, the US now has a requirement for a 'say on pay' by shareholders in the AGM. The vote is not binding, but if a substantial number of shareholders vote against the CEO's proposed pay package, this gives a signal to the board. An example is Citigroup, where, in 2012, 55% of the shareholders either voted against or abstained in the vote on the CEO's proposed pay package of $15 million. Citi investors had seen the share price decline 90% over a decade, but a generous cash bonus of $5.3 million and $8 million in deferred shares were proposed for the CEO. Even so, the vote came as a shock. One expert on shareholder voting said, 'we hadn't heard any drum beat about pay' (McCrum and Burgess, 2012). Citi's CEO resigned soon thereafter, but the company denied that his departure was precipitated by the shareholder rebellion over his compensation.

In the UK, the median earnings of a FTSE 100 CEO have risen 266% to £3.24 million in the last 13 years, while the median earnings of a full-time worker have risen 46% to £26,462 (Oakley, 2013). Commentators point to the fact that the people running companies 'do not live in the same world as the rest of us', in their 'sheltered lives of luxury' (Oakley, 2013). The

The people running companies 'do not live in the same world as the rest of us'.

CEO of Barclays, Mr Diamond, found in 2011 that his rise in pay of 25% to £25 million was criticized at a time when the company's shares were falling. The UK has now introduced a requirement that the shareholder vote on executive pay is binding. Boards have all along had the power to question pay and terms, but have been acquiescent. In other words, they have tended to go along with a view that there is now an international market in talented executives, and if the CEO feels underpaid (as Mr Diamond did), he or she might leave. In fact, many people would say that that would be a healthy sign. Although the finance sector has stood out, these levels of pay are not confined to financial services. Irene Rosenfeld, the Chairman and CEO of Mondelēz, formerly Kraft, which acquired Cadbury, received pay totalling $28.8 million in 2012, a rise of 31% on the previous year, despite the company's 28% fall in income.

Josef Ackermann, the outgoing CEO of Deutsche Bank, said that the bank's bonus pool had been reduced by 17% in 2011, following the rebellion in 2010 (noted in the previous section), but that year saw a slump of 42% in profits. Increasingly, executive pay is viewed in the context of income inequality around the world. The huge gap between total pay of CEOs and ordinary workers' earnings is evident in both advanced and emerging economies. Ratios of CEO pay to average earnings are shown in Figure 8.6. Executive pay in the US, already 500 times that of the ordinary employee, actually rose to 508 times in the years following the collapse of Lehman Brothers Bank and the ensuing financial crisis. The ratio also rose substantially in Germany, and, to a lesser extent, Hong Kong, where many mainland Chinese companies are registered. CEO pay came down significantly in Switzerland, where public opinion against high executive pay has been a factor. In a referendum in 2013,

Figure 8.6 *Ratio of average CEO pay to average wages*

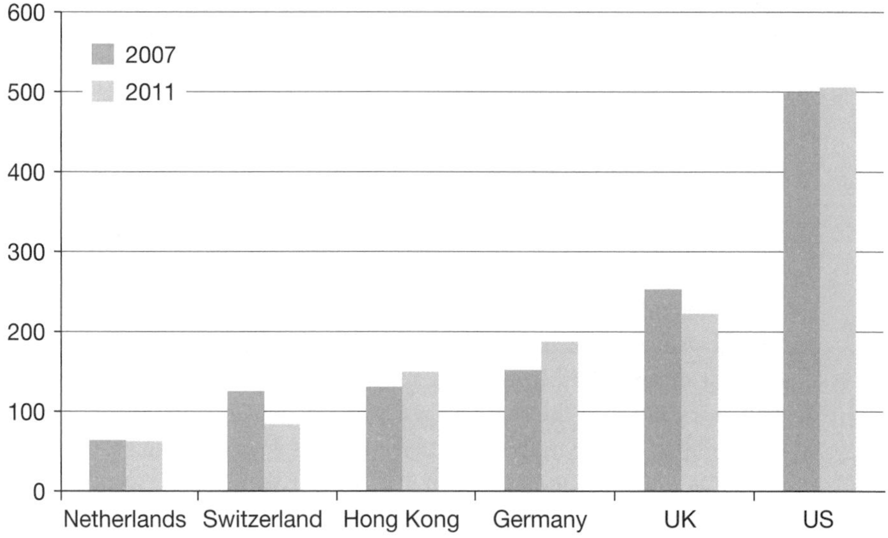

Source of data: ILO (2013) *World of Work Report 2013*, p. 83, at www.ilo.org (18/09/14).

68% of voters supported a binding vote on pay by shareholders, the abolition of 'golden' hellos and good-byes, annual re-election of directors and criminal sanctions for breaches. But in another referendum later in the same year, the Swiss voted against a legal cap on executive pay.

The EU has taken steps towards reining in executive pay across member states. The European Commission is implementing restrictions on bonuses of bankers and asset managers. The ratio of fixed salary to bonuses for these executives is being capped at 2 to 1. Critics say, however, that this will simply lead to higher fixed salaries. The EU is also proposing a clampdown on pay in companies which have received taxpayer-funded bailouts in the financial sector. This would affect numerous European banks, where executive earnings will be capped at no more than the higher of 15 times the national average salary or 10 times the wages of the average bank employee. The British government has opposed this measure, which would see severe cuts in pay from current levels.

Cutting bonuses and reining in overall remuneration might seem to be treating the symptoms rather than the disease of excessive executive pay. Media attention and political momentum have played roles in bringing in regulatory measures. Can highly-paid executives feel confident that the storm will blow over and business as usual will resume? The steep increases were triggered by agency theory views on how incentives work. But the use of market-based pay did not successfully align shareholders' and managers' interests as predicted. Instead, at the top level, it attracted individuals who relished the challenge of gaming the system. However, most people, including managers and shareholders, have both pro-social and ethical dimensions in their mental makeup. Research carried out by PwC in 43 countries, in which 1,106 executives were interviewed, suggests that current pay packages based on long-term incentives are not working. They found that executives work for other things than just money: 'Money is only part of the deal – and recognition matters as much as financial incentives' (PwC, 2012: 29). Most would take a 28% decrease in

'Money is only part of the deal – and recognition matters as much as financial incentives.'

pay for the 'ideal' job. Pay, the executives felt, is about fairness and recognition as much as incentives. By fairness, they mean that pay should be fair in comparison to others within the company, and among their peer group in the industry globally. The researchers found that there is no one-size-fits-all model of pay. The report concludes, 'We need to consign to the scrap heap the agency model approach to executive pay, based on "rational economic man", which has been so unhelpfully influential in current Western pay systems' (PwC, 2012: 30).

PAUSE TO CONSIDER...

Assume you are in the position of a highly-paid executive. Would you take a 28% cut in pay for the 'ideal' job? To what extent would you agree with the executives interviewed in the PwC survey, who said that fairness and recognition matter as much as money?

INTERCONNECTIONS: CSR, ETHICS AND CORPORATE GOVERNANCE

A strike of 5,000 workers at a tyre factory in Shandong province in China was a wake-up call in cross-border issues of corporate governance. After several months of unrest in 2013, the workers, who are unionized, stepped up their actions by 'locking out' their bosses, preventing them from entering the premises. The workers are employed by a joint venture company that is 65 per cent owned by Cooper Tire & Rubber of the USA and 35 per cent owned by the Chengshan Group of China, which manages the factory. Cooper agreed to be taken over by Apollo Tyres of India, but the Shandong workers objected to the takeover. They were not disputing their pay and conditions. They were objecting to the fact that they were not consulted before the takeover was agreed, and they felt the deal was unsound, as Apollo was financing the purchase of Cooper entirely by loans. The debt, they feared, would fall on their company's finances.

Employees are primary stakeholders, but in most systems have no direct role in corporate governance. Their interests should be taken into account in assessing the best interests of the company, but boards are more inclined towards shareholder value maximization, which usually implies a short-term perspective. The German model of corporate governance would take in the employees and their trade unions more directly. If Cooper were a German company, German workers would have a voice, but not those in another country. In fact, Cooper's American employees were not happy with the takeover either, but their objections centred on their pay and conditions. There appeared to be genuine financial concerns about the Apollo takeover, which might have weighed more with Cooper's board than employee concerns. The $2.5 billion they were offered seemed, on the face of it, to be decisive, but the deal was beset by troubles, including the debt financing, and fell through. A strong CSR approach might well have caused the directors to consider the wider stakeholder perspective, which would have involved consulting the workers and their unions in China. The workers were justifiably concerned over the high levels of debt involved in the Apollo deal. This is a long-term issue, and a CSR perspective would have taken such issues into account.

CSR concerns both social and ethical considerations, which, as this chapter has highlighted, tend to be underrepresented in corporate governance structures. They come into the 'enlightened shareholder' view of the company in the UK, but this is from the business perspective, not from a sense of moral duty. The UK code of corporate governance, which is held out as representing best practice, does not mention stakeholders other than shareholders. Under the Companies Act 2006, companies are required to submit CSR reports as part of their annual report. Moral problems are an aspect of corporate governance. An issue has been the failure of boards to monitor executives. In the USA, legislation following the Enron scandal, in the form of the 2002 Sarbanes–Oxley Act, was directed mainly at accounting and reporting issues. The CEO and Chief Financial Officer (CFO) are responsible for certifying the accounts, and the legislation increased the criminal penalties for reckless certification. The Act included no provisions on executive pay, but did require senior financial officers to disclose the company's code of ethics. The costs of compliance became significant. But have companies simply become more involved in compliance procedures, or have they become more ethical?

A driver of ethics in the corporate sphere is the concern for the company's reputation, among a variety of stakeholders. A survey of 230 senior finance executives in the USA and Europe has found that the main benefits of an ethical culture are in attracting the right employees and retaining them (CFO Europe Research Services, 2007). This was true for both US and European executives. Better relations with investors and greater attractiveness to customers were also seen as benefits of an ethical culture. However, the finance executives surveyed felt that competitive advantage and share price benefited less from an ethical culture. On these impacts, there was a gap between US and European perceptions: 66 per cent of US executives thought competitive advantage would be enhanced by an ethical culture, while only 41 per cent of European executives thought the same. Similarly, only 39 per cent of European executives thought ethics impacted on share price, while 53 per cent of US executives thought it did. A factor that should be taken into account is differing perceptions of an 'ethical culture'. Ethical codes are much more common in the US than in Europe.

Ethical codes tend to fall within two broad categories: those which are based on specific rules and those based on principles. Most American ones are rule-based, representing a regulatory approach to ethical issues. As we have seen, however, abiding by specific rules is not the same as being ethical. A person can do the right thing simply in order not to be caught, not due to a feeling of moral duty. It was for this reason that the Cadbury Committee, which reported on UK corporate governance in 1992, declined to recommend regulation. It feared boards would comply with the letter of the law, but not the spirit of the law. The UK's corporate governance code thus reflected this approach, which advocated trust rather than mechanistic rules. An ethical culture depends not just on adherence to rules, but on a sense of moral duty. Changing the culture of a company which has lost its ethical bearings is more difficult than changing structures and rules.

A person can do the right thing simply in order not to be caught, not due to a feeling of moral duty.

CONCLUSIONS

Corporate governance tends to be seen as a set of structures and processes which guide corporate decision-making and accountability at the highest level. We have highlighted in this chapter that these structures are just that, formal mechanisms which, to some extent, ensure stakeholders that monitoring of executives is taking place. But it has also become evident, especially following the financial crisis, that formal structures and processes can mask the realities in executive suites, where risk-taking and outsize rewards seemed to go unchecked, despite the formal procedures. Tightening up on corporate governance processes has been a common call among concerned shareholders and the public generally, and reforms have been put in place in many countries. Will they reassure a doubting public? Two themes highlighted in this chapter cast doubt on corporate governance structures. The first is that procedures are seen as box-ticking exercises, and what is actually needed is a change in corporate culture towards a more ethical and social perspective on what business is about. Much legislation, such as Sarbanes–Oxley, focusing on compliance measures, which have added cost burdens to public companies, have been among the factors contributing to a marked decline in the number of public companies. The number in the US has decreased by a third since 1997. Britain, similarly, has seen a decline. Public companies are more than ever inclined to de-list and go private, reducing the regulatory burden, but also reducing the amount of public information they must disclose.

The other theme that this chapter has highlighted is that corporate governance processes are generally based on a shareholder-centric view of the company. The reform of governance, including new requirements for votes on executive remuneration, is centred on accountability to shareholders. The legislation on duties of directors in the UK makes it clear that directors have duties towards the company as a whole, which includes stakeholders. However, as we have seen, this does not translate into the corporate governance codes, and, in practice, executives persist in viewing their duties in terms of shareholder wealth maximization. The consequences are that CSR and ethical considerations are relegated to the sidelines. The German approach to corporate governance does take a stakeholder perspective, but it is a limited one, and does not ensure a focus on the best interests of the company as a whole. Corporate governance should reflect a CSR approach to the purpose of the company. A focus on ethical issues would thus underpin the thinking of both executives and those sitting on boards, who are entrusted with oversight of the company's long-term well-being.

REFERENCES

Berle, A. and Means, G. (1932) *The Modern Corporation and Private Property* (New York: Macmillan).

CFO Europe Research Services (2007) *Corporate Ethics and the CFO: Balancing Principles and Profits in the Public Eye* (London: CFO Publishing).

Collison, D. (2011) *Shareholder Primacy in UK Corporate Law: An Exploration of Rationale and Evidence*, ACCA, at www.accaglobal.com (18/09/14).

Companies Act 2006, at www.legislation.gov.uk (18/09/14).

Elhauge, E. (2005) 'Sacrificing corporate profits in the public interest', *New York University Law Review*, 80(3): 733–869.

Fama, E. and Jensen, M. (1983) 'Agency problems and residual claims', *Journal of Law and Economics*, 26(2): 327–49.

FRC (Financial Reporting Council) (2012) *UK Corporate Governance Code*, at www.frc.org.uk (18/09/14).

Harris, J. (2009) 'What's wrong with executive compensation?', *Journal of Business Ethics*, 85: 147–56.

Hill, A. (2012a) 'Bonuses of contention', *Financial Times*, 4 February.

Hill, A. (2012b) 'Lofty aspirations', *Financial Times*, 16 July.

Jensen, M. and Meckling, W. (1976) 'Theory of the firm: managerial behaviour, agency costs and ownership structure', *Journal of Financial Economics*, 3: 305–60.

Jensen, M. and Murphy, K. (1990) 'Performance pay and top-management incentives', *Journal of Political Economy*, 98(2): 225–64.

Kay, J. (2012) *The Kay Review of UK Equity Markets and Long-term Decision Making*, at www.parliament.uk (18/09/14).

Kay, J. (2013) 'Directors have a duty beyond just enriching shareholders', *Financial Times*, 6 June.

McCrum, D. and Burgess, K. (2012) 'Shareholders lose patience on executive pay', *Financial Times*, 21 April.

Milne, R. (2013) 'Model management', *Financial Times*, 21 March.

Murray, S. (2013) 'Short-term tone in traditional MBA teaching begins to fade', *Financial Times*, 8 July.

Oakley, D. (2013) 'Up in arms', *Financial Times*, 8 April.

PwC (2012) *Making Executive Pay Work: The Psychology of Incentives*, at www.pwc.com (18/09/14).

Stout, L. (2012) *The Shareholder Value Myth* (San Francisco: Berrett-Koehler).

The Economist (2011) 'Milton Friedman goes on tour', *The Economist*, 27 January, at www.economist.com (18/09/14).

Yermack, D. (2006) 'Flights of fancy: Corporate jets, CEO perquisites and inferior shareholder returns', *Journal of Financial Economics*, 80(1): 211–42.

REVIEW QUESTIONS

1 Compare the private company and the public company in terms of corporate governance.

2 What are the characteristics of the shareholder primacy model of the company?

3 What are the main tenets of agency theory that support the shareholder primacy model? What criticisms can be made of agency theory in this context?

4 In what ways has shareholder primacy undermined business ethics?

5 What is the US view of company directors' duties, and to what extent does it support business ethics?

6 Why do some company founders opt for two classes of shares when they launch IPOs? Do you approve or disapprove of this policy?

7 How has the profile of the shareholder in British equities changed over the years?

8 What is the 'enlightened shareholder' view of directors' duties in Britain? How could it be interpreted as incorporating stakeholder concerns?

9 How does a dual board structure promote a stakeholder model of corporate governance? What are its drawbacks?

10 What are the pros and cons of market-based forms of remuneration, such as stock options, for executives?

11 Should shareholders have a binding vote on top executive pay, and why?

12 What are the arguments in favour of having an ethical code of practice in an organization, in order to promote an ethical culture?

SINGAPORE AND TEMASEK: A MODEL FOR SOVEREIGN WEALTH?

CLOSING CASE STUDY

Since its independence in 1965, the city state of Singapore has become one of Asia's most stunning economic success stories. It has risen from the ranks of developing countries to global economic status, with GDP per capita over $50,000, making it one of the world's richest economies. Among its location advantages are an open economy, which welcomes foreign investors, and its business-friendly environment, with low taxation and a burgeoning financial services sector. With its growing strength in trade, Singapore has benefited from strong economic growth in Asia. It is perceived as politically stable and enjoys a high ranking of 5 in the corruption perceptions index, above Switzerland, its more established rival in attracting global wealth (Transparency International, 2012). Mirroring Singapore's surging economy has been the growth of its sovereign wealth fund, Temasek Holdings, founded in 1974. Temasek's rise, like that of Singapore as a country, has been impressive. However, national economic success is not measured merely by corporate performance, but should be viewed in the context of the social, economic and political realities of the society. In these respects, Singapore and Temasek present a mixed picture.

Photo 8.2 Business and political élites in Singapore have enjoyed the prosperity and stability prevailing in the city-state, exemplified by its impressive skyline, but there are signs of tension in society and a questioning of what interests companies should be serving. (PhotoDisc/Getty Images)

Temasek prides itself on having grown with 'Singapore's transformation from third world to first' (Temesek, 2013). It was founded to take over government-controlled businesses from the Ministry of Finance. Temasek is registered as a commercial company in Singapore, but is wholly owned by the Singapore government. It has only one shareholder, the Ministry of Finance, which reaps all shareholder returns. It is a private company under Singapore law, and is therefore not required to make financial disclosures. However, it has taken the initiative to issue limited financial statements to the public. Its investment portfolio now totals the equivalent of US$173 billion, mostly in equities, and it also issues bonds. At the outset, its holdings were mainly in Singapore, where it is a major shareholder in leading industries, but it has turned its investment strategy towards Asia with the rise of these emerging economies. Other Asian countries now account for 41% of its portfolio. It is a major investor in Standard Chartered Bank, and an investor in several large Chinese banks. Temasek describes itself as 'an active owner and investor', and it commits itself to long-term goals in the

companies in which it invests, which have been mainly in sectors such as finance, trade and services. However, it does not seek representation on the boards of the companies it invests in (Temasek, 2013). Temasek has become more globalized in its investment strategy in recent years, widening its portfolio to companies around the world, notably in North America and Europe. Despite its globalization in terms of strategy, however, its governance roots lie in Singapore, where links between leading business families and the state remain the dominant forces in business.

Corporate governance in Singapore, as in other countries, was shaken by the financial crisis of 2008. Temasek saw a decline of $85 billion in its share portfolio as the world's stock markets plummeted. The country has adopted corporate governance codes which echo UK counterparts, aiming to ensure investors that boards of listed companies have a mix of executive and independent members. The latest version of its code of corporate governance dates from 2012 (MAS, 2012). It includes a general code and one for financial institutions. These codes help to give the country top ranking in Asia for corporate governance, but still raise doubts when judged by global standards (KPMG, 2011). The 'independent' director must be independent of major shareholders in the codes of the UK, Australia and Hong Kong, but not in Singapore. There, connection with a shareholder owning under 10% of the company's equity is considered independent. While these other countries require half the board to be independent, Singapore's rule is that only one-third of directors need be independent, except in exceptional circumstances, where, for example, the chairman and CEO are the same person or are in the same immediate family.

It is often the case in corporate governance structures that the formalities present an ideal picture, but the reality behind the forms tells a different story. This observation, made by the chairman of Singapore's Institute of Directors, is particularly relevant in Singapore (KPMG, 2011). Robert Zoellick, the former head of the World Bank, was made an independent non-executive director of Temesek in 2013, and commented at the time on the high standards of its corporate governance (Reuters, 2013). Temasek's board of 10 members has five independent directors, but most of these, and its executive directors, have Singapore backgrounds. Temasek's CEO, Ho Ching, is the wife of the Prime Minister. She announced she was stepping down in 2009, a difficult period following the global financial crisis. Chip Goodyear, former CEO of Australian mining giant BHP Billiton, was appointed as Temasek's new CEO, but three months before he was due to take over, his appointment was cancelled, and Ho Ching continued in office. The appointment of the company's first foreign CEO would have reflected Temasek's growing global ambitions, but it seemed that political pressures came into play to veto the appointment (Businessweek, 2009). Singapore's political establishment has dominated state institutions since the country's independence.

Singapore as a state is formally democratic, but it has been dominated by a single political party for over five decades. The People's Action Party (PAP), under the founding leader, Lee Kuan Yew, has promoted huge economic progress and also improved quality of life for Singapore society, especially evident in its education system. However, these successes have come at a cost of suppression of political freedom and rising inequality. Freedoms of speech, association and religion are guaranteed in the Singapore constitution, but all have suffered from authoritarian incursions. In terms of media freedom, Singapore ranks 149 out of 179 in the world, according to the Press Freedom rankings of Reporters Without Borders, which charts the levels of freedom of information around the world (RWB, 2013). Singapore's ranking places it in a similar position to Russia, Burma and Gambia. Suppression of freedom of expression is a worrying indicator for a country which considers itself on a par with other developed countries. Government controls of press, radio, television and internet have curtailed the activities of civil society organizations such as political parties which seek a democratic voice. Nonetheless, the opposition Workers Party took 8 seats out of the total of 87 in elections to the parliament in 2011. The PAP took 81 seats, although it had only 60% of the vote. Its declining popularity is an indication of grassroots dissatisfaction with manipulated elections in a country with no independent election monitoring. It is thought that, despite government censorship of the internet, the use of social media has helped opposition political parties to spread their views.

Growing unease is also evident in society, as the gap between the very rich and the rest widens (OECD, 2011). The country's education system and cultural heritage stress meritocracy in education, but its economy has seen growing inequality. Economic growth has encouraged immigration, often from poor countries, for example, construction workers from Bangladesh. The plight of poor immigrants, often hired through employment agencies, has come to the attention of human rights NGOs. Human Rights Watch has highlighted the fact that Singapore's hundreds of thousands of domestic workers working for families, do not have recognized employment rights. They are almost all women and are mostly from poor countries such as the Philippines and Sri Lanka. Although a new law entitles them to one rest day per week, this still does not bring Singapore up to international standards as set out in the ILO convention of 2011. Singapore has sought to attract immigrants to fuel its growing economy, but the government is concerned that they should not be so numerous as to pose a threat to Singapore society. A strike by Chinese bus drivers for better pay and conditions in 2012 was perhaps a sign that these groups wish to exert a voice and assert claims to a slice of the prosperity which economic growth is bringing the country. Four of their leaders were jailed.

Singapore's prime minister has said that if he could persuade another 10 billionaires to move to Singapore, this would be a good thing, even if it worsened income inequality, as billionaires bring the businesses that will create new jobs (Grant, 2013). Singapore's billionaires are enjoying the benefits of low tax and a banking system which is actively seeking wealthy individuals. The country has successfully transformed itself into a location which both foreign businesses and wealthy individuals find attractive. There have been setbacks, such as the intense smog which blanketed the city state in 2013, generally thought to have been caused by forest clearance in nearby Indonesia. A number of the companies cited as instrumental in the fires are registered in Singapore. Corporate governance codes in Singapore focus on shareholder relations and wealth maximization, rather than stakeholder concerns. The notion of CSR for Singapore's companies is focused on philanthropic activities, which are voluntary. A prominent Singapore businessperson has said, 'Corporate governance has nothing to do with other stakeholders' (KPMG. 2011). The corporate governance codes reflect this view, as other stakeholders are hardly mentioned. As a sovereign wealth fund, Temasek might be expected to view CSR as responsibility to the Singapore society, but its focus is framed in terms of shareholder returns. It speaks of communities in terms of its philanthropic activities associated with its investments. Good corporate governance is as much about values and culture as it is about forms. A highly unequal society with limited political freedom and suppression of freedom of expression has some distance to go in establishing corporate governance which recognizes social and ethical dimensions.

Sources: Transparency International (2012) *Corruption Perceptions Index 2012*, at www.transparency.org; Temasek (2013) *Beyond Investing: Review of 2013*, at www.temasek.com; KPMG (2011) *Singapore's Corporate Governance Transformed: The Strategy to Get it Right*, at www.kpmg.com; Reuters (2013) *Former World Bank President Robert Zoellick is to Join the Board of Singapore State Investor Temasek Holdings, 31 July*, at www.reuters.com; Businessweek (2009) *Goodyear's Shock Exit from Temasek*, 22 July, at www.businessweek.com; RWB (2013) *Press Freedom Index 2013*, at www.rsf.org; OECD (2011) *Society at a Glance: Asia Pacific*, at www.oecd.org; Grant, J. (2013) 'Billionaires add to Singapore inequality concerns', *Financial Times*, 8 July; MAS (Monetary Authority of Singapore (2012) *Code of Corporate Governance*, at www.mas.gov.sg (18/09/14).

DISCUSSION QUESTIONS

□ What are the pros and cons of Temasek's corporate governance?

□ It what ways are inequality and weakness in CSR perspectives linked?

□ Do you agree with the view of Singapore's prime minister in his wish to attract more billionaires? Why?

CHAPTER 9
HUMAN RIGHTS AND
ETHICAL BUSINESS

OUTLINE OF THE CHAPTER

Introduction

Ethical foundations of human rights

- From natural law to human rights
- The concept of human rights

Human rights in the global context

- Balancing state and international frameworks
- A legal turning point: the Universal Declaration of Human Rights

Evolving frameworks for business and human rights

- Companies and human rights obligations
- Comparing CSR and legal frameworks

Corporate responsibility: the legal routes

Human rights in business contexts

- The right not to be subject to inhuman treatment
- Reducing child labour
- Right of association and membership of trade unions
- The living wage: a human right?

Conclusions

ETHICAL THEMES IN THIS CHAPTER

- Interplay between the individual and society
- Businesses as part of society

THE AIMS OF THIS CHAPTER ARE TO

- Trace the ethical foundations of human rights
- Appreciate international and national human rights frameworks in relation to businesses
- Assess corporate legal and moral responsibility in human rights
- Apply human rights law in a variety of key business contexts

A BETTER LIFE FOR WALMART WORKERS?

Walmart has one mission: 'save money; live better' (Walmart, 2013). As the world's largest retailer, cost-cutting has been the centrepiece of its business model since it was founded in 1962. This message has resonated in America's poorer areas, mostly rural, where its roots lie. It has also spread to a wider spectrum of American consumers as the financial crisis squeezed household budgets. While many businesses suffered from reduced consumer spending, Walmart gained new customers. However, cost-cutting is multifaceted, benefiting consumers but at a cost to workers. While it claims to help consumers to 'live better', those consumers are often people employed in low-paid jobs with little prospect of a better life. Moreover, consumers as taxpayers help to fund the schemes such as food stamps which are needed to supplement the low wages of Walmart workers. Walmart has thus come under fire for its employment practices, both at home and in its supply chain.

Photo 9.1 *Workers whose wages are below the poverty line highlight a new awareness of the links between a living wage and human rights.*

In 2001, a Walmart cashier, Betty Dukes, launched a case against the company for sex discrimination, claiming that, despite good performance reviews, she was left behind for promotion while men were promoted. She was not alone. Hers was a class action lawsuit on behalf of many other women in a similar position across the US. Her lawyers pointed to evidence that the company systematically underpaid and underpromoted women in comparison with male colleagues. The case was successful in the lower courts of the judicial system, but Walmart appealed every decision. The case reached the Supreme Court in 2011, where, by a majority of 5 to 4, the judges decided the class action lawsuit could not be heard. The majority judges held that individual cases are all different and cannot therefore be dealt with as a class. The court also said that the complainants must prove the company had a general policy of discrimination, which had been impossible to show (Mears, 2011). The legal precedents for class actions have been well established, as the minority judges pointed out, and this new stricter interpretation of what plaintiffs must prove, seems intended to limit future class actions generally. This decision, which was welcomed by businesses generally, lowers the prospects of success in discrimination cases filed by all those who suffer discrimination, including people of colour and Hispanic

people. Walmart denies discrimination. However, under Walmart management practices, local store managers take decisions over pay and promotion, and their decisions can reflect their own personal views as much as objective criteria.

Walmart is America's largest private-sector employer. Its 1.3 million employees, known as 'associates', are among the lowest paid workers in the US. Hourly rates vary, but are usually in the region of $8, slightly over the federal minimum wage of $7.25. The federal minimum wage has not been changed for four years, and it is generally accepted that it is too low to live on. Individual states set minimum wages themselves, but most are not much above the federal minimum. In the last two years, Walmart workers in many cities across the US have staged walkouts and protests, calling for a minimum hourly rate of $12, which would amount to annual pay of about $25,000, still below the poverty line, but better than the norm for most of these low-paid workers. In 2013, 200 workers demonstrated with banners asking for respect outside the headquarters of Walmart in Bentonville, Arkansas, as shareholders were gathering for the AGM. Workers who strike are perceived as trouble-makers and commonly face either dismissal or disciplinary action, although the company invariably claims sackings and disciplinary actions are for other reasons. Walmart has a record of dealing harshly with those who strike, attempt to organize trade union activities, or even raise grievances. One worker, Raymond Bravo, employed as a janitor in a California Walmart store, was sacked after going on strike. He says he took part in protests because he saw co-workers suffering: 'Three days before payday I would see people who normally eat not eating', he said (McVeigh, 2013). He goes on to say, 'I was fired for going on strike, for speaking out … They told me it was for missing days, but in America you can go on strike and you are protected' (McVeigh, 2013).

In theory, American workers have labour rights guaranteed in legislation going back to 1933, but Walmart and other large employers are able to flout the law because sanctions are minimal. Employees making complaints can go to the National Labour Relations Board with their complaints. There are many complaints pending against Walmart, but the process can take years, and, if the worker wins, the result is a relatively modest fine for the company – a weak deterrent for a multi-billion dollar company like Walmart. It might be required to reinstate an employee, but would not be liable for back pay.

The council of the District of Columbia, in which Washington, the capital, is located, voted in 2013 to raise the minimum wage for workers in large retail stores to $12.50 an hour, which was intended to be a 'living wage'. This was double the city's minimum wage in other types of employment. At the time, Walmart was building three new stores, which would potentially offer employment to hundreds of people. The company announced that it would not go through with the projects if the living wage bill was passed. The mayor vetoed it.

Walmart's low-pay strategy benefits consumers through low prices at the tills, but the costs to consumers through taxes are less obvious. Walmart employees are one of the largest groups of people in receipt of food stamps, which is a federal government scheme to subsidize food for the poor. These low-paid workers are also more likely than others to make use of state health funding such as Medicaid, a federal health insurance scheme for the poor. A new compulsory healthcare insurance programme is designed to provide safety-net insurance for these vulnerable people, but has been resisted by many large companies such as Walmart, which would have to pay into the scheme.

Walmart's profits are generated mainly by its 4,600 stores in the US, which yield 70% of its sales. Its cost-cutting strategy has involved it in adverse publicity over the harsh conditions in supplier factories, including manufacturers in China and garment factories in Bangladesh, where many workers have lost their lives in unsafe buildings and fires. Should the company be responsible? A traditional view is that it is the job of the government to deal with safety issues and employment practices such as child labour. However, western consumers increasingly blame western brand owners. Walmart's expansion in the fast-growing emerging markets has also given rise to scrutiny of its expansion policies. It has faced bribery allegations in Brazil, China, India and Mexico, where it has been accused of paying bribes to acquire permits for new stores.

Employees calling for a living wage and a voice are forming a growing chorus for human rights in an increasingly unequal society. Walmart's dominant owners, the Walton family, are America's richest family, worth an estimated $100 billion. Through astute manipulation of inheritance tax rules, this vast dynastic wealth is passed on to future generations of the family, with minimal tax bills to pay (Mider, 2013). Against the background of the Walton fortune, reminiscent of the nineteenth-century resources barons, there is the growing scandal of poverty among low-paid workers, along with breaches of both ethical standards and labour law, national and international. Two European pension funds decided in 2013 to divest their stakes in Walmart on the grounds that the company does not treat employees in accordance with international standards of freedom of association. Many other investors around the world are now querying Walmart on ethical grounds.

Sources: Jopson, B. (2012) 'Walmart extends corruption inquiries', *Financial Times*, 16 November; Mider, A. (2013) 'How Wal-Mart's Waltons maintain their billionaire fortune', *Bloomberg News*, 12 September, at www.bloomberg.com; Walmart (2013) *Annual Report 2013*, at www.walmart.com; Mears, B. (2011) 'Supreme Court rules for Wal-Mart in massive job discrimination lawsuit', *CNN News*, 21 June, at www.cnn.com; Edelson, J. (2013) 'How Wal-Mart keeps wages low', *The Washington Post*, 12 September, at www.washingtonpost.com; McVeigh, K. (2013) 'Walmart workers protest over minimum wage in 15 US cities', *The Guardian*, 5 September, at www.theguardian.com (18/09/14).

DISCUSSION QUESTIONS

▫ Can a living wage be considered a human right, and if so, is the employer responsible for providing it?

▫ Compare Walmart's low-cost strategy with a strategy which would focus on CSR. What changes would be entailed in the ways Walmart is run?

▫ To what extent could reputational damage affect Walmart in terms of the areas of human rights and ethics highlighted in this case study?

INTRODUCTION

Human rights are closely associated with notions of justice. They are key to relations between the individual person or a group of people and the state. The state has a responsibility for implementing human rights. Businesses have often taken the approach that the laws of states therefore define the human rights obligations they owe in their differing national locations. This narrow view of human rights is undergoing transformation in two ways which are highlighted in this chapter. The first is the recognition of ethical principles in relation to business activities, with or without legal backup. The second way is the increasing importance of legal and regulatory frameworks at a global level. International law and governance frameworks to which states commit themselves impose obligations on all organizations. The business can no longer defend the use of child labour by saying that it is legal in a particular country. If it is prohibited in international law, these higher standards should guide the business, underpinned by inherent ethical principles.

This chapter begins with a discussion of the ethical foundations of human rights and examines the different ways of classifying the wide range of rights. It then looks at the relationship between CSR and stakeholder approaches to human rights obligations. We turn next to the ways in which these principles apply in practice. We will find that legal as well as moral liabilities are becoming important for corporate strategists. The final section focuses on key human rights in business contexts, where we find that companies still have much to do to bring their practices into line with their stated principles.

ETHICAL FOUNDATIONS OF HUMAN RIGHTS

Of the ethical theorists discussed in the first chapter, the one which is perhaps most closely identified with an idea of human rights is Kant. His focus on human dignity as framed in the categorical imperative encapsulates human rights as a concept. Every rational being, he said, exists as 'an end in himself, not merely as a means for arbitrary use by this or that will' (Kant, 1948: 105). This he describes as the dignity of every human being and the basis of morality. The idea of human dignity is often found in religions, and for many, religious beliefs are the source of duties towards other people. For Kant, the source of moral duty is universal law. Kant falls within the broad group of philosophers who believe in natural law, a law which is essentially moral and transcends the law of states. This tradition has a long history, and includes distinguished religious writers among their number. From their beginnings in

Greek philosophy, natural law theories have evolved over the centuries. Only in more recent eras, notably the seventeenth century and the era of revolutions, has natural law come to be linked to rights. Kant was not a revolutionary thinker in the way that Locke was (see Chapter 3 for a discussion of Locke). But Kant's views on human dignity have an affinity with those of Locke and his theory of natural rights.

The idea of a higher moral law is the foundation of today's thinking on human rights. This way of thinking has often been challenged. To some, it seems to be simply abstract ideals, and, although claiming to be universal, is clearly the product of particular western thinkers, who reflect their own ideas of right and wrong. There is a tension between the believers in universal law and those who deny its existence. The latter group includes positivists, who view only positive laws as 'real', and cultural relativists, who say that there is no universal right and wrong, only moral norms in particular cultures. The tension between the universalists and their opponents is not confined to philosophical circles. It influences thinking on social issues, and has impacted on businesses in their ethical policies. We will consider both sides in this debate, but look first at how thinking on human rights has evolved.

FROM NATURAL LAW TO HUMAN RIGHTS

Ancient Greece is thought of as the home of citizenship rights. Citizens of its city states enjoyed equality before the law and freedom of speech, both of which we value today. But we would consider these to be human rights, not just citizenship rights. The Greeks, too, had a notion of rights that belong to all people, simply because they human and rational (Lauterpacht, 1943). In *Antigone*, Sophocles wrote of rights that exist independently of the state: if what the state commands is wrong, then there is no obligation to obey (Cranston, 1973). There is thus a potential conflict between 'what is' and 'what ought to be'. Higher law came to be referred to as natural law. It was recognized in Roman legal doctrines, and it was adopted by medieval Christian thinkers. Aquinas saw natural law as the law of God, but stresses its universality. He said, 'the law of nature, as far as general first principles are concerned, is the same for all as the norm of right conduct and is equally well known to all' (Aquinas, 1965: 123). In the centuries which followed, ideas of natural law became decoupled from religious beliefs.

'The law of nature, as far as general first principles are concerned, is the same for all as the norm of right conduct and is equally well known to all.'

Natural rights theorists concentrated on individual rights, especially the rights referred to as 'negative freedoms', discussed in Chapter 3. Locke's notion of the right to life, liberty and property sums up the goals of the growing bourgeoisie, accumulating personal wealth and wishing to enjoy it, but encountering resistance from an entrenched establishment. The convulsions of revolutionary Europe and America overthrew a world of hereditary entitlement, aspiring to enshrine in its place systems which rewarded individual endeavour. Hand in hand with the new liberal view of the dignity of the individual were the beliefs that governments should allow people maximum freedom in which to pursue their goals, and that governments should be accountable to the people. The social contract, which has featured in numerous theories discussed in this book, signifies an agreement between the individual and the state, in which obligations and rights arise on both sides. The familiar freedoms, such as freedom of speech, the press and religion, are legacies of this period. They signify areas of individual freedom in which states should not interfere. Also important were ideas of due process and the rule of law.

The individualistic perception of human nature became a pillar of utilitarian thinking, despite the fact that Bentham viewed natural rights as 'nonsense on stilts' (Cranston, 1973: 13). Rights, he held firmly, were confined to those recognized in law, not those claiming moral status. However, as we have seen in Chapter 1, other utilitarian thinkers, such as John Stuart Mill, considered that moral and social dimensions are integral to human nature. Mill was concerned that the egoistic view of human nature espoused by the utilitarians was too narrow, and that the development of the individual encompassed ideas of morality and justice. The egoism postulated by the utilitarians was highly influential in the ethical foundations of capitalism, as we have seen in Chapter 2, but criticisms of this view of human nature have long existed. Natural rights in the Locke tradition derive from individualist thinking, but remain underpinned in their ethical foundations by natural law. This heritage is often overlooked, probably because we tend not to speak of natural law any longer. However, the concept remains alive and relevant, in that it invokes a sense of moral authority which is universal.

Individualist societies tend to place individual natural rights over community values and ideas of social justice. Rawls is a striking example of a modern liberal theorist who stresses that social justice is inseparable from natural rights. The tension between western liberal views of rights and the more collectivist view of rights in terms of social needs is a thread that has run through post-war human rights discourse. This tension was particularly evident in the cold-war era. With the collapse of the Soviet Union, the tension now resides more in conflicts between individualism, sometimes depicted as western cultural imperialism, and value systems that retain an emphasis on the person as belonging to a collective identity. That identity can be cultural, as in Asian cultural environments, or religious, as in Islam (Steiner and Alston, 2000: 368). Human rights are now viewed in a social context, which has contributed to an extension of the concept, to cover rights which are identified with peoples and societies.

PAUSE TO CONSIDER...

Compare Kant's view of natural rights with that of the utilitarians. Which, in your view, is closer to a concept of 'human rights'?

THE CONCEPT OF HUMAN RIGHTS

The idea of human rights rests on the premise that all people have human rights simply because each is a person. They rest on the assumption that some things are inherently bad and some inherently good. It is probably easier to identify things which are bad for every human being than to identify those that are good (Perry, 1997). The extreme cultural relativist takes the view that good and bad exist only as defined in particular cultural contexts. This position is difficult to defend when one looks at types of activity such as murder, torture, genocide, slavery, starvation and homelessness. These wrongs are wrongs to all human beings, regardless of culture.

'These working conditions and astonishing number of deaths of vulnerable people go beyond forced labour to slavery of old where human beings were treated as objects.'

The plight of the world's millions of migrant workers highlights these issues. Migrant labourers are to be seen in the large construction projects throughout the Middle East. In Qatar, human rights investigators have found that some Nepalese constructions workers working in 50-degree heat are being denied drinking water. They suffer from lack of food and squalid living conditions; their pay is often withheld; and many have had their passports confiscated, to prevent them leaving the country

(Pattisson, 2013). No one would deny that such treatment is in violation of their dignity as human beings. The head of an anti-slavery group has said, 'These working conditions and astonishing number of deaths of vulnerable people go beyond forced labour to slavery of old where human beings were treated as objects' (Pattisson, 2013).

The ILO has observed that Qatar ratified the convention against forced labour in 2007, but has not taken steps to enforce it in respect of the living standards and working practices which should apply to migrant labourers (Booth et al., 2013). The Nepalese workers are hired through middlemen and are employed by companies which are subcontracted by western companies that manage the projects. Lawyers in London have launched legal proceedings for human rights breaches against some of the British companies involved. Both Qatari and Nepalese governments have denied the accusations of human rights violations. Nepal is in an ambivalent position. Over 300,000 Nepalese work in Qatar, and their remittances to families back in Nepal amount to 25% of GDP (World Bank, 2013). As this example shows, enforcing human rights in a globalized business environment can be complicated. The rights are universal, but the legal processes are based in national systems. National governments are key players in the recognition and enforcement of human rights, often working in co-operation with private-sector companies. However, from the point of view of victims, the multiple centres of responsibility make it more difficult to find any one of them ultimately liable.

Every society, whatever the culture, has values and norms which people are expected to abide by. Even in Hobbes' state of nature, characterized by the war of all against all, people as rational beings could perceive that society would be destined for self-destruction if they did not co-operate to protect property and people from invasion by others. The social contract theory of Donaldson and Dunfee (introduced in Chapter 7) highlighted basic 'hypernorms', on which all are agreed, and other areas of behaviour, which are moral free space (Donaldson and Dunfee, 1994).

Donaldson and Dunfee show that while ideas about what is bad for all human beings stand out, ideas about what is good, by contrast, are more varied. The vision of a good life in one culture is not shared by others. Perry makes the point that pluralism exists happily alongside universalism (Perry, 1997: 473). All people have social and biological needs. All people desire recognition for achievement, co-operation from others, a place in the community, and a wish to be respected as a person. Kant, a universalist, noted that – with no sense of strain – people have varying ideas of happiness. Perry says, 'a conception of human good ... can be, and should be, universalist as well as pluralist: it can acknowledge sameness as well as difference, commonality as well as variety' (Perry, 1997: 473). Universalism and cultural relativism are therefore not as antithetical as they might seem. Wide acceptance of international human rights conventions shows there is a consensus on universal wrongs, and all societies share at least some ideas about what a good life is. However, countries diverge in interpreting the very broad principles in which human rights are set out, and in how they are implemented in practice. Indeed, some countries seem to tolerate blatant violations of human rights conventions which they have ratified. Human rights violations occur worldwide, despite the proliferation of international conventions.

In the case of migrant workers on construction sites such as those in Qatar, which parties are most to blame, in your view, and why?

Photo 9.2 These migrant construction workers in Dubai, mostly from India, Pakistan and Bangladesh, endure 12-hour working days, often in searing heat, and live in cramped conditions in camps far from the construction sites.
(© iStock.com/EdStock)

HUMAN RIGHTS IN A GLOBAL CONTEXT

The place of human rights in international legal and political frameworks is constantly evolving. As this section will show, international governance is gaining in legitimacy, but state authorities remain powerful, creating a continuing sense of tension.

BALANCING STATE AND INTERNATIONAL FRAMEWORKS

The UN Charter affirms in its preamble a faith in 'fundamental human rights, in the dignity and worth of the human person, in the equal rights of men and women and of nations large and small'. It also states a commitment to establish means for maintaining 'justice and respect for the obligations arising from treaties and other sources of international law'. The Charter notably does not rely on any justification in natural law or religion. It simply affirms the existence of fundamental human rights. A further point to note is that it expresses a commitment to the means for implementing them in practice. In citing both treaties and other sources of international law, it paved the way for developments which would gradually lead to greater international authority in human rights. State autonomy has been a foundation principle of the UN, but international frameworks are evolving, as shown Figure 9.1.

Figure 9.1 *International human rights frameworks*

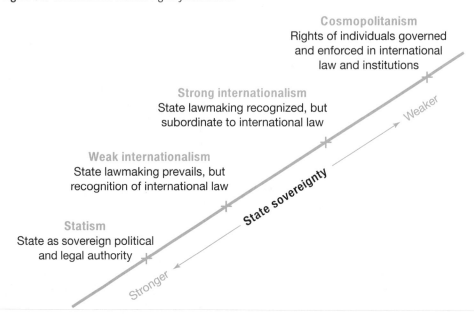

Figure 9.1 shows a continuum from statist to international frameworks. The statist position is based exclusively on state sovereignty, with no recognition of international authorities which can bind state players (Donnelly, 1998). Sovereign political and legal institutions prevail in every jurisdiction. This extreme position has probably never existed in the pure form depicted in the figure. At the opposite extreme is the cosmopolitan position, which envisages a global community and global institutions in which state actors have receded into the background. Cosmopolitanism is associated with extreme views of globalization, in that state sovereignty is seen as losing its force and its authority. Some theorists of cosmopolitanism see cultural differences melting away as people acquire a sense of global community. In reality, cultural differences remain potent forces, and state actors remain significant, but international institutions are also gaining in authority. There is thus a balance between global and state-centric outlooks, represented by the two middle positions in the continuum. The middle positions are both forms of internationalism. Where internationalism is weak, state institutions prevail, but international law can play a role, influencing the direction of national law and constituting moral standards against which national law is assessed. Where internationalism is strong, international law is binding on states, and there are legal institutions such as international courts, through which people can bring cases of violations of human rights. The decisions of those courts would then be binding on state actors. In today's world, the international framework for human rights probably lies in the range of weak internationalism, as states assert sovereignty but recognize international norms.

A LEGAL AND MORAL TURNING POINT: THE UNIVERSAL DECLARATION OF HUMAN RIGHTS

At international level, multilateral human rights treaties are a core source of law and are also important for articulating ethical principles. Legally, they are supplemented by other sources of international law, including customary law (which was noted in Chapter 4). The area of human rights law is relatively recent. The first important instrument is the Universal Declaration of Human Rights (UDHR), approved by the UN General Assembly in 1948. It remains the benchmark statement of principles, which are shown in Figure 9.2. It was not designed to be a legal instrument itself, but was the basis of the two main human rights conventions, the International Covenant on Civil and Political Rights (ICCPR) and the International Covenant on Economic, Social and Cultural Rights (ICESCR). Their provisions are set out in Chapter 4. The three documents together are often described as the International Bill of Human Rights. The UDHR is the foundational document and perhaps the most highly regarded of the three as an authoritative statement of rights. The two covenants followed much later. Only in 1976 were they ratified by enough states to become international law. As the original statement of principles, the UDHR has come to be regarded as legally binding. Some have said it has achieved the status of customary international law, which rests on state practice recognized over time (Steiner and Alston, 2000: 143). However, given the relatively short space of time in which it has been in existence, it might be more appropriate to attribute its legal authority to the consensus which it enjoys among states (Henkin, 1995).

The main areas covered by the UDHR are shown in Figure 9.2. In addition to the traditional natural rights, there are social and economic rights, which appear in the two boxes on the right of the figure. They represent a positive view of rights in comparison to the negative freedoms of traditional rights discourse. It is noteworthy that rights of democratic political participation are included in the declaration. The UDHR seems particularly relevant in today's world. It stresses that any limitations of rights and freedoms are justified only insofar as needed to ensure the rights of others in a democratic society, warning that, even in a democracy, the state can become oppressive and risk undermining the democratic values on which it is based. The UDHR imposes obligations to respect human rights of

Figure 9.2 *The Universal Declaration of Human Rights: one concept, many rights*

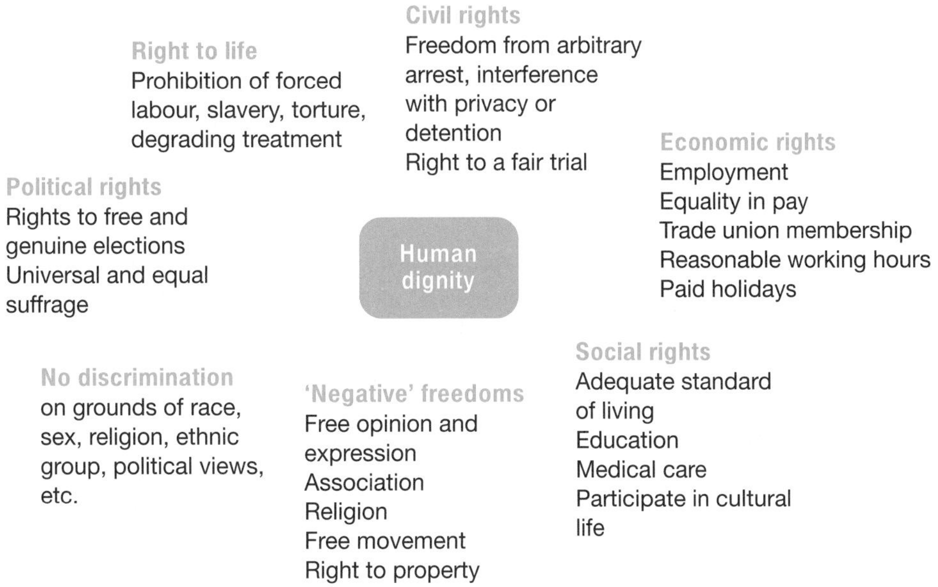

Right to life
Prohibition of forced labour, slavery, torture, degrading treatment

Civil rights
Freedom from arbitrary arrest, interference with privacy or detention
Right to a fair trial

Economic rights
Employment
Equality in pay
Trade union membership
Reasonable working hours
Paid holidays

Political rights
Rights to free and genuine elections
Universal and equal suffrage

Human dignity

No discrimination
on grounds of race, sex, religion, ethnic group, political views, etc.

'Negative' freedoms
Free opinion and expression
Association
Religion
Free movement
Right to property

Social rights
Adequate standard of living
Education
Medical care
Participate in cultural life

'every individual and every organ of society', which would encompass various types of organization, including corporations (Muchlinski, 2001: 40). In terms of enforcement, it states that 'everyone is entitled to a social and international order in which the rights and freedoms set forth in this Declaration can be fully realized'. This statement that people individually should be able to enforce rights turned out to be rather optimistic: it was deleted from the two covenants which followed.

The delegates to the UN who drafted and promoted the universal declaration saw enforcement as a priority, advocating an international court of human rights, which would preside over cases of alleged violations. Moreover, they stipulated that individuals and organizations, as well as states, would have access to the court. In 1950, the UN Commission on Human Rights was to proceed with formulating these enforcement measures. But opinion shifted, and, in the course of drafting the two covenants, it became clear that leading countries would not support such radical proposals, which appeared to encroach on state sovereignty. In the end, the US and UK both opposed setting up the court and allowing individual legal actions for violations. They considered that only states should be parties to international law, and that, if individuals are allowed rights of petition, this would constitute a threat to national sovereignty.

These arguments now look rather thin. The European Convention on Human Rights, which dates from 1950, did provide for the setting up of a court, which could hear petitions from individuals and companies. International law recognizes wrongs by individuals and against individuals, as shown in the Nuremberg trials, which tried former Nazis for war crimes (Clapham, 1993: 95). The Nuremberg court said, 'crimes against international law are committed by men, not by abstract entities, and only by punishing individuals who commit such crimes can the provisions of international law be enforced' (Clapham, 1993: 96). The delegates would have been familiar with these proceedings. Sovereign states regularly recognize obligations under treaties, and because this commitment is voluntary, it does not constitute a limitation of sovereignty. The proposed court could have been based on the principle of complementarity, by which national courts and international courts complement each other in human rights cases. This principle was put into practice decades later in the International Criminal Court in 1998 (see Chapter 4). In the covenants, upholding state sovereignty won out over enforcing human rights at international level. This might also explain why the delegates inserted into the two covenants rights to self-determination, which had been absent in the UDHR. The recoiling from international enforcement machinery, with hindsight, seemed to be a loss in terms of promoting recognition and enforcement of human rights in the world. As delegates would have been well aware, some of the most egregious violations of human rights are carried out by states. This remains true today.

'Crimes against international law are committed by men, not by abstract entities, and only by punishing individuals who commit such crimes can the provisions of international law be enforced.'

The universal declaration envisages all people being able to enforce human rights in an 'international order' (UDHR, Article 28). The two covenants which followed, by contrast, state that all state parties to the covenants undertake to introduce legislation to give effect to the rights. Cultural relativists would have been encouraged, as the notion of universal law appeared to have been diluted. Human rights were acknowledged, but the role of state actors remained crucial to their interpretation and enforcement. These developments were to have an enduring impact on the enforcement of human rights globally. For international business, they presented a situation in which companies could claim to be upholding human rights by adhering to national law in particular locations, even though national law and enforcement in some countries fell below standards stipulated in the UN conventions.

One might think that, as they are by definition universal, human rights would find a fuller recognition in a globalized world than in a fragmented world of sovereign states. However, as we have seen in looking at global corporate strategy, local differences are a source of competitive advantage. This strategy impacts on human rights. The two covenants have different perspectives. As noted in Chapter 4, the covenant on civil and political rights (the ICCPR) has been ratified by 167 states, but not China, while the covenant on economic and social rights (the ICESCR) has been ratified by 160 states, but not the US. Nonetheless, people in China are making their voices heard at grassroots level in areas associated with natural rights, such as freedom of expression and due process. At the same time, people in the US are increasingly concerned with welfare issues such as poverty, malnutrition, access to healthcare and decent working conditions, all of which feature in the ICESCR.

With hindsight, would it have been better to create an international court of human rights, to which anyone can come, or are human rights better protected through state authorities?

EVOLVING FRAMEWORKS FOR BUSINESS AND HUMAN RIGHTS

The idea that a business is part of society is one of the core precepts of CSR. This involvement in a society brings rights and also responsibilities. For large international businesses like MNEs, these relationships can become complicated, as they are involved in numerous societies, each of which has its own legal system and cultural context. Human rights are universal, but, for individuals who wish to bring claims, there is no global institution which is the ultimate interpreter, arbiter and enforcer. A citizen can bring claims for violations of citizenship rights in state courts; although many of these rights overlap with human rights, many do not. It has been said that human rights 'fit uncomfortably' with a system of sovereign states (Donnelly, 1998: 28).

We found in the last section that, although the rights declared in the UDHR were conceived as being enforceable in international institutions, the two covenants which followed re-affirmed a system of state sovereignty. Nonetheless, there has been a trend towards greater accountability for human rights violations at international level. This includes legal accountability and also moral responsibility, which increasingly plays a part in determining how businesses behave in situations involving potential violations of human rights.

COMPANIES AND HUMAN RIGHTS OBLIGATIONS

A company can be a beneficiary of human rights, and can seek redress if those rights are infringed (D'Amato, 1995). An example is intrusion by a state into its property rights. We have seen that companies in the US have been held to enjoy the right to free speech (see Chapter 3). Corporations have also been held to be entitled to a fair trial and privacy (Muchlinski, 2001: 33). Traditionally, states are parties to human rights conventions, and only states can be liable. However, increasingly companies are coming into the frame of liability for human rights violations. Here are some of the reasons:

○ The importance of human rights law outside the conventions, such as the UDHR, is growing. This trend is broadening the scope of authoritative international law, although, as noted below, there are contradictory precedents on whether companies are liable under customary international law in this area.

○ There is a growing perception that companies are social organizations with social responsibilities, as evidenced by, for example, the ILO Tripartite Declaration on MNEs and Social Policy of 1977 and the OECD Guidelines for MNEs of 1976. Neither of these is legally binding, but both create expectations of ethical behaviour. There are also UN Guiding Principles on Business and Human Rights, discussed below.

○ Many MNEs voluntarily adopt codes of conduct, some referring to the UDHR, which create expectations among consumers that standards will be observed. Ethical supplier standards adopted by retailers fall into this category.

○ National laws are becoming more stringent in implementing human rights conventions and enforcing them. Although the weak enforcement provisions of the two main covenants is an issue, the very fact of a state having to report and possibly be 'shamed' for non-compliance is a factor which weighs with governments (Henkin, 1995).

○ A shift in the view of the MNE as a private legal person is taking place, blurring the boundaries between public and private (Clapham, 1993). The global power exerted by some large companies, which see themselves, economically at least, as ascendant over states, has led to a perception that the power enjoyed by these companies should involve public accountability.

The blurring of public and private capacity is most obvious in situations where governments outsource public services to private-sector companies (see the Serco case study at the close of Chapter 7). State officials are directly liable for abuses in their prisons and centres for asylum seekers. But what is the position when the government outsources the operation to a private-sector company? The company might claim to be outside international law, but this claim will not constitute a defence. If the company's employees are accused of human rights abuses, they and the company are liable under the country's criminal and tort laws. In the UK, they would be liable under the Human Rights Act 1998, which incorporates the European Convention on Human Rights (ECHR).

States have responsibility under international human rights conventions to implement their provisions domestically. The state could be considered liable for infringements by a non-state actor with whom it collaborates, but states diverge on whether to recognize such liability. Some states have been accused of outsourcing activities to private-sector companies in order to distance themselves from human rights violations. As for the companies involved, they have indirect responsibility. But indirect responsibility is more akin to moral responsibility than legal liability. The victims might have little connection with the contractor. In the case of migrant labourers in Qatar, large construction companies registered in the UK and other western countries have numerous contracts with Qatari officials for building projects. But these companies contract with a plethora of small building companies in the location, many registered in foreign countries, including India and Egypt. These SMEs employ the labourers through agents (Booth, 2013).

Western MNEs tend to have in place policies such as CSR codes of conduct, which state that they do not tolerate human rights abuses. They also have supplier codes of conduct.

However, in practice, they might have little control over the various subcontractors and suppliers in foreign locations, and, if challenged in a legal claim for human rights violations, would argue that they had no direct knowledge or liability. MNEs would not have liability under the two main conventions, but it could be argued they have liability under evolving customary international law, especially the UDHR, which recognizes corporate liability. There are thus differing ways of looking at companies' responsibilities in the area of human rights.

COMPARING CSR AND LEGAL FRAMEWORKS

Most companies recognize the importance of human rights in principle, and would say they are against corporate activities involving breaches of human rights, such as forced labour. What is the best approach to ensure that human rights abuses do not occur? Divergent approaches are broadly depicted in Figure 9.3. On the left of the figure is a legal framework at international level, which involves penalties for non-compliance and legal liability for breaches. It would cover activities of subsidiaries and suppliers. Such a regime would run counter to the existing balance between sovereign states and international institutions. On the right is an approach which relies on companies' voluntary CSR policies. As the figure shows, the voluntarist approach is one in which companies have duties more associated with CSR. CSR tends to be viewed as management driven, focusing on considerations such as business reputation. This voluntary approach is arguably not appropriate in area of human rights, as human rights should not be viewed as voluntary (McCorquodale, 2009). A stronger approach is therefore called for, somewhere between the strict mandatory and the voluntary. For example, international standards backed up by monitoring by a UN agency would strengthen a voluntarist approach without overriding state authority. The UN has been active in attempting to bring MNEs within human rights frameworks, but challenges lie in achieving greater corporate accountability while retaining the state-centric framework of international human rights law.

Figure 9.3 *Divergent approaches to corporate responsibility in human rights*

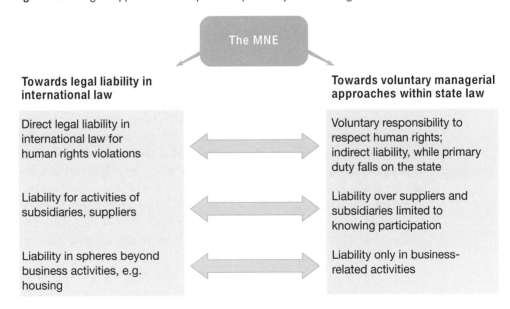

The UN launched a proposal for a robust regime for corporate liability in 2003. It was a set of guidelines known as the UN Norms on the Responsibility of Transnational Corporations and other Business Enterprises with respect to Human Rights. Drawing heavily on the UDHR, these norms would have fallen into the approach on the left in Figure 9.3, making companies directly liable for human rights violations, independently of states. A UN regime of enforcement was envisaged. The proposed norms, while welcomed by many human rights advocates, were resisted by many businesses and by many states (Bachmann and Miretski, 2012). The norms were seen as displacing the role of states in protecting human rights. They also sought to break new ground by creating liability of an MNE for activities within its 'sphere of influence', a term which was criticized for being too vague. This term was meant to pertain to suppliers and to other activities in which the company was involved, even if indirectly. These proposed norms were withdrawn in 2005.

Following this failed initiative, the UN appointed John Ruggie as Special Representative of the Secretary-General in the area of business and human rights. He carried out considerable research and produced a new document on guidelines, which was accepted by the Human Rights Council. A fierce critic of the failed proposal on norms, Ruggie based the new guidelines on his 'Protect, Respect and Remedy Framework' (Whelan et al., 2009). Ruggie's approach favoured a voluntary regime which relied on self-regulation, and was thus more in line with that shown on the right in Figure 9.3.

The Guiding Principles on Human Rights (UNGPHR) were issued in 2011 (UN Human Rights Council, 2011). The UNGPHR takes the view that companies have corporate responsibility associated with 'expected conduct' in respect of human rights. This would be 'over and above' what is required in national laws. Referring to the 'due diligence' expected of companies, it says companies should take care to ensure that they identify, prevent and mitigate adverse impacts. They should provide that victims have access to remedies such as grievance mechanisms. It urges companies to have a stated policy on human rights. On the problems of extended supply chains, the Guiding Principles state it might be 'unreasonably difficult' to identify all the possible adverse human rights impacts. In these situations, companies should identify the areas where the risk is most significant, and focus on them. Advocates of stronger action against MNEs whose suppliers are accused of human rights abuses would be disappointed that this statement seems weak, allowing companies to escape liability for wrongs which occur in the manufacture of their products. The statement acknowledges that in some national law, a company which outsources manufacturing could be held to be complicit in the committing of human rights crimes. It states, however, that it would only be found guilty if it had knowingly contributed to the commission of a crime. The authors of the principles are implying that a company would be unlikely to be found complicit if it has no actual knowledge of the wrongs committed in the supply chain. The document affirms the view that the state is not responsible for human rights abuse by private actors. It expressly states that it is affirming existing obligations, not contributing to any new international law. This statement could be read as implying that it rejects notions of developing customary international law.

The Guiding Principles stress the need for companies to take care in situations involving possible human rights abuse, but highlight limitations on legal liability in these cases,

The authors of the principles are implying that a company would be unlikely to be found complicit if it has no actual knowledge of the wrongs committed in the supply chain.

even though there are legal precedents for holding companies liable. The stress on policies which are voluntary, including offering grievance procedures, would appear to be weak in the context of human rights. These are frequently cases of violence against the person, sometimes resulting in death. The UK government, in its action plan to implement the principles, seems to go further than the UN document (UK Foreign and Commonwealth Office, 2013). It begins by stating the 'business case' for upholding human rights, and acknowledges the need to reduce litigation. It goes on to state that the UK is subject to customary international law and conventions. It also notes the liability under the UDHR of companies in the private sector which carry out public services. It further notes s. 172 of the Companies Act 2006, which stresses the duties of directors to promote the interests of the company as a whole, including those affected by its activities (see the discussion in Chapter 8). Finally, it urges businesses to treat the area of human rights as a 'legal compliance issue', acknowledging the possibility of legal liabilities (UK Foreign and Commonwealth Office, 2013).

In highlighting the duties of directors and urging businesses to behave as if human rights are a matter of legal compliance, the relatively strong UK response has revealed potential weaknesses of the Guiding Principles. Two weaknesses emerge. First, there is the 'due diligence' approach. Due diligence derives from commercial contexts such as a proposed takeover, when a company must carry out audit procedures to assure itself that the investment is advantageous. This is a risk assessment exercise. Such a process does not seem to be suited to human rights issues, which are essentially moral (McCorquodale, 2009). It is possible that due diligence exercised by directors could be adapted and expanded to cover human rights, which might be seen as a stakeholder issue (Muchlinski, 2012). However, this would seem implausible in the context of corporate governance frameworks built on shareholder value. As we saw in Chapter 8, despite the nod in the direction of other stakeholders, UK company law and corporate governance are based ultimately on enlightened shareholder value.

A second weakness is the vagueness of the notion of 'expected conduct' in defining the company's responsibilities (McCorquodale, 2009). For the MNE with operations – either directly or indirectly connected to its activities – in numerous societies, social expectations will differ widely. National laws and cultural differences come into play. In some countries, child labour is seen as acceptable, whereas it stands condemned on ethical grounds and in ILO conventions. Human rights cover a wide range of rights, including economic and social rights. All forms of discrimination come within human rights conventions, including discrimination on grounds of race, ethnic origins, sex, religion and political views. Wages that are too low to live on would be a breach of human rights. The Guiding Principles recommended the use of grievance procedures, but victims might be sceptical that these would suffice, especially if they are administered by the companies which have vested interests in the outcomes. Legal remedies, too, have many drawbacks. Access to courts is hardly a realistic possibility for the very poor. And in many human rights cases, the harm suffered cannot be put right by monetary compensation.

PAUSE TO CONSIDER…

Do you agree with the approach taken in the Guiding Principles for business and human rights? If not, how would you change its principles?

CORPORATE RESPONSIBILITY: THE LEGAL ROUTES

There is now some legal precedent for holding companies directly responsible for violations of human rights. In the case of *Doe v Unocal*, a case heard in the US, it was held that an MNE could be directly liable for violations of human rights (Muchlinski, 2001). This case, begun in California in 1997, involved claims on behalf of a group of Burmese villagers for torture, forced labour and other human rights violations, against Unocal, a US oil company. Unocal was a joint-venture partner with the military government in Burma in a project to build an oil pipeline.

The Unocal case raised the profile of a long-dormant US law, the Alien Tort Claims Act (ATCA) of 1789, which allows foreign plaintiffs to bring claims in US courts for breaches of international law. The claims may be brought against foreigners or US nationals. Unocal could have been liable for the forced labour on the pipeline, which it knew about, but the court held that it was not directly involved in the abuses. In a further twist, the judge asked for and received advice from the US government to the effect that US interests would be harmed by allowing the lawsuit. The US government had advised in an earlier case that this type of litigation would harm US interests, specifically in terms of opportunities for US investment abroad (Davis, 2008: 124). From the point of view of victims of human rights abuse, the court's recourse to advice from the executive branch constituted a limitation in the application of ATCA. Furthermore, other limitations have emerged in similar litigation.

It has been held that the plaintiffs must prove that the company 'purposefully' took part in the human rights abuse, in order to be found liable under ATCA. This was decided in *The Presbyterian Church of Sudan v Talisman Energy* (2009), a case in which Talisman Energy was alleged to have participated in ethnic cleansing in Sudan (Adamski, 2011). In a landmark case, *Kiobel v Royal Dutch Shell* (2013), the US Supreme Court decided that on the issue of 'extraterritoriality', claimants cannot bring claims against companies for activities which took place in other countries unless the company has a strong connection with the US (CJA, 2013). The mere fact that the company had a presence in the US was not enough. In this case, Nigerian victims of torture claimed damages in the US for human rights abuse carried out by the Nigerian military, aided by the company. Although they failed in these claims, it should be noted that some of the judges stated that extraterritorial claims for breaches of international law are allowed in other countries, and that legislation in the US also recognizes extraterritorial claims. Nonetheless, the cumulative effect of these decisions has been severely to limit the chances of victims of abuse making claims under ATCA in the US. Following *Kiobel v Shell*, they could make claims in cases where there is a stronger connection to the US. They could also still make claims under tort law, but these cases pose numerous obstacles.

In theory, a person alleging violation of human rights can bring a claim in the country where it occurred against the company alleged to have been responsible. The victim usually seeks compensation in the civil courts of the country. This assumes that the wrong is established in the national law of that country. The law in question is usually in the area of tort, often negligence, which involves failure to uphold a duty of care (see Chapter 4). In serious cases, it can involve criminal liability. In practice, the situation is usually far more complicated, mainly because of globalized business operations. The company could well be a subsidiary of a company registered elsewhere. For victims, launching proceedings usually involves financial resources beyond the reach of ordinary individuals. Moreover, in many countries, especially developing and emerging countries, legal processes, although recognizing equality before the law in principle, are difficult for the uninitiated to navigate. Moreover, human rights violations tend to affect large numbers of people. Their chances of redress depend in on whether class action lawsuits are permissible in the country.

A **class action** lawsuit allows one victim to bring a claim on behalf of many others in a group, who will all benefit from a successful verdict. Class actions are highly developed in the US, although with limitations highlighted in the opening case study. They are not so developed elsewhere, and not legal at all in some countries. A group of victims in a developing country might have a claim against their employer, which is a subsidiary of a US company. They might bring a claim in their own country, but, even if successful, would receive little compensation, and often court judgments are not enforced. Instead, they might try to launch a claim against the parent company in the US. However, this is likely to fail, as the court tends to find that the more appropriate forum for the case is the local court of the victims, in a rule known as the *forum non conveniens* doctrine. These factors were considered in the case of *Lubbe v Cape* (2000), in which victims of asbestos injuries in South Africa brought legal claims in the UK against the parent company of their employer. The UK judges held that the victims would not have received justice in South Africa, and also, importantly, that the parent company was liable for the harms inflicted by its South African subsidiary (Meeran, 2002).

The UK judges held that the victims would not have received justice in South Africa, and that the parent company was liable for the harms inflicted by its South African subsidiary.

In contrast, Bhopal victims attempting to bring claims in the US were unsuccessful. In that case, a gas leak at a pesticide factory in Bhopal, India, claimed the lives of 3,800 people. The company running the factory was a subsidiary of Union Carbide of the US. Litigation against Union Carbide in the US failed on grounds of *forum non conveniens*. The cases went back to India, where the government took over the litigation through a statute which allowed it to reach a settlement with Union Carbide. However, there was widespread dissatisfaction with this solution, and litigation continued. Dow Chemical, the company which absorbed Union Carbide, was sued for contamination of the soil and water in the area. This action failed too, because it was covered by the settlement. The case highlights the use of human rights law in respect of incidents of environmental degradation. MNEs have impacts in societies far beyond the workplace. In some cases, they provide accommodation and other services. In unstable environments, MNEs employ other companies as security contractors. We look next at the business contexts in which MNEs are involved in human rights issues.

HUMAN RIGHTS IN BUSINESS CONTEXTS

Building an oil pipeline, extracting oil and operating a chemical plant: these are some of the contexts featured so far in connection with abuse of human rights. All involved relatively hazardous activities in developing countries where the lead investor was a western company. All involved weak human rights protection in national law, and also government involvement. Developing countries have long sought to attract foreign investors, whose expertise in vital industries exceeded their own domestic capabilities. These investors bring numerous benefits, as we have seen in earlier chapters, especially Chapter 2. They help to exploit natural resources, generate wealth and provide jobs. Host governments offer incentives, and are inclined not to pry into the day-to-day running of operations. Neither are they inclined to pass stringent new safety or employment legislation: relatively lax standards are one of the attractions for foreign MNEs. Many global brands have signed up to the Ethical Trading Initiative (at www.ethicaltrade.org), which brings together businesses, trade unions and NGOs in an alliance to raise standards in supply chains through voluntary codes of conduct. As we saw in the last section, however, there is a possibility of workers mounting legal cases against foreign investors in the investor's home country. This involves extended costly litigation, even if the company can escape liability. It also involves reputational damage. Some of the main areas are examined in this section.

THE RIGHT NOT TO BE SUBJECT TO INHUMAN TREATMENT

Inhuman treatment covers a wide range of possible violations of human rights, including torture (both physical and mental), physical assaults, humiliating or degrading treatment. It is to the forefront in the UDHR and in the ICCPR, which also prohibits the use of forced labour or slavery. The UN convention on torture and other cruel, inhuman or degrading treatment or punishments dates from 1987, and has been ratified by 154 countries. These treaties focused on human rights violations by states, but the types of activities they cover can also be committed by companies, and sometimes companies in co-operation with states.

Ikea is a highly successful brand associated with flatpack furniture, popular in middle-class homes around the world. Its Swedish origins and image as a company suggest wholesome family values. However, Ikea used prison labour in the German Democratic Republic (GDR), communist East Germany, to make its furniture in the 1970s and 80s. GDR citizens imprisoned for activities such as distributing anti-communist leaflets, worked in factories producing Ikea flatpack furniture. Following a report that revealed the details of these factories, the company has admitted that it is true. One former prisoner who has come forward said that he was forced to do in a single day a workload equivalent to two-and-a-half days' work in a normal factory. If he fell short of this target, he was sent to an isolation cell. Ikea's CEO has stated that the use of political prisoners was unacceptable. He has apologized and assured today's consumers that nothing like this is now happening in the company's many global locations. But how can he be sure? The company says that in the 1970s and 80s, it took steps to ensure that political prisoners were not used, but is clear that the company did know of the practice (Connolly, 2012). The company was allowed to visit most factories, but there were restrictions on inspecting those in East Germany, which should have raised suspicions. Former political prisoners are now coming forward to seek compensation from Ikea. They have said that other companies were also involved, and that these, too, should be 'named and shamed' (Connolly, 2012).

China's system of prison camps, known officially as 're-education through labour', have long been criticized for forced labour, torture and inhumane treatment. People can be sent to prison for up to four years for minor crimes, political dissent and religious offences, such as membership of banned sects. China's new leadership seeks to implement the rule of law, and there are now numerous voices within China calling for the abolition of the camps, which are a legacy of the Maoist era. While much of the work carried

Whenever we were making goods for export, they would say, 'you better take extra care with these'.

out by these prisoners is on goods like military uniforms, there is evidence that goods for western brands have been made in these prison camps. One former inmate recalls, 'Whenever we were making goods for export, they would say, "you better take extra care with these"' (Jacobs, 2013). Another recalls coat linings with labels which read, 'made in Italy'.

Vulnerable people in low-wage jobs are among the most likely to be victims of inhuman treatment in any country. Companies often use the services of agencies to hire migrant workers, as was noted in relation to outsourced manufacturing in China (see Chapter 2). But similar practices can take place in other countries, developed and developing. A television documentary in Germany in 2013 featured the plight of foreign temporary workers hired by a subcontractor of Amazon, to work in its warehouses in the busy pre-Christmas period. These workers were housed in poor conditions and overseen by a security company hired by the subcontractor, whose heavy-handed methods were criticized. It was pointed out that the initials of the company's name, Hensel European Security Services, were the same as Rudolf Hess, a deputy of Hitler. Furthermore, the security guards wore black uniforms reminiscent of Nazi uniforms. The company denied any far-right connections. The German government said it would withdraw the licence of this company to operate if the allegations of mistreatment were found to be true, but Amazon pre-emptively fired the security company (Bryant, 2013).

Expressing expectations concerning subcontractors is not the same as accepting moral responsibility, let alone accepting legal liability.

Amazon is the world's biggest online retailer. It said its policy was one of zero-tolerance of intimidation and discrimination, and stressed it expected the same approach from the companies it works with (Bryant, 2013). However, expressing expectations concerning subcontractors is not the same as accepting moral responsibility, let alone accepting legal liability. In the event, the company sacked the security firm in order to limit reputational damage.

MNEs which outsource manufacturing are increasingly viewed as responsible for the inhuman treatment of workers who make their products. Mass-produced toys, the apparel industry, leisure goods and electronics are among the industries affected. MNEs such as Apple and Walmart have supplier codes of conduct, and they carry out audits of supply chains. The standards they seek to apply are those of national law, for example, on limitations of working hours. However, the MNEs themselves are partly to blame for excessive overtime, in that they put pressure on contractors to fill large orders of goods at short notice. They are thus aware that manufacturers are compelled to exceed legal hours of work to complete orders. As we found in Chapter 2, only 38% of Apple's suppliers keep within legal limits on overtime. MNEs drive hard bargains over price, and companies compete fiercely for these contracts. US-registered Jabil Circuit is one such company, which makes parts for iPhones. Jabil has factories in a number of countries, including China. Workers in these factories are within the protection of national law, but in cases of alleged human rights violations, they might consider pursuing human rights claims in the US under ATCA, as Jabil is based in the US.

Should brand owners be legally liable for human rights abuses committed by contractors making their products? If so, should lawsuits be allowed in the home countries of MNEs?

SPOTLIGHT ON ETHICAL BUSINESS

Garment workers in India *Dr Jean Jenkins*

Dr Jean Jenkins
*Senior Lecturer in
Employment
Relations, Cardiff
Business School, UK*

Jean Jenkins teaches modules in employment relations and the business environment at Cardiff University in the UK. She is an active researcher, looking at industrial relations in the international clothing sector, work-life integration and decent work, and union-management partnership.

Visit **www.palgrave.com/companion/morrison-business-ethics** to watch Jean talking about garment workers in Bangalore, in the context of global supply chains. She probes into working conditions and relations between workers and managers in the factories, which raise a number of human rights issues. She offers insight into a recurring question in regions which are becoming industrialized: Is regular paid work like this improving the human well-being of workers and those who depend on them? Finally, she explains why it is so important for students of business and management to study business ethics.

Before watching this video, take time to look at the background on human rights in Chapter 9. Also, look again at related sections earlier in the book. These include the discussion of CSR in Chapter 7, and case studies on Bangladesh (Chapter 1) and H&M (Chapter 7). There is also a discussion of the foundations of human rights law in Chapter 4.

When you have watched the video, think about the following questions:

1 Which situations described in the interview give rise to concerns about human rights? Remember to consider not just in the factory workplaces, but also the wider context of home life and social environment.

2 What is being done to improve the working conditions in the garment factories? What are the difficulties highlighted in terms of relations between managers and workers?

3 What is the role of the global brands mentioned in the video? Should more responsibility fall on them?

REDUCING CHILD LABOUR

The ILO Convention on the worst forms of child labour dates from 1999, and has been ratified by 177 states. An earlier convention, on the minimum age for entry into employment, dates from 1976. It stipulates a minimum age of 15 for a child to work, with an exception for developing countries, where 14 is the allowable minimum. For hazardous work, the minimum is 18, but there is again an exception for developing countries, in which 16 can be the legal minimum. The exceptions for developing countries should be allowed only under strict conditions, prioritizing the health of the child. Another convention, the UN Convention on the Rights of the Child, which took effect in 1990, complements the other conventions, and covers a wider range of issues, such as rights not to be subjected to cruel and unusual punishment, including the death penalty and life imprisonment. It also includes the rights of children involved in conflict. The Convention on the Rights of the Child has been ratified by 193 countries. There are only three which have not ratified it: Somalia, South Sudan and the US. Obstacles to US ratification have included the imposition of the death penalty on children, but this has now been held unconstitutional by the US Supreme Court, as has life imprisonment of children without the possibility of release.

In spite of overwhelming international support for these treaties, child labour is widespread. The good news is that it is declining. The ILO collects data on the extent of employment among children aged 5–17 in all the world's regions. The two main categories are, first, 'child labour' which is employment in an environment such as a factory or farm, for hours equivalent to those an adult would work, leading to detrimental effects on the child's education. Such work is more strenuous, therefore, than light work for a few hours a week. The second category is 'hazardous work', which is 'work that adversely affects the child's safety, health and moral development' (ILO, 2013: 16). It might involve work with dangerous machinery, handling dangerous substances, or working long hours. It is considered the worst form of child labour. Such work has long-term detrimental effects on the child's health and personal development.

There are now 168 million children working in the category of child labour. This figure represents a decline from 215 million in 2008 (ILO, 2013). The numbers involved in hazardous work have also declined, from 115 million in 2008 to 85 million in 2012. Despite these declines, about 11% of all children aged 5 to 17 are employed in some form of child labour, as shown in Figure 9.4. More than half of all these child labourers are engaged in hazardous work.

The Asia and Pacific region has more child labourers than any other, numbering 77 million children, but this region has seen a steep decline in numbers from 114 million in 2008. In this region, the percentage in labour, at nearly 10%, is considerably lower than in Sub-Saharan Africa, where 21.4%, approximately one in five children, are in employment, amounting to 59 million children (see Figure 9.5). About 35% of all child labourers in the world are in Sub-Saharan Africa. While the incidence of child labour is greatest in the poor

Figure 9.4 *Child labour and hazardous work: percentages employed worldwide*

Percentages of all children aged 5–17

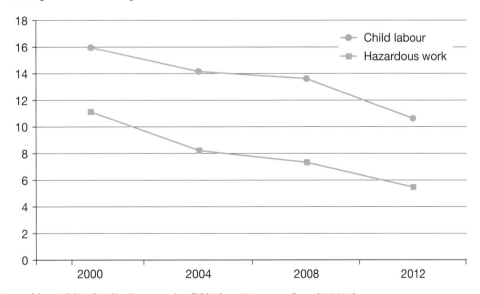

Source of data: ILO (2013) *Making Progress against Child Labour, 2013,* at www.ilo.org (18/09/14).

Figure 9.5 *Percentage of child labourers in selected regions of the world*

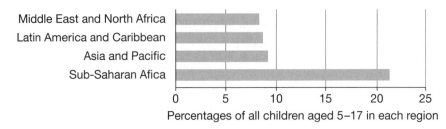

Source of data: ILO (2013) *Making Progress against Child Labour, 2013*, at www.ilo.org (18/09/14).

countries of Sub-Saharan Africa, the largest numbers of child labourers are in the middle-income countries of the Asia and Pacific region. About 93.6 million child labourers are in middle-income countries. The practice of child labour, therefore, is not confined to the poorest countries. It is commonly thought that in poor families, it is perceived as a necessity for children to work. But there are cultural issues involved as well, which come into focus in the countries with higher incomes.

Eliminating child labour is closely linked to the provision of compulsory education for all children. Without universal education, a country can make little progress, as the government will struggle to enforce laws against child labour (Weiner, 1994). India, which has a long history of tolerating child labour, is introducing reforms. Its Child Labour Act of 1986 prohibits children under 14 from working in hazardous work, such as mining and work in chemical plants. Children in India are predominantly employed in agriculture, but many work in catering and as domestic servants. A law in 2006 attempted to ban children working in catering, such as tea shops, and in domestic service. These practices, however, remained tolerated. In 2009, a Right to Education Act took effect, providing that all children from 6 to 14 should have free, public education. The government in 2012 proposed to criminalize those who hire child labourers. A three-year jail sentence could be imposed on someone employing a child under 14 in any type of work, or a child under 18 in a hazardous industry. Sceptics doubt whether India can wipe out child labour, which has for so long been tolerated. One official of a human rights organization observes that wealthy Indians who employ children say that they are providing 'better food and better shelter for a child, who would be otherwise in a much more deprived situation, and therefore they justify employment of a child' (Kazmin, 2012).

Wealthy Indians justify employing children, saying they provide better food and shelter ... otherwise these children would be in much more deprived situations.

PAUSE TO CONSIDER...

Cultural relativists might observe that child labour is part of the culture in many countries, and that international laws against child labour are based on a western view of childhood which is biased. How would you respond to this viewpoint?

THE RIGHT OF ASSOCIATION AND MEMBERSHIP OF TRADE UNIONS

The right of association is recognized in the UDHR and the covenant on civil and political rights (the ICCPR). The right of workers to organize in the workplace is expressly recognized in the covenant on economic and social rights (the ICESCR) and in ILO conventions. These include a convention of 1948, the Freedom of Association and the Right to Organise Convention, and a convention of 1949, the Right to Organise and Collective Bargaining

Convention. The conventions aim to facilitate dialogue with employers and to ensure that employees can organize themselves voluntarily, without pressure or intimidation from employers. As has been seen in Chapter 7, employees are primary stakeholders. Their roles are crucial in economic terms, but, above that, employees are the focus of legal and ethical responsibilities. Good employee relations involve employers and employees treating each other with respect. The right of association and trade union membership is seen as key to employee voice within a company. An independent trade union is an organization of workers that is not under the control of the employer or any connected entity such as a government department. To be independent, it must not be liable to interference by the employer and is not financially supported in any way by the employer. Trade unions which are 'in-house' staff associations or are controlled by the employer or the government are therefore non-independent, and would not meet the standard set out in the conventions.

A significant development in industrial relations in China was the launch of an independent trade union at Foxconn in 2013 (Hille, 2013). The company has had unions dominated by management in the past, in which workers have played little role. The new arrangements will see worker representatives elected to union committees, with no management influence. The catalyst for change has been an audit carried out for Apple by the Fair Labor Association, a US NGO, which found that workers had little prospect of airing their grievances under the existing arrangements. The new committees should result in better dialogue between workers and managers. It is no guarantee that problems such as excessive overtime will not occur, but it should provide more co-operative and peaceful means of resolving problems and airing grievances. Globally, labour relations in many countries have often been acrimonious, punctuated by strikes, sometimes long and bitter, which have a socially damaging impact not just on employees, but on families and communities.

Despite their historical connection with the founding human rights conventions, the conventions on workers' rights of association have not been adopted by some of the larger member states of the UN, as Table 9.1 shows. All the EU member states have ratified both conventions, but the large emerging economies of China and India have not. Neither has the US. Many US companies take an anti-union stance, as shown in the opening case study. In the US, the National Labor Relations Act of 1933 recognized the right of workers to join trade unions and to bargain collectively. In the era of growing mass production in sectors like the motor industry, the trade unions became powerful forces, speaking for workers whose jobs on assembly lines could be arduous and repetitive. This era came to be associated with confrontational labour relations. The unions succeeded in securing advantageous pay and conditions for their members, including generous healthcare and pension schemes. However, as costs spiralled, many companies, including the large car manufacturers,

Table 9.1 *Ratifications of two major ILO conventions on right of association and trade union membership*

Convention	Selected states that have ratified	Selected states that have not ratified
Freedom of association and right to organise	All EU, Bangladesh, Indonesia, Japan, Russian Federation, South Africa	Brazil, China, India, Qatar, Singapore, US, Vietnam
Freedom to organise and collective bargaining	All EU, Bangladesh, Brazil, Indonesia, Russian Federation, Singapore	China, India, Qatar, US, Vietnam

Source: ILO (2013) *International Labour Standards on Freedom of Association,* at www.ilo.org (18/09/14).

blamed much of their waning competitiveness on the welfare burdens imposed by union agreements. Foreign car-makers who invested in the US stayed away from the regions where the trade unions were entrenched, preferring to set up greenfield operations in non-union environments.

When US companies operate in other countries, they can be faced with a dilemma over recognition of trade unions. Many US companies see trade unions as disruptive forces, largely as a legacy of America's acrimonious labour relations. Amazon found that in Germany it was up against the Verdi union, which sought better pay and conditions for staff at its distribution centres. Collective bargaining for whole sectors is widely recognized in Germany, but Amazon objects to it. Verdi argues that Amazon's workers are in e-retailing, while Amazon says they are logistics workers, who receive lower wages and fewer entitlements than e-retailing workers. Amazon's operations in Germany have been disrupted by strikes over issues of pay and conditions at two centres, Bad Hersfeld and Leipzig. Amazon's business model prioritizes cost-cutting. The working conditions in its warehouses are often criticized as harsh, for example, in placing workers under intense pressure to meet targets. It is also criticized for its tax avoidance policies. On the other hand, it is popular with consumers, and has provided employment in areas of where old industries and mining have shut down. Examples in the UK are South Wales and the East Midlands, both former mining areas. Amazon warehouses in these areas have been called the 'mines of the 21st century' (Usborne, 2013). But, with bitter strikes persisting in Germany, Amazon announced the construction of three new distribution centres in Poland (Bryant and Cienski, 2013). Observers of globalization trends might conclude that the company is planning to shift some of the work currently done in Germany to these new centres, attracted by lower wage bills and weaker trade unions.

THE LIVING WAGE: A HUMAN RIGHT?

The authors of the UDHR included a category of rights which gave a positive focus to the meaning of human dignity. As shown in Figure 9.2, they included employment, a decent standard of living, adequate housing and medical care. These were elaborated in the second follow-up covenant, the covenant on economic, social and cultural rights (ICESCR). They provided a social counterweight to the traditional natural rights. In fact, they have a long pedigree in western thought and politics. Kant is perhaps the foremost proponent of the idea of positive liberty as human development. John Rawls, who was in the liberal tradition, viewed social justice as a priority. Socialists in Britain and New Deal advocates in the US both viewed social welfare as essential in democratic society. These ideas became part of international human rights law through the International Labour Organization (ILO), founded in 1919. Its aims were to abolish the 'injustice, hardship and privation' which workers endured (Steiner and Alston, 2000: 242). The ILO focused on conditions in the working environment, including unhealthy and unsafe factories, low wages and excessive hours. These types of hardship are linked to inadequate housing, poor health, poor diet and poor life prospects for workers and their families.

In the US today, manufacturing as a sector has shrunk, and with it, the generous benefits enjoyed in manufacturing's heyday. The service sector is now the largest source of employment, and the bulk of new jobs are in low-pay work such as fast-food outlets and supermarket work (see Figure 9.6). These jobs are poorly paid, offer few benefits such as health insurance and are mostly non-unionized. As the figure shows, retail cashiers and people

Figure 9.6 *Where are the low-paid workers in the US?*

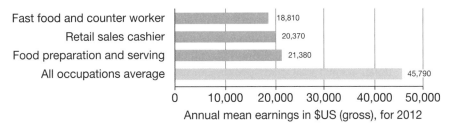

Source of data: US Government Bureau of Labor Statistics (2013) *Occupational Employment and Wages, 29 March,* at www.bls.gov (18/09/14).

working in fast-food outlets earn less than half the national average over all occupations. Companies in these sectors have long taken a strong stance against union membership (see the opening case study). Despite the legal right to join a union, employees who do so typically face recrimination and sometimes sacking. Even speaking up about poor conditions in some companies is likely to lead to punitive action.

Among the largest employers are Walmart and the fast-food chains, including McDonalds and the Yum Brands (Taco Bell, Pizza Hut and KFC). These low-paid jobs have long been taken by younger people who look to move on to better jobs as opportunities arise. But the opportunities seemed to dry up from about the 1990s onwards. Since then, the US middle class has seen declining prosperity, and many older, qualified people are now finding the only jobs available are in low-paid services. Workers in these jobs now tend to be older people with family responsibilities. Whole families struggle to make ends meet on minimum wage rates. The annual earnings of the jobs set out in Figure 9.6 are all well under the official poverty line. Protests against pay and conditions spread across the country in 2013. These workers' calls for a living wage can be seen as akin to the Occupy protests, highlighting the injustice and affront to human dignity in the employment practices of the large corporations they work for (see Chapter 5). But they differ from the Occupy protests, in that they are direct action against specific employers (Helmore, 2013).

Fast-food outlets tend to be franchises, which are independent businesses, whose owners work under franchise agreements with the company owning the brand. McDonald's and others stress that they do not determine wages; each business owner does. However, the company exerts considerable control over all aspects of the business, and its policies and strategies for the company pervade the individual franchise businesses. At the time protests were brewing, McDonald's issued a guide budget for its workers, in order to demonstrate how they could live on the minimum wage paid by the company. Soon attracting media attention as the McBudget, this attempt was a public relations disaster, as the company had

McDonald's had to admit it was impossible to live on its minimum wage without a second job, unless the employee went without a necessity such as heating or food.

to admit it was impossible to live on its minimum wage without a second job, unless the employee went without a necessity such as heating or food (Helmore, 2013). One 34-year-old father of three who works two jobs, at Burger King and Pizza Hut, makes about $8 an hour, which is just over the federal minimum wage of $7.25. He joined the one-day strike organized in Kansas City, saying he was striking for a living wage of $15 an hour, but also for 'respect'. He said, 'We don't have a voice' (McVeigh, 2013). That day saw similar strikes in 60 cities across the US. The federal minimum wage has not been changed since 2009. Adjusted for inflation, it is now worth 20% less than it was worth in 1967.

By comparison, McDonald's CEO received remuneration of $13.8 million in 2012, which was 558 times what it expected its employees to live on. McDonald's saw rising profits throughout the years of the financial crisis, in large part because during hard times, the 'dollar menu' is all many people can afford. McDonald's has long attracted criticism for contributing to America's obesity epidemic (discussed in the next chapter). Its website even reminds its employees that fast food is an 'unhealthy choice' (Johnston, 2013). It offers healthier options, but healthy eating costs more than traditional fast food. Fast-food workers are among the chief recipients of government food stamps (see Chapter 2, Figure 2.5), a programme which benefits the very companies that employ some of the lowest paid workers.

The UN conventions envisage economic and social rights as mainly issues of government protection. Employment, access to medical care, enough to eat, adequate housing, education: these are all obligations of the state. But the UDHR states plainly that the responsibility falls on any 'organ of society', which includes companies. Starvation wages would arguably amount to a breach of human rights, even when companies adhere to the legal minimum wage. Is this the responsibility of companies, or should it be the responsibility of governments to raise the minimum wage? A CSR approach would urge that the liveable wage is an ethical imperative, if not a legal one. The strikers and protesters in low-paid jobs in the US have raised the public's awareness of the ethical issues which go to the heart of corporate strategy of some of America's largest companies. Whatever the law, they are laying blame on their employers, whose billions in profits would easily cover a living wage, but whose executive directors choose to reward themselves and shareholders.

Reducing labour costs through flexible working has gathered momentum in the UK, through the use of the 'zero hours' contract, a device now used by a number of employers, in both private-sector companies and public services. They range from McDonald's to Buckingham Palace. This type of contract bears little resemblance to a traditional employment contract. It does not commit the employer to providing regular work or a stable income. Neither is the employee likely to receive sick pay or holiday entitlement. It has emerged that 82,800 workers at McDonald's in the UK are on zero-hours contracts. This is 90% of the company's entire workforce in the country. The sandwich company, Subway, also uses such contracts. The following is an extract from an employment contract issued by Subway:

> The company has no duty to provide you with work. Your hours of work are not predetermined and will be notified to you on a weekly basis as soon as is reasonably practicable in advance by your store manager. The company has the right to require you to work varied or extended hours from time to time. (Neville, 2013)

Subway's contract also provides that employees must waive their right under regulations to work no more than 48 hours per week. In jobs where there is steady work, the zero-hours contract is seen as a device to avoid paying sick pay and holiday pay. The worker is paid only for the hours worked, must always be available for work, and is not free to work elsewhere. The worker who is unable to attend work when called is likely to be sidelined and not called when future needs for work arise. This type of arrangement might be suited to people who simply want casual work, and are not dependent on the work for a living. However, for most people, this is not a satisfactory substitute for full-time employment. The benefits of the arrangement go entirely to the employer. The UK's Institute of Directors has defended zero-hours contracts (Neville, 2013). However, UK trade unions have objected to these contracts (Butler, 2013). Workers likely to be subject to a zero-hours contract are in some of the most lowly-paid sectors, notably, accommodation and food services, where workers have the lowest gross weekly earnings (ONS, 2013).

Employment practices involving precarious employment and low wages feature more prominently in the liberal market economies than in the social market economies. Companies would argue that they must be globally competitive, which entails every possible cost reduction. But where the employee is viewed simply as a pair of hands rather than a human being there is a loss of human dignity. The detriment to the employee is greater than simply the meagre wages and uncertain conditions, as it undervalues the respect which each person should enjoy in the workplace as in society. There is also a business case. The company might take a short-term view of the benefits of reducing labour costs, but in the long term, it is fostering poor employee relations which could easily lead to strikes and loss of production. The media attention which has focused on employment practices in many large companies has also arguably led to criticism on ethical grounds. McDonald's states that it has a 'culture of inclusion and respect' (McDonald's, 2013: 5). It is not alone. Companies almost invariably say in their publicity material that employees are their most valued assets, but when their actions do not match their stated principles, they invite even more criticism for hypocrisy.

PAUSE TO CONSIDER...

Would you go along with the zero-hours contract offered by Subway, and why?

CONCLUSIONS

Human rights have come more into focus for international business as globalization has deepened and competitive advantage has become a strategic imperative. Companies are constantly on the lookout for ways to reduce costs. Using cheap labour is accepted as a legitimate strategy, but there has been growing ethical criticism as well as accusations of circumventing relevant law. Mostly, cheap labour is found in developing and emerging countries. Exploitation of workers is now increasingly seen as the responsibility of western brand owners whose products are made in outsourced factories. However, as we have seen, legal liabilities do not mirror moral responsibilities. MNEs are seldom connected sufficiently directly with contractors' operations to be found legally liable in national law. On the other hand, they are criticized on moral grounds, and also on the basis of the norms of international law.

Human rights for international businesses do not start at the entrance to the factory or mine. They pervade the working and living environment of workers. Increasingly we see the damage of human rights violations spill over into the conditions in which workers live, with impacts on families and societies. These issues are not confined to developing and emerging countries. This chapter has emphasized that the attractions of cheap labour – and the social consequences – are highly visible inside developed western economies such as the US and UK. These countries pride themselves on individual freedoms and democratic values, but here, too, the living wage and worker voice are precarious. Global companies espouse the importance of employees as stakeholders, but in practice tend to see employees, especially in low-skilled jobs, in terms of costs. Their executives, meanwhile, receive remuneration in multiples of millions. While shareholders see the benefits of maximizing shareholder value, they are also aware that a poor human rights record can lead to unrest, loss of production, falling share price and reputational damage. Ideally, companies would turn their attention to human rights on ethical grounds. They feel they can fend off ethical criticism because they are successful financially and are confident they can withstand legal challenges. But with lawsuits mounting against companies for human rights abuse, who knows what company will be next?

REFERENCES

Note: The UN Charter and human rights conventions are available at www.un.org. They are listed under documents and human rights portals.

Adamski, T. (2011) 'The Alien Tort Claims Act and corporate liability: A threat to the United States' international relations', *Fordham International Law Journal*, 34(6): 1502–43.

Aquinas (1965) *Selected Political Writings*, edited by A. P. D'Entreves (Oxford: Basil Blackwell).

Bachmann, S., and Miretski, P. (2012) 'Global business and human rights – the UN Norms on the Responsibility of Transnational Corporations and other business enterprises with regard to human rights – a Requiem', *Deakin Law Review*, 17(1): 5–41.

Booth, R. (2013) 'Qatar World Cup: UK firms urged to do more to protect workers' rights', *The Guardian*, 3 October, at www.theguardian.com (18/09/14).

Booth, R., Gibson, O. and Pattisson, P. (2013) 'Qatar under pressure over migrant labour abuse', *The Guardian*, 26 September, at www.theguardian.com (18/09/14).

Bryant, C. (2013) 'Amazon fires security firm after documentary', *Financial Times*, 19 February.

Bryant, C. and Cienski, J. (2013) 'Amazon lines up low-cost Poland', *Financial Times*, 8 October.

Butler, S. (2013) 'Zero-hours contracts: 5.5 million Britons "are on deals offering little guaranteed work"', *The Guardian*, 8 September, at www.theguardian.com (18/09/14).

CJA (Centre for Justice and Accountability) (2013) *Kiobel v Shell: Light Dims on Human Rights Claims in the US*, at www.cja.org (18/09/14).

Clapham, A. (1993) *Human Rights in the Private Sphere* (Oxford: Clarendon Press).

Connolly, K. (2012) 'Ikea says sorry to East German political prisoners forced to make its furniture', *The Guardian*, 16 November, at www.theguardian.com (18/09/14).

Cranston, M. (1973) *What are Human Rights?* (London: The Bodley Head).

D'Amato, A. (1995) 'Human rights as part of customary international law: A plea for a change of paradigms', *The Georgia Journal of International and Comparative Law*, 25: 47–98.

Davis, J. (2008) *Justice across borders: The struggle for human rights in US Courts* (Cambridge: Cambridge University Press).

Donaldson, T. and Dunfee, T. (1994) 'Toward a unified conception of business ethics theory: Integrative social contracts theory', *Academy of Management Review*, 19(2): 252–84.

Donnelly, J. (1998) *International Human Rights*, 2nd edn (Boulder, CO: Westview Press).

Helmore, E. (2013) 'US fast-food workers in vanguard of protests at "starvation" wages', *The Guardian*, 10 August, at www.theguardian.com (18/09/14).

Henkin, L. (1995) 'Human Rights and State "Sovereignty"', *The Georgia Journal of International and Comparative Law*, 25: 31–46.

Hille, K. (2013) 'Foxconn workers in landmark China vote', *Financial Times*, 4 February.

ILO (2013) *Making Progress against Child Labour*, 2013, at www.ilo.org (18/09/14).

Jacobs, A. (2013) 'Behind cry for help from China labor camp', *The New York Times*, 11 June, at www.nytimes.com

Johnston, I. (2013) 'Fast food is an "unhealthy choice", McDonald's tells its own staff', *The Independent*, 25 December, at www.independent.co.uk (18/09/14).

Kant, I. (1948) *The moral law: Groundwork of the metaphysic of morals*, translated by H.J. Paton (New York: Routledge).

Kazmin, A. (2012) 'India plans child labour reforms', *Financial Times*, 30 August.

Lauterpacht, H. (1943) 'The law of nations, the law of nature and the rights of man', *Transactions of the Grotius Society*, 29: 1–33.

McCorquodale, R. (2009) 'Corporate social responsibility and international human rights law', *Journal of Business Ethics*, 87(2): 385–400.

McDonald's (2013) *Annual Report 2012*, at www.aboutmcdonalds.com (18/09/14).

McVeigh, K. (2013) 'US fast-food workers stage nationwide strike in protest at low wages', *The Guardian*, 29 August, at www.theguardian.com (18/09/14).

Meeran, R. (2002) 'Cape pays the price as justice prevails', *The Times*, 15 January, at www.thetimes.co.uk (18/09/14).

Muchlinski, P. (2001) 'Human rights and multinationals: is there a problem?', *International Affairs*, 77(1): 31–48.

Muchlinski, P. (2012) 'Implementing the new UN corporate human rights framework: Implications of corporate law, governance and regulation', *Business Ethics Quarterly*, 22(1): 145–77.

Neville, S. (2013) 'McDonald's ties 9 out of 10 workers to zero-hours contracts', *The Guardian*, 5 August, at www.theguardian.com (18/09/14).

ONS (Office for National Statistics) (2013) *Patterns of Pay: Results from Annual Survey of Hours and Earnings, 1997–2012*, at www.ons.gov.uk

Pattisson, P. (2013) 'Revealed: Qatar's World Cup "slaves"', *The Guardian*, 25 September, at www.theguardian.com (18/09/14).

Perry, M. (1997) 'Are human rights universal? The relativist challenge and related matters', *Human Rights Quarterly*, 19: 462–509.

Steiner, H. and Alston, P. (2000) *International Human Rights in Context*, 2nd edn (Oxford: Oxford University Press).

UK Foreign and Commonwealth Office (2013) *Good Business: Implementing the UN Guiding Principles on Business and Human Rights*, Cm 8695, at www.gov.uk (18/09/14).

UN Human Rights Council (2011) *Guiding Principles on Business and Human Rights*, at www.ohchr.org (18/09/14).

Usborne, S. (2013) 'Thinking outside the box: the amazing world of online retail giant Amazon', *The Independent*, 9 October, at www.independent.co.uk (18/09/14).

Weiner, M. (1994) 'Child labour in developing countries: the Indian case', *International Journal of Children's Rights*, 2: 121–8.

Whelan, G., Moon, J. and Orlitzsky, M. (2009) 'Human rights, transnational corporations and embedded liberalism: What chance consensus?', *Journal of Business Ethics*, 87(2): 367–83.

World Bank (2013) *Migration and Remittance Flows: Recent Trends and Outlook 2013–2016*, October, at www.worldbank.org (18/09/14).

REVIEW QUESTIONS

1 On what grounds do positivists challenge universal principles of human rights such as the categorical imperative?

2 Theories of natural rights are famously within the tradition of the 'negative' concept of liberty, but do they also encompass 'positive' notions of liberty? Explain.

3 In what ways does the plight of migrant workers highlight the nature of human rights?

4 What are the main differences between a statist view of rights frameworks and a more cosmopolitan view?

5 In what ways was the Universal Declaration of Human Rights (UDHR) very forward-looking?

6 What are the changes taking place which make MNEs more likely to be found liable for international human rights breaches?

7 In what ways is a voluntarist approach inadequate to deal with human rights abuses by companies?

8 Critically assess the main provision of the UN's Guiding Principles on Human Rights (UNGPHR) for businesses. What are its weaknesses in promoting greater respect for human rights in international business?

9 What is the importance of the Alien Tort Claims Act (ATCA) in the US, and why have cases brought under the statute suffered setbacks?

10 Should a western brand owner be liable if child labour is found to be used in Asian factories where its products are made? Consider both the legal and moral positions.

11 Why is the right to join an independent trade union important in employee protection?

In what ways has this right been weakly recognized in practice? Give examples.

12 What are economic and social rights in international law? To what extent can they be enforced against a company as employer?

Photo 9.3 *Poor living conditions in unsound dwellings like these were one of the factors that contributed to demands from South Africa's miners for better pay and conditions.*
(© iStock.com/fivepointsix)

HUMAN RIGHTS OF MINERS IN SOUTH AFRICA

Rich in gold, platinum and other minerals, South Africa has been home to a large mining sector since the 1880s, when Cecil Rhodes founded De Beers. Mining in South Africa has relied on abundant cheap labour in the poor black population. Miners are mostly migrant workers, living in poor conditions and working in dangerous deep mines. The exploitation of these workers was a legacy of the apartheid era in South Africa. Many of the country's current leading mining companies date back to this era. With the end of apartheid in 1994, ushering in a democratic government, the new South Africa enshrined human rights in its constitution, adopting a bill of rights mirroring the Universal Declaration of Human Rights. It was thought that this new era would see greater regard for human needs, including economic and social rights as well as civil and political rights. However, the system of migrant labour remained intact, and with it, the persistence of poverty and poor living conditions. The mining industry is important in the South African economy, accounting for 60% of the country's exports and 10% of its GDP. The industry employed over 500,000 people in 2011. The government, dominated since the first democratic elections by the African National Congress (ANC), has adopted an accommodating approach to the large mining companies, stemming largely from their economic importance. However, simmering labour tensions and growing dissatisfaction with the government over slow progress in dealing with social deprivation, have led to industrial unrest.

Wildcat strikes erupted in the closing months of 2012 in platinum mines belonging to Lonmin, a London-listed company whose roots go back to Lonrho, the former mining empire founded in 1909. The strikes soon spread to other platinum mines and to gold mines. Striking miners protested with traditional weapons such as spears, but were met with brutal force by the South African police. At the Marikana mine owned by Lonmin, police with machine guns shot and killed 34 miners; another 78 were wounded. This event marked a low point in South Africa's post-apartheid history.

Despite the hopes of a better life under democratic government, little has changed for most miners. Under the migrant labour system, the mining companies recruit tens of thousands of workers to live in rudimentary housing, sometimes hundreds of kilometres from their families and home communities. The poor living conditions and poor pay have bred unrest. The companies have offered miners an option of taking a 'living out allowance' in addition to their pay, enabling them to find their own accommodation, but the result tends to be that they concentrate in slum-type housing which lacks basic services such as clean water and sanitation. Trade unions are active in the mining industry. The oldest is the National Union of Mineworkers (NUM), which is associated with the ANC and has collective bargaining rights in the gold mining sector. At platinum mines, the unions negotiate company by company. The Association of Mineworkers and Construction Union (Amcu) has sprung up recently.

A rival of the NUM, Amcu is more militant, and has made gains in membership from many disaffected workers, especially following the Marikana shootings. Amcu called the Lonmin miners out on strike. It has now eclipsed the NUM, and represents the majority of Lonmin workers and workers in mines owned by AngloAmerican Platinum, the largest of the platinum producers. Following weeks of strikes which closed mining operations for both these companies, they have increased the wages of miners by 11–12%. The companies warn, however, that their costs have also risen, at a time when they have lost revenues because of the closures. AngloGold had to suspend its operations for an entire month because of strikes. Its CEO has observed that it needs a new model of working relations. He said, 'As an industry we have not understood our workforce as well as we should' (England, 2012). He also said, 'We have done terrible damage to South Africa as an investment destination' (England, 2012). Lonmin had taken a hard line against strikers, going so far as to ask the Ministry of Justice for the state to use its full force against the strikers (Hain, 2013). This request was made three days before the shootings occurred. At a commemorative ceremony to mark one year since the massacre, the CEO of Lonmin said, 'It should not have taken the loss of so many lives for us as a company, as employees, as a community, and as a nation to learn that this should never have happened and that it should never happen again' (BBC, 2013). The government did not send representatives to the ceremony.

One year on from the shootings, no member of the police forces has been arrested. However, 270 miners were charged with 34 counts of murder, on the basis of the 'common purpose' law inherited from the apartheid era. The police argued that they were acting in self-defence, although video evidence seemed to show unarmed miners being shot. The South African government responded to growing public disquiet over inaction by setting up a commission of inquiry to try to establish the truth, following which, police officers could be charged if there was sufficient evidence. However, to the disappointment of the South Africa Human Rights Commission, the Ministry of Justice has stopped the legal aid funding for those injured and arrested to have legal representation to put their cases before the commission (South African Human Rights Commission, 2013). The Human Rights Commission pointed out the inherent unfairness of the process. The victims and accused, who have no resources, were up against a police establishment with abundant resources and legal expertise. As proceedings progressed in September 2013, the commission of inquiry became disturbed by mounting evidence that the police had withheld documents, tampered with evidence and not told the truth. The commission thus took the unusual step of halting the proceedings, with a hope of resuming at a later date, when the police would be expected to present more credible evidence.

South Africa is one of the world's most unequal societies. Although it is classified as a medium-income country, the level of poverty is more like a poor country. South Africa has made strides in improving basic services for its majority black population, but for many, little progress is evident. The élite business establishment, while formerly white only, now includes new black business leaders as well, but the fundamental inequality remains. High levels of corruption have become a worry, draining resources which could be used for meeting social needs. South Africa has fallen from a rank of 32 in the Corruption Perception Index of 1998 to 69 in 2012 (Transparency International, 2012). The rule of law and the promotion of human rights were goals of the new democratic era in South Africa. While the country has made economic progress, its progress in human rights seems more elusive.

Sources: England, A. (2012) 'Mine strikes to hasten sector shake-up', *Financial Times*, 8 November; BBC (2013) *Marikana Shooting: Lonmin Apologises for South Africa Deaths*, 16 August, at www.bbc.co.uk; Hain, P. (2013) 'Marikana mine death casts long shadow', *BBC*, 20 April, at www.bbc.co.uk; South African Human Rights Commission (2013) *Marikana Statement: SAHRC Disappointed at Lack of Funding*, 22 August, at www.sahrc.org.za; South African Government (2012) *Development Indicators 2012*, at www.polity.org.za; Transparency International (2012) *Corruption Perceptions Index 2012*, at www.transparency.org (18/09/14).

□ List the human rights discussed in this case study, describing each in the context of South Africa.

□ What factors led up to the strikes and shootings at Marikana?

□ Why is there cause for concern that the rule of law is at risk in South Africa? How would this affect potential investors?

CHAPTER 10

SUSTAINABILITY AND THE ETHICAL BUSINESS

ETHICAL THEMES IN THIS CHAPTER

◻ Businesses as part of society

◻ Sustainability guiding business and state actors

THE AIMS OF THIS CHAPTER ARE TO

◻ Identify the multiple dimensions of sustainability

◻ Assess how businesses are addressing climate change and other environmental impacts

◻ Appreciate the links between sustainability and human well-being

◻ Explore ethical initiatives in social enterprises

CANADA'S OIL SANDS: AN ENERGY SOURCE, BUT AT WHAT ENVIRONMENTAL PRICE?

OPENING CASE STUDY

Canada has long been aware of the possibilities for exploiting oil sands which stretch over a vast area of northern Alberta. The Great Canadian Oil Sands Company, now Suncor Energy, embarked on mining in the area in 1967. But the huge potential of the oil sands were only fully appreciated in recent years, as fears grew that it might not be possible to meet global demand for oil from more conventional oil reserves. The Alberta oil sands have now seen huge investment and increasing production, making Canada

Photo 10.1 *Canada's surface mining of tar sands creates a barren landscape, affecting water, wildlife and land.* (© iStock.com/ Dan Barnes)

the fifth largest oil producer globally, and one of the biggest oil exporters. But success also depends on transport infrastructure. The US is Canada's biggest oil customer, and Canadians are hopeful that a new north–south pipeline, the Keystone XL across the US, will facilitate rising exports. They also aspire to ship more oil to Asian emerging economies from Canada's west coast. The environmental impacts, however, are a cause of concern, both for the extraction industry and the proposed Keystone XL pipeline. The steps being taken to address environmental issues seem to be falling behind expectations, and the proposed pipeline has led to controversy. Can Canada realize the economic benefits from its oil reserves while also protecting the environment?

Unlike many of the world's big oil producers, such as those in the Middle East, Latin America and Africa, Canada is perceived as a stable energy exporter. Political instability, weak institutions and corruption are aspects of many oil-rich countries, which pose risks for foreign oil companies. By comparison, Canada is politically stable, has relatively advanced infrastructure, and has established market institutions. As an established democracy, it is proud of the rule of law, and companies can feel confident that contracts and legal obligations will be observed. From the operational perspective, Canada poses many challenges, however. Surface mining of the type that is needed to extract oil from the tar sands is environmentally damaging. The operations themselves cover a huge area, approximately 54,000 square miles (140,000 square kilometres). This is an area the size of England or Florida. Research has suggested that the operations have caused pollution in the freshwater ecosystems in the region, evidence of which goes back to the 1960s (Kinver, 2013).

The petroleum is bitumen, which is heavy and relatively low grade compared with the light crude produced in other oilfields. It must be mined and converted to thinner fuel for transporting. These

processes generate large amounts of greenhouse gases and also use large amounts of water. Emissions and water use are more detrimental in environmental terms than in conventional oil extraction. Canadian authorities have undertaken to monitor emissions, but monitoring seems to have become a source of political tension between the federal government and the provincial government of Alberta. A federal report in 2010 found there were shortcomings in the environmental monitoring, and it was decided to create a joint monitoring programme, to monitor air, water, wildlife and land. However, this plan was still being discussed in joint talks in 2013 (Wingrove, 2013). The prominent participation of a representative of the oil companies' association, who was the only non-government member in the talks, seemed to suggest a degree of lobbying influence which dismayed environmentalists. Canada's federal government, although initially signing up to the emissions reduction targets in the Kyoto Protocol, withdrew from the treaty in 2011. While it had been committed to reducing emissions to 5% below 1990 levels, in fact, its carbon emissions had risen one-third by 2011. Rising carbon emissions are a growing concern, and oil sands exploitation is a major source of Canada's emissions.

Institutional investors in the oil companies which operate in Alberta have set up a loose grouping to exert pressure for improvements in environmental performance, warning that 'environmental impacts could create a significant threat to future earnings' (Crooks, 2012). This could happen if water shortages become a problem or if regulations controlling greenhouse gas emissions make excavating in the oil sands uncompetitive. These investors manage about $2 trillion in investments in Canada's oil sands, through holdings in the numerous companies which operate in the region, including BP, Royal Dutch Shell, Statoil and Total. There is already a group formed by 12 oil companies in the region, which focuses on environmental issues. The Canada Oil Sands Innovation Alliance (Cosia), as its name suggests, seeks innovative ways to improve environmental performance, but it does not set targets for cuts in water use or reductions in emissions. The institutional investors would like to see a more robust approach to environmental problems. They also have cause to be concerned about the transport bottlenecks which threaten to slow production.

There are already oil pipelines connecting Canada and the US. The proposed Keystone XL pipeline would offer an improved direct pipeline, taking diluted bitumen from Alberta to refineries on the US Gulf coast. Owned and built by the Canadian company, Trans Canada, the pipeline would pass through areas of the US which are considered environmentally sensitive. There is always the risk of an accident, such as the burst pipeline belonging to Exxon Mobil, which resulted in thousands of barrels of Canadian oil spilling into a residential area in Arkansas. The US president has been reluctant to give approval for the Keystone XL pipeline.

A factor weighing with authorities in the US is that the production of oil from Canada's oil sands accounts for about 14% more carbon emissions than the oil produced by other countries from which it imports, including Saudi Arabia, Venezuela and Nigeria. Given the need to reduce emissions globally in light of climate change, increasing Canadian imports is seen as a step in the wrong direction. The US is seeing increasing production of its own shale oil deposits, such as Bakken crude from North Dakota. This domestic production is making the need for imports from Canada seem less urgent, but they are still considered desirable from the point of view of US energy security. Trains and trucks already carry large amounts of oil, but they are also significant emitters, and accidents are also a risk. In July 2013, there was a derailment of a train in an urban area in Québec. It was carrying Bakken crude, and in the fires which engulfed the train, 50 people lost their lives.

Canada remains committed to exploiting its oil sands and enhancing its position as a global oil producer, but it remains beset by environmental and transport concerns.

Sources: Vaughan, A. (2011) 'What does Canada's withdrawal from Kyoto Protocol mean?', *The Guardian*, 13 December, at www.theguardian.com; Kinver, M. (2013) 'Oil sands "toxins" accumulate in freshwater ecosystems', *BBC*, 8 January, at www.bbc.co.uk; Wingrove, J. (2013) 'Files show how Ottawa and Alberta haggled over oil sands monitoring', *The Globe and Mail*, 15 October, at www.theglobeandmail.com; McElroy, M. (2013) 'The Keystone XL pipeline', *The Harvard Magazine*, November–December, at www.harvardmagazine.com (18/09/14); Crooks, E. (2012) 'Investors push for greener oil sands', *Financial Times*, 22 October.

▫ **What are the pros and cons for exploiting Canada's oil sands, and which set of arguments is the stronger, in your view?**

▫ **What are the difficulties in monitoring and regulating environmental performance?**

▫ **In your view, are Canada's oil sands a sustainable source of energy?**

INTRODUCTION

Most businesspeople would like to see their enterprises thriving not just in the immediate future, but into the more distant future, continuing beyond the careers of the people who are currently in charge. Simply to stay financially viable requires business skills, innovative capacity and also plain luck. The idea of sustainability goes beyond just existing into the future, pointing towards investment decisions today that will yield benefits for the future. This is true whether it is applied to the single business or to a whole economy. It suggests that the firm's or the economy's goals and ways of doing things should not just allow it to survive, but should cause as little harm as possible and produce outcomes that are as good as possible for the long term. These are essentially ethical concepts, covering many aspects of a business. They include impacts on the environment, impacts on finite resources, impacts on people and societies. Sustainability thus covers a variety of contexts, and demands that businesses think about all aspects of their activities from a critical perspective.

This chapter begins with an overview of the different facets of sustainability as a concept, tracing its ethical links. We look particularly at sustainable development, which is now broadly conceived as representing a range of economic and social goals. Environmental issues were the first to be specifically identified with sustainable development. Issues such as climate change, emissions and use of resources are discussed in the following section. We then look at sustainability in the context of agriculture and the food chain, highlighting human needs as an aspect of sustainability. The next section looks at social enterprises, which combine business objectives with social aims. While they are driven by ideals, they also point the way for more mainstream businesses to combine sustainable strategies and CSR.

THE MULTIPLE FACETS OF SUSTAINABILITY

Sustainability as a concept applying to the global economy came to prominence following its emphasis in the Brundtland Report of 1987, which was endorsed by the Rio Summit of 1992. The Brundtland Report defined sustainable development as 'development which meets the needs of present generations without compromising the ability of future generations to meet their own needs' (UN, 1987). It linked development with intergenerational equity, calling on the current generation to behave in ways that enable future generations to live as well as they do themselves. Also sometimes called 'intergenerational justice', this is essentially an ethical duty, which the Brundtland authors are urging should be adopted and implemented by states. The report recognized states' rights to development, but coupled them with obligations towards the environment. Development at the time was seen mainly as economic development, and concerns about damage to the environment were framed in terms of states' obligations. These remain vital elements, and, to many, they remain central. But this is a narrow view of development, and its focus on states is inappropriate in assessing and dealing with global issues. Sustainability has now come to be seen in a wider context than envisaged two decades ago. We look first at the view of sustainability which focuses on economic and environmental facets.

ECONOMIC AND ENVIRONMENTAL SUSTAINABILITY

Development has long been identified with industrialization and capital formation, resulting in growing labour markets and growing national income. In the economist's view, well-being for human beings is equated with economic well-being. However, it has broader implications than the merely economic. Benefits which come with growing economies include improving standards of living, providing jobs, improving education and reducing poverty. These gains are made possible by economic development, in particular, economic growth. Without growth, the economist sees little prospect of reducing poverty. The economist who is concerned about sustainable development looks at the ways in which an economy can be managed so that productive capacity will last into the long-term future (Solow, 1992). This involves making decisions about the using scarce resources and giving priority to investment, with a view to maintaining living standards for future generations (Solow, 1992). Many would consider this perspective one of weak or basic sustainable development, as shown in Figure 10.1. It takes a rather optimistic view that intergenerational equity can be met by more efficient use of resources, the discovery of new resources and technological innovation. It assumes that current material standards of living are not at risk, and does not see the need for any radical change in lifestyles and patterns of consumption (Williams and Millington, 2004).

International businesses play important roles in this basic approach to sustainable development, as shown in Figure 10.1. They carry out much of the research into cleaner technology, and they do much of the exploration and research on new sources of energy. Much of this activity is fostered by governments, which help with funding incentives. For an MNE, this type of investment makes business sense, even leaving aside the question of whether the

Figure 10.1 *Sustainability: economic and environmental perspectives*

company itself is committed to sustainability as an ethical principle. The grouping of oil companies featured in the opening case study exemplifies this basic view of sustainability, focusing on innovation to deal with environmental challenges. In fact, most companies now accept the need for framing strategy along sustainable lines. For many, this is an aspect of risk management, ensuring that products and operations are in conformity with environmental standards which are either part of national law or international conventions. Many adopt standards in accord with a CSR perspective, going beyond legal requirements, and including sustainability reporting in their annual reports. A widely adopted reporting framework is that of the Global Reporting Initiative (at www.globalreporting.org), which has widened its sustainability reporting guidelines to include anti-corruption and ethics in supply chains. This view of sustainability, nonetheless, is the moderate one of adapting current business models.

Proponents of **strong sustainable development**, by contrast, urge that patterns of consumption as well as production need to change to meet goals of sustainability. They would say that sustainability is a misleading term, implying that we need simply to maintain ways of doing things (Dower, 2004: 403). In fact, much of what is being done in the global economy is damaging, and needs to be changed. They would say that both consumption patterns and production strategies must change. Some take the view that

The proponents of a stronger approach to sustainability urge preserving ecosystems and biodiversity not simply because of the benefits to humans, now and in the future, but because of their inherent value.

our approach to the environment is too **anthropocentric**, that is, assuming the only interests that matter are those of human beings. On this view, steps to protect the environment are justified only insofar as they serve human interests. Ecosystems are seen as having instrumental value only, not inherent value (Shue, 1995). The proponents of a stronger approach to sustainability urge preserving ecosystems and biodiversity not simply because of the benefits to humans, but because of their inherent value. For example, this would be an argument behind a sense of responsibility to preserve species threatened with extinction (Sen, 2010: 251).

This stronger view, held by many ecologists, urges that the consequences of climate change, pollution and depletion of resources demand alterations to consumer lifestyles. Between the basic and strong views of sustainability there are numerous gradations. A moderate view of sustainable development holds that we should focus both on using resources more efficiently and reducing demand. This moderate approach is one which is more likely to be welcomed by governments. However, the focus remains a kind of trade-off between development goals and environmental protection. A practical difficulty for the proponents of the stronger view of sustainable development is implementation. Governments do not wish to court unpopularity or to risk growth. In particular, they are reluctant to undermine businesses which generate profits in lucrative consumer sectors. Governments tend to be locked into a perspective of national competitive advantage.

Consumers in the emerging economies are rapidly gaining a taste for western lifestyles, eating more meat, buying cars, and having long-distance holidays. These growth industries all put pressures on the environment, adding to challenges posed by industrialization and urbanization. Governments in emerging economies are likely to see sustainable development as economic sustainability in the weak sense. Their concern is increasing economic growth and productive capacity to generate jobs. They tend to speak of sustainable economic growth, implying a rate of growth commensurate with delivering jobs and economic well-being expected by their increasingly urban populations. Political leaders, whether elected or not, wish to avert social instability. Providing conditions in which the material expectations of the populace can be met is seen as the surest means.

PAUSE TO CONSIDER…

Which of the two approaches to sustainable development do you support: the basic approach or the stronger approach? Give your reasons.

SUSTAINABILITY AS HUMAN WELL-BEING

Human well-being has multiple dimensions, including material aspects of a decent life and capacity for moral development. These facets are related. For children, healthy diet, education and healthcare in their first few years pave the way for a healthy and fulfilling life as adults. The world's population at present is about 7 billion, and it is expected to reach 9 billion by 2050. Most of this population growth is taking place in poor countries (UN, 2011). The UN estimates that 1.4 billion of the world's people, or one in five, live in absolute poverty, defined as living on $1.25 or less a day. A billion people live in hunger, and 2.5 billion lack sustained access to improved sanitation (UN, 2012). Marking the 20th anniversary of the first Rio Summit, the UN held a second Rio Summit, the Rio+20 Summit, in 2012. Its two main themes were how to achieve sustainable development through green measures to lift people out of poverty, and how to improve international co-ordination for sustainable development. The issue of poverty and associated aspects of human deprivation was thus given prominence at the top of the agenda. The second theme, international co-ordination, impliedly acknowledges the lack of strong international institutions which can exert pressure on states.

The **UN Millennium Development Goals (MDGs)**, devised in 2000, represent a broad view of human well-being, including meeting basic human needs and environmental goals. They are shown in Figure 10.2. Each goal was conceived as subject to a target to be achieved in 2015. Their implementation depends on government action within states. States with poor governance and weak accountability struggle to achieve these targets.

Figure 10.2 *The UN Millennium Development Goals*

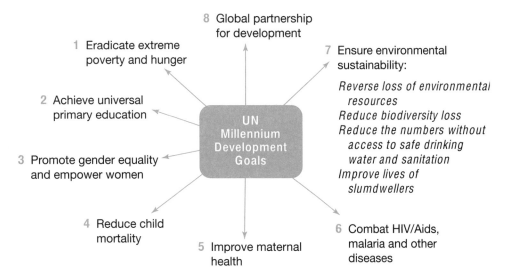

Source: UN (2013) *Millennium Development Goals 2015 and Beyond, 2013 Factsheet*, at www.un.org/millenniumgoals (18/09/14).

The seventh MDG, on sustainability, is detailed in Figure 10.2. It links environmental goals and goals associated with human well-being. It asks governments to take action to make positive changes, not simply to maintain the status quo, as would befit a weak view of environmental sustainability. This was echoed in the Rio+20 Summit, which pointed out the risks of climate change due to rising levels of greenhouse gases. It noted that a third of known species could become extinct if climate change is not addressed. We noted in Chapter 2 that the UN now looks at human development as a broader measure of human well-being. It encompasses economic indicators, education and life expectancy. These give a broad indication of quality of life. It now also has an index which takes inequality into account. The importance of social justice is thus acknowledged. However, human development also involves access to means of moral fulfilment. Education is a necessary step. Through education, we acquire knowledge, judgment and skills to make the most of our lives, and also the capacity to develop morally.

The uniqueness of the human being lies in autonomy of will and moral capacity. We noted above that a duty to future generations is essentially ethical. From the sustainability perspective, what is it that we should be conserving and building in terms of moral capacity? Sustainable development has tended to focus on economic capacity. From a deeper ethical perspective, sustainability is about sustaining the means by which each person can attain a good life. It includes not just economic well-being and environmental conservation, but values such as promoting peace, ensuring social justice and observing human rights.

Material well-being, it could be argued, rather than being an end in itself, should be seen as one of the means towards the end of enhancing human self-fulfilment in a moral sense. This view of sustainability takes a potentially stronger position on environmental protection, arguing that, for example, while destroying ecosystems to build factories brings jobs and greater prosperity to a region, it should be seen in a bigger picture of improving human well-being. Thus, a sustainability risk assessment for a new factory would include a wider range of issues than might be assumed. Here are some of the questions that might be asked:

- What ecosystems would be affected, and with what consequences?
- What sort of jobs would be created? Would they use migrant labour or local labour? Will workers receive living wages or national minimum wages?
- Does the company wishing to build the factory have strong stakeholder management practices and CSR? What is its record on ethical business practices and corporate governance?
- What products are to be made, and what health risks are involved for workers? How recyclable are the products?
- What types of pollution and waste risks are involved?
- How energy-efficient would the factory be, and how water-efficient would it be? Would it divert water needed by communities in the area?
- What legal liabilities does the owner of the proposed factory owe to the community and workers, and are they enforceable in practice?

Sustainability viewed as promoting human well-being broadens the range of issues addressed to the potential investor. Beyond economic and environmental issues lie the questions about human rights, respect for workers as people and the engagement with the community. For the business contemplating new investments, the assessment of sustainability becomes more nuanced, and also rather more tilted towards ethical considerations.

For example, H&M, the retailer featured in the opening case study of Chapter 7 (on CSR) should be uneasy with some of these questions. It publishes a sustainability report each year, much of which focuses on conditions within its supplier factories. Confronted with this list of questions, the prognosis would not look good for sustainability in terms of human well-being in places such as Bangladesh and Cambodia. Wages are typically the national minimum, conditions are dangerous, pollution is a health risk, and factory owners pay little heed to worker voice. There are legal liabilities, but they are weakly enforced. Fast fashion has a short lifespan: new products enter the market every few weeks, tempting consumers to throw out the old and buy new, even though the older garments are still wearable. On these criteria, these operations would not be considered sustainable.

The UN has found that poor countries have become a dumping ground for toxic e-waste, an increasing problem caused by mountains of discarded electronic goods, from old computers to smartphones. Consumers are encouraged to change their gadgets frequently, to benefit from the latest technology. Few probably consider the problems created by the accumulation of e-waste, but, globally, 50 million tonnes of e-waste are discarded annually. Shipping containers of discarded electronics are exported to poor countries in large numbers, much of it illegal. These goods should be recycled, but to avoid the costs of recycling, companies ship them labelled 'used goods' to landfills in poor countries (Vidal, 2013). It is estimated by Interpol that nearly one in three containers leaving the EU contains illegal e-waste destined for developing countries. Electronic gadgets contain a cocktail of toxic substances, including lead, mercury and cadmium. Once in a landfill, they seep into the soil, water and air. Most phones also contain precious metals such as zinc, gold and copper, which could be recycled. This would relieve the pressures on supply as well as helping to stop the dumping of toxic e-waste.

ETHICAL FOUNDATIONS OF SUSTAINABILITY

The notion of human dignity is the basis of ethical theories of sustainability. They hold that avoiding harm to others and promoting human values entails duties to people alive today and also future generations. Sustainability thus involves notions of rights and duties. There are moral duties towards the natural environment and towards other human beings. In a sense, respect owed to the natural environment reflects the fact that we share the planet with other living creatures: the lives of all are enhanced by efforts to preserve rather than destroy life. This ethical stance features in a number of religions, but does not depend on a belief that nature is endowed with religious significance. It can simply be viewed as an ethical principle.

Human beings have rights such as the right to life, and also the 'negative' rights like freedom from harassment and discrimination. There are corresponding duties: the duty to respect life and the duty not to harass others. These are, in a sense, two sides of the same coin. Removing an impediment such as discrimination allows a person to pursue individual fulfilment. This view of moral self-realization stems from a Kantian view of human dignity, whereby people are treated as ends rather than means (Dower, 2004).

Justice is a moral concept which features strongly in discourses on sustainability. As we have seen, it is used to signify duties to future generations, and features in the analysis of sustainability identified with economic well-being. However, ethical theorists view justice in terms of means as well as ends. Removing obstacles in the way of people realizing their

Figure 10.3 *Sustainability: human well-being*

goals takes a view of justice as focusing on the negative rights. Liberal theorists would say that this is the extent of what justice requires. This point of view is shown on the left in Figure 10.3. But a liberal theorist such as John Rawls would say that this is not enough. Justice is about sustaining the means of attaining a good life for all. This entails positive duties to meet the basic needs of people in society (Rawls, 1971). A liberal like Rawls would tend to think that this duty is focused on the specific society, holding that countries should aim to improve living standards and safeguard freedoms for their own people, including future generations. In the international sphere, the liberal would believe in a negative duty not to violate rights of others, but would say that people in one country do not owe positive duties to people in other countries, such as poor people in Africa. However, human well-being is universal, and would justify interpreting sustainability in a global sense. The more universal approach is shown on the right side of Figure 10.3. It takes the view that human rights are matters of global concern, not just the concern of states. As the figure suggests, international institutions would be needed, whereas the liberal approach would advocate merely international standards, without the institutions to enforce them against states.

The economic and social rights in the Universal Declaration of Human Rights (UDHR) are stated to be universal, not contained within states' boundaries. The UDHR envisaged that international institutions should come into play to realize human rights, but, as we saw in the last chapter, the state-centric system prevailed in the later covenants. This does not mean that there is no duty, for example, for rich countries to come to the aid of poor ones. But such a duty would be derived from ethical principles, not law. The government within a society feels obliged to lessen the impacts of inequality within the country, but obligations need not stop at the state's border. In a sense, Rawls' view of justice can thus be globalized

(Pogge, 1988). There is a parallel here with the question asked in relation to the duty of care owed to other people. As we found in Chapter 4, the key question is 'Who is my neighbour?' My neighbour could be anyone that I can reasonably foresee would be affected by my actions. The manufacturer of an unsafe product owes an obligation to consumers, wherever they are in the world. A global approach to justice implies that basic needs should be met everywhere, and international measures should be used to achieve these goals. In reality, however, states control the policies and means of implementing them.

PAUSE TO CONSIDER...

Look again at Figure 10.3. Assess the pros and cons of each ethical approach: the liberal approach which focuses on society and state, and the more internationalist approach.

ENVIRONMENTAL CHALLENGES AND SUSTAINABILITY

The MDGs envisaged a role for private-sector enterprises through the Global Compact (see Chapter 7). The Global Compact was intended to allow companies to work with NGOs and governments to promote basic principles derived from the UDHR and the Rio Summit. This initiative helps companies to frame ethical arguments for a broader perspective on sustainability, and it does seem to act as a catalyst for CSR. Importantly, it presents a view of CSR which takes in both global and local dimensions.

Every company must assess the risks that are posed in its business, both currently and for the future. Although companies are inclined to look at short-term impacts on profits, corporate strategy must also look ahead to future risks. Environmental challenges are not always easy to assess. For the company with a CSR focus, these considerations are part of its ethical responsibility and are subject to changing legal obligations. They are also aspects of economic responsibility, as environmental constraints can impact directly on costs and operations. For example, rising energy costs can have drastic effects on the company's business model. The company which focuses exclusively on economic considerations and takes a minimalist view of legal obligations risks underestimating the risks to its existing business model. What is more, that company is not actively seeking opportunities to promote sustainability. In this section, we look at some of the more pressing environmental concerns which impact on businesses.

CLIMATE CHANGE

Climate change, or, more specifically, global warming, is a multi-faceted phenomenon. A general rise in the earth's temperature is now seen by scientists as well established. They predict possible temperature rises of 3°C or 4°C over pre-industrial levels by the end of this century. This is far greater than any rise that has occurred in human history. Scientists are 95% certain that human activity is the main cause of current global warming (IPCC, 2013). Concentrations of greenhouse gases, notably carbon dioxide (CO_2), are chiefly to blame. The UN's Intergovernmental Panel on Climate Change (IPCC) has found that CO_2 concentrations have increased 40% since 1750, which was roughly the beginning of the industrial era. This increase is mainly due to fossil-fuel emissions.

Rising CO_2 emissions are associated with rapid industrial growth fuelled mainly by energy derived from coal. China is now the largest emitter, followed by the US and India (see Figure 10.4). China is now responsible for 29% of global carbon emissions. If we look at per capita emissions, China is rapidly rising, and now stands at 7.2 tonnes per capita. This

Figure 10.4 *The world's top three carbon-emitting countries*

Billions of metric tons of CO_2

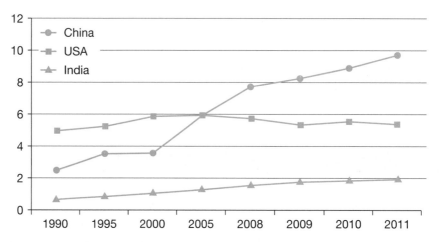

Source of data: EU Commission (2013) *Emissions Database for Global Atmospheric Research (EDGAR)*, at edgar.jrc.ec.europa.eu (18/09/14).

is similar to European countries and is classified in the range of major industrialized coun-tries. US per capita emissions remain much higher, at 17.3 tonnes per capita, despite the effects of recession (EU Joint Research Centre, 2012). China's levels of pollution are danger-ously high in some regions, especially in the north of the country. The effects on human health and the environment can be devastating, especially during spells of thick smog. China's pollution is not contained within its boundaries. It travels to other parts of Asia, and even continents further afield.

The Kyoto Protocol, a UN convention which dates from 1988, committed developed countries that ratified the treaty to reduce carbon emissions to 5% below 1990 levels by 2012. These targets were not imposed on developing countries, in keeping with a view that their right to growth should not be fettered in this way. Since 1998, the US, an original signatory, has unsigned the treaty, and China, still technically a developing country, has become the biggest emitter by far. The Kyoto framework has not been renewed, and there is little prospect of new agreed targets for either developed or developing countries. Instead, it is likely that future climate change negotiations will go along with each country setting its own targets. Industrialization in earlier eras caused environmental degradation and suffo-cating pollution. Governments in many developed countries, both local and national, have taken steps to reduce pollution and increase the use of clean technology, for the sake of human health as much as to protect the environment. Slower economic growth has also had environmental benefits in slowing pollution. Today's emerging economies have tended to stand by their growth models, arguing that they are as entitled to industrialize as earlier industrializing countries. However, climate change science now shows that the risks are much greater, and that the need for 'substantial and sustained' reductions in greenhouse gas emissions is imperative (IPCC, 2013: 14). The Rio Summit of 1992 had stressed the need for development to be sustainable, but this message was not heeded by the emerging economies, whose governments pursued rapid growth in the following two decades. What of the role of businesses?

'Substantial and sustained' reductions in greenhouse gas emissions are imperative.

We might say that businesses, even in emerging economies, should take the lead in reducing emissions. Many have been pioneering clean technology, but these are not mainstream activities. Google, Lego and Ikea, all in different sectors, have in common the fact that they are investing significantly in windfarms. This investment in renewable energy could be simply a peripheral activity, but it could also signify a genuine shift in corporate strategy towards sustainability (Clark, 2012). Still, these are small initiatives when seen from the standpoint of a whole economy. Significant greening, most would agree, requires government direction in the form of law and regulation. Companies exist to make profits, not to save the planet. In general, only when governments change the rules for everyone, do mainstream companies adopt new strategies. They respond to legal obligations rather than merely ethical ones. In mainstream economic activity, companies have had few incentives to adopt greener strategies. The financial crisis and recession in the US and Europe has forced economic issues to the top of the agenda for companies and governments, while environmental concerns have slipped back.

An external shock is sometimes the catalyst. The oil crises of the 1970s saw oil quadruple in price. California had become notorious for its heavy smogs, but decision-makers, in both government and business, decided that economic activity would have to adapt to changes in energy use. One environmental expert has said that, crucially, they took the decision to rely on gas rather than coal for energy generation (Clark, 2012). Looking at the current situation in China, she ponders how long China can carry on with its dependence on coal. Clean technology has greatly progressed since the 1970s, and China can benefit from these developments to maintain growth which would have been less sustainable in earlier eras. But the data above suggest that China is not prioritizing sustainability. Would its businesses take initiatives without government incentives? The dominance of huge state-controlled enterprises in key sectors, along with the influence on governance exerted by the party leadership in ostensibly private-sector companies, suggests that businesses follow government leads. China is not immune to environmental shocks connected with climate change. Severe storms, drought and flooding are examples, and their impacts can be significant in the rapidly-expanding urban landscape.

The influences of climate change can be widely ramified, and also contentious. It is established that rising sea levels are connected with climate change. Coasts and low-lying regions are particularly vulnerable. Extreme weather conditions such as damaging storms and flooding are associated with climate change, as are severe heatwaves and desertification in some regions. Some of the most extreme impacts of climate change are being felt in the poorest, most vulnerable countries, which have limited resources for ameliorating the problems. The results can be devastating. Land which once supported life and agriculture can become arid, causing inhabitants to move on to other places, which, in turn, can also become precarious. Governments are aware of the risks from storms and flooding. They invest in flood defences and draw up emergency plans for major storms. But the risk of storms has always existed, and it is difficult to say to what extent any given storm is caused by general weather patterns or climate change. It is generally held that more frequent and more severe storms are attributable to climate change. Poor countries such as Bangladesh, low-lying and at risk from flooding as well as at risk from rising sea levels, are particularly vulnerable. Over ten thousand people lost their lives when the biggest storm ever recorded struck the Philippines in 2013. At the opposite end of the

Some of the most extreme impacts of climate change are being felt in the poorest, most vulnerable countries.

wealth spectrum, New York was shown to be highly vulnerable when it was struck by superstorm Sandy in 2012.

Sandy caused the deaths of at least 117 people and left a path of devastation, through both commercial areas and poor residential districts, where inhabitants lost their homes. It also caused a breakdown of the transport system. A month after the storm, the Wall Street financial district was still without mains power and relying on emergency generators. One year on from the disaster, New York's subway system was still not fully restored (BBC, 2013).

The US president wishes to introduce regulations to reduce emissions from coal-fired power plants, both new and old, but faces political opposition in getting such legislation onto the statute books. Since 2008, the US has been using less coal to produce power, and increasing its use of oil and gas from new domestic sources of shale oil and gas. This has been made possible by technological advances in hydraulic fracturing (fracking). These advances have moved quickly, thanks to the rapid rise of numerous entrepreneurial SMEs. While this is good news from the standpoint of developing new resources, the processes of fracking and horizontal drilling are themselves controversial from an environmental perspective.

MEETING ENERGY NEEDS SUSTAINABLY

In areas like clean energy, companies are more inclined to invest money in solving immediate problems than in making long-term investments with high technological risk and uncertain costs. However, sustainability as a goal is about future generations, demanding long-term projects that carry big risks. Governments can provide incentives to some extent, but, as we noted above, a difficulty is that new technology might not be enough to solve the problems of scarce energy resources and a growing world population. Governments tend to be preoccupied with energy security, by which they mean that the country should have either its own accessible energy reserves for the foreseeable future, or have access to stable supplies from other regions of the world. International relations and foreign policy decisions are often determined by these considerations. Unfortunately, the priority given to energy security sometimes leads to territorial incursion into other countries. Colonialism, as we found in Chapter 6, was largely fuelled by the wish to control resources. It can lead to exploitation which is questionable on ethical and environmental grounds, causing potential damage in communities and habitats. Of considerable help is the fact that new technology is making it possible to tap new sources of energy and also to use energy more efficiently. It has been estimated that, while global GDP will expand 135% between 2013 and 2040, energy demand will grow by only 35%, most of it in developing countries (Chazan, 2013). Increasing energy efficiency is the reason for this discrepancy. Nonetheless, the money invested in energy efficiency is exceeded many times over by the amounts ploughed into finding and maintaining new sources of fossil fuel.

Oil-rich North African and Middle Eastern economies have long benefited from increasing global demand, and their reserves of oil and gas continue to make them important players in global energy (see the closing case study). But new sources of oil, like shale oil in the Americas, have gone some way to diversifying sources of oil and gas. Instability in a number of oil-rich countries, coupled with regional conflicts and religious conflicts between Shia and Sunni Muslims, have been factors in prompting resource exploration in other areas of the world. Some of the newer sources, however, bring new environmental risks. While fracking technology is improving, it brings risks of contaminating water resources and causes air pollution. Some countries, notably in Europe, currently ban fracking, despite the possibilities that they might have substantial oil reserves. Offshore sources of oil are also being explored off the coasts of Brazil and Mexico. Brazil's oilfields lie beneath a two-kilometre layer of salt under the seabed. There are huge technological challenges for Petrobras, the state-owned oil company. Mexico is also producing oil. Its state oil company, Pemex, has a monopoly over Mexico's oil industry, enshrined in its constitution, but steps are now being taken to bring in expertise from the private sector, which could potentially transform its oil industry. The world's large oil companies, such as BP, Shell, Total and Chevron, are important players, and it is their expertise which can be crucial in some of the harsher, more technically challenging environments. Gazprom, the state-owned Russian gas giant, has ambitious plans for extracting oil from the harsh Arctic, and has embarked on co-operative ventures with large oil companies. These can be uneasy alliances, as national oil companies are never far removed from the political leadership of a country.

Oil and gas resources can help to bring the energy security that countries desire, but they also involve environmental risks. There are risks of accidents, spillages and pollution of air, soil and water. Spillages have led to some serious disasters. Among them is the 2010 Deepwater Horizon disaster at Macondo in the Gulf of Mexico, for which BP is being sued in the US for many billions of dollars. That case involved other companies in addition to BP, and a number of criminal prosecutions are taking place in addition to civil proceedings. Shell has been involved in proceedings connected with its operations in the Niger delta in Nigeria (see Chapter 9). Its difficulties in Nigeria are due mainly to organized theft from pipelines, stemming from social and political unrest. Nigeria has huge oil reserves, and has been a major exporter to the US. Nigeria's government faces challenges in dealing with social and ethnic unrest. Potentially, its oil wealth should pay for better services to meet the needs of its people, but corruption and conflict have set back progress. Shell faced lawsuits in connection with human rights claims, where it was alleged to have acted in co-operation with the government (see Chapter 9).

Extraction industries generally involve environmental degradation. In the worst cases, they can affect whole communities, causing harm to human health and the ability of inhabitants to meet basic needs, such as water and food. Nuclear power, often considered a viable alternative to non-renewable resources, was set back by the tsunami which struck Japan's Fukushima power station in 2011. The disaster highlighted the risks of radiation leaks from nuclear power. Following the disaster, the Japanese power company and the government struggled with the fallout, as other governments watched nervously. The German government announced the winding down of its nuclear generation. But a result has been increased use of coal.

Contamination of soil and water are long-term legacies of oil drilling and other extraction activities. Investing companies have contracts with governments in these locations. When damage results, who should pay? The Rio Summit echoed the legal principle that the polluter pays, but it is not easy to assess liability in many cases. The answer depends in large part on where the damage is caused, and how. The Macondo disaster saw BP paying out many billions of dollars to businesses in the coastal region of Louisiana which claimed economic losses from lost business. A number of other companies were involved in those operations, and litigation continues.

Going back two decades, indigenous people in Ecuador claim their health and well-being suffered from the environmental impacts caused by the oil operations of Texaco, a US oil company. High rates of cancer and other diseases were a result. In the 1970s and 80s, an area of 1,500 square miles of Amazon rainforest was affected, particularly from the dumping of toxic waste, which turned the area into a wasteland by the time Texaco left in 1992. The rainforest victims pursued their claim for damages in the US, but lost on the principle that it should have been heard in Ecuador (see Chapter 9).

The Ecuadorians then took their legal battle back to Ecuador, where they were awarded damages of $19 billion by the local court. The defendant in that case was Chevron, which had taken over Texaco – and its legal liabilities – in 2001. Chevron has robustly refused to pay, maintaining that it had nothing to do with the damage, and has no assets in Ecuador. It launched a lawsuit against the Ecuadorians' lawyer in New York, for $19 billion. Chevron argued that he was part of a fraudulent conspiracy with the Ecuadorian court. Chevron sought and obtained a court judgment in New York which would prevent the Ecuadorians from collecting their damages award anywhere in the world. This case ultimately went to the US Supreme Court.

Chevron received considerable support from US business interests in its efforts to persuade the Supreme Court judges that the Ecuadorian court hearing was invalid and that a global ban on paying victims the award should be imposed. However, the US Supreme Court refused to hear the case. This has opened the way for the Ecuadorians to seek payment in other jurisdictions where Chevron has assets, including Brazil, Canada and Argentina (Barrett, 2012). A court in Argentina has granted an order against Chevron, but the company maintains it has no legal liability to pay. It said on the eve of the court case in Ecuador, 'We are in the business of producing energy for the future, not the cleaning up after other companies' (Laing, 2009). However, it cannot avoid the legal liabilities of Texaco, just as Dow Chemical, the new owner of Union Carbide, is still being pursued by Bhopal victims. US oil companies in the 1970s were less conscious of environmental and human rights concerns in the Amazon than we might expect today. Part of the reason would lie in the fact that corporate behaviour is now publicized extensively in global media. But it is also the case that oil companies are now scrutinized more than ever over CSR policies and practices, as the opening case study showed. In its corporate responsibility report of 2012, Chevron boasts of its gasfields in Bangladesh, stating that it is helping Bangladesh to achieve energy security, rather than to rely on imports (Chevron, 2013). However, such is the growing demand for energy in the country that, without continuing discovery of new wells, gas reserves could be exhausted in ten years. It is arguable that constantly striving to keep ahead of demand is not a sustainable approach to energy, especially in light of the perils of climate change. Changing patterns of resource use and consumption would be more sustainable, but such a policy would not be welcomed by profit-conscious oil companies.

'We are in the business of producing energy for the future, not the cleaning up after other companies ...'

PAUSE TO CONSIDER...

If a global sustainable energy policy were being devised, what should be its components, in your view, and why?

AGRICULTURE AND FOOD: MOVING TOWARDS SUSTAINABILITY?

Like energy, food security is a concern of governments. Another two billion people will inhabit the globe by 2050. Most of this population growth is taking place in developing countries, as shown in Figure 10.5. To feed all these people, production of food will have to rise 70% (Lucas and Fontanella-Khan, 2013). This poses serious challenges for all in the agriculture and food sectors. By 2050, nearly 90% of the world's population will live in developing countries, and 22% of the world's people will live in the least-developed countries, where most of the people suffering from hunger are located. By 2050, five least-developed countries – Bangladesh, the Democratic Republic of Congo, Ethiopia, Tanzania and Uganda – will be among the world's 20 most populous countries (UN, 2011). In this section, we look at the perspectives of both producers and consumers.

Figure 10.5 *Projected population growth to 2050*

Millions of people

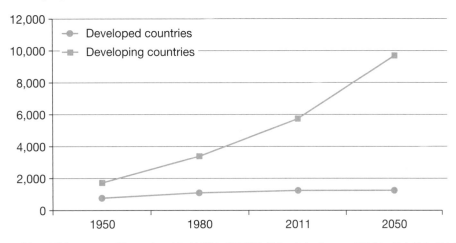

Source of data: UN Department of Economic and Social Affairs (2011) *World Population Prospects 2010* (New York: United Nations).

PRODUCERS' PERSPECTIVES

Agricultural yields have become less predictable in recent years, largely due to the effects of climate change, including drought and flooding, that have taken their toll on food production. Price volatility has been a result. Rich countries are better able to maintain food supplies than poor countries, even though most poor countries are predominantly agrarian. Fragile agricultural lands and subsistence farming in developing countries are a concern to governments, added to which are the vagaries of natural disasters and volatile market prices. Chapter 6 highlighted that trade in commodities, including agricultural commodities, is dominated by a few giant companies. Four dominate agricultural commodities. Known as the ABCD companies, they are Archer Daniels Midland, Bunge, Cargill and Dreyfus. They are now in dominant positions in global food supply chains, co-ordinating production, processing and shipping, in addition to their traditional roles in trading. Although most consumers are not familiar with their names, these food giants are among the most powerful players in global food supply, markets and pricing.

Urbanization is adding to the pressures in developing countries, as rural dwellers are driven from fragile lands to the cities. There are numerous causes of problems associated with hunger. One observation sometimes made is that there is more to go around than might appear. The food is just in the wrong place, and much is wasted. In the rich countries, about a third of food production ends up as waste. In India, the lack of adequate storage facilities means that a third of the grain produced either rots or is attacked by rodents. China stockpiles up to 300 million tonnes of grain for food security, but the exact amount is not publicized. As China's food imports grow, its leaders are preoccupied with sustainable supplies. China has about 9% of the world's farmland, but consumes 20% of the world's food supply. Its rapid industrialization has resulted in a growing urban population and fewer people on the land producing food. Environmental deterioration and pollution have led to even greater concerns about sustainable food supplies as demand continues to grow.

China and some other food-importing countries have taken the radical step of acquiring control of land in other countries for the purpose of producing crops for export to their own populations. Known as 'land grab', this is a controversial practice almost always involving powerful players in a richer country acquiring land through leasehold in a poorer country. It might be assumed that the poorer country would be using the land to grow food for its own people. But governments are sometimes tempted by the deals offered, which promise investment, development and often infrastructure projects. The attractions for the acquiring country lie in control over supplies and avoidance of price volatility in global markets. Steep rises in food prices in 2008, due largely to drought in key global agricultural regions, led to a growth in land acquisitions.

China, the rich Gulf states and South Korea have been among the leading acquirers of agricultural land, and much of the land targeted is in Africa and Southeast Asia. These projects can meet with hostility, including protests in the target country. One

'This reminds us of a colonial process even when there is no colonial link between the two countries involved.'

of the most ambitious so far is a 50-year plan by a state-owned Chinese company to lease a huge tract of land in Ukraine. The land leased to the Chinese amounts to 3 million hectares, or 9% of Ukraine's arable land (Spillius, 2013). It is not surprising that Ukraine has been targeted. It exports huge amounts of grain already, and would have plenty for its own population. Still, there are social and environmental concerns. The land deal would result in small local farmers losing their livelihoods, with consequences for existing communities. While the Chinese have promised new technology and greater efficiency to achieve greater productivity, environmentalists have questioned the sustainability of these proposals. What the area needs, they say, is investment in sustainable rural development, focusing on people as well as the environment. One expert has said, 'This reminds us of a colonial process even when there is no colonial link between the two countries involved' (Spillius, 2013).

The role of science and technology figures strongly in meeting demand for food worldwide. Science has contributed to increasing crop yields through the use of genetically-modified (GM) crops. GM crops have been developed to produce greater yields, resist diseases, resist pests, thrive in drought, or, alternatively, thrive in flooded fields. While this sounds like remarkably good news, it raises broad sustainability issues. Environmentalists are concerned about the loss of biodiversity and possible long-term effects on ecosystems. Conventional plant breeding is a traditional way of dealing with problems, and preserves biodiversity. Traditional farming provides livelihoods and supports communities, with both employment and food. Many countries express concerns that the industrial approach to farming will be socially and environmentally destructive. The US has been at the forefront of GM production, and US companies, notably Monsanto, are among the dominant companies in GM cultivation. The power of Monsanto is a factor which weighs with many critics of GM crops. In India, Monsanto in effect gained a monopoly, buying out most of the local Indian competitors. When committing to GM cultivation, the farmer is contractually committed to using Monsanto's patented seeds, fertilizers and pesticides. The costs soon mount up for poor farmers, and indebtedness has grown. Critics of GM crops, such as the environmentalist, Vandana Shiva, say bluntly that they are 'anti-life' (Shiva, 2013). Whereas the farmer using traditional methods relies on the seeds from this year for next year's crop, with patented seeds, the farmer must buy new seeds every year, and, crucially, buy them only from Monsanto. She says, 'Nature is impoverished, biodiversity is eroded, and a free, open resource is transformed into a patented commodity' (Shiva, 2013).

'Nature is impoverished, biodiversity is eroded, and a free, open resource is transformed into a patented commodity.'

Monsanto sues farmers for patent infringement when they grow plants from seeds they have gathered. In a noteworthy case, a farmer in Indiana in the US obtained seeds cheaply from grain in a grain store, intended for animal feed. The seeds were patented Monsanto soya seeds. He grew and harvested the crop in the way that farmers have done for millennia, gathered the seeds and grew further crops. He was sued by Monsanto, in a case which eventually reached the US Supreme Court in 2013. The judges held that, unlike other types of patent, over which patent rights become exhausted when the product is put into the market, the Monsanto patents gave the company what was in effect infinite legal protection, so patent infringement occurs when the product replicates itself (Liptak, 2013). While the judges made it clear that they were giving their judgment only in the case of seeds, it has repercussions in any area where the product is self-replicating, such as cell lines and even software. The case was therefore of wider potential relevance than might appear. For environmentalists and consumer groups, Monsanto's legal victory was a cause of concern. GM crops are pervasive, and they are displacing traditional farm practices such as crop rotation and timing of chemical use. Worryingly, it has been found in the US that one of the main pests that attack corn is becoming resistant to GM crops (Batchelor, 2012).

While the judges made it clear that they were giving their judgment only in the case of seeds, it has repercussions in any area where the product is self-replicating, such as cell lines and even software.

The world's largest agricultural chemicals company, Syngenta, has, perhaps counter-intuitively, created a new strategy which involves asking farmers to use less fertilizer and less pesticide. Syngenta has expressed concern that the business models of the big multinationals are putting at risk the smallholder farmers who grow most of the world's food. Their research has found that while people accept the importance of technology, they wish to reduce the use of pesticides, GM seeds and fertilizer. The company has expressed six aims in its Good Growth Plan (Syngenta, 2013):

- To raise productivity without using more land, water and inputs
- To improve fertility of farmland
- To enhance biodiversity
- To help smallholders to increase productivity
- To train farm workers in developing countries
- To encourage fair labour conditions throughout the supply chain

These goals exemplify sustainable agriculture, taking account of environmental protection, farming livelihoods and consumer concerns. The latter are increasingly important in alerting companies to how they might adjust their business models towards more ethically-oriented and sustainable practices.

An example is farm animal welfare, an issue of concern to consumers, which led to alarms about safety in 2013, when the presence of horsemeat in products labelled 'beef' came to light. Companies in meat supply chains, including producers, retailers and restaurants, have tended to underestimate the need for policies, commitments and monitoring of animal welfare. This could well be changing, with the publication of a Business Benchmark on Farm Animal Welfare (Amos and Sullivan, 2013). Among the issues surveyed were close confinement of animals in intensive farms; cloning of animals, which has detrimental effects on the animals and their descendants; the use of growth-promoting substances and antibiotics; routine mutilations; and long-distance transport. Cloning and growth hormones are banned in the EU, but used in some large producing countries, such as the US (see Chapter 6). The authors of the benchmark report found that, of the 68 large companies surveyed, only 36% had a comprehensive policy statement on animal welfare, and another 12% had a basic one. Even among the companies which have policies, less than half applied their policies to all the products they produced, including ones from other suppliers in their supply chain. Only 7% reported on how they had performed against their animal welfare policy commitments.

Only 7% of companies surveyed reported on how they had performed against their animal welfare policy commitments.

Consumers and investors would be disappointed with these findings. Consumers are concerned about safety as well as the ethics of animal welfare. Shareholders, of course, are also consumers, and, additionally, they are concerned about impacts on corporate reputation. The companies surveyed are now more alert to the issues. Celebrities campaigning against the poor treatment of pigs bred by a Walmart supplier have made a video in the US, vividly showing the distress and pain of extreme confinement. Walmart, which was found to have no policy of animal welfare in the benchmark report, has responded, saying the practices are unacceptable, and have promised a review (Child, 2013).

The multinationals engaged in industrialized farming have urged that it is only through their innovation and technology that the world's growing population can be fed. In pressing for liberalized trade agreements with the EU and Asian countries, the US is aiming to open these markets to many of its agricultural exports which are currently considered problematic, including GM products and chemically-injected meat. In the debate, the issues of sustainable production and the impacts on societies and communities must also be taken into account. The US government generously subsidizes its leading exporters of agricultural commodities. These subsidies are criticized for distorting global markets and placing poorer exporting countries, such as those in Africa, at a disadvantage. Governments, NGOs and international bodies such as the UN Food and Agricultural Organization (FAO), discussed in the next section, have roles to play in achieving a balance of solutions which achieve public goods as well as sound business outcomes.

PAUSE TO CONSIDER...

Assess the pros and cons of GM crops in terms of sustainability.

CONSUMERS' PERSPECTIVES

The discovery of horsemeat in supermarket ready-prepared dishes and restaurant meals alerted consumers in Europe to the complexity of food supply chains, and also their extended geographic scope, routinely crossing national borders. The difficulties of finding the sources of the contamination and putting it right were highlighted, and consumers were left thinking that the problems are possibly too complex to resolve. Who is to blame? The producers were cutting corners to keep costs down, as horsemeat is cheaper than beef, and they knew they were unlikely to be caught. Should government inspectors have spotted the problems? Government inspectors cannot catch every unsafe practice. Like all regulation, they rely on companies observing legal obligations as a matter of course. But if regulation is lax, companies are tempted to compromise on standards. We look at both corporate behaviour and the role of regulation in this section.

Global multinationals are the most powerful players in the supply chains in food and beverage sectors. The industrialization of food and beverage manufacturing has brought huge benefits to consumers in developed countries, and there is a growing presence of these companies in emerging markets, where future demand will be greatest (see Figure 10.6). There are huge challenges. Technology and large-scale food processing have benefited consumers, allowing people to obtain safe, nutritious products in convenient packets that are relatively cheap. In any case, that is the theory.

In practice, the large food empires have been built on selling products which have been less about nutrition and more about using fats, sugar and salt, sourced as cheaply as possible, to produce pleasant-tasting products which are cheap to make and sell in large volumes. These ingredients are cheaper than fruit, meat or vegetables, and they have a long shelf life. It is no wonder that they are the main ingredients in much processed food. But long-term nutritional harm can be a consequence, especially when products such as sugary drinks are consumed instead of fresh fruit. Excessive fats and sugar in the diet lead to obesity. Obesity is a form of malnutrition, as the extremely overweight person is not consuming enough nutrients. The proportion of people malnourished due to obesity is higher than the numbers of undernourished very poor people in the world (UNFAO, 2013). Reducing the numbers of undernourished people is the first MDG, discussed above, and progress is gradually being made through food aid and improved agriculture.

The scale of the obesity problem in some countries, and the costs in terms of health problems, are causing alarm. The fact that a person living in a rich country where there is abundant food can be both obese and malnourished is a challenge to governments and health authorities. Moreover, the trend can be observed in poor countries too. Mexico now has a greater proportion of obese people (32.8%) than the US (31.8%) (UNFAO, 2013). Although they are very

Figure 10.6 *The world's population in 2050*

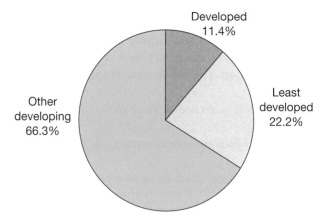

Developed
11.4%

Least
developed
22.2%

Other
developing
66.3%

Source of data: UN Department of Economic and Social Affairs (2011) *World Population Prospects 2010* (New York: United Nations).

Mexico now has a greater proportion of obese people (32.8%) than the US (31.8%).

different economically, they are similar in that food retailing is dominated by large multinationals and that processed products such as sugary drinks and fat-laden snack foods have replaced traditional foods. Alarmed at the obesity statistics, the Mexican president has announced new taxes on sugary drinks and 'junk' food (Boseley, 2013a). He has been prompted in part by the soaring costs of heart disease and diabetes, which are linked to obesity. About 9.2% of Mexican children have diabetes, mainly because of high consumption of soft drinks. Mexicans consume soft drinks like Coca-Cola in vast quantities. Here, and in other poor countries, the uncertainty of supplies of safe drinking water is a contributing factor.

Mexico is not the first country to impose special taxes on unhealthy food, but these measures are usually relatively low-key. Large food companies are powerful lobby groups. They lobby governments against mandatory measures of various kinds, arguing that the effects of mandatory regulation will damage their economies (Lucas et al., 2011). Besides taxes on unhealthy foods, other regulatory tools are labelling requirements and controls on advertising, especially advertising aimed at children. Food companies take the view that self-regulation is preferable, but the steps which they take voluntarily tend to be slight, and not all companies implement them. For example, chocolate makers in the UK promised to cut levels of saturated fat in their products in a voluntary move (Boseley, 2013b). Nestlé, the biggest producer, Mondelēz, the owner of Cadbury, and Tesco, the supermarket chain, all committed themselves to reducing fat levels. Nutritionists welcomed the move, but expressed disappointment that sugar and salt levels were not included. The consumer is still being encouraged to consume snacks such as KitKats, which are part of the health and nutrition problem.

Saturated fat, of which the most prominent is palm oil, is a major ingredient of processed food, including cakes, biscuits and confectionary. Palm oil is criticized on grounds of sustainability as well as health. Palm plantations are created by cutting down forests and destroying ecosystems. They are concentrated in Indonesia and Malaysia, and are now becoming widespread in Africa. While many food companies commit themselves to sourcing sustainable palm oil, the structure of the processing industry makes it unlikely that such guarantees are deliverable in practice.

Food companies would argue that they have implemented numerous measures to make their products healthier. But, it is asked, 'Can an industry that is seen as a big part of the problem also be part of the solution?' (Lucas et al., 2011). Although large food and drink companies assure the public that they take nutritional concerns seriously as part of their CSR policy, research suggests that implementation is well behind their stated commitments. In research carried out by Access to Nutrition, companies were ranked according to their positive contributions to improving nutrition. The top sixteen companies are shown in Figure 10.7.

The rankings shown in Figure 10.7 cover six sets of criteria. They are:

- ○ Governance and strategy – The extent to which the company has a nutrition strategy and reports on its implementation.
- ○ Products and accessibility – Nutritional profile of products; affordable pricing; audit of compliance with its policy.
- ○ Marketing – Responsible approach to marketing, advertising; audit of compliance with its policy. Responsible policy towards marketing to children, with audit process in place.

Figure 10.7 *Access to Nutrition rankings*

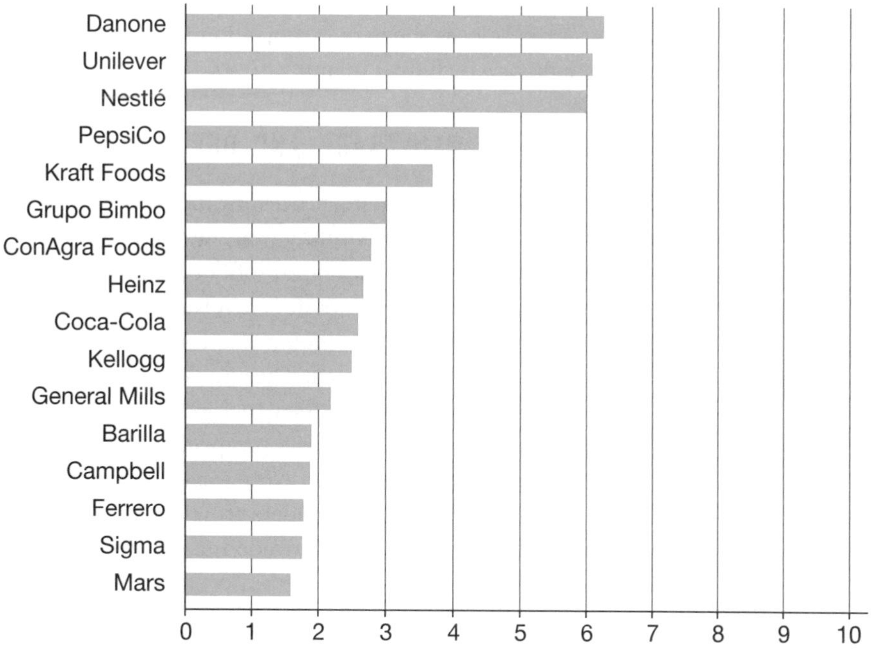

Source of data: *Access to Nutrition Index 2013*, at www.accesstonutrition.org (18/09/14).

- Lifestyles – Support for healthy diet and active lifestyles.
- Labelling – Informative labelling of products on nutrition; appropriate health and nutrition claims.
- Engagement – Engagement with policymakers and other stakeholders.

For each company, the highest possible score was 10, but, as the results show, corporate performance on these nutrition indicators was disappointing. Many had policy commitments which were not followed through. Many provided little information. Only three of these companies scored over 5. Many scored under 2, indicating little or no regard for nutrition in strategy or practice.

The UN Food and Agriculture Organization has urged that sustainable consumption should go along with sustainable production. A difficulty is that people in western markets, and, increasingly, those in emerging markets, are being offered products with weak claims to be sourced through sustainable supply chains. The FAO offers an outline of what a 'sustainable diet' would look like (UNFAO, 2013). It would have 'low environmental impact, offer nutritional security and a healthy life for present and future generations' (UNFAO, 2013: 4). It should:

- Protect and respect biodiversity and ecosystems; have lower environmental footprint
- Be culturally acceptable
- Be accessible, economically fair and affordable
- Be nutritionally adequate
- Reduce loss and waste through the food system

The FAO acknowledges that moves towards realizing these goals are progressing only gradually. It stresses that efforts from both producers and consumers are needed. Moreover, governments play a key role, as they are in a position to regulate both agricultural production and the food industry, including manufacturers and retailers.

ETHICAL INITIATIVES: FAIRTRADE AND ORGANIC FARMING

Ethical initiatives in agriculture, including processing industries and trade, are now making an impact globally, as consumers become more aware of the issues and the risks in extended supply chains. Fairtrade International, a non-profit organization, has as its primary purpose a fair deal for poor agricultural producers. It is involved with producers around the world, working mainly in developing countries, where the world's most disadvantaged farmers are located. The aim is to achieve a more sustainable livelihood for small farmers than that available from the mainstream trading system. It has broadened its perspective to encompass workers' rights in farming, and is devising a living wage benchmark. Fairtrade International point out in their annual report that 'smallholders grow 70% of the world's food, but still make up half of the world's hungriest people' (Fairtrade International, 2013: 4). The organization reaches over a million farmers, many grouped in over a thousand producer organizations. While this represents only a tiny proportion of global farming, the numbers grow every year, and consumers are becoming more aware of the issues. The Fairtrade label is now widely recognized by consumers in western countries. Consumers pay a premium price for Fairtrade-labelled products, knowing that the money will go back to producers to fund more sustainable farming communities. There are over 30,000 Fairtrade-labelled products, from bananas to sugar, being sold to consumers in 125 countries. They remain premium products, sold to consumers who are concerned about the ethics of both production and consumption.

'Smallholders grow 70% of the world's food, but still make up half of the world's hungriest people.'

Figure 10.8 *Percentage of organically farmed area in the EU-15 states' total utilized agricultural area*

The EU-15 states are member states before the accession of 10 new members in 2004 (that is, Austria, Belgium, Denmark, Finland, France, Germany, Greece, Ireland, Italy, Luxembourg, Netherlands, Portugal, Spain, Sweden and the UK).

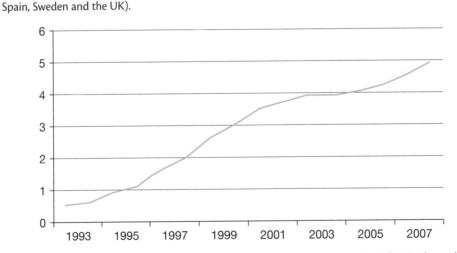

Source of data: EU Commission (2010) *An Analysis of the EU Organic Sector*, at www.ec.europa.eu/agriculture/markets-and-prices/more-reports/pdf/organic_2010_en.pdf (26/09/14).

SPOTLIGHT ON ETHICAL BUSINESS

Sustainability and Fairtrade   *Richard Anstead*

Richard Anstead
*Head of Product
Management, Fairtrade
Foundation, UK*

Richard has worked for the Fairtrade Foundation since 2005, and is its Head of Product Management. He and his colleagues look at the supply chain implications of every Fairtrade-certified product, from the producer to the ultimate consumer. He has been involved in many projects with producers in poor countries, where farmers and their families face numerous challenges, including precarious economic livelihoods, needs to improve human well-being, sustainable production, and impacts of climate change. He and his colleagues have worked with a wide variety of companies and brands including Divine Chocolate, Ben and Jerry's, and Nestlé UK.

Visit **www.palgrave.com/companion/morrison-business-ethics** to watch Richard talking about the work of the Fairtrade Foundation and about the growing importance of ethics in business globally. He discusses the ways in which consumers have become more conscious of how products are sourced, while businesses have become more focused on sustainability issues in their supply chains. While there are notable small businesses that have long been at the forefront of ethical sourcing, he now sees sustainability concerns rising up the agenda in mainstream businesses, often as a result of consumer pressure. Reflecting its growing importance, business ethics is now becoming a core subject in business and management education.

This interview draws mainly on material in this chapter, but you will find it helpful to look at other sections of the book which focus on related topics. These include the subsection on 'Ethical investing' in Chapter 5; and the sections on 'World trade and ethical dimensions' and 'Trade and globalization' in Chapter 6.

When you have watched the video, think about the following questions:

1 What are the three pillars of the Fairtrade Foundation highlighted at the start of the interview? Give some examples from each of these areas, which are mentioned in the course of the interview.
2 Describe the characteristics of the ethical consumer who is drawn to Fairtrade products as part of an ethical lifestyle. In what ways have grassroots pressures helped Fairtrade values of sustainability to become more widely recognized?
3 How are initiatives between the Fairtrade Foundation and big businesses contributing to a rethinking of mainstream business values? Give some examples.

Those same consumers are likely to be attracted to organic products. **Organic production** is agriculture which does not rely on synthetic fertilizers or pesticides. It can be commodity crops, fruit and vegetables, eggs, dairy products or meat. Organic production takes place all over the world, and much of it relies on traditional farming methods. For the consumer who wishes to buy organic products, there are labels which certify the product is organic. However, there are numerous organizations which have certification schemes, each with its own set of criteria. The EU Commission has sought to achieve some consensus within the EU, and has its own organic label. It publicizes its criteria, helping to inform consumers, who are increasingly concerned about ethical issues involved in the production of food. Food safety is a major concern, as we noted above, and the consumer is likely to feel that meat produced organically from a named local farm is a safer purchase than that offered by a large organization of meatpackers. The EU organic criteria include animal welfare criteria, such as adequate space and organic feed. Within the EU, nearly 200,000 farm holdings are certified organic, and the overall area under organic cultivation is gradually growing (see Figure 10.8). In Austria, it represents 15% of agricultural land. Still, like Fairtrade products, organic production is a small sector in terms of overall consumer spending on food, as these products are more expensive than their mass-produced counterparts.

PAUSE TO CONSIDER...

To what extent is your diet sustainable, including Fairtrade and organic products? Is an ethical approach to consumption a priority in your view, and why?

SUSTAINABILITY VERSUS PROFITS

CSR initiatives often founder when companies discover the costs involved, and the bottom line wins out over a sustainability initiative. Executives see the need for strategies which incorporate sustainability objectives, but, more pressingly, they see the need to generate profits. Those with a longer vision of corporate purpose would argue that sustainability needs to be wired into the company's long-term strategy as an imperative, not simply as a voluntary element. There is some evidence that companies are taking this message seriously. More than 8,000 businesses in 113 countries have signed up to the UN's Global Compact. The Compact embraces principles in four key areas: human rights, labour, environment and anti-corruption. Its 2013 report on progress on these objectives was based on a survey of over a thousand of the CEOs whose companies are participants in the Compact. We would expect that these companies would rise above others in their sector, displaying commitment to sustainability goals in both strategy and practice.

Figure 10.9 Sustainability risk assessment and risk impact among Global Compact participants

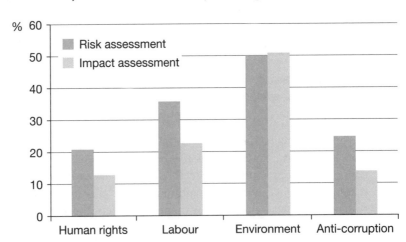

Source of data: UN Global Compact (2013) *Global Corporate Sustainability Report 2013*, at www.globalcompact.org (18/09/14).

The results of the Global Compact survey revealed above all the gap between what executives say and what they do. For example, 65% have sustainability policies at CEO level, but only 35% train managers to integrate these policies into strategy and operations (UN Global Compact, 2013). The first steps, to commit and define commitments, are taken by these companies. However, they fall down in the follow-up steps. These are the steps needed to implement, measure and communicate their achievements. They involve training, having appropriate systems, measurement tools and public disclosure of performance. While 66% have environmental systems, 54% monitor environmental performance and only 35% report on emissions data. Similar results obtained under all the headings. Less than one-third communicate on human rights and anti-corruption. In these categories, companies were particularly weak in risk assessment and impact assessment (see Figure 10.9). Tellingly, the report found that only 8% of company boards link executive remuneration packages to sustainability performance.

MANDATING CSR

Following the financial crisis, governments have seen the need for greater regulation in the financial services sector. They have also been persuaded by the abundant analysis of the causes of the crisis that high executive rewards and the culture of profit maximization have been factors. The EU has imposed a cap on bonus pay for bankers. Perhaps not unexpectedly, many have adopted measures to get legally round the new cap while still paying the bonuses. This highlights the difficulty of changing the culture of an organization from one based on profits-at-all-costs to one in which profit is one goal among many. Could governments help to bring about a change of culture by compelling companies to adopt CSR?

In India, legislation has been passed which requires businesses to give 2% of their net profits to CSR projects. The rule is not mandatory, but under the legislation, companies not doing so will have to explain the reasons in their annual reports, or face being fined. This might be seen as governments 'nudging' business towards more ethical behaviour, seeking to persuade them to adopt ethical behaviour voluntarily. In India, there is a strong case for more businesses to adopt CSR policies. India has widespread poverty and social problems. It has also suffered from weak education and health provision. At the same time, it is home to many successful companies. India's government is often accused of inefficiency and heavy-handed bureaucracy in delivering social programmes. Businesses might well be more efficient in these areas. Tata and Birla, two large Indian conglomerates, have notable records of charitable projects in the country (Crabtree, 2013). Often their motivation has been more business-oriented than charitable. Companies need educated, healthy workers. Building schools and hospitals themselves is a more efficient means than waiting for governments to act. Other companies could do likewise, it is argued. However, in the business environment in India, most companies are family owned and run. While they do give to charities, often these are offshoots of family organizations. They vary in community engagement, but some are devised as means to cultivate local politicians, a perceived necessity in India. Encouraging, and even mandating the giving to CSR projects, might, it is feared, lead to more such projects, well-intentioned on the surface, but serving economic and political purposes at base. And there is always the problem that legal measures cannot change the culture of an organization. It is suggested that greater transparency, the encouragement of CSR projects and a focus on outcomes might provide the basis of more genuine conversion to CSR.

SOCIAL ENTERPRISE

The for-profit business can be contrasted with the not-for-profit organization, such as a charity. The one exists to make money for its owners, and the second exists to serve good causes and makes no profit. In reality, the distinctions are not as clear-cut as this. Many for-profit businesses adopt CSR goals, which include social responsibilities, while charities, such as foundations, are investment vehicles which in fact make money from their investments. In theory, they plough this money into good works, but in practice, much goes into investments. In some less-than-scrupulous charities, relatively large sums go to owners and associates in the form of fees and expenses. Charities have tax advantages in all jurisdictions – a status which is much used by businesses and individuals in their financial arrangements. It is thus imperative to look behind the structures to what organizations are actually doing in terms of their purposes and financial arrangements.

Many people who start up businesses are motivated by social goals as well as a desire to make money. The social entrepreneur has in mind a good cause, such as a service in a local community, and seeks to turn this into a business which is on a sound enough financial footing to survive, but does not seek to extract significant profits. The social enterprise is thus in the area between a for-profit business and a charity. There is an array of business models available today. The line between the social enterprise and the for-profit business has become blurred. Microfinance is an example of a sector which has grown to encompass a variety of organizations offering financial services to poor people who fall outside mainstream banking. Microfinance institutions have become popular in developing countries, where large numbers of poor people, many with small businesses, can tap into loan funding which they would not get from an ordinary bank. The microfinance institution is often backed financially by a charity or charitable donor, but aims to be sustainable financially. Some have evolved into for-profit businesses, but this is unusual. For most, the social aim is the driver, rather than profits.

Still, for a social enterprise to succeed, it helps if some of the people involved have business skills and financial expertise. Access to finance, especially in the early stages, can be an obstacle for the social entrepreneur. For people who are motivated by ethical and environmental goals, it is often more rewarding to become involved in a social enterprise than to join a large company. The hands-on feel of doing good is evident in the social enterprise, whereas in a large business, CSR may well not be seen as a core aspect of the business.

In the UK, there are an estimated 70,000 social enterprises, which employ a million people (Pozniak, 2013). There is also a trade body for these organizations, Social Enterprise UK. Initiatives in funding are helping social enterprises to meet the funding challenges. A private equity fund, the Global Health Investment Fund, is helping to finance the provision of medical products for poor people in the world. Investors are asked to invest in the fund, for which they receive a modest return on their investment. This socially focused investment fund disperses invested funds in companies and non-profit organizations which are pioneering new products. The Global Health Fund was launched at a time when governments were feeling the strains of demands on public funding. The fund links wealthy investors with businesses in the health sector which are in need of funding. In fact, not just wealthy individuals are investing in the fund. GSK, the global pharmaceutical company, has invested $10 million. For GSK, the investment makes business sense, as the innovative work it funds can feed into the mainstream pharmaceutical industry (Jack, 2013).

In the US, the benefit company is a corporate form available to people wishing to set up a business with social goals or convert an existing company to a socially-oriented one. The benefit corporation can be registered in 19 states in the US. It is established for social purposes, and has its own regulatory framework. The latest state to legislate for the benefit company is Delaware. As half of all listed companies in the US are registered in Delaware, the state is highly influential in US company law (see Chapter 8). In Delaware, it is now possible to register a public benefit corporation, the purpose of which is to operate in a 'responsible and sustainable manner' (Fisher, 2013). This might look slightly weak: should not all companies operate responsibly and in sustainable ways? Some states do specify a stronger purpose in their legislation, stating that the company should have positive social goals. But the new Delaware law still establishes the point that the benefit company operates in the context of the triple bottom line, mindful of profits, social goals and sustainability.

It is useful to recall the prevalent thinking on corporate purpose in the US, where the accepted view is that the company's sole legal duty is to pursue profits. In law, this is erroneous, but nonetheless dominates corporate thinking. As we noted in Chapter 8, Delaware recognizes the business judgment rule, by which directors are able to act in the interests of the company. This means that directors can give money to charity rather than pay a dividend, and can defend their position if they are sued by unhappy shareholders. This might not seem very different from what the new benefit company would do. But the benefit company is required to pursue social goals as a mainstream activity, and is also required to carry out triple bottom line reporting. Under the new Delaware law, a for-profit company can transform itself into a benefit company if 90% of the shareholders agree. While this will probably happen only rarely, it is worth noting that hundreds of US companies have either registered as benefit companies or become certified under the 'B corporation' certification scheme, which focuses on social goals. Some well-known companies, such as Etsy, the internet marketplace, align themselves with social goals and have become certified B corporations, even though not registered as benefit companies. For Etsy, supporting micro-enterprises and sustainable communities is central to their social purpose, 'redefining success and helping to build local, living economies' (Etsy, 2013).

The benefit company is required to pursue social goals as a mainstream activity.

CONCLUSIONS

Sustainability implies thinking long-term about business models, resources and environmental impacts. It also involves thinking about human well-being both in today's businesses and the evolving social impacts that are unfolding into the future. Businesses which focus wholly on shareholder value are not well placed to respond to these sustainability issues, as their focus is almost exclusively short-term profits. To what extent can they adapt to more long-term perspectives within their current business models? This chapter has shown that many of the world's leading companies have little in the way of a strategy for sustainability, even though the issues, such as climate change, are urgently in need of being addressed. Part of the blame lies with governments.

As the chapter has pointed out, international frameworks for mandating sustainability goals are weak, deferring to sovereign states to initiate changes. States, however, have been slow to adapt resource-greedy models of economic development, largely because they are locked into thinking in terms of national competitiveness rather than global threats and universal values. How can both corporate and governmental priorities be refocused on sustainability goals? As we have seen, the message that long-term survival depends on rethinking current ways of doing things appeals to companies' and countries' self-interested outlooks. But sustainability has always had an ethical dimension as well: social justice requires an intergenerational approach. Sustainability matters because it provides the guideposts to the right way to behave towards others and towards the environment. This message is increasingly being appreciated by companies that espouse CSR strategies, often because stakeholders are urging that ethical considerations need to rise up the agenda, even in companies which cling to shareholder primacy.

REFERENCES

Amos, A. and Sullivan, R. (2013) *The Business Benchmark on Farm Animal Welfare: 2012 Report*, at www.bbfaw.com (18/09/14).

Barrett, P. (2012) 'Chevron fails to squelch $19 billion verdict', *Bloomberg Businessweek*, 9 October, at www.businessweek.com (18/09/14).

Batchelor, C. (2012) 'Report calls for more use of research to improve crops', *Financial Times*, 21 November.

BBC (2013) *Superstorm Sandy: US Marks One Year Anniversary*, 29 October, at www.bbc.co.uk (18/09/14).

Boseley, S. (2013a) 'Mexico to tackle obesity with taxes on junk food and sugary drinks', *The Guardian*, 1 November, at www.theguardian.com (18/09/14).

Boseley, S. (2013b) 'Saturated fat to be cut in chocolate products, makers pledge', *The Guardian*, 26 October, at www.theguardian.com (18/09/14).

Chazan, G. (2013) '"Invisible fuel" promises more secure future', *Financial Times*, 4 June.

Chevron (2013) *Annual Report 2012*, at www.chevron.com (18/09/14).

Child, B. (2013) 'Babe star James Cromwell attacks Walmart supplier's treatment of pigs', *The Guardian*, 30 October, at www.theguardian.com (18/09/14).

Clark, P. (2012) 'Capitalist conservationists', *Financial Times*, 5 June.

Crabtree, J. (2013) 'Take a closer look at the hand that gives', *Financial Times*, 15 August.

Dower, N. (2004) 'Global economy, justice and sustainability', *Ethical Theory and Moral Practice*, 7(4): 399–415.

Etsy (2013) *Etsy Joins the B Corporation Movement*, at www.etsy.com (18/09/14).

EU Joint Research Centre (2012) *Per Capita CO_2 Emissions in China Reach EU Levels*, at www.ec.europa.eu (18/09/14).

Fairtrade International (2013) *Annual Report 2012–13: Unlocking the Power*, at www.fairtrade.net (18/09/14).

Fisher, D. (2013) 'Delaware public benefit corporation lets directors serve three masters rather than one', *Forbes*, 16 July, at www.forbes.com (18/09/14).

Jack, A. (2013) 'Pioneer medical fund takes in $94m', *Financial Times*, 23 September.

IPCC (2013) *IPCC Report: Summary for Policymakers*, at www.ipcc.ch (26/09/14).

Laing, A. (2009) 'Ecuador's Amazonians sue Chevron over poison waterways', *The Daily Telegraph*, 15 November, at www.telegraph.co.uk (18/09/14).

Liptak, A. (2013) 'Supreme Court supports Monsanto in seed-replication case', *The New York Times*, at www.nytimes.com (18/09/14).

Lucas, L. and Fontanella-Khan, J. (2013) 'Dampened prospects', *Financial Times*, 26 January.

Lucas, L., Rappaport, A. and Jack, A. (2011) 'An ever heftier problem', *Financial Times*, 28 October.

Pogge, T. (1988) 'Rawls and global justice', *Canadian Journal of Philosophy*, 18(2): 227–56.

Pozniak, H. (2013) 'Social enterprise is the way forward', *The Telegraph*, 30 October, at www.telegraph.co.uk (18/09/14).

Rawls, J. (1971) *A Theory of Justice* (Oxford: Oxford University Press).

Sen, A. (2010) *The Idea of Justice* (London: Penguin).

Shiva, V. (2013) 'How economic growth has become anti-life', *The Guardian*, 1 November, at www.theguardian.com (18/09/14).

Shue, H. (1995) 'Ethics, the environment and the changing international order', *International Affairs*, 71(3): 453–61.

Solow, R. (1992) 'An almost practical step toward sustainability', *Resources for the Future* (Washington, DC: Butterworth/Heinemann).

Spillius, A. (2013) 'China to rent 5% of Ukraine', *The Telegraph*, 24 September, at www.telegraph.co.uk (18/09/14).

Syngenta (2013) *Good Growth Plan*, at www.syngenta.com (18/09/14).

UN (1987) *Report of the World Commission on Environment and Development: Our Common Future (the Brundtland Report)*, at www.un-documents.net (18/09/14).

UN (2011) *World Population Prospects 2010 Revision* (New York: UN).

UN (2012) *The Future We Want, UN Conference on Sustainable Development 2012*, at www.un.org (18/09/14).

UNFAO (2013) *The State of Food and Agriculture 2013*, at www.fao.org (18/09/14).

UN Global Compact (2013) *Global Corporate Sustainability Report 2013*, at www.globalcompact.org (18/09/14).

Vidal, J. (2013) 'Toxic e-waste dumped in poor nations, says UN', *The Observer*, 14 December, at www.theguardian.com (18/09/14).

Williams, C. and Millington, A. (2004) 'The diverse and contested meanings of sustainable development', *The Geographical Journal*, 170(2): 99–104.

REVIEW QUESTIONS

1 Is intergenerational justice a valid basis for sustainable development in an ethical sense? What objections to it can be raised?

2 A weak view of sustainable development is often criticized by environmentalists, but it is perhaps all that can realistically be contemplated in today's world. Do you agree or disagree with this statement, and why?

3 What are the elements of human well-being?

4 What are the differences between negative rights and positive rights in terms of human development?

5 Multilateral negotiations on what should replace the Kyoto Protocol are unlikely to commit to mandatory emissions reductions. Explain why there is a wide divergence in positions.

6 Companies exist to make profits, not to save the planet. How, if at all, can these goals be reconciled?

7 What are the ethical issues involved in the exploitation of energy resources in poor countries? What are the elements of an ethical approach for a foreign oil or mining company in these circumstances?

8 From an ethical perspective, why are there concerns over the power of the large commodities companies that dominate global food supply?

9 Why are 'land grab' policies of some countries considered controversial? How can they be defended?

10 One of the objections raised to the use of genetically modified (GM) crops is the dominance of a handful of powerful agribusiness companies. Do you agree or disagree, and why?

11 Global food companies are criticized for contributing to health problems such as obesity. To what extent are these criticisms justified?

12 How can legislation be used to promote healthier eating?

13 In what ways can the social enterprise be considered a viable business model over the long term?

14 Should triple bottom line reporting be compulsory for all companies, not just benefit companies? Why?

ASSESSING TURKEY'S SUSTAINABLE DEVELOPMENT

CLOSING CASE STUDY

In the last decade, Turkey has joined the ranks of leading emerging economies. Industrialization, urbanization and growing services industries have contributed to high growth rates reaching 8% or more in a period when European growth was stumbling. GDP per capita has doubled during the decade to over $10,000, reducing poverty and creating a middle class with growing aspirations for better living standards. Better housing, education and healthcare are part of this picture, but so are cars and consumer goods, which also make up a middle-class lifestyle. These changes have taken place in a predominantly Muslim country with secular institutions and democratic government. Turkey has been perceived as relatively stable in a region of the world marked by social and political instability. Turkish society, however, has diverse cultural groups. The main ones are the socially conservative Sunni Muslims, westernized secularists, and minority Kurdish groups. Will Turkey's development bring sustainable benefits to all in society?

Photo 10.2 *Marchers in Istanbul in 2013 protested against the construction of a shopping centre in one of the city's few remaining green areas, but their protests run deeper, to authoritarian tendencies in Turkey's government.* (© iStock.com/ petekarici)

The driving force behind Turkey's decade of growth has been its prime minister, Recep Tayyip Erdoğan, of the moderate Islamic party, the Justice and Development Party (AKP). Muslim entrepreneurs led the way in economic drive, 'combining capitalism with piety' (Hakura, 2013: 3). They benefited from Islamic social networks, including returning migrants from Germany, keen to bring business ideas back to their home country. These businesses grew rapidly, and helped to transform the country from a mainly agricultural one to one with a relatively modern industrial sector, supporting growing export industries. Mr Erdoğan has been successful in nurturing relations between these business leaders and the government. A construction boom, including huge numbers of new houses and commercial complexes, has ensued. But much of this development has been financed largely through borrowing in global financial markets, and Turkey is thus vulnerable to any volatility in these markets.

While bringing material prosperity, the growing industrial and construction sectors have heightened concerns about energy and resources. These sectors are heavy users of energy and are responsible for nearly 30%

of Turkey's emissions. Turkey's carbon emission rose 143.5% between 1990 and 2011 – a period when, under the Kyoto Protocol, developed countries were committing to reductions (UN Climate Change Secretariat, 2012). Like other emerging economies, it has prioritized economic growth over climate concerns. It belatedly ratified the Kyoto Protocol in 2009, a move likely to have been linked to its application for EU membership. Turkey has wavered on whether to look towards the west and the EU or to look towards Russia, which looms large. Energy concerns come into these considerations. Turkey has few energy resources of its own, and depends heavily on neighbours in the region. However, it has strained relations with many of these, including Iraq, Iran, Saudi Arabia and Israel. It imports gas and oil from Iran. It is frowned on by the US for doing so, because of American sanctions against Iran for its nuclear programme, but Turkey's government has little choice, as 90% of its oil must be imported. Turkey wishes to develop new coal-fired and nuclear power plants, although these would rely on outside investors such as Russia. With advice from American experts, it is also exploring fracking in the interior of the country, where there are possible reserves of shale oil. A domestic oil supply would be welcome, but Turkey is in an earthquake zone, and fracking could pose risks to its sensitive geology. The last big earthquake in the country was in 1999, when 25,000 people lost their lives. Turkey thus faces challenges in energy security and meeting increasing energy demands, but it also faces criticism for its weakness in addressing climate change.

Turkey's development model also depends on social factors such as education, as education is a key to employment for all sections of society. Turkey is a young country: half its 76 million people are under 30. The number of working-age people is set to rise to 65 million by 2030. The government has made strides in providing basic education, but educational achievement at higher levels has been disappointing when compared with other countries. It was ranked 65 out of 148 countries by the World Economic Forum (WEF) in terms of higher education and training (WEF, 2013–2014). While the manufacturing sector has relied on semi-skilled workers in industries such as car assembly plants, the country needs development in high-tech sectors like electronic machinery, which would produce value-added exports and improve productivity. This requires improvements in education and research, to equip people with innovation skills.

Turkey is among the world's weakest countries for gender equality. In rankings on gender equality compiled by the WEF, Turkey is ranked a lowly 124 out of 135 countries (WEF, 2012). These rankings are based on health, education, economic opportunity and political empowerment. Education is satisfactory, but in other categories, the gender gap is wide. The participation rate for women in the workforce is only 31.2%, which contrasts poorly with the OECD rate of 60%. Poor childcare services is one of the factors holding back women, but there are also fewer job opportunities and little prospect of promotion. Women's pay on average is less than half that of men (WEF, 2012). Not only is society missing out on huge potential enrichment, women as individuals are missing out on the personal prospect of a fulfilling career.

Approaching the end of his maximum tenure of three terms as prime minister, Mr Erdoğan set his sights on the presidency, and was duly elected in 2014, giving further cause for concern among those who fear his dictatorial tendencies. Economic growth slowed to 2.2% in 2012. Uncertainty hangs over the prospect of sustainable development. His legacy has been formidable, but many in society now have doubts about what the future holds. Many people had hoped that the greater freedoms would be introduced in society. But Mr Erdoğan has taken a hard line on political dissent, and a number of journalists have been imprisoned. In the summer of 2013, thousands of people converged in Taksim Square in Istanbul, to protest against government-backed plans to develop Gezi Park, one of the few green spaces left in the city. The protesters included people from diverse cultural backgrounds and occupations, sending a message of general disquiet with Mr Erdoğan's tendency towards authoritarian rule. A carnival atmosphere erupted, with impromptu skits mocking the prime minister. Riot police were dispatched, using tear gas and water cannons against demonstrators, whom he called 'riff-raff' (Traynor, 2013). The protesters were put down, but the groundswell of opinion favouring more freedom within society continues to simmer under the surface. The Gezi Park development was stopped by the courts because of lack of consultation, but the developers appealed against the decision, indicating that legal uncertainty will hang over the project for a time. Not many days after the protesters left, builders' cranes were observed at work on the Gezi Park site.

Sources: UN Climate Change Secretariat (2012) *Summary of Greenhouse Gas Emissions for Turkey*, at www.unfccc.int; Traynor, I. (2013) 'Erdoğan's split personality: the reformer v. the tyrant', *The Guardian*, 30 September, at www.theguardian.com; Gardner, D. and Dombey, D. (2013) 'A change of tempo', *Financial Times*, 8 June; WEF (2012) *The Global Gender Gap Report 2012*, at www.weforum.org; WEF (2013) *The Global Competitiveness Report 2013–2014*, at www.weforum.org; Dombey, D. (2013) 'Sleeping giant of old stirs amid fiery rhetoric', *Financial Times*, 1 October; Hakura, F. (2013) 'After the boom: risks to the Turkish economy', Briefing paper, *Chatham House* (the Royal Institute of International Affairs), at www.chathamhouse.org (18/09/14).

- **Describe Turkey's development model.**

  - **What are the external risks to Turkey's sustainable development? What are the internal risks?**

- **What are the prospects for Turkey in evolving a more sustainable economic model and promoting sustainable well-being for all in society?**

CONCLUSIONS: BUSINESS ETHICS AND GLOBAL CHALLENGES

ETHICAL THEMES IN THIS CHAPTER
- Synthesis of the six themes in the book

THE AIMS OF THIS CHAPTER ARE TO
- Review ethical themes in business contexts
- Highlight changes in the international environment which impact on business ethics
- Critically consider the role of regulation in international business
- Appreciate the ethical challenges facing business, and how they can be addressed

SPAIN REJECTS LAS VEGAS-STYLE CASINO PROJECT

The prospect of a multi-billion-dollar development, potentially employing hundreds of thousands of people, and attracting huge numbers of tourists, was one that had electrifying appeal for the Spanish government. The offer came from the American casino tycoon, Sheldon Adelson, who proposed to have built a Las Vegas-style complex in Spain. Spain's economy has been mired in recession for years, and has been considered among the 'sick' economies of the eurozone. When the proposal from Adelson was received by the Spanish government in 2012, it was warmly welcomed as a rare piece of good news. Adelson's company, Las Vegas Sands, had a track record of building and operating casino complexes, initially in Las Vegas itself, but more recently in Macau, the special administrative region on the Chinese mainland, and also in Singapore, where the Marina Bay Sands opened in 2010.

Photo 11.1 *Gaming has become a global industry. Casino complexes are bigger than ever, but not all governments are willing to bow to the demands of powerful casino owners.* (PhotoDisc/Getty Images)

Adelson's proposal, like his other developments, was conceived on a big scale. This would be an investment of $30 billion, consisting of 12 hotels, six casinos, a conference centre, shopping malls and golf courses. He projected that 250,000 jobs would be created. The big issue in 2012 seemed to be simply which location in Spain should be selected for the project. The two contenders were Barcelona and Madrid. Barcelona in Catalonia receives regular visits from large cruise liners, whose passengers would enjoy the entertainments on offer. On the other hand, Madrid receives more tourists arriving by air. Madrid won out over Barcelona, but when detailed discussions got under way, issues emerged that began to cloud the prospect of EuroVegas, despite Spain's desperate need for foreign investment and jobs.

The collapse of a debt-fuelled construction bubble in the mid-2000s had devastating impacts on Spain's economy. Bankrupt builders led to banking woes as debt mounted. The government had to seek a bailout for four failed banks from fellow members of the eurozone, amounting to 37 billion euros. Corruption between the building sector and many regional and local authorities, also themselves teetering on the edge of bankruptcy, contributed to the financial crisis. As unemployment rose and salaries fell, Spanish standards of living fell. Unemployment has remained at about 25%. More than half of these people have been unemployed for two years or more. It has been estimated by charities associated with the Catholic Church that three million people in Spain are living in extreme poverty, on less than 307 euros per month (Buck, 2013). Spain had a thriving manufacturing sector until the early years of the new millennium, but many of these jobs migrated to lower-cost locations, especially in Central and Eastern Europe and Morocco. Spain's high social charges on employers and employment protection laws were factors which led to investors departing, and discouraged new investors. Spain rapidly lost in competitiveness, just when the construction bubble was on the verge of bursting.

Would the casino complex on the outskirts of Madrid go some way to turning things round, at least in that region? Adelson had a list of demands which he presented to the Spanish government. It is common for foreign investors to seek incentives from host governments, but his demands proved controversial. He demanded guaranteed compensation in the event of legislative changes in Spain which could adversely affect his business. He asked for a reduction in the social security charges which are paid by employers in Spain. He also wished for immigration laws to be relaxed in relation to this project, so that he could bring in workers from other countries. Finally, he demanded an exemption from Spain's laws banning smoking in public places, so that smoking would be allowed in his casinos.

Faced with these demands, and objections from many groups in Spain, the government rejected the terms demanded by Adelson, and he withdrew from further negotiations. It is probable that the EU competition authorities would have rejected the proposal for guaranteed compensation as being anti-competitive. Religious groups had objected to EuroVegas on the grounds that gambling brings social problems, rising levels of crime and prostitution. Environmentalists objected to the adverse impact of the huge development on the natural environment in the region. Many businesses, such as hotels, had mixed feelings about the project, as the concessions, if granted, would have given the Sands businesses advantages over domestic ones. Other businesspeople were lukewarm, noting that, although Adelson had promised a large number of jobs for local people, he was wishing to bring in migrant labour from abroad.

Moral issues are tied up in these considerations. Despite the hotels, restaurants and entertainment, gambling is by far the biggest moneyspinner for Las Vegas Sands. The company's fortunes have risen considerably with growing Asian markets, and these are the focus of the Sands business. The Catholic Church in Spain commented that it would support projects 'to create wealth and employment, but not at any price' (Kassam, 2013). Ambitious construction projects were largely to blame for Spain's economic woes in the first place, and it is perhaps not advisable to go down that same road again.

Sources: Buck, T. (2013) 'Economy strengthens, but gloomy mood lingers', *Financial Times*, 29 October; Kassam, A. (2013) 'Spain's EuroVegas plan: US casino operator pulls plug', *The Guardian*, 13 December, at www.theguardian.com; Burridge, T. (2013) 'Spain's dilemmas over EuroVegas mega-casino plans', *BBC News*, 12 March, at www.bbc.co.uk; Minder, R. and Kartner, J. (2012) 'Spanish banks agree to layoffs and other cuts to receive rescue funds in return', *New York Times*, 28 November, at www.nytimes.com (18/09/14).

- Would you have advised the Spanish government to accept Adelson's terms or reject them? Why?

- What are the ethical concerns raised by large casino projects such as those run by Las Vegas Sands?

- What types of investment would Spain be better advised to seek?

INTRODUCTION

This chapter looks back to discussions of concepts, theories, key players and key locations highlighted throughout earlier chapters. Some concepts, such as human rights, have arisen in a range of different contexts, and, some players, such as CEOs and other decision-makers, have been seen in a number of different roles. This concluding chapter does not aim to summarize all these earlier discussions, but to highlight key issues which illuminate the ways in which ethics is becoming more widely ramified in international business. These issues are revisited, bringing together earlier insights and looking forward to future challenges.

The chapter begins with a review of the ethical themes which have recurred throughout this book, pointing out how they might play roles in business ethics in the future. We then review the actors, concepts and contexts of business ethics. As the book's chapters have unfolded, it has become clear that improving adherence to ethical standards is not a matter simply for businesses. Governments, civil society organizations, and also stakeholders like employees and consumers, all have roles and responsibilities. We then draw conclusions on meeting the ethical challenges in today's world, which were highlighted in the book's introduction. Among these, inequality is singled out for its relevance in social, business and political contexts. Regulatory reform is now seen as playing an increasingly important role in guiding principled behaviour of key players, but it is not a solution to dealing with the many areas of ethical failings. Corruption, human rights abuses, unsustainable business models: all present ethical challenges for business and for regulators.

REVIEWING THE ETHICAL THEMES

Six ethical themes were highlighted in the introduction to this text. They have provided insights through discussion of issues and examples, which are reviewed in this section. Ethical themes were grouped under three headings, which are reproduced in Figure 11.1.

Ethical principles are the guiding beacons for taking the right decisions and actions in international business. The individual in society has been at the heart of ethical theories over the centuries. Human dignity is the basis of the core foundation theories of business ethics. These have guided our assessment of businesses in relation to employment conditions, labour practices, supply chain responsibilities and human rights. We have emphasized diverse cultural backdrops in assessing how ethical principles can be applied effectively in the huge variety of social contexts. We have seen the application of ethical principles in highly diverse contexts, including Brazil, the US, and South Africa. As highlighted in the introduction, business ethics is often about identifying, understanding and respecting the divergences, while being able to identify the right ethical approach which transcends cultural boundaries.

Changing economies and societies in a globalized world are presenting ever more ethical challenges. Most countries seek the benefits of economic development, and market

Figure 11.1 *Ethical themes in the book*

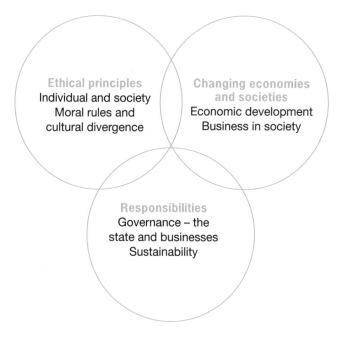

reforms have played an important part in transforming many of those featured in this book, including countries as diverse as China, Qatar, Bangladesh and Turkey. Industrialization, resource exploitation, changes in the nature of work and changes in social interactions have resulted. Many benefits have resulted from these transformations. They include reducing poverty and creating jobs. But negative impacts have also been aspects of development, raising ethical issues, including social justice and human rights. The business as part of society plays economic roles, but also social roles. These roles, often depicted in terms of stakeholder relations, involve taking decisions which have unavoidable ethical implications. Recall the retailers who source goods from Bangladesh factories or Lonmin, the owner of the Marikana mine in South Africa.

Governance and responsibilities form the final set of ethical themes. Governance is not limited to governments and regulators, but encompasses the broad range of processes, formal and informal, which determine how societies are run. They also determine how business goals and societal values can be harmonized to achieve long-term benefits to all in society. Issues such as food security, energy, water and other vital resources have gained a sense of urgency, raising the importance of sustainability for both businesses and governments. Steering a sustainable course is a responsibility of state actors, including governments. But, increasingly, business leadership is also seen as essential to the attainment of sustainability objectives. Sustainability in both long-term goals and day-to-day decision-making is central to the thinking of the ethical business in all its international activities.

KEY ROLES AND HOW THEY ARE CHANGING

This book has highlighted actors, concepts and contexts in business ethics, in a figure which appeared in the Introduction. That figure reappears here as Figure 11.2. In this section, we look at the first of these headings – key actors. The figure poses the question, 'Who decides what and how?'

Whereas business ethics textbooks typically focus on management issues in western companies, this book has taken a broader approach, addressing ethical issues that arise in a globalized world and in all types of organization, whether private, publicly-listed or state-owned. Globalization is often described in terms of ascendant multinational companies contrasted with weakened states and governments. However, the interactions of different players globally are more complex than this simple dichotomy. FDI, the main driver of globalization, has been driven largely by MNEs. While this has remained true, the nature of these companies and the destinations of FDI have undergone changes. FDI outflows used to be mainly from MNEs based in advanced economies to other advanced economies. In these cases, the parties are based in economies that are broadly market-based, institutions are based on the rule of law, societies are relatively stable, and political systems are broadly democratic. Examples are Japanese and, later, German car-makers setting up in the US. The fall in FDI flows to the US has been dramatic – from 37% of the total in 2000 to just 17% in 2012 (Politi, 2013). Foreign investors and host countries are now far more diverse (see Chapter 2). There is growing outward investment from emerging economies, and the destinations of FDI are increasingly developing countries. In developing economies, as we have seen, numerous ethical issues arise. They include unsafe working conditions, weak employment protection, the use of underage workers and poor environmental protection. What is

Figure 11.2 Actors, concepts and context in business ethics

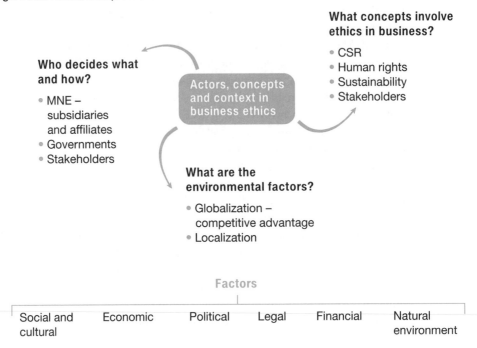

Who decides what and how?

- MNE – subsidiaries and affiliates
- Governments
- Stakeholders

Actors, concepts and context in business ethics

What concepts involve ethics in business?

- CSR
- Human rights
- Sustainability
- Stakeholders

What are the environmental factors?

- Globalization – competitive advantage
- Localization

Factors

Social and cultural	Economic	Political	Legal	Financial	Natural environment

more, low-cost developing countries often have weak rule of law, high levels of corruption, social instability and poor governance in their political institutions.

The challenges in these environments multiply when we consider that the people who run factories that manufacture for western brands are often themselves foreign investors, such as Foxconn, which is a Taiwanese company running factories in China and other locations to make western-branded products for global markets. Untangling the ethical and legal responsibilities in cases such as this – which are common – is one of the major ethical challenges associated with globalization. While western brand owners have persisted in treating local law as being their benchmark, we have found that ethically they bear responsibility, as party to the arrangements under which their products are made. Furthermore, as international legal norms increasingly envelop corporate players, it is not too far-fetched to say the western brand owner is potentially liable for breaches of international human rights law, regardless of the applicable national law and the fact that the workers are secondary stakeholders, not directly employed by the brand owner.

Consumers in today's world are becoming more aware of the nature of supply chains, with responsibilities spread across different companies and different country jurisdictions. It is often observed that consumers are ambivalent: they want to purchase goods at competitive prices, but they expect ethical standards to be upheld. The two are not easy to reconcile, and this is one of the ethical challenges faced by companies in international business. Law and regulation in the world's developing countries tends to be weak, often because countries are keen to attract foreign investors who bring employment. If these countries' governments strengthen employment protection and wages, workers benefit, and with them, the whole society. But a perceived risk for host governments is that the wealth-creating activity, such as textile manufacturing, will shift elsewhere. Can this spiral, described as the 'race to the

Can this spiral, described as the 'race to the bottom', be broken?

bottom', be broken? It can, if enough host countries adopt a pro-social approach to FDI, setting and enforcing international human rights standards. As we have seen, producers might see profit margins slip, but the businesses can remain well in profit, and be more sustainable. This might seem idealistic, mainly because of the predominantly profit-seeking ethos of corporate decision-makers.

As it has unfolded, globalization has seen increasing participation of MNEs from emerging economies such as the Bric countries (Brazil, Russia, India and China). Many of them, like many of their western counterparts, are family or insider dominated, despite being listed companies in most cases. But state-dominated or state-owned MNEs are also prominent in emerging economies. They have a national vision wired into their cultures, and their home environments are not the institutional rule-based frameworks that are the basis of company law in most western countries. Most have opaque corporate governance, which is the norm in their home countries. These countries, moreover, all fall within the broad group of state capitalist economies, although India and Brazil have moved away from this model in recent years. MNEs from emerging economies have invested heavily in developing countries, where the weak institutional environment and personalized governance chime with their own. They have also gained in confidence in investing in advanced western economies. We have seen some examples, such as Chinese investment in the US. In China, the state is both an active economic player and a regulator. Indeed, as a one-party state, the party leadership takes all major decisions, whether in businesses it dominates, the regulatory framework, or public spending decisions. To the western businessperson, this situation suggests numerous cross-cutting conflicts of interest, which would be likely to lead to corruption.

The market economies of the advanced countries, although taking different views on the role of state, tend to see regulators in a more independent light, upholding the rule of law and fair treatment of all under the law. In practice, as we have seen, there is still considerable scope for evading and avoiding the law. Businesses are also active in lobbying lawmakers for changes which benefit their particular interests. The emphasis on 'self-regulation' and 'enlightened self-interest' in the UK (discussed in Chapter 8) is appropriate where executives and managers are broadly prudent and motivated by ethical principles, but where they are motivated only by greed, and see laws simply as obstacles to get round, as in the years leading to the financial crisis, the deficiencies of both the corporate ethos and the regulatory authorities became apparent. A result has been a renewed vigilance in devising and administering regulatory frameworks, although it is acknowledged that a change of culture towards ethical principles is the key to changing corporate behaviour.

A point that has been stressed from the beginning of this book is that while we refer to companies taking decisions, the reality is that there are real people who take decisions, and holding them accountable to high ethical standards is crucial for business ethics. This highlights the role played by governments and regulators in laying down ethical benchmarks and enforcing them against both companies and the individuals behind them.

PAUSE TO CONSIDER...

In what ways do the roles of governments remain crucial in today's world, despite the predictions by some commentators that globalization would lead to a reduction in state power?

ETHICAL CONCEPTS IN PRACTICE

The second heading in Figure 11.2 focuses on key concepts relevant to business ethics. The first of these is corporate social responsibility (CSR). It starts from the idea that business is part of society, with responsibilities which those relationships entail. The concept has developed into various approaches to business in practice, including corporate social performance, but always referring back to the basic concept. The origins of CSR theories lie in western contexts, mainly the liberal market economies, where the idea of CSR was a counterbalance to free-market assumptions about the role of business and views of 'economic man', focused on material self-interest. The shareholder primacy model of corporate purpose evolved from these assumptions. They remain powerful, and, indeed, many companies which profess to embrace CSR see it as a voluntary add-on to existing market-oriented business models. This book has taken the view that CSR implemented as a core strategy shifts the purpose of the company towards social values, and that this shift is compatible with a capitalist system. CSR acts to bring back social values to capitalist enterprise, which have been recognized but lost sight of in the last three decades. Capitalist competition from the days of Adam Smith was conceived as tempered by a sense that businesses should refrain from behaviour that is excessively predatory (Gambetta, 1988). Some have called for 'retooling capitalism' to reflect social values, in the ways that the benefit corporations in the US are now doing (Freeland, 2013). This is not as radical as it might seem, as it involves restoring the moral dimension capitalism once had. It is already happening.

Social values that feature in a CSR approach include human rights, sustainability and stakeholder concerns. These have seen resurgent emphasis as elements of business ethics in the last two decades. Human rights are now broadly interpreted to cover all aspects of human well-being (see Chapter 9). Similarly, sustainability has come to be interpreted broadly as including a range of social values as well as environmental issues. We now find reports on welfare conditions in outsourced manufacturing as part of corporate sustainability reports, impliedly acknowledging the importance of workers as stakeholders. However, the companies which use outsourcing models, such as clothing retailers, tend to see the ethical dimension in terms of issuing supplier codes of conduct. They also tend to emphasize compliance with national laws. In fact, these human rights issues are covered extensively in international law and are increasingly being applied to organizations in society – not just governments.

Companies have been reluctant to confront the fact that they can be complicit in human rights abuse, but consumers are increasingly connecting global companies with breaches of human rights in both their direct operations and their supply chains. In its sustainability report, H&M acknowledge human rights as important in their ethical policies, which are based on the UN's Guiding Principles (H&M, 2013). The limitations of these Principles were highlighted in Chapter 9, noting their state-centred, voluntarist approach rather than an internationalist approach. H&M, in fact, recognizes education and health as human rights, reflecting the broader perspective of economic and social rights in the Universal Declaration of Human Rights (UDHR). Associated British Foods, the owner of Primark, one of H&M's rivals, takes a rather weaker perspective in its corporate responsibility report, expressing an aim to be guided by the UDHR (Associated British Foods, 2013). These companies have been in the ethical firing line over conditions in factories in Bangladesh where their branded clothes are made. They take the view that expressing a sense of responsibility for improving conditions over time is enough to satisfy critics, while consumers are more focused on low prices than on ethics.

PAUSE TO CONSIDER...

How can capitalism be re-tooled, to reflect social values and to become more sustainable?

THE CHANGING INTERNATIONAL ENVIRONMENT

Environmental contexts, the final element in Figure 11.2, were explored in Part 1 of this book. Chapters 1 to 5 highlighted cultural, economic, political, legal and financial contexts, while Chapter 6 examined trends in global trade, which were found often to reflect influences mentioned in the earlier chapters. The chapters in Part 1 revealed that globalization occurs not just despite local differences but *because* of them. We found that crucial differences are linked to opening markets and opportunities in different countries. Globalization sees the spread of capitalist enterprises and also the deepening of capitalist values. In this section, we review these trends, and their ethical implications for business.

GLOBALIZATION

As the example of textile manufacturing in Bangladesh in the last section showed, globalization has brought opportunities but also risks. Bangladesh is populous, mainly Muslim, poor, and prone to flooding and other disasters associated with climate change. Its democratic system has suffered setbacks and is unstable, with parties disagreeing over the basic constitution. Factory owners are part of the political scene, making it difficult to bring about legislative changes to improve conditions. It could well be said that Bangladesh has benefited from globalization. Some four million workers, mainly women, work in the textile industry, producing goods mainly for export, which brings in valuable income. Workers from Bangladesh are to be found on construction sites in the Middle East and elsewhere. But in both these examples, the workers in question face serious risks to their health and well-being, make little money and have few legal rights. The wealth generated goes mainly to corporate owners and middlemen, many of whom have political ties. A number of other developing countries have become integrated into the global economy through global supply chains and migrant labour. Other Asian countries and, increasingly, African countries, are viewed as promising for foreign investors. FDI in Africa has been rising.

Much FDI in Africa is in energy and natural resources, sectors in which foreign investment has long played a key role. However, for many countries, such as oil-rich Nigeria, benefits from oil wealth have not led to improvements in well-being for the population. South Africa (see closing case study in Chapter 9) has seen GDP rise from $136 billion in 1994 to $385 billion today. That is a tripling during the two decades of democratic rule. There have been improvements in electricity, sanitation, health and education over this period. However, resource wealth still dominates the economy, and inequality is still high. While in 1993, 70% of the black population lived below the poverty line, that percentage is now 81%. By contrast, 87% of white citizens are middle or upper class (Goldman Sachs, 2013). Unemployment was 23% in 1994, and is 25% today. Among those aged 15–34, unemployment is 70%. South Africa has enjoyed strong growth, but faces huge problems of unemployment, inequality and poverty.

Globalization has brought investment, both foreign and domestic, and promoted economic growth in emerging economies. But economic growth in itself does not lead to sustainable development or human well-being in society. Decision-makers in government play important roles in determining what foreign companies are welcome and on what terms, as the opening case study showed. Where the government is controlled by a dictator or military junta, a deal with a foreign investor is likely to be lacking in transparency, designed to benefit the authoritarian leadership and the foreign investor above all. The experience of Guinea, one of Africa's poorest countries, is salutary. Guinea has one of the world's largest undeveloped iron-ore deposits, but developing it would cost an estimated $20 billion, which is more than triple Guinea's GDP (Burgis, 2014). Mining rights to the iron ore were awarded in the 1990s by the ruling dictator to mining company, Rio Tinto. But in 2008, half those rights were transferred by the government to Beny Steinmetz Group Resources (BSGR), a Guernsey-registered company which is part of a large conglomerate. It set up a joint venture with Brazilian mining giant, Vale, to exploit the rights. A military overthrow of the government ensued, followed by a return to civilian rule, with an elected government installed in 2010. The new government paid off Rio Tinto in an agreement over its earlier rights, and set up an inquiry into possible corruption in the award of the mining rights to BSGR. BSGR insists that it acquired the rights legally, but the inquiry found in 2014 that the process had been corrupt. This would invalidate BSGR's agreement, and would also lead to more delays in developing the resources. Mineral riches can be a curse rather than a saviour for poor developing countries. In Africa, natural resources amount to two-thirds of exports, but many of the exporting countries remain poor, socially divided and politically unstable.

Mineral riches can be a curse rather than a saviour for poor developing countries.

MNEs seek the best deal they can achieve in each location. Mining and oil companies are in the spotlight. Here, we highlight the issues in the economies which *The Economist* expected to have the highest growth in 2013 (see Table 11.1). The rates of growth forecast are perhaps higher than other expert forecasters would expect, but they give an indication of where the strongest growth was expected globally.

The countries listed in Table 11.1 are mostly resource-rich economies with fragile institutions. All of these economies attract FDI, and most depend on foreign investors for their economic viability. Energy and other resources are dominant in Mongolia, Libya, Bhutan, Timor-Leste, Iraq, Mozambique, Rwanda and Ghana. In Bhutan, the main industry is hydro power, exploited by neighbouring India. Casinos and gambling dominate the economy of Macau, a special administrative region of China. Chinese gamblers are swelling the profits of American casino tycoon, Sheldon Adelson, the owner of Macau's largest casino complex and prominent Republican donor mentioned in Chapter 3 (see also the opening case study in this chapter). In the resource-rich economies on this list, large MNEs such as oil companies must reach terms with

Table 11.1 *Forecast growth rates for the ten fastest growing economies in 2013*

Economy	Forecast percentage rate of growth
Mongolia	18.1
Macau	13.5
Libya	12.2
China	8.6
Bhutan	8.5
Timor-Leste	8.3
Iraq	8.2
Mozambique	8.2
Rwanda	7.8
Ghana	7.6

Source of data: The Economist (2013) *The World in 2013*, at www.economist.com (18/09/14).

national governments, most of which have had periods of conflict in the recent past and are struggling to establish authoritative institutions. These are mainly poor countries, despite resource riches, and their societies demand to see the benefits of the resource wealth in terms of improved standards of living.

Timor-Leste, a country only just over a decade old, is an example. Having recently emerged from years of domination by Indonesia, its new democratic government is seeking to rein in the large oil companies, including Conoco Phillips, Shell and Eni, in order to direct oil wealth towards societal goals. But these goals clash with the oil companies' aims of extracting the best deal for their shareholders. This presents an ethical dilemma in which a CSR approach would be relevant, taking into account societal goals as well as corporate profits. Companies wish to maximize profits, and national goals of state building might not seem to be in their interests, but these goals are relevant for the long-term sustainability of the foreign oil companies' activities, as they help to deliver prosperity and stability to society. International organizations have stressed the social contract between state and society, but MNEs also have responsibilities.

THE SPREAD OF MARKETS

Capitalism rests on individuals and companies pursing self-interested goals. The cultural environment in which the capitalist thrives is one of economic freedom and minimal intrusive regulation. Globalization has been driven mainly by capitalist enterprises, although state-owned companies and other types of state-controlled entities are now active players in the global economy. The liberal market economies in which laissez-faire capitalism has flourished, notably the US and UK, fall culturally in an individualistic tradition, and have also evolved democratic institutions based on the rule of law and thriving civil society organizations. There is a deeply rooted belief that the good of all in society is served both by the free market and democratic institutions. This belief has been shaken in recent years by the financial crisis of 2008 and growing inequality, which have undermined markets and led to disillusionment with political institutions. However, several decades of relative prosperity constituted a persuasive example of the benefits of markets to other countries, even though most of these are very different in cultural background than the capitalist heartlands.

Economic and political systems globally are more diverse than the model of liberal democracy enshrined in the western foundations of capitalism. Still, capitalism as an enterprise model has spread relentlessly. Even business sectors in China are sometimes described as the 'wild west' in terms of rampant capitalism (Hochberg, 2012). But the systems in which these enterprises develop are anything but the American's picture of a capitalist enterprise. Intrusive bureaucracy, orders from party leadership, regulatory inflexibility – these are aspects of state capitalism familiar in China, while issues such as quality control, product safety checks, environmental protection and employment protection are lax. 'China Inc.' is a hybrid, combining markets with a vision of national development. Ning Gaoning, a director of a state-owned agribusiness company says, 'We have a very strong sense of responsibility and sense of mission' (Rabinovitch, 2012). He is one of many Chinese businesspeople who are reluctant to embrace more market reform, but this is not necessarily just because of his own self-interest. Mr Ning has a strong faith in the state model of

'China Inc.' is a hybrid, combining markets with a vision of national development.

development, which has delivered spectacular growth. China's authoritarian model has attracted many admirers among emerging and developing countries.

An inherent weakness, nonetheless, is that China's development model, which has served during two decades of rapid growth, must change as growth slows. A difficulty for China is that, although growth has now slowed, there is still much unfinished business left in order to bring a level of human well-being to the whole of its vast and disparate society. Herein lies a major challenge. Many, like opponents of Mr Ning, urge more open capitalist reforms, but existing leaders take a cautious approach to reform which might undermine their political control. Many private-sector companies in China, while emulating the 'wild west' approach, have been caught up in a number of scandals, including food safety standards, exacerbated by a lack of regulatory standards. Political leaders are also aware of the need for jobs: state-owned companies, although many are environmentally dangerous and have poor working conditions, are a vital source of employment. Closing down a pollutant factory would benefit the environment but could be devastating in a city dependent on the factory for jobs. The fear of social unrest is never far beneath the surface. Feelings of discontent are fuelled by the social media in China, which increasingly highlights luxurious lifestyles of party leadership. The rich–poor divide is accentuated by the fact that the party leadership in China still boasts, implausibly, of its commitment to Marxism-Leninism. Deng Xiaoping, who initiated China's market reforms, announced that 'to get rich is glorious', but the greed-is-good attitude can go too far, as has been evident in a backlash against the rich which has become global (Rachman, 2012). In moves announced to reduce corruption, the new leadership in China banned lavish banquets and luxury gifts among the higher echelons of the party. However, it was suspected that banquets simply become more discreet affairs held in private locations.

Capitalist enterprises are not compelled to adopt a profits-at-all-costs approach. Indeed, this is often a recipe for failure. Companies which collapsed and had to be bailed out in 2008 were companies which had taken excessive risks to boost profits. In countries where social values are actively promoted by governments and where the model of corporate governance is based more on stakeholder participation, there is less inequality and greater levels of human development. Denmark is an example.

We have discussed the shareholder primacy model of the company, noting its shortcomings, in Chapter 8. If businesses take an aggressive, profit-maximizing stance, disregarding worker concerns, relations with the workforce and with other stakeholders are likely to be adversarial, each side seeking gains at the expense of the other, with no shared sense of purpose. The shareholder primacy model of corporate governance tends to undervalue the role of stakeholders, seeing their role in an instrumental way, contributing to the creation of shareholder value, rather than as ends in themselves. In many companies, notably technology companies, the shareholder primacy model has been adapted to perpetuate the control of founders, even though these companies are listed public companies. Mark Zuckerberg, a Facebook founder, owns the bulk of Facebook's B shares, which are not traded and have 10 times the voting strength of A shares, which are traded. Facebook is, in fact, the opposite of the modern capitalist company described by Berle and Means, in which ownership and control are separated. Zuckerberg both owns and controls the company, and is closer in practice to the role of the all-powerful tycoon of earlier capitalist eras than the image of the modern CEO who is accountable to a range of shareholders. Insider domination of companies, however perpetuated, is a common feature of businesses the world over. It has contributed to the rising wealth of the top 1% in society – and also widening inequality.

PAUSE TO CONSIDER...

Do you consider Mark Zuckerberg a good role model of the modern capitalist, and why?

MEETING THE CHALLENGES

Four challenges were highlighted in the Introduction to this book. These are migrant labour; privacy and data protection; climate change; financial crises and inequality. The chapters which followed presented a more vivid picture of these challenges, their ethical dimensions and how business responses to them are evolving. Here, we draw together some conclusions.

Migrant labour – It is extraordinary to think that, although the global economy depends on millions of migrant workers, these people are viewed mainly in economic terms by the companies and governments who depend on them. The human well-being of these vulnerable workers is only gradually being addressed, and in many cases this is only in response to revelations of inhuman conditions which emerge through the media. As this book has shown, however, the very essence of migrant labour involves denying basic rights to people – rights at the heart of human dignity. These workers typically have no freedom over employment terms, little freedom of movement, little freedom of association, substandard housing, little scope for human relationships, harsh working conditions and risks to health. In Chapter 6, I highlighted the affront to human rights which characterized colonial regimes, but many aspects of slavery which are now recognized as unethical (and illegal) are being perpetuated in more nuanced ways. Most are illegal within national laws, but weak enforcement helps to perpetuate infringements of human rights. We have seen examples of garment factory workers in Bangladesh who come from rural areas, miners in South Africa, construction workers in the Gulf states and manufacturing workers in China. Addressing their employment and living conditions should be a primary concern for companies involved from the outset of their operations, not a response to complaints after operations are in full swing. In all of these examples, unfortunately, it has taken deaths to bring the plight of these workers to the attention of those who operate the systems that employ them. The message of business ethics is that business models which rely on migrant workers are unsustainable on ethical grounds. Companies should look from the outset at sustainability from the standpoint of human well-being.

Privacy, data protection and surveillance – It is not surprising that some of the biggest, most successful companies are in the high-tech sector. Global companies such as Google and Microsoft have not just economic power, but immense capacity for data collection and use. This gives them sweeping power on a global scale: over other businesses, over government information systems and over the ways in which people go about their daily lives, especially through mobile technology. Systems are vulnerable to criminal actors and terrorists, but also to practices which fall into a more ethically 'grey' area. As we have seen, the US government has pursued programmes of bulk collection of private data from internet and telephone systems, with the co-operation of many businesses in the technology sector. Now being questioned in the Congress, the US executive has acted under questionable legal authority and safeguards for individuals. While US citizens stress their worries about constitutional rights, the broader issue is human rights, which is the concern of everyone. Governments justify their surveillance activities in terms of national security, but drawing the line between warranted intrusions into privacy and infringement of human rights has become more difficult – and more urgent. The involvement of technology companies makes this a matter of business ethics, just as much as their own collection of personal data for commercial uses.

Climate change – Although reducing emissions is overwhelmingly recognized as necessary to slow climate change, most governments, businesses and individuals remain reluctant to act decisively. Climate change is a global issue, and the Kyoto precedent of agreed emissions reductions indicated that concerted action was possible. But since then, divisions among governments at international level have probably set back the prospect of international agreement. There is a split between developed and developing countries as to who should bear responsibilities for reducing emissions. Developing and emerging economies point to the fact that the developed countries bear historic responsibilities for climate change, while developed countries point out that current emissions are growing most rapidly in the developing world (see Chapters 4 and 10). Businesses need not wait on governmental leads, but are in a position to take initiatives on grounds of CSR. The challenge for businesses is to endorse sustainability as a strategic imperative. This has been a forceful message put forward in the UN Global Compact. It does not entail forgoing economic goals. On the contrary, economic goals are only achievable in a context of sustainable use of energy and resources. Moreover, the strength of the human rights case in sustainability becomes ever stronger, as this book has highlighted. The devastating impacts of climate change, especially in poor and vulnerable countries, is a human rights issue as much as an environmental issue.

Financial crises – The impacts of financial crises have been evident throughout this book. Whereas financial crises are not new, the rapid rise of globalized financial flows has led to increased risk that a financial crisis, such as the banking crisis of 2008, will have global repercussions. In Chapter 2, we saw the impacts of financial crisis on societies. The financial services sector was examined in detail in Chapter 5, looking at the risks and instability in global markets, and the consequences for societies. The relationship between legal and ethical dimensions came into focus: although legal regulation and reform are recognized as necessary, an underlying culture of personal reward-seeking and profit maximization has been at the heart of rising financial instability globally. As highlighted in Chapter 7, where regulation is implemented, financial professionals find ways around it, and financial activities tend to gravitate towards markets and environments where there is less regulation – and usually greater risk. Future financial crises are always brewing, even as the litigation from earlier crises proceeds through judicial systems. Challenges remain in designing and implementing regulation to facilitate fair markets, preferably in a context of global co-operation such as the G20 and IMF. However, the bigger challenge is shifting the mindset of financial actors towards a more sustainable, and therefore more ethical, view of financial services.

Inequality – The last of the challenges, inequality, is entwined with the previous three. Migrant labour is a stark reminder of the vulnerabilities of the weakest workers in labour markets. Cross-border migrants inevitably travel from poor countries to rich ones. The climate change debate has opened up wide gaps in global perspectives, developing countries looking back at historic responsibilities, and developed countries looking forward to what

Photo 11.2 *The simple message of protesters in Amsterdam in 2011 echoes those of the Occupy movement in New York.* (© iStock.com/VLIET)

now needs to be done. Some of the most severe impacts of extreme weather events such as storms and flooding are in poor countries that are least able to cope. The financial crisis of 2008 saw the bailout of banks deemed to be too big to fail, but in the economic recession which followed, there were no bailouts for the ordinary businesses which collapsed and only crumbs for workers who lost their jobs. As we saw in Chapter 2, at the heart of capitalism lies the basic assumptions that 'greed is good'. Supporters of markets urge that inequality is not a bad thing: the rags-to-riches story is part of the capitalist's thinking. However, we also saw that rising inequality can leave many millions of people behind, with little prospect of economic betterment or improvement in well-being. In ethical terms, as Rawls would remind us, this amounts to injustice. The Occupy movement, highlighted in Chapter 5, targeted the concentration of wealth in the top 1%. Its message was that capitalism is not working. The Occupy movement spread out from New York to other cities in the US and around the world, striking a chord among the 'other 99%' in locations far beyond Wall Street. Deteriorating human development can destabilize societies and threaten governance systems in the long term. The world now faces extreme inequality, not just in one country, but throughout the world. The rich are getting richer almost everywhere, in both advanced and emerging economies.

INEQUALITY REVISITED: THE ETHICAL DIMENSIONS

Inequalities exist in all aspects of life, not just business. Some children have greater aptitudes than others and are better achievers in the school system. The higher achievers usually go on to have more fulfilling careers than students who struggled in school. Every society contains inequalities: some people have more power and authority than others, whether because of inherited status, elected office or just wealth. Supporters of liberal principles, such as John Rawls, would argue that inequality is inevitable, but it is possible to have a system of equality of opportunity, so that all people are able to fulfil their potential. Inequality leads to injustice in societies where a good education and healthcare depend on having the money to pay for them.

As discussed in Chapter 2, capitalism depends on some people selling their labour for a wage, and owners making a profit. While some staunch anti-capitalists would see this arrangement as essentially unethical, most people would accept that arrangements between workers and owners can be designed as mutually beneficial and ethically grounded, with a recognition of human dignity and principled dialogue between the two. It is when the relationship becomes exploitative that it undermines human dignity. Exploitation of workers is unlikely in situations where workers and managers enjoy a constructive dialogue and share a vision of the purpose of the company.

An enduring assumption of capitalism has been that society would ultimately benefit from free markets based on individuals and corporations pursuing their own self-interest. We have seen in the chapters of Part 1 that many people in societies around the world have

Figure 11.3 The many sides of inequality

International trade
Unequal bargaining
power among nations
in trade deals

Economic inequality
Widening income
gaps within countries

**Access to education
and healthcare**
The poor
and minorities
disadvantaged

Many sides of
inequality

**Exploitation of
natural resources**
determined by
powerful interests,
but communities
and natural
environment at risk

Legal systems
biased towards
rich and powerful

Public voice
Governments tilt
towards rich and
powerful groups

Financial markets
Favoured treatment
for powerful interests,
but crises impact
disproportionately
on the powerless

benefited from market reforms and economic development. MNEs as the drivers of FDI and supply chains were at the forefront of these developments, which surged ahead in the 1990s. While economic development has been applauded, it is now clear that globalization and capitalist development have produced a mixed set of outcomes, raising issues of sustainable development which are now being addressed. Sustainability takes an essentially ethical perspective, valuing human life and the natural environment both for the present and into the future. It is now evident that many people, like rural dwellers and the very poorly paid in developing countries, have seen few gains in human well-being from globalized production. Inequality associated with globalization has been on the rise both within and between countries. Human rights of workers are at risk not just in the poor factory conditions of developing countries but in the retail parks of the US and other advanced economies. In the US, the share of total income of the top 1% was 9% in 1976, and 20% in 2011, which is the same as it was in the 1920s (Alvaredo et al., 2013). In situations of inequality, whether between a factory owner and a worker or in a trade agreement between a rich country and a poor one, inequality tends to equate with injustice. Wherever inequality is pervasive, ethical behaviour is under threat. The mentality of 'might is right' is the antithesis of right actions taken on ethical principles.

Figure 11.3 highlights seven dimensions in which inequality benefits the rich and powerful and disadvantages the poor and weak. It reveals the damaging impacts of inequality within societies and between countries. We look first at inequality within countries.

INEQUALITIES WITHIN COUNTRIES

There is a widening income gap in almost all societies. The rich are getting richer everywhere, a trend reported annually in the World Wealth Report (Capgemini, 2013). The numbers of millionaires and billionaires are growing on every continent. The wealth of

Photo 11.3 *Companies are lured to offshore havens, and so are rich individuals. The Principality of Monaco, on the French Riviera, is famed for attracting the super-rich, as evidenced by the luxury yachts that dot its harbour.* (PhotoDisc/Getty Images)

these individuals rose 10% in the year to 2012, to $46.2 trillion. That is just over half of world GDP. The number of very rich individuals also grew, at 9.2%, to reach 12 million globally in 2012, the highest rise being in North America, at 11.5%. The super-rich are concerned above all to preserve their wealth for future generations of their families (Capgemini, 2013). Where markets function in the ways posited by capitalism, the theory is that the people who earn high incomes are those who create the economic value, which ultimately benefits all. This is not what is happening in today's world, despite the spread of capitalist thinking.

The income share of the rich is growing, and is being successfully transmitted to future generations, thanks in large part to the opportunities presented by global financial planning. Capitalism should, in theory, create value, but in today's world, much productive activity is, instead, channelled towards protecting the assets of the wealthy. A growing branch of the financial services sector, for example, is in running 'family offices', firms of professional fund managers who serve a single family or a group of families. In the more unequal developed countries, the US and UK, the transmission of wealth from one generation to the next is stronger than in more equal societies, such as Denmark (Harford, 2013). Intergenerational income mobility has diminished in the US, perpetuating inequality (Corak, 2013). It has been observed that, 'the more unequal a society, the greater the incentive for the wealthy to pull up the ladder behind them' (Harford, 2013). Partly,

'The more unequal a society, the greater the incentive for the wealthy to pull up the ladder behind them.'

this is because the super-rich have reason to fear democratic politics. After all, in a system of one-person-one-vote, candidates advocating redistribution stand to benefit. On the other hand, as was pointed out in Chapter 3, in the US, both Democrats and Republicans derive their major funding from wealthy donors, making redistribution policies less likely (Bonica et al., 2013). Moreover, favoured investments of the rich are media, newspapers and internet technology, which are powerful tools for influencing political debate. Where that debate is seriously curtailed, as in China, there is a greater risk of upheaval. China's rich–poor divide has risen to a level 50% above that associated with unrest, according to a Chinese central bank survey (Bloomberg, 2012).

While the numbers of people globally living in absolute poverty (less than $1.25 a day) decrease, now standing at 1.4 billion, the numbers of people just above that level are finding it more difficult to rise above their relative poverty and precarious livelihoods. Education and healthcare both contribute to achieving better long-term life prospects. Education is a key not just to employment, but to a fulfilling life. The same is true of basic health. Providing universal access to basic education should be a priority of governments, but public provision is weak in many countries, including rich ones, leaving the poor and those in minority groups educationally disadvantaged. In some countries, such as India, discrimination against girls in educational opportunities is widespread.

Equal political voice for all in society is a mainstay of ensuring that government is accountable to all the people. Yet in many countries, democracies among them, political power rests less on the voice of the people and more on the sway of powerful elements in the society, often business interests. We have seen widespread erosion of trust in politicians as promoters of the public good. Where politicians are perceived as using public office for their own personal gain, ordinary voters feel that their voices do not count. Low electoral turnouts are a consequence. But, at the same time, in many instances people take to the streets in movements and demonstrations to make their views known. Recall the example of Turkey (the closing case study of Chapter 10), where a democratically-elected government was widely perceived as serving the business élite rather than the broader interests of society. It has been said that we live in an age of 'individual empowerment', in which technology gives people unprecedented ability to communicate with each other and gain knowledge (US National Intelligence Council, 2012). Certainly, governments have all become wary of the power of social networks, but the tools of technology have also given governments and corporations the ability to gather vast amounts of personal data on people everywhere, which is arguably in breach of human rights.

Where politicians are perceived as using public office for their own personal gain, ordinary voters feel that their voices do not count.

The rule of law in principle implies that all should be equal before the law, whether rich or poor or whatever a person's racial background, sex, nationality or ethnic origin. However, even in countries which proclaim adherence to the rule of law, such as the US, the reality is a legal system which serves the powerful, wealthy and mainly white population, while the poor and minority groups are disadvantaged (Stuntz, 2001). 'Too big to jail' is an accusation often made against leading figures in global finance, whose activities contributed to the crisis of 2008. Global financial markets enriched bankers, hedge fund managers and traders, most of whom have escaped unscathed. However, the lives of many ordinary people were ruined, as they lost their jobs and homes when businesses collapsed.

ECONOMIC INEQUALITIES BETWEEN COUNTRIES

Inequalities in economic power and trade among countries have made the principle of the sovereign equality of states sound hollow. The rich and powerful nations have long used their position to extract terms of trade from weaker countries, which are skewed towards their interests. Recall that trading interests within countries are often highly concentred in a few large companies, which tend to receive favourable treatment by governments, often in the form of protections, because of their export prowess. The WTO, most of whose 159 members are developing countries, aimed to make multilateralism a reality, but it has struggled to bridge the gap between the powerful trading interests and the developing countries. Its achieving a conclusion to the Doha round in 2013, following 12 years of repeated failures, was seen as an impressive achievement, due in large part to the skills of its new director general, himself from an emerging country (Brazil). However, it is widely acknowledged that the chief beneficiaries of the deal are powerful business interests, rather than the interests of poor developing countries (see Chapter 6). It has been suggested that the world is becoming multipolar, with power shifting away from the US towards the large emerging economies, commensurate with their growing global economic power (US National Intelligence Council, 2012). The Doha conclusion reflects this trend. As the US has been aiming to conclude trade deals with Asian and European partners, many emerging countries saw the risks of being left out. China, India, Brazil, Russia, Indonesia, Nigeria and South Africa – all saw the benefits presented by a Doha multilateral agreement.

Poor developing countries, however, remain vulnerable to the bigger economic powers, whether from the older advanced economies or the new emerging economies. The BRICs are all active in pursuing trade and other opportunities in Africa, as we have seen. Poor African countries, although rich in minerals, tend to be the losers in the exploitation and protection of their own natural resources. As discussed in the last section, many factors come into play, including poor governance, weak institutions and social instability. Where accountability is weak, leaders and their associates can capture benefits for themselves. Communities and the environment are at risk, despite the fact that governments, often elected, should be focusing on public goods as the means of achieving sustainable well-being for societies. Governments or poor countries come under a great deal of pressure. The countries of Africa are seeing rising levels of FDI, which is good news, but large companies such as Coca-Cola and IBM do not offer the benefits to local economies which feature in headlines. Large foreign companies typically channel flows through offshore centres, resulting in reduced tax liabilities, as the investor is resident in a low-tax jurisdiction, such as Luxembourg or Singapore. While this benefits the investor, it effectively deprives the host country of valuable tax revenues.

Foreign investors often insist on a Foreign Investor Promotion and Protection Agreement (FIPA). This is a bilateral investment treaty (BIT) between governments, which gives investing companies a right to an ad hoc arbitration tribunal to challenge domestic laws in the host country if it feels its interests are being prejudiced (see Chapter 6). A fear in host countries is that the investing company can use this mechanism to avoid legitimate social and economic laws. The FIPA is also a feature in international trade agreements, where it is sometimes referred to as an 'investor–state dispute settlement mechanism', which is proposed by the US for inclusion in both the Trans-Pacific Partnership (TPP) and the Transatlantic Trade and Investment Partnership (TTIP). Canada has a seen both the benefits and the drawbacks of such agreements. It has FIPAs with a number of countries where its mining companies are active investors. But it has also been on the losing end of legal actions taken by US companies on a number of occasions, under the FIPA contained in the North American Free Trade Agreement (NAFTA). China has now invested in Canada, and is also seeking protections under a FIPA. As the weaker partner in the agreement, Canada has cause to be concerned about the power of foreign companies, which could enjoy greater legal protection than domestic Canadian companies (Herman, 2013).

Australia's law on the plain packaging of cigarettes (discussed in the opening case study of Chapter 1) prompted the large tobacco companies to pursue legal challenges under bilateral treaties, which it had entered with a view to protections for Australian companies in their foreign investments. Australia's government probably would not have foreseen the legal challenges it now faces from tobacco-related lawsuits, and has objected to including in the TPP a right for tobacco companies to pursue lawsuits which override national laws.

HOW FAR CAN REGULATION RAISE ETHICAL STANDARDS?

In the three decades leading up to the financial crisis, markets had been thought to be the solutions in just about every sphere of life, from consumer goods to services such as healthcare, education and prisons (Sandel, 2012). Sandel refers to the commodization not just of the economy, but of society (see Chapter 2). The trend started in the 1970s, when President Ronald Reagan in the US and Prime Minister Margaret Thatcher in the UK ushered in a period of deregulation, lower taxes – and rising inequality (Rachman, 2012). Deng Xiaoping even joined in the market thinking, with his exhortation to get rich. When Mrs Thatcher came to power, the top rate of income tax in Britain was 83%. She cut it to 60% and then 40%. Similarly, Mr Reagan reduced the top rate of income tax from 70% to 50%, and then to 28%. The top rate in the UK in 2013 was 45%, and in the US, 39.6%. The rich in today's globalized world are highly mobile: most already avoid existing rates through offshoring and investment vehicles. This highlights the eternal problem of regulation: whatever legal steps are taken, people affected will make every effort to sidestep the rules if they can. In matters of tax, the most powerful are able to escape, while the weak are not. Where an activity is made more expensive or forbidden, it will retreat into the shadows or be redesigned to get round the rules.

This book has highlighted a number of examples of the regulator's dilemma. Shadow banking was discussed in connection with China in a case study (Chapter 5). It has grown up in order to get round regulatory constraints, and similar arrangements exist in most countries. But the risks lurking in unregulated shadow markets could potentially bring down whole financial systems. As part of the Dodd–Franks reforms in the US, public companies face new regulatory hurdles, and a response for many has been to delist and go private. Similarly, any stock exchange that introduces more stringent rules will find that IPOs migrate to other exchanges. Alibaba's founder, Jack Ma, wished to launch an IPO in Hong Kong in 2013, but the exchange would not allow his dual-share structure in the Facebook mould. He therefore sought a listing in New York. Hong Kong was criticized for turning away the business, as if its principled stance was wrong, and the rules should be bent for Ma. The London Stock Exchange went through a troubled spell, having waived its rules to attract poorly governed mining companies. It then regretted it when fraud allegations compelled some companies to delist, and the LSE responded by tightening its rules. Again, critics expressed concern that by tightening the rules, the LSE might turn away business. On principles of upholding public confidence in fair markets, *all* exchanges should turn away insider-dominated companies which lack transparency. In this way, investors can be confident that companies which come to market meet minimum standards of governance.

Regulation which takes the form of legal frameworks and sanctions stems from national law. Examples we have seen in this book include environmental law, food safety law, employment law, tax law and competition law. In these – and many other – areas, companies are bound by national laws. But, that said, enforcement is sometimes weak, and countries in fact compete on the friendliness of their business environment. We have noted the attractions of Singapore in this regard (case study in Chapter 8). It is because of this sense of national competitive advantage that corporation tax rates have declined markedly in many countries (see Chapter 5). The lack of regulation at the global level has been a factor in allowing MNEs great scope to locate operations in places which are advantageous, often avoiding obligations such as taxes through offshoring. Organizations such as the G20 (see note in Chapter 7) have pledged to act to deter offshoring, but these initiatives depend on the will of national governments. Among the few global bodies that are in a position to exert regulatory authority, there is the World Bank, which is pursuing a strong policy against fraud and corruption in the many projects which it helps to fund in developing countries.

The World Bank has dispersed over $200 billion in funds to finance development projects over the last five years. These projects, such as large infrastructure projects, have long been seen as opportunities for bribery and corruption by unscrupulous businesses. The World Bank has powers to launch investigations and to debar companies from future contracts, or to impose other sanctions on them in cases of wrongdoing. In 2012, it imposed a record number of debarments and other sanctions (see Figure 11.4). In a report on its

Figure 11.4 Debarments and other sanctions issued by the World Bank for corruption and fraud (number)

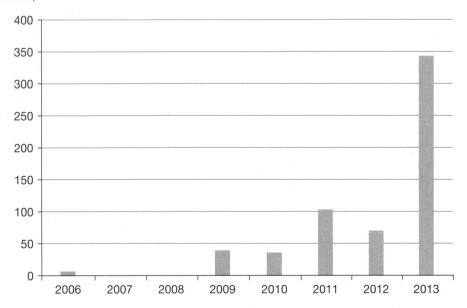

Source of data: Freshfields Bruckhaus Deringer LLP (2013) *World Bank Sanctions Investigations: Blacklist Revisited,* at www.freshfields.com (18/09/14).

'We're not a global policeman, but what we can do is facilitate the global conversation against corruption.'

sanctions and investigations, the point is made that the corruption uncovered has led to the theft of some $40 billion in funds from some of the world's poorest countries (World Bank, 2013). A total of 250 companies have been barred, most of which are North American and Caribbean. The largest number of entities barred were connected with a Canadian company, SNC Lavalin, in connection with a bridge being built in Bangladesh (McArthur, 2013). SNC Lavalin is debarred from tendering for any World Bank project for ten years. Canada has had an anti-corruption statute in its domestic law for over two decades, but has brought under 12 actions against companies in that time. The World Bank's debarment has been a wake-up call to national authorities, as it has been in other countries. The World Bank recognizes its responsibility in fighting corruption, but also its limitations. Its director of integrity says, 'We're not a global policeman, but what we can do is facilitate the global conversation against corruption' (Binham, 2013).

PAUSE TO CONSIDER...

Explain the regulator's dilemma. In your view, what are the best ways to overcome it?

MEETING ETHICAL CHALLENGES IN INTERNATIONAL BUSINESS

The comments of the World Bank's director of integrity echo the problems faced by regulators everywhere. Passing stringent laws to stamp out corruption or other unethical practices does not result in the end of corruption. What it does achieve is to make ethical behaviour a matter of rules and compliance. Knowing that there are never enough officials to uncover all wrongdoing, the regulator hopes that actors will comply out of a sense of moral obligation. But many actors will comply with the law simply for fear of being caught. Many will not, considering it unlikely that enforcement will be effective, and many will carry on as before, but disguise payments to avoid raising suspicion. In all but the first group, who comply out of a sense of morality, behaviour is not based on ethical principles, but on expediency and self-interest. Businesses with this attitude treat their obligations in terms of law, not ethics. Such a view would reflect the view of corporate purpose enshrined by the profit-maximizing model of the company. As we have seen, however, this view of business represents a set of assumptions which are acknowledged, even by advocates, to be too simplistic in practice (Stout, 2012). It has also been revealed as flawed, in that companies obsessed with profits at all costs, which had been held up as global leaders, have spectacularly failed.

Everyone has a multiplicity of motivations, some self-interested, others pro-social and altruistic. The person dominated by rational calculation of self-interest is a construct which is used to explain how markets work in economic theory. In reality, businesses see the importance of ethics in their activities, even if they do not acknowledge it. They appreciate that when a deal is done with another party, each trusts the other to abide not just by the letter of the agreement, and also to be co-operative in carrying out the deal (Gambetta, 1988). This is increasingly the case in a globalized environment, where in many emerging countries, business is thought to be about personal relations, not just formal contracts. Increasingly, a co-operative element is a necessary part of any deal. Businesses which are motivated only by material self-interest are rather like Hobbes' inhabitant in the state of nature: insecure and afraid. The result is a war of all against all in which none is secure and none actually achieves any personal goals. In practice, businesses value employees, customers and other stakeholders, not just shareholders. One could take the view of stakeholder theorists who argue that these groups are important from an instrumental perspective because they are essential to achieving business goals. But there are also elements of trust and respect. Trust between managers and employees implies each respecting the human dignity of the other, apart from what is written in the employment contract. Trust between a company and its customers also matters. Consumers everywhere want not just safe products and services, but brands they can trust. Thanks largely to social media, consumers feel empowered as never before, speaking out against companies perceived as arrogant and greedy. Starbucks has pursued a supremely effective tax-avoidance policy, which would, in theory, please shareholders, but the company has alienated consumers in large markets such as the UK, who feel it is unfair that Starbucks is allowed to escape taxes while rivals pay theirs.

Consumers are unimpressed when Starbucks claims it is a good corporate citizen and pays all the taxes it owes. Extensive media coverage has ensured that public knowledge of tax avoidance schemes is widespread. Especially in communities where unemployment is high and wages low, few would sing the praises of the shareholder primacy model of the company. They have seen the outcomes in practice, and they almost inevitably threaten ethical and social values. This is one of the reasons why a CSR approach represents a more balanced and realistic approach to the company than a fixation on profit-maximizing. Far from being aspirational – 'a good idea if we can afford it' – it actually represents a picture of most people's values, whatever the national culture, incorporating pro-social as well as self-interested motives. People need meaningful jobs and fair incomes, but they need much more, as the UN's ideas of human development remind us. People are concerned about communities, education, health and housing. They also need a natural environment in which food is safe and nutritional, the water is safe, the soil supports crops and the air is clean. Moreover, they are concerned that future generations will see similar aspirations fulfilled. International businesses have been slow to take this message on board. They have embraced the rhetoric in many cases, but their actions have lagged behind. Now, they face the hardest tests of all, not those of stock markets and boardrooms, but from the rest of us.

REFERENCES

Alvaredo, F., Atkinson, A., Piketty, T. and Saez, E. (2013) 'The top 1 percent in international and historical perspective', *Journal of Economic Perspectives*, 27(1): 3–20.

Associated British Foods (2013) *Corporate Responsibility Report 2013*, at www.abf.com (18/09/14).

Binham, C. (2013) 'World Bank sanctions hit record', *Financial Times*, 16 September.

Bloomberg (2012) *Heirs of Mao's Comrades Rise in New Capitalist Nobility*, 26 December, at www.bloomberg.com (18/09/14).

Bonica, A., McCarty, N., Poole, K. and Rosenthal, H. (2013) 'Why hasn't democracy slowed rising inequality?', *Journal of Economic Perspectives*, 27(1): 103–24.

Burgis, T. (2014) 'Steinmetz unit won Guinea mining riches corruptly, says inquiry', *Financial Times*, 10 April.

Capgemini (2013) *World Wealth Report 2013*, at www.worldwealthreport.com (18/09/14).

Corak, M. (2013) 'Income inequality, equality of opportunity, and intergenerational mobility', *Journal of Economic Perspectives*, 27(1): 79–102.

Freeland, C. (2013) *Retooling Capitalism for the Social Good*, at www.reuters.com (18/09/14).

Gambetta, D. (1988) *Trust: Making and breaking cooperative relations* (Oxford: Basil Blackwell).

Goldman Sachs (2013) *Two Decades of Freedom*, at www.goldmansachs.com (18/09/14).

Harford, T. (2013) 'How the rich are making sure they stay on top', *Financial Times*, 16 August.

Herman, L. (2013) 'Time to rethink foreign investment protection agreements? Perhaps', *The Globe and Mail*, 4 May, at www.theglobeandmail.com (18/09/14).

Hochberg, F. (2012) 'State capitalists work out a new wild west', *Financial Times*, 11 July.

H&M (2013) *Conscious Actions Sustainability Report 2012*, at http://about.hm.com (26/09/14).

McArthur, G. (2013) 'Businessman charged in SNC-Lavalin probe turns himself in to RCMP', *The Globe and Mail*, 3 December, at www.globeandmail.com (18/09/14).

Politi, J. (2013) 'US opens arms to foreign investors', *Financial Times*, 31 October.

Rabinovitch, S. (2012) 'Scandals fail to dent faith in China's state-led capitalism', *Financial Times*, 21 November.

Rachman, G. (2012) 'The backlash against the rich has now gone global', *Financial Times*, 7 August.

Sandel, M. (2012) *What Money Can't Buy* (London: Allen Lane).

Stout, L. (2012) *The Shareholder Value Myth* (San Francisco: Berrett-Kohler).

Stuntz, W. (2001) 'The pathological politics of criminal law', *Michigan Law Review*, 100(3): 505–600.

US National Intelligence Council (2012) *Global Trends 2030: Alternative Worlds*, NIC 2012-001, at www.dni.gov (18/09/14).

World Bank (2013) *World Bank Sanctions Investigations: Blacklist Revisited*, at www.freshfields.com (18/09/14).

REVIEW QUESTIONS

1 In what ways have the ethical themes throughout this book illuminated the debate on the impacts of globalization?

2 Governance is not limited to governments, but involves a range of business and other organizational players. Is this a positive development towards social well-being, or a setback, reflecting the rise of particular interests which can capture governments?

3 What is the role of consumers in bringing about shifts towards CSR in global supply chains?

4 What evidence is there that capitalism is failing? Can it be reformed from within, and who should take the lead in bringing about reforms?

5 What are the main ethical issues which arise in the context of African development? What recommendations would you make to African states to reap the benefits of foreign investment while also benefiting society?

6 How is China's development model changing? Are these changes pointing towards a more ethically attuned economic model such as CSR, or simply towards maintaining short-term social stability?

7 What are the risks in a society where there is a wide gap between rich and poor?

8 Can a highly unequal society be democratic? Give your reasons.

9 National competitive advantage has played a big part in globalization by attracting FDI, creating a kind of 'race to the bottom'. How can this downward spiral be broken on ethical grounds?

10 Why is trust an important ingredient in implementing business ethics?

GLOSSARY

agency costs – in agency theory, the costs incurred by a person (the principal) in hiring an agent to carry out a task on the principal's behalf, arising, in particular, because the agent is inclined to behave opportunistically rather than in the interest of the principal

Alien Tort Claims Act (ATCA) – in the US, a statute of 1789, which allows foreign plaintiffs to bring claims in US courts for breaches of international law

alienation – concept whereby the worker sees both the product of his work and the process of production as externalized, or standing outside himself like hostile forces

annual general meeting (AGM) – in a company, a formal meeting of shareholders, legally required to take place annually under national law

anthropocentric – view that the interests of human beings are the only interests that matter

arbitration – means of settling a dispute by bringing the parties together through the offices of a third party

authority – the rightful exercise of power; can apply to a group, organization or the state

authoritarian – rule which is unaccountable to the governed; usually involves a repressive regime and few civil liberties

autocracy – rule by a leader unaccountable to those ruled; usually involves personalized rule and authoritarian means

barter – transaction in which goods are exchanged for other goods

basic sustainable development – view that intergenerational equity can be met by more efficient use of resources, the discovery of new resources and technological innovation

benefit corporation – a company established for social purposes, which can be registered in 19 states in the US

bilateral trade agreement – a treaty between two countries on the subject of trade and related issues

branch office – in relation to a company, an office in a different location from the company's headquarters, from which it operates in that location; the branch office does not constitute a separate legal entity, in contrast to the subsidiary company

BRICs – reference to the loose grouping of Brazil, Russia, India and China, which are all emerging economies

business – all types of economic activity carried out commercially, including agriculture, manufacturing, energy industries, trade and financial services

business ethics – the study of ethics as applied to business

'business judgment rule' – in the US, rule which holds that company directors are entitled to use their own best judgment in deciding what is best for the company

capitalism – economic system based on market principles, entailing an exchange of something of value, such as labour, for something else, typically a 'price' in the form of wages

casino capitalism – likening companies in the financial sector, especially global banks, with gambling; stems from the trend towards increased risk-taking and increased financial rewards for leading players

categorical imperative – principle associated with Kant which holds that each person should always treat other people as ends in themselves and never as means

checks and balances – in political systems, institutions which are designed to achieve a balance between the different branches of government

chief executive officer (CEO) – a company's highest executive officer, accountable to the board of directors for the management of the company

child labour – employment of children between 5 and 17 in an environment such as a factory or farm, for hours equivalent to those an adult would work, leading to detrimental effects on the child's education

citizenship – legal status which connects a person to a particular country, involving rights and duties

civil law – system of law based on legal codes handed down by the sovereign

civil society – the multiplicity of associations which people are free to join in a society, including interest groups, trade unions, religious groups and political parties

class action – lawsuit in which one or more persons brings a claim on behalf of a larger group of people with similar claims

climate change – any change in climate over time, whether from natural causes or human activity; usually refers to a rise in the earth's temperature, or global warming

'co-determination' – principle of corporate governance which holds that employees should have a say at the highest levels of decision-making in the company, along with shareholders

colonialism – expansionist rule by a stronger power, usually a state, over a weaker power; often involves taking over the territory and government of the weaker power

common law – legal system based on judge-made law, that is, decisions handed down by judges in dealing with the cases that come before them

company – legal entity which is an artificial person with separate legal existence from the people who form it and own it; also known as a 'corporation'

competition law – body of law designed to curtail monopolies and restrictive business practices; called 'antitrust' law in the US

competitive advantage – concept that economic advantages flow from competitive strategies; often used with reference to countries competing to attract foreign investment

compulsory licence – in patent law, awarding a firm the right to produce a medicine although it is under patent to another firm; awarded to resolve a public health need in a particular country

consequentialism – principle associated with the utilitarians, which holds that whether an action is good or not depends on the consequences

'constituency statutes' – statute laws in states of the US which provide that, in corporate decision-making, directors can take into account other stakeholders besides shareholders, including employees, customers and suppliers

constitution – the basic law of a state, setting out rules on how the system of government should function, and including rights and duties of both rulers and ruled

contract law – the area of law that covers most business transactions, such as buying and selling, employment and insurance

Convention on Contracts for the International Sale of Goods (CISG) – convention of 1980 which aims to harmonize contract law among differing legal systems

conventions – in international law, multilateral treaties, usually agreed through UN sponsorship

copyright – type of intellectual property which comes into existence automatically on creation of the original work, such as a literary or musical work

core values – in a company, the values which are central to the company's purpose, guiding its activities and culture

corporate bonds – fixed-term debt instruments which pay investors a fixed rate of return

corporate citizenship – view that a company is a member of society in a way analogous to the individual citizen

corporate governance – a company's structures and processes for decision-making at the highest level

corporate social performance (CSP) – concept associated with CSR, which focuses social responses in practice, bringing in all the ways in which a firm goes about meeting challenges for business in society

corporate social responsibility (CSR) – concept that the company as part of society has a broader range of roles and responsibilities than merely economic ones, notably including ethical responsibilities

cosmopolitanism – in international relations, an approach which envisages a global community and global institutions, in which state actors have receded into the background

cronyism – networks of personal relations and economic ties between political and business leaders; tends to be associated with corruption

cultural relativism – approach to ethics which holds that the moral values in any culture are as valid as those in any other, and refrains from making any ethical judgments among different cultures

customary law – type of law that draws on cultural values and norms in the community for maintaining continuity and social cohesion

debtholder – person or organization that has lent money to an organization

de-industrialization – decline in manufacturing in a country, which occurs as a result of companies shifting operations to more advantageous locations, especially to countries with lower labour costs

democracy – political system which recognizes accountability of governments to the people, through free and fair elections, backed by civil liberties

democratization – building democratic institutions in countries with an authoritarian past

deontology – philosophical tradition which focuses on the intrinsic nature of right and wrong

derivatives – financial instruments that depend on the value of another asset; involves risk in that the other asset can be difficult to measure

developed economies – economies which have reached high income levels, usually through industrialization

developing economies – economies which, starting from low income levels, are pursuing economic growth, usually through industrialization and exploitation of natural resources

direct democracy – political institutions in which people participate directly in governance

directive – type of EU law which obliges member states to incorporate it in domestic law

directors – in companies, the highest decision-makers in corporate governance structures, entrusted with safeguarding the best interests of the company as a whole

dividends – in companies, authorized payouts to shareholders from profits, which must be declared by the board of directors

due process – aspect of the rule of law, by which all people are entitled to fair, unbiased judicial proceedings

dumping – sale of goods in foreign markets at below the price charged for comparable goods in the producing country

economic freedom – freedom defined specifically as the maximum scope to pursue economic goals

economic responsibilities – in relation to for-profit companies, responsibilities of generating profits, maintaining a strong competitive position and maintaining a high level of efficiency

egoistic hedonism – view of human nature associated with Hobbes, which holds that people pursue self-interested goals, and desire a maximum amount of freedom in which to do so

emerging economies – term used loosely to describe developing countries with relatively strong economic growth, rising incomes and growing consumer markets

energy security – policy that a country should have either its own accessible energy reserves for the foreseeable future, or have access to stable supplies from other regions of the world

enlightened shareholder value – in corporate governance, concept that shareholder value includes the interests of other stakeholders and also the reputation of the company

equity – in companies, the share capital; shares (stocks) are sometimes called 'equities'

ethical absolutism – philosophical position which holds that human nature is universal, and that there exist ethical rules which apply universally

ethical investing – an approach to investment which weighs ethical concerns about the target company more heavily than monetary returns; often called 'socially responsible' investing

ethical responsibilities – in relation to companies, responsibilities to adhere to ethical principles of right and wrong, despite possible economic costs

ethics – the study of basic concepts of good and bad, right and wrong, which relate to all people as human beings

exports – products sold in countries other than the one in which they were made

Fairtrade International – a non-profit organization, which has as its primary purpose a fair deal for poor agricultural producers

federalism – constitutional arrangement by which regions or other units have some autonomy under a central government which has ultimate control

filial piety – notion of loyalty of the child to parents, associated with Confucius, which became a metaphor for rule by any superior over subordinates

finance – business function which involves money transactions and arrangements; includes buying, selling, lending, investing and also arrangements such as tax planning

financial globalization – increasing interconnectedness between financial markets, facilitated by advances in IT and communications

foreign direct investment (FDI) – acquisition, usually by a company, of productive assets in a foreign country, with a view to gaining operational control

Foreign Investment Promotion and Protection Agreement (FIPA) – bilateral or multilateral treaty under which foreign investors from one member country can have recourse to an arbitration tribunal to settle disputes in another member country

for-profit enterprise – business that aims to make money, allowing the gains to be used as owners desire

fracking – method used for extracting oil and gas deep beneath the earth's surface by hydraulic fracturing, which involves injecting chemicals through high-pressure horizontal drilling

fragile state – any state which struggles to carry out basic governance functions and whose governance is characterized by weak relations within society

fundamentalists – usually in relation to a religion, believers who practise strict adherence to rules, beliefs and practices, and tend to be hostile to more relaxed adherents within the same religion

G20 – group of 20 developed, developing and emerging economies, brought together by the IMF in 1999, which meets regularly, focusing mainly on financial stability

GATT (the General Agreement on Tariffs and Trade) – series of post-war trade agreements which aimed to reduce trade barriers; culminated in the Doha round, concluded in 2013

general will – in democratic thought, a focus on the common good of society, which is higher than the particular wills of individuals; associated with Rousseau

generic medicines – medicines whose patents have expired, leaving manufacturers other than the patentholder free to produce them for markets

genetically modified (GM) – with reference to crops, plants altered by genetic engineering, to adapt them for specific purposes, such as making them resistant to pesticides, able to withstand drought or increasing their nutrient values

Global Compact – UN initiative which brings together companies, governments and NGOs to promote basic principles in four key areas: human rights, labour, environment and anti-corruption

global warming – a general rise in the earth's temperature, caused by the build-up of heat-trapping gases, or 'greenhouse gases', in the earth's atmosphere

globalization – the lowering of barriers to the movement of people, financial flows, goods, services and information around the world

golden rule – maxim that people should treat others as they would wish to be treated themselves

governance – in general, processes by which rule-governed behaviour takes place; can apply to organizations, communities, states and in the international sphere

government – in the political sphere, the institutions by which rule is exercised, usually including lawmaking bodies and an executive branch to administer the law

greenfield investment – type of foreign direct investment which involves setting up operations from scratch in the host country

gross domestic product (GDP) – the value of the total economic activity produced within an economy in a year

guanxi – a Chinese cultural approach which values inter-personal relations

Guiding Principles on Human Rights (UNGPHR) – UN guidelines for companies in respect of human rights; issued in 2011

hazardous work – in relation to child labour, work involving dangerous machinery or dangerous substances, that adversely affects the child's safety, health and moral development

hedge funds – investment funds that generally have a short-term investment horizon, and whose managers are noted for their aggressive investment strategies

hegemony – the existence of a dominant power in international relations

human development – a view of improvement in human well-being which comprises health, education and standard of living; used as an indicator by the UN

human dignity – notion that human beings uniquely possess rationality, freedom and moral capacity

human rights – rights people hold by virtue of their inherent human dignity

human well-being – broad view of what contributes to a meaningful life, which includes material aspects of a decent life and capacity for moral development

hypernorms – principles so fundamental to human existence that they serve as a guide in evaluating moral norms of different cultures

imperialism – the domination and exploitation of a weaker state by a stronger one

imports – products entering a country from abroad

independent trade union – an organization of workers that is not under the control of the employer or any connected entity such as a government department

individualism – concept that moral value resides in the individual human being, rather than in a collectivity

inequality – in economic terms, the gap between rich and poor within a country or other area, usually measured in terms of income

inhuman treatment – term used in UN human rights conventions which covers torture (both physical and mental), physical assaults, humiliating or degrading treatment

initial public offering (IPO) – the first offering of a public company's shares to potential investors on a stock exchange

insider dealing or trading – in the trading of shares in public companies, the use of information not available publicly to gain a financial advantage over others in the market

intellectual property (IP) – property rights in intangible assets, that is, products of human mind rather than physical property; includes patents, copyright and trade marks

integrated social contracts theory – a normative approach to business ethics which focuses on ethical principles as well as the role played by local community norms in business relations; devised by Donaldson and Dunfee

intergenerational equity – principle that the current generation should behave in ways that enable future generations to live as well as they do themselves

intergenerational justice – fair system of co-operation over time between generations

Intergovernmental Panel on Climate Change (IPCC) – UN body which brings together research on climate change and makes recommendations for action by member states

International Bill of Human Rights – common collective reference to the three leading UN documents on human rights: the universal declaration of human rights; the covenant on civil and political rights; and the covenant on economic, social and cultural rights

International Covenant on Civil and Political Rights (ICCPR) – UN human rights convention dating from 1976, ratified by 167 states

International Covenant on Economic, Social and Cultural Rights (ICESCR) – UN human rights convention dating from 1976, ratified by 160 states

International Labour Organization (ILO) – UN agency which brings together member states to agree, implement and apply international conventions on labour standards and human rights; it has 185 member states

internationalism – in international relations, the predominance of state institutions, but with a role for international law, influencing the direction of national law and constituting moral standards against which national law is assessed

internationalization – strategy of companies to expand into other countries, usually through export or foreign investment

Islamic finance – area of finance designed to comply with Islamic law, through the application of specific rules to commercial transactions

Islamic law – the law which guides followers of Islam, known as Sharia law and based on the Qur'an

joint-stock company – historically, the corporate form which allowed people to come together as investors, each owning shares or stock in the company; now simply referred to as a 'company' or 'corporation'

justice – in ethics, the concept which focuses on the value of each individual human being, implying that all in society are morally equal; in law, justice refers to fairness and procedural correctness in applying laws

Kyoto Protocol – UN convention which committed developed countries that ratified the treaty to reduce carbon emissions 5% below 1990 levels by 2012

laissez-faire capitalism – model of capitalism in which there is a maximum of enterprise freedom and minimum of government intervention

law – rule or body of rules perceived as binding because it emanates from the state's sovereign authority

leftwing political parties – parties whose political beliefs rest on social priorities, usually involving a pivotal role of government in social spending

legal responsibilities – in CSR theory, a broad duty to comply with relevant national and international law

legal rights – rights recognized in law, often called 'positive' rights, such as the right to own property or to vote

legitimacy – in the political sphere, a government which is perceived as having authority to govern, usually through democratic institutions

lex mercatoria – body of law based on custom and practice among traders engaged in commercial activities across national boundaries; dates from the medieval period

liberal democracy – democratic system based on individual freedoms such as freedom of expression and association, which support free and fair elections; also includes respect for majority rule and minority rights

liberal market economy – type of market economy which balances individual freedom and the need for government intervention to promote public goods

liberalism – focus on individual rights in economic, political and social thinking (but note, in American political terminology, tends to have the opposite meaning, that is, a focus on social justice)

liberty – derived from the notion of human dignity, the capacity of people to pursue goals and achieve personal moral fulfilment; combines 'negative' freedoms such as freedom of movement, and 'positive' freedoms such as individual self-determination

limited liability – in companies, the principle that a shareholder is liable only for the amount invested in the company, and not liable for debts incurred by the company (as the company is a separate legal entity); also pertains to limited partnerships

lobbying – activities of businesses and other interest groups to influence politicians and political decision-making

localization – for international business, the strategy of seeking particular advantages presented by one location over another

location advantages – in international business, the advantages, such as low-cost labour and access to resources, which distinguish one country or region from another

malnutrition – condition of consuming insufficient nutrients to sustain a person's life; can be caused by hunger or by obesity

managers – employees responsible for day-to-day running of an organization's activities; in a company, they are accountable to the CEO and board of directors

market – bringing together of buyers and sellers in exchange transactions, in either regulated or unregulated settings

mercantilism – in international trade, the approach of a country which sees trade mainly as promoting its own economic gains; associated with high tariff barriers on imports and also, historically, colonialism

merger and acquisition – in relation to corporate control, the coming together of two or more companies, either as equals (merger) or as a purchase of one by the other (takeover)

microfinance – sector which encompasses a variety of non-profit and social enterprises offering financial services to poor people who fall outside mainstream banking

mixed economy – an economy with elements of both open markets and state direction or ownership

monopoly – domination by one firm in the market for particular goods or services, enabling that firm to determine prices and supply

moral hazard – in decision-making, a sense of freedom from responsibility which encourages a person to take risks, knowing that others will have to bear any losses

moral self-realization – view of human dignity which is associated with Kant and the positive concept of liberty

morality – rules and norms of behaviour derived from cultural values

multilateral agreements – in international law, treaties to which there are many ratifying parties

multinational enterprise (MNE) – a company which owns or controls other business entities and co-ordinates activities across national borders

multipolar – reference to the shift from American hegemony towards a global environment in which there are numerous powerful players, notably including the large emerging countries

mutual fund – a type of investment which consists of a bundle of investments managed by fund managers

NAFTA (North America Free Trade Agreement) – regional trade agreement between the US, Canada and Mexico

national culture – distinctive set of values and norms by which a nation or people feel a sense of identity and cohesion nationalism – political thinking based on a national culture which sees itself as superior to others; can be the basis of political parties

natural law – universal rules which are binding on all people as rational beings

natural rights – rights that all people are said to have by nature; associated with natural law theories and the political thought of Locke

negligence – in the law of tort, breach of a duty to take reasonable care, which causes injury or other harm to others

neoclassical school of economics – influential school of economic thought based on values of laissez-faire capitalism, including economic freedom and limited government interference

non-executive – in a company, part-time directors who take no part in the day-to-day running of the company, but nonetheless have legal responsibilities as directors

non-governmental organizations (NGOs) – voluntary organization formed by private individuals for a particular shared purpose

not-for-profit organization – organization such as a charity, which exists for the purpose of promoting a good cause rather than to make a profit

non-tariff barriers – in trade policy, barriers to imports, such as safety requirements, which do not involve import duties

'nudging' – measures used by governments to persuade businesses to adopt more ethical behaviour voluntarily

obesity – condition of having excess body fat to an extent that becomes harmful to a person's health and life expectancy

OECD (Organisation for Economic Co-operation and Development) – organization of the world's main developed economies

organic production – agriculture which does not rely on synthetic fertilizers or pesticides

outsourcing – in business operations, shifting an operation or an entire production process, such as manufacturing, to another company and, often, another location, usually for reasons of cost savings

partnership – people entering business together for common gain; the partnership is not a separate legal entity like a company; partners share liabilities, except in the case of a limited liability partnership

patent – type of intellectual property which covers inventions, giving the owner extensive rights over the exploitation of the invention for a specified duration of time

philanthropic responsibilities – in CSR theory, the discretionary spending by a company on good causes, such as donations to charity or the setting up of charitable foundations

pluralism – the multiplicity of groups and interests in society, which is grounded in freedom of association and is central to democracy

plurilateral trade agreement – treaty among a number of countries on trade and related issues

polis – in ancient Greek ethical theory, a political association, such as the Greek city state; more akin to 'society' in modern contexts

political power – the exercise of power over others in the political sphere, usually connected with offices of state

politics – processes of allocating power in any social group or organization, but used most commonly in relation to power wielded in public life, as in a state

portfolio investment – type of investment in international business which focuses on financial investment and returns, rather than ownership and control of foreign assets

positive law – law, often termed 'written' law, enacted by state law-making authorities; can be contrasted with natural law, conceived as a higher moral law

primary stakeholders – stakeholders directly involved in a firm's business

principal–agent model – in a company, a model of corporate governance which holds that the shareholders are the principal and managers are agents; although legally flawed, the model has been highly influential

private company – registered company, usually with limited liability, in which owners are not allowed to offer shares to the investing public

private law – body of law concerning families and individuals; includes property law and the law of obligations, covering contracts and torts

privatization – the conversion of state-owned entities into listed companies which offer a portion shares to private investors, although the state often retains a controlling stake

property theory – in relation to a company, an approach to corporate governance which holds that the shareholders as owners have rights analogous to owners of other types of property; although a flawed analogy, it has become highly influential

protectionism – government trade policy of favouring home producers and discouraging imports

public benefit corporation – in the US, registered public company which is legally committed to act in a socially responsible and sustainable manner

public limited company (PLC) – registered company which offers a portion of shares to investors through a listing on a stock exchange, and whose shares are then traded on that exchange; the PLC is a private-sector company, although in some cases the state owns a significant stake

public–private partnership (PPP) – contractual arrangement between a public-sector authority and a private-sector company (which can be a PLC) to provide a service such as healthcare or prisons, which had previously been a purely public-sector service; also used for capital investment projects such as hospitals rational choice theory – the approach to human behaviour, derived ultimately from utilitarian thinking, which assumes all people seek always to maximize benefits to themselves and minimize costs; central to neoclassical economic thinking

rationality – in philosophy, autonomy of will which distinguishes human beings from other living creatures; in economics, associated with self-seeking behaviour as in rational choice theory

regional trade agreement – multilateral trade agreement by countries in roughly the same geographical region

regulation – in general, rules backed by state authority, often in the form of enacted laws, which govern the conduct of business activities, such as finance; in EU law, enacted laws directly applicable in member states

religious law – body of law pertaining to a particular religion, derived from sacred documents and interpreted by jurists steeped in the relevant religious tradition

renewable energy – creating energy from sources which do not become depleted over time; examples are wind turbines, solar panels and hydro-electric power generation

rent-seeking – making a gain, such as a financial gain or political benefit, at the expense of someone else; rent-seeking is considered exploitative behaviour in that the benefit, such as a payment, is in excess of what is needed in the circumstances

representative democracy – indirect democracy whereby electors vote for office holders to represent them in assemblies which have lawmaking authority

research and development (R&D) – in business, seeking new knowledge and applications which can lead to new and improved products or processes

rights-based theories – ethical theories that adopt a view of individual human dignity as their starting point; often referred to as theories of natural rights

rightwing political parties – political parties which, in economic terms, tend to favour greater economic freedom, lower taxes and lower social spending; often labelled 'conservative', but the 'right' can also refer to religious-based parties and nationalist parties

rule of law – principle of the supremacy of the law over both ruler and ruled; entails equality before the law and an independent judiciary

'say on pay' – in relation to corporate governance, the requirement, notably in the US, that shareholders in the AGM have a right to vote on executive remuneration, although the vote is not binding

secondary stakeholders – stakeholders indirectly involved in a firm's business, in contrast to the direct influence exerted by primary stakeholders

shareholder primacy model – in relation to for-profit companies, model which holds that the sole purpose of the company is maximizing returns to shareholders as owners; also called the 'economic model' of the company

shareholders – investors in a company, who acquire an ownership stake in it and are known legally as 'members' of the company; also known as 'stockholders' in America

small-to-medium-size enterprises (SMEs) – businesses ranging in size from micro-enterprises of one person to firms with up to 249 employees

social contract – in political theory, an agreement among free people to engage in social relations and to set up a government which is accountable to them

social democracy – political system which combines socialist ideals, such as equality and solidarity, with democratic government

social enterprise – business established mainly for a social purpose; lies between a for-profit business and a charity

social justice – concept of inherent duties towards others in society to act in a way that reflects basic human dignity

social market economy – economic system which sees a positive role for the state in fostering social goals within a market economy

social responsiveness – element of theories of corporate social performance, whereby the company engages with social issues and stakeholder concerns

socialism – economic model which rests on the belief that societal goals rather than private profit should be the basis of the economy

sovereign debt – the accumulated national debt of a country

sovereign wealth fund – in finance, an entity owned by the state or an arm of the state, whose main activity is investing and managing funds on behalf of the owners

sovereignty – supreme legal authority in a state, under which laws are made and institutions are set up to administer and enforce the laws, backed up by coercive force

stakeholders – a wide range of groups, individuals and interests which interact with a company and exert influence on it

state capitalism – economic system where the state is the main economic actor in the country, either through direct ownership or indirect control

state-owned enterprise (SOE) – entity established for economic purposes which is owned or controlled by the state; can be a listed company

state-planned economy – economic system run by the state, including collectivization of production and collectivized farms; the antithesis of capitalism

statism – in international relations, an approach based exclusively on state sovereignty

strong sustainable development – view that that patterns of consumption, as well as innovations and efficiencies in production, need to change substantially, in order to meet goals of sustainability in society

subsidiary – a registered company which is wholly or majority owned by another company, known as the parent company; usually treated in law as a separate company from the parent

supervisory board – in two-tier boards of directors, the higher of the two boards, which takes the major strategic decisions of the company

supply chain – production process broken up into separate stages, co-ordinated by a lead company; can involve numerous different companies located in different countries

sustainability – the principle of taking into account the needs of today's inhabitants of the planet in ways which do not constitute a detriment to the ability of future generations to do the same

sustainable banking – approach to banking as a business model based on ethically sustainable principles of serving society

sustainable development – view of economic development involving continuing investment for future generations, taking into account the long-term viability of industries, both in terms of human values and environmental protection

sustainable diet – a diet which has low environmental impact, offers nutritional security and fosters a healthy life for present and future generations

tariffs – taxes imposed by governments on traded goods, usually imports

tax avoidance – arranging financial affairs to reduce tax liabilities, which is considered legal

tax evasion – financial arrangements which have as their only purpose the avoidance or reduction of tax liabilities; can be treated as a breach of taxation laws

tax havens – locations, usually small offshore jurisdictions, which have low or no taxation and seek to attract individuals and companies wishing to avoid the higher taxation and greater disclosure rules which characterize most countries

theocracy – legal and political system in which sovereignty rests in religious rule, and laws are based on religious law

tort – in countries within the common law tradition, the area of law which covers obligations owed by individuals and organizations in society not to harm others

trade – exchange transaction whereby goods or services are sold for some price, although not necessarily money; international trade is between a buyer and seller in different countries

trade deficit – in a national economy, the importation of more goods and services than the country exports

Trade-related Aspects of Intellectual Property Rights (TRIPS) – multilateral treaty which aims to achieve harmony among states in the legal protection of intellectual property; involves the raising of legal protection in developing countries to the level of developed countries

trade surplus – in a national economy, a surplus of exports over imports

trademark – a type of intellectual property consisting of a logo or name which identifies a brand; it can be registered under national law in each market

transfer pricing – in international business, the arrangement of transactions by an MNE among its units in different countries to suit its tax objectives

transition economies – economies making the transition from state-planned to market-based economies, along with supporting institutions; also often refers to political transition to democracy

treaty – in international law, an agreement between sovereign states which obliges state parties to implement its provisions in their territories

'triad' countries – advanced economies of North America, Europe and Japan

triple bottom line reporting – company reporting which takes in financial, social and environmental performance

trust – in interpersonal relations, the belief or expectation that another person will act in a morally responsible way

UNIDROIT Principles of International Commercial Contracts – UN-sponsored statement of principles of international contracts which has facilitated international transactions

United Nations (UN) – intergovernmental organization to which most of the world's countries belong, and whose authoritative instruments are a source of international law

UN Convention on the Rights of the Child – UN human rights convention which covers a wide range of rights regarding children, including civil, social, health and cultural rights; took effect in 1990 and has been ratified by 193 countries

UN Millennium Development Goals (MDGs) – devised in 2000, eight goals representing a broad view of human well-being, including meeting basic human needs and environmental goals

Universal Declaration of Human Rights (UDHR) – the UN's landmark statement of human rights in 1948, which has been followed up in later human rights conventions

universalist – ethical perspective based on principles which transcend differing cultures

universalizability – precept that a person's moral decision-making and actions should always accord with the principle that they could become universal law

utilitarians – broad grouping of theorists who are noted for a view of human nature based on the self-interested pursuit of pleasure and avoidance of pain, along with a view that morality of an action depends on its consequences

utility – the principle that government should seek the greatest happiness of the greatest number within the population

'veil of incorporation' – the legal divide between the individual member of a company and the company itself;

in cases of suspected misdeeds or misuse of the corporate form, courts can 'lift the veil', holding owners personally liable

virtue – quality of goodness in the human being, which, for Aristotle, includes human achievement of any kind, as well as upright behaviour

virtue ethics – ethical focus on the qualities of virtue in the person, rather than simply on ethical actions

WTO (World Trade Organization) – successor organization to the GATT, which took over the oversight of multilateral agreements and also established a trade dispute resolution procedure; it has 159 member states

'zero hours' contract – a device used in employment by which the worker is required to be available for work, but the employer is not required to provide either regular work or stable income

INDEX

Notes: bold = extended discussion or term highlighted in text; f = figure; n = endnote or footnote; t = table; * = photograph.